Penguin Handbooks

Equal Opportunities

Ruth Miller was born in Hamburg. She left school and Hitler's Germany and came to this country 'au pair' shortly before the war. In 1944 she became a journalist, obtaining a job on *Leader* (an illustrated magazine, stable-mate of *Picture Post*). Soon after *Leader* folded, she became a full-time freelance writer.

She is a founder member of the Careers Writers' Association and has written on careers and related subjects for *The Times*, *Good Housekeeping*, the *Daily Telegraph*, *The Times Educational Supplement*, *Where*, *Woman*, as well as for the Careers Research and Advisory Centre and specialist careers publications. She is the author of *Careers for Girls* (1966), the forerunner of this book.

Ruth Miller is married to an engineer and lives in Hampstead.

Anna Alston took a degree in English at Oxford and qualified as a careers officer. She was senior careers officer in Waltham Forest for several years. She is married, has a daughter at primary school and is now a freelance careers writer. She was co-author of *Working in the Travel Business*, *Working in Photography* and *Working in the World of Music*, and has written articles for the *Daily Telegraph* and specialist publications. She writes a careers column for *Company* magazine and has worked with Ruth Miller on previous editions of this book. She is a member of the Careers Writers' Association.

Ruth Miller and Anna Alston

EQUAL OPPORTUNITIES

A Careers Guide for Women and Men

Seventh edition
Revised and expanded

Penguin Books

To Ken and Gordon,
without whose practical commitment to equal opportunities in the home this book could not have been finished on time

Penguin Books Ltd, Harmondsworth, Middlesex, England
Viking Penguin Inc., 40 West 23rd Street, New York, New York 10010 U.S.A.
Penguin Books Australia Ltd, Ringwood, Victoria, Australia
Penguin Books Canada Ltd, 2801 John Street, Markham, Ontario, Canada L3R 1B4
Penguin Books (N.Z.) Ltd, 182–190 Wairau Road, Auckland 10, New Zealand

First published as *The Peacock Book of Careers for Girls* 1966
Second edition published in Penguin Handbooks as *Careers for Girls* 1970
Third edition 1973
Fourth edition 1975
Fifth edition published as *Equal Opportunities: A Careers Guide for Women and Men* 1978
Reprinted 1978
Sixth edition 1981
Reprinted with revisions 1982
Seventh edition 1984

Made and printed in Great Britain by
Cox & Wyman Ltd, Reading
Filmset in 8/10 pt Linotron Times by
Rowland Phototypesetting Ltd, Bury St Edmunds, Suffolk

Contents

Main Careers in Alphabetical Order
(See index for all careers mentioned)

This book uses only the feminine pronoun though the information, unless otherwise stated, applies to both sexes.

Acknowledgements

We would like to thank the statisticians in the Universities Central Council on Admissions, the Department of Education and Science, the Statistical Sub-Committee of the Association of Graduate Careers Advisory Services, the Department of Employment and the Manpower Services Commission for letting us have up-to-date figures for the Sex Balance sections on pp. xxxiii–x, and for their patience in explaining statistical method, and jargon, to a layperson.

We would also like to thank the 120-odd organizations who answered our many questions, especially about the details we wanted for the **Position of women** paragraphs. Special thanks are due to Pam Morton of Thames Polytechnic and Jan Harding of Chelsea College for helping with the computing and science sections.

Finally, we would like to thank careers and educational advisers for suggesting improvements in the presentation of the information.

Introduction to the Guide

What are its aims?

Firstly, to *provide unbiased accurate careers information.* Hard facts like entry and training requirements are checked with relevant organizations. Descriptions of the work involved – necessarily brief and only highlighting vital aspects – and descriptions of the sort of person likely to be good at/happy in the work, are based on practitioners' experiences and views and on our own observations over many years of interviewing people at work.

We believe this is the most important difference between this Guide and organizations' own careers literature. To give just one example: before finally going to press each entry is sent to the relevant organization. Again and again organizations ignore our request to check only *the facts*, and they add 'integrity' to **Personal attributes**. Can you imagine anyone saying to her/himself 'I haven't got integrity, so career XYZ is not for me'?

Who is it for?

The Guide is likely to be used mainly by young people between fourteen and twenty. However, it should be equally valuable to the increasing number of people in their twenties, thirties or forties who want to, or have to, change their occupation. Whether the contemplated change is the result of having made the wrong choice first time round, or whether it is due to people's change of interests, or to skills and occupations no longer being in demand, it is essential to realize that in many careers maturity is an asset; training facilities are available, and entry qualifications demanded of young entrants may be relaxed for older ones (see **Second Start in Education**, p. xli).

What About the Changing Job Scene?

Young people choosing their first career should prepare for the probability of having to learn new techniques, update skills and adapt to changed working environments in the future. We've all been told over and over again that technological developments, and resulting organizational ones, will have affected all our working lives by 2000 AD

– but nobody knows how quickly, and to what extent changes will affect individual jobs. Informed guesswork suggests that, while most craft-level jobs will change out of all recognition, not *all* engineering works, for example, will install robots overnight. Copy-typing will all but disappear, new information-storing and retrieval technologies have already drastically reduced tasks like filing and the looking-up of information. Doing away with dreary routine jobs will free staff to deal with customers'/clients' queries, say the optimists. No, say the pessimists (or should one say the realists?), it will lead to fewer jobs for people qualified only to do routine jobs.

To minimize the shock when change becomes necessary and to maximize the options open for changing to something that will be both in demand and congenial, people choosing careers now would be wise to go for as broad-based an initial training as possible, and be wary of jobs where initial pay is fine but no systematic, or only job-specific, training is given. What is absolutely vital to bear in mind throughout the choosing process is that it is mostly the unskilled jobs, needing little or no training, which are disappearing. The lower the qualifications, by and large, the greater the likelihood of unemployment. So it's important to stay in the education system, full- or part-time, as long as possible and to remember that, apart from CSEs, GCEs and further and higher education, there are alternatives such as BTEC, City and Guilds Foundation and other courses (see p. xvi), and other vocational courses.

What's a Career?

Careers in this Guide are listed alphabetically. However, many if not most 'careers' are really 'areas of work'. Look in the index and you see how many more jobs than career sections there are. Usually, one kind of training leads to jobs in a variety of settings, and you can usually mould training plus experience to the kind of job you will want to do when you know more about the whole spectrum and about your own likes, dislikes, strengths and weaknesses. For example, an engineering degree can lead to the top in the Civil Service or in industry, i.e. into prestigious, well-paid jobs where an understanding of new technologies helps with decision-making; it can lead to academic research; into exploring new export markets; to partnership in a professional consultancy or to setting up your own business, and so on. In each case the job's ingredients and the personal qualities required are different. The same goes for a first job in retailing: it can lead to a comfortable 9-to-5 office job or to hectic travelling across Europe checking trans-continental truck-drivers' schedules – quite apart from obvious retailing jobs like store-management and buying.

Use this Guide as a springboard, a first lap on the lengthy and possibly bumpy ride from vague first idea – design engineer or TV reporter? – to final choice. Use the Guide in conjunction with the 'How to Choose' aids (p. xlviii), combined with discussion with careers advisers and parents, and if possible with people in the jobs you'd like to do.

A Special Plea to Girls and Their Parents

The book's other main purpose is to encourage girls to widen their career choice and speed their progress towards equality in the job market. Women now account for about 43% of the total workforce in this country, but only about 2% are senior managers. Many more women manage, say, launderettes or small offices; many more men than women are bank managers or senior executives in industry. In the professions, women are beginning to make some progress (see list, p. xxxix), but having started from a very low baseline, they are still a tiny minority.

Because job segregation is still so strong, Equal Pay legislation (p. xxx) isn't helping women much; average earnings per hour for women are less than three quarters of the earnings for men. The reason is not blatant flouting of the letter of the law, but the fact that women are still clustered in a narrow range of industries (especially catering, textiles, distribution) and in a narrow range of occupations, doing mainly unskilled or semi-skilled work which needs little training and therefore offers poor promotion prospects.

At a higher educational level tradition still puts women at a disadvantage: physiotherapists, for example, earn far less than electronics technicians; yet physiotherapists, nearly all women, need higher entry qualifications for a longer and more wide-ranging training than do electronics technicians who are nearly all men.

When Sex Discrimination legislation (see p. xxix) was first passed nearly ten years ago few people realized how many intractable, persistent hurdles women had (and still have) to negotiate before 'equal opportunities' became more than a pious hope and a slogan. Legislation, we now know, merely set the stage – the action hasn't yet reached the end of the first act.

Why Do Women Lag Behind?

Very briefly, three main factors combine to keep women down, and out of most prestigious, well-paid and influential jobs. Firstly, *traditional career structures*: men's careers tend to have built-in training and promotion plans; women have to make it known to employers that they want a career, not just a job, even though they may be busy having children just at the time men are forging ahead. Secondly, *entrenched assumptions* which don't stand up to being tested: it is still widely assumed, for example, that women aren't worth training because they leave before they have repaid the time and money invested in that training. However, respectable academic research has proved that that is just not so. ('Young men don't stay in jobs longer than young women,' says the Chief Executive of one of Britain's most successful marketing companies, 'that's been proved beyond doubt. Besides, I'd much rather lose a member of expensively trained staff after five or seven years because *she*'s having a baby than because *he* is going to the competition.') Other disproved assumptions: women don't *want* responsibility; women aren't prepared to travel; women are absent more often than men. The last assumption is in fact a misleading sweeping statement: women *as a whole* are absent from work more often. But the level of absenteeism for men and for women depends on the level of responsibility involved in the job; the lower down the ladder, the higher the absenteeism rate – and far more women than men are on the lower rungs. In professional and management jobs, absenteeism does not differ significantly between the sexes.

The third factor lies in the *girls and women themselves* – their lack of confidence in their abilities; their apparent lack of 'venturesomeness'; their low job expectations. Social conventions and conditioning still make most girls into dear little stereotypes by the time they are thirteen – the vital stage when they choose their exam subjects. By choosing traditional girls' subjects girls limit their career choice *far* more than do boys who choose typical boys' subjects (see Sex Balance in Education, p. xxxiii).

Why 'She'? The Importance of 'Role Models'

This Guide is trying to re-condition careers advisers, parents, and career-choosers. This is why the female pronoun is used throughout, although the information applies to both sexes. That sounds like a gimmick – but why should it? Using the male pronoun when text applies to both sexes is normal practice: it is precisely this kind of social and semantic convention which is responsible for the snail's pace at which ideas are changing on what is and what is not a Good Job for a Girl.

How can girls be expected to see themselves as chartered engineers, TV service people, surgeons or bank managers while nearly all the chartered engineers, TV service people, surgeons or bank managers they see on TV or in real life, and whom they read about, are male? Until girls have more female 'role models' – women in traditionally male jobs with whom they can identify – the equal opportunity concept remains a vast oversimplification. There are indeed no medical school quotas now, and neither builders nor barristers may use the old 'we-have-no-ladies'-lavatories' excuse for keeping girls out of builders' yards or barristers' chambers. But that sort of thing is only the tip of the iceberg of discriminatory traditions.

Equal Opportunities? Yes *and* No

In terms of access, opportunities are theoretically pretty equal, but they are still totally unequal in the demands they make on boys' and girls' motivation, determination and self-confidence. To choose surveying, engineering or a management traineeship with one of the multi-national companies, boys mainly need certain academic qualifications. Girls need those, plus the guts, the self-confidence, to stand out in a crowd, to differ from their peers, to put up with boring jokes about women's lib, and to be prepared to be asked personal questions about marriage plans at interviews. In other words, to make what would be a perfectly ordinary choice for an ordinary boy, a girl or young woman has still to be a bit extra-ordinary. That's why girls need positive encouragement from parents and careers advisers; but often the best they can hope for is amused acquiescence or raised eyebrows.

This Guide is trying to de-stereotype jobs and people, and to chivvy girls off the tramlines. (But a TV series about a perfectly ordinary couple where the husband is a nursery teacher and the wife a chartered engineer would be a lot more effective!)

Checklist

Initials, Qualifications and What They Mean

'O-level' in the General Certificate of Education normally refers to pass-grades, i.e. grades 1, 2 or 3 (or A, B, C). It covers O-level equivalents – such as CSE Grade 1, or Ordinary Grades in the Scottish Certificate of Education.

BTEC

BTEC is the Business and Technician Education Council and offers a range of nationally recognized qualifications (other than degrees) in a wide range of subjects. BTEC took over responsibility for all former BEC (Business Education Council) and TEC (Technician Education Council) courses when these two bodies merged. The merger took place in October 1983 and the only change so far has been in the titles of the awards. All students gain a BTEC award (see below for levels of award). There has been no change in the structure or content of the courses, and there is unlikely to be in the next couple of years at least. This leaves a rather confusing situation. Any two students who gain a BTEC National Diploma may not have studied the same type of course, and indeed might have had completely different entry qualifications. This is because the BEC and TEC systems differed quite a lot. Therefore, the sections below have been split up to take account of this. All former BEC courses are given the general term 'Business Studies Course' (including computing) and all former TEC courses are called 'Technician' courses (although they include courses in hotel and catering and design).

BTEC courses cover:
Business Studies courses: business and finance, computing and information systems, distribution, public administration.
Technician courses: engineering, construction, science, hotel and catering, design, agriculture.

Business Studies Courses

There are four main categories of Certificate and Diploma Award – General, National, Higher National and Post-Experience.

Awards are given to students who have completed a course; courses are made up of individual 'modules' – packages of skill and knowledge within a subject area. A certain minimum number of modules, at one of the three levels of attainment, adds up to a Certificate; if more modules are added, a Certificate is converted into a Diploma. As with technician awards, diplomas indicate a wider spread of knowledge than certificates; the mode of attendance is immaterial; students may study part-time, full-time, or mix modes of attendance.

All students take certain 'core modules': all learn a bit about the inter-relationship between the various business functions and specializations (see Management, p. 269). But right from the start students choose programmes in one of the following career areas:

General business studies – for students who intend to go into or are working in a medium-sized concern but do not, or at least not yet, want to specialize;

Financial studies – for students who intend to work in or are working in banking, accountancy, insurance, etc.;

Distribution studies – for students who intend to or work in retail or wholesale distribution;

Public administration studies – for students who intend to or work in local or central government, the police, the health services or other public body.

Within each of the four areas, students add modules relevant to their job or prospective job; awards are tailored to individual students' needs. Students may take different lengths of time to collect the modules necessary for completion of an award course. Minimum durations are:

For first-level award: 1 year part-time for General Certificate; 1 year full-time or 2 years part-time for General Diploma;

For second-level award: 2 years part-time for National Certificate; 2 years full-time or 3 years part-time or sandwich for National Diploma;

For third-level award: 2 years part-time for Higher National Certificate; 2 years full-time or 3 years part-time or sandwich for Higher National Diploma.

Entry requirements are fairly flexible: with fewer than 4 O-levels, students first work for General (first-level) awards; with at least 4

O-levels (normally including English and maths) or a General BEC award, students work for National (second-level) awards; with at least 1 A-level and 3 O-levels (including English and maths) or with a National award, students work for a Higher National award.

Students without formal qualifications may be admitted at the discretion of the college Principal.

BTEC National and Higher National Certificates and Diplomas in Computing: Entry requirements for National award: 4 O-levels or BTEC General or 4 BTEC level 1 units. For Higher National: 1 A-level and 3 O-levels (including maths) or BTEC National.

BTEC Post-Experience Certificate in Business Administration
Students should be at least 21 and have appropriate business experience. It is intended for people who want to extend or update their knowledge and skills; for people in employment and for those temporarily not in employment, such as women returners. This certificate is made up of 5 separate units which can be taken over a period of time or simultaneously in about a year. Content and organization vary from one college or polytechnic to another. In exceptional cases colleges will accept students with alternative qualifications or give credit for relevant experience. Check with your local college first.

Technician Courses

There are three main categories of Certificate and Diploma Award – National, Higher National and Post-Experience. Courses leading to awards are called 'programmes'. Programmes are made up of 'units', each dealing with one aspect of a course subject. A certain number of first-level units add up to a National Certificate; with additional first-level units a National Certificate can be converted into a National Diploma; if second-level units are added a Certificate can be converted into a Higher Certificate and then, by adding more second-level units, into a Higher Diploma. (In the past, *technician certificates* were usually awarded after part-time study, *diplomas* after full-time study. A diploma indicates a wider spread of knowledge than a certificate; the student's 'mode of attendance' is immaterial.) All students take 'essential units' within a subject area – say sciences – and then add optional units according to interests/job – for example, hospital technicians would take different optional units within their sciences programme from those taken by science technicians in a university lab (see Science Technician, p. 441).

Awards lead to partial exemption from relevant bodies' examinations, such as the Institute of Medical Laboratory Sciences, Institute of Building, Institution of Electrical and Electronic Incorporated Engineers, etc.

There are no rigid *entry requirements*: The scheme is flexible and programmes are tailored to fit entrants' educational level; the higher the entry-level, the quicker students will get their awards; but there is no time-limit within which programmes must be completed. There are no 'courses' which last a definite number of years.

For example, students with four relevant O-levels including maths, a science and English or 'a subject requiring English as a means of communication' (i.e. history, geography, social studies, etc.) can complete a Certificate programme by two years' part-time study. But students with fewer entry qualifications will take longer. The statutory minimum entry qualifications are three CSE Grade III, in maths, a science and English 'or a subject requiring English as a means of communication'; but individual colleges and employers can, and do, set higher entry requirements in many cases. The scheme is still so new that no national pattern, covering all the various technician subjects, has yet emerged.

Although, theoretically, students can switch from full-time to part-time study and vice versa, in practice Certificate programmes are part-time; Diploma programmes are usually full-time. Most Diploma programmes last two years and entry requirements – set by colleges – tend to be three or four O-levels in relevant subjects. However, students with fewer entry qualifications should nevertheless apply; acceptance for individual courses depends so much on supply and demand, course directors' views, and programme content. It is also sometimes possible for students to catch up on missing GCE subjects while following a Diploma programme.

One relevant A-level generally qualifies for entry to Higher National Diploma courses; for Higher National Certificate courses one A-level passed and another studied, or even 2 A-level passes, may be required.

Post-Experience Studies/Individual Unit Scheme

It is possible for students to take individual units from a technician course and certain units on the business studies side. These students do not have to study a full course so this scheme is useful for people who want to update a particular skill, or extend their knowledge in order to change to a new occupation. It is very useful for women wanting to return to work after a gap. Subjects offered include: Microelectronics, Word Processing, Information Technology and so on. Students are awarded a Record of Success for individual units, but if they study a coherent group they could be awarded a Post-Experience Certificate or Diploma.

Recognition of BTEC Awards
Many professional bodies recognize BTEC awards for entry/exemption purposes. BTEC National awards meet most CNAA and many university degree general entry requirements.

Further information from:
For England and Wales: BTEC, Central House, Upper Woburn Place, London WC1H 0HH
For Scotland: Scottish Technical Education Council (SCOTEC), 38 Queen Street, Glasgow G1 3DY
Scottish Business Education Council (SCOTBEC), 22 Great King Street, Edinburgh
SCOTEC and SCOTBEC are amalgamating in August 1984 to form SCOTVEC (Scottish Vocational and Educational Council).

City and Guilds

Apart from the basic skills schemes offered under the Youth Training Scheme (see p. xxvii) there are two main kinds of awards: *general* vocational preparation and *specific* vocational preparation.

Under the first heading come foundation and vocational preparation (general) schemes. City and Guilds Foundation Certificates are usually awarded after one year's full-time integrated education and introduction to one of a large number of occupational areas. These include Agricultural Industries; Commercial Studies; Community Care (nursing, nursery nursing, residential social work, etc.); Computing Studies; Construction; Distribution (mainly retail); Engineering (the largest area); Food Industries; Science Industries; and Technology.

No entry requirements; Foundation courses are held in further education colleges, in schools, or as 'link courses' between school and further education college and practical experience at work. Courses are intended for young people (mainly sixteen- to eighteen-year-olds) who are interested in an area of work but do not know what specific jobs involve, and who also need to improve their 'communication skills' (written and spoken English and numeracy) before embarking on a career. A Foundation Certificate is not a formal qualification, rather proof of 'vocational preparation'. However, all school-leavers without academic qualifications, or only a few poor CSEs and just a vague idea of what they want to do, are likely to stand a far better chance of getting a job with a Foundation Certificate than without one. The Certificate may also lead on to further education courses or apprenticeships for which some CSEs or even GCEs are expected or preferred (for example, BTEC courses for which admission of students without GCEs is at the discretion of the college).

City and Guilds also offers a broad-based general vocational preparation scheme. Both these schemes form part of the CPVE (Certificate of Prevocational Education) administered jointly by City and Guilds and BTEC. Under the second heading come City and Guilds Certificates (at three levels) awarded after part-time day- or block-release study to operatives and craftswomen/men in a vast variety of practical and technical subjects. No entry requirements for Certificate exams, but colleges and employers may require some CSEs (usually in maths and/or a science). (City and Guilds *technician* certificates generally have been phased out and replaced by BTEC awards.)
Further information: City and Guilds of London Institute, 46 Britannia Street, London WC1X 9RG

Diploma of Higher Education (Dip.HE)

Dip.HE – Diploma of Higher Education: Courses started in the seventies; they take two years full-time, some three years part-time, and are held at Institutes/Colleges of Higher Education and Polytechnics. Entry requirements for school leavers: 2 A-levels (but A-level grades accepted are lower than most degree students'). Mature entrants – who account for a large proportion – are admitted according to 'suitability'; this could mean having taken a re-entry course (see Second Start in Education, p. xli), or merely experience of life and proof of appreciation/essential basic knowledge of subject to be studied.

Courses vary enormously in content, organization and in vocational and academic value. Most Dip.HEs are modular; students build up their own course from a range of options within an area of study: for example in sciences, social sciences, humanities. Many are identical to the first two years of a related degree course in the same institution. Some courses guarantee 'Diplomates' entry into the third year of that course. Students on Dip.HEs which are not linked to a degree course may have difficulty in finding degree courses which will accept their two years' study as equal to the first two years of that course. If they are accepted only on to the second year they may well have problems getting a grant for the extra year (see Grants, p. xxv). Experimentally, some Dip.HEs are preparing students for local employment opportunities, but it is too early to say whether this will work.

The main advantage of the Dip.HE is that students can defer final career and course decisions – for example whether to take a BEd or a science degree (assuming the Dip.HE modules were science ones), or leave the education system altogether after two years.

Although the Dip.HE was intended to be a qualification in its own right, its value in the job market is not very great. Few employers have heard of its existence or understand where it fits into the academic hierarchy; others think that students chose the Dip.HE because their A-levels were not up to degree course requirements, or because they wanted a soft option in higher education.

Diplomates are not normally accepted for graduate trainee schemes in industry nor for graduate jobs in the Civil Service. Most professional bodies grant exemption from their own exams in exactly the same way they grant exemption to (lower-entry-level) BTEC Higher National award holders. There are no Dip.HE courses in Scotland.

Colleges and Institutes of Higher Education

Colleges and Institutes of Higher Education developed in the seventies when teacher training was being reduced and changed. Most of the new establishments are amalgamations of former colleges of education; some are old colleges of education with a new title.

They still train teachers (BEd and post-graduate certificate courses), but in order to use spare capacity and staff and also to enable teaching students to work together with other students, they have 'diversified' their courses. Students can now choose from a range of Dip.HEs and degrees and, in some establishments, they can also train for social work and some other professional qualifications.

Most of the establishments' titles and range of courses owe more to the whims of local education authorities and principals than to any concerted national education policy. The only feature all establishments have in common is that 'study programmes' are flexible. Courses often start with a 'common year' during which students can sample various subjects, and they can postpone both subject-choice and choice of qualification (Dip.HE, BA, BEd) till the end of the first academic year.

These establishments may be first choice for A-level leavers to whom universities and polytechnics seem frighteningly large and high-powered places, or who want to take a higher education course locally. Mature students make up a rather larger proportion of students than they do at university.

CNAA (Council for National Academic Awards)

Awards degrees at polytechnics and other non-university educational institutions. Most of these degrees – for example in business studies, engineering – are sandwich courses, with periods in employment.

CNAA degrees are comparable in academic standard to university degrees; their content and approach tend to be more directly geared to employment (i.e. vocational) in industry. Therefore, their value on the job market in subjects such as computing or business studies may be greater than their university full-time equivalent.

Pay

The categories 'low', 'medium' and 'high' may be irritatingly vague. But a rough indication of relative earnings is the nearest one can get to being accurate and helpful. Precise figures would be misleading, not only because rates of pay change frequently, but because individuals with different priorities, abilities, and luck tend to earn different amounts in the same type of work, after the same amount of time. Even in jobs with fixed salaries, like the Civil Service, nursing, or air traffic control, speed of promotion depends on luck as well as ability (and mobility).

But above all, most jobs can be done in many different settings, each with different scope for earning and promotion – and different attractions for different people. For example psychologists in the prison service probably earn less than those in advertising; newly-qualified engineers in local government earn more than those with consultant engineers; with a few years' experience, engineers willing to move to where the demand is greatest – perhaps the Middle East – earn more than those who prefer to stay put; a hairdresser in London's West End earns more than one who prefers a cosy suburban salon; an electronics technician in a factory earns more than one who wants to meet people and services TV and hi-fi equipment for a neighbourhood shop.

Another point about earnings: jobs which are well paid to start with, but which require little or no pre-entry training, tend to be dead-end (and usually dull in the long run). Trainees – whatever their title – who are given day-release and/or other systematic training are naturally paid less than employees who are at their employers' disposal throughout the working week. Differentials between skilled and unskilled (or qualified and unqualified) people at the moment may be small, but the person who has had systematic training and understands the 'why' behind the 'how' is immeasurably better able to change the nature of her work, to switch jobs, and to adapt to the technological and organizational changes which will affect everyone during the rest of this century.

Prospects

Comments under this heading throughout the book may seem rather optimistic, but they assume that by the time today's career-choosers are qualified, some way of sharing out the available work more fairly may have been found. Perhaps shorter working hours all round, or a working life interspersed with educational leave, or with updating courses, or just longer holidays, will become normal procedure. Also prospects are always relative; for example, not every engineer will be able to get the ideal job anywhere she likes – but engineers generally have far better prospects than, say, town planners or clerks.

Two general points: firstly, in many jobs a foreign language is a great asset as it enables people to work abroad; and secondly, the broader-based the qualification, the better the chances of being able to adapt to changes in the employment market. Throughout the recession, unemployment among skilled people, whether craftspersons, technicians, or graduates, has been far lower than among unskilled people.

Part-time and Job-sharing

Part-time work tends to be available only at the lower ends of career structures. Nursing sisters who want to work part-time have to take jobs as nurses; in jobs like the law, medicine, surveying or the Civil Service, etc., *very* few senior or even middle-level jobs are open to part-timers. So a few years ago women from various professions thought up *job-sharing*. As there are no longer enough jobs to go round, the job-sharing concept is spreading, men as well as women are now sharing jobs, and institutions as traditional as the Stock Exchange are employing job-sharers in responsible positions.

In job-sharing schemes, two people with the same qualifications and similar experience take full responsibility for one job. They share pay, holidays, fringe benefits on a pro rata basis. Most job-sharers work half a week each; some work alternate weeks or fortnights – it varies according to the needs of job and job-sharers. In some cases the sharers overlap, either to cover busy periods, or to 'hand over'. For the scheme to work, sharers have to be compatible, conscientious, and flexible. They probably pay for the privilege of working part-time in a job of their choice, with giving a little extra of their time and commitment.

The scheme benefits employers, too. Though administrative costs may be marginally higher, they get two brains for (almost) the price of one; part-timers spend less time taking coffee and other breaks (that has been proved); and job-sharers stand in for each other when one is ill or on holiday.

As the idea is still new and viewed sceptically by traditional employers, the initiative to share a job has usually to come from job-applicants – which means individuals have to find a suitable partner and then jointly apply for a job. For details on job-sharing write to New Ways to Work, 347A Upper Street, Islington, London N1 OPD.

Grants (see also TOPS, p. xlvi)

Further education up to age 18 (in some cases 19) is free, provided the student attends a local college. Help with fees, travelling expenses, etc. for a course outside the area is up to the discretion of the local education authority.

Most students who have been offered a place on a 'designated' course are eligible for 'mandatory' awards, usually payable by the local education authority (where the student *lives* not where the course is). 'Designated' courses are generally post-A-level; they include *full-time* first-degree, Dip.HE, BTEC Higher National Diploma and equivalent courses. However, mature students (see p. xliii) who have been accepted on a designated course are now eligible, whether they have A-levels or not. Courses in the Long-Term Adult Residential Colleges (see p. xlv) also qualify for mandatory grants.

Mandatory grants are intended to cover fees and term-time maintenance. Additional allowances may be payable to mature students and for certain courses. Grants are means tested, the amount paid out depending on parents' or, in the case of married students, spouse's, income. Basic rates change every year.

All other students, i.e. all those not on designated courses, e.g. BTEC National, and people who have had mandatory grants in the past, may be paid 'discretionary' grants. The size, and indeed the award of any discretionary grant at all, depends on the economic situation, the policy of the local education authority, and on the student's suitability, in the council's view, for the course.

Careers Advice for School and College Leavers

Young people who have left school, and later if still in full-time education outside the universities, can go to *any* careers office for information and advice. So for any young person who is not happy with the careers service provided at school or at college, there is an alternative source of help. They may also use Jobcentres (a few have job libraries).

Graduates, whatever their age, can use university and polytechnic careers advisory services. Recent graduates, or those still on their degree courses, should go first to the service provided by their own institution. Those who graduated some years ago may use their nearest service.

Educational Guidance Services for Adults (EGSAs)

There is currently no statutory educational or careers guidance service for adults. Concern about this situation in many quarters has led to the setting up and gradual expansion of a network of local advisory services; titles vary, but most are known as EGSAs. Many are in adequately funded and rely on voluntary, as well as paid professional, staff; however, they offer free information and advice to clients of all ages and from all educational backgrounds. The emphasis is on education and training opportunities – anything from evening classes to degree study – and they will refer clients to other agencies where appropriate. Anyone wishing to find out if there is a service available locally should ask at the local education authority office, library, Citizen's Advice Bureau, or write to one of the following: *for England and Wales*: Linda Butler, ECCTIS (see below). *For Scotland*: Anne Docherty, NETWORK, 74 Victoria Crescent Road, Glasgow G12 9JQ. *For Northern Ireland*: Dr Dorothy Eagleson, EGSA, Room 208, Bryson House, 28 Bedford Street, Belfast BT2 7FE.

ECCTIS (Educational, Counselling and Credit Transfer Information Service). This is a new computerized information service for potential students and for students considering transfer from one course to another. The database holds information on two groups of courses: all courses of higher education throughout the UK, together with general entry requirements; and all other courses of further education leading to recognized qualifications (except GCEs) in South West England. Enquirers should either telephone Milton Keynes (0908) 71131, or write to: ECCTIS, PO Box 88, Sherwood House, Sherwood Drive, Bletchley, Milton Keynes MK3 6DL.

The New Youth Training Scheme

The government's Youth Training Scheme was launched in 1983 and replaced the Youth Opportunities Programme. It forms part of a wider government-backed New Training Initiative (see Adult Training, p. xvii). The aim of YTS is to ensure that as many young people as possible are given the opportunity of a year's good quality, planned training and work experience. The majority of those completing the scheme should have their chances of long-term employment enhanced, while those who do not get jobs straight away should be better prepared to plan their lives and use their leisure time constructively. During the first two years of YTS the following groups are guaranteed a place on the scheme:

All 16-year-old school leavers (i.e. those of statutory minimum leaving age);

Those who have stayed on at school or college for an extra year after the minimum leaving age and then cannot find a job, or who become unemployed during their first year out of school;

Disabled 18-year-old school-leavers;

Certain categories of young offenders.

YTS provides for up to one year's integrated training, education and work experience, including a minimum of three months off-the-job training (by day- or block-release). The Manpower Services Commission has laid down minimum requirements relating to the design and content of programmes. For example, they must include training in both specific and broad groups of skills (so that trainees become more employable and adaptable than they would have been in the past). Certain 'core' skills must be included, e.g. numeracy, communication, manual dexterity, problem-solving and introduction to computer literacy. Existing apprenticeship schemes which already provide sufficient off-the-job training, such as those run by the Engineering Industry Training Board, form part of the scheme. Most schemes are employer-based and -run, the rest are administered by the MSC, through the use of sponsors and schemes linking small firms, community projects, training centres and ITECS (Information Technology Centres). Trainees taken on by companies in addition to their normal intake of recruits will be trained alongside them. Although there is no undertaking that these trainees will be employed by their company at the end of the year, it is hoped that some will be absorbed and others will be much more employable. Trainees are paid £25 a week.

Whether or not YTS will be seen by young people and their parents to be more successful than was YOP in increasing their chances of employment remains to be seen. Much will depend on the quality of training offered. Hopefully it will provide a really constructive and forward-looking alternative to being 'on the dole', especially as it covers a very wide range of industries and occupations (anything from deep sea fishing to clerical work, retailing to construction, travel firms to football).

YTS and Equal Opportunities

YOP was, with a few exceptions, unsuccessful in persuading boys and girls to consider work traditionally associated with the opposite sex. It is very much to be hoped that YTS will achieve some breakdown of traditional barriers and open up new horizons for girls. Any girl who finds herself being unwillingly channelled into a particular scheme because it is 'more suitable for girls' should resist and, if necessary, complain to the local MSC Area Board. The organizers of YTS have pledged themselves to implement an equal opportunities policy and it would be extremely disappointing if such a genuine chance to broaden young people's occupational knowledge and lessen demarcation should be lost.

Sex Discrimination Legislation

Brief Summary of Main Provisions Relating to Employment and Education

The *Sex Discrimination Act* makes it unlawful to treat anyone on the grounds of sex (and, in the case of employment, on the grounds of marriage) less favourably than a person of the opposite sex.

Employment

The Act defines two kinds of discrimination:
DIRECT discrimination, for example sending boys but not girls on day-release courses when both are doing similar jobs; or *not* promoting the person next in line *because* she is a woman (or a man).
INDIRECT discrimination: applying the same conditions to both sexes which favour one sex rather than the other but are not justified. For example if an employer, when recruiting an *office* manager, demands that the candidate must have served a *technical* apprenticeship, he or she is discriminating against women because they are far less likely to have served an apprenticeship – which is irrelevant to the job to be done; or if an employer only recruits people aged 20–30, it indirectly discriminates against women who are likely to rear children during those years.

The Act's main exemptions apply:
to employment in private households*;
to firms employing not more than five people*;
where sex is a genuine occupational qualification (known as a GOQ), for example in acting or modelling (neither strength nor stamina are GOQs);
where one sex is required for reasons of decency, for example in an Asian all-women's hostel;

* The European Court of Justice has now issued proceedings against the UK saying that these exemptions must be removed.

in certain jobs providing care and/or supervision;
to jobs which genuinely involve work abroad in countries where women in such jobs are not acceptable. However, if, for example, an employer persistently employs men because he or she claims the job *might* take them to a country where women are unacceptable, but in fact few male employees are sent to such countries, the employer would be illegally discriminating;
to the Armed Forces, the Churches, competitive sports and charities, work in mines, certain shift and night work.

Equal Pay Act

The Equal Pay Act stipulates equal treatment as well as equal pay for the same or broadly similar work or for work that is judged to be of equal value. It covers all conditions and benefits contained in a contract of employment, for example holiday entitlement and the payment of bonuses. Being able to claim your work is of equal value has only been allowed since 1 January 1984 when the government amended the original Act after the European Court of Justice decided it did not go far enough in awarding women genuine equal pay. Women's average earnings are still less than three quarters those of men; the change in the law may alter that by allowing a woman to claim her job is of equal value to any other job in the same firm being held by a man – for example, a woman secretary could ask for equal pay with a male clerk, a woman machinist in a textile factory with a male cutter or a woman checkout cashier at a supermarket with a male shelf filler. At the time of going to press no court cases had been argued under the re-drafted Equal Pay Act. The Equal Opportunities Commission and the TUC are two of the most outspoken critics of the new law, complaining, among other things, that it is too complex, time-consuming and costly to enforce.

The *Employment Protection Act* says that a woman may not be dismissed because of pregnancy; she is entitled to 6 weeks' maternity pay and to reinstatement for up to 29 weeks after the birth of the baby. These provisions apply only if the employee works till 11 weeks before the baby is due and if she has worked for the same employer for at least 2 years full-time or 5 years part-time; if she wants to resume work, she must have told her employer so *in writing* before leaving.

Positive Discrimination

The Sex Discrimination Act specifically permits 'positive action' to be taken by employers, employers' organizations, education and training establishments, in two kinds of situations:

1. Where in the past jobs (and training schemes) were available only or mainly to one sex, special training may be provided for the other

sex, to redress the balance and improve job and promotion prospects for the hitherto under-represented sex;
2. Special training may also be provided to help women who wish to return to work after a gap.
Disappointingly little use has so far been made of the 'positive action' provision. Few women probably know that they could press for 'catching-up' courses and training.

Complaints concerned with employment matters are dealt with by Industrial Tribunals.
(Leaflets setting out rights and procedures in full available from Job Centres.)

Education

Discrimination is unlawful in admission to and provision of education facilities in both the public and private sectors. A few exceptions relate to establishments which are single-sex. All other classes and establishments must be open to all pupils/students regardless of sex. Girls who want to take technical drawing, and boys who want to do cooking, must not be discouraged; medical schools may not operate a quota system, etc.

It is not only discriminatory to refuse entry, but also, for example, gently to persuade girls *not* to choose physics or craft, design and technology where laboratory and workshop facilities are restricted, and instead let them take biology which is less useful later. It is also discriminatory to give boys more chance of work-experience schemes than girls, or to differentiate between the kind of schemes offered (for example to arrange that all girls work in hospitals once a week, all boys in engineering works).

To observe the spirit as well as the letter of the law, careers staff have a duty to widen the girls' careers horizons and to ensure that they are fully aware of all the opportunities, including the non-traditional ones, which are open to them.

As Sex Balance in Education figures (see p. xxxiii) show, changes in boys' and girls' exam subject choices are not encouraging. While the letter of the law *is* observed, in many schools the spirit of the Act is ignored.

Complaints about discrimination in education must first be made to the appropriate Secretary of State (for England and Wales or Scotland) for Education. If no satisfactory conclusion has been reached within two months, cases must be taken before county courts in England and Wales, sheriff courts in Scotland.

Advice and information about all sex discrimination matters is available from the Equal Opportunities Commission, Overseas House, Quay Street, Manchester M3 3HN. Advice on employment matters is also available from the Advisory, Conciliation and Arbitration Service (addresses from local employment offices). Also, local Citizens' Advice Bureaux, such women's organizations as Townswomen's Guilds, and the National Council for Civil Liberties, 21 Tabard Street, London SE1 4LA, will advise and/or provide leaflets.

Women's Rights: A Practical Guide, by Anna Coote and Tess Gill (Penguin), contains full details on anti-discrimination legislation, including complaints procedure.

Sex Balance in Education

Some Facts and Figures

Absolute equality in education is essential if women are to be equal at work. But traditional attitudes and assumptions still steer boys and girls into choosing different subjects at 13+. Girls' choices are far less useful in terms of further and higher education, job opportunities, and generally coping with technological developments.

Proportion of Total O-level Passes Gained by Boys and Girls

	1982		*1979*	
	Boys	*Girls*	*Boys*	*Girls*
Engineering Workshop	98·7	1·3	99·4	0·6
Maths	57	43	61·5	38·5
Physics	73	27	75·2	24·8
Biology	39	61	40·2	59·8
Chemistry	61	39	64	36
Technical Drawing	96	4	97	3
Craft Design and Technology	96	4	97	3
Sociology	24	76	24·6	75·4
Commercial Subjects	38·5	61·5	34·7	65·3
Cookery	2	98	2	98
Computer Studies	72·4	27·6	72·9	27·1

The proportions are changing at an elderly snail's pace, despite rapid changes in women's life styles and later job aspirations. It is particularly disappointing that such a small proportion of girls is taking Computer Studies, a new subject where there cannot be any traditional barriers to break down. (Computer facilities in schools are still limited; perhaps not all schools comply with sex discrimination legislation – see p. xxxi – about equal access to facilities.)

Marginally more girls than boys leave school without A-levels but with 5 O-Levels, Grades A–C, or CSE Grade 1 – 10·8% of girls and 8·5% of boys. But boys' choices include more 'useful' subjects, and so girls still limit their career options long before they can possibly know what they will want to do eventually. Most boys with several O-levels have at least one physical science and/or a technical subject apart from maths. If girls do choose a science, it is often biology which rarely fulfils later course or job entry requirements.

Only 7% of girls against 20% (1981) of boys left with O-level physics (which is essential for most technical traineeships). 24% of girls and 30% of boys had O-levels maths – here the gap *is* narrowing.

After O-levels, girls are still more likely to leave school than boys. In 1981 14·2% of boys and 12·6% of girls left with at least 2 A-levels, 10·4% of boys and 8·2% of girls left with 3 A-levels – the crucial number for getting into the most prestigious and most sought-after degree courses. Girls are less likely to use their science A-level potential. 63% of the boys and only 33% of the girls with O-level maths took A-level maths. 58% of the boys and 43% of the girls with O-level physics took the A-level. 0·1% of boys and 5·2% of girls went on to secretarial courses.

Higher Education

In 1982, girls made up 43.9% of first-year full-time or sandwich higher education students; 9·1% of boys and 6·9% of girls taking degree courses. 93% of boys and 80.5% of girls *qualified* to do so – i.e. leaving with at least 2 A-levels or 3 Scottish Higher levels – chose higher education as the next step.

The gap between numbers of men and women is steadily narrowing – but very slowly – by just under 1% a year. In 1974, out of every 100 candidates for admission to university, 65 were men and 35 were women. In 1983, out of every 100, 58 were men and 42 were women.

Until recently women had a marginally better chance of acceptance than men. Of all male candidates in 1978, 54% were accepted; of all women candidates 56% were accepted. In 1983 only 44% of both male and female candidates were accepted. Women's equal acceptance rate is interesting because, proportionately, far more women try for over-subscribed, difficult-to-get-into courses such as Law, Medicine, English; far fewer apply for often undersubscribed engineering and science courses. For example 4,158 women applied for Medicine for which only 40% of applicants were accepted; only 528 women applied for Physics for which 74% of applicants were accepted.

However, although numbers were still small, proportions of applications from women in some subjects showed encouraging increases since 1978: e.g., Electrical Engineering: 4·9% from 2·2%, Production Engineering: 6% from 5·5%, Maths: 35% from 32·7%.

Men are much more career-minded. Degree subject choices are of course limited by candidates' A-level passes, but these alone cannot explain all disparities. Women are far less likely than men to opt for degree courses which have a high value in the job market and for which *any* 2 A-levels are acceptable: 2,170 men (2·39% of male applicants) and 860 women (1·2% of female applicants) chose Accountancy; 2,444 men (2·7% of male applicants) and 906 women (1·4% of female applicants, half the proportion of men) chose Economics; 723 men (0·8% of male applicants) and 1,904 women (2·9% of female applicants, or over three times the proportion of men) chose Sociology; and 2,310 men (2·5% of male applicants) and 4,765 (7% of female applicants) chose English.

Women as Percentage of all Entrants by Subject Groups

	1983 Universities	*1982 Polytechnics (all advanced courses)*
Education	74·8	58·5
Medicine, Dentistry & Health (includes ophthalmic optics, pharmacy, etc.)	49·3	31·9 (excludes Medicine & Dentistry)
(Medicine only, included in above)	(44·7)	—
Engineering & Technology	10	6·5
Agriculture, Forestry, Veterinary Science	38·4	—
[1]Science	32·9	30·2
[2]Social, Administrative, Business Studies	45·8	38·6
[3]Architecture & other professional/vocational studies	40·2	32·1
Languages, Literature, Area Studies	68·4	59·6
Arts other than Languages	53	56

1: Much smaller proportion of women in physical and computer sciences where prospects are good; far more in subjects like botany and biology where prospects are poor.

2: Far more women in non-vocational, poor-job-prospects subjects such as sociology and anthropology; more men in management-oriented, vocational subjects like accountancy and economics.

3: More women in catering, institutional management; far more men in architecture.

Differences in Subject Choices, Universities

	(1983) Men %	Women %
Education	1·4	3·6
Medicine, Dentistry, Health	9·4	12·5
Engineering & Technology	20·3	2·4
Agriculture, Forestry, Veterinary Science	2	1·8
[1]Science	25	16·3
[2]Social, Administrative, Business Studies	26·3	29·8
[3]Architecture & other professional/ vocational subjects	2·7	2·1
Languages, Literature, Area Studies	6·8	21·4
Arts other than Languages	6·2	10

1: Much smaller proportion of women in physical and computer sciences where prospects are good; far more in subjects like botany and biology where prospects are poor.

2: Far more women in non-vocational, poor-job-prospects subjects such as sociology and anthropology; more men in management-orientated, vocational subjects like accountancy and economics.

3: More women in catering, institutional management; far more men in architecture.

Sex Balance in Employment and Training
(see also Introduction, p. xi)

Women now account for about 43% of the total workforce. About 63% of women between 16 and 60 work,* but about 40% of them part-time. Two thirds of women at work are married. One in 7 of families with children under 16 has a woman as main provider. The proportion of women working, and the extent of part-time work, varies with age. Almost 70% of women aged 35 to 54 work; under 60% of those between 25 and 34 do so. The higher their educational qualification and/or specific job training, the shorter the 'domesticity gap', i.e. the sooner they want to return to work.

Despite the increase in numbers of women at work, there has been no corresponding increase in the spread of jobs they do or the industries they work in. Over half of all women in manual work are still concentrated in a narrow range of low-paid, low-skill industries and occupations – mainly in textiles, catering, hairdressing, laundries, cleaning, and light engineering assembly work. (No single industry employs more than 10% of working males.)

Sex Distribution in the Main Non-Manual Occupational Groups, 1981

	Men %	*Women* %
Managerial	12·4	5·2
Clerical & related	7·2	30·7
Professional & related in health, welfare, education	4·6	12·7
Literary, Artistic, Sport	0·9	0·8
Selling	4·2	9·5
Professional & related in technology, engineering, science, etc.	6·3	0·8
Professional & related supportive management and administration	5·4	2·2

Clerical and Selling, the two groups in which women predominate spectacularly, are those in which jobs are most seriously threatened by

* By 'work' is meant 'economically active', i.e. includes those seeking work.

chip-based technologies. The Professional/Technical and related work groups, which have the lowest proportion of women, offer the best employment scope.

About 37% of boys and 8% of girls take up formal apprenticeships (Dec. 1980) – and most of the girls go into hairdressing. In engineering (which includes electronics – clean light work and a growth industry – see Engineering, p. 175) 26·7% of the operatives (semi- and unskilled work) are women; they have little hope of promotion. Only 2·4% of technicians and 4% of trainee technicians are women (1982 figures). This is the area where job segregation is most disturbing; technicians in engineering and related fields (which include computer manufacture and servicing) are in demand whatever the unemployment figures elsewhere. But technicians need maths, and usually physics or at least a technical subject (see Sex Balance in Education; and **Position of women**, Engineering, p. 189, for the industry's efforts to attract more women).

More boys than girls go straight from school into employment (i.e. without first taking a full-time further or higher education course), but far more boys than girls get systematic on-the-job training. In 1981 19% of boys and only 5% of girls aged 16 to 18 were on non-advanced day-release courses; most of the girls took 'job-specific' subjects such as shorthand or hairdressing; most boys were on courses which extended their skills range – and their job opportunities.

In the professions, the vast majority of women are still in traditionally female jobs. However, more women are now training for professions (i.e. are on relevant degree or similar courses) – and so they are beginning to catch up.

University Graduates (first degree) Entering Different Types of employment, 1982
(% of total home employment)

	Men	*Women*
Public Service	22·5	35·1
Education	3·5	8·5
*Industry	37·9	15·5
Chartered Accountancy	11	8·3
*Banking & Insurance	6·7	5·5
*Other commerce	10·9	17·3
Private practice (e.g. solicitors)	2·6	2·3
*Other employment	5	7·3

* Includes graduate secretaries

Proportion of Women in Some Top (and Other Good) Jobs, 1983		
Bank Managers	Just over 1%	
Members of Institute of Directors	2·9%	
British Institute of Management members	2·32%	
Institute of Chartered Accountants full members	5%	(student members: 28%)
Institute of Cost & Management Accountants full members	2%	(student members: 15%)
Institution of Civil Engineers full members	well below 1%	
Institution of Electrical Engineers full members	below 1%	(student members: about 3%)
Institution of Mechanical Engineers full members	well below 1%	(student members: about 3%)
Dentists – practising	18%	(dental students: about 35%)
General Practitioners – practising	18%	(entrants to medical school, 1983: 45%)
Surgeons – practising	1%	(registrars: 35%)
Barristers – practising	10%	
Solicitors – with practice certificates	12%	(law students about 45%)
Royal Institution of Chartered Surveyors full members	well below 1%	(student members: 7%)
Society of Surveying Technicians	well below 1%	
Engineering Technicians	2%	(trainees: 4%)
Architects – practising	7%	
Veterinary Surgeons	10%	(students: about 35%)
Advertising Account Executives	20%	
Air Traffic Control Officers	5%	(trainees 5%)
Driving Examiners	well below 1%	
Local Authority Chief Executives	well below 1%	
University Professors	3%	

Proportion of Women in Some Top (and Other Good) Jobs, 1983	
Civil Service (1982/3):	
Executive Officers (fairly junior grade)	40%
Under Secretaries (senior grade)	5%
Administration Trainees (high-flyer graduate entrants)	40%

Second Start in Education

A Variety of Routes for 'Returners'

There are plenty of opportunities for catching up on missed educational opportunities. Adults who need GCEs, technical or commercial certificates, or simply more knowledge, for courses or careers they want to start after a gap of some years, can join any further education college for part-time day or evening, or full-time, courses. Most of these are intended for school leavers, but adults are welcome.

Students can take as many subjects as they like; just one, or several, building up their own full-time course. Most people take 1, in some cases 2, sessions a week, for 3 terms, to get an O-level, and about twice as long to get an A-level.

It is also possible to take GCEs by correspondence course (but correspondence courses should be chosen with care!). If you cannot get advice from someone in education, go for a non-commercial organization, e.g. National Extension College, 18 Brooklands Avenue, Cambridge CB2 2HN.

Then there is a wide variety of *non-examination* courses. These include the traditional evening classes in all sorts of subjects, and various 're-entry' courses. These may be called *Wider Opportunities for Women*; *New Opportunities for Women* (men are rarely excluded, but most re-entry courses were started by women, for women wishing to return to work); *New Directions*; *Fresh Horizons*; *Return to Study*, etc. Courses vary in content, organization, level and quantity of work expected. Some are mainly confidence-restoring and 'diagnostic'; they help students to sort out their aims, motivation, level of confidence, circumstances, and then balance these with the available job opportunities, and the obstacles which may arise. Some courses teach only study technique: learning how to study is very important for people who left school years ago and/or never took studying very seriously. Other courses combine study technique with specific subjects.

Courses may be held on 1, 2, 3 or 4 days a week; day-time classes are morning only or between 10 and 3, to fit in with school-hours. Length varies from 8 weeks to one academic year (in a few cases two years).

There are also some 'access' courses; these do not lead to A-levels, but successful completion is usually recognized as equivalent to degree course GCE requirements. A few courses lead on to science degrees – helpful for people who want to switch to or start a technological career.

A useful innovation for people who cannot commit themselves to attending classes regularly is the *FlexiStudy* scheme. Briefly, it is a combination of correspondence course with personal contact with a tutor by letter or telephone, and occasional face-to-face tuition. FlexiStudents have access to college laboratory, library and social facilities. Write for free leaflet, 'FlexiStudy', to National Extension College (address above).

In several parts of the country adult and further education institutions have combined to form Open Colleges. These vary enormously in organization. All enable more people to make use of educational facilities, including non-examination courses, and provide alternative routes into higher education and the professions – i.e. alternatives to orthodox O- and A-levels. Open College courses are geared to mature students' needs and take account of students' 'life experience'. Course structures usually include FlexiStudy or a variation on that theme, i.e. supplementing attendance at college with 'distance learning packages' (souped-up correspondence courses) and occasional contact, possibly by telephone, with tutors. Some students take 'access' courses which lead to specific degree courses; some take 'return-to-learning' courses; others accumulate 'credits' by taking as many separate courses as they may need to reach a certain level, usually O- or A-level equivalent. People who start from scratch and want to get into higher education as well as people who only want a bit of additional information or to stretch their minds are all provided for.

Some Open Colleges intend to build on students' existing but so far unrecognized skills. For example, a secretary without GCEs but experience of running computerized office equipment might be given a credit which entitles her to get into an O- or A-level-entry technology course. Recognition of Open College awards in lieu of GCEs is by no means automatic. Because the concept is so new, most higher education establishments and professional bodies have yet to be convinced that the system works. However, the OC movement is rapidly gaining momentum. At the time of writing – February 1984 – a National Federation of Open Colleges, and a Conference to thrash out common patterns are being planned. To find out whether an Open College scheme exists locally, ask at an educational guidance service, or a further or adult education establishment.

Whether there are courses locally depends entirely on whether there is someone in the education system with enthusiasm for helping potential returners. Many classes start in response to demand from potential students (please note!).

Mature Students and Higher Education

Universities and polytechnics can waive normal entry requirements for mature students (usually people over 21, sometimes over 23). The extent to which this is done varies enormously: again there is no national pattern. Most admissions officers want 'evidence of ability to benefit from and cope with sustained post-A-level study'; but there are no generally agreed methods of assessing such evidence, nor of the standards required. Applicants may be accepted on interview only, but usually they have to write an essay as well; some universities accept only on results of special mature-entry examination. All higher education establishments welcome mature students, who tend to make up in enthusiasm and motivation what they lack in GCEs.

There are no establishments which will *not* consider mature entrants; one college (Lucy Cavendish, Cambridge) is for mature women graduates and undergraduates only.

Part-Time Degree Study

These were originally intended only for people in jobs, with all or most tuition in the evenings. Part-time *day* courses were pioneered by Hatfield Polytechnic and then Kent University. Most polytechnics and many universities now have part-time day degree courses, or are planning them. If there is no such course locally or within commuting distance, there are alternatives:

Associate Students

These sign on for a part or parts of full-time courses. They *must* do course work and can, but need not, take exams and earn 'credits'. If, having tested the water, they decide to take the plunge and enrol as full-time students, any credits gained may count towards the degree. The Associate Student scheme was initiated by Hatfield Polytechnic some years ago, but now many Polytechnics accept Associate Students.

Occasional or Special or Non-degree Students (titles vary)

These schemes exist at most universities in one form or another, basically for the benefit of students from abroad. They come for a term or a year or a particular course of lectures. Arrangements vary enormously from one university to another. For example at University College London, there are 4 categories of 'special students', ranging from a year's full-time attendance including tutorials, etc., to not more than 6 hours' attendance a week at lectures only; while at Lancaster University most lectures are now open to outsiders. This type of part-time work does not necessarily lead to degree entry, but some students have switched to undergraduate status. As most universities are now trying to 'reach out into the community', requests for participation from local residents are likely to be sympathetically considered. Anyone who wants to do some degree-level work locally should read relevant prospectuses and then write to the registrar. It is up to individuals to take the initiative.

Open University

No entry requirements; admittance is mainly on first-come first-served basis. To be able to cope with the course, most people find some preliminary GCE or other re-entry study necessary. OU students 'build up' degrees by completing a number of 'course credits'. It is possible to accumulate the 6 credits required for a degree (8 for an honours degree) in 3 years; in practice most people take longer. There is no time limit; dropping out for a year or longer presents no problems.

There are now transfer agreements with CNAA and many university degree courses. These enable OU students with a certain number of credits to slot into the second year of a relevant full-time course. The other way round, students who had to drop out of full-time higher education (for other reasons than failing their exam!) may be able to finish in the OU. These arrangements are specially useful for temporarily housebound people.

The OU also runs an *Associate Student Programme* for people who do not want to embark on a degree course or feel they are not up to degree standard. There are about 150 short courses, lasting from a few weeks to a year, to choose from. Some are actually undergraduate course units and later count towards a degree if a student – as often happens – decides to take a degree after all. Some are updating courses for social workers, managers, technologists (several microprocessor/computer subjects are covered), teachers, etc. One course is specially designed for women engineers and technicians who want to return to work after a break. Then there is large variety of courses, under the general heading *Community Education*, which deal with practical everyday problems rather than academic education. Titles include child development, consumer decisions, planning for retirement, governing schools.

For details of degree courses write for Guide for Applicants, for non-degree courses write for Associate Student Programme, to the Open University, Walton Hall, Milton Keynes, MK 6AA.

London University External Degrees

Students study by themselves, with a little tuition at some (not many) FE colleges, or with correspondence course. The National Extension College (Brooklands Avenue, Cambridge) has a tuition package which includes correspondence material, personal contact with a tutor and a student-to-student service intended to minimize the loneliness of the distance-learner.

OU and London External degrees do not overlap – they serve different types of students: OU degrees are broad-based and cover an 'area of study'; London External degrees cover specific subjects in depth; for example, modern languages (a great many), law, economics. One big drawback for mature entrants: of all universities, London is the most rigid in its entrance requirements and makes fewer concessions to mature students than other universities. Details from University of London, Senate House, Malet St, London WC1E 7HU: 'General Information Leaflet for External Students'.

Residential Colleges

There are eight 'Long-Term Adult Residential Colleges' – and despite the title students do not necessarily have to live in. They are for people with few or no GCEs who want to go on to higher education or professional training, or who merely want to stretch their minds. One college is for women only, one for men only; the others are mixed, and want more women students: only between a quarter and a third of applicants are women. Most students take 2-year courses, some take shorter ones; subjects so far covered are a mix either of liberal studies or of social studies; Hillcroft runs a computer studies course and is hoping to start soon a Living with Science and Technology course, to enable women to get into the expanding computer-associated job area. Details from Hillcroft, Surbiton, Surrey (women only); Newbattle Abbey, Dalkeith, Midlothian; Coleg Harlech, Gwynedd, Wales; Co-operative College, Loughborough; Plater College, Oxford; Ruskin College, Oxford; Fircroft College, Selly Oak, Birmingham (men only); Northern College, Wentworth Castle, Barnsley, Yorkshire.

Government Training Schemes

MSC 'Bridge' Courses

These are intended for unemployed and redundant managers and professional people aged 21–60. They are part-time and free, so do not qualify for TOPS allowances (see below), but travelling expenses may be paid. Approximately 30 programmes are run throughout the country under various titles (e.g. Prospect, Crossroads, Job and Career Change), but all offer individual counselling and workshops and facilities for job-searching (e.g. CV writing and self-presentation). Details from Manpower Services Commission local Training Division office or PER (Professional and Executive Recruitment) office.

TOPS – The Training Opportunities Scheme

TOPS is run by the Manpower Services Commission and helps people over 19 who have been out of full-time education for at least 2 years (it does not matter how much longer) and who want to learn new skills or update, or add to, old ones.

TOPS is flexible. Almost any full-time course which lasts at least a month and not more than a year and is likely to lead to employment may qualify for a TOPS grant (but for post-graduate university courses applicants must be at least 27). The final decision as to whether a person is given a TOPS grant is up to MSC and possibly course administrators. It is up to individuals to make out a case for their sponsorship – so it pays to do careful research about likely employment opportunities resulting from the course for which a grant is wanted.

Craft courses, in anything from welding to catering, heavy goods vehicle driving to agriculture, TV servicing to carpentry, are at Government Skill Centres; most last 6 months and are followed by at least a year's 'learnership'. Technician courses in a vast variety of subjects, including BTEC (see p. xvi) courses in things like microprocessor applications, are normally at Further Education Colleges. At management level, TOPS grants are available for courses – usually at Polytechnics – in, for example, Personnel, Transport, Marketing Management, and the Diploma in Management Studies (see Management, p. 274).

Proportion of Women on TOPS Courses 1982/3

Clerical, commercial and office services	71%
Shorthand typing and office machinery	96%
Craft courses in skill centres, e.g. bricklaying, engineering, joinery	3·5%
Electrical/electronic (e.g. radio and TV servicing and electrical installation)	0·6%
Science and technology (includes computer science)	3%
Management and business training	19·7%

The vast majority of women still apply for clerical courses but these are now being drastically reduced (see Secretarial and Clerical Work for poor prospects for clerks, typists, etc.). TOPS organizers would greatly welcome more women on craft, technician and management courses (see **Prospects**, Engineering Technician, p. 185).

TOPS grants are higher than students' grants and are paid regardless of spouse's or own income and may include dependants' and other allowances (see also Grants, p. xxv).

There are only a few part-time courses.

TOPS details from Jobcentres and Employment Offices.

White Paper 'Training for Jobs', January 1984

At the time of going to press (February 1984) the government had just announced changes in the future provision of adult training and retraining. The Manpower Services Commission is to act as a national training agency and will oversee the new programme, which will supersede the present TOPS scheme. No precise details have yet been announced, but courses will fall into two main groups. The first will consist of vocational training geared to local employment needs, i.e. they will teach specific skills known to be in demand by local employers (such as computer-related qualifications). They are likely to incorporate the more successful elements of existing TOPS courses, but will lay greater emphasis than did TOPS on skills likely to be needed in the future and on higher level technician training. Another difference is that the emphasis will be on enabling individuals to add to, or upgrade, their existing skills rather than learn from scratch. The second group of courses will be aimed at the unemployed, by helping them to retain their employability and to improve their basic skills. Pilot schemes will run during 1984/5 and the full programme should be under way by 1985/6.

Details of all schemes from Jobcentres and Employment Offices.

Some Useful Publications

(Should be available in schools' and careers offices' libraries or public reference libraries)

'How to Choose' Aids:

Beyond School
Decide for Yourself
Choosing and Finding a Job
Male and Female
Careers and Jobs without O-levels
Your choice at 13+
Your choice at 15+
Your choice at 17+
Your choice of A-Levels
Your choice of Degree and Diploma
Jobs and Careers after A-Levels
all published by CRAC, Bateman Street, Cambridge CB2 1LZ
Which career for you? by Catherine Avent, published by Robert Hale.

Reference Books:

A Compendium of Advanced Courses in Colleges of Further and Higher Education (full-time and sandwich), published annually by DES Regional Advisory Councils, Tavistock House South, Tavistock Square, London WC1. (Post-A-level courses, including 'one-off', BTEC Higher Diploma, and Professional Examination courses.) Similar information on part-time and 5th-form leavers' courses is published regionally (details from local careers offices/teachers).

Careers Encyclopedia, published by Cassells. Most detailed reference book available.

Polytechnic Courses Handbook, published annually for Committee of Directors of Polytechnics, 309 Regent Street, London W1. Details of individual polytechnics and their varied courses.

Higher Education – Finding your Way, published by Department of Education and Science, Information Division, Elizabeth House, York Road, London SE1.

Directory of Further Education, all FE courses; including new 'distance-learning'/second-chance (see Second Start in Education, p. xli) courses as well as BTEC, City and Guilds, day-release, full- and part-time ones. Published annually by CRAC.

Which Degree, covers all degrees and gives full course and institution details; now published annually by New Opportunity Press.

Degree Course Guides, booklets comparing individual courses within disciplines, published bi-annually by CRAC.

Directory of First Degree and Diploma of Higher Education Courses, published annually by CNAA (344–54 Gray's Inn Road, London WC1). CNAA course details only.

Directory of Postgraduate courses (CNAA – as above).

Graduate Studies, published annually by CRAC – details of postgraduate courses in: Humanities and Social Sciences; Biological, Health and Agricultural Studies; Physical Sciences; Engineering and Applied Sciences.

The Handbook of Degree and Advanced Courses in Institutes/Colleges of Higher Education, Colleges of Education, Polytechnic and University Education Departments, published annually by National Association of Teachers in F and HE. Covers wide range of courses and all BEds, PGCEs and courses for qualified teachers.

The Compendium of University Entrance Requirements, published annually for Committee of Vice-Chancellors and Principals. Essential information on varying entry requirements. Useful section on mature students' entry.

Grants to Students: a Brief Guide, published annually by DES.

COIC (Careers and Occupational Information Centre) publishes an annual Careers Guide and a wide variety of leaflets and booklets, including the 'Working In . . .' and 'Close up' series. All these, and Information Sheets specially for graduates, should be available in schools' and careers offices' libraries.

Especially for Job-changers and Late Starters

COIC Routefinders

Returners, by Elizabeth Dobbie, National Advisory Centre on Careers for Women, Drayton House, 30 Gordon Street, London WC1H 0AX.

1 Some Useful Publications

Second Chances, published by National Extension College; all types of courses for late starters; mid-career changers; women returning to work.
Access to Higher Education, published by the Open University.
What Else Can a Housewife Do?, published by COIC.
Never Too Late to Learn, published by Longman.

Accountancy

Accountants in: public practice – industry and commerce – public sector; accounting technicians

Professional Accountant

Entry qualifications 2 A-levels and 3 O-levels including maths and English language. Over half the entrants (about 80% of Chartered Accountants) are *graduates* (any discipline). In Scotland, Chartered Accountancy trainees *must* be graduates. (See also *Accounting technician* route below, p. 8.)

The work The image of accountants as deskbound figure-crunchers is quite wrong. An accountancy qualification leads to a vast variety of jobs, in virtually any environment: heavy industry or television; retail or merchant banking; professional consultancy; public service. There is scope for accountants interested in the intricacies of accounting procedures and their technological development, or in high finance, or as a way into general management, and also for people who intend to become entrepreneurs. (See Working for Oneself, p. 560.)

Work falls broadly into three categories:

1. *Public* (illogically also called 'private') *practice*
2. *Industrial accountancy*
3. *Public sector accountancy*.

Public Practice Accountants

They work in firms of partners or 'principals'. They are consultants, and employ qualified assistants, trainees and technicians (see below). Firms vary in size from one to well over 100, and in type from high-powered international practices which deal mainly with large companies and are at the very centre of the country's commercial activities, to small suburban practices which function at a gentler pace and deal mainly with private clients and local 'small traders'. Normally each accountant deals with particular clients' affairs so that there is personal (at least written or telephone) contact with individuals.

As the financial scene becomes ever more complex, accountants now often specialize in one particular accountancy aspect; for example, computer systems, inflation accounting, mergers, corporation finance. However, the bulk of public practice work is taxation and auditing (which is increasingly computerized). Auditing means analysing and verifying clients' books and ensuring that the annual balance sheet presents a 'true and fair' picture of the client's financial affairs. Auditing is done on clients' premises so it involves meeting people and possibly travelling. Audits take anything from a few hours to several months, depending on the client's size and type of business. Audits may be done in streamlined offices using the latest technologies, or it may mean having to create order out of chaos when, for example, a farmer's 'office' consists of a drawerful of bills. Auditing is largely desk- (or desk-top computer) work, but it also involves discussions with clients – anyone from clerk to managing director – if specific items in the books are not clear. Accountants also advise their clients on personal and business financial matters, from how to invest a small legacy to setting up a business or liquidating one.

Increasingly, large accountancy firms provide *management consultancy* services. Management consultants are called in, for example, to investigate the reasons for a firm's decline and to advise on ways of improving profitability. They may also undertake investigations into, for example, the pros and cons of proposed mergers or takeover bids. In the course of their work, management consultants collect information on individuals' working patterns and established but perhaps outdated ways of working. Management consultancy involves interviewing people at all levels in an organization rather than mainly figure- and desk-work. It requires considerable expertise in business organization and practice.

Industrial Accountants

They work for an employer on a salaried basis. They can be divided into *financial* accountants, concerned largely with internal audits, taxation, wage and salary structure, financial record-keeping; and *management* accountants. This is the fastest-growing accountancy specialization (and it overlaps with management consultancy work). Management accountants assess the relative importance, value and cost of all aspects of a business (or public enterprise) – equipment, labour, raw materials, transport, sites, administration, marketing, etc. Every person's, machine's, department's, vehicle's, etc., contribution to the effectiveness of an organization, and their interdependence, can, with the help of computer systems and mathematical models, be assessed separately and as part of the whole operation. Management accountants might, for example, compare the relative cost of using a cheap new raw material which would necessitate more expensive machine maintenance and require mounting a marketing campaign to launch the changed product, against the cost of going on using the more expensive traditional raw material – taking into account, among other factors, what the competition abroad might do, and how staff would feel about the change. Or they might assess the cost of moving a factory to a cheaper site, considering increased transport cost, recruiting and training new staff. Like management consultants, their work requires interviewing all the people whose work affects the efficiency of the organization concerned. Having compared the financial results of alternative courses of action, management accountants present the information to the decision-makers at the top of the organization.

Management accountants need a broader understanding of business organization in general and of the type of business with which they are concerned than do financial accountants. They often move from salaried employment into public practice, or into *management consultancy* (see page 281).

Public Sector Accountants

Accountants working for local government, the nationalized industries, the Health Service, etc., have much the same function and aims as industrial accountants: i.e. the most efficient use of resources. Only the emphasis is different: instead of improving profitability, public sector accountants are concerned with control and management of public authority finance. They advise on the financial implications of various courses of action and help sort out priorities when, with limited financial resources, new schemes or improvements or existing services have to be abandoned or curtailed.

Whereas accountants in industry present their information to business people who are themselves often knowledgeable about business matters, public sector accountants advise and explain things to professional colleagues from other disciplines and to elected councillors who may know very little about finance.

Prospects Generally good. Demand equals supply even during a recession but jobs are not as easy to get as they were a few years ago. However, because of the increasing complexity of financial management and planning, accountants are needed, whether business is good or bad.

Accountants can remain specialists and move up the ladder to financial controller (titles vary) in industry or in the public sector; they can move sideways and up into general management (see Management, p. 269), into accountancy teaching, into systems analysis (p. 133) or into management consultancy. At middle level there are a vast variety of jobs in all types and sizes of business and public enterprise. An accountancy qualification is also an excellent preparation for jobs in merchant and other banking, insurance, the Stock Exchange.

There are some opportunities for employment (but *not* in public practice) in the EEC, and in most other countries.

Pay: Very high (but low while under training contract) (see p. xxiii).

Training There are six main professional qualifications, each awarded by a different body:

1. Institute of Chartered Accountants of England and Wales;
2. Institute of Chartered Accountants of Scotland;
3. Institute of Chartered Accountants of Ireland;
4. Association of Certified Accountants;
5. Institute of Cost and Management Accountants;
6. Chartered Institute of Public Finance and Accountancy.

The differences between the syllabuses are small – there is a basic body of accountancy knowledge which all accountants must master.

Accountancy courses all cover economics; statistics; computer applications and systems; corporate finance; financial management; inflation accounting; taxation; trustee work; share organization; management accounting; relevant law; EEC accountancy implications; auditing. The emphasis on different aspects of accountancy differs in the various professional bodies' examinations; some syllabuses overlap more than others. The reason for the existence of several accountancy bodies is historical rather than logical and a merger has often been discussed.

It is generally believed that chartered accountants get all the best jobs, or indeed that all qualified accountants are 'chartered'. But that is not so at all. The various qualifications, with the exception of 6, are equally marketable. Choice of one qualification rather than another only partly depends on the ultimate career aim: it also depends on what training is available locally; and on the type of training method preferred.

Main differences in various qualifications' usefulness in the job-market:

Only *Chartered* and *Certified* accountants may, by law, audit limited companies' accounts. People who want to go into public practice *must* therefore choose one of these two qualifications. *Chartered* and *Certified* accountants can also go into industry and commerce so these two qualifications leave the widest range of options open. (More than half of all qualified accountants work in industry and commerce.)

Cost and Management Accountants are the most commercial and profit-orientated. This training concentrates more on running a business and planning its future than do the others. So people who definitely want to go into industry/commerce might choose this qualification.

The *Chartered Institute of Public Finance and Accountancy* qualification differs from the others in that it leads only to work in the public sector – nationalized industries; national health service; local and central government. But for this – very large – sector, the CIPFA qualification is, usually, essential.

Accountancy training requires intelligence, determination, motivation, staying-power and a logical mind. It does not require exceptional mathematical ability, nor academic brilliance.

Training methods vary between the various bodies, and they are complicated. (Candidates should read carefully all the accountancy bodies' training literature.)

All non-graduates may, and Institute of Chartered Accountants and Chartered Institute of Public Finance and Accountancy *must* take a 'Foundation course', usually at a Polytechnic. Candidates who are not sure which qualification they will ultimately want to take must ensure they take a 9-month full-time 'common' Foundation course: most prepare students for any of the accountancy bodies' examinations, but some lead only to one or two bodies' exams. The Foundation course syllabus covers accountancy principles, law, economics, statistics, taxation, computer applications.

The essential differences between the various bodies' training methods are:

Institute of Chartered Accountants

Students enter into a 'training contract' with a firm of chartered accountants. They train with the same firm throughout. *Graduates* train for at least 3 years. If they do not hold an approved (by the ICA) accountancy degree they take a 'conversion course' during the early part of their training. If theirs is a 'related degree' (business studies, economics, etc.) they may be granted partial exemption from the conversion course.

Non-graduates (who must have taken a Foundation course) train for at least 4 years. BTEC HND holders also train for 4 years, but they do not have to take the Foundation course.

All trainees take the ICA's Professional Examinations. They are entitled to 22 to 26 weeks' study leave but they must also do a considerable amount (on average 2 to 3 evenings a week) of studying in their own time. Most students take 'link' courses at polytechnics or private tutorial colleges.

As they are *trainees* ICA students usually get less pay than other accountancy learners.

Association of Certified Accountants

Training is the most flexible. Students do not have to enter into training contracts but train while in salaried employment. They may change employers, and type of employer, during their training and thus can get varied experience. They need not make up their mind at the outset whether they wish to go into industry/commerce or into public practice. However, a certain period in public practice is obligatory for persons who ultimately want to go into public practice. ▸

ACA examinations consist of three 'levels' – Preliminary, Professional and Final. *Graduates* are exempt from the Preliminary level. Graduates with relevant degrees and BTEC HND holders (Business and Financial Studies) may also be exempt from parts of the Professional examination. Training – called 'required accountancy experience' – normally takes at least 3 years for graduates and persons who have taken at least 2 consecutive levels of the examinations on a full-time course, and at least 4 years for others (including *Accounting Technicians*, see below, p. 8).

ACA students are not automatically *entitled* to study-leave, but many companies run training schemes with study-leave. ACA students may have to spend more of their own time studying than do ICA students, but ACA students usually earn more while training.

About half of all accountancy students now choose Certified accountancy.

Institute of Cost and Management Accountants

Training is flexible. Students do not enter into training contracts but train while in salaried employment. Students may change employers during training. They train entirely in industrial and commercial enterprises. Training takes at least 3 years for *Graduates*, BTEC HND holders and *Non-graduates* who have taken a 9-month full-time Foundation course, 5 years for others. ICMA exams consist of 5 parts. Partial exemptions are granted to graduates and BTEC HND and Foundation examination holders. Some employers run training schemes and grant day- or block-release; other students must study entirely in their own time, and take evening and/or correspondence courses to prepare for the exam. The *minimum* time taken to complete training is 3 years.

Chartered Institute of Public Finance and Accountancy

CIPFA exams are taken by students employed in public sector organizations. Before starting professional training, A-level students must complete a 9-month full-time or 2-year part-time day-release course.

Graduates with a non-relevant or partially relevant degree must attend an approved graduate conversion course.

During the 3-year professional education and training programme trainees attend 39 weeks' approved educational courses but this training programme is reduced for graduates with a specially relevant degree. It is possible (but in practice difficult) to move from one public sector employer to another during training.

Personal attributes Academic ability; numeracy; ability to speak and write concisely; business sense; logical mind; ability to negotiate without self-consciousness with people at all levels within an organization; tact in dealing with employers and clients; a liking for desk-work.

Accountants in public practice: a confidence-inspiring manner; ability to put things clearly to lay people.

Industrial accountancy: ability to communicate with and extract information from people at all levels of intelligence and responsibility; enjoyment of decision-making.

Late start No significant GCE concessions, but cases judged on merit individually. It may be difficult to find training vacancies, but there are opportunities.

Position of women Proportions are still surprisingly low:

	Qualified Members	*Trainees*
Chartereds	5%	28%
Certifieds	7%	28%
ICMA	2%	15%
CIPFA	5%	23%

There is little prejudice in accountancy generally except perhaps in some City firms and at the top in local government (see Local Government, p. 265). The reason for low proportions must be: (a) tradition, (b) the image of accountancy as totally desk-bound work without contact with people, and (c) the fact that fewer girls take O-level maths. Yet accountancy training helps women to get into senior *management in industry* (see p. 269). A fair proportion have done extremely well in, for example, financial journalism, and some in *management consultancy* (see pp. 2 and 281).

Career-break: Should be no problem with ICA and ACA. There are lectures and journals which help to keep accountants up to date with developments. It is possible to work in most parts of the country and also to run a small practice from home. More difficult with other two bodies.

Part-time: Opportunities increasing.

Further information Institute of Chartered Accountants of England and Wales, PO Box 433, Chartered Accountants' Hall, Moorgate Place, London EC2R 6EQ

Institute of Chartered Accountants of Scotland, 27 Queen Street, Edinburgh

Institute of Chartered Accountants of Ireland, 7 Fitzwilliam Place, Dublin 2
The Association of Certified Accountants, 29 Lincoln's Inn Fields, London WC2A 3EE
The Institute of Cost and Management Accountants, 63 Portland Place, London W1M 4AB
The Chartered Institute of Public Finance and Accountancy, 1 Buckingham Place, London SW1E 6HS

Related careers *Actuary – Banking – Company Secretary – Computing – Insurance – Management in Industry – Purchasing and Supply – Statistics (Science) – Tax Inspector*

Accounting Technician

Entry qualifications 4 O-levels including an English and a numerate subject, and not more than one non-academic one; or BTEC National award in Business Studies (financial studies). Requirements may be reduced for older students.

The work There is no legal requirement for accountants to be professionally qualified; 'accountant' is not a 'protected title' in the way 'solicitor' or 'architect' is. The Association of Accounting Technicians was set up a few years ago, and this 'second tier' qualification was created, because there is so much accountancy work which while being highly responsible and requiring expertise and training, does not require the breadth of *professional* accountancy education (see above, p. 4).

Broadly, professional accountants conduct audits (which technicians are not empowered to do) and deal with high-powered financial management and advice, etc.; accounting technicians collect the information on which professional accountants base their decisions, and deal with straightforward accountancy. This involves more desk-work than does professional accountancy, but it also involves contact with clients.

The vast majority of accounting technicians work in professionally qualified accountants' (all types) offices. However, some are 'sole' or 'company' accountants in firms too small to warrant employing a professional accountant, and some accounting technicians set up on their own, dealing with private clients' (individuals, shopkeepers, etc.) VAT, income tax and similar matters. Some keep small firms' books and visit such clients at regular intervals on a contract basis. Others put advertisements in local papers and do 'one-off' jobs for people who need some straightforward accountancy advice, or help with tax returns. So accounting technicians can choose whether to take on secure employment and do mainly desk-work, or to have contact with a variety of clients and be their own boss (see Working for Oneself, p. 561).

AAT members who want to become professional accountants (see above) normally get exemption from the professional accountancy bodies' (see above) Foundation examinations.

Prospects Good. There is an increasing demand for accounting technicians as the still fairly new qualification is becoming more generally recognized; scope for self-employed technicians seems to be good though it varies from one area to another.

Pay: Medium to high (see p. xxiii).

Training Either 2 years' full-time or 3 years' part-time (day-release usually) for the BTEC National Diploma for Accounting Technicians or by correspondence course for the AAT Membership Examination. Students must spend at least 3 years in 'approved practical experience' before they can become members of the AAT.

Personal attributes A methodical approach; liking for figure, computer and desk-work. There is room in this work for those who prefer to work on their own but with limited responsibility as support staff to more highly qualified/ experienced colleagues, and for those who, though unable to take the professional examination, wish to do responsible work and have contact with colleagues and clients. For AAT members who want to set up on their own: confidence-inspiring manner; self-confidence; ability not to worry as work may be sporadic rather than regular (see Working for Oneself, p. 561).

Late start Very good scope for various kinds of older entrants such as unqualified but experienced accountancy staff, returners to office occupations, mid-career changers. O-level entry requirements waived for people with relevant experience or knowledge.

Position of women Women are doing well as accounting technicians, both in employment and working on their own. In 1983 14% of Senior Members (i.e. with 5 or more years' AAT experience), 23% of Members and 36% of Student Members were women.

Career-break: Unlikely to present any problems as long as people keep up with changes in taxation and other accountancy matters. Evening classes and correspondence courses (including Open University) can act as refresher training.

Part-time: Very good scope, both in employment and working on one's own.

Further information

Association of Accounting Technicians, 21 Jockey's Fields, London WC1R 4BN

Related careers

Banking – Insurance – Purchasing and Supply – Shipbroking – Stock Exchange

Acting

Television – theatre – commercials – films – drama therapy

Entry qualifications

No rigid requirements. See **Training**.

A career only to be contemplated by those who feel they could not possibly be happy doing anything else. Complimentary notices for school or college plays are rarely pointers to professional success, because being the best of a group of local performers is irrelevant when competing with the best from all over the country. In addition, luck plays a large part: being known to the right employer at the right time is as important as being good at the job.

Entry to this overcrowded profession is extremely difficult. There are 'casting agreements' between theatrical, TV, film and commercials producers which control the employment of actors and virtually restrict employment to Equity members. Equity (the actors' trade union) in turn strictly controls the entry of new members.

Television

The work

Provides well over half the total of acting jobs, and is not easy to get into either: producers can pick and choose, and tend to choose players who have had repertory experience or have done exceptionally well at drama schools or in fringe theatre work. TV plays are video-taped (recorded), they are shot in 'takes' which are longer than film-takes, but not long enough to allow players to 'get into' the part as stage performances do. TV acting is more of a strain than filming or the theatre: rehearsal time is always cut to a minimum (3 weeks at the most), so it is impossible to have as many re-takes as in filming, yet there is no hope of doing better the next night, as in the live theatre. The TV studio atmosphere is hectic and tense. The majority of players prefer the stage, whatever their public utterances; but television provides their bread and butter and helps them to get known nationally.

Theatre

Performers usually give 8 performances weekly. In repertory, there are often morning rehearsals as well, which leaves little free time.

Reasonably priced digs near the theatre are rarely luxurious; theatre dressing-rooms tend to be cramped and uncomfortable.

Only a minute proportion of actors ever have a 'secure job' – contracts may be as short as 2 weeks; never longer than a year.

Apart from the conventional theatre, there has in recent years been a considerable growth in 'fringe theatre'. Companies are often set up by young players working as cooperatives (for a very small wage), taking plays into small halls, pubs, schools, etc. This type of acting – without proper stage – requires adaptability, devotion and special technique: it is not much easier to get into than conventional stage work.

Commercials

Work comes through theatrical casting agencies or some of the big advertising agencies. Work is never regular; TV commercials producers always look for fresh faces, and an actor or actress who is currently advertising, for instance, a baby food, is unlikely to be used for some time, either for a competitor's food or for, say, a sophisticated drinks or fashion advertisement. Once established, actors and actresses sometimes appear in commercials which are written to suit their particular style, or they do 'voice overs' – the speaking but not the visual part of the commercial. Commercials are not a way into acting, but useful bread-and-butter jobs.

Films

The film industry is very small. There is very little work; nobody can hope to be a *film* actress or actor today. Engagements tend to come at short notice. The decision whether to accept a tiny part in a TV soap-opera serial or wait for a hoped-for break in a film is always a difficult one. Once a performer has accepted a part, she must stick to it and not let a producer down if something better turns up – otherwise she loses her agent's or casting director's goodwill, which is fatal.

Acting is never easy, however good a player is. It gives great satisfaction, however, to people with stamina, real talent and lots of luck.

Prospects Very poor indeed except for the outstandingly talented and lucky. A recent survey showed that at any one time over two-thirds of professional actors and actresses are out of work. An inquiry also showed that the chances of success are immeasurably better for students who have attended one of the established acting schools (see **Training**) than for those who have been to one of the 'academies' which are totally out of touch with the changing needs and techniques of the theatre and broadcasting, or those few who somehow slipped in without any systematic training at all.

'Graduates' from established drama schools do not normally have great difficulty in getting their first job. They are usually fixed up within a few months of leaving drama school. It is the second step into bigger and better repertory, or into TV, West End, etc., which is the problematical one – and which vast numbers never manage to take at all. It means coming to London, finding a good agent who will take a newcomer, and earning a living, yet being available if the hoped-for audition comes.

Pay: Depends too much on luck and talent to generalize about.

Entry requirements and training

No rigid GCE requirements; acceptance at good drama schools depends on audition, but candidates considered suitable almost invariably have several O- and often A-levels, especially in English language and/or literature. The average ratio of acceptance at good schools is about 12 to 1; for women candidates it is about 45 to 1.

About 85% of players who earn their living at acting have been to schools which belong to the Conference of Drama Schools and one or two other well-known ones which for various reasons do not belong to the CDS (careers officers have lists of these schools). The overwhelming majority of students from other schools and academies fall by the wayside because they are not trained adequately.

Performers' courses last 2 or 3 years. Students unlikely to succeed are asked to leave, or leave of their own accord, well before the end of the course. Courses prepare students for all types of work, but individual schools' curricula vary considerably. All cover the three main aspects: *movement*, *voice production* and *acting studies*. All students do all types of parts, from musical to mime, Shakespeare to Stoppard. Courses include general stage-craft, play-construction, etc.

Drama can also be taken as part of a first degree course, but the primary purpose of these courses is the study of literary criticism, history and literature of the theatre; not vocational acting training. Graduates from these courses usually go into teaching or possibly into drama production (mainly TV); but there are far fewer such openings than there are drama degree students.

Post-graduate drama courses are usually academic, not vocational.

Personal attributes

Good health; well-cut features, but not necessarily beauty; the ability to learn lines quickly; a good memory; great self-confidence; imagination and sensitivity to interpret any part; resilience, to ignore or benefit from the constant and public criticism from teachers, producers, directors, colleagues, and the critics; an iron constitution; a sense of rhythm, at least (preferably an aptitude for dancing and singing); outstanding acting talent and a 'stage personality'; grim determination.

Position of women Only about 1 woman applicant in 45 is accepted at drama school: the ratio of female to male students training is 3 to 1. Although there are *far* more parts for men than for women, more women graduate every year. In this profession it is of course not a question of discrimination at the employment stage, but entrenched tradition makes even women dramatists write more parts for men than for women. Actresses are therefore strongly advised to have a second string to their bow. Secretarial training is useful here, as 'temping' and part-time jobs enable an actress to be available for auditions while earning her living.

Further information National Council for Drama Training, 5 Tavistock Place, London WC1H 9SS

Conference of Drama Schools (enclose sae) for list of member schools, c/o Rose Bruford College of Speech and Drama, Lamorbey Park, Sidcup, Kent DA15 9DF

Related careers *Barrister – Broadcasting – Speech and Drama Teaching, p. 527 – Speech Therapy. Arts Administration – Recreation Management*

Drama Therapy

Drama therapy aims to use various dramatic techniques (including mime and improvisation) to provide meaningful and therapeutic experiences for mentally and physically handicapped and psychiatric patients. It is practised by both specialist drama therapists and other professional staff involved in the care and treatment of such patients.

Training Either via part-time course while working in the health or community services (for details write to the British Association for Dramatherapists, 7 Hatfield Road, St Albans, Herts) or via the 1-year full-time course, Drama and Movement in Therapy, operated by Sesame (a charity) at Kingsway-Princeton College. Students should have had previous relevant experience, e.g. psychiatric nursing, teaching, social work or drama. For details write to the Department of Creative and Vocational Studies, Kingsway-Princeton College, Hugh Myddleton Centre, Sans Walk, Rosoman Street, London EC1R 0AS.

Actuary

Entry qualifications *England and Wales*: 2 A-levels, one of which must be at least grade B in a maths subject or grade C in further maths, the other at least grade C, and 3 O-levels including one English subject.
90% *graduate* entry, most graduates have degrees in a mathematical subject.

The work Actuaries use the theory of probability and the theory of compound interest together with statistical techniques to highlight and if possible solve financial problems; to suggest appropriate courses of action and to predict the financial implications of such actions. In other words, they 'work out the odds'. Their work has a strong mathematical bias and is essentially desk-work performed in a variety of settings. The majority of actuaries work for insurance offices, concentrating on the technical side of life assurance and pension funds, investigating such matters as relative life expectancies of various groups in the population, and assessing the effects of life-styles and characteristics on premiums and policies and investment. In other insurance branches – accident, fire, motor – actuaries assess risks and pin-point variables in the light of changing conditions and life-styles, and advise on reserves necessary to cover long-term liabilities. In government departments actuaries advise on public service pensions and insurance schemes. Though they are concerned with various aspects of people's lives and welfare (cushioning of the effects of old age, accident, sickness being the reasons for insurance schemes), actuaries do not usually have much contact with people outside their own office.

For actuaries who want to have more contact with people outside their own profession and perhaps apply maths to wider commercial matters, there are some opportunities in commerce and industry as financial analysts, advisers, planners. About 15% are in consulting practice, advising mainly on private pension funds. Consulting actuaries may negotiate with solicitors, tax inspectors and trade union officials concerned with pensions. There are also openings in merchant banks, the Stock Exchange and other financial institutions.

Prospects A small profession, but steady demand for qualified people.
Pay: High (see p. xxiii).

Training 6–7 years' part-time study for school-leavers, 1 or 2 years less for graduates. No formal articles or apprenticeships. Training is on-the-job plus correspondence study (and discussion classes) for Institute of Actuaries' (England and Wales) or Faculty of Actuaries' (Scotland) examinations. Employers may give time off for day-time study, but considerable evening work is necessary too.

Students with good degrees in mathematics, statistics or economics qualify for exemption from parts of the Group A examinations, which include computer application; probability; statistics and compound interest; principles of actuarial treatment of statistical data; use of statistics in the study of population changes; finance and investment. The final examination covers life offices, pension funds and friendly societies, finance and investment, general business insurance.

Personal attributes Liking for concentrated desk-work; an analytical brain (actuaries tend to be good and devoted bridge-players); probing curiosity; pleasure in solving complicated problems; ability to interpret and express in clear English results of mathematical and statistical analysis; business sense for those who want to go into private practice.

Late start Only advisable for brilliant mathematicians because of the long training; also difficulty in finding training posts.

Position of women Of 3,448 fully qualified members of the Institute of Actuaries only 108 are women; but of 2,153 students, 235 are women, so the proportion is going up. No difficulties getting jobs and promotion.

Career-break: Possible for experienced actuaries who have kept up with developments, especially relevant legislation and data processing application (see p. 131). Temporarily retired members pay a reduced subscription which nevertheless entitles them to receive all journals and attend meetings.

Refresher courses: Correspondence courses can be adapted.

Part-time: In theory work could be done part-time, and by freelances; in practice no concentrated attempts to organize this seem to have been made by prospective part-timers.

Further information Institute of Actuaries, Staple Inn Hall, High Holborn, London WC1V 7QJ

The Faculty of Actuaries, 23 St Andrew Square, Edinburgh EH2 1AQ (Scottish training and educational requirements differ in detail from the above)

Related careers	*Accountancy – Banking – Civil Service – Insurance – Stock Exchange*

Advertising

AGENCIES: Account executive/account planner – media executive – market research – creative department; ADVERTISERS; MEDIA

Entry qualifications No rigid requirements; in practice usually at least A-level English or BTEC award (see p. xvi). Most entrants are now graduates.
Graphic design, *typography*, etc., require art-school training (see Art and Design, p. 58).

The work Advertising specialists work in:
1. Agencies
2. Company advertising departments
3. The media and for suppliers of advertising services (e.g. studios, film production, market research)

Agencies

Agencies plan, create and place advertisements on behalf of advertisers who appoint them to handle their 'account'. This may be a detergent, a package holiday, government information, or a nationalized industry. Only 40% of advertising expenditure is concerned with persuading people to *buy*; advertisements are also used to get money for charities, votes for political parties, support for seat belts, to encourage energy saving or investment, to fill jobs.

Agencies vary in size and scope. Some employ up to 600 people, most under 50. Some specialize: for example, in technical or recruitment advertising. The largest agencies have a range of specialist services such as package design (see p. 58), film production (see Television, Radio and Films, p. 543), market research and marketing (see pp. 19, 283) and public relations (see p. 398).

Account Executive/Account Planner

Agency staff work in groups on individual accounts. Responsible for each account group of specialists is the *Account Executive*. They are usually in charge of several accounts, each dealing with a different product, and are the link between clients and agency. They must acquaint themselves thoroughly with each client's product: this may involve asking Research (see below) to identify the 'target group' (the people at whom the advertisement is to be aimed); to investigate the competition's product; to ensure the client's claims for the product can be substantiated. After the initial research, the group decide on a 'campaign theme', then the Account Executive discusses it with the client. When the brief and the budget are agreed, work on 'creating the advertisements' starts.

The Account Executives coordinate the work, control the budget and present progress reports to the client. Their work involves travelling if clients are scattered over the country or abroad.

Some agencies split the job into *Account Executives* and *Account Planners*. The executives' main responsibility is liaison with the client; the planners' with organizing research into consumer attitudes and views.

The executives' job requires self-confidence and diplomacy, as clients often have to be persuaded that the type and tone of a campaign suggested by the agency will be more effective than the client's own idea. Planners' jobs tend to be more academic in approach.

Media Executive and Buyer

Media planners' jobs are crucial to the success of any campaign. They choose the channels of communication – newspapers, magazines, radio, television, posters and so on – which are most appropriate for any particular campaign and reach the target group most economically. Media planning decisions are based on information and statistics provided by *media research.* Computers are widely used to compare effectiveness and costs, but creative requirements – for colour, movement or sound – require subjective judgement.

Media buyers are responsible for the purchase of press or air time.

Planning, research and buying are the three media functions; they may be carried out by different people within the department, or the whole media operation may be the responsibility of a group of individuals assigned to a particular campaign.

Market Research

Before an advertising campaign is planned, facts are compiled about the product's uses, its advantages and limitations, competitors' products, distribution and so on. Facts and opinions are also gathered about its potential users – the target group: not just in terms of who they are, how much money they have and where they live, but in terms of their attitudes and behaviour. Some facts come from desk research, collecting information from a variety of published sources and the client's own records. Others may need specially commissioned research, ranging from statistics compiled by part-time interviewers questioning members of the public, to sophisticated behavioural studies involving trained psychologists.

Creative Department

Once the account group has been briefed and a strategy agreed with the client, the *copywriter* and *art director* together develop the advertisement.

The advertising 'message' is translated into a 'communication' that makes an instant impact on the target group. Words and pictures must complement each other.

Copywriters must be literate and imaginative, but they must choose their words under considerable constraints – from the disciplines of the brief and the restrictions of the space or time available, to the obligations of the Code of Advertising Practice and legal requirements. An interest in commercial success and an understanding of people's ways of life and priorities are far more useful than literary leanings.

Television and cinema commercials may be created jointly by copy-writers and producers, or written by specialist scriptwriters to the producer's brief. There is no hard and fast rule about who exactly does what, and whether the visual or verbal aspect is the more important.

The *Art Director* (see Art and Design, p. 58) is responsible for the physical appearance of print advertisements, deciding whether to use photography or illustration, commissioning and supervising its production and the type selection and typography. The typographer chooses type which is easily readable, fits the layout and reflects the character of the product.

The atmosphere in agencies is often relaxed and informal, but the pace and pressure are very demanding indeed. The decline in the number of people in agencies means fierce competition for any openings. Considerable talent, the right kind of personality and commitment are needed to survive and succeed.

Advertisers

Many advertisers incorporate advertising into marketing (see p. 283). *Brand managers* are responsible for the marketing policy for a product, including its advertising. Others have their own advertising departments, which vary in size. If a manufacturer creates and places all the advertising directly, the department may be much like a small agency. There is less scope for employees to work on different types of products simultaneously, but there may be a broader range of work.

Retailers' advertisement departments may deal with store and window displays, exhibitions, fashion shows, promotions and public relations, for example, using an advertising agency only for display advertisements.

Advertising departments are useful training grounds, giving experience in a range of work. There are more opportunities for junior copywriters in advertising departments than within agencies.

Media

Advertising departments are responsible for selling space or air time to advertisers, directly or through agencies. The *research section* provides information about readers or viewers; it helps advertisers pin-point target groups. The *promotions section* may have its own creative department, which works in three areas: projecting the medium to advertisers, to distributors, and to retailers on behalf of advertisers. *Sales representatives* are responsible for selling advertisement space or air time; this may include telephone canvassing, trying to get classified advertisements (which may involve having to put up with being rebuffed, and trying again). *Media Managers* are responsible for ensuring that advertisements comply with the Code of Advertising Practice, which may involve checking copy claims and possibly asking for changes to be made before accepting copy.

Prospects Now more limited than they used to be; the advertising industry has contracted considerably in the last few years. Considerable persistence – apart from talent – is needed to get a job. Virtually all jobs are in London.

Pay: High (see p. xxiii).

Training A combination of practice and theory. Examinations are set by the CAM (Communication Advertising and Marketing Education Foundations) and by the (newer) International Advertising Association (IAA).

1. CAM examinations

Entry requirements for CAM Certificate: 5 GCEs (including English language), two must be at A-level; *or* BTEC or SCOTBEC National award (see p. xvi); *or* London Chamber of Commerce and Industry Higher Stage Group Diploma in Marketing or Public Relations; *or*

International Advertising Association Basic Certificate in Advertising (see below); *or* 1 year in full-time employment in the communications business and 5 O-levels including English language. People who have been in the communications business for at least 3 years may be considered for the CAM Certificate with fewer than the above qualifications.

The Certificate covers marketing; advertising; public relations; media; research and behavioural studies. It normally takes about 2 years' study, usually at evening classes, occasionally by day-release.

Certificate holders can go on to take the CAM Diploma and specialize in a specific aspect of the communications business.

Partial or even total exemption from the Certificate stage is granted to holders of relevant BTEC awards (see p. xvi), or degrees in Business Studies or Communication Studies, Diploma in Marketing or Management Studies and post-graduate degree in Business Administration.

2. International Advertising Association's Certificates, Advanced Certificates and Diplomas

These qualifications are fairly new. There is some overlap with the CAM awards (and CAM is responsible for administering the IAA education in this country). The basic difference is that the IAA, as the title implies, takes a global view of advertising and looks at various countries' approaches to communicating the advertising message to the public. IAA awards are, of course, recognized internationally – but they are still very new and may not in practice carry more weight with job-seekers abroad than the established CAM awards.

There are 3 awards:

(a) The IAA Basic Certificate. No entry requirements are laid down, but colleges may well set their own requirements before enrolling students. Students who do not have the CAM course entry qualifications can take the IAA Basic Certificate (by day-release, evening study or correspondence course), and *then* take the CAM Certificate (see above).

(b) The IAA Advanced Certificate. Study by day-release or evening study – details from CAM.

(c) The IAA Diploma in International Advertising launched in 1982. Students must have the IAA Basic Certificate plus 3 years' experience, *or* the CAM Diploma *or* the IAA Advanced Certificate, *or* be exempt from the above by virtue of having a relevant degree or similar qualifications, *or* have had a senior position in advertising and at least 7 years' work experience.

Qualifications are not obligatory in advertising, but their importance is increasing, and promotion is more likely with than without.

There are few in-service training schemes, but some agencies take several graduates (any discipline) each year; many advertisers have management training schemes which can lead to advertising jobs.

Secretaries occasionally progress to executive or copywriting positions; their chances are better with a small specialist agency (for example, a recruitment agency) or in an advertising department, but they are never great.

Personal attributes Business acumen; interest in social and economic trends; flair for salesmanship; communication skills; ability to work in a team; ability to stand criticism whether justified or not; ability to work under pressure; resilience; persistence.

For creative people: discipline; originality; strong feeling for uncomplicated images and 'messages'; willingness to produce the kind of words/artwork that are best for the campaign, whether artistically first-rate or not.

For research: objectivity; a logical, analytical brain.

Late start Little opportunity unless there has been previous relevant commercial experience.

Position of women Although the majority of advertisements are aimed at women, only about 1 in 5 account executives are women, and about 1 in 5 copywriters; women do best in research, and an increasing number of brand managers (see Marketing, p. 283) are women. Though the Women's Advertising Club keeps an eye on women's promotion, they have not been able to do much about unequal promotion at senior level. It is an area where discrimination is difficult to prove, as there is no career-structure; promotion does not depend on qualification and experience but on 'suitability' for any particular job.

Career-break: Prospects only reasonable for experienced researchers or for successful executives who have 'kept their hand in' with freelance work.

Further information CAM Foundation, Abford House, 15 Wilton Road, London SW1V 1NJ

Institute of Practitioners in Advertising, 44 Belgrave Square, London SW1X 8QS

IAA Education Secretariat, c/o CAM

Related careers *Management in Industry – Marketing – Public Relations – Retail Management*

Agriculture and Horticulture

PRACTICAL WORK: *Agriculture*: livestock – farm mechanic – general farm work; *Horticulture*: commercial horticulture – amenity horticulture

ADVISORY WORK, TEACHING, MANAGEMENT; RESEARCH; FRINGE SPECIALIZATIONS: conservation – forestry – agricultural engineering – fish farming – horticultural therapy

Entry qualifications Entry at all levels from no qualifications to degree.

The work Agriculture and horticulture cover a wide range of jobs. There is scope at all educational levels. Jobs range from work for the loner who chose agriculture for the peace of working on the land, or horticulture for its scope for beautifying the urban environment, to work for people primarily interested in using the latest technologies to improve the world's food crops, or who want to work with animals. To be commercially viable, units are increasing in size, and mechanization and use of management techniques and specialization within both agriculture and horticulture are now usual. All levels of work need greater technical knowledge than previously.

Practical Work

(Usual qualifications: Apprenticeship or Craft training, National Certificate or BTEC National Diploma.)

Agriculture

1. Work with Livestock

(a) *Beef Cattle*: Work varies according to size and type of farm. Some farms rear calves and feed some mature animals; others fatten cattle through to slaughter.

(b) *Dairy Herd*: A 50-cow herd can be worth £50,000, so this is highly responsible work. Work involves rearing, feeding, milking and following strict hygiene maintenance routines.

(c) *Pigs*: Some farms breed pigs for sale; others buy young pigs and fatten them for sale as bacon or pork; yet others both breed and fatten.

Extent of automation varies: on some pig farms feeding and cleaning of pens is mechanized, on others it is not.
(d) *Poultry*: Highly specialized: holdings concentrate either entirely on egg production, or on hatching – often in fully automatic giant incubators where thousands of chicks are hatched at the same time; or on rearing table birds, mainly broilers, which are chicks fed scientifically specified diets to reach exact weights within a defined period. Some poultry units resemble a cross between a laboratory and a modern factory, with indoor, clean work. There are few farms where looking after poultry means feeding birds in the farmyard.
(e) *Shepherd*: Hill farms usually concentrate on large numbers of sheep: on lowland farms sheep may form part of a unit and shepherds spend a lot of their time helping with other farmwork. Shepherds work with (and may train) dogs.

On the whole the larger and/or more mechanized the farm, the greater the degree of specialization. Individuals need not stick to one specialization throughout their career, though some prefer to do so. Livestock workers are expected to drive tractors.

2. Farm Mechanic
All farmworkers must be able to cope with running repairs; many arable units which use machinery worth thousands of pounds employ farm mechanics who are in charge of machinery maintenance, repairs and adaptation of all types of mechanical gadgets. On large units there may be several mechanics; usually there is only one.

3. General Farm Work
People who do not want to specialize and take responsibility for animals or machinery can carry out general duties. They may drive tractors, operate machinery, help with livestock, repair buildings, clear ditches, etc. The range of jobs depends on the type and size of farm, as do working conditions. Some workers live in the farmhouse, others in digs in the village. Some are near towns or Young Farmers' Clubs; others may be isolated. On large farms there will be colleagues; on small farms there may be only one young worker. Hours are generally long and irregular, especially on small farms where there are not sufficient staff to work a rota system, and where there are no holidays during the summer months. Although all farmworkers are on their own for some of the time, only hill farm shepherds are alone all day.

Horticulture

This can be divided into *Commercial Horticulture* and *Amenity Horticulture*. Horticulturalists may work in tiny nurseries or large commercial establishments; as the only employee or as one of a large staff; on the outskirts of a town, or in the depths of the country. Hours are sometimes irregular, and it is usually impossible to take a holiday in the summer. The former is much more competitive and staff often work under pressure to meet deadlines (e.g. flowers for Mother's Day) or to beat the weather. They also have to try accurately to anticipate demand, whether for cut flowers or cucumbers.

Commercial Horticulture

(a) *Market gardens*: Vegetables, salad crops, tomatoes and flowers are grown. Market gardens are 'cultivated intensively', which means the land is used to grow more than one crop a year. This makes the work varied. Harvesting, planting and ploughing are increasingly mechanized, but delicate tasks like thinning out and disbudding are normally done by hand. Grading, washing and packing may all be done by hand, or may be mechanized.

(b) *Nurseries*: Some grow a variety of herbaceous and other plants, ornamental trees, shrubs, bushes, fruit trees, etc.; others specialize in one or two. Nursery workers learn propagation (increasing plants by collecting and sowing seed, grafting, taking cuttings); soil preparation; pest and disease control; they dig up plants and pack them for dispatch. They may also sell produce and advise customers on how to look after it.

(c) *Glasshouses*: These form part of most nurseries and market gardens, for the production of out-of-season and delicate plants; some concerns consist almost entirely of glasshouses. The work is usually the least hard physically. Those in charge of a glasshouse must understand ventilation, temperature control, etc.

(d) *Fruit Farms*: Work consists of pruning, grafting, cultivation and spraying of trees. In orchards, the autumn and most of the winter is spent grading and packing. (Poultry-keeping may be done as a sideline.)

Experienced horticultural workers can become plantation assistants on fruit research stations; quality inspectors and crop estimators for canning and quick-freezing stations run by large commercial firms.

Garden Contractors

The work may overlap with landscape architecture (see p. 237). It may include design and construction of private gardens; planting; maintaining gardens on contract. Owing to weather conditions jobs are more plentiful in summer, when firms may take on jobbing gardeners (who may also work for themselves at other times). These days contractors sometimes work in amenity horticulture on mowing or tree surgery contracts with local parks.

Garden Centres
This is a combination of selling, advising, growing. Staff answer customers' queries and they grow the produce they sell. Garden centres are busiest at weekeneds. They are in town and on the outskirts.

Amenity Horticulture
This is a relatively new specialization. Its purpose is to provide and maintain pleasant open-air environments for townspeople to relax in: parks in towns; country parks; picnic areas off motorways; National Trust properties; nature trails. Work involves maintenance of ornamental gardens and, often, nursery work. It may also include maintenance of bowling greens, golf courses, tennis courts, etc. Staff have to cope with sometimes conflicting demands of the gardening programme and public events held in the park. A park manager may spend a large proportion of time on such non-horticultural activities as paperwork and rubbish disposal. Current reductions in staffing levels often affect types of planting, e.g. bedding plants may give way to grass and shrubs. Amenity gardeners are usually employed by public authorities rather than by commercial enterprises. The work involves contact with the public and often helping with recreational activities, such as sitting at cash-desks for open-air concerts, usher and patrol duty, although in some parks these duties are carried out by keepers with no horticultural training (see also Diploma in Management Studies, Recreation Management, **Training**, p. 411). There is more of a career-structure (and day-release) in this type of horticulture than in commercial concerns.

Prospects In horticulture prospects are better than in agriculture where numbers of full-time workers have been steadily falling; poultry work, especially the broiler industry, offers the best opportunities. Setting up on one's own, whether in market gardening or poultry farming, demands considerable capital and experience.

Pay: Low to medium (see p. xxiii).

Advisory Work, Teaching and Management

Entry qualifications Higher National Diploma or degree (see below).

The work

Advisory Work

The Agricultural Development and Advisory Service (includes horticulture) and commercial firms employ specialist advisers who visit individual growers and farmers to help them with production problems. Advisers also lecture to allotment societies, farmers' clubs, women's organizations and schools. The work combines meeting people with work in the country – an unusual combination.

Horticultural specialists advise, for example, new and inexperienced growers on where to plant what. They may diagnose plant disease and type of soil and advise on marketing questions.

Poultry specialists discuss the best type of breed for farmers' individual purposes, advise on feeding and housing problems, and help farmers keep abreast of developments in poultry technology.

Livestock and Dairy specialists advise on such matters as grass production, silage, making the proper use and choice of feeding stuffs and balancing rations, and on new milking equipment. Dairy specialists can also become *milk officers*, taking samples of milk at farms for laboratory testing. Milk Marketing Boards employ staff to inspect producers' herds, milk and milking parlours.

Teaching

Work is in secondary schools (mainly in rural areas), in technical and agricultural colleges, and as Rural Economy Instructors travelling round a county lecturing to women's organizations, allotment societies, etc. The work in schools may be combined with running school gardens, or with teaching other subjects. Teachers sometimes teach part-time in several schools. Subjects include processing farm produce; farmhouse budgeting; dairying and poultry-keeping; cheese-making; horticultural practice; environmental studies. Not all subjects would be taught to the same form or even in the same school; the rural studies teacher's work is much wider in scope than it used to be.

Management

Practical work shades into management. The first step on the management ladder may be supervising several dairy-herd workers or being in charge of quality control of the cut-flowers section in a nursery.

As farms – and horticultural units – are growing in size, the range *but not the number* of management jobs is increasing. At the top of the ladder are *farm managers*, who are responsible for the day-to-day running of the farm, control of staff, marketing of produce, record-keeping, farm accounts, dealing with suppliers. Work, and level of responsibility, vary according to type (privately owned or belonging to food manufacturers and other commercial concerns) and size of farm.

A small but growing number of farmers now use microcomputers to help monitor individual cows' milk yields and fertility cycles, deal with accounts and in other ways help plan the farming programme.

On small and medium-sized farms, managers may also be practical farmers and help out in whatever section help is needed; in other jobs, the work is entirely administrative, though the 'office' may be makeshift. On larger farms, *farm secretaries* (see p. 454) may be employed.

Prospects 1. *Advisers*: good only for those with good qualifications who are willing to move round the country.
2. *Teachers*: Some form of 'rural studies' is now taught in about half the country's schools. The work is ideal for those who like teaching (see p. 520) and who want to do work which is connected with the country, if not entirely a country job.
3. *Management*: Jobs are very difficult to get especially for those without a farming background – there is very stiff competition.

Abroad: Some opportunities in developing countries; amenity horticulturalists may be able to work in EEC countries; agricultural engineers in developing countries.

Pay: Low to medium (see p. xxiii).

Personal attributes *Practical work*: Attention to detail; reliability; good powers of observation; ability to work without supervision; commonsense; adaptability; manual dexterity; willing to work long and irregular hours.
Advisers: Very much the same as for practical work because practical work has to be done during training: ability to get on well with all kinds of people and to convey practical and factual information clearly; diplomacy when attempting to persuade growers to try new methods.
Teachers: Much as for advisers, with, of course, an interest in children. See also personal attributes for teachers, p. 527.
Managers: Ability to recruit and cope with permanent and seasonal labour; ability to take decisions, knowing that these are subject to the vagaries of nature; enjoyment of responsibility.

Research

Entry qualifications Degree.

The work Research is usually concerned with a particular aspect of crop production or of animal husbandry. Work may be largely or entirely theoretical, involving study of scientific journals and papers as well as collaboration with scientists from other disciplines; it usually involves experimental work in the laboratory and may involve practical work observing animal behaviour, plant growth, effects of climatic conditions, etc. (see also Research and Development, p. 428).

In horticulture most of the work is connected with pest control, plant diseases, soil chemistry, cultivation methods, crop suitability for canning and freezing.

In the poultry and dairy industries the main fields of research are genetics, biochemistry, nutrition, stock management, and breeding principles and methods.

In the poultry industry and in horticulture there is research into taste preservation after freezing and into producing the right kind of product for processing. Researchers work closely with technologists in food processing (see Food Science and Technology, p. 447).

Researchers work for research establishments, botanical gardens, in industry, in the Civil Service Science Group.

Training

Training patterns can be adjusted to fit individual requirements. It is possible (though it takes a long time) to start without any GCEs and eventually get a degree. The main types of course for those with fewer than 4 O-levels or CSEs are:

1. The Agricultural Training Board's or similar *Local Government Training Board (Amenity Horticulture) Apprenticeship Schemes*.

Three years' supervised practical training in one branch (either horticulture or agriculture). These schemes normally include day- or block-release and may also include a 1-year full-time certificate course (see below). This type of training leads to a Craftsman's Certificate and possibly to City and Guilds Certificates or, if the 1-year full-time course is included, to the National Certificate in Agriculture or Horticulture. There is no need to decide on any specialization within either agriculture or horticulture before starting initial training.

2. *New Craft Training Scheme*. This is a 2–3-year training agreement with a farmer, but no time limit is fixed. Trainees are able to take the same qualifying tests as apprentices do, but can choose whether or not to attend college.

NB: The majority of school leaver entrants will be recruited onto the standard YTS scheme for the industry. This will count as the first year of an apprenticeship.

3. Full-time or sandwich courses at Colleges of Agriculture.

(a) *National Certificate courses*: Normally 1 year full-time.

Entry requirements: At least 1 year's practical work on farm or holding (which may have been part of the apprenticeship scheme); and evidence of having studied English, maths and a science (O-level or CSE passes are not essential; but college places are often scarce: GCEs or CSEs help to get a place).

Most courses are in general agriculture or in general horticulture, but a few are specialized, for example in poultry husbandry, in amenity horticulture and in commercial horticulture. On the whole, specialization starts *after* the general course: in 'supplementary' courses, for example, in dairy husbandry, grassland farming, glasshouse production, etc.

(b) From 1.10.1983 the administration of diploma courses has been taken over by BTEC. The former OND and HND courses have been re-named BTEC National and BTEC Higher National Diplomas.
BTEC National Diploma Courses: 2 years full-time or 3 years sandwich.
Entry requirements: 4 O-levels, including 1 science, and 1 year's practical work (or National Certificate credit standard). Courses are available in several specializations and in general horticulture and general agriculture.

These lead to 'technician' level and eventually to supervisory and, with further training and/or experience, possibly to management level.

(c) *College awards*: A variety of specialized (varied length) courses, usually for post-Diploma students or those with Certificates with credit. These courses are useful for students who during training decide on a specialization they had not previously thought of.

(d) *Amenity horticulturalists* may take further training in *recreation management* (and manage sports centres, etc., see p. 410).

(e) *BTEC Higher National Diploma*: 3 years sandwich.
Entry requirements: At least one science A-level with at least 3 O-levels normally including maths and an English subject and preferably a science, or a good BTEC National Diploma, Agriculture or Sciences. Candidates must normally have had a year's practical experience.

BTEC Higher National courses are concerned with the managerial, scientific and technological aspects of agriculture and horticulture; they are intended for people who will go into management or advisory work (in industry: ADAS now takes only graduates). Courses are available in amenity horticulture, commercial horticulture, general agriculture, agricultural or horticultural marketing/business administration, poultry husbandry, dairy technology. Further specializations may be introduced.

Post-diploma courses are also available, mainly in new technologies, in management and farm organization. These courses may be taken after some time at work.

4. Degrees: 3 or 4 years.
Entry requirements: 2, or more often 3, A-levels, including at least 1,

usually 2, sciences, and 3 O-levels, or good BTEC National Diploma Agriculture or Sciences, and 1 year's practical work.

Degree subjects, apart from general agricultural and horticultural sciences, include *forest science*; *agricultural engineering*; *agricultural economics* and *agricultural business management*. Little actual farm work is included in degree courses, which are intended for future advisers, researchers, teachers or managers.

5. Royal Horticultural Society's training scheme at Wisley. 2-year full-time, mainly intended for those with fewer than 4 O-levels.

6. Kew Diploma. 3-year full-time. Entry with either 4 O-levels, including maths and science, plus 1 A-level (preferably botany) plus minimum two years' work experience in horticulture, or some horticultural qualification, e.g. City and Guilds or a BTEC Diploma. A small number accepted straight from 6th form.

Fringe Specializations

Conservation

Concerned with the preservation of the country's plant and animal life.

Conservationists research into and try to balance the long-term effects of modern aids to farming such as pesticides, and of changes in the use of land. The removal of a hedge – for more efficient ploughing, for example – may destroy shelter for certain animals which then disappear from the area but had previously been useful in keeping down other harmful animals. Conservation takes in *ecology*, which is the study of how plants as well as animals exist together and act and react upon one another in their natural surroundings, and what happens when the natural balance is disturbed through intervention by man in order to use land and resources for more immediately efficient purposes.

The greatest demand is for graduates with degrees in horticulture, botany, zoology or geography. Conservationists work mainly for research organizations, specially the Natural Environment Research Council (see Science, p. 435).

Forestry

This is a small specialization. The Forestry Commission and, increasingly, large companies and private owners' cooperatives, employ *forestry officers* who plan afforestation programmes and are responsible for the management of groups of forests. Though an administrative job, it also involves driving and walking through forests. It includes responsibility for fire protection; wildlife protection; disease identification and control; recreation-area planning and control; possibly marketing management (the production of home-grown timber is increasing). *Foresters* (supervisors) are responsible for the day-to-day management of individual forests. They have more direct contact with the general public – they are often asked by children and their teachers about plant- and wildlife.

Forestry Officers must be graduates in forestry. Foresters may now take one of two Ordinary National Diplomas in Forestry (one is administered by BTEC). There is also a 2-year basic training for forest workers leading to City and Guilds qualification.

Forest work usually involves living in or near the forest all the year round; being on one's own for days on end and yet being good at dealing with the general public.

Agricultural Engineering

Agricultural engineers apply engineering principles to food production. As the world's non-renewable and slowly-renewable resources are being rapidly used up, it is essential to make the most efficient use of natural resources. This involves recycling processes; exploring and using new sources of energy and, above all, incorporating new technologies in the design, manufacture and maintenance of agricultural equipment. Agricultural engineers may be involved in 'environmental control' – providing the right housing for livestock; in product planning; mechanizing procedures; crop storage and processing. The work is related to food technology (see p. 447) and professional engineering (p. 168). There is ample scope for work abroad, especially in developing countries.

Training Either a BTEC HND or a first degree in agricultural engineering (it is possible to start without A-level maths as long as students had good O-level grades and take a special maths course during their first degree course year); or BTEC HND or degree in related subjects (geography; sciences; agriculture), followed by 1- or 2-year post-graduate courses at Silsoe College (formerly the National College of Agricultural Engineering) which is part of the Cranfield Institute of Technology.

Fish Farming

Breeding and rearing fish for food or sport. Most fish farms (there are approximately 400) are one- or two-person businesses, but there are some large-scale fish farms. Like all animal husbandry, this is usually a 7-day-a-week job and involves unsocial working hours. There is no

prescribed training and entry; the usual ways into this new and growing industry are:
1. For day-to-day management: 1-year full-time gamekeeping and fishery management course. People with practical farming experience are given preference for course places.
2. For unit-managers, forewomen, own-business fish farmers: 2-year full-time Diploma in Fishery Management. Minimum age 17; 4 O-levels, preferably including chemistry, and 12 months' practical fishery experience required.
3. For research and management: degree in biological science or agriculture, usually followed by post-graduate course.

Details from Institute of Fisheries Management, 36 Springfield Road, Wallington, Surrey; and Ministry of Agriculture, Fisheries and Food, Whitehall Place, London SW1.

Late start On the whole this is not advisable, as trainee vacancies tend to go to young applicants. However, 1-year courses for horticultural Certificates are available under TOPS (see p. xlvi).

Position of women Women form just over a quarter of the labour force. Of these a large proportion are unskilled farm workers, but very few are apprentices or on full-time courses. Women are still found mainly in the traditional areas of horticulture, poultry and other livestock, but more now work on arable farms where mechanization has lessened the need for brute strength. Farm management is an almost totally male preserve: farmers tend to be traditional in outlook, and while there are more male applicants than jobs women are unlikely to get farm management posts. Farmers genuinely believe that women would not be able to help with the tough work, and managers, at least on small and medium-sized farms, do occasionally help with whatever needs doing. Up to now, very few women have taken the long training required for management, which is necessary to convince farmers that they are able to cope with all the work. Women tend not to apply for forestry work, mainly because of the need to live in often isolated areas and to be able to do physically hard work, although some are employed, e.g. by the Forestry Commission. In amenity and commercial horticulture, and especially in agricultural engineering, they have equal opportunities of getting top jobs.

Career-break: There should be no problem for those who progressed into management level jobs before the break.

Part-time: Teaching is virtually the only job in agriculture and horticulture in which there is any opportunity for part-time work. Casual (i.e. short-term) work is sometimes available in horticulture.

Further information

Agricultural Training Board (includes horticulture), Bourne House, 32–34 Beckenham Road, Beckenham, Kent, BR3 4PB
Women's Farm and Garden Association, c/o Lilac Cottage, Birch Green, Colchester, Essex, CO2 0NH
Royal Botanic Gardens, Kew, Richmond, Surrey TW9 3AB
Royal Horticultural Society's Garden, Wisley, Woking, Surrey GU23 6QB
Forestry courses: Cumbria College, Newton Rigg, Penrith, Cumbria CA11 0AH

Related careers

Animal Nursing Auxiliary – Landscape Architecture – Science Technician – Scientist – Veterinary Surgeon

---

Horticultural Therapy

This covers the use of horticulture and agriculture in the treatment, education and recreation of people suffering from handicaps or other disabilities. Most therapists work in hospitals, residential homes or training centres. There is as yet no career structure and much of the work is carried out by volunteers with a horticultural training.

Further information

Horticultural Therapy, Goulds Ground, Vallis Way, Frome, Somerset BA11 3DW

Animals

Animal nursing auxiliary – dogs – horses – veterinary surgeon (or veterinarian) – zoo keeper

Animal Nursing Auxiliary

Entry qualifications 4 O-levels, including English language and a physical or biological science or mathematics.

The work Animal nursing auxiliaries assist veterinary surgeons in their surgery and occasionally on visits. They hold and pacify animals during examination and treatment; in the surgery they sterilize and look after instruments. They collect and analyse specimens, prepare medicines, and take out stings and stitches. Auxiliaries also clear up after un-housetrained animals and after operations; they may assist in the reception of patients. They work in 'small-animal' practices, i.e. those dealing with domestic animals, and for the RSPCA and other animal welfare and research organizations.

The hours are usually long and irregular. Animals have to be cared for at weekends which may mean going to work on Saturday and Sunday, perhaps just to feed them.

Some veterinary surgeons' practices employ only one auxiliary, so she may be rather isolated from her contemporaries and have little companionship. Most of the working day will be spent with her employer.

Prospects Poor on the whole, but once trained, auxiliaries have a much better chance of congenial work than untrained girls. There is no career ladder though – no promotion prospects.

Pay: Low (see p. xxiii).

Training Minimum age for enrolment as trainee is 17; practical work may start earlier.

Training is on-the-job, plus private study. There are some day- or block-release courses.

A potential trainee must first find a job with a veterinary practice or hospital approved by the RCVS as a training centre and must then enrol with the RCVS as a trainee. The syllabus covers anatomy and physiology, hygiene and feeding, first-aid, side-room techniques (analysing specimens and preparing slides), and the theory and practice of breeding and nursing. Finals may be taken after at least 2 years' traineeship.

Trainee vacancies are sometimes advertised in the *Veterinary Record*, and prospective trainees may themselves advertise for jobs. Letters to local veterinary surgeons and animal research and welfare societies may also bring results; and the RCVS will provide a list of those veterinary practices and centres which are approved as training centres.

Personal attributes A love of animals and a scientific interest in their development, behaviour, and welfare; lack of squeamishness; a willingness to take orders, and yet to act independently when necessary; readiness to work well both alone and with others; a sure, firm, but gentle grip; patience.

Late start Difficult to find training vacancies as surplus of young applicants who are satisfied with very low wages. Ability to type and drive is helpful.

Position of women This is still a female preserve: out of 1,845 ANAs, 7 are male; out of 791 students, 5 are male.

Career-break: This is a young woman's job.

Part-time: No part-time training, a few part-time jobs.

Further information *Animal Nursing Auxiliaries Guide*, price £1.25 plus letter postage from Royal College of Veterinary Surgeons, 32 Belgrave Square, London SW1X 8QP

Related careers *Animal Technician, p. 445 – Dogs – Horses – Veterinary Surgeon*

Dogs

Entry qualifications None required.

The work There are two kinds of work with dogs: (1) breeding, boarding, greyhound training, and quarantine kennels (licensed by the Ministry of Agriculture, Fisheries, and Food); (2) dog beauty parlours.

Kennels

The work Work is always hard and usually dirty. The kennel maid's day starts at 8 a.m. and usually ends at 5 p.m. but she must be prepared to stay up all night, for example when puppies are about to be born. Regular time off is difficult to arrange except in large establishments; someone is always needed to feed the animals. Quarantine and greyhound kennels are usually run on more professional lines than small private boarding and breeding kennels, with more regular working hours.

A kennel maid cleans kennels, grooms the dogs, and deals with minor ailments. Dogs who are really ill are looked after by full-time attendants (see Animal Nursing Auxiliary, p. 36). In breeding kennels, she trains puppies and learns all about preparing for dog shows. In greyhound kennels, exercising the dogs is an important part of the work.

Prospects There are far more applicants than jobs. Poor ratio of managers to kennel maids.

Considerable capital and experience are needed to set up boarding kennels. A good deal of land is required for exercise yards. Breeding pedigree dogs must be done on a big scale to be really profitable.

Pay: Very low (see p. xxiii).

Training Two methods:

(a) 6–12 months as working pupil in a kennel. Pupils learn grooming, handling, training, stripping, clipping, diagnosis of sickness symptoms; first-aid; nutrition; breeding principles. Courses are usually residential and cost around £10 to £60 per week. Teaching kennels must be chosen with great care – some teach little, and use pupils as cheap labour.

There are no set courses or examinations.

(b) On-the-job. Starting as a junior in good kennels can lead to just as good jobs in the future, if the junior does some private reading, and asks questions of senior staff.

Personal attributes An unsentimental affection for dogs; a placid but firm manner; patience.

Dog Beauty Parlour

The work Pet shops and dog beauty parlours (sometimes attached to department stores) employ girls to clip, groom, and strip poodles and other breeds. Usual shop working hours, with occasional weekend duties.

Prospects Fair only for the really good trimmer and clipper. Setting up on one's own requires great business sense and knowledge, and capital.

Pay: Very low to high (see p. xxiii).

Training Two methods:

(a) 6–12 months as working pupil in breeding kennels specializing in show animals (poodles usually). Pupils learn general dog care as well as shampooing, handling scissors and electric clippers, and learning how and when to give various types of trim (details as in **Training** (a) under Kennels).

(b) On-the-job, 2–3 years as junior. Leads to just as good a job eventually.

Personal attributes Patience and firmness; dexterity; imagination to show off the animal's best points and hide its weaker ones; a good appearance and a pleasing manner; ability to deal with dogs' owners; for the better paid jobs, organizing ability.

Late start No.

Position of women This is almost all female work; kennels are also usually run and owned by women; but dog beauty parlours (more profitable) are sometimes run and/or managed by men.

Like all jobs with animals (except veterinary surgeon) this is largely a young woman's job: only those with management experience are likely to be able to return after *Career-break*.

Part-time: No.

Further information Jobs and courses advertised in *Dog World* and *Our Dogs*.

Horses

(Riding instructor; groom; stable manager)

Entry qualifications 4 O-levels, including an English subject but requirements waived for entrants over 20.

The work Physically hard, outdoors in all weathers, and varied depending on the type of stables, i.e. looking after hunters in the winter and children's ponies in the summer. Thus hours are often long, including weekends, especially during the summer (sometimes up to 14 hours a day).

Accommodation varies, 2 or 3 working pupils or grooms may have to share a room. Grooms usually live in (unless their home is near the stables) because their working day may start at 6 a.m. Instructors are not usually obliged to do so.

Riding Instructor

The work She teaches children and adults, both in private lessons and in classes, and accompanies riders who hire horses by the hour. She starts early and may finish late, because many pupils come before or after their work. She may also train horses and ponies, and she usually has to spend some time looking after the horses, and cleaning tack and stables. Senior instructors are also responsible for general stable management.

Prospects Good, but although opportunities are increasing, there are still more candidates than good jobs. Setting up on one's own requires considerable capital, experience, and business knowledge. Good instructors are wanted frequently for work in equestrian training centres, and quite a few work on travel organizations' pony-trekking holidays (summer only).

Pay: Low to medium (see p. xxiii).

Training Three methods of training for the British Horse Society's Assistant Instructor's, Intermediate Instructor's and Instructor's Certificates:

(a) *At a fee-charging school*

Courses last about 3 to 15 months; fees vary enormously.

(b) *As working pupil*

Courses last normally 1 year and usually consist of 9 months' stable routine and management: i.e. mucking-out, feeding, and watering, riding exercise, and some instruction; and a 3-month concentrated course of instruction while still doing light stable duties. Working pupils may receive pocket money but usually pay for their board and lodging (around £10–£50 a week). After at least a further year's work and at a minimum age of 22, they can take the BHS Instructor's Certificate.

(c) At a College of Further Education where 1- or 2-year courses include business and other subjects.

NOTE: Some establishments call themselves schools but are stables which hire out horses. They tend to use working 'pupils' as cheap labour. Pupils should choose a school which is 'Approved' by the

British Horse Society, and is a member of the Association of British Riding Schools.

Personal attributes Authority; physical agility; the ability to express oneself clearly; patience; a liking for children; not too much ambition.

Groom/Stable Manager

The work A groom works in and may eventually manage hunt, racing and show jumping stables, private stables, livery stables (which look after horses for private owners), riding schools, or stables with horses for hire, or at a stud.

She cleans stables; looks after the well-being of the horses – feeds them, and watches out for and reports any symptoms which make her suspect that a horse is sick; and keeps the saddle and the rest of the tack in perfect condition.

At a horse or pony stud, the groom also looks after the brood mares and cares for their foals. She may also break in ponies.

Prospects Though opportunities are increasing, there still are far more candidates than good jobs. Plum jobs, such as travelling with show horses, are very rare indeed.

Pay: Low (see p. xxiii).

Training Training is usually as a working pupil, and lasts from around 6 months to over 1 year. Students usually first take the BHS Assistant Instructor's Examination, or the Certificate of Horsemastership Examination. At age 22 they would then go on to take the BHS Stable Management Certificate.

There is also a 1-year course in *Horse Management* at the Warwickshire College of Agriculture. Candidates must have had one year's practical experience with horses. The course is intended mainly for people who hope to manage studs or large stables or riding schools. The syllabus covers basic principles of planning a stud as well as looking after the animals' welfare. There are options in either teaching riding and in office practice for entrants who have 4 O-levels.

Personal attributes Physical stamina; liking for being out of doors in all weathers; indifference to getting dirty; willingness to work irregular hours, often by oneself.

Position of women About 10 times as many women as men are instructors, but the majority of grooms and the vast majority of stable managers are men. This is largely a young woman's field, as far as jobs are concerned, but quite a few women own their own riding schools or stables.

Part-time: There may be some part-time work for riding instructors at local riding establishments; payment by the hour is anything from £3 to £10.

Further information

British Horse Society, The British Equestrian Centre, Kenilworth, Warwickshire CV8 2LR

Related careers

Agriculture and Horticulture – Animal Nursing Auxiliary – Animal Technician, p. 445 – Dogs – Sport – Veterinary Surgeon

Veterinary Surgeon/Veterinarian

(General practice; official appointments; commercial organizations; teaching)

Entry qualifications

3 good science A-levels chosen from chemistry, physics, biology and maths. The subject not offered at A-level to be offered among the 6 O-levels usually required. Entry to veterinary courses is the most competitive of all UCCA courses. Individual veterinary school requirements vary, but all ask for very high grades. Experience of work with animals is also essential.

The work

General Practice (including work for animal welfare)

Work includes carrying out operations in the surgery as well as visiting patients in their owners' homes. In urban practices vets are concerned with small animals; in country practices with small as well as with farm animals.

Veterinary surgeons are expected to provide a 24-hour service, but most practices are organized so as to provide reasonable time off, and holidays.

It is usual to start as an assistant in an established practice and later either become a partner or set up on one's own (which makes time off more difficult to arrange).

Official Appointments

Officers in the Animal Health Division of the Ministry of Agriculture, Fisheries and Food, and in the Agricultural Research Council cover a wide range of duties:

(a) *Field Service*: Practical experience elsewhere is essential for acceptance as Veterinary Officer.

The Ministry's Field Service Officers are stationed throughout the country, usually in county towns, and deal with the prevention and control of notifiable diseases of animals and poultry, the tuberculin testing of cattle, the inspection of animals on farms and in markets, and other duties in connection with government regulations and schemes for the maintenance and improvement of farm-animal health standards. The work involves a considerable amount of visiting farmers, markets, etc., and therefore dealing with people as well as with animals.

(b) *Research Officers* and *Scientific Officers* are employed by the Ministry's Central Veterinary Laboratory as well as by the Agricultural Research Council. Officers are concerned with causes, treatment, and prevention of animal diseases; with the development, production, and uses of biological products for the diagnosis of such diseases, and for immunization against them; and with the effects of modern agricultural practice on animal health and production. Immediate practical farming problems as well as long-term applied and fundamental research projects are dealt with.

(c) *Officers in the Veterinary Investigation Service* of the Ministry carry out laboratory tests for the diagnosis of disease on carcasses and organs from cattle, sheep, pigs, and poultry submitted to Veterinary Investigation Centres by veterinary surgeons in practice all over the country. The Veterinary Investigation Service also takes part in field investigations into outbreaks of disease among farm animals in consultation with local veterinary surgeons in general practice, and advises on the most suitable treatment.

Commercial Organizations

Work with manufacturers of agricultural products, feeding stuffs, fertilizers, pharmaceutical products, etc., is similar to that of research officers in the Scientific Civil Service.

Teaching

At universities; usually combined with research work.

Prospects *General practice*: Good.
Official appointments: Limited.
Commercial organizations: Fair.
Universities: Poor.
Abroad: With post-graduate experience some openings on short-term contracts on schemes of technical assistance in developing countries.

Pay: High (see p. xxiii).

Training

Degree courses usually last 5 years and are divided into *pre-clinical* (anatomy, physiology, biochemistry, pharmacology) and *clinical* (animal husbandry, medicine and surgery, veterinary public health).

During training, usually in their vacations, students must spend at least 6 months with a veterinary surgeon, to gain practical experience.

In some veterinary schools training is shortened by one year for science graduates.

Personal attributes

Scientific interest in animals and their behaviour and development, rather than sentimental fondness for pets; powers of observation; a firm hand; the ability to inspire confidence in animals (i.e. total absence of nervousness) and in their owners; self-reliance and adaptability; indifference to occasional physically disagreeable conditions of work.

For some posts: organizing ability and powers of leadership; for others, ability to work as one of a team.

Late start

As there is such stiff competition for degree course places, it is unlikely that anyone over 30 would be accepted, though there is no official upper age limit.

Position of women

15% of registered (practising) veterinary surgeons are women, and about 39% of students. In the past it was believed that veterinary departments, like medical schools, operated (unofficial) quota systems, but now the proportion of women students *admitted* is slightly higher than that of applicants, compared with men. Women who get as far as filling in UCCA forms are known to be more highly motivated than men: they know the hard physical work they will have to undertake. Even if they eventually set up an urban practice, dealing mainly with pets, they have to deal with all kinds of animals and diseases during training.

Career-break: May present problems. Veterinary practice changes rapidly: young graduates are preferred to 'returners'.

Part-time: Some opportunities as assistant in general practice; very occasionally in research; by running small practice from home; or as Temporary Veterinary Inspector with Ministry of Agriculture, Fisheries and Food.

Further information

Royal College of Veterinary Surgeons, 32 Belgrave Square, London SW1X 8QP

British Veterinary Association, 7 Mansfield Street, London W1

Civil Service Commission, Alencon Link, Basingstoke, Hampshire

Agricultural Research Council, Cunard Building, 160 Great Portland Street, London W1

Related careers *Agriculture and Horticulture – Animal Nursing Auxiliary – Animal Technician (p. 445) – Dogs – Environmental Health Officer – Horses – Medicine – Science (Biological, p. 433)*

Keepers in Zoos and Safari Parks

No specific entry qualifications; no career structure. Keepers are recruited locally as temporary/weekend helpers in the first place, so that they themselves and employers can assess their suitability for the job. There are always far more applicants than vacancies even though many helpers change their minds after a few weeks' work when they find out that they cannot look after the type of animals they want to look after, the long hours they want to work and the dismal promotion prospects.

Only London and Whipsnade Zoos run a training scheme in conjunction with a Further Education college; a small proportion of students who pass the Zoo's examination become Senior Keepers.

Details from individual zoos and safari parks.

See also *Animal Technician* in *Science Technician*, p. 445.

Archaeology

Entry qualifications 2, often 3, A-levels and 3 O-levels. Maths or a science and modern language at O-level normally required.
For classical archaeology, Latin or Greek at O- or A-level.
For conservation, chemistry at A-level.

The work Excavation work is only one aspect of this science of gaining knowledge of the past from the study of ancient objects. Though archaeologists need a broad knowledge of the whole field they may specialize in one geographical area. For example there is Norse, Ango-Saxon, and classical archaeology. Most archaeologists also specialize in particular objects of study, for example coins, weapons, sculpture, or deciphering inscriptions. Excavation technique is another, highly technical, specialization.

Many archaeologists work in museums (see Museums, p. 310). Others work for the Ancient Monuments division of the Department of the Environment, the Royal Commission on Historical Monuments, the archaeological section of the Ordnance Survey, a few for country and regional units and local authorities.

Because of new technologies being used in excavation and in dating 'finds', two archaeological specializations have developed: *Environmental Archaeology*, concerned with scientific examination of remains and artifacts and with changes in the environment as they affect previous cultures; and *Archaeological Surveying* which combines *surveying* (see p. 504) with archaeology. Archaeological surveyors use sophisticated instruments to locate and plot sites and to draw up maps. Most archaeological surveyors took land surveying training (see p. 509) and then a post-graduate course in archaeology or the CBA's Diploma (see **Training** below). (A surveying qualification leaves rather more options open than an archaeology degree.)

Prospects Very limited. There are many more archaeology graduates than jobs.
Pay: Medium (see p. xxiii).

Training BA in archaeology, ancient history, anthropology, or classics with archaeology, or any honours degree followed by a 2-year archaeology diploma; or, with A-level chemistry, BSc in Conservation of Archaeological Materials.

The Council for British Archaeology (the professional organization) awards a Diploma in Archaeological Practice. The CBA does not arrange teaching – candidates, both amateurs and graduates, study for a number of certificates, on their own. There are no correspondence courses but a few local education authorities run suitable courses and so do some extra-mural and continuing education departments at universities. The Diploma is not an *academic* qualification, but it proves job applicants' commitment and knowledge to 'dig' directors and others choosing people for jobs in archaeology – so it is a useful vocational qualification.

Personal attributes Deep curiosity about the past; intellectual ability well above average; artistic sensibility; patience; manual dexterity (for handling delicate and valuable objects). For excavation, physical stamina.

Late start Advisable only for people who already have a relevant degree and/or hobby experience, and see **Prospects**.

Position of women About 20% of archaeologists are women, most of them working in museums. Women have reasonable chances of directing excavation work.

Career-break: Prospects for returners depend on previous experience.

Part-time: Probably more on a short-term project basis than regular part-time work.

Further information The Council for British Archaeology, 112 Kennington Road, London SE11 6RE

Related careers *Archivist – Museum Work*

Architecture

Architect – architectural technician

Architect

Entry qualifications 2 or 3 A-levels and 3 O-levels. Individual Schools of Architecture have widely differing requirements, ranging from *any* 2 A-levels, and maths merely as one of the 3 O-levels, to 3 specified mixed science/arts A-levels.

The work The challenge of architecture is to produce, within a given budget, an aesthetically pleasing design which will stand up to wear and tear and which is the kind of building in which people will want to live or work. Architects must fully understand traditional and new building methods and materials and appreciate their potentialities and limitations. But above all, they must understand and be interested in contemporary society and changing lifestyles, the community's expectations and needs, and social problems which may lead to loneliness, mugging and vandalism. The sociological aspect of architecture is much more important now than it was even a decade ago. The reason for that is that what were hailed as architectural successes when they were first put up – high-rise blocks and vast council-flat complexes – have turned out to be disasters in social terms. Architecture today requires a combination of artistic, technological and sociological expertise. Architects have always questioned householders, hospital staffs, teachers, office workers, etc. to find out what they 'expected' from a new building, and what they criticized in existing ones. But now, architects do much more systematic social research when they tackle a project. They listen to managers, workers, sociologists, social psychologists, social workers, etc. to ensure that future buildings, and complexes of buildings, 'work' more satisfactorily than many post-war creations have done. This, together with strict financial constraints, makes architecture a more demanding discipline than it has ever been. However, not all architects have to aim at being responsible for designing and implementing projects. Tasks range from converting houses into flats to designing hospitals or council houses or factory complexes. But basically, the method of working is the same, whatever the size of the project.

Architects receive instructions from their clients or employers on the type, function, capacity and rough cost of the building required.

Then they do their research – and at that stage they may question the social decisions on which the client based the brief.

When the type of the building has finally been decided upon, the design work begins. This starts with producing, perhaps jointly with colleagues, a sketch scheme of the floor plans, the elevations, and perspective drawings. Several such schemes may have to be produced before one is finally approved.

The next stage is to prepare contract documents, which will include detailed drawings and specifications, and estimates of cost. At this stage, if the scheme is a big one, consulting engineers (see p. 173) and quantity surveyors (see p. 506) may be appointed. Necessary planning consents must have been obtained from the local authority.

When the contract for the work has been awarded to a building contractor, the architect is in overall charge. She is responsible for certifying payment to contractors, and for inspecting the work in progress. She regularly visits the building site, issues instructions to the contractor's agent or foreman and discusses any difficulties with him. Site visits involve walking through mud and climbing scaffolding. The architect is normally also responsible for the choice or design of fittings and the interior design of the buildings she undertakes. (See Art and Design, p. 60.)

An architect can work in different *settings*: in private practice; in the architects' and planning departments of a local authority; with a public body such as a new-town corporation; with a ministry; or in the architect's department of a commercial firm large enough to have a continuous programme of building or maintenance work.

In private practice her client may be an individual, a commercial firm, a local authority or other public body. It is usual for private practices to specialize, but not exclusively, in houses, schools or offices, etc. In private practice architects normally work only on design and not, as in other categories, on design and maintenance.

In local authorities the architect works on a wide variety of buildings, such as one-family houses, blocks of flats, schools, swimming-baths and clinics. Usually she also collaborates with private architects employed by the authority for specific schemes.

For other public bodies such as nationalized boards or ministries, the architect's work is less varied and is largely confined to the organization's particular building concern: for example hospitals for the Department of Health and Social Security.

The same applies to an architect working for a commercial concern. Her work is confined to that organization's particular type of building: for example, hotels and restaurants for a large catering organization; shops for a merchandising group.

The majority of architects are salaried employees, but they may become junior partners and later principals in a firm, or set up on their own. But to start a firm requires a good deal of experience, capital and contacts.

Since 1982 architects are permitted, under RIBA rules, to become directors of building and development companies. They can now combine professional work with running their own business.

Prospects They fluctuate according to economic climate. Apart from joining architects' firms or departments, there is also limited scope in interior design studios, designing interiors of shops, hotels, aircraft, etc.

Abroad: Limited opportunities to set up in practice in the Commonwealth or to work (not set up in practice, though) in EEC countries.

Pay: Medium to very high (see p. xxiii).

Training The normal pattern of training is a 5-year full-time course, with 1 year of practical experience after the 3rd year and a second year of practical experience at the end of the course, making a minimum of 7 years. There are a few part-time (day-release) courses, but this method of training is not recommended: it takes even longer than the normal training and the failure rate among part-time students is higher than among full-time students. Subjects studied include history of architecture, design and construction, town planning, environmental science, some sociology, economics, traffic studies.

For interior designers, architectural training need only be up to RIBA Part I standard. It must be followed by a specialized art-school course (part- or full-time) and practical experience.

NOTES: (1) Architecture, Planning and Landscape Architecture are closely related disciplines. There are some courses which start with a combined studies year so that students can delay specialization until they know more about the whole field. But courses must be chosen with care: practising architects whether in private practice or public employment must be on the Register of the Architects Registration Council of the United Kingdom. Only 'recognized' courses lead to Registration. Up-to-date lists of 'recognized' courses are available from the RIBA (which 'recognizes' courses on behalf of the ARCUK) and from the ARCUK. Course titles can be misleading, for example 'Architectural Studies' may or may not be a 'recognized' course.

(2) For candidates who are not quite certain whether to commit themselves to a 7-year training it is useful to know that the first 3-year stage of training, on most courses, leads to an Honours degree in its own right, and therefore to all the 'graduate jobs' for which no particular discipline is specified.

Personal attributes A practical as well as creative mind; an interest in changing life-styles and social priorities; self-confidence to put over and justify new ideas; mathematical ability; some dexterity in drawing; the ability to deal with legal and financial questions; a reasonably authoritative personality; an aptitude for giving clear instructions and explanations; good health; good eyesight.

Late start There are special provisions for members of allied professions and people with degrees in related fields to apply to the RIBA Special Entry Panel and then to take whatever training may be deemed necessary before sitting the RIBA's own Examination. However, practical training and first jobs for people over about 35 are difficult to get.

Position of women 7% of registered architects and 30% of 1st-year students are women. Proportions have risen slowly in recent years. It seems that the image of architecture as being mainly concerned with building and technical matters generally keeps women from applying even to schools of architecture which do not require A-level maths. See **The work** for the sociologically based content of the job which is as suitable for women, however traditional in outlook, as for men.

At present, far fewer women than men are principals in private practice – most women remain assistant architects; in public service the vast majority remain in middle-level jobs. However, this may change as more women qualify.

Refresher training: No courses, but *ad hoc* arrangements for returners to work in architectural offices. Some returners take post-graduate courses and specialize in something like traffic planning, urban design, planning, etc.

Career-break: Opportunities for those who have kept up by way of reading journals, attending occasional lectures and seminars. Architects are strongly advised to 'keep their hand in' and do *some* work throughout the break, however sporadic.

Part-time: A fair proportion of women architects work part-time, virtually all of them in private practice. There is little opportunity in the public sector, but heads of departments agree that up to middle-level jobs it should be possible to organize job-sharing and other part-time schemes.

Further information The Director (Education and Practice), Royal Institute of British Architects, 66 Portland Place, London W1N 4AD

Royal Incorporation of Architects in Scotland, 15 Rutland Square, Edinburgh

Architects Registration Council, 73 Hallam Street, London W1N 6EE

Related careers *Architectural Technician – Design – Engineering – Landscape Architecture – Surveying – Town and Country Planning*

Architectural Technician

Entry qualifications In theory 3 CSE including a science, maths and a subject involving the use of written English; in practice 4 O-levels including the above subjects. For membership of the Society of Architectural and Associated Technicians (SAAT), BTEC Higher National Award in Building Studies or degree in Building, plus two years' practical experience.

The work Architectural technicians work in architects' and planners' offices both in private practice and in public employment. Duties vary considerably according to the size and the structure of the office. They may include any or all of the following: collecting, analysing and preparing technical information required for a design; preparing technical drawings for the builder and 'presentation' drawings for the client; administration of contracts; liaison with clients and with specialists such as, for example, quantity surveyors; taking notes at site meetings; site supervision; collecting information on performance of finished buildings (which means contact with satisfied and possibly dissatisfied clients); office management. Technicians often do responsible work but not normally any creative designing. Technicians with a few years' experience in employment can set up on their own and, working for private clients or building contractors, design conversions; or make working drawings for firms of architects who need occasional extra work done.

Prospects Vary according to economic climate but during the recession technicians suffered less than architects; many architectural technicians do much the same work as architects in junior positions but they are paid less than fully-qualified architects. Contractors and individuals often now employ technicians rather than architects for the more routine type of work. Technicians who want to become architects must take the full architectural training; their BTEC award is normally accepted in lieu of A-levels. Few technicians however switch to architectural training: if they are good enough to take the architectural training, they usually do very well as technicians.

Pay: Medium to high (see p. xxiii).

Training Normally on-the-job with day-release for the BTEC National Certificate in Building Studies with architectural option, or the equivalent full-time BTEC National Diploma (see p. xvi). To qualify for membership of the SAAT, technicians must go on to take a BTEC Higher award. Entrants with A-levels can take a degree in Building Studies which qualifies them for membership of the SAAT.

Personal attributes Accuracy; ability to draw; technical ability; interest in architecture and environment; liking for teamwork; some design flair.

Late start Not advisable, as young trainees, of whom there are sufficient, are preferred.

Position of women Only about 5% of SAAT members are women; no figures for trainees are available but it is believed that also only about 5% are women. Yet the job is highly suitable for women who are interested in housing and the environment but are put off by the long full architectural training (or have not got the necessary A-levels). It is the image of architectural technicians' work as something highly technical (reinforced by the words Building Studies, the title of the course trainees have to take) and the lack of role-models (women technicians who can talk about their work) which keeps the proportion of women so low. The few women who have taken this training are doing very well, both in jobs and in their own small practices. They had no special problems getting training vacancies or places on full-time BTEC courses.

Career-break: Theoretically no reason why qualified technicians should not return. BTEC training system can be adapted to help with updating skills.

Part-time: Not much opportunity in employment, but possible as self-employed technician.

Further information The Secretary, Society of Architectural and Associated Technicians, 397 City Road, London EC1 1NE

Related careers *Surveying Technician*

Archivist

Entry qualifications Usually A-level Latin and a reading knowledge of French, and an arts degree (preferably in history).

The work The archivist's work combines scholarly research with the selection, preservation, arrangement and description of documents, such as official records of central and local government and courts of law, or private documents such as title deeds, business records, family papers. The archivist assesses the value for posterity of papers being currently produced and she preserves and puts in order, for reference purposes, all types of records which were produced in the past. She helps members of the public with their research, whether they are professors of history, solicitors in search of evidence, students working on projects, or genealogists. She must understand methods of preservation and repair, of microfilming and new technologies.

Archivists work in central and local government record offices; for industrial and business firms; for professional institutions; for universities; and for a wide variety of other institutions, including ecclesiastical foundations; hospitals and charitable organizations; and specialist museums, libraries and research bodies. The work involves contact with a vast variety of members of the public.

Prospects The supply and demand for archivists are about even. It is usually necessary to go wherever there is a vacancy, both for the first job and later for promotion.

Pay: Medium (see p. xxiii).

Training 1-year post-graduate full-time course for the Study of Records and Administration of Archives Diploma. Subjects include palaeography, record office management, research methods, editing, some history and law.

Personal attributes A strong sense of history; liking for painstaking research; curiosity; ability to communicate with wide variety of people when researching.

Late start Probably difficult, for above reasons and see *career-break*.

Position of women Just over half of Britain's archivists are women; but 33 county archivists are men, 15 female – men have a greater share of top jobs.

Career-break: Return difficult, as there are always sufficient young (and cheaper) job applicants.

Part-time: Training: possible. Work: not many opportunities at present, but theoretically it should be possible to work part-time.

Further information Chairman, Training Committee, The Society of Archivists, Hampshire Record Office, 20 Southgate Street, Winchester SO23 9EF

Related careers *Archaeology – Librarian – Museum Work*

Art and Design

FINE ART; DESIGN: graphic design or visual communication – 3-dimensional design – textiles/fashion; ART THERAPY; ARTS ADMINISTRATION

The work Covers two distinct fields: ART, which is largely painting and sculpture and is not a career in the usual sense; and DESIGN, which could be called 'applied art': it covers design for industrial and commercial application and industrial engineering. The terminology can be confusing. For example *industrial design* (engineering) is also called *product design*, and comes under the broader heading *3-dimensional design*. Similarly, *graphic design*, with all its sub-categories – illustration, typography, photography, etc. – is also called *visual communication* or *communication design*.

In the Art and Design CNAA degree (see below), the areas of specialization are: (1) fine art; (2) graphic design; (3) 3-dimensional design; (4) textiles/fashion. Within these broad categories there are many specializations.

Fine Art

An extremely small number of artists are talented enough to make a living by painting and sculpting alone. Anyone determined to paint or sculpt for a living must have a private income, a second string to her bow, or be prepared for a precarious existence.

Commissions for murals and sculptures for public buildings are extremely rare, and private commissions even more so.

The majority of painters and sculptors also teach, and for that they need art teacher training. Part-time teaching is now *very* difficult to get. Others combine fine art with design in overlapping areas, for example, studio-based craft, or such graphics specialization as book illustration or advertising. But in these areas opportunities are also rare. A few artists do picture restoring or copying, but again there are few openings.

Design (see also Engineering Design, p. 169)

The function of the designer, who is, broadly, a specialist combining artistic talent and training with sufficient technical and business knowledge to appreciate the requirements of an industry, is still evolving. There is no career structure; no particular qualification leads to any particular level of responsibility or type of job. But most designers start as assistants and work first in the area of specialization in which they trained. Later, with experience and evolving interests, they can switch specializations, or at least sub-specializations. For example, a 3-dimensional designer might switch from light engineering to furniture or interior design; a graphic designer from typography to photography; a fashion/textile designer from fashion (see p. 197) to floor-covering or wallpaper, etc. Sometimes 3-dimensional-trained designers switch to visual communication – but the switch the other way round is less likely. A few later combine several design categories.

Titles in industry are arbitrary and mean little; an assistant designer may have more scope for creativity and decision-making than a designer or even design director. Many industrial employers are not yet used to working with designers; the contribution the designer is expected or indeed allowed to make varies from one job to another. For example, sometimes the bias is towards technical expertise: the designer is expected to state, through design, exactly how a product is to be manufactured or printed; sometimes the bias is towards creativity, and the designer is expected to put forward ideas for totally new products. Most frequently she is responsible for the visual appearance of the product.

She usually works with a team of experts from different disciplines – both technical: engineers, printing technologists, etc., and business: buyers, marketing people, etc. This teamwork is one of the important differences between artists and designers: designers cannot just please themselves: their ideas on what is 'good design' and what is not have to be adapted to fit in with commercial and technical requirements.

Though the designer's work varies from one field of design to another, the end-product always has to fulfil at least three demands: it must look right, perform its function adequately, and be economically produced so that it is profitable. For example, a poster must attract attention and be easily readable; a tin-opener or a fridge must work well, look good and last; a biscuit pack must attract attention, fit into shelf-displays, keep its contents fresh, and open easily; a machine tool must serve the engineer's stated purpose, be easy and safe to handle and clean, and all these products must be manufacturable within given cost-limits. Designers must fully understand the purpose of the product they are designing and its marketing and manufacturing problems. They must know the limitations of and potentialities of materials and machines available for production.

At first as design assistant, the trained designer gains useful experience when carrying out rather simple 'design-technician' rather than design tasks. For example she may translate a designer's idea for a product into detailed working drawings: this requires technical know-how rather than creativity. In furniture design, for example, she would specify how to fix A satisfactorily to B in manufacturing terms without spoiling the appearance.

One designer usually has several design assistants (now sometimes called design technicians) working for her; the size of design teams varies greatly. Designers and design assistants work in various settings: in advertising agencies; manufacturing concerns' design departments; architects' offices; interior design studios; design consultancies, and many others. Organizing freelance work either on one's own or with colleagues on a design consultancy basis is complex and requires experience: newly-trained designers should try and gain experience as staff designers first. They need to know a lot not only about production problems and organization, but also about how to deal with clients and finance.

Graphics or Graphic Design or Visual Communication

This is concerned with lettering; illustration, including photography; the design of symbols or 'logos'. It ranges from the design of books, book jackets, all kinds of advertisements (posters, packaging, etc.), to the visual 'corporate identity' symbol of organizations, i.e. presenting the image of that organization in visual, instant-impact-making terms; for example a logo might be required for use on all of an airline's, hotel chain's, local authority's or company's equipment and property; from planes to cutlery, letter-heads to delivery vans and perhaps even items of clothing.

Visual communication includes 'visual aids' for industrial and educational application. This is an expanding area: instructions and/or information are put over in non-verbal language, with symbols taking the place of words. Symbols are used as teaching aids in industrial training; as user-instructions in drug and textile labelling; as warning or information signs on machinery; on road signs. Symbols may be in wall-chart or film-strip form, or on tiny labels as on medicine and detergent packages, or on textile labels, or on huge posters.

Symbol design, whether single or in series, requires great imagination, social awareness, logical thinking.

Visual communication also includes TV graphics: captions, programme titles, all non-verbal TV presentation of information, election results, trade-figure trends, etc.; packaging, publicity and advertising; stamp and letter-head design. Graphic designers work in advertising agencies, in design units, or in manufacturing firms' and other organizations' design departments. Television absorbs only a tiny proportion.

There are few openings in general book and magazine illustration and design, but there is considerable scope in technical and medical graphics, which require meticulous accuracy rather than creative imagination. There is also some scope in the greeting-card trade and in catalogue illustration. Much of this is considered hackwork by creative artists.

3-Dimensional Design

This can be divided conveniently into *Product Design* and *Interior Design*. The former embraces the design of such things as furniture, jewellery, pottery, silver, etc., as well as the design of certain aspects of products made by the engineering industries. The latter is usually referred to as Industrial Design (Engineering). Interior design embraces the design of office, domestic, hotel, aircraft and airport interiors; exhibition and window display and sets design.

Product Design

This covers the design of all kinds of consumer goods (for example domestic appliances, or suitcases), and of machine tools, mechanical equipment, cars.

It is fairly generally agreed now that manufacturing industry must pay more attention to design than it has in the past. But there is no general agreement on how this is to be brought about. Many engineers and manufacturers still believe that with a bit more design training, engineers can cope with the aesthetics and ergonomics (ease of handling and cleaning, convenience in use, legibility of instructions). But most progressive manufacturers now agree that engineers must work *with* design specialists who, for their part, must have a thorough understanding of engineering principles and production constraints.

The proportion of 'design input' and 'engineering input' varies from product to product. Designers talk about a 'spectrum' – for example, in the manufacture of a plastic egg cup the 'engineering input' is very small, the 'design input' large; at the other end of the spectrum is a gas turbine, where the design input may be confined to the lettering of the instructions and the colour (which is, however, important, as it affects the 'work environment', which affects industrial efficiency). In between the two extremes are appliances such as food mixers, record players; the engineer designs the components and says how they must be arranged to do the job; the industrial designer is primarily concerned with the appearance and ergonomics of the product.

Between the first sketch and the final product there may be many joint discussions, drawings, modifications, working models and prototypes. The designer negotiates with the engineer; design technicians develop the product through the various stages. Designers and engineers work in teams – whether the team leader is an engineer or a designer varies according to the type of product, the firm's policy and, last but by no means least, to the engineer's and designer's personalities.

Product designers need such extensive knowledge of relevant engineering and manufacturing processes that they tend to stay within a particular manufacturing area. The greatest scope is in plastics, which cover a wide range of products, from toys to complex appliances and equipment.

Interior Design

Interior designers work in specialized or general design consultants' studios; large stores; for a group of hotels or supermarkets; in private practice or local authority architects' offices. A considerable knowledge of architecture is required in order to know how to divert drains, move walls safely, or enlarge a shop window satisfactorily. The job of the interior designer, besides being responsible for such things as the management of contracts, is to specify the nature of an interior – how it is made, built and finished – as well as selecting the finishes and fixtures and fittings.

Planning interiors for a hotel, shop, liner, etc., needs research before designing starts. Beginners often spend all their time on fact-finding: the different items of goods to be displayed; the number of assistants required in a new shop; the kind of materials suitable for furnishing a ship cruising in hot climates. They also search for suitable light fittings, heating equipment, furnishing materials, and they may design fixtures and fittings.

The term 'interior design' is often interpreted rather loosely, and some jobs require less training and creativity. This applies particularly to work done by assistants in the design studios of stores or architects' offices, in showrooms of manufacturers of paint, furniture, furnishings, light fittings, wallpaper, etc., and in the furnishing departments of retail stores, and in specialist shops. In these settings, interior designers may advise customers or clients on the choice and assembly of the items needed. This may mean suggesting colour schemes, matching wallpaper and curtains, sketching plans for room decoration, or advising on the most suitable synthetic fabric for a particular furnishing purpose. As stores estimators and home advisers, they may go to customers' houses to give advice or even only to measure up for loose covers and curtains. Some stores employ interior designers as buyers in furniture and furnishing departments, and paint, wallpaper and furnishing fabric manufacturers may employ sales representatives.

Set Design
The work requires a knowledge of period styles, structures and of lighting techniques, and a wide range of interests, to help visualize the right kind of set for any particular play or TV programme. Limited scope.

Design for Exhibitions and Display
Combines some of the work of interior and set designer with model-making and graphic design. Exhibition design is usually done by specialist firms. Exhibitions are often rush jobs, and designers may help put up stands and work through the night before opening. Exhibition designers also work in museums (see p. 310). Limited scope.

Window Display
Closely allied to exhibition design, but can be specialization on its own. The essence of window and 'point of sale' design is communication: the display designer must present the store's or shop's image, attract attention and persuade the passer-by to buy. Window display can consist of merely putting a few goods in the window or a show case, or it can be a highly sophisticated exercise in marketing, using specially designed models (see Model-Making below) and specially chosen merchandise to convey a 'theme' and marketing policy. In stores there may be a *display manager*, a *display designer* and several display assistants or technicians who make/arrange the props and merchandise. Reasonable scope.

Studio-Based Design (glass, jewellery, silverware, stained glass, etc.)
Design and production by designer-craftspeople who run their own small-scale studios or workshops where each article is made individually. This is almost as precarious a way of making a living as painting or sculpting. However, some studios survive, selling to local shops and individual customers, they have 'studied the market', and perhaps compromised, producing designs which sell rather than those which they would ideally like to produce.

Model-Making
This includes the design and/or making up of models for window and exhibition display, and the making of scale models for architects, planners, and interior-design and product-design studios. Many designers, architects, etc., find that their clients are better able to judge a

design if they see it in 3-dimensional model form rather than as drawings.

Model-makers use the traditional materials – wood, plaster, fabric, etc. – and also the new synthetics. They usually work in specialist studios and firms, but some work in other types of design studio. There is more scope here for manual work requiring some creative ability than for pure artistic design. This is an expanding field.

Textiles/Fashion (see also Fashion, p. 197)

Textile design includes printed and woven textiles, carpets, lino, wallpapers, and plastic surface coverings and decoration. There are few openings in manufacturing firms. One of the difficulties is that thorough knowledge of manufacturing methods is essential, but it is difficult to get a job with suitable firms.

Textile designers work on their own more frequently than do other designers. They usually work through agents who show their designs to manufacturers. Fashion collections are held 2 or more times a year, furnishing collections usually twice.

Prospects all design

As in all creative work, success depends on ability, luck, personality and such imponderables as current taste and economic conditions. Few designers ever make a name for themselves.

The ratio of opportunities to qualified applicants is more favourable in the less glamorous and more technical field of *product design* than in *interior*, *set*, or *textiles* and *fashion design*.

There will never be as many creative top-level jobs as there are aspiring designers, but there is scope for 'design assistants' or 'technicians' whose work varies in level of creativity and responsibility; such work as making working drawings from designers' scribbled outlines; model-making; or, in communication design, trying to get as near the designer's intended effect with restricted number of colours and within printing constraints; and there is a vast range of jobs in product design which require technical competence, an appreciation of what constitutes good design and *some* creativity rather than creative genius.

Prospects are reasonable for people who *want* to design for industry and appreciate that it is teamwork, but *not* for failed artists. Many of the best product and fashion designers go abroad where British training is greatly appreciated.

Training

No particular level of qualification is indispensable for, or guarantees access to, any particular level or type of job. Course choice needs very thorough research: no two courses, even at equal level, have exactly the same aim and content, whatever their title. A BTEC award (see below) plus experience may lead to as good a job as a degree – in some cases even to a wider choice of job. It depends whether employers want as many people with exceptional creativity as people with thorough industrial training and technical skills – people who put the end-product's marketability above aesthetic considerations. What matters in the job-market above all is the portfolio of work, and experience. To get the first job – i.e. experience – *some* systematic full-time training is essential in all but exceptional cases. Methods of training:

4-Year Sandwich or 3-Year Full-Time CNAA Degree in Art and Design at Colleges of Art, Polytechnics, Colleges of Higher Education
Entry Requirements: *Either* 5 O-levels plus Foundation course lasting 1 or 2 years; *or* 1 A-level and 3 O-levels plus – normally but not invariably – a 1-year Foundation course; or DATEC Certificate or Diploma (see below). Individual colleges vary in their precise requirements; some demand, for example, O-level maths or craft design and technology and English. Acceptance also depends on applicant's portfolio, i.e. on proof of creative ability.

Degrees are normally awarded in 4 separate areas of specialization: fine art, graphic design, 3-dimensional design, and textiles/fashion. Within their specialization, students normally study one principal and one or two subsidiary subjects. In graphic design, for example, typography may be the principal subject with photography and lettering as subsidiaries. In 3-dimensional design, product design may be the principal, with ceramics and/or silversmithing as subsidiary.

Students sometimes work for some weeks in a studio or design department in industry. Contact with whatever branch of design they hope to take up should play a vital part throughout the course. All students spend 15% of their time on complementary studies which may include History of Art and/or Management.

Within these broad outlines, individual courses vary greatly.

Courses are normally preceded by a full-time Foundation course which should be 'diagnostic' to help students decide on the specialization in which to qualify. There are many aspects of design which school-leavers cannot know about, and this course is expected to lead many students to one of the less well-known design fields. However not all Foundation courses give such broad training and candidates should find out something about the courses. Acceptance for the Foundation course is no guarantee of acceptance for the degree course itself.

There are some art/technology, art/management, creative arts and similar 'mixed' degree courses (2 A-level entry) but they are *not* intended for potential designers.

Post-graduate training is almost always required for designers who aim at top jobs. There are post-graduate full-time courses (1 to 3 years) in most design specializations, for example, in film, in TV graphics or in Graphic Information for Technical, Scientific and Educational Application. The highest qualification is the Royal College of Art Master's Degree (M.Des.RCA).

University Courses

Very few universities offer degree courses in design, but there are plenty of university courses in fine art, history of art and, for students with arts degrees, post-graduate courses in history of art. Fine arts and history of art qualifications lead to work in museums and art galleries, in art publishing, in research and teaching. Prospects are severely limited.

See also Arts Administration, p. 69.

Vocational Courses – many leading to BTEC awards (see below)

These vary considerably. Some are almost indistinguishable from degree courses, but they do not necessarily contain so many complementary studies, and can therefore devote more time to professional design studies. Many vocational courses are approved by the Chartered Society of Industrial Artists and Designers (which is the professional association for designers), and they may be as useful in career terms as degree courses (possibly even more so). The Society approves only courses which have up-to-date equipment at their disposal and which include professional practice. This covers client contact; administration; designing to cost; manufacturing processes.

Other vocational courses are chosen for their relevance to the student's objectives. Some are suitable for the student who wishes to concentrate on, for example, lettering or typography, costume jewellery, glass decoration, photography, model-making, interior decoration, window display, book-binding, picture restoring, etc., but who does not aim to be a designer responsible for the creative conception of projects and products. Other courses, for example ceramics in Stoke-on-Trent, or corsetry and lingerie in Leicester, are geared to local industries. They cover a particular design field in depth and may lead to top jobs in those fields. In some specializations, for example, model-making, window display, picture restoring, it is also possible to learn on-the-job as trainee, sometimes but rarely with day-release. It is essential, when taking such a post, to make sure that it includes some kind of training and is not a dead-end unskilled job.

DATEC Courses

Until recently, these courses varied enormously in aims, quality, content and entry requirements. Courses have now been 'rationalized'; many have disappeared, those remaining are validated by DATEC, the Design and Art Committee of BTEC (see p. xvi). There are four types of award:

(a) *National Certificate* – entry at 16+, with, in theory, 3 CSE Grade 3; in practice, colleges often ask for higher qualifications and/or evidence of skill.

(b) *National Diploma* – entry at 16+ with, in theory, 3 O-levels; in practice, often 4, possibly including maths or art or craft design and technology and/or evidence of ability. Again, colleges may set their own requirements. About 90% of Certificate and Diploma courses are full-time; they last 2 years.

(c) *Higher National Certificate* – entry at 18+, usually with Certificate or Diploma, occasionally with Foundation course or, exceptionally, with 5 O-levels or 3 O-levels and 1 A-level and evidence of relevant skills. Courses are normally full-time and last 1 year.

(d) *Higher National Diploma* – entry as for Higher Certificate; length 2 years, full-time (Higher National Diploma courses only started in 1982). They qualify for mandatory awards; Higher National Diploma holders will compete in the design job-market on equal terms with Art and Design graduates.

National Certificates and Higher National Certificates, and National Diplomas and Higher National Diplomas respectively, are intended to lead to the same level of achievement, but the two types of award emphasize different design aspects. Certificate and Higher Certificate courses teach technical skills and procedures within one, or possibly two, sub-specializations. For example, within graphic design, typography and photography; within 3-dimensional design, model-making and window-display. A Higher Certificate holder who specialized in photography, for example, would be able to brief photographers to carry out work required for a mail order catalogue, as requested by the chief designer; but she would not be a top-rank photographer.

Diploma and Higher Diploma courses are more broadly based than Certificates, and they place more emphasis on creative aspects and design problem-solving. A Higher Diploma holder in graphic design would be expected, for example, to see through the production of a mail order catalogue from the marketing manager's brief right up to the finished product.

For people who are not sure which aspect of design attracts them, there are *General Art and Design* or *General Vocational Design* (the latter title may be phased out) courses. They are 'diagnostic' (rather like Foundation courses) for 16- and 17-year-olds, and normally last 2 years. In some cases students with A-level art may enrol for the second year of the course. Some students get 'design-related' jobs immediately after the course – i.e. clerical work in a studio; or simple lettering or model-making, etc.

There are only *very* few part-time day-release courses.

In job-getting terms, certificate courses – both levels – may be more useful than same-level diploma courses, because there are more jobs for technically skilled than for creative/design-management people.

DATEC courses are totally industry-orientated. Students are taught by staff with industrial experience (though how recent that experience is varies from one course to another). All courses include 'professional practice'. That covers 'client-contact', i.e. communication with people who want work done (and who do not necessarily understand art-course jargon); business administration; design-management. Colleges which cannot guarantee work experience in a commercial studio must simulate such real world-of-work pressures as working to absolute dead-lines; coping with late or non-delivery of materials; absence of vital colleagues; last-minute changes in design-brief; working to stringent cost-limits.

In future there are probably going to be more courses which integrate business and design practice, and courses which move across the traditional design specialisms, training 'multiskilled' designers who can adapt to changing industrial demands. Students will also all have to learn to work with the many new visual-communication technologies.

Choosing the right course is difficult, terminology is very vague and course-titles can be misleading. For example, a Graphic Design and a Visual Communication course could both cover exactly the same ground. Equally, Graphic Design could be much narrower, or indeed much broader, than Visual Communication; also the approach to the work and sub-specializations and options within courses vary enormously. Candidates must study *Design Courses in Britain* (published annually by the Design Council, current price £3.00), then send for prospectuses of likely-sounding courses. If at all possible, colleges should be visited before deciding on any particular course (although for 16+ Certificate and Diploma courses choice will be restricted to what is available locally; no awards are normally paid to students on these courses).

Subjects in which courses can be taken (not usually at all levels) full-time or part-time day-release or evening classes

Antique restoration
Book design and production and bookbinding
Book illustration
Ceramics
Conservation
Decorating and sign-writing
Display and exhibition design
Dress design and manufacture
Embroidery – hand and machine
Enamelling
Etching
Fashion
Film
Fine art

Furniture design
Glass design and decoration
Interior decoration
Interior design
Jewellery
Lettering and illumination
Lithography
Metalwork
Millinery
Modelling and sculpture
Model-making
Mosaic
Package design
Painting
Paper conservation
Photography
Picture restoring
Product design or industrial design (engineering)
Sculpture
Set design
Shoe design
Silversmithing
Stained glass
Technical graphics
Technical illustration
Textile conservation
Textile design (including carpets and lino, synthetic surface coverings)
Toys
TV design
TV graphics
Typography

Art Therapy

Work and training This is a growing field. Its purpose is twofold: painting and other art forms help withdrawn patients to express themselves and relieve tension, and seeing patients' work helps psychiatrists pinpoint patients' thoughts and problems. The majority of art therapists work – usually on a sessional basis – in psychiatric and mental handicap hospitals with children and with adults, individually and in groups; some work with maladjusted and some with physically handicapped children. Art therapy is not so much a career in itself as a field in which practising artists with the necessary human qualities can do useful work. Post-graduate 1-year special training is essential.

Personal attributes All careers in art and design require resilience, self-confidence and exceptional talent.

Especially for design: ability to work as one of a team; creative sensibility and imagination coupled with a logical analytical mind; an interest in science and technology; curiosity and a desire to solve technical problems; perseverance; an interest in the social environment and in the community's needs, tastes and customs; the ability to take responsibility, and criticism; willingness at times to lower one's artistic standards in the interests of economic necessity or technical efficiency.

For freelances and senior staff jobs: business sense; the ability to communicate with employers and clients who commission the work but are possibly not themselves interested in art.

For 'technician' jobs: considerable manual dexterity, technical ability and some creativity.

Late start If to earn a living, advisable, if at all, only in strictly limited areas – perhaps in typography.

Position of women Only a small proportion of designers are women. In the most promising specialization, *product design*, the proportion of women is minute; very few women take up this specialization – largely, probably, because of the considerable engineering content during training (and maths O-level requirement). A woman in a manufacturing industry design-engineering team needs special drive and self-confidence to overcome traditional resistance to (a) designers in industry and (b) women in manufacturing industry; but those who have tried have done quite well – at home and abroad.

In set and exhibition design women still have to persuade employers that they are able to cope when in an occasional rush designers have to put up sets and display stands.

There is no logical reason whatever why there are so few women in good jobs in graphics; more women than men take the appropriate training.

In fashion/textiles again more men than women succeed. Design is one of the areas where discrimination is difficult to prove but it seems to exist.

Career-break: If experienced and established, designers can take up freelance work; some return to work, but competition from recent art school leavers is likely to be stiff.

Part-time: As freelance.

Further information Design Council, 28 Haymarket, London SW1

Chartered Society of Industrial Artists and Designers, 12 Carlton House Terrace, London SW1Y 5AH

British Institute of Interior Design, Lenton Lodge, Wollaton Hall Drive, Nottingham NG8 1AF

Art and Design degrees: Art and Design Admissions Registry, Imperial Chambers, 24 Widemarsh Street, Hereford HR4 9ET

British Association of Art Therapists, 13c Northwood Road, London N6 5TL

British Display Society, 24 Ormond Road, Richmond, Surrey

DATEC Courses: BTEC, Central House, Upper Woburn Place, London WC1H 0HH

Related careers *Advertising – Architecture – Cartography – Engineering – Fashion – Landscape Architecture – Museum Work – Photography – Teaching (Art, p. 528) – Television, Film and Radio*

Arts Administration

The City University, London, runs courses in Arts Administration both part-time, for people in relevant employment, and full-time, with a one-year Diploma course. At Leicester Polytechnic the Performing Arts CNAA degree course includes Arts Administration. Courses combine box office management; planning exhibitions; orchestral management. The great majority of students are graduates, and most have had some administrative or secretarial experience in something connected with the visual or the performing arts. Students must have extensive knowledge of whichever type of artistic activity they wish to administer; music graduates go into symphony orchestra administration; fine arts graduates into art gallery or similar administration. But for regional arts centre work any form of experience/training in the arts may be acceptable. Scope, however, is very limited indeed, for training and for work, but women are doing well.

See also Music Administration, Recreation Management.

Banking

Entry qualifications 4 O-levels, including an English and a numerate subject, or BTEC General Award (see p. xvi); A-level holders and graduates slot in higher up the training ladder.

The work There are three main types of banking: *domestic*, *international* and *merchant*. The major clearing banks operate in the domestic and international fields.

Domestic (or Branch) Banking

Many jobs involve dealing with people as much as dealing with figures. Trainees start in the general office, where they learn how to deal with payment and collection of cheques and other basic banking procedures. Routine figure work is now largely done by machines: trainees spend some time in the Machine Room (see Computing/Information Technology, p. 131). First important promotion is usually to cashier (at least in clearing banks, in which the majority work). Cashiers are often called a bank's ambassadors – like sales staff in stores, the impression they make determines the bank's image.

After a spell at the counter, trainees are moved around the various departments and then decide whether they would like to specialize (or stay cashiers). The main specialist departments are: *Securities*, which deal with investments (stocks and shares, mortgages, etc.) – work involves advising customers, keeping up with economic trends, discussion with businessmen, City experts; *Foreign Exchange*, dealing with travellers' cheques and foreign transactions generally; *Trusts*, dealing with trusts and wills in which customers have appointed the bank to look after their own or their dependants' interests; advising people who have been left money how best to invest it; explaining intricate money matters to bewildered heirs.

Advisory services (various titles): banks are increasingly involved in commercial planning, advising, for example, when mergers, takeovers or liquidations are negotiated. Small and medium-sized businesses often rely on banks for financial advice. Branch managers, acting within the policy laid down by Head Office, have powers to decide what overdrafts to grant to individuals and firms. This requires considerable commercial expertise and judgement, and may involve research into, for example, the viability of a particular type of venture which a customer wants to start, or into the housing situation to determine whether a customer's proposal to convert an old house into flats makes commercial sense.

International Banking

In the international division of a clearing bank work includes arranging finance for the import and export of goods; advising customers on foreign trading conditions; handling shipping documents; dealing in foreign stocks and shares. Those with a flair for the buying and selling of large amounts of foreign currency can become foreign exchange dealers on the international money market (which operates 24 hours a day). The pattern of training is similar to that for branch banking, but there are fewer openings.

Foreign-owned banks also employ British staff, but do not usually offer the same training structure. Many of these operate as merchant banks.

Merchant Banking

Most are based in the City of London and are small compared with clearing banks. They provide services to companies and are involved with a wide range of activities: advising on mergers; managing large investments; financing imports and exports; foreign currency dealing; and insurance broking.

Prospects Banking is one of the employment areas where chip-based technology is likely to reduce the demand for all but management staff.

Smaller branches are being closed, while at the same time banks are expanding their range of activities (e.g. providing mortgages).

The first few years in banking are largely routine, with little scope for initiative. Trainees who do not lose heart, and who pass their exams, stand a fair chance of promotion to middle-management (head of section or small department) and to sub- or assistant manager of a small branch. Promotion to senior management – branch or assistant manager – depends on candidate's willingness to move to wherever there happens to be a vacancy, ability and luck. The clearing banks all prefer to promote from within: there is hardly any movement from one of the Big 4 to another. The staffing structure is very much a pyramid – very few at the top, large numbers at the bottom (60% of staff are under 23). The merchant banks and the Bank of England recruit mainly graduate trainees, although there are a few openings for O- and A-level entrants.

Note: Girls and women who enter as clerks or secretaries are not 'banking trainees' and are unlikely to be granted day- or block-release for the exams which are necessary for promotion in professional banking. (See Secretarial and Clerical Work, p. 451.)

Pay: Medium to occasionally high (see p. xxiii).

Training

Domestic and International divisions: on-the-job training with day/block-release. (Time off may only be granted automatically to A-level entrants. O-level entrants have to show keenness and motivation.)

New structure of Institute of Bankers' examination:

Stage 1: BTEC National Award in Business Studies (O-level entrants) or a one-year 'Conversion Course' for those with one or more A-levels. Those with two or more relevant A-levels (Law, Economics, Accountancy) and graduates go directly into

Stage 2: Eight papers set by the Institute leading, after banking experience, to Associateship (AIB).

Stage 3: Financial Studies Diploma: a degree-level qualification for those expected to achieve senior management.

Entry requirements: Associateship or Degree plus two direct entry papers. This Diploma is useful only in Banking. BTEC Higher National Award (see p. xvi) or a degree or Accountancy qualification may lead to wider choice of management jobs.

Merchant banking: trainees may study in their own time for IOB examinations. They may be given day-release for short specialized courses being developed at City University.

Personal attributes

Meticulous accuracy; a clear, logical mind; tact; courtesy; a feeling for figures and interest in work with data-processing equipment (see p. 131). For senior jobs: ability to deal with many different types of customers, sometimes in difficult situations.

Late start

It is unlikely that over-25s would be taken on as trainees.

Position of women

Banks need large staffs for routine work which, traditionally, women have done. Far fewer girls than boys are granted day-release right from the start; possibly because fewer *ask* for it. It is up to girls to take only jobs as trainees (and not as clerks or secretaries), and to make sure they are granted day/block-release on the same basis as boys. 16% of Institute of Banking members but under 2% of bank or senior departmental managers are women. This may partly be due to the fact that women are sometimes not as willing as men to move to wherever there is a vacancy one step higher up the ladder (although men are not expected to be as mobile as previously), but banking is certainly one of the careers in which opportunities are not equal. Women have to be considerably more determined, and more intelligent, than men, to be given equal chances of promotion to senior management. A few banks have started initiatives to try to 'develop' women managers.

American-owned banks offer better prospects for women in some cases.

Career-break: Probably no problem at lower and middle levels; but so far no woman who has interrupted her career seems to have got anywhere near the top.

Part-time: Not in professional banking – only as clerk or secretary.

Further information

Banking Information Service, 10 Lombard Street, London EC3V 9AS
Institute of Bankers, 10 Lombard Street, London EC3V 9AS
Accepting Houses Committee, Granite House, 101 Canon Street, London EC4N 5BA (for merchant banking)

Related careers

Accountancy – Actuary – Insurance

Beauty Specialist

Beauty therapist (including beautician and electrologist) – sales consultant

Entry qualifications For school leavers, 2 or more O-levels depending on course, but some schools ask for chemistry; see **Training**. Minimum age for employment as beauty therapist – 18+; as consultant usually about 24.

The work There are two types of job: beauty therapist and sales consultant (or 'beauty consultant' or 'sales representative').

Beauty Therapist

A *beauty therapist* uses the full range of available treatments on the face and body. These extend from make-up, facials and wax or electric depilation (removal of superfluous hair) to massage, saunas, diet and exercise. She knows when to deal with a skin complaint herself or when to advise her client to see a doctor. It is possible to learn one or two techniques only, e.g. a *beautician* works on the face and neck only; a *manicurist/pedicurist* on the hands/feet; the *electrologist (or electrolysist)* uses various means to remove unwanted hair; a *masseuse* on face/body massage.

Beauty therapists work in private high street salons (sometimes combined with hairdressers), in health farms or cosmetic firms' salons. The majority of clients are middle-aged and some are men.

Sales Consultant

Usually works in the perfumery department of large stores, occasionally in luxury hotels (at home or abroad), on liners, or at airports. She is usually under contract to a cosmetics firm and travels round the country, working for a week or two each in a succession of stores or shops.

She sells and promotes her firm's products and tries to win regular customers. She answers questions on skin-care and make-up problems, and may give talks and demonstrations.

Prospects Poor to fair for gaining experience. More girls take the expensive training than can find jobs. For *experienced* women there *are* good jobs: cosmetics buyers for stores, at the head offices of cosmetics firms, training consultants, and travelling for cosmetics firms. For those also trained in hairdressing there are some opportunities in television (see p. 538) and as hairdresser/beauty specialists in psychiatric hospitals which recognize the importance of beauty care in rehabilitating patients.

Pay: Medium to relatively high (see p. xxiii).

Working for Oneself

Some beauty specialists set up on their own. The initial financial outlay on equipment can be quite high. The town hall will advise on necessary licences.

Income: Low to very high (see p. xxiii).

Training

Professional Training

1. 2-year (1-year for over-21s) full-time course for City and Guilds Beauty Therapy Certificate. 3 O-levels preferably, including a science.
2. Courses leading to one of the qualifications of the International Health and Beauty Council or Confederation of Beauty Therapy and Cosmetology. Minimum age usually 18. Most good courses last from 5 to 12 months (some are longer). Courses are divided between theory – anatomy, physiology, diets, salesmanship, salon organization, and sometimes electrical treatments – and the practical work: giving facials, different types of massage, make-up, etc. Some are offered by further education colleges, some by private schools (fees start at around £1,000).
3. Higher Diploma in Beauty Therapy. Courses last 2 years full-time; special emphasis on TV make-up requirements, and remedial aspects. 4 O-levels and 1 A-level in approved subjects which must include at least 1 science subject.

Courses Given by Cosmetics Houses for Sales Consultants Only

Minimum age depends on age range at which product is aimed, e.g. teenagers or mature women. Majority need to be 24+ and must have several years' selling experience and must be good saleswomen. Training is mainly in-store and lasts a few weeks. Subjects dealt with are facials, simple massage, eyebrow shaping and make-up, both for day and evening. These courses qualify students as sales consultants, but *not* as beauty specialists.

It is useful to take a hairdressing training (see p. 211) as well as beauty training. It widens the choice of jobs later.

Personal attributes

A liking for women of all ages; a friendly, confident manner; tact; courtesy; an attractive, well-groomed appearance; *naturally* good skin; cool dry hands; good health; business sense; ability to express oneself easily; foreign language sometimes an asset.

Career-break: No special problem, but see **Prospects**.

Late start Beauty specialists' work is very suitable for late entrants. Many salons prefer women who are nearer in age to the majority of clients than young school-leavers are.

Part-time: Fairly easy to find for the over-30s.

Further information City and Guilds of London Institute, 76 Portland Place, London W1N 4AA
Confederation of Beauty Therapy and Cosmetology, 5 Greenways, Winchcombe, Cheltenham, Glos.
International Health and Beauty Council, PO Box 36, Arundel, West Sussex BN18, 0SW

Related careers *Television (Make-up, p. 538) – Hairdressing*

NOTE: BTEC validation is being sought for Higher Diploma Courses.

Bookselling

Entry qualifications None laid down, but good general education essential.

The work The accent is on selling and keeping stock moving, rather than on literary pursuits, yet staff must be well read and keep on reading books and reviews in order to be able to advise customers and answer queries. Reading should cover a wide field rather than only one's own interests, but in large bookshops staff usually specialize in one or two subjects. Customers are often left to browse undisturbed amongst the stock but must be offered help and advice when they want it.

Assistants' duties include daily dusting and filling and tidying shelves and display-tables. This also helps them to learn the stock and remember where titles are shelved. Assistants also write out orders, keep records and may do some book-keeping. In many bookshops ordering, etc. is now computerized. They may pack and unpack parcels and perhaps carry them to the post. Bookshop work is physically quite hard.

One of the most interesting and most skilled parts of the job is helping customers who have only a vague idea of what they want or cannot explain what they have in mind. It may involve tracing titles in bibliographies and catalogues.

Book-buying – selecting a small proportion of the vast number of new titles published each month – is a highly skilled and often tricky task. Several members of staff may be responsible for buying within one or more subject areas. They have to be able to judge what will interest their particular customers, whether to buy a new title at all and how many copies to order. New titles are ordered before reviews have appeared so staff must trust their own judgement. They must also judge how much reliance to place on the recommendation of publishers' representatives.

Managers may take part in or do all the buying – it depends on how experienced their staff and how large the shop. Above all, the manager tries to give her shop an 'image' to attract a nucleus of regular customers. This is done partly by the choice of books in stock and partly by the method and type of display and arrangement of the shop as a whole. The manager is also responsible for the stock control system (as she would be in any other kind of shop).

Prospects Not very good. Far more people want to work in bookshops than there are vacancies. Bookshops thrive only at Christmas, but some owner-managers of small bookshops nevertheless do reasonably well if they research the market thoroughly before buying/renting premises.

Pay: Low to medium (see p. xxiii).

Training Staff learn mainly on-the-job but good bookshops and departments encourage staff to take the Booksellers' Association's qualification. This has just changed. The old Diploma in Bookselling is being replaced in 1985 by the Certificate in Bookselling Skills, the syllabus of which is more up-to-date. It includes, for example, computerized ordering and cataloguing systems, present-day marketing and customer-relations principles. The Certificate syllabus, therefore, contains 'transferable skills' which may be useful in other retail spheres. On-the-job training is complemented by Open University-type 'distance learning' packages. Students have a tutor, seminars and tutorials; self-help groups complement the training. An outside examiner assesses students' work before the Certificate is awarded.

Personal attributes An excellent memory; commercial sense; wide interests and extensive general knowledge; pleasure in reading and handling books; a liking for meeting people with various interests; a helpful friendly manner and the knack of making diffident customers who are not well-read feel they are welcome; the ability to work well in a large team or in a very small shop or department; a calm temperament; good health and strong feet.

Late start No greater problem than young entrants, but see **Prospects**.

Position of women A large proportion of staff and managers, but not of owners, are women. The proportion of part-time staff – mainly women – has increased recently, but their pay is low.

Career-break: Should not present any problems, but see **Prospects**.

Further information Booksellers' Association of Great Britain and Ireland, 154 Buckingham Palace Road, London SW1W 9TZ

Related careers *Librarian – Publishing – Retail Management*

Building

Building crafts – Building management

Entry qualifications

Craft training: average ability in maths, a science (other than biology or domestic) and English language.
Technician (management jobs) training: see BTEC, p. xvi.
Degree: 2 A-levels, 3 O-levels, including maths, or a physical science.

The work

The building industry is made up of companies ('contractors') of all sizes, from international giants employing thousands of staff, including architects, chartered surveyors and chartered engineers, to small 'jobbing builders' employing one or two craftsmen/women and taking on additional people as required. Many small builders work part of the time on their own and part of the time for larger contractors. Large companies have their own design departments and execute large-scale projects such as housing estates, large office blocks, hospitals etc. Smaller firms – and often large ones too – work to plans drawn up by the client's architect. Firms may subcontract work to specialist firms of plumbers, tilers, smaller general builders etc. On large projects the client, or the client's architect, appoints a *clerk of works* (see below).

Levels and organization of work are very much less well-defined than, for example, in the engineering industry. Many contractors start at craft level and build up their own business, but they need to understand the new technologies and materials, and know how to organize work efficiently and to work to given standards. There is, therefore, increasing scope for people with specialist qualifications, but there will always be scope for craftsmen and craftswomen who are good at their job and also have organizing ability to build up their own business. Knowledge of basic crafts like bricklaying is useful even for managers; knowledge of new materials and technologies is essential.

Building Crafts

The main trades or crafts are:
1. *Bricklaying*: measuring and marking out a job; checking verticals and horizontals with guide and plumb lines and spirit level; laying the bricks using mortar and trowel. Bricklayers must be able to read drawings.
2. *Carpenter and joiner*: laying floorboards; hanging doors and fitting window frames; erecting roof timbers and staircases; making built-in

furniture; knowing about the qualities and uses of different types of timber. Carpenters must be able to read drawings.
3. *Plastering*: preparing surfaces of inside walls and ceilings; making up the plaster; applying and spreading it evenly; using moulds for decorative work.
4. *Roof slating and tiling*: fixing roofing felt and battens to timbers of sloping roofs; fixing slates or tiles to the battens; fixing slates or tiles to walls.
5. *Painting and decorating*: knowing about different types of paints and finishes; preparing surfaces; painting; hanging wallpaper.
6. *Plumbing*: installing, maintaining and repairing water supply and waste systems; understanding complicated plumbing systems in houses where the system has been changed or added to after conversion.
7. *Heating and ventilating fitter*: installing heating and ventilating (including air conditioning) systems; understanding constantly changing heating, etc., systems.

In most of these trades craftsmen and women may work, on their own at times, in people's homes as well as on new constructions.

Building Management

The term is used to cover a wide variety of jobs and skills. It includes responsibility for seeing that the work is carried out in the right sequence with the right materials at the right cost, for organizing the labour force and for the supply of materials. It may include organizing the financial side (paying wages, paying for materials, etc.) but that depends on the size of the firm. Some building management jobs are site-based (there may be a site-office), some are office-based; nearly all jobs involve some site-visits; and many jobs – at least for large firms – involve working away from home at times. Building management jobs normally involve dealing with labour; to succeed in this kind of job – to be respected by the labour force – building managers, whatever their specific job, must understand the rudiments of building crafts. Job titles and specializations (which vary very much between firms) are:
1. *Buyer (Purchasing Officer)*: selects from the design drawings the materials and services needed; contacts suppliers and subcontractors to obtain the most competitive prices; ensures materials are available at the right time.
2. *Estimator*: calculates the likely cost of materials (from door handles to concrete), labour and plant, and the time needed for the project when the firm is tendering for a contract. Also analyses costs of existing projects to provide guide to future estimates.
3. *Planner*: at pre-tender stage is involved in the decision about how the tender can be adjusted. When tender is accepted, she produces charts showing sequence of operations. Works closely with contracts

manager. In large companies will use computer for this (see p. 131). She will have had experience of estimating, buying or contracts management.

4. *Site engineer*: in charge of technical side of an individual project. Sets out the positions and levels of the building to ensure it is placed in the correct position in accordance with the designs. Oversees all the work on site, including quality control (see Structural and Civil Engineering, p. 175).

5. *Site manager (site agent)* (used to be called 'general foreman'): in charge of the contract. Ensures the designs and specifications are understood by the foremen; plans and coordinates materials and labour. Sees that building keeps to the plan and time schedule (see *Building Surveying Technician*, p. 513). May have young engineers under her control.

6. *Production controller (Productivity)*: works on incentive schemes; measures work done by operatives as part of productivity control; takes part in construction planning at site level. Some specialize in work study, and/or industrial relations.

7. *Contracts manager*: oversees several projects. Moves from site to site ensuring that work is progressing according to plan. Plans movement of machines and labour to minimize delays and time wasting. Has overall responsibility for completion of projects to correct standard at the right time.

8. *Clerk of works*: Other building management specialists work for the contractor; the clerk of works is employed by the client (or client's architect). She may be employed full-time by a local authority or, in the private sector, on a contract basis. She works from an office on site and is responsible for seeing that the work is carried out according to the architect's specifications. As the only person on site not working for the contractor she can be rather isolated, so needs to be confident and self-sufficient. On large schemes she may supervise several other clerks of works specializing in, for example, heating and ventilating or electrical installation.

Training

Crafts: School leavers are strongly advised to train with firms operating National Joint Training Schemes for skilled building operatives. There are two training schemes available:

Either MSC/CTIB Youth Training Scheme. The first year consists of full-time training in college or training centre for up to 24 weeks plus work experience in company workshops or on sites. If the firm has vacancies a service agreement will be signed for a further 2½ years' training on site and in college to study for craft qualifications;

Or trainees serve a 3-year apprenticeship with a company which provides training on site and day- or block-release for City and Guilds Craft Certificates.

Management: BTEC National and Higher National Certificate; or Diploma in Building Studies with appropriate units (see BTEC, p. xvi), usually on-the-job with day-release. Successful completion leads to licenciate and associate membership of the Chartered Institute of Building.
For jobs with big building organizations, 3-year full-time or 4-year sandwich degree in building/building technology/building construction and management. Most give exemption from Institute of Building's Final examinations parts 1 and 2.
Clerk of works: as above, followed by evening or correspondence course for Institute of Clerks of Works' Intermediate and Final examinations. (BTEC certificate or diploma in Building Studies gives some exemptions.) Membership of the Institute of Clerks of Works is compulsory before sitting the examinations. Some local authorities give day-release.

Personal attributes

Building crafts: see Electrician, p. 166.
Building management: technical and practical aptitudes; good at organization; willing to work outdoors in all weathers; ability to manage the work force; commercial sense.

Prospects

There is a shortage of skilled craftsmen and women in most areas. Trained and experienced managers are also in demand, but large-project building fluctuates with the economic situation.
NOTE: Building management overlaps very much with surveying and civil/structural engineering technician jobs.

Pay: Low for crafts when training; medium to occasionally high for crafts and management when qualified (see p. xxiii).

Late start

Possibilities with related experience and/or qualifications, i.e. as *surveying technician*, p. 512.

Position of women

There are as yet few craftswomen; more women have entered building management and are proving very successful. There is no reason why there should not be many more at all levels.

Further information

Chartered Institute of Building, Englemere, King's Drive, Ascot, Berks SL5 8BJ
Institute of Clerks of Works of Great Britain, 41 The Mall, London W5 3TJ
Construction Industry Training Board, Radnor House, London Road, Norbury, London SW16 4EL

Related careers

Agriculture and Horticulture (Engineering) – Architecture – Engineering Crafts and Technician – Surveying Technician

---

Building Society Management

Entry qualifications 2 A-levels, 4 O-levels, including English and a subject proving numeracy, or BTEC National award in Business Studies or Financial Studies. Also *graduate* entry.

The work There are over 150 members of the Building Societies Association, but there is no uniform building society organization. In the 'Big 5', each of which has its own distinctive structure and policy, management trainees tend to go up the promotion ladder within that society. Then come about 30 societies in which branch management is sufficiently similar for management staff to move between these societies for promotion. The remaining societies are small and mostly local ones. They do not usually have an organized management and training structure. It is almost impossible to move 'up' from management in a small, local society into one of the bigger ones. So people who want to make a career in building society management should try for a job in one of the Big 5 or in one of the medium-sized societies.

In practice, in the large and the medium-sized societies there is now a two-level entry. Clerical staff may do some counter-work and deal with clients, but few manage the leap into management. Trainee managers who must have the required entry qualifications (see above) do some counter-work to begin with to learn how to deal with clients, but most of their time is spent on such building society work as mortgage principles and processing; assessing applicants' suitability for mortgages; and liaising with surveyors, estate agents, solicitors and investment specialists. Increasingly, they learn how to adapt traditional office procedures to new technologies. After 2 to 3 years, trainee managers are expected to be fully-fledged managers of small branches, or they may become assistant managers in a bigger branch. The branch managers' main job is 'getting business': 'selling' *their* branch and society in competition with other societies. This means managers must make contact with solicitors, estate agents, large local companies, etc.

In a large branch an assistant manager would be responsible for the administration of the office and for interviewing all but the most important clients. The manager is responsible for finding out why, for example, a client might be taking his/her business elsewhere: she may arrange to visit such a client and find out in what way her branch or society has displeased a client. But much of the manager's time is spent on routine mortgage processing.

Building Societies are widening their activities – issuing cheques in some cases; looking into various aspects of house-buying and house-building. There are therefore more planners and researchers now than there used to be. Most new opportunities are for graduates.

Prospects After the rapid expansion of the 1970s, building societies are 'consolidating'; new branches are not opening in such great numbers as they did a few years ago. Also, as fewer clerical staff will be employed as office technologies change, there is a reduction in junior management/supervisory staffs. However, prospects are fair, and promotion prospects to bigger-branch management and regional management are also reasonable, but only for people willing to move to wherever the next step-up vacancy happens to be.

Training Trainee managers work for the examinations set by the Chartered Building Societies Institute. The big societies run their own in-house training courses and there are some CBSI residential courses. The bulk of exam-preparation has, however, to be done by private study; day-release is granted by some societies.

Personal attributes Ability to inspire confidence in clients; organizing ability; numeracy; communication skills; liking for routine desk-work.

Late start At present, societies take on trainee managers up to about 30; but it seems that no older women with relevant previous experience have tried for trainee management jobs.

Position of women So far there are few women branch managers; about 10% of students for the CBSI exam are now women. Building societies tend to be conservative bodies; discrimination is difficult to prove but male trainee managers progress more quickly. As the various societies' policies on everything vary greatly, prospective trainee managers could 'shop around' and find out which society has a significant proportion of women trainee managers.

Career-break: No evidence yet of any woman manager having tried to come back; it is likely that young trainees are preferred as technologies and policies change rapidly.

Part-time: Not at the moment. No reason at all why it should not be tried.

Further information

Chartered Building Societies Institute, Fanhams Hall, Ware, Herts.
Building Societies Association (for member societies), 34 Park Street, London W1Y 3PF
Individual Societies.

Related careers

Banking – Insurance – Management

Careers Officer

Entry qualifications Degree, Dip. HE, teaching or comparable professional qualifications, or industrial experience.

The work Careers officers' main job is helping school children make wise career-decisions, but they also deal with adults: anyone who is in full- or part-time education, or any adult who wants or has to change careers, is entitled to go to the local education authority careers office for information and advice. (See Careers Advice, p. xxv.)

Careers work in schools is a long-term process. Ideally it should start early enough to discuss the career implications of dropping and taking up particular subjects for O-levels or CSE and to stress the importance of leaving as many options open as long as possible. Careers officers also help young people, possibly using interest and aptitude questionnaires and tests, to clarify their thoughts about their own personalities, abilities, career expectations and desired life-style. They normally give individual or group vocational guidance interviews to fifth formers, whether they are leaving school or staying on, and follow-up interviews where necessary.

Careers programmes are planned to suit the various age and ability groups and may include a variety of media and methods. A careers officer may give talks or hold discussion groups in school. She may organize or help to organize careers libraries; arrange talks by specialists in schools or at careers conventions; arrange for individuals and groups to visit places of work. She may also arrange work experience periods to give children who are interested in a career but vague about the actual work and/or environment a chance to get first-hand information, and to widen others' career horizons. Films, TV, tape-recordings are also used in careers programmes.

Careers officers work closely with careers teachers. Some specialize in work with pupils who leave with few or no qualifications; others in work with those who go on to higher education, or with the physically handicapped; some work entirely with further education and polytechnic students. An important aspect of the work is finding suitable jobs for school leavers. Employers notify the careers services of vacancies which are circulated to careers officers. Careers officers also 'canvass' employers and other careers officers for young people where necessary; for example, if the individual wants a job which is only available in certain areas, such as apprentice jockey.

These days many specialize in work with unemployed young people. They are also closely involved in administering the government's Youth Training Scheme.

In order to inform pupils adequately, careers officers must themselves be well informed about developments, trends and impending changes in education, training, the job market. They divide their time between giving out information and collecting it: they visit employers, they talk to personnel officers and to the people who are actually doing the work; they attend meetings where they are told about the industrial and the further/higher education scene; and they visit colleges and other educational institutions.

Like teaching, careers work must not be judged by one's own personal experience of it. It would be wrong for a pupil who had no or poor advice at school to dismiss careers work as nothing but giving routine talks and handing out careers literature. The quality of careers work varies enormously from one area to another; there are still not enough careers officers to make the service work as well as it is intended to.

Prospects Reasonable; though there is a shortage, employment prospects depend on level of public expenditure. Promotion prospects are good for those who are able and willing to move around the country to get varied experience.

Pay: Medium (see p. xxiii).

Training 1-year full-time (2-year part-time) courses at universities and polytechnics for Diploma in Careers Guidance. Trainee careers officers may be seconded on a course by a local education authority. The syllabus includes organization of education services; occupational and social psychology; public and social administration; organization of industry; counselling aims and methods; practical work with pupils; visits to a variety of places of work and talks with/by employers. The course is followed by a probationary year.

Personal attributes Ability to get on with and understand people of all levels of intelligence and temperaments; interest in industrial and other employment trends and problems; sympathy with rather than critical attitude towards other people's points of view; organizing ability; willingness to work in a team; ability to put facts across clearly and helpfully; ability to gain young people's confidence and to put them at ease however shy and worried; insight and imagination to see how young people might develop.

Late start Those over 25 with five years' relevant work experience are exempted from normal entry requirements. Relevant jobs are those which involve dealing with a variety of people, preferably in a work situation. Maturity and variety of experience can be an asset.

Position of women About half of all careers officers are women, but a very much smaller proportion are in senior jobs, let alone at the top. Women careers officers feel that there certainly has been discrimination in the past: women have had to be better qualified and have wider relevant experience than men for the same type of promotion.

Career break: Should not present any problems (but see **Prospects**).

Part-time: Not at the moment, but no reason why this work could not be done on a part-time basis.

Further information Institute of Careers Officers, 37a High Street, Stourbridge, West Midlands
Careers Service Training Committee, Local Government Training Board, 4th floor, Arndale House, The Arndale Centre, Luton LU1 2TS

Related careers *Management in Industry – Personnel Management – Teaching – Youth-and-Community Work*

Cartography (Map Making)

Cartographer – cartographic draughtsman

Entry qualifications Depends on type of work – from 3 O-levels to degree. See **Work** and **Training**.

The work Cartography is concerned with the evaluation, compilation, design, reproduction, draughting and editing of maps. A map in this context covers any type of chart, plan or three-dimensional model representing the whole or sections of the earth or of other parts of the universe.

Both cartographic data collection and map reproduction methods have changed drastically in the last few years. Apart from traditional land survey techniques and aerial photography, such advanced technologies as satellite photography, seismic sensing and electrostatic mapping are being used. But cartography does *not* involve exploring uncharted territory, taking photographs from helicopters or setting up satellite photography! It is an indoor desk job though very occasionally cartographers may accompany the information gatherers. While the cartographer determines what data are needed for any particular map and may discuss which type of data collection is best in any particular case, the actual collection is done by specialists such as *surveyors* (see p. 503), *specialist photographers* (see p. 370), *computing people* (see p. 131) or by historical or archaeological researchers. *Cartographers* interpret the information collected by other specialists, *cartographic draughtsmen/technicians* represent the information in three-dimensional or graphic form. Apart from tracing and drawing, draughtsmen use highly sophisticated reproduction methods and materials.

The largest single employer is the Ordnance Survey. Other employers include various Ministries (Defence and Environment particularly), nationalized industries, local authorities, commercial map publishing houses, motoring organizations and exploration departments of oil companies.

The varieties of maps which are produced can include: cartographic portrayals of airfield approaches with landing charts for pilots; maps showing traffic flow or the distribution of population, housing, employment and industry for planning purposes; maps for the Forestry Commission showing the progress of land acquisition, planting, thinning, and felling; maps of the surface of the moon and maps of ancient Rome.

Prospects Limited. Jobs are mainly in London and Southampton (Ordnance Survey).

Training *Cartographer*: Degree in Cartography with related subject, or degree in Geography or Topographic Science or Mapping Sciences, or a postgraduate Diploma in Cartography. *Minimum entry requirements*: 2 A-levels normally in geography and a science subject, plus 3 O-levels one of which must be maths.

For work with the Ordnance Survey, Southampton:

Cartographic Assistant: Maximum age 19; 2 O-levels including either English language or mathematics, geography, art or technical drawing or comparable subject, a science or a language.

Cartographic Draughtsman: Maximum age 25, 3 O-levels (chosen from the same as above), 4 months in the Ordnance Survey Department's Drawing School.

For work with other employers, draughtsmen now work for a BTEC award in Cartography, Planning and Land Use. Entry is flexible (see BTEC, p. xvi) but in practice cartography employers demand 4 O-levels including mathematics and a 'subject demonstrating facility in the use of English'. Trainees complete the Certificate course in 2 years' day-release. Entrants with lower qualifications take at least 3 years.

Personal attributes Patience; great accuracy; good colour vision; keen interest in physical surroundings; powers of observation.

Late start Very few opportunities.

Position of women *Cartographers*: Comparatively few women have qualified, but those who have had no special problems.

Cartographic draughtsmen: About one in six are women.

Career-break: Should be no problem for qualified cartographers who keep up with technological changes; but see **Prospects**.

Part-time: Not normally; but graduate cartographers might be able to get sporadic rather than part-time project work.

Further information British Cartographic Society, R. W. Anson, Department of Construction, Oxford Polytechnic, Headington, Oxford OX3 0BP

Related careers *Architectural Technician – Art and Design*

Catering

Fast foods – industrial catering – school catering – restaurant management – hospital catering – transport catering – professional cooks – freelance work; HOTELS; INSTITUTIONAL MANAGEMENT

Entry qualifications All educational levels.
Considerable graduate entry: See **Training**.

The work Catering is the umbrella term for providing accommodation and/or food and drink services. It overlaps with Recreation (see p. 410) and is sometimes referred to as the 'hospitality industry'. It covers a vast array of totally different types of concern. The main branches are: *hotels* – vast number of small ones, small number of large and/or luxury ones, motels, pubs; *restaurants* – all types and sizes; *industrial catering* – staff canteens, restaurants and overlapping with *contract catering* which overlaps with *institutional catering*. The last is also called '*institutional management*' (see below, p. 101), but there is not necessarily any greater difference between jobs in commercial and in institutional (i.e. non-profit-making) catering than there is between individual jobs *within* commercial and *within* institutional catering. The continued use of 'institutional management' owes more to tradition than to logic. The difference is in emphasis on various aspects rather than in operation and management methods.

People switch from one branch of catering to another. But for senior hotel management, experience in food and drink services *as well as* in accommodation services is necessary; for non-residential catering, experience of accommodation services is *not* necessary.

Job titles often mean very little: two jobs with the same title may involve totally different tasks and levels of responsibility. Catering does not have a clear-cut career structure; there are several overlapping levels of skilled work: *craft level*: cooking, housekeeping, junior reception, etc.; *supervising* a small number of people doing cooking, housework, etc.; *junior and middle management*: in charge of a section or department in hotel, restaurant, etc.; and *senior management*.

In senior management, work often overlaps with other managerial jobs and does not necessarily involve any contact with the public (the reason which brings most entrants into this industry). Senior managers in a fast food chain may, for example, work entirely at head office; in industrial catering they may be responsible for a group of catering units; visit individual managers and liaise with head office; or they may investigate latest 'catering systems' (see below). Job content varies according to catering branch and to type and size of unit. Concerns range from the small and/or old-fashioned hotel run by an individual with total disregard for current catering practice, to units and chains run with the latest technological aids.

The majority of catering jobs involve work at 'unsocial hours'. Success in most jobs depends largely on motivating others to do their jobs well, and on efficient utilization of equipment and deployment of staff.

As in other industries, technology is 'de-skilling' many jobs and introducing new skills in others. Large industrial and institutional catering concerns and speciality restaurants increasingly use *systems catering* or *catering systems* instead of letting the chef decide what is for dinner and then getting her staff to prepare the meal. There are variations on the catering systems theme, but broadly this is how it works. Market research (see p. 283) identifies the most popular dishes within given price-ranges for given consumer-groups. Dishes are part- or fully prepared, and often even 'trayed up' in vast production kitchens. Then they are transported, frozen or chilled, to the 'point of consumption', which may be many miles away. Finally, at the point of consumption, food is 'reconstituted', for example in an aircraft galley. That may mean instant cooking in a microwave oven, or merely taking the food out of the container into which the dish was put in the production kitchen, and serving.

Managers must understand the technologies involved and their effects on ingredients, and they must be good organizers, but 'reconstituting' the food means merely setting dials and turning knobs rather than cooking.

Production kitchens leave little scope for creative cooking; every dish is prepared to recipes specifying such details as the size, weight, colour and often even the position on the plate of meat or cucumber slices, of sprouts or strawberries. But in experimental kitchens where new dishes and technologies are tried out, the work combines creative cooking skills, an understanding of the effects on the ingredients of being prepared in these unorthodox ways, and above all, managerial skills.

Fast Foods

The products of this expanding part of the industry range from fish and chips to baked potatoes, pizzas to hamburgers. Outlets may be independent businesses, part of a large chain or franchises (the parent company, or franchisor, supplies materials and services and the right to use a trade name, in return for which the franchisee invests her own capital and pays a levy). Some sell takeaway food only, others also provide table service; all resemble small factories with a retail counter. The actual cookery is 'de-skilled' and all operations can be learnt quickly. Most chains run their own training centres as well as providing training 'on the job'. In what is very much a young person's environment promotion from school leaver entrant to supervisor level can be rapid. Management posts are filled either by very successful supervisors or by people with degrees or diplomas in catering, business studies or even arts subjects. The latter have to learn all the basic operations at first hand before undergoing management training. The fast food industry is highly competitive and requires considerable business expertise in order to maintain cash flow and to control stock. Success depends on high turnover, which in turn involves very unsocial hours. Many managers hope to run their own business eventually.

Industrial Catering

This covers the provision of meals at places of work. Service is provided either by staff employed by the organization itself, or, increasingly, by *catering contractors*. These run 'catering units' on clients' premises in factories, offices, schools, leisure centres, motorway restaurants, at airports, and, with mobile units, on racecourses, agricultural shows, etc. Contractors' staff can change the setting in which they work without having to change employers. Middle and senior managers are in charge of a number of units; junior staff work on the same premises regularly for a period.

The unit manager's job is administrative. She only cooks herself if fewer than about 20 meals are being served. Her main task normally is trying to achieve as even a flow of work as possible – though peaks and valleys of activity and therefore occasional frayed tempers are unavoidable. Other management tasks include: *menu-planning* – the complexity of this varies according to the range of meals to be provided, from a narrow range of unexciting standard dishes to a wide selection including directors' dining-room 'specials', and according to the importance attached to nutritional values and tight budget control. Caterers must be able to provide at least 2 weeks' changing menus within several given price ranges and at different grades of sophistication. *Costing* – ingredients, labour costs, etc. *Purchasing*, which includes negotiating with suppliers and specifying, for example, the uniform size and weight of each lamb chop in an order of several hundreds.

Managers normally attend meetings with directors and/or personnel managers and also discuss improvements or complaints with staff representatives. They must keep up with technological developments and may be responsible for, or advise on, purchasing new equipment; but that work may also be done by specialists. Managers are usually responsible for, or for advising on, type of service, purchase of equipment and other maintenance.

There is a wide choice of jobs: from preparing sophisticated snacks for a West End showroom, or a dozen *haute cuisine* lunches in a stockbroker's office with one or two assistants, to feeding 2,000 a day with a staff of 50 – including 2 or 3 assistant managers.

Fair prospects.

School Catering Service

Basically the same as in industrial catering, with special emphasis on catering for children's tastes, nutritional values and strict budget control.

After training, caterers supervise the preparation of dinners, either at school kitchens or at centres from which up to 1,000 meals are distributed to a number of schools.

Promotion is to school meals organizer, advising on buying, planning, staffing, kitchen management, nutrition, etc. Organizers cover part of or the whole of a local education authority area and do a good deal of travelling. Some kitchens are antiquated; some up-to-date.

School meals staff are employed by local education authorities, not by individual heads of schools, with whom, however, they work in close cooperation. They do not, as a rule, have anything to do with supervising children during meal-times. During school holidays such work as stock-taking is carried out; in depressed areas a skeletal meal service is often provided during holidays.

The service has contracted severely recently. Often, only snacks are provided.

Restaurant Management

Eating places range from wine bars to large 'popular' and to exclusive *haute cuisine* restaurants. Restaurant managers must know how to attract and keep customers. Budgeting is often not as tight as in industrial and institutional catering. Menu-planning complexity depends on type of restaurant, with special scope for culinary creativity, for example, in vegetarian and in luxury restaurants, for management skills in narrow-range large or chain restaurants.

Catering for fluctuating numbers of customers with the minimum of waste is a highly skilled job. Rush hours tend to be more hectic than in industrial catering because it is impossible to have enough staff for busy days without being overstaffed on slack ones.

Managers' responsibilities vary greatly according to type and size of restaurant. For example, if the restaurant is one of a chain, overall planning and ordering may be done at head office; in other places the manager may be given a very free hand to 'give the restaurant that personal touch', as long as she keeps menus within a given price-range and reaches the profit target.

According to type of restaurant, managers spend varying amounts of time on 'customer contact'. Except in lunch-only restaurants, working hours, though not necessarily longer, are more spread out, with some evening and weekend work.

Pub ('Licensed House') Management is almost invariably done by couples. It is a way of life rather than a job, as it means being tied to the bar during licensing hours, 7 days a week. Most managers work for breweries which own pubs; some own or manage 'free' houses. Work involves purchasing, stock- and record-keeping as well as bar service. Thorough knowledge of licensing laws is essential. Interest in entertainment trends and more than just a 'liking for people' of all kinds are essential. Specialist training and experience in bar and cellar work required.

In some leisure centres (holiday camps, race courses, etc.), bar staff are the licensees and have their own 'franchise' – they run their own bars, i.e. instead of working for a salary they 'rent' the bar on the premises.

Hospital Catering

Hospital catering officers organize provision of meals for patients and staff, which means meals for between 200 and 3,000 people, many of whom need meals round the clock. They usually prepare diets under the overall direction but not day-to-day supervision of dietitians. Unlike other catering managers who may have learnt largely on-the-job, hospital catering staffs (management level) invariably have had systematic specialist training. This is the only catering specialization with a career structure (apart from school meals). At the top *catering advisers* work as National Health Service Regional Officers (see Health Service Administration, p. 214), i.e. not actually in hospitals. They advise on planning kitchens, catering technologies (see Systems Catering, above), staff training and staffing requirements, etc. *Catering managers* are responsible for the catering arrangements in a group of hospitals. *Catering officers* are responsible for provision of meals in individual hospitals. (See Dietetics, p. 157, for dietitian catering officers.)

Assistant and *deputy catering officers* are steps on the ladder to catering officer. In small hospitals, *catering supervisors* may be in charge of the whole catering operation; in larger hospitals they are responsible for a section.

Experience in hospital catering is very useful training for other specializations.

Some hospital catering is 'contracted out' to industrial caterers.

Transport Catering

This is often done by contractors using *catering systems* (see p. 92). In airline catering for example, all meals are prepared, and many 'trayed up' in production kitchens on or near airports, for consumption hundreds of miles away. Menu planning involves taking into account climatic conditions at point of consumption; commercial facts such as air commuters' 'menu-fatigue' (business people travel the same routes regularly; frequent menu changes must be made or customers are lost to the competition); research into which dishes and wines 'travel well'. *Airline catering* is very tightly cost-controlled; but in *marine catering* priorities are different: for passengers and crews at sea, meals are the highlight of the day. Proportionately more money is spent on food at sea than in the air, so sea-cooks and chefs have greater opportunities for creative cooking, and therefore for getting good shore-based jobs later.

Victualling ships – ordering supplies for trips sometimes several months long – is another catering specialization. Work is done in shipping companies' offices. Previous large-scale catering experience is essential.

All Catering Establishments

Assistants – various titles and various levels of responsibility – may be in charge of one catering function – purchasing, budgeting, food preparation for example – or of several functions.

Cooking always involves some physically hard work – the larger the kitchens, the tougher the job often is. Even with modern design and equipment kitchens still tend to be hot, noisy, and damp, and at times very hectic.

In large kitchens there are many cooking jobs without managerial responsibilities, but anyone who wants to progress beyond the kitchen-hand stage must take systematic training; home-cooking experience is not enough. It is important to distinguish between courses for professional cooks and for *haute cuisine* for home cooking. Cookery classes and schools do not always make this difference quite clear.

Professional Cooks

A variety of openings at various levels of skill and responsibility. For example, in large-scale *haute cuisine*, a chef heads a hierarchy of assistant chefs, each responsible for one type of cooking – meat, vegetables, pastry, etc. The chef may be responsible for budgeting, buying, planning – or this may all be done by a food and beverage manager, or at head office; responsibilities depend on type and size of organization worked for. In small *haute cuisine* restaurants, 2 or 3 cooks may do all the work. In simpler restaurants, convenience foods are used extensively and cooks' ability to produce palatable, inexpensive yet reasonably varied menus is the most important aspect of the work. It is no easier than, but very different from, *haute cuisine*.

Freelance Work

For *directors' lunches*, for example, one cook prepares up to about 12 lunches a day, single-handed. This may be part of the company's industrial catering unit with planning, shopping, etc., done centrally, or it is done by *freelance cooks*, who do their own planning, budgeting, shopping. They may have several lunch-time clients each requiring service on 1 or 2 days a week. Freelance cooks also cook for private dinner parties and, on a regular or occasional basis, they cook evening meals for families (one or several), usually to relieve working mothers of shopping and cooking chores. They need their own car to transport equipment and shopping. They must be able to budget and cook within various price-ranges.

Sometimes they cook for families on holidays abroad, or for travel agents' chalet-party package tours, working in ski resorts all winter, at the seaside all summer. This type of work usually includes general housekeeping.

Personal attributes *For all catering (in varying degrees)*: organizing and administrative ability; ability to discuss matters with all types of people – unskilled kitchen staff and managing directors, salesmen and shop stewards, committee chairmen and colleagues; interest in people as well as in preparing food and in management; some manual dexterity and visual imagination; ability to remain unruffled in inevitable crises; physical stamina. For *Freelance Cooks*: as above, plus business acumen.

Hotels

Manager

The work The manager's work varies enormously according to size and type of hotel. In large hotels, the general manager is coordinator and administrator. Departmental managers are in charge of specialist services:

reception, sales, food and bar service, housekeeping, etc. The manager deals with correspondence, has daily conferences with departmental managers and may be in touch daily or weekly with head office. Although she tries to be around to talk to guests (not only when they have complaints), most of her time is spent dealing with running the business side, making decisions based on information given her by accountants, personnel manager, sales manager, accommodation manager, etc.

She does not normally have to live in, though she may have a bedroom or flat on the premises. Her working hours are long, and often busiest at weekends and during holidays. Managers are expected to speak at least one foreign language. They must be able to switch from one task to another instantly, and change their daily routine when necessary – which it often is.

Among the manager's most important tasks: creating and maintaining good staff relations, as success depends entirely on the work done by others under her overall direction; giving the hotel the personality and the character which either the manager herself, or more often her employers, intend it to have; and being able to make a constantly changing clientele feel as though each of them mattered individually, though the extent of emphasis on personal service varies according to the type of hotel.

In small hotels the manager may have a staff of about 15 to 30, and instead of several departmental managers, possibly 1 general assistant. She often has to live in, and she usually has less off-duty time than managers in large hotels. There are *far* more small (and unglamorous) hotels than large or small luxury ones. Many small and medium-sized country hotels are owned by companies and run by married couples (who have little time off together). In the past the husband was invariably the manager, the wife assistant or housekeeper or receptionist. Under equal opportunity legislation, women must be given equal opportunities on companies' training schemes; in practice there seems to have been little change.

General Assistant – Assistant Manager

The work In small hotels she helps wherever help is needed most – in the kitchen, in the bar, in housekeeping. Although the work is extremely hard, it is the best possible experience, some hotel managers say the only valuable experience – better than theoretical training (though the ideal is a sound basis of technical training complemented by experience). In large hotels she assists the manager and may be entirely responsible for certain departments: housekeeping, reception, food and drink service, etc. Some remain assistants, either by choice or because managers' jobs are not available.

An assistant departmental manager may be as responsible and as well paid as a general manager: it depends on size and type of hotel.

Personal attributes

For top jobs: exceptional organizing ability and business acumen; outgoing personality; the wish to please people, however unreasonable customers' demands may seem; an interest in all the practical skills – cooking, bar-management, housekeeping, etc.; willingness to work while others play; ability to shoulder responsibility and handle staff; tact.

For assistants/managers of small hotels: partly as for managers, but exceptional organizing ability is not necessary; instead, a liking for practical work is essential, and willingness to work hard and get things done without taking the credit.

Receptionist/'Front Office'

The work

Head receptionists are assisted in large and medium-sized hotels by *junior receptionists*. They keep the chart or 'bedroom-book', which shows at a glance provisional and definite bookings. To steer a course between unnecessary refusal of bookings and over-booking is skilled work. Receptionists deal with correspondence; they must be able to do straightforward book-keeping, type and compose their own letters: they notify other hotel departments of arrivals and departures, and keep the Tabular, or 'tab. sheet' (a ledger into which all charges are entered to the relevant room numbers), which involves collating chits handed to reception by the kitchen, hall porter, bar, etc., and transferring charges to guests' accounts and on to the Tabular.

Many hotels have computerized reservations and accounts systems, which give instant information on a whole hotel group's vacancies; on guests' accounts; and possibly supply position regarding clean linen, beverages, etc.

Receptionists also act as general information office, answering guests' queries, such as train times, or the address of a good hairdresser. In motels, guests 'buy keys' as they arrive to rent a suite with garage for one night at a time. Receptionists explain the procedure and hand over the keys.

They work in or near (and sometimes do the flowers for) the entrance hall, and are always at the centre of activities. They work shifts. Especially in country hotels, they may live in; meals on duty are supplied free, sometimes in the restaurant, more often in the staff dining-room with other senior staff.

Head receptionists are usually responsible directly to the manager; theirs is considered one of the most important posts in the hotel business and can be a stepping stone to general management.

Personal attributes A friendly, helpful personality; an uncritical liking for people of all types; a good memory for faces – visitors appreciate recognition; ability to take responsibility and to work well with others; considerable self-confidence; a methodical approach; a liking for figures; meticulous accuracy. *For top jobs*: business acumen; good judgement of people; leadership.

Housekeeper

The work Except in small hotels, housekeepers do not do housework, but supervise domestic staff. Other duties include: checking rooms – for cleanliness, general comfort, bedside lamps, etc.; laundry – giving out clean linen, seeing to its repair and replacement; pass-key control; room service organization and supervision; discussions with heads of other departments; training and engaging staff and arranging work schedules. In a large hotel a head housekeeper may have a staff of 200 under her.

In small and medium-sized hotels the housekeeper may be responsible for choosing and maintaining the furnishings, decoration and general appearance of bedrooms and lounges. In large hotels there may be one assistant or floor housekeeper to every floor, or every two floors; the head housekeeper's job is therefore more onerous. She is immediately responsible to the manager.

Housekeepers generally only have direct contact with guests when there are complaints, or when special attention is needed – if guests fall ill, for example. Success depends largely on ensuring that the domestic staff do their work well.

There are similar housekeeping jobs in halls of residence and especially in the *Health Service*. Career structure is better in the latter than in hotels.

Personal attributes Organizing ability; practical approach; an eye for detail; practicality; ability to handle and train staff.

Hotel Sales Management

A fringe hotel management career. Hotel sales managers work for large hotels and hotel groups. They sell 'hotel facilities' – efficiency, service, atmosphere, as well as conference and banqueting facilities. A hotel sales manager for example may approach large business concerns and try to fix contracts for business executives to stay regularly at her hotels and, jointly with tour operators (see Travel Agent, p. 554) and airlines etc., she 'builds' package tours.

No career structure or definite way in yet. Hotel sales managers come either via hotel management, or marketing (p. 283) or any other type of business experience. (BTEC diplomas with Tourism specialization are useful preparation.)

Personal attributes Business acumen; numeracy; extrovert, friendly personality.

Institutional Management

The work This is management in non-profit-making, mainly residential establishments: halls of residence, hostels; the domestic side of hospitals; as well as, increasingly, in commercial conference and training centres. It also includes non-residential work: school catering; meals on wheels; social service departments' day centres.

Managers may be called bursar, warden, domestic superintendent, institutional manager. Titles are arbitrary and do not indicate any particular level of responsibility, status or duties.

There are almost as many different types of 'institutions' as there are of hotels, and there is considerable overlap between catering and institutional management. The difference is one of emphasis and setting in which the work is done. Some jobs in institutional management have more in common with running a hotel – for example running a large conference or management training centre – than with other institutional management jobs, in which residents' general well-being and emotional needs as well as their creature comforts have to be considered (such as old people's homes, where the job is part catering, part social work). In hospitals, institutional managers are level-pegging with senior nursing officers.

An *institutional manager* may be responsible for all or some of the following aspects of a community's creature comforts: general management; meals service; budgeting; purchase and maintenance of kitchen equipment; planning or having a say in the planning of additional building; furnishings and decoration; making arrangements, in establishments with long vacations, for residential conferences, vacation courses, etc.; dealing with residents' and staff's suggestions and complaints; helping to establish a friendly atmosphere both among staff and among residents; in small establishments, first-aid and home-nursing (but *not* responsibility for sick residents); acting as hostess and as general information bureau; dealing with committees.

Most jobs are entirely administrative, but in small institutions the manager occasionally has to help out with housework or cooking. Many (by no means all) jobs are residential; accommodation varies from bedsitter to self-contained flat for couples (with spouse not necessarily working in the organization concerned).

Institutional managers are occasionally expected to spend a good deal of their time in the common or public rooms with the residents – the degree of privacy varies.

Assistant institutional managers – often means housekeepers – are usually beginners seeking experience or those unwilling or unable to take the more responsible jobs, but in large organizations, especially hospitals, it is a step on the ladder.

Personal attributes

A sociable temperament; ability to get on with all kinds of people as well as a liking for things domestic; a practical approach; ability to handle staff and willingness to lend a hand wherever necessary; calmness in crises; disregard of criticism – institutional managers are often blamed for domestic hitches beyond their control.

Prospects catering generally

Fluctuates according to economic situation. There is more scope for 'doers' – i.e. cooks, housekeepers – than senior managers. The higher the level of management, the stiffer the competition. There is no rigid career structure, except in hospitals and school catering. Promotion depends on experience, luck, personality and mobility: experience in variety of type of establishment is essential for work with some large companies.

Pay: Varies. The luxury hotels do not necessarily offer better-paid or more varied jobs than large limited-menu restaurant chains.

Training

This is rather haphazard with a variety of courses and qualifications. Large catering organizations now often expect specific qualifications for the various levels and types of jobs, but there is still no universally applicable career structure. Below degree-level entry, on-the-job training, with day- or block-release, is probably as useful a preparation for advancement as full-time training. But day-release is not easily granted in catering and employment *without* day-/block-release is not recommended.

Pre-entry courses

1. For entrants with at least O-levels in English, maths and a science: 2-year full-time courses for BTEC National Diploma (see p. xvi) in *Hotel, Catering, Institutional Management and Food Technology*. Students take 'core units', which give them a broad-based catering training, and special option units to prepare them for a specific aspect of catering. BTEC National Diploma leads to 'technician' level, i.e. practical/supervisory jobs, but a first job depends on the individual, type of organization and supply and demand.

2. For entrants with *either* 1 A-level (and possibly another subject

studied to A-level) and 3 O-levels (including English, maths and a science) *or* with a BTEC National Diploma (with relevant option units): 2-year full-time or 3-year sandwich BTEC Higher Diploma courses. BTEC Higher awards probably lead to junior/middle management jobs.

3. For entrants with at least 2 A-levels and 3 O-levels (including English, maths and a science and, for some courses, a modern language (whether a BTEC National Diploma is acceptable in lieu of A-levels depends on relevance of units studied – there is no blanket acceptance as with old OND)): 3-year full-time or 4-year sandwich degree courses. These vary in emphasis on differing catering aspects but include supervision of food and beverage preparation (and some practical work); catering management principles and practices; catering technologies (for example, equipment and processes used in 'fast food' restaurants, 'systems catering'); specialist work such as airline catering; sales management and marketing; accounting; computer application; the various aspects of tourism; the implications of the growing recreation and leisure industries.

4. For graduates with *either* a relevant degree or comparable qualification, *or* any degree plus proof of interest in/experience of catering: 1-year full-time courses for post-graduate diplomas (old HND/Cs are acceptable too, BTEC Higher awards *may* be).

Both catering degrees and post-graduate diplomas lead to exemption from Professional Examinations of Hotel Catering and Institutional Management Association (HCIMA), the professional hotel and catering organization.

Courses for people in relevant employment

1. For entrants with *either* 4 O-levels (including subjects demonstrating command of English and numeracy and a science) *or* with 3 years' relevant work experience and minimum 1-year full-time or 2-year part-time course: 2-year part-time course for HCIMA Part A examination, leading to HCIMA membership.

2. For students with at least 12 months' responsible work in the industry and, usually, Part A: HCIMA Part B (former Final) examination: 1-year full-time, 2-year sandwich or 3-year day- or block-release course. (Whether BTEC awards will qualify for entry to Part B courses will not be known until BTEC courses have run for some years.)

NOTE: It is usually possible to study for BTEC awards by full- or part-time study but very few colleges run part-time BTEC catering courses.

3. Mainly for people in relevant employment with few or no O-levels: 2-year part-time City and Guilds Craft Certificates in *General Catering*, *Basic Cookery* and various other hotel/catering subjects such as

Housekeeping/Cleaning Science, *Food Service* and *Reception*. In some colleges City and Guilds courses are also available full-time. These courses may also qualify, with experience, for BTEC and HCIMA courses.

In some Further Education Colleges and 6th forms, City and Guilds Foundation courses combine general educational subjects with an insight into, or preparation for, jobs in the broad hotel and catering area. No entry qualifications.

Personal attributes *For all catering management (in varying degrees)*: organizing and administrative ability; ability to discuss matters with all types of people – unskilled kitchen staff and managing directors, salesmen and shop stewards, committee chairmen and colleagues; interest in people as well as in preparing food, and in management; a certain amount of manual dexterity and visual imagination; the sort of temperament which remains unruffled in inevitable crises; physical stamina.

Late start No problem. Admission to courses depends on experience and motivation rather than age and GCEs. 6-month and 1-year catering courses are available under TOPS (see p. xlvi).

Position of women Traditionally, and illogically, catering and hotel-keeping (not institutional management) have been a man's world. In hotels until very recently there were hardly any women above departmental or assistant or small-hotel management. As yet no woman is manager of any of the well-known large luxury hotels; very few are near the top in spite of the fact that more women than men take advanced catering courses. Women traditionally only run hotels in which there is no management hierarchy. To break the tradition, women have to be exceptionally well qualified and they must be mobile: companies say that the reason for not promoting more women is that women are not willing to gain varied experience by moving around the country.

This is a career area where discrimination is difficult to prove; qualifications do not always prove suitability for individual jobs.

In up-market restaurants, men are traditionally managers; women chefs are still very rare indeed, and most managers have *been* chefs at least for a time. In large commercial kitchens, most of the staff are men, but in school and hospital kitchens, where the work is just as arduous, there are mainly women cooks.

In industrial catering, women are beginning to have equal chances at all management levels and are, in fact, encouraged to move up the management ladder. Just over half are women. In hospitals, institutional-management-trained women have top jobs in domestic management, but top catering officers – concerned with food and drink, not housekeeping – are more frequently men. 70% of schools and institutional catering managers are usually women. The fact that women do hold large-scale catering management jobs in some areas shows that it is only tradition which has kept them out of other catering management areas. A scheme has been run recently by the industry to develop women managers in the hotel and restaurant branches.

Career-break: No problem in institutional management for women who can live in and/or work irregular hours; nor in industrial and schools catering.

Refresher training: Most catering courses can be adapted.

Part-time: Very limited opportunities at management level, good opportunities at craft level (i.e. cooking, housekeeping, junior reception). Freelance catering offers possibilities.

Further information

The Hotel, Catering and Institutional Management Association, 191 Trinity Road, Tooting, London SW17 7HN
Hotel and Catering Industry Training Board, PO Box 18, Ramsey House, Central Square, Wembley, Middlesex HA9 7AP

Related careers

Dietitian – Food Technology – Home Economics – Services (Catering Corps) – Teaching – Travel Agent and Tour Operator

Chartered Secretary and Administrator

Entry qualifications 2 A-levels and 3 O-levels or 3 A-levels and 2 O-levels; or BTEC National Certificate/Diploma in Business Studies or Public Administration. See **Training** for *graduate* entry, and **Late start**.

The work The work is very different from that of the secretary to an executive (see Secretarial Work, p. 451). Instead, 'administration' overlaps with 'management' (see Management, p. 269). The distinction between the two terms, and indeed the concept, is blurred. It used to be clearer: 'administrators' in the public sector used to do very similar work to 'managers' in industry. Now 'management' is an important function in the public service, but it is likely to be carried out by 'administrators' (see Local Government, Health Service Administration, pp. 265, 214), while in industry, 'administration' is often seen as one of the separate 'functions' (see Management, p. 269). It is all rather confusing. From the career-chooser's point of view, professional administration can be one of the specialist activities carried out in the public service *or* in industry and commerce.

The main element in professional administration, wherever it is carried out, is coordinating (and possibly also controlling) various individuals and/or departments within an organization. Administrators are the link between people and their separate activities; they make sure that different sections or departments dovetail, and fit into the whole. At senior level, administrators have an 'overview' over whatever their organization does; at junior level, they may, for example, coordinate the work of, say, the accounts department; at middle level they ensure that, for example, production, distribution and personnel departments are informed of each others' needs. Professional administrators often work for a time in the various departments, to find out how each works and where it fits into the whole. Like other professional qualifications, professional administration can lead to the top in whatever the type of organization. The work is immensely varied, and so are the top jobs. There is no rigid pattern.

Chartered secretaries, i.e. ICSA Diploma holders (see **Training** below) can become company secretaries: public companies are by law required to have company secretaries, i.e. people who have either a legal, an accountancy or the ICSA qualification. According to type and size of company, company secretaries can be chief executives – possibly called director, or secretary-general – responsible only to the Board or whoever are the policy-makers; or they can be the chief administrative officer responsible to the director or chief executive. The ICSA Diploma is now the professional qualification for administrators in Local Government (see p. 267).

Prospects Good, as it is an adaptable qualification.

Pay: Medium to high (see p. xxiii).

Training The Institute's examination is in four parts, each part divided into two modules and each module consisting of two subjects. Students who fail one subject retake the module, not the whole examination part, as in the former structure. The Part I examination gives a general grounding in administrative techniques and covers communication, principles of law, economics and statistics. Parts II, III and IV are geared to the type of setting in which the student intends to work. The three options are (a) the *company secretarial* stream, (b) the *general and financial administration* stream, and (c) the *public service* stream.

Such subjects as personnel management, economic policies and problems are studied in all streams. Company secretarial students take for example a taxation module; general and financial administration students take a management administration module.

The differences in the syllabuses are not very great and it is likely that whatever stream a student chooses to study, she could later switch to work in one of the other settings.

There are various ways to study:

1. Best for school-leavers, as it does not require a final career decision at the outset, is to take a Higher BTEC award in Business Studies or Public Administration followed either by employment plus part-time study (day-release is generally granted by public employers and large companies) or by a 1-year full-time course for Parts II, III and IV. Subject-for-subject exemptions are normally granted to BTEC Higher award holders.
2. By taking a degree (in any subject) followed either by a full-time 1-year course for Parts II, III and IV or by employment plus part-time study. (Graduates are granted subject-for-subject exemption.)
3. Entirely by part-time study while in appropriate jobs. This takes at least 4 years: it is advisable to choose a job with day-release.
4. Entirely by correspondence study perhaps supplemented by evening classes.

Personal attributes A flair for administration; common sense and good judgement; numeracy; interest in current affairs; tact; discretion.

Late start Good opportunities. Mature students with previous experience in administrative, accounting or secretarial work do not need to have the normal entry qualification. Full-time 1-year courses may qualify for TOPS grants (see p. xlvi).

Position of women About 6% of *all* Institute members, but 34% of under 30s, are women. Though there are no doubt pockets of resistance to women in many companies, women who have qualified have had no problem getting jobs – more often in public service and general administration than as company secretary.

Career-break: Should be no problem for people who had responsible jobs *before* the break. There are 'Revision Courses' which can be used as *refresher* courses. Also, there is no time limit for completing the 4-part examination; so it is possible either to resume studies after returning to work, or to study by correspondence course, preferably with evening classes, while housebound.

Part-time: Fair possibilities. Many professional associations and institutions want only part-time secretaries. It may also be possible to attend the part-time day-release courses while *not* in employment – depends on individual colleges' policy.

Further information The Institute of Chartered Secretaries and Administrators, 16 Park Crescent, London W1N 4AH

Related careers *Accountancy – Health Service Administration – Secretarial and Clerical Work*

Chiropody

Private practice – hospitals and health authorities – industry

Entry qualifications Minimum age 18. 2 A-levels and 3 O-levels.

The work Chiropodists diagnose and treat foot diseases and functional and constitutional foot disorders; they inspect children's and adults' feet to prevent minor ailments from growing into major ones. When patients need their shoes adapted, chiropodists give the necessary instructions to surgical shoemakers or shoe-repairers; they also construct special appliances themselves. Chiropodists can choose the environment in which to work:

1. *Private practice*: This is the most remunerative work. The chiropodist treats patients in her own home and, occasionally, may visit patients in their homes. Private practice can be lonely work (even though patients are seen all day) but group practices are now being set up in some areas, partners renting premises jointly or using rooms in one of the partner's homes as a surgery.
2. *Hospitals and district health authority clinics*: Chiropodists are employed on a session (3-hourly) basis or full-time.
3. *Industry*: Concerns where staff are on their feet all day often employ full- or part-time chiropodists.

In both (2) and (3) chiropodists enjoy the companionship and social facilities of a large organization. Some combine part-time work with private practice, to have a small regular income which supplements private practice income.

Prospects Good. In employment, only fair chances of promotion to senior appointments.

Pay: Medium (see p. xxiii).

Training For State Registration, which is essential, 3 years, full-time, at chiropody schools which prepare students for the Society of Chiropodists' examinations. Two-thirds of the training is practical and includes treatment of patients under the supervision of experienced chiropodists, the preparation of appliances and shoe-fitting. The theoretical training includes the life sciences, anatomy, physiology. Candidates must make sure that a chosen course is recognized by the Society of Chiropodists (the Society is the qualifying body); other courses are useless.

Personal attributes A high degree of manual dexterity; ability to get on with people greatly affects chances of promotion and of having a flourishing private practice. However, unlike many other careers with patients, a shy, retiring person may get on well, providing she is even-tempered.

Late start Good opportunities, with relaxations in GCE requirements. Upper age 37, but, exceptionally, older entrants may be accepted for training. 15% of entrants are over 25.

Position of women At the moment, 55% of practising chiropodists, and 73% of students, are women. Proportionately there are more men than women in senior jobs and in private practice.

Career-break: No problem if kept up with developments. Reduced 'non-practising membership' subscriptions are available.

Refresher courses: *Ad hoc* arrangements with 1 month 'up-dating' can be made.

Part-time: Ample scope for work, no part-time training.

Further information The Society of Chiropodists, 8 Wimpole Street, London W1M 8BX
The Institute of Chiropodists, 113–115 Oxford Street, London W1R 1TD

Related careers *Physiotherapy*

Civil Aviation

Air traffic control officer – cabin crew – ground staff – pilot

Air Traffic Control Officer

Entry qualifications 5 GCEs including English language and maths; 2 must be at A-level (or 3 Scottish Highers) of which one must be maths, geography or a science subject. A few entrants are graduates.

The work Teams of ATCOs control and monitor the movements of aircraft taking off, landing and when *en route* in designated controlled airspace. An aircraft leaving a controller's area of responsibility is coordinated with the next ATC unit, which may be an airfield or an air traffic control centre in the UK or in Europe. Pilots of aircraft are, in fact, in two-way radio communication with controllers from the time they request permission to start engines until the engines stop at their destination.

The work is responsible and highly skilled; it may involve the safe 'stacking' of aircraft in an airfield's 'holding area' while awaiting approach, the 'sequencing' of aircraft using radar to maintain a safe distance between them, and ensuring that aircraft flying the same routes at varying speeds, heights and directions are always safely separated horizontally and vertically. ATCOs are often assisted in their calculations by computers, and must be aware of the relevant data fed to these computers. After gaining operational experience, a small proportion of ATCOs specialize in ATC computer work.

An ATCO spends most of her time – normally wearing earphones – monitoring data about relevant aircraft, either looking at a radar display or out over an airfield. The international language of ATC is English, so the UK ATCO talks and is talked to in her own language; but foreign pilots sometimes have problems expressing themselves clearly, especially when under pressure. The ATCO must make up her mind quickly, but can ask the pilot to repeat anything which she may not immediately understand.

The great majority of operational ATCOs work shift duties, and all ATCOs must be prepared to do so; as far as possible these are planned well in advance, but last minute changes are sometimes necessary.

Prospects Fair.

Pay: Good.

Training The 2¾-year course consists of periods of academic and simulation training at the College of Air Traffic Control near Bournemouth, alternating with spells of practical training at operational units. Training is given in all aspects of ATC, and in basic meteorology, navigation, telecommunications and principles of radar and associated techniques; flying experience is also given, and this at the moment includes learning to fly to Private Pilot's Licence standard.

Personal attributes A calm cool temperament; ability to conceal and control excitement in emergencies; ability to concentrate both in busy and in quiet periods; a good quick brain, with quick reactions and the ability to be decisive; the ability to work as part of a team.

Late start Normal maximum age 25; with substantial relevant experience, this is raised to 34.

Position of women In 1983 3·5% of qualified ATCOs, but nearly 20% of those under training, were women. The number of women who apply for ATCO posts is increasing, and a slightly higher proportion of women than of men applicants is accepted for training.

Career-break: Re-training could in theory be given to women who have left ATC and wish to return; the number who have done so is tiny.

Further information Civil Aviation Authority Personnel Services, Room T1220, CAA House, 45–59 Kingsway, London WC2B 6TE

Air Traffic Control Assistants (ATCAs)

Entry qualifications Minimum age 17.
GCE O-level or equivalent passes in 4 subjects including English language and either maths or a science subject; substantial flying experience may be accepted in lieu of some educational requirements.

The work Assisting ATCOs in their tasks by undertaking certain routine functions, particularly with data preparation and display, at both airfields and airways control centres. This usually involves using computer terminals.

All ATCAs must be prepared to work shifts.

Prospects Limited, because between one-third and one-half of candidates accepted for ATCO training start as ATCAs.

Pay: Fair

Training 4 weeks at the College of ATC, Bournemouth, followed by practical 'hands-on' training lasting up to a year at an operational unit.

Personal attributes Ability to work as part of a team; a liking for routine but responsible work.

Late start No maximum age but late-starters need to have relevant experience, probably in the Armed Forces.

Position of women Between 20% and 25% of ATCAs are women.

Career-break: Re-training at an operational unit can be given. Opportunities for returners depend on supply and demand. Young entrants are given preference.

Further information As for ATCOs.

Air Traffic Engineering Cadetships
About 30 cadets with entry qualifications of at least BTEC National Diploma in Electronics and Communications and preferably GCE O-levels in English undertake a 1-year full-time training course at the Authority's College of Telecommunications Engineering, Bletchley, Bucks, on sophisticated electronic navigational aids and radar equipments. Successful completion of training can lead to a career as an Air Traffic Engineer at the CAA's National Air Traffic Service units throughout the United Kingdom.

Cabin Crew (Stewardess and Steward)

Entry qualifications Minimum age usually 21. Upper age limit about 30.

No qualifications laid down; usually O-level standard (not passes) in English and French, German, Italian or Spanish, some catering or nursing experience, or 1 year in a responsible job which involved dealing with people.

The work The cabin crew welcome passengers, supervise seating and safety-belt arrangements, and look after air-sick travellers, babies, and children travelling alone. Stewards and stewardesses serve meals (but do not cook them), and sell drinks, cigarettes, etc. in a variety of currencies.

They 'dress the plane' to see that blankets, head-rests, magazines, cosmetics, etc. are available and in good order, and make necessary announcements over the public-address system. They deal with any emergencies and write reports after each flight, with comments, for instance, on the behaviour of unaccompanied children.

Most of the time cabin crews are airborne waiters and waitresses. From the moment the plane is airborne they are continuously busy, working at great speed in a confined space.

Duty hours vary from one airline to another and are likely to be changed at the last minute because of weather and other 'exigencies of the service'. Normally on European routes cabin crews are 'on' for 4–6 days with a good deal of night duty; they are then off-duty for 2–4 days. On long-distance trips they may be away from home for 3 weeks, but that would include several days' rest at a foreign airport.

The farther the destination, the more chance of sightseeing. On short routes cabin crews may fly backwards and forwards for a month without seeing more than the airport at their destination. On long-distance trips crews often change planes at 'slip-points' and stay for a few days' rest, living in luxury hotels at their airline's expense.

Prospects Vary according to economic climate. British-trained crews are in demand by American and other foreign airlines if they speak the appropriate language.

Pay: Medium (see p. xxiii).

Training About 6 weeks with Europe-only airlines to about 8 with transatlantic ones. Subjects include meal-service, first-aid, airborne procedure, emergency drill with swimming-bath lesson in the use of the inflatable dinghy and life-jacket.

Personal attributes A likeable personality; calmness in crises; common sense; efficiency; sensitivity to anxious passengers' needs.

Position of women See p. 116.

Further information Individual airlines.

Ground Staff (some examples)

Passenger Service Assistant (titles vary)

Entry qualifications

Usually O-level standard English and maths and geography. Minimum age usually 18.

The work

Passenger service assistants see that passengers and luggage get on to the right plane, with the minimum of fuss. They check-in luggage, which involves checking travel documents; check-out passengers at boarding gates. They answer passengers' questions on travel connections and similar matters.

Other duties carried out by experienced PSAs include: load-control – preparing information for aircraft loaders on luggage weight; cargo documentation for Customs clearance; checking that planes leave with the right meals, cargo, baggage.

PSAs work in uniform, and do shift work. They move about the airport all day, rarely sit down.

Sales Staff (again titles vary)

Entry qualifications

Usually O-level standard English, maths, geography, a foreign language.

The work

Sales staff sit in airport and city offices and answer questions on international flight connections; make fare calculations (in various currencies); sell tickets over the counter and over the phone. Bookings are made to and from all over the world; each reservation must be related to reservations made elsewhere and reservation vacancies available for any particular flight at any given moment. This is called 'space control'. Reservations staff use computerized information systems: at the push of a button they can see, on their computer terminal, exactly what the present reservation situation is on any flight.

Senior sales staff may call on travel agents, business houses and other important customers to explain ancillary services such as car hire, hotel accommodation, package holidays, and 'sell' their own particular airline, both passenger and cargo services.

Sales staff may do shift work, though less so in senior positions.

Training

Short on-the-job training with some lectures.

Personal attributes An orderly mind; communication skills; a liking for meeting people very briefly; a calm, helpful manner; good speech and appearance.

Commercial Management, Flight Operations and Flight Planning

Entry qualifications Vary with different airlines and according to supply and demand. Some promotion from sales staff; most entrants have A-levels; many have degrees or BTEC Business Studies.

The work The administration of flight programmes, which cover many thousands of flight-miles, millions of tons of freight and ever-growing 'passenger throughput' is a highly complex undertaking. Staff organize the airline's fleet of planes over its network, making the most efficient use of each aircraft, e.g., ensuring that as far as possible outgoing freight is replaced with return-flight freight, and that the 'turn-round' time in airports is as short as possible, while allowing time for maintenance, loading, etc. 'Aircrew management' involves arranging individual crew members' schedules, taking into consideration maximum flying hours allowed; rest-days ('stop overs') abroad, etc.

Apart from this planning work, staff are also responsible for ensuring that at all times aircrew have all the information they need before each take-off, throughout the planned itinerary. This involves discussions with a variety of departments and individuals; keeping detailed records; being prepared for emergencies.

Prospects Vary according to economic climate.

Pay: Low to medium (see p. xxiii).

Training Through airlines' own training schemes, lasting 2 to 3 years, *or* BTEC Higher awards or degree, followed by shorter airline training. Schemes vary between companies and according to expansion or contraction rate of airline industry.

Personal attributes Drive; organizing ability; liking for working under pressure.

Position of women *Air stewardesses and stewards are all 'cabin crew'*; a woman is quite often in charge of an aircraft's cabin crew. *Ground staff* examples: traditionally mainly women. *Commercial management*: so far very few women have tried. Equal chances of promotion.

Further information Individual airlines.

Related careers *Linguist – Management, Hotels and Catering – Travel Agent*

Pilot

Entry qualifications 2 A-levels and 3 O-levels; subjects must include maths and English language, and either physics or chemistry or physical science; in practice at least 1 scientific subject must be at A-level.

Graduates, preferably in science or engineering, stand the best chance of acceptance. Upper age limit: 26 (25 for Helicopter Training Scheme).

The work The pilot's most taxing task is assimilating a mass of separate bits of information presented to her by an array of indicators on the instrument panel and by colleagues, to 'process' it in her mind, and to take whatever action may be necessary. Procedures during the flight and specially during take-off and landing are complex enough, but what makes the pilot's job the arduous one it is is the fact that she must at all times be prepared for the unexpected. Instrument failure may require her, instantly, to override whatever the computerized equipment's instructions are, or evasive action may have to be taken to avoid a mid-air collision. Throughout her working life a pilot probably never has to cope with such 'incidents', but she must be *able* to do so.

Her first job for at least 2½ years is as *co-pilot*. Then, as *pilot*, she has total responsibility for the aircraft, crew, passengers. Navigators are now rarely employed, and flight engineers not on all aircraft: the pilot must in any case be able to perform navigating and engineering tasks.

Her work starts at least an hour before take-off, when she either prepares her own or is presented with a detailed flight plan. This gives such information as exact height at various stages on her precisely defined route; meteorological information; take-off and landing weights which are vital data in case of emergency action.

On 'short hauls' (in Europe) pilot and crew are busy all the time. On long hauls there can be long hours with only routine checks to go through. This can be difficult in an unexpected way: pilots get bored, because there is no real work to do, yet the need for alertness is as great as ever.

Prospects As the last of the war-time pilots – who make up a large proportion of present pilots – are retiring, demand was expected to increase. However, because of the world-wide recession this increase has not materialized. There is some small demand for other types of pilots (plane or helicopter): on air taxis; crop spraying; aerial photography; oil rig supplying; weather and traffic observation; flying privately or company-owned planes and helicopters, and especially for instructors in flying clubs. In recent years a few pilots have managed to pay for their own initial training and then 'built up' the number of flying hours needed to be eligible for a Commercial Pilot's Licence (see **Training**) while working as an instructor.

Pay: High (see p. xxiii).

Training The overwhelming majority of students at the recognized air training schools are sponsored, but the only regular sponsor of any number of pilots, British Airways, has discontinued its sponsorship schemes for the time being. Basic training lasts at least 20 months for non-graduate entrants, about 1 year for graduates. The syllabus includes aerodynamics, meteorology, electrical engineering and electronics, aircraft design and systems, flight procedures and aviation law. Flight training starts on the ground, in simulators.

The first qualification is the Commercial Pilot's Licence (CPL), but to fly in an airliner as co-pilot the basic requirement is the CPL plus Instrument Rating. Ratings are qualifications in particular aspects of flying and in flying particular types of aircraft; the types of aircraft a CPL holder may co-pilot depends on her Ratings. Before a pilot is qualified as Captain of an airliner she must have the Airline Transport Pilot's Licence (ATPL) and many thousands of flying hours.

Full-time, non-sponsored training to CPL costs about £30,000 but quite a lot of people now get only a Private Pilot's Licence (PPL). They then gain sufficient hours to take an Instructor's Course; as Instructors they are paid and they can accumulate the 700 hours' flying-time necessary to qualify for exemption from the full-length, full-time CPL training. This roundabout way of qualifying is *very* much cheaper and can be done while, most of the time, earning a living in part-time employment.

Personal attributes Above-average intelligence; ability to fight boredom and be alert at all times; mental agility; self-confidence; leadership qualities; ability to take instant decisions; total unflappability; very well balanced personality; desire to break down traditional sex-barriers.

Position of women There are about 60 female professional pilots (1983) employed with airlines, and on air taxis, crop spraying, etc., and especially as instructors in flying clubs. Once trained, women have no more problems getting jobs (*outside airlines*) than men. But despite the Sex Discrimination Act it is unlikely that women will have equal opportunities as airline pilots for a long time to come, as many men learn flying in the Services, and companies say that all pilots must be able to work on all routes and in some destination countries there is no accommodation or provision for, and/or reluctance to deal with, women pilots.

The British Women Pilots Association has about 200 members and helps with advice and (small) scholarships (Hon. Sec.: Mrs M. E. Tucker, BA Terminus, PO Box 13, London, SW1).

British Airways opened its training sponsorship scheme to girls in 1977, but none has been sponsored yet.

Further information

Civil Aviation Authority, FCL 3, Aviation House, 129 Kingsway, London WC2B 6NN (licensing inquiries only)
British Women Pilots Association (address above)
British Airport Authority, Gatwick Airport, West Sussex RH6 0H2

Related careers

Air Traffic Control Officer – Engineering – Surveying

Civil Service

Despite recent cuts the Civil Service is Britain's largest employer. It offers opportunities at all educational levels, in virtually all career fields. There is a tradition of training and encouragement to use day-release facilities which enables ambitious entrants to proceed in easy stages up the Civil Service hierarchy.

For *graduates* the Civil Service has one of the most sophisticated training programmes anywhere.

There are two main categories of entrants:

(a) Specialists with professional or other qualifications or skills, who follow the career for which they trained *before* joining the Civil Service. They include architects, economists, psychologists, scientists, engineers, computer scientists, librarians; and also secretaries, word processor operators, caterers (details under individual career headings).

(b) School-leavers and graduates of any discipline. They enter one of the general Civil Service groups or grades.

This section deals mainly with the second category – the non-specialists.

The work The type of work done is immensely varied: virtually every facet of contemporary life has some connection with a government department; only a few examples of the vast number of subjects dealt with by Civil Servants can be given. In the Home Office, for example, staff, at any level, might be concerned with the administration of prison and borstal management and reform; or with the award of orders and other decorations. The Central Office of Information is concerned with projecting Britain's image abroad through films and feature articles on life in Britain and British institutions, and it also produces reference and publicity material for use in this country on anything from home safety to new methods of bee-keeping. In the Department of the Environment staff liaise with local authorities on, for example, housing policies and environmental health matters and traffic policies. The Department of Education and Science is concerned with the overseeing of the work of local education authorities, and is responsible for long-term policy on museums, art galleries, sports facilities in the 'leisure society', when more people spend less time working and more time on leisure pursuits. The Department of Industry organizes research into the application of information technology. It runs laboratories and research establishments. Other Ministries deal with transport, defence, agriculture, etc. In the Department of Employment and in the Manpower Services Commission for instance, Civil Servants are concerned with the efficient use of manpower and productivity. They deal with the training and retraining needs of people whose jobs are changing as a result of new technologies in industry, with the YTS (see p. xxvii) and with industrial tribunals. At executive level, Department of Employment Civil Servants are in contact with the general public at Jobcentres and Employment Offices; at administrative level, the work is mainly policy-making which involves investigation and report-writing.

Most vacancies up to and including O-level standard candidates are filled by departments recruiting locally. Others are filled by admission (see below) into a 'grade'. Candidates can express a preference for any particular Department, and the Civil Service does its best to fit them in. It is possible to transfer from one Department to another later on.

The atmosphere in individual offices depends as much on the person in charge as it does in any department in any large organization. As a rule, public servants, except at the top, do not work under as much pressure as many people in industry, but the work is no less stimulating. At administration trainee (see below) level and above it is likely to be intellectually more challenging: complex policy matters are discussed and the consequences of alternative decisions and policies assessed. An important difference between Civil Service and private-sector management careers: Civil Servants are always primarily advisers – someone higher up and finally a Minister takes the final decision; in industry, executives at comparable level are more likely to be responsible for the consequences of their own decisions. However, managerial skills are now much more important for promotion than they were even a few years ago.

Social and welfare facilities vary in extent and quality, but they always exist. Sports grounds and social clubs are available in larger centres. Civil Servants working away from home are helped with accommodation problems.

Holidays are often better than in industry. 4 weeks is usual, 6 weeks for those in the highest posts.

Administration Trainee (leading up the administrative hierarchy)

Entry qualifications

Maximum age: 28.

First- or second-class honours or post-graduate degree or comparable post-graduate qualification. In the past senior Civil Servants usually had arts degrees; now the need for relevant, expert knowledge in top-level administration is generally accepted, science and technological qualifications are equally welcome.

Method of entry and training: Written examination and series of tests and interviews, lasting 3½ days in all, at Civil Service Selection Board. Successful candidates are told the initial estimate of their potential at the time of selection; this assessment is progressively revised. Trainees spend 2 to 4 years (the first 2 are probationary) in this grade and during that time they have several 'postings' to different types of work and 4 to 5 months of formal training at the Civil Service College. Throughout the trainee period they are supervised, and their progress is monitored. There is a shortage of top-level applicants, especially of people with science-based degrees.

The work Senior Civil Servants are responsible, under Ministers, for policy-making and laying down broad lines of organization and development. In an industrial or commercial organization this would be the function of senior executives. They thoroughly familiarize themselves with their particular subject, whether an aspect of industry, health or whatever, and then advise Ministers on policy; they are often involved in legislation which gives effect to that policy. They assemble material for Ministers' speeches in the House and draft replies to Parliamentary questions. They reply to letters from MPs about the work of the Department, and may represent the Department in negotiations with other governments, other Departments, outside organizations, and occasionally members of the public.

Prospects Those who successfully complete their probationary period (normally 2 years) will be promoted to Higher Executive Officer (Development). They can expect further promotion after 2–4 years. The speed of advancement then depends not only on ability and performance, but also on the number of vacancies. Administrative Civil Servants become responsible for controlling progressively larger and/or more important sections of the work of their Department. The proportion of desk and paper work, of dealing with committees and attending meetings with other Civil Servants and/or people outside varies greatly between and within Departments. Administrative Civil Servants may switch Departments, but more often they move on to different sections within their Department. Individuals' preferences and abilities are taken into consideration.

Pay: High (see p. xxiii).

Personal attributes High intelligence; capacity to grasp all issues involved in a problem, to weigh up facts, conflicting opinions and advice and to make decisions; ability to extract the main points from a mass of detail and to write balanced and concise reports; ability to hold and delegate authority;

the art of inspiring loyalty, stimulating and guiding enthusiasm; tact for dealing with Ministers, staff and outside parties; enjoyment of responsibility.

Executive Officer

Entry qualifications

Maximum age: 44.

Two A-levels and 3 O-levels or BTEC National award in approved subjects which must include English or English language, or promotion from Clerical Officer grade. A large proportion of entrants are *graduates*.

Method of entry: Competitive interview and tests.

The work

Executive officers are either 'general executives' or 'departmental executives'. Departmental executives are only employed in certain Departments and have special titles, for example Immigration Officer (see p. 225).

General executives work in most Departments. Their work varies widely. An executive officer may be in charge of a group of clerical officers assisting more senior officers, or she may be responsible for work of her own. This ranges from the granting of import and export licences (according to laid-down criteria) to acting as secretary (which is *not* the same as doing 'secretarial work') to a committee, which may deal with anything from transport to ancient monuments or housing policy. An executive officer might also work on individual 'cases', seeing a case through from beginning to end; such work might bring her into contact with the general public. HM Customs and Excise offers a wide range of casework in connection with the detection of contraband at ports, and visiting manufacturers of dutiable goods.

In the Department of Health and Social Security she might be visiting hospitals to discuss, for example, proposals for using new technologies in kitchens or intensive care units. She would be a link between specialists at the hospital, and administrators, as well as specialists in her Department. In this type of work, the executive officer's and administrative Civil Servant's (who started as administration trainee) duties overlap. People in charge of Jobcentres are often Senior Executive Officers.

In level of responsibility, executive officers' work is broadly comparable to that of junior to middle management in industry. Some executive officers specialize in computer work.

Prospects

Fair for promotion to Higher and Senior Executive Officer. After 2 years Executive Officers may be considered for selection as Administration Trainees along with graduate entrants.

Pay: Medium to high (see p. xxiii).

Personal attributes Organizing ability; a liking for paper work or for dealing with people; enjoyment of a measure of responsibility; ability to manage staff.

Clerical Officer

Clerical officers are employed in most government departments. In addition, there are departmental clerical officers who work mainly in branch offices, such as Job Centres, Tax Offices, and Offices of Customs and Excise.

Entry qualifications 5 approved O-levels, including English language. Many candidates have A-levels or BTEC National award (see p. xvi).

The work A clerical officer does much the same wide range of jobs as a clerk in industry and commerce. She deals with incoming correspondence, sees that it is distributed to those concerned, writes letters or drafts them for a senior officer, handles correspondence with and telephone inquiries from the public, assembles statistics and keeps records.

There is often more variety of work than in comparable jobs in a private firm. For example, in the Immigration Department of the Home Office, a clerical officer may deal with students visiting this country, with permits for employment, and with aliens whose residence permits have expired. Clerical officers may also interview the general public who call into the office for information or papers.

Prospects There are opportunities for promotion to executive officer. Clerical officers are given day-release to study for examinations. But see Clerical Work (p. 457) for effect of 'chip' on office work.

Pay: Medium (see p. xxiii).

Personal attributes Accuracy and a liking for desk-work. There is room both for good mixers and for those who prefer to work on their own.

Clerical Assistant

Entry qualifications *Either* O-level English language and 1 other subject; *or* short test. In practice, most entrants have several O-levels or BTEC General (see p. xvi).

The work A clerical assistant or junior clerk does routine work for clerical officers: filing, sorting, keeping records. She may also deal with inquiries from the public.

Prospects Clerical assistants are encouraged to take day-release classes and prepare for examinations. Promotion prospects are excellent, but see Clerical Work (p. 456) for reduction in clerical jobs due to the 'chip'.

Pay: Medium (see p. xxiii).

Personal Secretaries

Entry qualifications Minimum age: 18. 3 O-levels, including English or English language or equivalent, i.e. BTEC General award or RSA Certificates. Shorthand and typing speeds of 100 and 30 words per minute or an audio test of 360 word tape transcription at speed of 120 wpm in 20 minutes. Equivalent word-processing skills are valuable and may be preferred. No speeds/tests have been defined yet. Many posts are filled by promotion from the clerical grades.

The work Personal secretaries work for senior Civil Servants; their duties cover the usual secretarial functions (see Secretarial Work, p. 451). Occasionally there are opportunities for travel, especially in the Diplomatic Service (see below), but they are few.

Prospects There are posts of great responsibility as secretary to heads of Departments, and opportunities for promotion to supervisory duties.

Pay: Medium (see p. xxiii).

Typing, Shorthand-Typing and Word-Processing Grades

Entry qualifications For typists, a typing speed of 30 words per minute; for *shorthand-typists*, shorthand speed of 100 words per minute, or equivalent audio-typing or word-processing skill. Good typists may be given word-processing training. Various office machine operating skills may also be accepted as entry qualification.

The work As in any office – see Secretarial and Clerical Work, p. 451.

Prospects With good shorthand and typing or word-processing, prospects of promotion are good. Study by day-release is strongly encouraged. But see Clerical Work (p. 456) for changes due to the 'chip'.

Pay: Medium (see p. xxiii).

The Diplomatic Service

Entry is to Grade 7 or 8 (Administrative), to Grade 9 (Executive) and to Grade 10 (Clerical) as follows:

Grade 7 and 8: As for administration trainee but maximum age 32, plus proof of ability to learn languages.

Grade 9: As for executive officer, but with evidence of command of a foreign language.

Grade 10: As for clerical officer. Preference given to candidates with O- or A-level in a foreign language.

The work Staff work in foreign and Commonwealth countries as well as in London. During a working life-time usually about 8 to 10 tours are served abroad, each lasting 2 to 5 years, i.e. roughly two-thirds of an officer's career is spent abroad. Work is very varied. Staff may work on trade, political, cultural relations, general administration, aid administration, or the dissemination of information. They meet many inhabitants of the country they work in and are expected to know or learn the relevant language. However, knowing one particular language well does not mean that all the career will be spent in the country where that language is spoken. Members of the Diplomatic Service must be prepared to serve anywhere in the world. Those who cannot or do not want to do so are usually asked to resign.

Prospects The functions of the different grades overlap. Promotion prospects from one to another are good. Promotion from Grade 10 to Grade 9 is usually by examination; promotion to higher grades, and for those with some experience, is on merit without further examination.

Pay: High (see p. xxiii).

Training The Diplomatic Service attaches great importance to proper training. New entrants at any level usually have a short course of lectures and visits designed to acquaint them with the organization and working of the Service and its place in the machinery of government. Specialized courses are also arranged in most types of work with which members of the Service will be concerned. Great importance is also attached to language study; even when no full-time language training is given, officers are expected to learn something of the language of the country in which they are serving and are given encouragement and assistance to enable them to do so. (Language allowances are paid to officers who reach certain levels of proficiency.)

Personal attributes An officer must be part salesperson, part political analyst, part public relations person; she must have a calm and reliable personality; a persuasive, confidence-inspiring manner, have the ability to make friends easily and to put down roots instantly, yet not mind being uprooted at short notice. The Diplomatic Service is not so much a job, more a way of life; it needs balance, staying power, great curiosity about the way other nations live, without having any preference for any particular nation.

Departmental and Specialist Posts

Apart from the posts for professional specialists mentioned earlier and careers described under separate headings, there are some other posts of interest to graduates, though only limited numbers are recruited each year.

For example, in the Department of the Environment some Civil Servants are concerned with the preservation of ancient momuments and historic buildings. This includes inspecting and reporting on the conservation and restoration work done by the Department, and general inspection of monuments which are, or should be, scheduled under the Ancient Monuments Act. Such monuments may be of any date from the neolithic period to the last century. Candidates must therefore have a thorough knowledge of history; preferably also experience of archaeological field work and some knowledge of architecture. They may research and write guide books and reports and may also appear in courts of inquiry. They also do general administrative work and answer questions sent in by students, etc. Candidates should have a relevant first- or second-class honours degree – or a post-graduate qualification (for example a diploma in the history of art).

There are also opportunities in the Information Group where Information Officers and Assistant Information Officers maintain a flow of information about the policies and activities of their Departments and advise on relations with the public. Many of those appointed are graduates, but at Information Officer level some relevant experience or training is essential. There are also opportunities at both levels for non-graduates especially if they have had a basic grounding in public relations or journalism.

Pay: Medium to high (see p. xxiii).

Research Posts

Research officers are recruited for various Departments, usually for specific projects. Virtually any type of subject may have to be researched. Research officers collect, analyse, and assess information, and prepare reports and surveys on the basis of which reports are drawn up and policy decisions made by senior Civil Servants.

Research projects vary vastly. For the Diplomatic Service they might include collecting information about foreign countries' economic structure or agricultural resources. For the Home Office, cooperating with university sociology departments on inquiries into the causes of delinquency and the treatment of offenders – just about every Department needs researchers occasionally.

Entry requirements First- or second-class honours degree. For some posts degrees must be in relevant subjects. This could be economics; sociology; physics or computer science or agriculture. For others degree subjects are not specified. For posts in the Diplomatic Service reading knowledge of a particular non-European language may be required. Technological/science degrees are now often specially useful, even if the degree subject is only used as background knowledge.

Science Group: covers both science and engineering work

Most scientists in the Civil Service are concerned mainly with research and development (see Science, p. 426, for definition of types of work). They work in about 100 government or government-sponsored research establishments. Research covers a wide spectrum – from projects concerned with defence to projects concerned with 'improving the quality of life': here scientists may be engaged on research into improving building methods; nutrition (to increase food supply in developing countries as well as food production yields in this country); transportation; long-range weather forecasting; conservation and recycling resources. Physicists, mathematicians, electronics engineers, computer scientists, statisticians, seem to be in steadiest demand, but demand levels for the various disciplines change frequently.

Entry qualifications *Either*:
(1) With 4 O-levels, often now 1 A-level and/or more O-levels, including an English, a science and/or mathematical subject, as *assistant scientific officer*. Like other Civil Servants they may take day-release to continue their studies for BTEC awards (see p. xvi) or equivalent. Recruitment at this level is straight into particular jobs, as vacancies arise. *Or*:
(2) With BTEC Higher Award or, in practice, now Honours, degree as *scientific officer*. This is the main recruitment grade, and entrants are recruited either centrally, much as administration trainees, or by individual research establishments.

There are also opportunities for entry for those with post-graduate qualifications and/or research experience in industry.

Late start There are some opportunities for people with managerial/professional (especially technical/scientific) experience. Interchange between the public and the private sectors at middle and senior level is encouraged now.

The age limit for Executive Officer entry (regardless of relevant experience) is now 45. There is no age limit for clerical staff. Opportunities depend on local supply and demand.

Position of women

The Civil Service was the first large-scale employer to accept that there is a case for adapting traditional employment patterns to women's career patterns. A report, *Women in the Civil Service*, said that 'conditions of service ought to reflect the different social patterns under which most men and women live their lives'. The report's recommendations were accepted in principle as long ago as 1971 but little progress has been made in implementing them although in 1982 another report, *Equal Opportunities for Women in the Civil Service*, reinforced and extended the 1971 report's recommendations. The second report also recommended that there should be joint management/union monitoring of women's career paths and that an 'awareness programme' should be mounted to help overcome traditional assumptions among senior officials about women's lack of ambition and suitability for senior jobs. An 'exploratory study', identifying the hurdles women have to overcome to progress at the same rate as men, is in progress: interviewing techniques on recruitment; annual 'reporting' on staff; types of 'posting' (jobs offered within the Service); are the sort of matters being dealt with by the study. Statistics show that there *are* invisible barriers. Comparing like with like – i.e. entrants with equivalent qualifications – women have about 60% less chance of promotion to senior jobs than men.

Women now constitute just under half the non-industrial Home Civil Service, but they are clustered in the lower grades. In 1983 there were 57,901 female and 27,604 male clerical officers (see p. 124); one notch up, at Executive Officer level, the ratio was 17,807 women and 26,514 men. A few grades higher, at Senior Principal level, there were 623 men and 12 women.

But the Civil Service is at least recognizing and tackling a problem which bugs women throughout the working world – the problem of reaching middle-level jobs, and rising above them at the same speed as men. For example, since 1982, the Civil Service College has been running management courses for women only – mainly, but not only, for Clerical Officers. It is thus one of the very few employers which is making use of the 'positive discrimination' clause in equal opportunities legislation. This permits training for one sex only in areas of work where that sex is severely under-represented.

Job-sharing schemes and *part-time work* are however still almost exclusively limited to clerical grades, and promotion prospects for part-timers are bleak. Reinstatement after the *career-break* is not a right – only a 'right to apply'.

Women themselves can help to change the situation to a certain extent. They can ask for 'hard' or 'crunchy' (CS jargon) jobs: finance rather than personnel; the Treasury rather than the Department of Health and Social Security. It is true that women tend to be shunted into 'soft' jobs and Departments, but they can try harder to assert their preferences. At promotion Boards, having held a 'hard posting' helps enormously.

It is generally accepted that only a lack of applicants keeps the women in the science group so low. In 1983 there were 2,202 male and 635 female Scientific Officers (graduate entrants); of new entrants that year 159 were men, 39 were women. This reflects the low proportion of women with science/technology degrees.

However, among Administration Trainees (potential high-flyers) women are catching up. In 1980 there were 48 male and 12 female AT recruits, in 1983 12 males and 8 females. Recruitment ratios reflect application ratios.

Further information

Civil Service Commission, Civil Service Department, Alencon Link, Basingstoke, Hampshire RG21 1JB

Related careers

See those mentioned in the text – Local Government

Computing/Information Technology or IT

Systems programmer/software designer/engineer – systems analyst/designer – applications programmer – computer operator – user support staff – sales and marketing – technical writing – service engineers – consultants

Entry qualifications Nothing rigid; depends on job-type (see below). Ability to think logically and computing hobby experience more important than specific O- and A-levels. For trainee programming jobs, in practice, at least 2 A-levels or degree (any subject); for Software Programming/Engineer usually Computing Science degree – Computing Science A-level not essential for most of these courses. Sandwich (i.e. CNAA) Computing Science degrees more helpful than full-time degrees.

The work Wanting to work with computers is by no means a reason for choosing a computing career. In virtually any job, whether it is clerical, technical, professional; whether it is in banking, manufacturing, retailing or medicine, computers are used extensively. They are tools with which to process information, measure, assess, monitor facts, figures, progress, procedure; they are information-processing devices. The information or 'data' may be in the form of numbers, words or graphs. Strictly speaking, the term 'computer' is out of date. It was correct when, in the early days, computers merely performed complex arithmetical operations with phenomenal speed and complete accuracy – when they were merely 'number crunchers'. Now that their capacity and use have widened so dramatically, 'Information Technology' or IT is becoming the accepted term. IT describes the 'convergence' of office automation, telecommunications and computing. However, 'computing' and 'computer' have become part of the language, and the terms have stuck.

People usually want to work with computers because they are fascinated by their versatility, their capacity to cut out drudgery and to achieve results which in pre-computer days were either impossible to achieve, or took a vast amount of time and trouble. Thanks to microprocessors, robots now perform repetitive manufacturing tasks; word-processors eliminate repetitive typing; data banks help solicitors keep track of caselaw without having to search through heavy tomes; management can base decisions on facts and figures rather than hunch.

In all these spheres people who use computers need not understand any more about the working of the computing device than car drivers need to understand about engines – and they are no more computer professionals than car drivers are engineers. There is a vast and sometimes under-rated difference between amateurs who program their computers and computer professionals.

Computing professionals comprise a range of highly-skilled specialists who have to acquire their expertise just as any other professionals have to. The demarcation between the various computer specialisms is blurred, and it is constantly changing for two main reasons: because devices are becoming ever more sophisticated, demanding new skills or newly-combined skills, and because this is such a new job-area that both computing-power providers and computer users are still experimenting with how best to use specialists to organize the work. To perform its information-processing tasks, the actual device, the 'hardware' (which is designed by engineers and computer scientists), relies entirely on 'software', the instructions or 'programs'. Hardware without software, computer people say, is as useless as a mousetrap without cheese or a TV set without the programme companies' wares. It is the software which enables the computer to enter into a dialogue with the people who want to use it, and to respond to their needs. The versatility of the tasks the computer can perform depends on the complexity and quality of the software, and on the size and sophistication of the computer's main memory and central processing unit (CPU).

Computing Jobs

Systems Programmer/Software Designer/ Software Engineer (titles are interchangeable)

These people produce the software which enables the otherwise inert hardware to provide the basic facilities – the 'controlling programs'. This has been likened to the electric power system into which users 'plug' various devices – it is the 'computer workhorse'. Whether it is a microcomputer which performs one task at a time, say word-processing or controlling a robot, or whether it is a system with 100 terminals, the controlling program, designed and developed by the Systems Programmer, makes the whole thing function. The work is a combination of applying computer science principles, creativity, high technology expertise and analytical reasoning. Software programmers work jointly with engineers, mathematicians, operational researchers, physicists and other highly-trained specialists. They are the only computer people who (a) *must* have a technological/scientific background (a degree normally) and who (b) work almost entirely with other highly-qualified experts and have little contact, at work, with non-computer people. Their work is basically Research and Design (see Design and Research and Development, p. 170, under Engineering).

Some develop existing Operating Systems, updating, extending, refining them; others work on software which will be ready for general use in a few or even 10 or 20 years' time. Theirs can be very much pushing-out-the-frontiers-of-science work. Most of the work requires high-calibre brains, but there is also scope for support staff (see Technicians, under Engineering, p. 182). Systems Programmers/Software Designers/Software Engineers work mainly for computer manufacturers, but all companies which have large computers employ some systems programmers. Of all computing jobs, theirs is the most theoretical/academic.

Systems Analyst and/or Designer

She identifies the problem and designs the solution to it. There are three stages to her job. First, she investigates and analyses the existing system – or lack of it – in the organization which is intending to instal a computer or system. In many organizations patterns of work have evolved haphazardly and in the process have become inefficient. For example, in a department store which has increased its volume considerably over the years, the method of recording sales, ticketing goods, making out bills, stock control and dealing with suppliers may be totally unsuited to the size of the organization today. The systems analyst spends several months getting to know the intricacies of the business, observing and talking to staff in all departments and at all levels – from junior clerk or packer to buyer or marketing and managing directors – to assess routines, bottlenecks, objectives. The work requires business acumen, knowledge of commercial practice and an ability to get people to talk freely about their work and to accept changes in old-established routines. When the systems analyst has reduced the old system into a logical sequence of procedures, she writes a report on how computerization would affect the organization's staff, and how it would improve efficiency and profitability. If the report is accepted by the management, the systems analyst completes the analysis and design, using structured procedures, and then hands over the program specification to the programmers. She probably supervises the subsequent implementation of the system and troubleshoots if necessary.

Analysis and design may be done by the same person, or the work may be split into two – the analysis being done by one person, the design by another.

The vast majority of analysts and designers work for computer users; 'in-house' analysis and design is now more usual than having the work done by software houses, i.e. consultancies which provide professional services for a number of clients. Some analyst/designers (with ample experience) work as freelances.

Analysts' and designers' work also covers advising their employers, or clients, on what systems to buy, so they must be knowledgeable about and critical of the various systems available. They must be very good at explaining complicated matters to lay people – the computer users.

The attraction and challenge of this computing job is the mixture of tasks and of talents required: applying highly specialized technical knowledge; improving an organization's efficiency; assessing competing computer manufacturers' claims for new products. On top of applying technical know-how, systems analysts/designers must be very good at dealing with people – communication skills are vital. They must make the computer acceptable to staff. Traditional working methods and hierarchies may have to change; retraining has to be arranged and accepted, and staff reductions may have to be faced.

In commercial computing – the vast majority of jobs are in this field – the jobs of analyst/designer and of programmer are now sometimes merged into *Analyst/Programmer*. This is one more manifestation of the constantly shifting computer job-scene. How much analysis and/or design, and how much programming each job entails varies enormously from one organization to another; usually the emphasis is more on programming than on analysis and/or design. It depends partly on the size of the computing system – or planned computing system – partly on policy. Also, within each project team the proportion of analysis/design and programming shifts as a project progresses. There is, obviously, more analysis/design work at the start of a project; more programming once the analysis/design has been completed.

(All these patterns of work apply only to commercial computing: in scientific/engineering organizations, a completely different working pattern usually obtains, with computing personnel normally having a technical background or working closely with technical staff.)

Applications Programmer

The relationship between systems analyst/designer and applications programmer has been likened to that of architect and builder. Applications programmers work to 'program specifications' – a description of what the program is to achieve – provided by the systems analyst/designer. There is a spectrum of applications programmers – senior ones, especially if they work with a 'business-expert' type systems analyst, do almost all their own 'systems design' (and may be analysts/programmers); some work to a 'loose specification', using great expertise and ingenuity; others work to a 'tight specification', need less expertise and have less scope for ingenuity.

Applications programming covers various stages. The Applications Programmer roughly assesses the time needed to complete the program, breaks down the program into separate components, and then breaks down each component into individual step-by-step sequences of instructions upon which the computer can act. All this needs logical, analytical reasoning, but *not* mathematical skills. Then comes 'coding', which is the conversion of each instruction step into the appropriate programming language (most of which are now easily learnt). So the job which laymen often think of as programming, i.e. writing in symbols in a given computer language onto coding sheets, or keyboarding (like typing) instructions straight into a computer terminal, is only part of the vast and varied programming skills area.

Applications programmers may produce programs to instruct particular machines to perform particular tasks: for example to enable a chain of hotels to keep a constantly updated record of vacancies, or a hospital group to keep a constantly updated record of the lengths of waiting lists within the various specialities and the various hospitals within the hospital group. In large organizations an applications programmer would deal with a variety of programs in succession – writing for new applications; updating existing programs, etc. Applications programmers can also specialize in 'applications packages'. These are programs, or 'program systems' produced 'for stock', to be bought off-the-shelf by users with run-of-the-mill requirements: programs for stock control; payrolls; personnel records; video games; office applications like word processing and file storage. As 'tailor-made' programs are very expensive – they take a long time to write – off-the-shelf programs are being produced in ever-growing numbers as more and more computers are being installed and therefore more users with similar requirements are being catered for. Writing applications package programs requires special skills: the programs must be 'user-friendly' (easy for laypersons to understand) and flexible enough to be adaptable to particular users' differing needs.

Applications programs are produced by software/systems houses, as well as by manufacturers, consultancies and, increasingly, by freelance programmers with considerable experience, as well as 'in-house'.

Applications and applications package programmers can therefore choose the environment and type of organization they want to work for. Programmers may have almost as much contact with non-computer people as have systems analysts; others, especially those who concentrate on coding, have little contact with the outside world.

There is usually a hierarchy of programmers, from trainee right up to project team leader, and then on to various management jobs. There is no universally accepted structure. As virtually everybody in computing, however high up, has to have had some programming experience, programmers have a choice of ladders. Most large installations have two branches, one dealing with the functions concerned with the system in operation – and another one dealing with developing systems and with those in the planning stage.

Computer Operator

She works almost exclusively on mainframe installations – very large computer installations with many distant terminals, often performing number-crunching rather than text-processing functions. The operator usually sits at a console in an air-conditioned room feeding instructions into the computer to 'run' a particular program, and then 'obeys' the computer's command (which appears on a TV-type screen) to 'load' a particular disc or tape next.

Computer operating usually consists of carrying out a sequence of operations with meticulous attention to detail. Computer time is expensive and an operator's mistake can be costly. Operators work in all types of large organization; they usually have to do shiftwork, as the computer, to pay its way, must be in use 24 hours a day. Operators with analytical reasoning ability (assessed by in-house tests) may be able to go on to applications programming – though this progression is now much less frequent than it used to be. Operators with organizing ability have rather more scope to go up the administrative ladder in operations management, or they may branch off into one of the many peripheral jobs, such as working in/managing the tape/disc library; organizing the work-flow, etc.

Data Preparation is not now, strictly speaking, a computing job. It is usually done by retrained clerical staff.

Engineers (various disciplines) and *Computer Professionals* design and develop computers and related products ('peripherals') for computer manufacturers (see Engineering, p. 175).

The people who design and develop the hardware – the equipment which houses the software, are engineers and scientists. Various specialists are involved, mainly but not only electronic engineers, physicists, mathematicians. *Computer engineers* and *computer scientists* are emerging as specialists in their own right. At the moment titles of relevant degree courses vary; computing hardware professionals of the future must carefully peruse degree course syllabuses. Terminology of job-titles and specific functions vary, too. Hardware manufacture is a fast-developing industry; in career terms it fits into high technology, highly competitive, high-risk manufacturing.

Some 'Spin-off' Jobs

With 'orthodox' (i.e. applications or software programming, systems/software design analysis) qualifications and experience, there are a growing number of opportunities in, as yet ill-defined, computer careers, suiting individuals with various bents, abilities, expertise. Information technology including as it does telecommunications (and office automation) is developing faster than any industry ever has done: new jobs are constantly emerging – but beware: the un- or semi-skilled ones may be short-lived: a few years ago there was a vast demand for computer operators and for so-called 'service engineers' who were often narrowly trained. Now, users themselves rather than specialist operators operate the majority of computers; and some large computers can diagnose and rectify their own faults: service engineers now are thoroughly trained to cope with serious faults.

User Support Staff

They provide a 'hand-holding' service to users who have bought a new system or updated and extended an existing one. Job content varies greatly. Support staff may be asked to provide training for everyone who will use or be affected by the new systems – from clerk to managing director; they may suggest additional or more efficient application of the system; or if they work for manufacturers or software houses, they may visit, at regular intervals, to see all goes well – and possibly keep the customer informed of new equipment or software. The job combines ability to communicate and establish good relations with people at all levels in an organization, with technical expertise to keep up with technological developments.

Sales and Marketing

For details of general *sales and marketing* see p. 283. However, in the computer hardware *and* software area specialist knowledge is vital. Computing is not only technologically the most sophisticated industry, it is also a highly competitive, cut-throat industry. Sales people usually specialize in systems for specific markets – i.e. commercial, scientific or educational.

Technical Writing

Writing manuals for – especially – mini and microcomputer users is a growing job area. It requires both the ability to put over complex information clearly, succinctly and unequivocally, and it requires thorough understanding of what the device described can and cannot do, and how it functions. Manual writers have to know very much more about their subject than the people for whom they are writing. Existing manuals are often criticized; manufacturers say they have difficulty finding people who combine the necessary technological expertise with the necessary communication skills. Technical writers may be employed by manufacturers or by consultancies or work as freelance or 'in-house'. 'End-user documentation' production is becoming a sophisticated area. Writers have to produce material – both in print and 'screen dialogue' – which is 'user-friendly', i.e. easily understood by amateurs, as well as documentation for experts.

Service Engineers

They work either for large users 'in-house' or for manufacturers and visit customers – often irate and impatient – whose equipment has broken down (or *apparently* broken down: often it is simply wrongly used). Service engineers must thoroughly understand the complexities of hardware and software to be able to diagnose and rectify the trouble. Unlike engineers at the hardware/software production end, service engineers get out and about and meet the users.

Consultants

Systems analysts and designers can ultimately become independent consultants – advising prospective users on whether a system would be of use to them, and if so which one. Considerable experience of the computer-scene, plus specialist knowledge in a commercial, banking, retailing, etc. or industrial or educational area is essential.

Training

This is still evolving. Experience is, on the whole, more important than paper qualifications but experience is often difficult to get without qualifications. It is still possible to start with a few O-levels as an operator and, with in-house training and preferably day-release, become an applications programmer and then a systems analyst – if the conditions and the personality and ability are right. Because of the quick expansion and rapid developments in the whole computer area, training is still disorganized and haphazard, with several overlapping types of qualifications. Many people at the top of the profession now are unqualified, because when they started their careers there were no relevant qualifications. Others have got on without qualifications because of the shortage of computer staff, but new entrants must aim at a qualification (though the only work for which a degree is invariably demanded is Software/Systems Programming). Training is also continuous, with the need for continuous updating.

There are various bodies which award computing qualifications. The main ones are:

BTEC (see p. xvi): National Certificates and Diplomas and Higher Certificates and Diplomas in Computer Studies; in Business Studies with Computer options; in Applications Programming and in Systems Analysis (titles vary and may change from one year to the next).

Royal Society of Arts: mainly in operating.

City and Guilds: in operating and in applications programming.

National Computing Centre: all levels and aspects of computer jobs.

British Computer Society: The main professional body; awards its own qualifications, from applications programming upwards.

These are now the most common and the recommended training routes:

Software or Systems Programmer/Software Designer/Engineer

Degree in computing science (titles vary – check that degree is concerned with the scientific software work and *not* with commercial computer applications/systems analysis); or in maths, electronics, physics. Science A-levels, preferably in physics and maths, are usually required for entry.

Systems Analyst/Designer, Applications Programmer, Programmer/Analyst

No one type of course. The following routes are *not* listed in order of merit; there is no 'best buy':

4-year CNAA sandwich degree in computing which includes a year's practical computing experience. Degree titles vary: it is essential to find out, for example, whether a 'Computing Science' course includes commercial computing application experience, or whether it is intended for software programmers/systems designers/engineers; *or*

3-year full-time university computing degree – again titles vary. Computing is probably the only career area in which a CNAA (sandwich) degree is likely to be of greater value in the job-market than a university (full-time) degree; *or*

Business Studies sandwich degree with computing option; *or*

BTEC Higher National Certificate (2-years' part-time day-release) or Higher National Diploma (2-years' full-time or, occasionally, 3-years' sandwich) in computing subject. *Entry* with either any BTEC National Certificate or Diploma, or with 1 A-level and 3 O-levels; maths to be included, at either level, in the GCE passes; *or*

Post-graduate or post-HND computing course, usually at Polytechnics; *or*
TOPS computing course (see p. xlvi for TOPS entry conditions); *or*
Accountancy qualification; *or*
Commercial work experience – for commercial computer application job; scientific/technical work experience for computing jobs in science/technology.

Some employers take 2 A-level entrants or graduates (any degree subject) for in-house training. COSIT (Computer Services Industry Training Council) started systematic in-house training only early in 1984. Most in-house training is still rather haphazard. Large concerns tend to do all the training, others then 'poach' trained staff. When applying for 'trainee programmer' jobs, applicants should make sure there is either some systematic in-house training, and/or opportunity for preparing for recognized qualifications. Some 'trainee programmers' are, and remain, 'junior programmers'. COSIT has laid down detailed guidelines for training, but at present the scheme applies mainly to trainees in software houses and consultancies. It is hoped 'user departments' will join the scheme in the future.

Operators
Employers' requirements depend partly on type of operating to be done and partly on supply and demand. Full-time pre-entry training is not as useful as on-the-job training but can be helpful if jobs are scarce. Many employers require 5 O-levels including a language and maths; others even require an A-level; yet others accept people with manual dexterity and practicality with lower entry qualifications – candidates are given aptitude tests.

BTEC National Certificates/Diplomas (see p. xvi) in Computer subjects normally require entrants to have 4 O-levels, including maths, but entrants with fewer O-levels (and no maths) may be taken on on basis of aptitude tests.

NOTE: Private schools diplomas (full-time courses) vary enormously in value. Check with National Computing Centre or British Computer Society before enrolling.

TOPS (see p. xlvi) course available.

For unemployed young people and school-leavers who pass an aptitude test (no specific entry requirements):
The Data Processing Threshold Scheme. This consists of 42 weeks of integrated practice (work with computer-users) and theory at technical colleges. Students work for the BTEC National Certificate in Computer Studies. Although the scheme was originally intended to lead to junior computer jobs only, many Threshold students have gone on to programming and some to systems analysis.
ITEC (Information Technology Centres) throughout the country offer

1 year's training plus work experience to school leavers without any qualifications. The training is an introduction to Information Technology rather than a preparation for specific careers but it leads on to further training and/or jobs. Details from Jobcentres and careers offices.

Prospects This is the fastest-expanding career area. Old – in computing terms – job categories are breaking down, but for computing professionals who are flexible and prepared to continue learning new skills and for constant change and challenge, scope is immense. Computing is expanding in two dimensions: (1) It is penetrating ever more areas of activity, with more and more workplaces within each area installing or expanding systems; and (2) devices and systems are getting ever more sophisticated and versatile (e.g. voice input, electronic mail and confravision systems are all in use on a small scale now and are likely to be in more general use soon). As one generation of computers comes onto the market, the next one is in production, and the one after that on the drawing-board (or rather the researcher/designer's VDU). So computing professionals of all kinds have a promising future.

About 80% of computing professionals now work with users – installing, programming, analysing/designing systems, controlling, managing, setting up project teams or computing departments, liaising with other staff, training existing staff to use the devices. So systems programmers, systems analysts/designers, analyst/programmers, well-qualified applications programmers, technical writers, user support staff are all likely to be in demand for the rest of this century (see display advertisements in the press for variety of job-titles, tasks to be performed and levels of responsibility/expertise). But the demand for operators and for not-very-highly-skilled programmers is dwindling fast as computers increasingly do their own operating and straightforward programming, or these tasks are performed by non-specialist staff – the users.

Manufacturers and software houses employ the remainder. Broadly, then, prospects are excellent for highly-skilled, highly-trained people and for support staff – i.e. technicians (see *Technicians* in Engineering, p. 182); but prospects are not so good for run-of-the-mill professionals who are lured into computing by the novelty of the work, and by the advertisements.

There is increasing scope for specializing within a work area: people with experience in, say, retail, banking, the law or agriculture may become computing professionals by grafting computing skills on to their particular expertise. (See TOPS courses p. xlvi and **Late start** p. 142.)

The prospects for people with engineering/science background plus computing experience/training are excellent.

Pay: Very high (see p. xxiii).

Personal attributes

All professionals: flexibility, willingness to adapt to new methodologies and to continue learning.
Systems Analyst/Designer: Well above average intelligence and powers of logical reasoning; imagination to put themselves into the shoes of the people whose jobs they may be 'analysing away' or at least changing; tact and diplomacy; ability to get on well with people at all levels in an organization's hierarchy; a confidence-inspiring manner; curiosity; creativity to visualize how old-established methods might be changed; ability to explain complicated procedures in simple language; ability to listen; ability to take an overall view of a situation and yet see it in detail; business acumen; numeracy.
Applications Programmers/Programmers/Analysts: Powers of logical thinking; numeracy; powers of sustained concentration; great patience and willingness to pursue an elusive problem till solved; liking for concentrated desk-work; ability to communicate easily with people in computing *and* with lay people. Programmers who hope to progress to systems analysis should note the different personal qualities required.
Systems Programmers/Software Engineers: Very high intellectual ability; originality; research-inclined mind; imagination; interest in high technology and its implications and rapid developments.
Operators: Practicality; liking for routine work; organizing/administrative ability for those wanting to get promotion.

Late start

Good opportunities, especially for people with business or related experience and for graduates. TOPS courses (see p. xlvi) in various computing subjects are available. For graduates, there are post-graduate courses. (Software/Systems Programmers need recent scientific work experience or degree.)

Position of women

This is a promising area for women. The 80% plus computing professionals who work with computer users (see above) are in 'dealing-with-people' jobs. Their computing expertise is the essential background which enables them to do their job. So the vast majority of computer people are doing work which even the most traditionally-minded would consider eminently suitable for women. It requires an interest in what makes people tick – to understand and know how to allay people's fear of new – and jargon-ridden – technologies. Women have shown that they appreciate employees' resistance to change and know how to work out changed working patterns which are both efficient and acceptable to staffs. In systems analysis/design women's knack of gaining staff's confidence at the investigation stage has proved particularly useful. One of the most prestigious and biggest software houses/consultancies is run and almost entirely staffed by women, many of them part-timers. So many women are freelance programmers working at home while raising a family that programming has been called the new cottage industry.

As the whole area is so new, there were no traditional barriers to break down. Nevertheless, there is evidence now that a disproportionate number of senior project leader and other management jobs are being filled by men, and that women are 'dropping back'. This could be due to senior managers' traditional attitudes to women in management jobs (see Management, p. 277). But there may be another reason: of the first generation of specially trained computing professionals, a sizeable proportion is at present either taking a child-rearing *career-break*, or experiencing the adverse effects of having taken such a break. In this fast-changing profession, it is essential to work continuously, or at least to keep one's hand in during the break. Women who take off more than a few months will inevitably be left behind. But as there are good opportunities for *part-time* work, possibly doing irregular project-based rather than regular work, there is no need for a long complete career-break.

So opportunities for women are excellent. But there are alarming signs that women are not making full use of these opportunities, and that computing is becoming a male-dominated area at an early stage. Parents are buying computers as toys for their young sons, not for their young daughters; in schools far more boys join computer clubs, and take (are persuaded to take?) computing at O- and A-levels (see p. xxxiii). At degree level, the proportion of girls taking computing science is actually declining; it was 25% in 1980 and about 19% in 1983. Computing professionals – both sexes – say that computer advertisers are projecting a false image. The emphasis, as computing skills are needed in virtually every area of work, should be on communication skills, not on mathematical/technological skills. There is no reason whatever why little girls should not see computing as a 'fun subject' just as young boys do, and why women should not do at least as well as men as computing professionals.

Further information

National Computing Centre, Oxford Road, Manchester M1 7ED
British Computer Society, 13 Mansfield Street, London W1M 0BD
BTEC, Central House, Upper Woburn Place, London WC1H 0HH
Computing Services Industry Training Council (COSIT), 73/4 High Holborn, London WC1V 6LE

Dancing

PERFORMING: ballet dancer – modern stage dancer. TEACHING: teaching children – teaching adults – teaching keep fit and exercise. CHOREOGRAPHY

Teaching and performing are two separate careers. There are two kinds of performer: (1) *ballet dancers*, and (2) *modern stage dancers*.

Performing

Entry qualifications No specific educational requirements, but a good general education is essential for ballet dancers.

Ballet Dancer

The work The ballet dancer leads a dedicated life. Her days are spent practising, rehearsing and performing. She has little spare time and may not indulge in such activities as cycling, riding, etc., lest they develop the wrong muscles. She will meet few people who are not in some way involved with ballet.

She is usually attached to one particular company and may be on tour for much of the year.

Prospects Not good. Ballet companies have only a few vacancies each year. Once she is a member of the *corps de ballet*, a talented dancer has a chance of rising to solo parts and understudying bigger roles, but it is rare indeed to rise to principal dancer status. Even a successful dancer's professional life is short; only the very exceptional still get engagements in their middle thirties. There are increasing prospects with contemporary dance companies for dancers not suited to classical ballet.

Pay: Medium to high for the few who do succeed (see p. xxiii).

Training Serious training must have started by the age of 10 with a professional teacher who prepares pupils systematically for one of the officially recognized major dancing examinations: e.g. those of the Royal Academy of Dancing, the Imperial Society of Teachers of Dancing, or the British Ballet Organization (RAD, ISTD, BBO).

The best training is given at professional schools which give general education for GCEs and a thorough drama and dance training.

Promising pupils usually take scholarship auditions held by the Royal Academy of Dancing. Under the Academy's scheme promising pupils are given free classes twice a week for up to 5 years (provided they keep up to standard, and don't grow awkward or too tall).

Full-time professional training must start not later than at 16. It lasts for about 3 years.

There are ballet schools all over the country but pupils from the London ballet companies' schools have a far better chance of eventually finding a place in these companies, which recruit most of their *corps de ballet* from their own schools.

Ballet training includes national and character dancing, mime, history, art and literature, and usually French (most technical terms are in that language).

Before accepting a pupil, good schools insist on a thorough orthopaedic examination, which is repeated at regular intervals throughout training.

Personal attributes Strong back, perfect feet; intelligence; intuition; emotional depth; musical talent; the ability to take criticism without resentment; a strong constitution; complete dedication.

Modern Stage Dancer

The work The modern stage dancer performs in musicals, pantomime, cabaret, on TV, and in light entertainment generally. She is not usually attached to a company, but appears in individual shows, usually with spells of unemployment in between. She does not work quite as hard as a ballet dancer – practising is not so all-important.

Prospects For the fully trained first-rate dancer (about 1 in 10) prospects are fair. But like other entertainers, a dancer must be prepared for months of 'resting', meanwhile earning a living in some other way yet being available to attend auditions. If she is lucky, she may get a long run in the West End, a tour, or a television series.

Unless she has made her name in her early twenties she will find it difficult to go on getting engagements, however competent she is.

Pay: Medium to high for those who do succeed (see p. xxiii).

Training 3 years full-time, preferably but not necessarily at one of the professional schools (see Ballet Dancer **Training**). At auditions, she must be able to demonstrate her ability to dance up to intermediate ballet exam level. The modern stage dancer should also have some training in voice production and drama. The latest starting age for serious, but not necessarily professional, training is about 14.

Personal attributes Attractive appearance, especially shapely legs; resilience; versatility; enterprise in tracking down jobs; sense of rhythm.

Teaching

Entry qualifications For qualified teacher status, training which is required for teaching in ordinary (i.e. not *dance*) schools: 2 A-levels and 3 O-levels (see Teaching, p. 520). Very exceptionally, 1 A-level may be acceptable.

The work A dancing teacher may teach both children and adults, or she may specialize in teaching one or the other.

Teaching Children

The teacher who specializes in teaching children works in 3 main fields: ordinary schools; dancing classes; specialized professional schools.

Ordinary Schools
Full-time or visiting part-time teachers teach dancing to O-level, mainly to improve children's poise and deportment.

Dancing Classes and Schools
These are intended for children who don't have dancing lessons at school. They may be run by a teacher who hires a hall for the purpose, or they may be in a dancing school which caters for both children and adults.

Children are usually prepared for 'Ballet in Education' exams or other officially recognized dancing examinations (see Ballet Dancer **Training**). This ensures that children are being properly taught even though they do not intend to become professionals.

Professional Schools
Dancing is an essential part of the curriculum; the teacher deals with specially talented children who hope to become professional dancers.

Prospects Excellent. More and more parents want their children to learn dancing.

There are also good opportunities for teachers in Europe where non-professional dancing for children is now very popular. Royal

Academy of Dancing and Imperial Society of Teachers of Dancing examiners often go abroad to organize, teach and examine.

Pay: Medium (see p. xxiii).

Training

Leading to qualified teacher status

This is changing at the moment; a new Council for Dance Education and Training has been set up. It issues up-to-date lists of 'accredited' courses which would normally lead to teaching in *dancing* schools; these courses do not lead to 'qualified teacher status' (nor do they usually qualify for admission to post-graduate teacher training). To teach dancing in ordinary schools, training is *either* a 4-year course at one of the few dancing schools *which have a link with a College of Education*; *or* a 3- or 4-year Bachelor of Education course which has a dance component – it is important to check prospectuses carefully before choosing such a course, as the 'dance component' varies from a few hours to a substantial proportion; *or* a degree in Dance or in Performing Arts (titles and course content vary) followed by a 1-year post-graduate teacher training course.

Personal attributes

The ability to explain and demonstrate steps and movements; a fine sense of rhythm and some proficiency at the piano; a liking for people of all ages; imagination; endless tact and patience; good appearance; graceful movements. (See also Teaching, p. 527.)

Teaching Adults

The work

Most adults and teenagers are interested in learning mainly ballroom dancing, including Latin-American and whatever may be the current craze.

A ballroom-dancing teacher may work either in a general dancing school, of which ballroom dancing is one department, or at a school which specializes in ballroom dancing. She may also teach in youth clubs and hold ballroom classes for children as a sideline.

Prospects

At the moment first-rate both for those who want to work as assistants in dancing schools, and for those who want to open their own schools, but the dancing boom may not last indefinitely. There are occasional, but very few, opportunities for dancing-teachers-cum-hostesses in hotels.

Pay: Medium (see p. xxiii).

Training

For ballroom specialists, training takes 1 year to 18 months, and can be taken on an apprenticeship basis. Students pay fees at first; later they receive a salary.

Personal attributes Much the same as for teachers of children; even more tact, patience, and self-confidence are needed.

Teaching Keep Fit and Exercise

This area has expanded rapidly in the last few years. Movement classes have mushroomed, changing their style frequently in order to follow the latest (often imported) fashion. Many people have cashed in on the dance/exercise craze without a proper knowledge of how the body works and what kind of movement is suitable for each type of student. The most suitable basic training for teachers in this area is either a proper dance course; or Physical Education teaching; or a 2-year part-time course organized by the Keep Fit Association and run in conjunction with local education authorities. (Keep Fit award holders are allowed to teach in local education authorities' adult education classes.)

Choreography

The work The dancer who has exceptional imaginative powers and the ability to interpret music in terms of dancing may ultimately do choreography. This is dance composition: the grouping of dancers and sequence of dances which make up the entire ballet. In modern stage dancing, a choreographer may direct within a wide range – from the production numbers on TV which involve scores of dancers, to the unexacting dances of a seaside concert party.

Choreography is not a career for which a novice can be trained. Years of experience of ballet and a thorough musical training are needed (see Music, p. 313).

Position of women *Performing*: Far more men are coming into the profession; there is now a far greater shortage of *first-rate* male than of first-rate female dancers.

Teaching: This is still a predominantly female occupation (especially teaching children) but there is no reason why more men should not train for teaching.

Part-time: Good opportunities.

Further information Council for Dance Education and Training, Room 301, 5 Tavistock Place, London WC1H 9SS (for addresses of accredited ballet schools)
Imperial Society of Teachers of Dancing, Euston Hall, Birkenhead Street, London WC1H 8BE

Central Register and Clearing House (qualified teacher status BEd and post-graduate courses), 3 Crawford Place, London W1H 2BN
The Keep Fit Association, 16 Upper Woburn Place, London WC1H 0QG

Related careers *Acting – Music – Remedial Gymnast – Teaching (Speech and Drama), p. 528*

Dentistry

DENTAL SURGEON: general practice – community dental surgeon – hospital dental surgeon; ANCILLARY WORK: dental therapist – dental hygienist – dental surgery assistant – dental technician

Dental Surgeon

Entry qualifications 3 good A-levels: if only 2 sciences at A-level there should be an additional science among the O-levels. Physics, chemistry and biology must always be included at either O- or A-level.

The work A dentist (or dental surgeon) preserves teeth by filling, crowning, and scaling. She extracts teeth and designs and fits artificial dentures. She also does surgical operations on the jaw, and orthodontics, which is the improvement of irregular teeth, mainly in children. The preventive aspects of dentistry are very important, involving regular teeth inspection for children.

General Practice

The majority of dentists are in general practice. Most of them treat National Health patients almost exclusively, though some treat both private and NHS patients. A minority treat only private patients.

A dentist in general practice has the best financial prospects and the greatest independence, but she is also likely to work the hardest. She may be in a partnership, or in practice on her own, working in her own premises with her own equipment, and employing her own dental surgery assistant (see p. 154).

It is usual to begin as an assistant or associate in a practice, with a view to becoming a partner later, but primarily to learn how a practice is run. This involves a good deal of organization, filling-in of forms, ordering stocks, and contact with technicians.

It is also possible to buy the 'goodwill' of a dentist who is retiring or moving away, or simply to put up a plate and wait for patients.

Community Dental Surgeon

The Community Dental Service is intended to foster the idea of dental care within the whole community through the dental inspection and treatment of priority groups such as school and pre-school children, expectant and nursing mothers, and, increasingly, elderly and handicapped people.

Hospital Dental Surgeon

In hospitals, a dentist looks after sick patients whose teeth need urgent attention, and does jaw operations and complicated extractions. Outpatients may need only ordinary dental treatment.

Dental work in hospitals has the usual hospital advantages of life in a community, colleagues to discuss difficult cases with, and social and sports clubs.

Prospects Good in all fields. Qualifications are now accepted in EEC countries. Some scope in Commonwealth countries.

Pay: Medium to high (see p. xxiii).

Training 5–6-year courses at dental schools attached to universities. The first year is a preliminary science course (as for medical training). Students with A-level physics, chemistry, biology, zoology or maths are exempt from it.

Some dental schools have discontinued this course. Even when dental schools do accept students for a preliminary year, local authorities do not always pay grants for what is in effect an A-level course.

Dental training lasts for 4 or 5 years. The syllabus covers anatomy and physiology, the uses of dental materials, design and fitting of dental appliances, pathology, some medicine, general as well as dental surgery, anaesthesia, orthodontics, children's and general preventive dentistry, radiology, dental ethics, and relevant law.

Practical work on 'phantom heads' normally begins in the second year, and work on actual patients during the second or third year of the dental course.

Personal attributes Manual dexterity; a methodical and scientific approach; and good health.

Left-handedness is not a disadvantage.

Dentist in general practice especially: The ability to establish easy relationships quickly with people, and give confidence to the nervous. (The growth of the practice depends almost entirely on the patients' personal recommendations.) Organizing ability.

Community dental surgeon especially: The ability to get on with children.

Hospital dentist especially: The ability to work well as a member of a team.

Further information General Dental Council, 37 Wimpole Street, London W1M 8DQ

Related careers *Dentistry: Ancillary Work – Medicine*

Ancillary Work

(Dental therapist – dental hygienist – dental surgery assistant – dental technician)

If you are interested in dentistry but do not have the necessary qualifications for dental training, there are 4 careers available in dental surgeries: dental therapist, dental hygienist, dental surgery assistant and dental technician.

Dental Therapist

Entry qualifications Minimum age for training 18.
4 O-levels, including English language, and a science subject, preferably biology.

The work Dental therapists do operative work; they work in the hospital, and community dental services, helping dentists to give treatment to children and to teach them how to care for their teeth. They work under the direction of a dentist who prescribes the treatment to be given; this includes simple fillings, extraction of deciduous teeth, and cleaning, scaling and polishing teeth. Dental therapists always work under supervision, mostly in double-surgery clinics. Their responsibility is therefore limited. Most of the patients are very young – in welfare clinics under 5, in school clinics mostly under 11. Dental therapists do not work for dentists in general practice.

Prospects The training of dental therapists has recently been reorganized, and there is intense competition for the *very* few training places per year.

Pay: Medium (see p. xxiii).

Training 2 years full-time, only in London. Practical training (on which more time is spent than on theory) is initially on phantom heads, so that students learn how to scale, polish, fill and extract teeth without worrying about hurting the patient; they also work on patients, under supervision. Theoretical training includes anatomy, physiology of the teeth and jaw, some radiography, some dietetics – enough to understand why some foods are good and some bad for the development of children's teeth.

Personal attributes Considerable manual dexterity; conscientiousness; some interest in science; good health, especially healthy feet; a way with children.

Further information General Dental Council, School for Dental Therapists, 37 Wimpole Street, London W1M 8DQ

Dental Hygienist

Entry qualifications Minimum age for training 17.
4 O-levels, preferably including English language and a science subject. Candidates are given a manual dexterity test, and are expected to have had experience as a *dental surgery assistant* (see below).

The work A dental hygienist also does 'operative work'. She does scaling and polishing under the supervision of dentists, but she does not do any fillings, etc. An important aspect of her work is preventive dentistry.

She works with adults as well as with children, and for dentists in general practice as well as in community health clinics.

Prospects Fair: more dentists in general practice, especially in partnership, are now also employing hygienists, but there are no promotion prospects.

Pay: Medium (see p. xxiii).

Training 9 months to 1 year full-time at dental hospitals. Training is similar to that of therapists, but the extracting and filling of teeth are not included. Some time is spent in learning how to talk about oral hygiene to children and adults.

Personal attributes As for therapists, plus the ability to express oneself lucidly.

Further information General Dental Council, 37 Wimpole Street, London W1M 8DQ

Dental Surgery Assistant

Entry qualifications None laid down, but most hospital training schools demand GCE passes, which should include English language and a science. Two O-levels are required for admission to the examination for the National Certificate of the Examining Board for Dental Surgery Assistants. Minimum age for training usually 17.

The work A surgery assistant does no 'operative work'. She is the dentist's 'third hand', handing her the right instruments at the right time; she also looks after her instruments, does sterilizing, gets out patients' treatment cards, helps with filling in forms and filing, and often does general secretarial work. She may act as receptionist.

Surgery assistants work wherever dentists work, i.e. in general practice, in community dental clinics and in hospitals.

Prospects Good.

Pay: Medium (see p. xxiii).

Training Most dentists train their own assistants, but some prefer those who were trained at a dental hospital, for a period varying from 12 to 24 months. The type of training differs slightly from one hospital to another, but it is mainly practical, with some lectures and demonstrations. The reason for variation in the length of training is that in some hospitals courses concentrate on training only. In others, assistants earn a little during training for help with routine work, looking after instruments, etc.

The majority of dental surgery assistants, however, learn on-the-job. They go straight from school or from secretarial college into a dentist's surgery and are trained mainly by her. They are advised to attend evening classes.

After the training, plus at least 2 years' work, they can take the examination for the National Certificate awarded by the Examining Board for Dental Surgery Assistants.

Personal attributes A polite, friendly manner; some manual dexterity; a well-groomed, neat appearance; good health.

Further information Association of Dental Surgery Assistants, DSA House, 29 London Street, Fleetwood, Lancashire FY7 6JY

Dental Technician

Entry qualifications None specified. Some knowledge of chemistry and physics desirable and, in practice, essential. Higher salary for students with 4 O-levels.

The work Dental technicians construct and repair dentures, crowns and other orthodontic appliances. They work either in commercial dental laboratories where work for individual dentists is carried out, or in hospital dental laboratories. It is highly skilled work.

Prospects Excellent. There is a great shortage of dental technicians.

Pay: Low to medium (see p. xxiii).

Training The present 5-year apprenticeship with day-/block-release for a City and Guilds Certificate is being phased out. It is being replaced by BTEC National Certificate training (see p. xvi). Training will vary according to type of course and entry qualifications. For example entrants with 4 O-levels including, normally, a science and English language can take either a 1-year full-time or 2-year part-time course; entrants with lower qualifications will need 3 years' part-time training.

Personal attributes Willingness to work as a woman in a mainly male laboratory; great manual dexterity; patience; accuracy.

Further information National Joint Council for the Craft of Dental Technicians, 64 Wimpole Street, London W1M 8AL

Late start *1. Dentists*

Dental schools vary in their attitude to mature students and judge each case on her merits – acceptance depends largely on the number of years students would have after qualifying: over-35s tend to have more difficulty getting a place than under-35s. There is, usually, no relaxation in GCE requirements – but prospective dentists can take missing A-levels at evening classes. No employment problem once qualified.

2. Ancillary work

Young students are given preference for training usually, but mature entrants are also considered. Mature entrants could try for training under TOPS (see p. xlvi) for Dental Hygienists' and Dental Surgery Assistants' 1-year full-time courses.

Position of women

1. Dentists

18% of practising dentists are women, but over 33% of students are now female. Of all the top professions, dentistry is the most promising for women. They have truly equal chances of promotion in the health services; they are welcomed in private practice by partners and by patients; and it is a profession which can be carried on anywhere in the country.

Career-break: No problem: there are refresher courses. The Dental Retainer Scheme encourages women dentists to work at least 12 sessions and attend 7 education sessions a year, while paying reduced membership fees.

Part-time: Excellent opportunities for employment, none for training.

2. Dental Therapists, Hygienists and Surgery Assistants

Predominantly female profession.

Career-break: Should be no problem.

Part-time: Excellent opportunities for employment – none for training.

3. Dental Technicians

Although most technicians are men, more women are now training and their position is much as for other dental staff now.

Career-break: No problem.

Part-time: No problem.

Related careers

Medicine – Nursing – The Services – Science Technician

Dietetics

Preventive dietetics – therapeutic dietetics

Entry qualifications 2 science A-levels, one of which must be chemistry; 3 O-levels which must normally include English and mathematics. See **Training**.

The work Dietitians apply scientific principles of nutrition to normal and to therapeutic diets. Their functions have broadened in the last few years as healthy eating habits become recognized as a vital part of preventive medicine.

Dietitians' work divides broadly into *preventive* and *therapeutic* dietetics.

Preventive work, mainly in the community: As food becomes ever more expensive and as more 'convenience' and other processed foods come on the market it is becoming more and more important that shoppers should be able to assess the nutritional values of various foods, and the possible ill effects on health. Preventive dietetics is part of health education. In preventive work the dietitian tries to get her message across to as many people as possible *before* they need therapeutic diets. To do this she works 'through' other professionals – those who reach wider sections of the community than the dietitian could hope to reach. She endeavours to keep nurses, social workers, health visitors, midwives, teachers and GPs up to date on nutritional matters; she gives talks in schools, to youth clubs, PTAs, Rotary Clubs etc. There is an element of public relations work in preventive dietetics: the dietitian has to make herself and her work known and get herself *asked* to speak to groups.

She also works out diets for special groups; for example cheap and simple-to-prepare meals for the elderly; for parents with large families, little time and little money; for people living alone; and for ethnic groups who have to observe certain dietary rules but cannot afford to buy their own food-stuffs here because they are too expensive.

Preventive dietetics overlaps with *therapeutic work* which involves advising individuals, mainly hospital in- and out-patients, on specific diets. For therapeutic work, the dietitian uses her expertise together with skill and imagination to make diets 'stickable-to' even when, for example, patients may have little understanding of the need to avoid certain ingredients in their diets and include others.

Dietitians do not normally do any cooking themselves; even direct supervision of diet-kitchens is now the exception rather than the rule. They act as consultants to catering managers in hospitals (or a group of hospitals) and other institutions. Most dietitians are employed by the National Health Service and are hospital-based. At the top of the NHS dietetics tree is the District Dietitian. She decides how to use her staff to best advantage – whether to designate one dietitian to do the health education work in the community and let the rest work with patients in hospitals, or whether to let everybody do a bit of everything.

Some local authority social services employ dietitians entirely for community work; some local education authorities employ them for work in the school meals services.

Dietitians occasionally become catering managers in hospitals or other large organizations either because they cannot get suitable jobs *in* dietetics, or because they prefer the possibly greater managerial content of large-scale catering management (see Catering, p. 91) to dietetics. Experienced dietitians may become lecturers, and/or do research in industrial or public sector jobs.

Prospects Fair on the whole. Experienced dietitians are usually in demand, but first jobs are not necessarily available where they are wanted. Industry now employs far fewer dietitians than in the past, but there are some openings in the developing countries and in the EEC (for dietitians who speak the relevant languages). British qualifications are not yet recognized in the USA, Canada and Australia but reciprocity of recognition may be obtained in the future.

Pay: Low to medium: possibly improving as profession now becoming all-graduate.

Training 4-year degree course. Titles vary; some courses including the term 'nutrition' are recognized by the Dietitians Board as entitling holders to State Registration, and some are not – Registration is essential for dietitians wishing to work in the National Health Service. Degree courses include at least six months' practical work. The syllabus includes physiology; biochemistry; microbiology; nutrition and food science; diet therapy; health education; large-scale catering systems and principles; economics of nutrition.

Graduates with relevant degrees (i.e. which include human physiology, human biochemistry and nursing at *degree* level only) may take a new 2-year postgraduate Diploma instead of the degree course.

Personal attributes *For all dietitians*: interest in science as well as in food; curiosity about and sympathy with other people's ways of life and standards of food preparation; ability to get on well with people of all ages, temperaments, backgrounds in one-to-one consultations. For dietitians who hope for promotion: sufficient self-confidence, intellectual ability and communication skills to fulfil the dietitians' new role as health educator and consultant to other professionals.

Late start No age-bar in jobs, mature students welcome on degree courses.

Position of women 90–95% female profession, but the proportion of male students is increasing. Proportionately more men than women in lecturing and other senior posts.

Career-break: Presents no problem; although there are no formal refresher courses, *ad hoc* arrangements are made by hospitals.

Part-time: Fair opportunities for work, none for training. Job-sharing has not been discussed in the Association but it should be a possibility.

Further information British Dietetic Association, Daimler House, Paradise Street, Birmingham B1 2BJ

Related careers *Catering – Food Technology – Home Economics – Medicine – Science (Biochemist, p. 433; Chemist, p. 432)*

Driving Instructor and Driving Examiner

Driving Instructor

Entry qualifications 4 years' full (not provisional) driving licence without disqualification: no minimum age but, in practice, licences rarely granted to anyone under 23.

The work The majority of instructors work on their own. This is more lucrative, but also more precarious, than working for one of the big driving schools. Hours are irregular and long: far more pupils want lessons after work or at weekends than during normal working hours. It is essential to have someone at home who will deal with telephone bookings, inquiries, cancellations. Most instructors teach between 6 and 12 pupils a day.

Being a good driver is not the most important aspect of instructing: instructors must like teaching and have the natural ability to do so; they must be able to put themselves into the position of a nervous, possibly not very talented, learner. They usually drive all day and every day through the same streets, which can be dull. The attractions of the work are, largely, being one's own boss; developing learners' road sense and driving technique; talking, during lessons, to a variety of people.

Prospects Depends on area: it is essential, before investing in a dual-control car, to find out whether the area is not already saturated with instructors.

Pay: Varies from low to medium (expenses are very high) (see p. xxiii).

Personal attributes Organizing ability, business acumen, ability to get on with all types of people and to put them at their ease; complete unflappability and fearlessness; mechanical aptitude; teaching talent; endless patience; ability to criticize tactfully and explain lucidly.

Training Instructors must pass the Department of Transport's stringent written and practical examination. There are instructors' schools, but potential instructors may learn as they wish. Syllabus covers driving techniques; teaching skills and practice; knowledge of design and mechanism of cars; road procedure as in Highway Code (but in very much greater depth) and the Department's manual, *Driving*.

Driving Examiner and Traffic Examiner

Entry qualifications

Minimum age 26; experience of having worked with the public, in a position of some authority; 6 years' driving licence without conviction for serious motoring offence, and wide experience of driving in last 3 years; active interest in and knowledge of all motoring/road/traffic trends and problems; some mechanical knowledge of cars and other vehicles; elementary knowledge of road transport law as it affects commercial, passenger and goods vehicles; preferably some experience of driving heavy goods or public transport vehicles and/or motor-cycles.

Acceptance is by competitive examination held, at irregular intervals, by the Department of Transport, plus interview, driving test and 4-week course followed by special test.

The work

Driving Examiners are Civil Servants. They test learner-drivers of cars and other vehicles. They work as members of a team under a senior examiner, attached to one of over 300 test centres throughout the country. They conduct normally 8 or 9 tests a day. During the test, when examinees tend to be nervous, examiners may not converse (to ensure that examinees are not, and cannot claim to have been, distracted); they make detailed notes on driving technique and road sense throughout each test-drive. Their decision is final; they must keep records of each test in case an examinee complains. The work is highly concentrated and, for work as responsible as this, can be rather repetitious.

Traffic Examiners, also Civil Servants, investigate, by observation on the road, by inquiry of operators and by examination of drivers' records, whether laws concerning operation of vehicles (such as hours a driver may be in charge of a vehicle without rest period) are being observed. Examiners do not have to examine vehicles' mechanical conditions.

Prospects

Fair. Recruitment is however only sporadic. For promotion examiners may have to move to another area.

Pay: Medium (see p. xxiii).

Personal attributes

Air of authority; patience; tact; ability to concentrate constantly; unflappability.

Late start

Most instructors and examiners have had some other job before; maturity is an asset.

Position of women

Driving Instructors
About 20% now are women (a great increase in the last few years). Women instructors have no special problem getting pupils.

Career-break: There is a danger that, during the break, another instructor may set up in the area. Continued driving during the break would be essential.

Part-time: It is possible to have a small number of pupils, but it is never possible to work during school-hours only. Summer months are the busiest time. So far no part-time examiners.

Driving Examiners
The first few women applied in 1977; by late 1983 only about 20 had been appointed. The Department genuinely wants to attract more women, but the 'preferred' experience (see above) makes it difficult for women to be eligible. Women who have had experience of driving heavy goods vehicles or buses stand a good chance. (*Note*: Heavy Goods Vehicle Driving instruction is available under TOPS (see p. xvi).)

Further information

Instructors: Department of the Environment (Register of Driving Instructors, or Driving and Traffic Examiners), Lambeth Bridge House, London SE1 7SB
Register of Approved Driving Instructors, 2 Marsham Street, London SW1 3EB
Examiners: Department of Transport, Common Services, Lambeth Bridge House, London SE1 7SB

Related careers

Motor Mechanic – Teaching

Economics

Entry qualifications Degree in economics; A-level maths or statistics preferred, but not essential, for all courses.

The work Economics is concerned with the organization, utilization and distribution of productive and financial resources, nationally and internationally. This includes the study of political, industrial and social relationships and interactions.

Economics comes under the Social Sciences umbrella, but it is not a science in the accepted sense. Economic theories are not 'correct' or 'incorrect'. Even if worked out on mathematical models and tested on the computer, premises are based on assumptions and imponderables rather than on unassailable facts and figures. Hence the variety of 'schools' of economists (e.g. Keynesian, monetarist), each with different answers to the same economic problems. Economics therefore involves making judgements, choosing to adhere to one set of principles rather than another.

Economists work in a wide variety of settings – in urban and regional planning, in industry, commerce, the Civil Service, in financial and industrial journalism, as organizers or researchers in trade unions and in management consultancies and overseas in development programmes. They try (but do not often succeed) to identify the causes of problems like inflation and unemployment, and suggest courses of action which might solve or ease the problem. Some economists specialize in, for example, the economics of energy resources, the car industry, agriculture, transport.

Extent of specialization varies enormously. Some economists become very knowledgeable about a particular aspect or part of an industry; others in an area of economics. For example, an economist who spent years in the catering industry then set up as a freelance consultant. A recent assignment required her to suggest sites for and types of new hotels which a major company wanted to build. Work involved research: what makes hotels successful at home and abroad? In what proportion do food, accommodation, hotel location, service, pricing, affect a hotel's profitability? What constitutes 'good' food, accommodation, etc? The economist spent a year asking questions in hotels – of guests and staff and management – analysing relevant companies' accounts, and then presented her report. Another economist who specialized in 'agricultural economics' prepared a report on measures to improve the productivity of an underdeveloped Third World country. New specializations emerge on society's needs, priorities and problems of change.

Economists who take jobs *as economists* act as advisers – whatever type of employer they work for. They do not normally take or implement decisions, and they have to be prepared for their advice to be ignored. Economists who want to be involved more directly with the work of the organization that employs them, would be wise to go into management in industry or commerce (see Management in Industry and Commerce; Banking; Accountancy).

An economics degree can be a general graduate qualification; and it can be a 'specialist' qualification – for work in systems analysis, statistics, market research, investment analysis, cybernetics, operational research.

Prospects Fair, as such wide application.

Pay: Depends largely on type of employer; medium to very high (see p. xxiii).

Training Most degree courses include as 'core' studies: micro and macro economics, economic and political theory and economic history. Specializations to choose from include agricultural economics, economic geography, urban development, industrial or financial economics, transport studies, operational research. Economics can be combined with accountancy, geography, computing, law, sociology, planning, maths or a physical science. The content of individual courses and the emphasis given to the many aspects of economics vary greatly from one course to another.

Personal attributes Numeracy; interest in political and social affairs; analytical powers. Resilience, to be able to persevere when events prove research and theories wrong, and when suggestions are being ignored; ability to explain complex research findings to lay people.

Late start Should be no problem for people who have commercial, financial or similar experience.

Position of women About 10% of economists, but over one quarter of economics students are women. They do not seem to have any special difficulties getting jobs. A comparatively large proportion do well in financial journalism and in investment analysis. The subject is adaptable enough to enable women to work in *some* area at all stages of their career. Instead of part-time work they do sporadic freelance work, *if* established and experienced.

Career-break: It is essential to maintain contact through reading journals, going to meetings and reading reports, etc.

Part-time: Freelance consultants for experienced consultants. Job-sharing should be possible though there are no precedents as yet.

Further information No central organization.

Related careers *Accountancy – Computing – Cybernetics – Information Work – Journalism – Management in Industry – Operational Research – Town and Country Planning*

Electrician

Entry qualifications For traineeships: in theory, an aptitude test. In practice, applicants with at least CSE in English, maths and/or a science are more likely to get a traineeship.

The work Electricians instal, maintain and repair a vast variety of equipment. Work varies enormously and includes repairing plugs or burglar alarms in people's homes; repairing domestic equipment brought into high street electricians' shops; working for Electricity Boards, for manufacturers, for organizations such as chains of hotels or stores which maintain their own electrical departments; and working on building sites as one of the team responsible for installing all electrical equipment from switch gear to central heating pumps. Experienced electricians often set up on their own (see Working for Oneself, p. 561), usually doing mainly domestic repair jobs. Electricians also work for small builders, for large electrical contractors or as self-employed sub-contractors.

Training Since 1983 traditional apprenticeships have been phased out. Most electrical contractors now take on trainees who are given practical training and block-release to take the City and Guilds Craft Certificate Part I, after one year, together with a practical test (Achievement Measurement 1 (AM1)). During the second, and possible third, year, trainees get day- or block-release (college–industry arrangements vary locally) for the Part II Certificate. Having passed the Part II City and Guilds exam and a practical test (the Achievement Measurement 2 (AM2)), trainees are graded (and paid) as electricians.

Local authorities, hospital boards and other public authorities may also use this new 'Joint Industry Board' trainee scheme. Some trainees take the BTEC (see p. xvi) modular Certificate by day-release or possibly evening class. BTEC Certificate holders can, through their employers, apply for registration as electrician. It is also possible, and often necessary, to take City and Guilds Craft Certificates at evening class.

Personal attributes Some manual dexterity; an inquiring and logical mind; willingness to work with the minimum of or no supervision with potentially dangerous equipment; a reasonably careful nature or at least awareness of dangers unless basic rules are observed.

Late start No age limit for traineeships as there used to be for apprenticeships but in practice young school-leavers are given preference. There are some TOPS (see p. xlvi) and similar training and retraining schemes for adults.

Position of women *Very* few women electricians at the moment, but no reason why this should remain so.

Career-break: Probably difficult without retraining (see TOPS, p. xlvi). So far nothing is known about returners (see Working for Oneself, p. 560).

Part-time: Possible if working for small contractor or shop or for oneself.

Further information Construction Industry Training Board (see telephone directory for area office).

Related careers *Engineering – Motor Mechanic*

Engineering

CHARTERED ENGINEERS: design – research and development – production – technical sales and marketing – consultancy
ENGINEERING DISCIPLINES; TECHNICIANS AND TECHNICIAN ENGINEERS

Chartered Engineers

Entry qualifications Degree: 2, often 3 A-levels including maths and physics, and at least 3 O-levels which should include English language and often a foreign language. Chemistry at O-level is often required; chemistry A-level is essential for Chemical and, usually, Agricultural Engineering. BTEC National Certificates and Diplomas are accepted for CNAA degrees if appropriate units were taken; their acceptance by universities is not automatic. ('Conversion' courses for people with the wrong A-levels are available at some institutions.)

The work Engineering is not so much one career, more an expertise which opens doors into a vast range of jobs. Engineers probably have a wider choice of environment in which to work, and of type of job, than any other professionals.

The purpose of engineering is the design and manufacture of the 'hardware' of life. Engineers have a hand in the creation of anything in use anywhere – from chips (both kinds) to chairs; cable TV to toys; motorways to kidney-machines; robots to milk bottles. They are the wealth creators without whom the country's economy cannot improve, and they are also a twentieth-century type of missionary: by designing irrigation and similar schemes for the Third World they reduce famine and poverty. So engineering can be the right choice as much for the person who wants to improve the quality of life all round as for the person who wants a prestigious top managerial or professional job.

There is a range of engineering functions (see below) each appealing to different temperaments and talents. Engineers can concentrate on, for example, creative design; on developing ideas, seeing them translated into the end-product and sold at a profit; on managing people and/or resources and/or processes; on research into, say, laser beam applications or into robotics.

Apart from the many aspects of practical 'active' engineering, there is the vital commercial exploitation of ideas and products. Technical sales and marketing (see below) are now often considered the sharp end of the profession, and engineers do well in both these areas.

The amount of time engineers spend at the drawing-board – or, rather, using a light pen on desk-top computer – varies, of course, with each particular job, but it is estimated that most engineers spend about one third of their time discussing work with colleagues, customers or clients, staff, bosses; but there are equally backroom jobs for loners. During their training all engineers spend some time supervising work – and usually doing some of the work themselves – on shopfloor, construction site or in the lab. Once qualified they can choose functions in which they do not have anything to do with the production/construction part of the job. Nor do professional engineers often do any physically heavy or dirty work.

An engineering qualification is much under-rated as a way into more glamorous-sounding (better paid) and more difficult-to-get-into careers – e.g. Marketing (see p. 283), Industrial Management (see p. 269), Public Relations (see p. 398), Television (see p. 534) and other graduate employment. Engineering is, in fact, very much a 'transferable skill' – and that is so useful at a time when everybody is likely to change jobs several times in a working life.

Employers who want graduates often now prefer science and engineering to arts graduates. Their specific knowledge can be useful in an age when technology has a bearing on virtually any type of business; their analytical approach to problem-solving is invariably useful, even when the problem is not a technical one. So even young people who are not planning to spend their lives as engineers, but want to go into anything from merchant banking to journalism, might well consider taking an engineering degree as a stepping-stone. Engineering need no more be a vocational course than an arts degree (engineering courses are much easier to get into than arts degree courses); the chances are that, during their course, students may find that engineering itself has more to offer than they thought.

There are degrees which combine engineering with management, economics, languages and other subjects, and there are post-graduate courses in Business Management, Systems Analysis, Transport, etc., which can be taken either immediately after qualifying or a few years later (after the *career-break*, p. 191).

Engineers normally specialize in two dimensions: in one *branch* or *discipline*, and then, after training, in one *function*, or type of activity. Function can be changed more easily than discipline. The main functions within each branch are:

Design

This is the most creative of the engineering functions and is the core of the engineering process. The design engineer creates or improves a product which can be manufactured and maintained economically, performs satisfactorily, looks good and satisfies proven demand. Looks matter more in consumer goods – freezers, cars – than, for example, in machine tools. She may also design a new, or improve an established, engineering process. Most designers work to a brief. For example, a car manufacturer's marketing department may request that next year's model within a given price range should incorporate fuel-saving and/or safety devices (which may have been perfected in Research or which Research may be asked to work on); and that the model should incorporate certain visual features which seemed to 'sell' a competitor's model; the design engineer may add her own, totally new, ideas.

Her job is to find efficient and economic solutions to a set of problems. She must investigate materials and processes to be used in the manufacture of the product, which means she has to consult experts from other disciplines; but *she* specifies what goes into the manufacture of the product and what processes are to be used.

Because the work of design engineers varies so enormously, the job is impossible to define precisely. Designing an aircraft which is a team effort has little in common with adding a feature or two to an established type of transistor. Most work is done in 'design offices', where several graduates assisted by technicians work under a *chief design engineer*; some designing, in electronics for example, is done in the laboratory. CAD – computer-aided design – is now used extensively. An experienced design engineer can choose whether to be part of a team that designs, say, a whole new airport, or whether to work on simple, straightforward design on her own.

Personal attributes High academic ability; an urge to put new technologies to practical use; creativity; imagination; ability to coordinate the work of others; interest in marketability of product; ability to work as one of a team *or* to lead it.

Research and Development

In some organizations research and development are two separate departments; in some the two, plus design, go together. But most typically research and development form one department, with design a separate, but very closely linked one.

Research and development engineers investigate, improve, adapt established processes, products and components of products, and they may create new ones. The work is essentially experimental, laboratory-based, but the 'laboratory' could be a skid-pan on which new tyre-surfaces are tried out, or a wind-tunnel in which to experiment with aircraft models. Whenever the product is not too unwieldy, research and development build (or let the technicians build) prototypes, which are then discussed with marketing and production colleagues.

While there is some extending-the-frontiers-of-knowledge kind of research, most of engineering research is 'applied', i.e. aimed at maximizing sales and profits; or at saving precious resources; or exploiting newly discovered materials or processes.

Work comes from several sources: *design engineers* may want to use a new material or process which they have heard of but they need to know more about its 'behaviour' before using it; *production engineers* may ask research and development to investigate why there is a recurrent fault in a particular production process or product; the *marketing* department may complain that a particular aspect of a competitor's fridge, aircraft, or traffic signal component makes the competitor's product sell better: research and development would investigate the better-selling product, and then try and come up with something even better. Research and development is very much team work. There is scope for specializing in the academic research or the practical development side of the work.

Personal attributes Practical bent; high academic ability; imagination; perseverance in the face of disappointing research results; interest in following up ideas which have profitable application; ability to work well with colleagues from other departments; willingness to switch from one project to another if Marketing or Production have urgent problems.

Production

Confusingly, this is both a *branch* with its own degree and Chartered Institution, and a *function*. In addition, terminology is vague. Some production engineers are not chartered engineers but became production specialists by working their way up from the shopfloor. Occasionally, arts graduates go into production – if they are practical, good at organizing and take (usually) post-graduate training and/or pick up the technical knowledge as they go along. Production engineers *may* be – and nowadays usually are – qualified production engineers, but people doing the work may also be called production planners or production managers. Titles vary and may or may not denote different levels of responsibility and qualification.

The production function broadly covers changing raw materials into all types of articles. This involves the selection of the most suitable material and the application of the manufacturing process and system in order to manufacture saleable commodities economically.

Production people use the most up-to-date manufacturing techniques including robotics and computers. 'Production' can mean producing a one-off product (e.g. a ship) or mass-produced commodities (e.g.

motor cars) or continuous flow-line goods (e.g. glass). The production engineer must see that labour, equipment and materials are used efficiently and that the product is completed at the correct quality and cost, in the right quantity, at the right time. The variety of settings in which production engineers work is enormous: it can be a huge (and noisy) heavy engineering plant; it can be a large, but very quiet, highly automated workshop; increasingly also small manufacturers in light engineering, clothing and food processing employ production specialists.

Production engineering invariably contains a large 'man management' element: as foreman or production supervisor, a junior (or trainee) production engineer might be in charge of a production line, responsible for the work done by perhaps 100 operatives; later, as production planner (or whatever her title) she might be responsible for ensuring that the right materials used in the production process are available on the shop-floor at the right time in the right quantities and that 'dispatch' is ready to receive the finished product: she might later be responsible for long-term production planning and development – that would be part of Management (see p. 269).

In the past, production engineering was usually done by practical people with some knowledge of engineering processes. As manufacturing processes become ever more sophisticated, and as industry recognizes the need for greater efficiency and streamlining, production engineering has grown in importance (and status). It is now an important equal of other engineering branches *and* functions.

Production managers often do work which has much in common with personnel management. An important part of their job is smoothing out problems on the shop-floor before they flare up into disputes; they deal with union officials, as well as with staff problems which might affect the department's productivity.

Personal attributes Organizing ability; practicality; ability to get on well with people of all types at all levels in the hierarchy – from operatives to heads of research and managing director; ability to keep calm under pressure and in inevitable crises; liking for being very much at the centre of action.

Technical Sales and Marketing

Sales engineers spend most of their time away from the office, meeting people. Selling engineering products ('specialist selling'), which may be selling anything from machine tools to oil rigs, domestic freezers to road maintenance equipment and service, combines salesmanship with technical knowledge. Customers may be lay people to whom the virtues of a product have to be explained, or highly professionally qualified people (more so than the sales engineer possibly) who ask searching questions about its performance and properties. Sales engineers also act as link between prospective customer and manufacturers, passing on criticism of and requests for products and changes. They must find out, for example, what features – design – after-sales service – cost – makes a competitor's product sell better in which country or at home: sales engineers use engineering expertise in a commercial context. The job requires communication skills as much as engineering knowledge. (See also Marketing/Selling, p. 283.)

Searching out new customers is an important part of selling. Some sales may take months of meetings and negotiating. Sales engineers may travel abroad a good deal, or they may have their own 'territory' near home – it largely depends on the type of product.

Personal attributes Outgoing personality; adaptability to use the right approach with different types of customers; perseverance, and indifference to the occasional rebuff; commercial acumen; interest in economic affairs; communication skills.

Consultancy

This function absorbs significant numbers only in civil and structural engineering, but numbers in other branches – notably mechanical, electronic and production engineering – are increasing. Consulting engineers work in partnerships in private practice, rather like accountants or solicitors. A few set up on their own; most work in firms of between 2 and over 50 partners. Firms vary in organization and extent of specialization. Basically, consultants provide specialist services for clients who are usually public authorities or architects in charge of large projects. Other engineers, for example chemical engineers erecting a large plant, or quantity surveyors, could also be clients. Consultants are commissioned to advise, provide feasibility studies, design to a brief, and, sometimes, to organize projects. They are *not* in the constructing/manufacturing business but may be in charge of putting work out to contractors and, as their client's agent, may then be responsible for supervising contractors' work, including authorizing payment.

Consultants may specialize: for example civil engineers may specialize in motorway or in oil rig design, or in traffic management; electronic engineers may specialize in telecommunications or in medical electronics or in instrumentation and systems. Consultants are usually *design engineers* (see above), but as they move up the ladder they spend more time dealing with clients and with getting business – i.e., the commercial side of the job. Some go into or specialize in *management consultancy* (see p. 281). Civil and structural consulting engineers work abroad a lot, especially in the Middle East, usually on contract for a fixed number of years.

Personal attributes As for design engineers, plus a confidence-inspiring manner, persuasive powers for dealing with clients and contractors; for senior jobs: commercial sense.

Engineering Disciplines

Considering the need for precision in engineering, job and function titles are often surprisingly vague and can, therefore, be misleading.

Apart from these specializations, there are many jobs which are, usually, carried out within one of the main functions. Titles and the work they describe vary. They include *maintenance* (work on employer's premises) and *service* (work carried out on customer's premises), *test*, *installation*, *quality assurance*, *systems*, *control* engineers. These functions may be carried out by graduates early in their career, they may be top jobs or they may be carried out by technicians (see p. 182).

The main *branches* or *disciplines* are:

Mechanical Engineering

Mechanical engineers work in all branches and all functions; they are concerned with the application of the principles of mechanics, hydraulics, thermodynamics, to engineering processes. They have a vast choice of end-product to work with and environment to work in: literally no industry is closed to them; they work in hospitals; in computer manufacture; robotics; all types of research establishments. The engineer who wants to help humanity as directly as possible, who wants to see the application of her efforts to the alleviation of suffering and discomfort, can work in *Medical Engineering* (see below); the engineer who wants to go into technical sales or into marketing, or general management can take her mechanical engineering training into anything from car manufacture to computers or North Sea oil extraction.

Environmental Engineering (Heating and Ventilating Engineering/Building Services Engineering)

This used to be part of mechanical engineering, but is now a specialization on its own. Environmental engineers are concerned with heating, lighting, acoustics, ventilation, air conditioning, noise and air pollution and its control. They are called in as consultants by civil engineers and architects on building projects from hospital to airport, office block to housing estate, chain store to underground station. This branch straddles mechanical, electrical and structural engineering.

Civil Engineers

They are concerned with the design, planning and construction of motorways, bridges, dams, large buildings (in conjunction with architects usually), waterways, sewage plants, oil rigs, and, increasingly, with traffic and transportation planning and management. More than any other branch of engineering, civil engineers tend to be consultants, called in by local authorities or architects for whom they plan and design projects. *Consultant engineers* design for and negotiate with clients and professionals from other disciplines – i.e. this is office and conference-table work rather than supervision on site. Civil engineers working for contractors supervise construction projects and deal with contractors' agents and foremen; they may also do design work.

Structural Engineering

This overlaps with *Civil Engineering*. Structural engineers may be called in as consultants by architects and by civil engineers – they are specialists in designing and choosing materials and processes used in large-scale constructions.

Electrical and Electronic Engineering

The two overlap. Broadly, *electrical engineering* is concerned with the use and generation of electricity to produce heat, light and mechanical power: electrical engineers work in generating stations, distribution systems and on the manufacture of all kinds of electrical machinery from tiny motors for powered invalid chairs to heavy motors for industrial plant. They are also concerned with research into the more efficient use of, and new sources of energy for, electrical power, for example for use in transport and heating systems.

Electronics is mainly concerned with *computers*, *telecommunications*, *automation/instrumentation and control.*

(a) *Computers*: The electronic engineering industry is concerned with producing the machinery – the 'hardware' – which gives houseroom to the software, i.e. the programs, and with producing the components and products which 'computer systems' (see Computing) need to perform their tasks. This includes microprocessors, visual display units, printers, mainframe, mini- and micro-computers. (For details of software/programming jobs see Computing, p. 131).

All engineering *functions* are carried out by electronics engineers, but the proportion of design, research and development engineers is greater in electronics than in other branches. To complicate a complex set-up even more, mechanical, electrical and chemical engineers, physicists, and computer scientists (see Computing) also work in computer manufacture. There is also some overlap between hardware and software production: computer manufacturers produce the 'controlling' or 'systems' programs which are built into – some – computers (see *Software or systems programmers/software designers* in Computing, p. 132).

(b) *Telecommunications* include, for example, the extension of old-fashioned telephony into 'multi-facility' services such as 'conference calls': that means facilities for telephone conversations between several participants in different locations; and for 'confravision': centres in various towns are equipped with close circuit television as well as with 'conference call' services, and are rented by the hour to business people who then 'hold meetings' with colleagues or customers without having to travel. Other telecommunications developments include the replacement of metal cable network with optical fibre systems; the extension of radio networks; satellite television; cable TV.

Telecommunication technologies in offices include electronic mail – devices which enable keyed-in messages and reports to be transmitted instantly from one computer to another, and teletex – the successor to telex, and facilities like Prestel, Ceefax, etc.

(c) *Automation, Instrumentation and Control*: This is concerned with automatic control devices, from the operation of equipment in space, by ground control, to nearer-home gadgets such as automatic ovens and central-heating time-clocks, and robotics.

Then there is the vast area of computer-controlled equipment. Anything from a factory mass-producing fish fingers or plastic cups to railway-signalling or supermarket re-ordering installations can be computer-controlled. (See Computing, p. 131.)

All this has become possible as a result of the development of *Microelectronics*; the most dramatically developing and expanding sub-section. Briefly, it is electronics writ small in terms of cost and size, and writ very large indeed in terms of present and potential uses and employment opportunities (at technician, technician engineer and professional levels). Microelectronics is concerned with the design, development and production of scaled-down, minuscule electronic circuitry – the 'chip' – and with its application. The chip affects virtually every industrial, commercial, scientific and professional activity but it can do nothing by itself: electronics specialists develop its potential and 'program' (instruct) it to perform the precisely defined task for which it is intended. (Programming in this context differs from data-processing programming: electronics and other engineers use their programming skill as an additional tool – they are not 'programmers'.)

Mass-produced, general-purpose as well as specialized chip-based equipment is now used (or soon will be) in such varied spheres as hotel, aircraft and theatre seat reservations; supermarkets (those bleeping checkouts keep the warehouse management informed of the precise level of stock of every item in every store at any time); document storage and retrieval systems (see Information Scientist, p. 256); in hospitals, libraries, banks, television production companies, commercial and professional offices. In manufacturing, 'robotics' – assembly-line work done by programmed robots – is developing fast. Scientific applications include weather-forecasting; computer-aided design in civil and structural engineering; dating archaeological discoveries. In hospital, a doctor's request to the laboratory for a blood sample analysis can soon be transmitted verbally instead of by writing out chits: voice recognition by machine is now possible but not yet in practical use.

Medical or Biomedical Engineering

This is a combination of electronic, electrical and mechanical engineering and physics. Medical engineers at the moment usually take a degree in either mechanical, electronic or electrical engineering (but there are also medical engineering options in electronic and mechanical engineering degrees) and then either take a post-graduate course or join a team working on medical engineering projects. These are often carried out jointly with consultants in hospitals, who specify what they want any particular equipment to do. Kidney transplants, heart surgery, and many less spectacular procedures are only possible thanks to the imaginative cooperation of doctors and engineers.

Medical engineers also design aids for severely handicapped people – for example, artificial, remarkably usable, limbs for thalidomide children, or custom-built 'transport' for severely handicapped patients.

Medical engineering is often overlooked as an alternative to medicine for people who want to be closely involved with alleviating disabilities.

Municipal or Public Service Engineers

They work for public authorities. (It is now not so much a discipline as an application of a discipline.) They do mainly *civil engineering* (see above), and are often also responsible for refuse collection and disposal, the maintenance of public parks and gardens, street lighting, and – a very important aspect of their work – highway planning, car parking, and traffic management schemes. Traffic/transport engineering is becoming an important specialization in itself with special post-graduate or first degree course training. While the majority of municipal engineers take civil engineering degrees, other engineering and some other degrees may be acceptable. This branch contains more administrative work than other branches.

Chemical Engineering

Chemical engineers are concerned with the design and development of laboratory processes, and with their translation into large-scale plant, for the production of chemicals, dyes, medicines, fertilizers, plastics, etc. Their expertise in designing and managing plant in which chemical processes take place is also used in food processing, brewing, paper, textile and other industries. They are also concerned with converting noxious waste into useful by-products (see Biotechnology, p. 434), or at least into harmless substances. Chemical engineering has far wider application than is often believed: many chemical engineers do work in oil refineries and other heavy industry, but there is wide scope elsewhere, for example in computer and silicon chip production.

Production Engineering

See *Production*, above, p. 171.

Production engineering covers all aspects of manufacture. It embraces knowledge of many aspects of engineering and ensures that labour, equipment and materials are used efficiently and economically.

The production engineer needs both technical and 'people management' skills, so that goods of the right quality are produced at the required time at the right price and quality. The production engineer plans the production methods and systems and liaises with other departments such as design, research and development, purchasing and sales to make sure that manufacture is as efficient as possible.

Naval Architecture

Despite the title, the work is engineering rather than architecture. Though it is concerned with the design and construction of craft which float on or under or hover just above the water, its main concern is with the efficient and economic operation of craft, of any size from sailing dinghy to supertanker, hydrofoil, oil rig, nuclear-propelled submarine and naval vessel. Naval architects work for the Services as well as for ship- and boat-building firms. A small branch.

Aeronautical/Aerospace Engineering

Concerned with aircraft design and construction and space and satellite research, as well as with planning, operation and maintenance of airlines' fleets of aircraft and aircraft components. They work for aircraft manufacturers, airlines and the Ministry of Defence. They are also involved with hovercraft and other high-speed transport systems, many of which are still on the drawing-board. This is a small branch of engineering, and a greater proportion work in research and development, fewer on production. People who want to work in this area can take electronics or physics – and leave more options open.

Agricultural Engineering

See Agriculture, p. 33.

Mining Engineering

What was said in the introduction about engineering being a door-opener into a wide variety of jobs applies to this branch only to a very limited extent. Mining engineers' training is very much more vocational than that of other engineers. The majority of mining engineers (it is a small branch) in this country work in the coal industry; a few in quarrying, rock, salt, and potash mining. There are opportunities abroad in ore extraction and other types of mining, but most jobs abroad require some experience at home.

Very broadly, work can be divided into mine management and mine development. Mine management includes coordinating and organizing the work of the various colliery activities – work at the coal face, distribution, etc. Above all it involves man-management, especially for junior managers. They go down the mine to ensure safety regulations are adhered to, work is carried out correctly, equipment is in order, etc. At a more senior level, management may involve responsibility for the whole of a colliery's work, or for several collieries – i.e. at that level, mine management involves mainly administration, no direct involvement with the work force. Mine development is team-work with electrical, electronic and mechanical engineers, geologists and surveyors. The mining industry has changed drastically in the last decade or so; pick-and-shovel work has virtually disappeared; mechanized cutters and conveyor belts have taken over. Development now involves the introduction of highly sophisticated technologies. Though basically planning, design and research work, testing new equipment and observing its use may involve some work down the mine.

Some engineering jobs described elsewhere (or advertised) have different titles from all those mentioned here. They may be jobs in small branches, or offshoots of, or options within, established engineering branches. Titles may describe jobs which can be done by people from various disciplines. Or, as in the case, for example, of *computer engineering*, they may describe emerging new branches which are also still under the umbrella of an established branch (electronics in this case).

Engineering can no longer be neatly categorized into the traditional disciplines. It is a fast-changing profession, developing as a result of scientific discovery (scientists discover; engineers exploit discoveries and make them work productively as well as in response to need). For example, new sources of energy will be needed next century: engineers are working on the development of wind, wave and solar energy – and become known as *energy engineers*. Technological tasks are so complex now that people from various disciplines have to pool their expertise: at the same time, some disciplines are becoming so unwieldy that they sub-divide. That applies specially in *electronics* and *mechanical engineering*. New titles do not have as precise meanings as have traditional engineering disciplines.

Here is a very brief (and superficial) guide to some of the current engineering job-titles and the – probable – umbrella discipline, or function, which should be the first port of call for information on what knowledge is required and what work involved:

Computer, systems, control engineering: umbrella discipline: *Electronics*.

Offshore, oil, fuel, energy engineering: umbrella disciplines: *Mechanical*, *Electrical*, *Electronic*, or *Chemical Engineering*. (Energy engineering can also describe the energy-saving function in large organizations.)

Nuclear engineering: umbrella discipline: *Physics* and *Electronics*.

Industrial engineering: umbrella discipline: *Production Engineering*, but can also be combination of management and engineering.

Manufacturing engineering: umbrella discipline: usually *Production Engineering*.

Process engineering: umbrella discipline: *Chemical Engineering*.

Plant, installation, test and commissioning engineering: umbrella discipline: could be *Mechanical*, *Production* or *Chemical Engineering*, but also used for functions carried out by *Mechanical* or almost any other specialist engineer.

Prospects (all Chartered Engineers) Good on the whole, because engineering is such an adaptable skill; the broader the areas of application of the discipline, the better the prospects; for example, mechanical and electronic engineers are needed in very many more areas of employment than are naval architects. Within electrical, electronic, mechanical and production engineering it is possible to switch from one branch to another. This usually requires taking a post-graduate course (possible part-time, while working). Many engineers, from any discipline, go into industrial and commercial management (see introduction, p. 168, and Management in Industry, p. 269) and into management consultancy (see p. 281). Others, especially electronics engineers, go into Computing (see p. 131). Chartered engineers can become maths, physics and engineering science teachers. There are opportunities in the EEC and elsewhere abroad; for civil and structural engineers especially, opportunities in the Middle East are good.

Pay: Medium to high (see p. xxiii).

Training Engineering degree which leads to 'professional engineer' status and usually to a first job as 'graduate trainee'. The degree can either be in one engineering branch right from the start, or it may be a course which starts with a general engineering first year, allowing students to postpone specialization until they know a bit more about engineering generally. There are also an increasing number of courses which combine engineering with another subject, for example economics, marketing, a modern language or especially management. Some last 4 years and have higher status. Courses, even within individual disciplines, vary in content, some being more industry orientated, others more academic in approach. Before choosing a course prospective students should first study CRAC *Course Guides* and *Which Degree* and then individual prospectuses.

Sandwich courses are particularly suitable for students who want to go into industry, as it gives them a chance to sample the industrial scene, and it is reassuring for the prospective employer if a job-applicant has had experience of the working world. Many of the large companies now sponsor students (i.e. pay them while they are studying). Sponsored students are 'industry-based', they spend all their work-experience periods with their sponsor's organization; 'college-based' sandwich students have their work-experience periods organized by polytechnic or university and may get experience of a range of employers during their course. There are 'thin sandwich' courses which last 4 or 5 years, with students spending alternately 6 months with employer and 6 months studying; 'thick sandwiches' are 5-year courses with a year each at the beginning and at the end with an industrial employer, and 3 years' studying in the middle. For top design jobs a post-graduate MSc or similar course is essential.

To be registered as a Chartered Engineer, graduates must have spent a few years (at least 2 usually) in 'a responsible position', and must normally have passed a 'professional interview' and been admitted to corporate membership of one of the member Institutions of the Council of Engineering Institutions (each branch of engineering has its own Institution; there are 15). Some Institutions now stipulate a first- or second-class honours degree for membership.

It is possible to switch to engineering with a 'related' degree, which may be, for example, in planning, physics, maths or, for certain branches, chemistry. Such graduates would have to satisfy the Institution they wish to join that they have acquired the necessary engineering knowledge (i.e. provide evidence of work done).

It is also possible to become a Chartered Engineer without joining one of the Institutions. The Engineering Council sets its own two-part examinations which lead to Registration as Chartered Engineer. Graduates in an engineering discipline normally qualify for exemption from the EC examinations but the EC has kept open a non-graduate part-time route to qualifying. It is possible to qualify via BTEC and Higher BTEC awards (or possibly by taking a special polytechnic course) and then to take the EC's own examinations. This route is not recommended: it is lengthy and the drop-out rate is very high. People who cannot take a full-time degree course, for whatever reason, are advised to qualify as Technician Engineers (see below).

Technicians and Technician Engineers

Entry qualifications

In practice normally 4 O-levels including maths and physics, but see **Training** and BTEC (p. xvi). Technicians can also start by training as craftsmen/women and through the YTS (see p. xxvii).

The work

Chartered and technician engineers' work overlaps in all branches, but more in electrical, electronic, mechanical and production engineering than in the others. It also overlaps in all functions (see above) but much less in design and research where graduates' depth and breadth of training, and their creativity, are usually essential. After a few years' work, though, applicants' experience and ability rather than their qualifications count. At that stage, experienced technicians are on a par with *average* graduates (not with high-flyers). Degrees for chartered engineers became the normal qualifications only about 15 years ago, when new technologies increased the complexities of engineering tasks (and as higher education became more accessible). But for every engineer who has the chance to make full use of degree-level knowledge, who is, say, responsible for the safe design of an oil rig or for a research project into the application of laser beams in surgery, there are hundreds of engineers whose jobs require sound professional expertise, but not the depth and breadth of knowledge needed for top jobs. Hence the increasing scope for technicians.

Technician engineers have never managed to put themselves across as a professional entity, although in most branches they have their own professional institutions, and, within the engineering profession, they are fully recognized as vital experts in their field and essential colleagues. According to experience and training, they are either left to get on with tasks on their own, or are support staff with limited responsibility (both apply to average graduate engineers as well). Job titles such as, for example, *plant*, *project*, *production*, *commissioning*, *development* or *sales* engineer can describe *either* a chartered *or* a technician engineer. There is nothing precise about titles and demarcation by qualification in the engineering profession which depends so much on expertise and/or experience.

The technician scene is very confusing indeed to anyone outside the industry. There are, officially – that is according to the Engineers Registration Board – two levels of technician: *Technician engineers* – those whose work overlaps with graduates and whose breadth of knowledge enables them to take responsibility for a wide range of tasks; and *Technicians* who take responsibility for jobs in a more narrowly defined area. In practice, however, the distinction is blurred. The term 'technician' is loosely used to cover a whole range of job levels. Very many 'technician' jobs are in fact done by graduates. Technicians become 'senior technicians' rather than 'technician engineers' in some organizations. Some go on to qualify as Chartered Engineers (see **Training**).

Work is as varied as that of chartered engineers and the settings in which technicians work are equally varied. They range from hospital to aerospace laboratory, from professional consultant's drawing office to large factory or local authority engineer's department.

Tasks include, for example:

In all branches: draughtsmanship (usually computerized) which may be routine work, but may involve using initiative and special knowledge, and producing working drawings from designers' rough notes and/or instructions; or assisting professional engineers in Research, Design, Development (see pp. 169–70); taking charge of *production processes* and procedures (see Production, p. 171); being responsible, for example, for one or several production lines or for continuity of supplies, or dispatch. Production functions are often subdivided and carried out by technicians under a production manager, who may also be a technician.

Mechanical engineering: as estimating engineer, responsibility for costing projects or parts of projects; supervision of installation of equipment on customer's premises or in firm's own factory; vast variety of *repair and maintenance* work and supervision and coordination of it in anything from garage to hotel, hospital to factory; *after-sales service* to investigate, for example, complaints when computer hardware has gone wrong.

Electrical and *electronic engineering*: probably the widest scope. Wherever there is electronic equipment, technicians are needed for installation, maintenance, monitoring, fault tracing, repairs, sales, servicing, and for explaining things to customers both in person and by writing manuals. This means they are needed in hospitals (see *Medical Engineering* above, p. 177); at airports; in places like the Stock Exchange; the Post Office – any organization which uses electrical or electronic equipment (see Computing, p. 131). While large organizations, for example, hospitals, supermarkets or factories, employ their own technicians, the majority are employed by equipment manufacturers and are sent out to service, sell, investigate and repair, which means they visit a variety of customers.

Technicians also work in broadcasting (see p. 534); for British Telecom; in hi-fi and similar equipment shops where they repair and service customers' equipment (this may involve visiting customers' houses); and in commercial recording studios – for example, *balancing engineers* (who must be able to read music and have a good ear) are responsible for producing the required levels of sounds from various sources.

Radio, television and video servicing is often a simple job; technicians employed by rental firms are trained to service one or two types of models and call on customers to repair equipment on the spot, or replace faulty parts. (It is important to find out, when taking this type of job, whether training (see below) is available or whether it is a dead-end job without prospects of progressing.)

Civil and *Structural Engineering*. Technicians in traffic management may be in charge of compiling a 'street inventory' prior to the installation of traffic signals (finding out where gas and electricity mains are; what shops/schools and other 'traffic generators' there are); they organize traffic counts and collate accident data. Others cost projects; supervise construction work; work out what equipment is required on bridge or road works; liaise with clients and, in municipal work, with local residents. They also become *building inspectors* for local authorities, or they specialize as design draughtsmen; they investigate new materials and processes; or assist with making land and site surveys (see Surveying, p. 503).

In *Production*, technicians work at all levels, from monitoring or servicing machinery to jointly with Personnel (see p. 358) working on job evaluation schemes, to being in full charge. Many *production engineers* or *production managers* have technician qualifications, plus experience. In *Marketing and Sales* where (see above) engineering knowledge is only one of the necessary skills, experienced technicians do very well indeed and can rise to the top. Finally, experienced technicians can set up their own workshops/business (see Working for Oneself, p. 560).

Prospects Good, especially for electronics, electrical and mechanical technicians. Even during the worst of the recession the demand for technicians often exceeded the supply. Experienced technicians are also often able to get work *abroad*. Technician training is broadly based and, once trained, technicians can switch type of work.

Pay: Medium to high (see p. xxiii).

Personal attributes A practical and methodical approach and an interest in technology are needed in all technician jobs. There is room for backroom types who like to get on with their work on their own, for those who like to work in a team, those who like to work in a drawing office or laboratory, and for those who enjoy visiting clients and customers. For some jobs, but by no means all, manual dexterity. For others, ability to explain technical points in plain language and liking for meeting people.

Training There are a variety of training schemes. It is important when getting a job as trainee or learner or junior (or whatever the title) to find out whether systematic training is given. Jobs which do not include systematic training are not 'technician engineer' or 'technician' jobs in the correct sense of the term.

The most up-to-date training pattern is that recommended by the Engineering Industry Training Board; it is widely adopted by employers.

Training starts with 12 months in a training centre which covers basic engineering processes including machining, fitting, welding, electrical wiring, electronic assembly, soldering and sheet metal work. About a third of the time is spent in college on learning the theory to complement the practical training. After the first year, specialized training starts. It is planned to enable the technician to master the six skills which are required in all technician jobs to a greater or lesser degree: choosing materials and components and understanding processing of materials; handling and using measuring tools or instruments; collecting and communicating information; understanding the manufacturing and commercial activities of the employer; planning and organizing one's own work as well as the work of others; diagnosing and solving problems and analysing faults.

Carefully worked out manuals explain, for example, how to consider when writing reports what the recipient's level of technical knowledge is, and what information should be transmitted in any particular situation to client and colleagues and how to transmit it; how to design specifications; how to plan projects; all tasks which are concerned with the organizing of work as much as with doing it.

The length of training varies, largely according to entrants' school qualifications, from 2 to 4 years. Examination structure has just changed (although the old method may still operate in some colleges).

The normal pattern of training is based on BTEC courses (see p. xvi). Length of training depends on entry qualifications and aim.

1. Entrants with CSE Grade 2 or 3 in maths, physics and English, and preferably, but not necessarily, in technical drawing or engineering, take a 3-year part-time day-release course leading to a BTEC National Certificate which, with practical experience, leads to registration as *Technician (Tech. (EC))*. Technicians can then go on to take a Higher BTEC National Certificate by two years' further part-time day-release training and become registered as *Technician Engineers (T.Eng.(EC))*. However, minimum entry qualifications are in practice set by colleges, and many require 4 O-levels.

2. Entrants with O-levels or CSE Grade 1 in maths, physics, English and one other academic subject normally take a 2-year full-time or a 3-year sandwich BTEC National Diploma, or a 2-year, part-time day-release Certificate, leading to Technician status. Then they do a further 2-year full-time or 3-year sandwich course for a BTEC Higher National Diploma (or they can take a Higher National Certificate – see above, under 1). Entrants with at least 1 relevant A-level (usually maths or physics) and at least 4 relevant O-levels or CSEs Grade 1 (maths or physics must be included at O-level or A-level) can go straight into a BTEC Higher award course (either part-time, full-time or sandwich). Most colleges require a second A-level subject to have been studied, but not necessarily passed.

BTEC courses, called 'programmes', are very flexible. Programmes are made up of individual 'units', a certain number of which add up to a Certificate; if more units are added, a Certificate becomes a Diploma. In practice, part-time day-release programmes lead to a Certificate; sandwich and full-time programmes lead to a Diploma. The procedure is the same at Higher National Certificate and Higher National Diploma level. A Diploma, at each level, denotes greater breadth of knowledge and skills than a Certificate.

Each programme within an engineering discipline contains 'essential units' taken by all students within the subject area – for example, electronic or mechanical engineering – and a number of additional optional units which fit in with the students' individual interests and job requirements.

Technicians and technician engineers are registered with the Engineers Registration Board.

Craft Level Entry

Entry qualifications Average ability in maths, science (*ex*cluding biology), technical/practical subjects (*ex*cluding domestic science). Employers normally test applicants' aptitudes. Many ask for CSE Grade 3 maths. Maximum age: normally 17 (but see TOPS, p. xlvi).

The work Engineering craftsmen and women do skilled work and need sufficient theoretical knowledge to understand the principles behind the operations they carry out and to solve basic problems. They work in all branches and may be in charge of semi- and unskilled workers. Their work, and their scope, is changing as a result of new technology. First of all, the distinction between craftspersons and technicians is narrowing, with craft-trained people becoming technicians more frequently than in the past; and secondly, as a result of automation in all engineering spheres, the distinction between the specialist trades is blurring. Craftspersons may switch trades more easily than in the past, as well as learn new ones. However, traditional crafts or 'trades' continue to be practised. Some of the commonest are:

Machine-shop Crafts

(a) *Toolmaking*: a highly skilled trade, involving the use of precision machinery and tools to make jigs, fixtures, gauges and other tools used in production work. Apprentices may start in the toolroom, or they are upgraded from other trades.
(b) *Toolsetting*: setting of automatic (such as computer/tape numerically controlled) or semi-automatic machines for use by machine operators in mass production.
(c) *Turning*: operating lathes which use fixed cutting tool(s) to remove metal/material from a rotating workpiece.
(d) *Milling*: operating milling machines where metal/material is removed from a fixed workpiece by rotating cutter(s).
(e) *Jig-boring*: highly skilled work in which very heavy articles are machined to a high degree of precision.
(f) *Grinding*: obtains a very accurate finish by removing small amounts of metal with rapidly revolving abrasive wheels. It is also used to sharpen tools.

Fitting

Fitters, whether working in mechanical, electrical or electronic engineering, combine the basic skills of the machine-shop craftsperson with the ability to use hand tools. In production work they may assemble cars, generators, TV sets, etc.; on customers' premises – private houses, factories, offices, etc. – they carry out maintenance and repair work: gas fitters install, service and repair gas-powered domestic appliances or industrial plant; marine engine fitters put together and repair ships' engines, etc.

Training Craftspersons serve an apprenticeship, preferably with a company which follows EITB (Engineering Industry Training Board) recommendations for Craft Training.

The first year ('Basic Engineering Training') is 'off-the-job', i.e. in a Training Centre, learning basic engineering skills. These include hand and machine skills, manipulation of sheet metal, welding and electrical/electronic skills.

Second and subsequent years (usually 2 or 3) are spent in the employing company on Module Training. A Module is a package of skill training and experience 'on-the-job' to nationally agreed standards. An EITB Certificate of Craftsmanship is awarded on successful completion of two Modules. A Certificate of Endorsement is awarded for each further Module successfully completed.

During both Basic Engineering and Module Training trainees attend a College of Further Education by day- or block-release to learn relevant theory.

The majority of engineering craft trainees now follow EITB recommendations. The remainder receive traditional training by doing a job and attending Further Education Colleges either by day-release or evening classes, usually for City and Guilds Certificates. EITB training is more likely to lead on to technician work and training (see above).

Craft training no longer lasts a given length of time as did traditional apprenticeships. Instead, Certificates of Craftsmanship are awarded when nationally-agreed standards have been reached – usually after 2 to 3 years' training.

Prospects These vary according to geographical area, economic climate and quality of training. However, there are skill-shortages and well-trained craftspersons have good prospects of becoming technicians (see above). Craft level jobs are diminishing in all manufacturing.

Pay: Low during training, medium to high as technician (see p. xxiii).

Late start (all levels)

Chartered Engineers: Only advisable for technicians and people with related degrees or at least good, and recently-acquired, science A-levels, or with very strong motivation plus recent relevant work experience.

Technicians: Good opportunities for people who have taken TOPS courses, especially in electronics and related fields or such specialized areas as TV and other electronic equipment servicing.

Craft level: Not advisable as there are more young applicants than apprenticeships; however there are some TOPS courses.

Position of women (all levels)

The proportion of women engineers is still woefully small. Under 1% of the main Chartered Institutions' members are women (figures refer to November 1983). Proportions very according to age-group: around 3% of student/associate members are women; minute proportions of Fellows or equivalent. However, there is a significant increase in the proportion of female university engineering students. 14% of chemical, 11% of 'general and combined engineering subjects', 10% of civil, 6% of mechanical and 6% of electrical engineering students who started courses in 1983 were women. The proportion of women electrical engineering students especially is still disappointingly small: electrical and electronic engineers are wanted in computing/information technology (see p. 131) – the fastest-growing career area and the one in which the dealing-with-people element is very great indeed. The old image of engineering as arid, only dealing-with-things-and-theories, figures, drawing-boards and workers in dirty overalls, still lingers.

The small proportion of women cannot be entirely explained by the still relatively small proportion who take physics and maths (see p. xxxiii for O- and A-level male/female proportions): 52% of ophthalmic optics first-year students are women, and they normally also need A-level physics and maths (and ophthalmic optics courses are usually more difficult to get into than engineering courses). Yet engineering generally, and electrical engineering especially, leads to a far wider job-choice and hence smaller risk of unemployment, than ophthalmic optics.

Women's career-choices cannot be blamed just on poor careers information; it must also be due to the fact that women are still less long-term career-minded than men.

At technician level (see p. 182) the situation is even worse. According to a late-1983 Engineering Industry Training Board survey, only 2·4% of technicians are women, and 4% of technician trainees. Not all trainees seem to be working for qualifications; BTEC (see p. xvi) has only 2% of women on its engineering programmes (at both National and Higher National awards levels). The largest technician institution, many of whose members work in information technology, the

Institution of Electrical and Electronics Incorporated Engineers, has 38 women among its 20,000 members. Yet the Institution has for five years now run an annual Girl Technician of the Year competition which always gets widely publicized and shows the wide range of jobs women do. (It is possible that women technicians are less willing to join institutions, but even allowing for that, the proportion is dismal indeed.)

Women who *have* gone into engineering are doing well. According to the Institution of Electrical Engineers' 1983 *Survey of Members* (the only such survey undertaken by a chartered institution), 'being female often helped gaining sponsorshop (for training) and jobs, as the minority was more noticeable at interview'. This statement has been corroborated by many young women engineers. Recruitment officers say they usually have 'more good and fewer average and plain hopeless' women than men applicants. They genuinely want more women chartered and technician engineers. The fact that a woman has the initiative to step off the tramlines and choose a non-traditional career shows she is more determined and interested than the average male who may have chosen engineering 'because it is there', and the obvious next step after school.

Promotion prospects, according to the IEE survey, are reasonable in the early stages, but opportunities at management level, and for management training, could be better (see Management, p. 277, for hurdles in women's promotion paths). Nevertheless, the small but growing number of women in senior-middle and senior jobs (including non-technical work such as marketing) say that attitudes *are* changing and that opportunities are there – especially in the wide-ranging information technology area where 'people-related' skills are specially important. In GEC, the largest British employer of electrical and electronic engineers, women now account for 8% of research staff. GEC has said they 'would be happy to see this rise to 50%'. They mean what they say: they have produced, and are distributing free of charge, a glossy brochure showing their women engineers' diverse activities.

It seems that in the mid-80s the worry is not so much lack of opportunities for women, but the slow change in parents', schools' and generally society's realization that there cannot be equality between the sexes if one sex almost monopolizes the skills which will matter most in the 1990s and beyond. As the IEE survey put it: 'Social prejudice against women in engineering should be tackled from, or even before, primary school level, because children base their ideas on models in the environment, in books . . . etc. Women seem to lack examples of other women's achievements, whereas men always have other men's achievement to inspire them.'

There is no shortage of initiatives from industry, the EITB, polytechnics and universities to attract more women. Conferences, seminars, residential weeks for sixth formers, have all been running for several years now. 1984 is WISE (Women Into Science and Engineering) year, with even more recruiting events showing the many types of jobs to which an engineering training can lead.

(At craft level, women account for well under ½%, but demand for craftspersons is falling. Good craftsmen get technician training so, as women who break into this male preserve are likely to be enterprising, they might as well go for technician training right away.)

Career-break: Because of the pace of technological change, a complete gap of even a few years would be difficult to bridge. But there are various schemes for enabling women to keep in touch. These include encouraging women to visit their former employers regularly during the break and, on their return, for them to have a 'mentor' or 'industrial tutor' who, in an informal way, helps them to catch up. During the break, women technicians and chartered engineers are encouraged to take the Open University (see p. xliv) 'Women in Technology' Associate Student programme. This has been specially designed for women who want to return to work after a child-rearing break.

Part-time: Very few part-time jobs at present, but some opportunities for engineers who have specialized or can specialize, in computing and related work. Job-sharing schemes do not seem to have been tried on any scale, but there is no reason why they should not work.

Further information

Engineering Careers Information Service, 54 Clarendon Street, Watford WD1 1LB

Engineering Council (for list of individual Institutions as well as general information), Canberra House, 10–16 Maltravers Street, London WC2R 3ER

Civil Engineering Careers Service, 1–7 Great George Street, London SW1P 3AH

For list of special courses (conversion and technician) for women: Equal Opportunities Commission, Overseas House, Quay Street, Manchester M3 3HN

BTEC (see p. xvi) Women's Engineering Society, 25 Foubert's Place, London W1

Related careers

Agriculture – Art and Design – Building Management – Computing/Information Technology – Science – Surveying

---

Environmental Health Officer

Entry qualifications 2 A-levels including a science, and 3 O-levels: in English language, maths and a second science subject.

The work Environmental Health Officers work for local authorities (see Local Government, p. 265). They are concerned with the prevention of disease and the enforcement of regulations designed to secure healthy living and working environments. They are responsible for:

(1) *Food*: Inspecting places where food is stored, prepared (including slaughterhouses), sold or served, to check that it is hygienically handled at all stages. Officers check cleanliness of equipment, washing facilities for staff, the state of the staff's overalls, etc. They also make spot-checks on different foods, taking away samples for bacteriological examination and chemical analysis. In cases of food poisoning officers trace the source of the trouble, which involves a good deal of detective work.

As well as visiting restaurants, shops, warehouses, etc., environmental health officers also check food at fairs, exhibitions and stalls. Some EHOs work for food manufacturers, ensuring efficient and clean handling and transporting of food, and investigating new technologies.

(2) *Housing*: An officer has powers to enter and inspect homes unasked if she 'has reason to believe that the premises are not fit for human habitation'. In most cases she calls only if there has been a request for advice. She helps to decide whether the premises should be repaired or modernized, or whether they are only fit for demolition. She must be able to discuss health and structural questions on equal terms with experts and to advise landlords and tenants, including those in overcrowded slum property, or owner-occupiers wishing to modernize their houses. Officers also check on conditions and facilities for caravan and houseboat dwellers.

(3) *Places of work*: Officers check on satisfactory working conditions: sanitary arrangements; overcrowding; temperature; ventilation; lighting; provision of seating in shops; closing hours; hours of work for juveniles. The extent of duties varies, and overlaps with Factory Inspection (see p. 195).

Environmental health officers are also responsible for implementation of anti-pollution legislation.

An officer spends more than half her time visiting, inspecting, discussing suggested improvements, etc.; desk-work consists mainly of record-keeping and report writing.

Prospects Good.

Pay: Medium to high (see p. xxiii).

Training *Either*: For the Diploma awarded by the Institution of Environmental Health Officers: 3-year sandwich or 4-year day-release course. Arrangements are made for students to get experience of work not carried out within their authority's area; for instance, students in suburban areas go elsewhere to see factories, caravans, etc.

Or: 4-year sandwich degree. Syllabus includes the basic sciences as applied to environmental health (control of infectious diseases and of vermin, for instance); physical aspects of housing (dilapidations, unfitness); public cleansing; water supply; drainage, sewerage and sewage disposal; procedures under Housing Acts; hygiene of buildings (standards of heating, ventilation and lighting); food (hygiene and inspection), etc.

Personal attributes Interest in people's living and working environment; ability to take decisions; sufficient self-confidence to go where one is not necessarily welcome, to be firm when necessary and to discuss complicated problems intelligently.

Late start Not much opportunity for on-the-job training. Some BTEC certificates and Open University foundation courses available for entry.

Position of women Only a relatively small proportion of women but applications from women are increasing rapidly. Over one third of student EHOs are women. However, this is one of the careers where legislation and changing attitudes should help a lot: there never was any discrimination at the *entry* stage, but, largely because women were assumed not to be able or willing to do the rough parts of the work (slaughterhouse and unfit-for-human-habitation dwelling inspection), women did not qualify for promotion – not having had all-round experience. Now women cannot be barred from that part of the work.

Career-break: Should be no problem if you have kept up with developments.

Part-time: Not at the moment, but it should be possible to organize it in this type of work.

Further information The Institution of Environmental Health Officers, Chadwick House, Rushworth Street, London SE1 0RB

Related careers *Factory Inspector – Food Technology – Housing Management – Trading Standards Officer*

NOTE: In Scotland education requirements and duties are slightly different.

Factory Inspector

Entry qualifications Honours or post-graduate degree (any subject) usually *plus* experience in industry, preferably in production or similar department. All candidates must have at least O-level maths.

The work A factory inspector is responsible for seeing that the standards required by the Health and Safety at Work and similar Acts are observed in factories and various other places of work. She deals with people as well as with technological problems. She used to be entirely concerned with physical conditions at work, but since the Health and Safety Executive was set up her responsibilities widened. She is now also concerned with the social and psychological implications of technological developments (for example, what leads to, and what situation or innovation diminishes, job satisfaction), and with the effects of industrial hazards on the public. She is very much concerned with the implications of 'chip-based' technologies; for example, the possible eye strain caused by looking at the VDU of the word processor (see p. 455); the monotony of monitoring machines in a highly automatic factory.

Her duties are varied. She advises employers on methods of safeguarding health from dust and fumes given off in industrial processes; she checks heating, ventilation, safety of equipment used and standards of hygiene, and she investigates accidents and their causes. Occasionally, she may conduct legal proceedings for which she collects the necessary evidence, prepares the case, and gives evidence. If at all possible she effects changes by persuasion and advice rather than legal action.

She visits places of work at fairly regular intervals, but it is up to her to decide which places need frequent visits and which do not, and she plans her own working day.

There is nothing desk-bound about this career. The work involves gathering first-hand information on conditions in factories, on construction sites, etc. Only about 2 days a week is spent in the office, when the inspector consults with her colleagues, writes up reports and reads technical literature; it is also part of her job to advise industry on new processes and equipment and on the lay-out of new factories. The work overlaps with Environmental Health Officer (see p. 192).

Prospects Fair. Factory inspectors are needed in many parts of the country.
Pay: High (see p. xxiii).

Training 2 years on-the-job, but including a 6-month full-time course for Diploma in Safety and Hygiene, as well as other shorter courses.

Personal attributes Self-reliance; interest in technical matters and in people; diplomacy; ability to get on well with all kinds of people; fitness; initiative; ability to take responsibility; ability to communicate easily. *For women*: self-confidence to work in male-dominated environments.

Late start Over 30s likely to be accepted for training only if they have had extensive industrial or other relevant experience.

Position of women About 11% of factory inspectors are women; too few apply. As the work is done in almost entirely male-oriented settings, women have to be willing to face occasional surprise or opposition when visiting factories, and have probably to be better qualified, in terms of work experience and personality, to get promoted on equal terms with male colleagues. However, the Inspectorate genuinely wants more women to apply.

Career-break: In theory, people who keep up with developments should be able to return, but work is not always available everywhere, and generally only in cities.

Part-time: Very little at the moment, though in theory no reason why it should not be possible to arrange small 'caseloads'; no promotion for part-timers; job-sharing should, in theory, be possible but has not been considered.

Further information Health and Safety Executive, 25 Chapel Street, London
Civil Service Commission, Alencon Link, Basingstoke, Hampshire RG21 1JB.

Related careers *Engineering – Environmental Health Officer*

Fashion – Women's and Men's

Design – production – sketcher, stylist, cutter, assistant designer, assistant designer-cutter, pattern-cutter, pattern-grader – fitter – hand – sample machinist. FASHION SIDELINES: lingerie, swimwear, gloves, shoes and knitwear – paper patterns – theatrical costume design – embroidery – millinery

Entry qualifications Vary according to the type of training from none to degree.

The work There is a good deal of confused thinking about careers in fashion, which is an industry, not an art. Very few designers create original models or launch a new line which shakes the fashion world. The majority spend most of their time and talent on translating famous designers' ideas and on adapting last year's best-sellers to suit this year's mood, and on producing clothes which are marketable and economic to manufacture.

The industry falls into overlapping sections: *haute couture* and bespoke tailoring – both tiny sections; 'up-market ready-to-wear' – medium-sized; mass production – a vast field; and an uncategorizable group of young determined designers who do not fit into the traditional pattern of the industry.

Women's Fashion

Haute couture
Houses show twice-yearly collections. No more than about two dozen copies of any one garment are made; each is cut and made up for individual customers almost entirely by hand. In the workrooms where this is done, the hierarchy is usually assistant designer, fitters, hands, junior assistants and learners.

A few designers/dressmakers work on much the same lines as couture, except that staff consists of only one or two hands.

Up-market ready-to-wear
Follows couture trends. Garments are made individually with a considerable but diminishing amount of hand-work; but graded into stock sizes and sold in limited quantities at home and abroad.

Mass production
Adapts high fashion within limits set by mass-production methods, costing and mass-appeal. Garments are sold in thousands at home and abroad. They are cut by machine, hundreds at a time, and made up with a minimum of hand finishing. By far the largest sector.

Many houses within each of the three categories now produce several types of collections, each under a separate name with its own style and price-range, each collection designed for a given market. Usually each of these collections has its own design team.

The best career opportunities are in the design rooms of wholesale and mass-production houses. Here sample garments and prototypes are worked out before garments go into production.

Young designers
Usually art and design graduates, with exceptional drive and determination, who set up on their own, with very little capital, possibly working from their homes, often a few friends working together and employing a few 'outworkers'. They usually make trendy clothes for men's, women's or unisex boutiques; some open their own boutiques; a few get some orders from enterprising store buyers; the majority give up after a few years (often heavily in debt). Only the exceptionally lucky, talented and hard-working survive. They either join an established house (but continue designing under their own 'label') or find financial backing to enlarge and put their business on a sound footing.

Men's Fashion

Bespoke tailoring
Equivalent in price range to *haute couture*, but the emphasis is on craftsmanship rather than original design. Bespoke tailors are highly-skilled craftspeople – hand-stitchers (most of them), cutters and fitters. Some specialize in cutting or in fitting, some combine the two. Some specialize in making one type of garment; most make all types. A few bespoke tailors also make women's clothes. Firms tend to be very small – and old-established. Very few tailors now set up their own workrooms.

Men's ready-to-wear and mass-produced garments
The 'engineered suit' is taking over from the small tailors' made-to-measure middle-price-range suit (and the increase in casual wear has reduced the market for ready-to-wear suits). Cutting and grading and even 'hand-stitching' is done by computer-controlled machines. Care-

fully researched sizing assures near-perfect fit for most shapes and sizes. This is much more clothing technology than fashion-design work. 'Design input' is small. Until recently most mass-produced men's clothing was produced in Scandinavia and Italy; the industry in this country is now growing. Scope mainly for technologists and technicians – few designers needed.

Leisure wear
Men's, women's and unisex leisure wear is a growth area. Although there is more 'design input' than in men's clothes, the emphasis still is on making mass-produced garments which, with minimum need for re-tooling and re-programming of machines, can be made to appear different from last year's. Mass-production houses also make some 'short runs'. Again, scope for clothing technologists/production managers is greater than it is for designers.

Different types of jobs:

Design

Titles give little indication of a job's creative content and status. An assistant designer or a pattern-cutter may have more scope in one firm than a designer in another in which the head of the firm has the creative ideas and employs the designer merely to interpret and modify his/her own sketches, or to carry out decisions taken jointly by a team including fabric buyers, production, and marketing specialists.

The designer's job always involves a variety of tasks but it varies enormously according to the size and organization of the firm for which she is working. Few designers spend much time creating styles and trends. Instead, the majority are 'creative technologists', using their creative ability, technical and marketing expertise to incorporate trends and their firm's 'hand-writing' into garments which sell to a given type of market (for example, trendy, classic, classy, young, elegant). Most designs are an amalgamation and adaptation of ideas from various sources: perhaps a sleeve the designer thought up herself; a skirt-front featured in a foreign magazine; a pocket-flap seen in a shop-window abroad, a collar sketched roughly by the head of the firm. The skill of the designer shows in how brilliantly she can adapt last year's best-seller to look entirely new, while incorporating features which made it a best-seller.

Designers may do their own *pattern-cutting*, which combines ingenuity – saving cloth yet retaining the design's essential features – creative ability and technical knowhow. They may also make working drawings of their own or someone else's designs, cut sample garments, drape and pin them on dress-stand or model, and make necessary adjustments to improve appearance or facilitate manufacture.

Designers work closely with *production managers* (see below) and must understand and be able to use the latest production processes and management principles.

Each garment is costed to fall into a given price range. This may involve working out a compromise, minimizing, for example, the number of operations and components while keeping the maximum similarity between the original conception of the garment and its eventual prototype for, say, 30,000 copies.

When a designer goes to dress-shows in Rome or Paris – by no means all do – she decides whether to buy an (expensive) toile (a draft model tacked up in muslin) for the wealth of its ideas, or whether she can memorize such details as the cut of a sleeve, the position of a dart in relation to the arm-hole, etc. (sketching is not allowed at dress-shows). Her job may include choosing – on her own or jointly with the buyer or merchandise director – the materials for forthcoming collections. This is a challenging task: she has to visualize the potentialities and limitations of materials in design terms, and to evaluate the properties of new fibres in production terms.

Designers work under many constraints, which is challenging, but is entirely different from drawing pretty sketches and either leaving others to translate the idea into something that is marketable, or making it regardless of the cost. That kind of designing is done by only a very few geniuses. Most jobs in fashion combine technical and creative elements – only the proportions of the two vary.

Production/Clothing Technologists

They are a fairly new breed of fashion experts. Work varies as much as, or even more than, designers'. They know exactly what each piece of manufacturing equipment can do; how to adapt garment design to the equipment's limitations; how to change details so as to reduce the number and complexity of operations needed to complete a garment and yet retain as much as possible of the designer's concept. For example, they may suggest a change in the shape or construction of a pocket or collar to ease the production process.

Whether the designer or the production manager decides finally on the detailed construction of a garment varies. In practice, a designer's success is ultimately judged by the profitability of her designs. She is therefore likely to take note of the production manager's suggested modifications even if she is, theoretically, not forced to do so (which, however, she might be).

The production manager is in charge of working out and managing production flow systems – ensuring that the manufacturing process, once it is broken down into a number of operations, will work smoothly, without bottlenecks, and keeping all the operators and equipment evenly busy. In houses which design and manufacture for the boutique trade, production management is particularly tricky as rush orders for short-run designs have to be fitted in at frequent but irregular intervals; the twice-yearly collection system does not apply here.

Production managers must be thoroughly conversant with constantly developing manufacturing technologies, with cutting and sewing-room organization techniques, with quality control methods. They may also be concerned with labour relations and other personnel matters (see Personnel Management, p. 358, Production Management, p. 171, and Production Engineering, p. 178), especially if – as is usual in the clothing trade – the unit is too small to have a personnel officer. In large units there are production supervisors under the production manager.

Sketcher, Stylist, Cutter, Assistant Designer, Assistant Designer-cutter, Pattern-cutter, Pattern-grader

Their work may be what the titles imply but exact functions and responsibilities depend on the size and type of firm and on the director's temperament and talent. A director of a small wholesale firm may theoretically do the designing herself, but in fact may give only a rough sketch to her 'assistant designer' or cutter who produces a workable design without getting the credit for having done so.

Pattern-cutting and the highly skilled (non-creative) pattern-grading can be stepping-stones to work with more creative content or more often to production management. Both cutting and grading are increasingly done with computer-controlled machines.

Fitter

The work possibly varies even more. One fitter may be entirely in charge of a workroom, organizing the work and seeing the buyers. Another may work on improvements to the original design before it is put into production. In retail stores, shops and bespoke tailoring a fitter's job is again different. She is in charge of all the alteration work, but does no designing. In this job there is considerable contact with the public.

Hand

In sample work- or design-rooms, a hand distributes work to the junior assistants and learners and does the most skilled parts of garment-making herself. The work is very important but not creative; again it may be a stepping-stone.

Sample Machinist

Exactly what the title implies: she runs up prototypes and samples and often suggests simplifications. Can be a stepping-stone to supervisory work and production management.

Fashion Sidelines

Lingerie, Swimwear, Gloves, Shoe and Knitwear Design

Competent but not necessarily brilliantly creative people have more chance of finding responsible, semi-creative jobs in one of the lesser-known offshoots of fashion: lingerie, swimwear, children's wear and especially shoe and knitwear design. This is part creative, part production technology work.

Paper Patterns

Designs are adaptations and simplifications of current fashion. Designers must be particularly highly skilled technically, and must be able to design patterns for various types of garments, though some specialize in one type of pattern, such as children's wear, or 'couture' patterns, particularly simple ones, etc. The work is highly computerized.

Designers with a flair for public speaking sometimes visit schools and women's organizations, to give talks on fashion and dressmaking.

Theatrical Costume Design

This is design and dressmaking plus historical research. The sixteenth-century dress or the war-time uniform must be accurate and the material must be suitable for its special purpose. For films or television the garments are not required to last but they must look right under the cameras. For the stage, dresses must be of particularly tough materials. Most of the work is done by specialist firms under the supervision of the designer of the show. Theatrical costume designers often merely fill in details and work to designs they are given. Only occasionally are they asked to 'dress' a show.

Film and television studios have their own art departments where costume supervisors and wardrobe mistresses are in charge of hiring, making, adapting, and maintaining costumes (see Television, p. 538). There are far more people who wish to do theatrical design than there are vacancies, but there is scope for exceptionally talented and highly trained designers.

Embroidery

Computer-controlled machine embroidery is extensively used in most sections of the fashion industry. Embroiderers usually learn on-the-job, and some eventually do simple embroidery designing. Most designing, however, is done by fashion designers. There is considerable scope for machine embroiderers, not so much for designers.

Millinery

Model millinery
Model hats are hand-made in workrooms attached to fashion stores, boutiques, etc. A model is rarely repeated more than thirty times. A worker spends up to 3 days making one hat from start to finish. The designer, called the 'milliner', is in charge of design, workroom organization, and of buying the materials. She may also be a boutique owner.

Mass production
Hats are mass-produced by machine, with the minimum of hand-finish. Mass-production firms buy originals from model milliners. 'Copyists' then adapt them to mass-production methods and price-range. Organizing production is highly skilled work, demanding knowledge of fashion production (see above).

'Copyists' also produce some designs of their own, incorporating the current fashion trends. Millinery is a declining industry.

Prospects *Design*: Not good. There is a great surplus of designers; many, with out-of-date technical training, have little hope of work in the fashion industry. Even those with up-to-date training need push, luck and outstanding talent. To set up on one's own needs exceptional talent, business acumen – and capital (see Working for Oneself, p. 560). Some opportunities abroad.
Production/Clothing Technology: Good, both at technician (cutting, grading, etc.) and at technologist/production management level for well-qualified applicants. The fashion industry is getting more automated and more highly capitalized; large houses take over small ones and install computerized machinery which can also cope with 'short runs'. Even medium-sized and small firms now often want production experts, possibly on a temporary/advisory basis. Production experts

can switch from one type of garment production to another, and those with design-flair can, and often do, either become designers or designer/production managers. Some opportunities abroad where British training is greatly appreciated.

Training

In theory, it is possible to train in a workroom, learning by working and watching. In practice, full-time college training is almost essential as more new fabrics are produced, each with its own limitations and possibilities, and as production methods and machinery become increasingly more sophisticated: for example some garments are now heat-sealed rather than sewn, pattern-grading is computerized; designers and production technologists must know what machinery can and cannot do with new materials, and how materials will react to given manufacturing processes. Designers and production managers must also understand marketing and general business aspects of the fashion industry.

No particular type of qualification necessarily leads to a particular kind or level of job; the value of a course depends largely on 4 factors rather than on the qualification it leads to:

(a) The college must have good connections with industry so that students may work in or at least regularly visit design-rooms and factories.

(b) The college must have up-to-date equipment.

(c) At least some of the staff must be working part-time in industry – to know what is happening in this fast-changing field.

(d) The syllabus must include production management and technology as well as design.

The various types of courses may and may not fulfil these conditions. Training is a jumble of courses and qualifications. Broadly, this is the picture:

Design and clothing technology/production courses overlap: all design courses include some technology; all technology courses include some design. The exact composition of courses, whatever their title, varies enormously and students should thoroughly study syllabuses, and if possible visit colleges before choosing a course. They should find out about courses' connections with industry, above all, and what kind of jobs recent students obtained.

1. *Degree courses*

Art & Design (see p. 56) *Fashion/Textiles specialization*. Emphasis very much on design; industrial relevance varies enormously.

Industrial Technology (clothing option) and *Clothing Studies*. Production/management orientated but some design content. Both 4-year sandwich courses.

2. *Courses for the Clothing and Footwear Institute Examinations Parts I and II*
Candidates should have 1 A-level and 4 O-levels, including an English and a maths or science subject. Courses are planned in collaboration with industry; numbers of students are kept down to the number of skilled staff which the industry can absorb. Courses take 4 years, including 1 year in the industry. The syllabus includes knowledge of materials, design, anatomy, translation of two-dimensional materials into a three-dimensional form, pattern construction, cutting-room and sewing-room organization and management; production management, work study, marketing; personnel management; basic engineering principles. Candidates must submit a management report based on their industrial experience.

Clothing and Footwear Institute examination courses put more emphasis on production management; degree courses more on design, but degree holders can eventually take jobs in which production management plays a more important part, and Clothing and Footwear Institute students can specialize in design. Having studied production management in depth they are qualified as designers in mass production fashion manufacture (where there is by far the greatest scope) rather than in couture.

Associateship of the Clothing and Footwear Institute (gained by passing its examinations), plus 2 years' industrial experience, confers 'degree equivalent' status for teaching purposes: useful at the return-to-work stage.

3. *BTEC and DATEC Higher National Diplomas* (see p. xvi)
1 A-level entry (in practice often 2). Higher National Diploma courses last 2 years, full-time. They overlap a great deal but emphasis differs: BTEC Higher is geared to clothing technology with some design input; DATEC Higher is 'design training with technical background'. BTEC Higher National Diploma holders have better job-getting records than DATEC Higher National Diploma holders. BTEC course content is more adaptable for non-fashion production jobs. Options vary from college to college, and include both specialization in type of garments and in type of work – i.e. 'product development' option covers sketching a garment and taking it right through the production process; 'manufacture' option includes virtually no original design-work.

4. *BTEC and DATEC National Diplomas*
3 O-level entry (in practice often higher). Courses also last 2 years; also overlap, but BTEC National Diploma geared more directly to one specific function – cutting, pattern-grading, etc.; DATEC to designing a particular type of garment and/or production function. Both courses

usually followed by Higher National Diploma (it is possible at that stage to switch from BTEC to DATEC and vice versa).

5. *Higher BTEC and DATEC National Certificates*
BTEC Higher is usually 2 or 3 years' part-time; DATEC Higher usually 1-year full-time.

6. *BTEC and DATEC National Certificates*
3 CSE or City and Guilds Certificate entry. May be 1-year full-time or 2-year part-time day-release. More basic/practical than Diploma courses; lead on to Diploma courses or to technician work in the industry. Certificates usually more specific than Diplomas, concentrating on one specific function – such as machine technology; cutting for bespoke tailoring etc.; sewing machine mechanics.

7. *Some specialist courses*
Whatever the level, these are often of the same value, in job-getting terms, as a degree – for example, DATEC Diploma in Embroidery (3 O-level or CSE entry); DATEC Higher Diploma in Theatrical Studies; certain courses in knitwear, shoe design and manufacture; lingerie design and manufacture. Awards may still be college rather than BTEC or DATEC though this is becoming rare.

8. *City and Guilds Certificate*
Craft courses in various specializations. Courses vary in length, some are 1-year full-time; some 2-year, part-time, day- or block-release. Variations also depend on local industry. Many clothing firms, specially small ones, do not grant day-release. There are some evening courses but it is important to choose a vocational one: some evening courses are intended for people who just want to make their own clothes. City and Guilds Craft and Advanced Craft Certificates lead on to BTEC/DATEC awards. School-leavers without any qualifications can, therefore, work their way right through the training ladder up to Higher BTEC/DATEC or degree.

9. *One-Year Full-time Course in Fashion Retailing*
At the London College for the Distributive Trades. Entry qualifications: 4 O-levels in theory; in practice, because of competition for places, 2 A-levels are usually necessary.

The course is geared to retailing, and covers properties and performance of textiles, colour and design, display, accounting, customer relations, retail organization, evolution and psychology of fashion. Students spend 1 day a week working in a variety of stores and boutiques. They also do 'projects' which involve research and writing up research results.

See also Fashion Writers' course (Journalism, p. 235).

10. *Workroom and Factory Training*
No educational requirements; there are now hardly any apprenticeships. *Workroom* and *factory* training are quite distinct and lead to different work:

Workroom training, 4–5 years, learning making-up by hand and sewing-machine. This *may* eventually lead to design-room work, but *not* to designing; or, in retail, to fitter. The individual has to make herself noticed so that she is given a variety of jobs and not left to sew in sleeves or do hems for years. Hardly any day-release; ambitious workers must go to evening classes.

Factory training teaches mass-production methods. With evening classes it may lead to supervisory posts, and to cutter and junior production management, but not to design-room work. There are few apprenticeships now.

Personal attributes

For top level designers: visual imagination and creative genius; exceptional business flair or a partner with business flair or unlimited capital; the power to make customers trust their judgement; a flair for sensing what people may be persuaded to buy next year and for making staff work devotedly; technical ability; absolutely unshakeable faith in their own talent; determination to overcome apparently insurmountable obstacles; (ability to draw beautifully is *not* necessary); lynx-eyes and a photographic memory for details once seen.

For others: visual imagination and colour sense; a good deal of creative talent but willingness to subdue this to the technical and economic necessities of design for a popular market; finding satisfaction in creating something which is firstly saleable and secondly artistic; adaptability; ability to work as one of a team; some manual dexterity; dry hands; good feet; self-confidence; ambition; determination.

For production management: as above, plus interest in the technology of fashion, and organizing ability; ability to delegate and deal with people. Enjoyment of trouble-shooting.

Late start

Depends on talent and drive: competition from young college-leavers is very stiff.

Position of women

TOP JOBS
Designers: In up-market ready-to-wear and mass production an increasing proportion of designers are women; but while there are lots of male designers in women's fashion, no woman has yet succeeded in men's fashion (which is big business too now).

Many small 'own label' businesses are run by women (but only women's wear).

Production managers: *Very* few women at the moment; more would be very welcome, because women production managers are more likely to want above all to work in fashion and choose production management as a way in. Male production managers tend to drift into fashion production as a production management job.

Career-break: *Designers*: Depends on how established before break. *Production management*: Probably no problem for women who have had good experience before the break. Changing technologies can easily be coped with by well-trained production managers.

Part-time: Not normally, except as freelance designer, or, *very* occasionally, as relief (holiday) cutter, etc.

Further information

Clothing and Allied Products Industry Training Board, Tower House, Merrion Way, Leeds LS2 8NY
The Clothing and Footwear Institute, 71 Brushfield Street, London E16 AA
City and Guilds of London Institute, 76 Portland Place, London W1N 4AA
BTEC/DATEC, Central House, Upper Woburn Place, London WC1H 0HH

Related careers

Art and Design – Television – Journalism – Photography – Public Relations

Floristry

Floral make-up – buying – outside work – hotel florist

Entry qualifications No specific requirements, but English language, art or science CSE or O-level advisable.

The work There are, broadly, four aspects:

1. *Floral Make-up*: consists of wiring, 'mossing and de-thorning' bouquets, wreaths, sprays, and a wide range of set table-decorations. Wiring a presentation bouquet or making a set piece may take anything from an hour to a whole day. Set pieces are usually made from sketched or detailed designs. For bouquets, makers-up are normally given the flowers and then use their own imagination.

The majority of florists work on making-up. Some combine this backroom work with selling in the shop; others who work in small shops or on their own also do the buying. The buyer often has to start work at 5 a.m. Making-up is usually done in damp, cool rooms, and the conditions are adjusted to suit the flowers rather than the staff. The work is hard on the hands, and most of it has to be done standing up. But the atmosphere in flower-shops is usually friendly.

2. *Buying Flowers*: from markets or market-gardeners which requires a thorough product knowledge and commercial expertise and flair.

3. *Outside Work*: involves regular trimming, watering and generally keeping in good order the window-boxes of office blocks and official buildings, making and arranging table decorations for private banquets; and flower work in hotels, exhibition halls, etc.

Outside work is often done at odd times depending on the type of work. Flowers may be needed just before a banquet, and window-boxes in busy streets may have to be watered late at night when the traffic is less heavy. The florist on outside work meets a great many people and sees many different houses, hotels, and exhibitions.

4. *Hotel Florist*: a minority of experienced florists are employed by chains of hotels and catering firms, etc., to run the 'flower side'. This is done either single-handed or as an organizer with a staff to do the actual making-up. The florist is part of the hotel staff and meets colleagues and guests from all over the world.

Prospects There is scope for making-up, but other jobs are not easy to find.

…ence and capital are essential for setting up on one's own. (See …king for Oneself, p. 560.)

Pay: Low to medium (see p. xxiii).

Either short courses at private floristry schools (expensive, grants not given);
Or as trainee with part-time (evening, day- or block-release) study for City and Guilds Certificate Parts 1, 2 and 3;
Or full-time 1- or 2-year courses (only a few available) for same City and Guilds Certificates;
Or (one only) 2-year full-time course in Floristry and Flower Production at Welsh College of Horticulture.

The Society of Floristry holds annual examinations for an Intermediate Certificate and a Diploma in Floristry. Candidates must hold *either* City and Guilds Part 2 Certificate with credit or distinction, or equivalent.

Personal attributes Nimble fingers; patience; good health (no tendency to chilblains); visual imagination; good colour sense; organizing ability for managerial posts; a friendly manner for shop, outside and hotel work.

Late start No traineeship, but private courses can be taken.

Position of women An almost all-female profession.

Career-break: No problem.

Part-time: Fair opportunities.

Further information City and Guilds of London Institute, 76 Portland Place, London W1N 4AA
British Retail Floristry, 24 Market Place, Sleaford, Lincs.

Related careers *Agriculture and Horticulture – Art and Design*

Hairdressing

Entry qualifications No rigid requirements, but science CSE at least an advantage when applying for jobs with day-release.

The work Both men and women work in men's, women's and unisex salons.

Hairdressers are on their feet almost all day. If well trained they can choose whether to work in an elegant salon, where the pay and tips are higher but the work probably harder, or in a small suburban hairdresser's, where they earn a little less but where the atmosphere is likely to be more relaxed. They can choose whether to work in men's, women's or mixed salons.

Apart from cutting, shampooing, tinting and styling, a hairdresser may also look after and order stores, keep the appointments book, do simple book-keeping, make out bills, measure clients for and 'dress' wigs, switches, and other kinds of 'made-up' hair. Wig-making is expanding, but wigs are made in special workrooms, not by hairdressers.

Prospects Fair but depend on locality and economic conditions. There are also a few jobs in hotels, hospitals and in television studios (see Television, p. 538) for experienced hairdressers.

There is scope everywhere abroad, except in the United States. Resorts in most tourist countries welcome experienced hairdressers who speak the relevant language. Hours in holiday places are long, but the pay is good. As there is always a slack time between the winter and summer seasons, it is difficult to get a permanent job abroad.

Pay: Low to very high (see p. xxiii) (see Working for Oneself, p. 560).

Training There are 3 ways; but only 2 lead to being eligible for membership of the Hairdressing Council.

1. *3-year indentured apprenticeship*

Supplemented by day-release and some evening classes. Good salons spend 1 night a week teaching cutting, scalp massage, tinting, etc.

At college, apprentices are taught hygiene, the nature of hair, and some chemistry, tinting and bleaching, the rudiments of wig-making. At the end of the training, apprentices sit for City and Guilds examination.

2. *2-year full-time course at colleges of further education*
The courses are recognized by hairdressing associations as the equivalent of an apprenticeship, and also lead to the City and Guilds examination. They cannot, of course, give the same opportunities for learning how to deal with clients. Technical college courses are the first choice for anyone too shy to ask questions and who finds it hard to pick up facts for herself.

Both day-release and full-time college courses deal with men's and ladies' hairdressing.

3. *6- or 12-month course at private hairdressing schools*
Pupils from private schools cannot normally sit City and Guilds examination. Schools' own diplomas are not recognized by the Hairdressing Council to which most good salons belong. Fees at private schools are high. There is no legal need for hairdressing schools to register or be licensed, and some give very poor training.

Anyone who joins as a 'junior' on a proper salary will usually be too busy to learn and is not entitled to the type of teaching given to an apprentice. However, though this method of learning is frowned upon by many hairdressers, some juniors who start in good salons where there are regular weekly 'practice nights' do eventually get good jobs. Only when registration of hairdressers becomes compulsory will all hairdressers have to train at recognized schools or as apprentices.

Personal attributes Fashion flair; some artistic ability; a friendly, outgoing personality; an unruffled manner; pleasing appearance; dexterity; good health, especially strong feet.

Late start Difficult to get apprenticeship and college vacancy, but scope once trained.

Position of women The top salons now welcome female stylists as they once only welcomed men.

Career-break: No problem. Many hairdressers work from home, taking on a few private clients.

Part-time: Plenty of scope.

Further information

Local F. E. Colleges; hairdressing establishments
City and Guilds Institute, 76 Portland Place, London W1N 4AA

Related careers

Beauty Specialist – Model-making, p. 61 – Window Display, p. 61

Health Service Administration

Entry qualifications Institute of Health Service Administrators. Examinations: 2 A-levels, 3 O-levels including English or English language, maths and a science (see **Training**).

The work The hospital, general practitioner and community health services form one administrative structure (it was reorganized in 1982). Health service administration covers a far wider field, and offers more scope for administrators' individual skills, qualities and preferences than did its predecessor, hospital administration.

Health service administrators are the non-medical staff responsible for the general management, coordination and smooth running of all services from cottage hospital to community nursing; GP services to family planning clinics. The work is varied and includes decision-making based on up-to-date management techniques and principles; the planning of future requirements (human and material); financial forward planning; as well as responsibility for maintenance of buildings; purchase and control of supplies and equipment; personnel management; and for the organization of support-services such as laundry, catering, domestic work and transport. Although ultimate responsibility for introducing sophisticated medical technologies like heart transplants rests with doctors, administrators are involved in allocating funds.

Individual administrators' functions vary according to specialist skills and interests as well as according to the level of the administrative structure at which they work. For example, at the 14 Regional Health Authorities' offices, administrators are primarily concerned with forward planning and with assessing needs and priorities. For instance, as the age-structure of the population is changing, more geriatric services are needed; as more emphasis is put on community care, more community nurses are needed. Because of financial constraints, economies have to be made somewhere.

The day-to-day managing is done by administrators at about 190 'districts', and in hospitals, health centres and family practitioner committee offices. Specialist administrators (see **Training**) are more likely to work at 'region' level. At grass-roots level, administrators have some contact with patients or more often, with relatives, and when things go wrong or something unusual happens, with the media.

There is also scope at junior level for those who prefer meeting the public to administration, for example, dealing with queries; and for those who prefer backroom work which also helps to improve the patient's lot.

Prospects Fair but depend on current levels of public expenditure. For promotion it is usually necessary to move around to get varied experience.

Pay: Medium to high (see p. xxiii).

Training Membership of Institute of Health Service Administrators is the normal route to top jobs; but there is also a trend for specialists with professional qualifications in, for example, chartered secretaryship, personnel, information systems, accountancy, to go into health service administration. Specialist qualifications can be as useful as Membership of the Institute of Health Service Administrators. Candidates who are interested in one aspect of administration can therefore train for appropriate qualifications and leave other options open. Those who are not sure which field interests them most and those who know they will want to stay in the Health Service should train for Membership of the IHSA.

There are various training schemes:

(a) For graduates and those with equivalent qualifications: 40-month training in financial administration (organized by the National Staff Committee in association with the King's College Fund, Nuffield Centre, at Leeds, Manchester and Birmingham Universities) leading to the Chartered Institute of Public Finance and Accountancy examinations.

(b) For those with 2 'A-levels and 3 O-levels: 3- to 4-year regional schemes leading to various professional or IHSA examinations.

(c) For those with at least 4 O-levels or BTEC award (see p. xvi): occasional regional schemes of varying length.

Staff may also attend short courses on specialist subjects, e.g. in computing or in supply, designed to develop potential for promotion to higher posts; administrators' Development Courses provide management training for trainees and other staff in the 23–35 age-group. At more senior levels, staff may attend multi-disciplinary management courses.

Personal attributes Efficiency; adaptability; the ability to discuss complicated issues with specialists at all levels; organizing ability; tact and diplomacy.

Late start Persons over 30 who work in, or have worked in, the NHS may become IHSA students with lower than normal entry requirements. For Graduate Training Schemes the upper age limit is 30. Specialists in Accountancy (see p. 1), Chartered Secretaryship (see p. 106),

Personnel Management (see p. 358), Work Study (sce p. 557) and Supplies (see Purchasing, p. 404) can go into health service administration up to about 50.

Administration and clerical staff over 30 can now study for the new (1983) IHSA's Certificate in Health Service Management. The Certificate may be a useful scheme for returners or career changers, as it can be studied by day-release *or* evening classes by anyone with some clerical health service experience. 'Distance learning' (i.e. correspondence courses, see p. xlii) is also available.

Certificate students cover 4 areas of study selected from: Principles of Organization and Management; Health and Social Services; Health Service Finance; Law Affecting Health Services; Personnel and Labour Relations; Health Service Building, Design and Construction; Health Service Supplies; Statistics and Information.

Position of women

Still far fewer women than men in senior administrative jobs, but now almost half of all IHSA students are women. Women still have to be more highly motivated than men.

Career-break: Should be no problem. Some health authorities are 'considering' refresher in-service training. However, promotion prospects are restricted in practice when competing with colleagues who have gained wider administrative experience. Seniority, rather than experience, counts in health service administration.

Part-time: Occasional opportunities; no reason why women administrators should not suggest job-sharing schemes.

Other non-medical health service work

Medical Records Officers deal with arranging appointments, patient registration, waiting lists, etc. The work is increasingly computerized. It may lead on to health service administration as this is a fairly flexible field. Entrants with at least English and one other O-level, preferably indicating numeracy, can work for the Medical Records Officers' Certificate. BTEC National award is also a useful entry qualification for adminstrative work.

Secretaries and receptionists in GP practices can now work for the Diploma in Practice Administration. See also Secretarial Work, p. 461.

Further information

National Staff Committee, Department of Health and Social Security, Hannibal House, Elephant and Castle, London SE1 6TE

Institute of Health Service Administrators, 75 Portland Place, London W1M 4AN

Related careers *Chartered Secretary – Institutional Management – Secretarial Work*

Home Economics

Entry qualifications None laid down; depends on **Training** (see below).

The work Home economists act as link between producers of goods and services and their consumers. This covers a wide range of jobs. Within industry they also act as link between technologists who design and develop new products but often know little about consumer preferences and requirements, and marketing and general management staffs. So home economics, at least at senior level, requires communication skills as well as an understanding of technological and of social trends.

Home economists work in various settings: industry, social services, public relations, public utilities, consumer advice and protection, the retail trade. There is nothing clear-cut about the professional home economist's work: people with related kinds of training may do the same, or similar, jobs; and qualified home economists branch off into related fields such as catering, marketing, journalism.

The majority work in manufacturing industry on development, quality control, promotion and marketing of products, appliances and equipment used, or services provided in the home. Before new or improved food and washing products, dishwashers, cookers, central heating systems, etc., are put into production, home economists discuss details of design and performance with engineers, scientists, designers, marketing people. They put the customers' point of view; they test prototypes in the laboratory under 'ideal conditions', and they also use them in the same way as the housewife might – being interrupted in their work and not always following the instructions as they should. For instance, they test whether a new type of butter-substitute creams easily, even if kept in the fridge too long and if clumsily handled; how a washing machine behaves if switches are turned on in the wrong order, or how easily a new cooker cleans when it is really dirty. As a result of laboratory and 'user' tests, alterations are often made before a product is put into production. In the retail industry, home economists work in, or manage, food- and textile-testing laboratories, some become management trainees and then go into store management (see Retail, p. 420).

For gas, electricity and solid fuel suppliers they work as 'home service advisers' (titles vary). They visit consumers in their own homes: this may be a straightforward 'after sales service'; more often it is to investigate a complaint, maybe about a central heating installation which is not working properly. The home economist must be able to diagnose the fault and perhaps then to explain tactfully that the instructions have not been followed. Increasingly they are involved with educating the public in the need for, and methods of, energy conservation (for example, home insulation and other fuel-saving devices). The work combines dealing with lay people who have much less technical knowledge, and with experts who have very much more.

Under the heading '*customer relations*' or '*marketing*', work involves writing clear, concise user-instructions for explanatory labels and leaflets which accompany fish-fingers, freezers, synthetic fibre carpets, babyfoods, etc., as well as dealing with inquiries and complaints correspondence.

Home economists also identify demand for new products or changes in existing ones. This may involve field work – interviewing potential customers in their homes (see Market Research, pp. 19 and 283) and thinking up innovations which could *profitably* be marketed.

In the *media* – magazines, newspapers, TV and radio – home economists prepare features and programmes: they cook and cost elaborate as well as very cheap dishes, or arrange and cost domestic interiors which are then photographed and described, or demonstrated on TV.

In local authority *social services departments* home economists advise low-income families on budgeting and general household management; and they may run the home-help service and advise on the efficient running of the authority's residential homes.

In *hospitals* home economists become domestic administrators at top management level.

They may also work in the Trading Standards Department (see p. 552) in the consumer advice services.

Experienced home economists can work as freelance consultants: firms may wish to research and/or promote a new product and need a home economist for a particular project rather than permanently. For example, home economists worked as freelances on metrication, writing explanatory leaflets, changing recipes and equipment, etc. Some prepare food for magazine photography or TV commercials; some write books.

Prospects Depend very much on economic conditions. Though the combination of technical knowledge and understanding of family and consumer needs can be useful in a variety of jobs, competition for jobs is very keen indeed. Jobs tend to be concentrated in cities. Greatest scope in food and domestic appliance manufacturing, and in retail.

Pay: Medium (see p. xxiii).

Training

No particular qualification leads to any particular type of job. It is possible for anyone with basic approved training or related training (see Catering, Institutional Management, p. 101) and the right experience and personality ultimately to do as well as a graduate. But the more thorough the training, the wider the scope of the job.

For candidates with 2 A-levels and 3 O-levels (no specific A-levels but maths, English language and a science at least at O-level): Degree (usually at polytechnic or college of higher education) in Home Economics or related subject such as Food, Textiles and Consumer Studies; Home Economics/Industrial Studies; Nutrition and Management Sciences; Hotel and Catering Administration; B.Ed. (Home Economics) (see Teaching, p. 520).

For candidates with 1 A-level and 4 O-levels (including maths, a science and an English subject): BTEC Higher National Diploma in Home Economics. Courses are full-time and last 2 or 3 years (colleges' course organizations vary, BTEC details, p. xvi).

Diploma and degree syllabuses include varying amounts of food and textile technology, business and marketing and social studies. Some courses include periods of practical work in industry/institutions.

For candidates with 3 (in practice often 4) O-levels including English language, maths and a science usually: BTEC National Diploma in Home Economics. Courses last 2 years, full-time. Syllabus covers broadly the same subjects as HND but not in such depth; some courses concentrate more on practical skills such as cooking; home management; care of textiles, etc.

For candidates with 3 CSE Grade 3 usually in maths, English language and a science: BTEC National Certificate in Home Economics. Courses may be part-time, 2 years, or full-time 1 year. Syllabus concentrates on practical skills.

For candidates without any or only a few CSEs or O-levels who prefer a course which concentrates entirely on practical skills: City and Guilds 2-year full-time course or similar part-time course.

Not all types of courses are available in all areas.

Personal attributes

Practicality and organizing ability; interest in consumer affairs and in streamlining housework; ability to understand both consumers' and manufacturers' points of view; ability to communicate easily both with more highly qualified professionals and with often poorly educated, possibly illiterate, consumers; a liking for working with and for women.

Late start Mature entrants are welcome on all courses but see **Prospects**. Young entrants preferred in industry; mature people in social services.

Position of women This is a virtually 100% women's occupation. Industrial and media employers of home economists tend to think of customers for whose benefit home economists work as housewives. Anyone who feels strongly about equality might not fit into many of the jobs done by home economists.

Career-break: Should be no problem for people who keep up with developments.

Part-time: Not normally except as freelance.

Further information BTEC Central House, Upper Woburn Place, London WC1H 0HH
City and Guilds of London Institute, 76 Portland Place, London W1N 4AA
For list of degree courses:
Dr E. Thorne, Roehampton Institute, Roehampton Lane, London SW15 5PH

Related careers *Catering – Dietitian – Public Relations – Teaching – Trading Standards Officer*

Housing Management

Entry qualifications 2 A-levels and 3 O-levels, including English language, *or* BTEC National award. Considerable *graduate* entry.

The work Traditionally, housing managers are responsible for the administration, maintenance and allocation of accommodation let for rent. In recent years their scope has expanded enormously and it is still expanding. It now also includes, for example, the running of Housing Aid Centres; the administration of rent rebate, and rent allowance and housing benefit schemes; housing research and the formulation of housing policy. The majority of housing managers and housing assistants work for local authorities; a growing number work for housing associations and a few for private property owners.

Day-to-day housing work adds up to an unusual combination of dealing with people, using technical knowledge and getting out and about. Duties include interviewing applicants for homes; visiting prospective tenants in their homes to assess their housing needs; inspecting property at regular intervals and arranging, if necessary, for repairs to be carried out; dealing with tenants' complaints about anything from noisy neighbours and lack of play facilities for children to leaking roofs or lack of maintenance. Rent collecting, which used to be the most important and time-consuming task, is dying out: most tenants now take or send rent to the housing office. But as soon as a tenant falls into arrears, the housing assistant still visits. As rent arrears are often the first sign of social distress, housing management is a preventive social service; there is a considerable element of social work in housing management; staff work closely with social workers. For example, if a housing assistant notices a disabled person's or an unsupported mother's need for help, she alerts the social services department. She herself might help, for example, if a family who move from a one-room hovel into their first adequate home need advice on how to budget for new furniture.

Housing staff try to establish or maintain good tenant–landlord relationships and try to forge a conglomeration of dwellings into a community. To this end they may try to involve tenants in managing their block of flats or estate, or they may set up tenants' management committees. In Housing Aid Centres, housing staff advise on any problem related to housing, from how to cope with an eviction order or how to get a rent allowance, to where to apply for a mortgage.

At senior level, the work involves top-level general and financial management using modern management techniques; the purchase of properties; the allocation of accommodation (which is the most onerous task); research into general housing needs and into such questions as 'How can we retain the neighbourliness of the slums in new developments?', 'What is a good environment?', etc.; advising architects and planners on social aspects of siting, design and lay-out of new developments.

Many housing managers prefer to stick to day-to-day management throughout their careers, because they enjoy dealing with people. At senior level the jobs can be controversial. Directors of Housing may have to implement policies with which they do not agree, e.g. sale of council houses.

In local authority departments which administer thousands of dwellings, staff usually specialize in one aspect of the work at a time. In housing associations, which manage a smaller number, one housing assistant or housing manager may deal with everything concerning a number of tenancies. While this makes for more variety of day-to-day work, there is usually more scope for promotion in local authorities.

Housing associations also increasingly provide facilities for special groups: for example, for the elderly, single-parent families; the disabled. Some are run as hostels for such 'special needs' groups as ex-prisoners or people who have been psychiatric patients and still need support while adjusting to living in the community.

Prospects Good normally but depends on current level of public expenditure.

Pay: Medium (see p. xxiii).

Training 1. The traditional method: on-the-job with day-release or correspondence course for the Institute of Housing Professional Qualification. Students are given experience in the various housing functions and may be seconded for a time to a housing association (or to a local authority if they are training with a housing association). Training takes about 3 years, less for graduates. The syllabus includes building construction and maintenance (to a standard which any interested woman can cope with whether technically-minded or not); landlord and tenant law; town planning and other relevant law; organization of social services and local government; estate records and accounts.

2. Degree in Housing Studies, which covers the wider social aspects of housing and includes some social administration; it leads to total exemption from the written examinations.

3. Social science degrees and diplomas which lead to partial exemption from the Professional Qualification.
4. For housing association work only: any degree or professional qualification, and learning on-the-job – not necessarily for the Institute of Housing qualification.

Personal attributes Getting on well with all types of people; an interest in social, practical and economic problems, and in planning; tolerance; ability to be firm; indifference to being out in bad weather; organizing ability and diplomacy for senior people.

Late start Late entrants welcome in theory, but training vacancies are often difficult to find for mature entrants. Untrained mature entrants often do the same work as trained younger people, without the chance of promotion. More opportunities in housing associations where aptitude and relevant work, as well as 'life experience', are more important than qualifications.

Position of women The proportion of women and men entering housing is fairly even, but *very* few local authority housing managers are women (see Local Government, **Position of women**). There is no reason whatever why women should not do better. They do very well in housing associations.

Career-break: Returners are usually welcome, but depends on level of unemployment.

Part-time: Fair opportunities; some job-sharing schemes in operation.

Further information The Institute of Housing, 12 Upper Belgrave Street, London SW1

Related careers *Environmental Health Officer – Local Government – Town and Country Planning – Surveyor*

Immigration Officer

Entry qualifications As for Civil Service Executive Officer. (See Civil Service, p. 123.)

The work Immigration officers are responsible for checking passports and credentials generally of persons arriving at and departing from sea- and airports. They carry out regulations governing the entry of persons to this country. The work can be tricky and distasteful when officers have to ask searching questions to try and ascertain personal details from arrivals, however sympathetic they may feel towards the individual they have to question; in the interests of upholding the law, officers may have to be suspicious and thus possibly embarrass the innocent in order to catch out the guilty. When necessary they have to take harsh action and refuse entry to would-be immigrants or visitors. (Senior officials take final decisions.) However, most of the time the work merely involves routine checking of documents.

The atmosphere at ports and airports is always lively (and noisy). Immigration officers meet large numbers of people – each usually very briefly.

Prospects Apart from promotion to Chief immigration officer at a port or airport, opportunities exist for promotion to higher executive officer and other posts in the Civil Service. In addition, after at least 2 years' experience, immigration officers under 28 can become administrative trainees and go up the administration ladder (see Civil Service, p. 120).

Pay: Medium to high (see p. xxiii).

Training Given after entry, largely on-the-job.

Personal attributes Aptitude for foreign languages; interest in current affairs; patience, tact and courtesy; quick judgement in order to make accurate assessments of people after a short interview; ability and willingness to stand the pressure of enforcing what may appear harsh regulations.

Late start See Civil Service, p. 128.

Position of women Women have only fairly recently been able to become immigration officers. About 12% are women.

Career-break and *part-time*: See Civil Service, p. 129.

Further information See Civil Service, p. 130.

Related careers *Civil Aviation (Ground Staff) – Civil Service*

Insurance

Entry qualifications For CII qualifying examination see **Training**: either BTEC National award (see p. xvi); or 2 A-levels and 2 O-levels, including English at either level and one A-level to be in one of the following: English, maths, geography, history, a foreign language, natural science, economics, public and economic affairs, British constitution, surveying, accounting, sociology, law.

Also *graduate* entry.

The work Insurance is a method of compensating for losses arising from all kinds of misfortunes, from the theft of jewellery to the loss of a ship at sea. It is based on the principle that many more people pay regularly into a common fund than ultimately draw from it, and thus the losses of the unlucky few may be made good. The organizers of the system are the insurers, i.e. the insurance companies or Lloyds' underwriters. Lloyds itself is not an insurance company, but a society whose members transact business as individuals, or as individual companies.

It is usual to specialize in one of the main branches of insurance: marine, aviation, life and pensions, property, accident, motor liability and reinsurance, although transfers are possible. Occupational pension schemes are a growth area.

Insurance *brokers* act as intermediaries, bringing together the insurers and those who wish to be insured.

In the office, risks are assessed by the *underwriting* department (see Actuary, p. 15), and according to the degree of hazard, a premium is agreed upon.

Surveyors (sometimes called *Risk Managers*) may report on the state of a building to be insured, its fire protection standards and give advice which will minimize risk. A contract is drawn up based on the premium, and arrangements are made for the premium to be paid regularly. When a claim is received, losses are assessed to determine the sum the sufferer should be paid in fairness to all parties. Sometimes outside intermediaries called *Loss Adjusters* are asked to assess the claim.

Other jobs involve visiting clients. *Inspectors* (or sales agents) have a good deal of independence: they are responsible for obtaining new business and ensuring that existing clients' cover is adequate in changing circumstances. They may sell directly to individuals or through agents or brokers. *Outside claims officials* are responsible for inspecting damaged property. The investment department decides how and when to invest the company's income to obtain the highest yield.

Prospects Prospects of promotion are best only for people entering with A-levels, HND or degree in Business Studies. There are increasing opportunities, particularly for graduates, in specialist fields such as insurance law. However, O-level entrants who show sufficient commitment and are willing to study part-time over a long period can still move up the ladder. Competition from better qualified entrants means fewer chances than before.

Pay: Medium (see p. xxiii).

Abroad: Possible in theory. There are branches of insurance in most parts of the world.

Training 1. *On-the-job*: with day-release for 3 years (evening study is also necessary) for Associateship of Chartered Insurance Institute, followed by one year (approximately) for Fellowship CII, or for BTEC Higher award. This leads to partial exemption from CII examinations, and leaves options open for work in other commercial fields. For some specializations, e.g. investment, loss adjusting and pensions management, the CII examination is followed by Fellowship examinations of a relevant institute.

2. *Pre-entry*: Degree in Business Studies with insurance options, *or* full-time or sandwich BTEC Higher award. (See p. xvi.)

Personal attributes Some mathematical ability; a liking for paper work; ability to grasp the essentials of a problem; sound judgement; determination and a certain amount of push; tact; a persuasive, confidence-inspiring manner; ability to communicate with people, often in difficult circumstances; for broking: an entrepreneurial flair.

Late start Possible, some relaxation of minimum qualifications, but training vacancies might not be so easy to find. Upper age limit in practice 30. People of all ages and different backgrounds recruited as sales agents.

Position of women Under 10% of qualified, but 25% of student, members of the Chartered Insurance Institute are women (1983). The tradition of men in senior jobs is still strong in this industry and women have to be very determined and very good indeed to get to the top. No problem at middle-level jobs.

Career-break: Previously qualified returners are usually welcome if they have kept up with developments. Retraining on an *ad hoc* basis.

Part-time: Few opportunities.

Further information

The Careers Information Officer, The Chartered Insurance Institute, The Hall, 20 Aldermanbury, London EC2

Related careers

Accountancy – Actuary – Banking – Computers – Stock Exchange

Journalism

Newspapers – Freesheets – Magazines

Entry qualifications *Newspapers*: 5 O-levels including English language for traineeship, but nearly all school-leaver entrants have at least 1 A-level, most have 2; 40% of entrants are *graduates*. For pre-entry course: 2 A-levels. Upper age limit normally 24.

Magazines: Depends on editor; for pre-entry course: 1 A-level, 4 O-levels.

The work Journalism covers a variety of jobs in a variety of settings (or 'media', which really should be 'media of communications'). Broadly, the main job groups are *reporter*; *correspondent* or *specialist writer*; *feature writer*; *news editor*; *editor*; *freelance*. Division of duties depends on paper's size and organization.

Newspapers

Virtually every journalist starts as trainee-reporter. *Reporters* cover any kind of event: from council or Women's Institute meeting to political demo, fire, or press conference for visiting film star or foreign statesman. Reporters 'get a story' by asking questions and listening to other journalists' questions and interviewee's answers at press conferences, or in one-to-one interviews with individuals. For such interviews, reporters have to do some preliminary 'homework' – to interview a trade union secretary or famous novelist, for example, requires some background knowledge.

Reporters must compose stories quickly, sometimes dictating them over the phone, sometimes typing them in a noisy office. Accuracy, brevity and speed are more important than writing perfect prose: reporting is a fact-gathering and fact-disseminating rather than creative job.

Occasionally, reporters may be on a particular story for several weeks, researching the background and/or waiting for developments. They work irregular hours, including weekends.

Specialist Reporter or Correspondent

'Hard news' is broadcast more quickly than it can be printed; to fight TV and radio competition, newspapers have developed 'interpretative' or specialist reporting. Specialists' titles and precise responsibilities and scope vary; the aim always is to interpret and explain news, and to comment on events, trends, causes and news behind the news. The number (and the expert knowledge of) specialists varies according to the type and size of newspaper. On the whole, only the nationals have specialists who concentrate entirely on one speciality; on other papers and in news agencies, reporters with a special interest in a particular field (or several) may do specialist along with general reporting. The main specializations are: parliament and/or politics generally; industry; finance; education; foreign news; local government and/or planning; social services; sport; science and technology; agriculture and food; motoring; fashion, women's/home interests; theatre; films; broadcasting. Financial correspondents tend to be economics graduates, science correspondents are science graduates, but education correspondents are not normally teachers: there are no hard-and-fast rules about how specialists acquire their specialist knowledge (and how much they need).

News Editor

Journalists with organizing ability may become news editors, controlling reporting staffs, allocating stories to individual reporters and attending senior staff's daily editorial conferences. It is an office job and normally involves no writing. The title usually applies on daily papers; titles and organization of work vary considerably from one paper to another.

Sub-editors

Sub-editors do the detailed editing of copy; they re-write stories to fit in with required length, re-write the beginning, and may 'slant' stories. They write headlines and, in consultation with the night or assistant editor, may do the layout of news pages. On large papers there are several specialist subs. Subbing is team-work and entirely desk-bound; it always has to be done in a hurry.

Feature Writers

Usually experienced journalists who can write lucidly and descriptively on any topic; but specialists may also write features. Reporters may combine reporting with feature writing.

Columnist

Like feature writing, a job for experienced journalists; there are specialists, for example financial or consumer affairs columnists, and general columnists. The work requires a wide range of interests and contacts.

Leader-writers

Leaders may be written by the Editor, or specialist correspondent, or other experienced journalists.

Editor-in-Chief, Assistant Editor, Deputy Editor

Editors (including departmental editors) are coordinators, policy-makers. The number of top jobs, and the amount of writing editors do, vary greatly: some editors write leaders on specific subjects, some write in crises only; some on a variety of subjects, others not at all.

The amount of freedom an editor-in-chief has to run the paper in the way she wants depends on the proprietor; policies vary enormously.

There is no set promotion structure on newspapers. Some journalists do all or several types of newspaper work in succession in preparation for senior editorial jobs (subbing is a vital step on the ladder), others become heads of departments (finance, fashion, home affairs, chief sub, etc.) fairly quickly. Many remain reporters.

Titles, functions, and division of labour are not consistent throughout the industry and often change with a change of editor-in-chief or proprietor.

Freesheets

Locally distributed 'giveaway' papers are the fastest-growing advertising medium and the only expanding type of newspaper. Called 'freesheets', they vary enormously in proportion and variety of editorial content. A few are much like small local weekly papers; most carry very little editorial matter. Some are published by established newspaper houses, some by members of the Association of Free Newspapers, yet others are run individually from tiny offices by a man/woman and a boy/girl. Jobs on freesheets with varied editorial content may be acceptable as traineeships (see below), but work on the majority is unlikely to lead to jobs on national or other prestigious local newspapers.

Magazines

Broadly there are two types:
(1) Trade, technical, professional and 'house' journals, geared to a particular profession, trade or organization.
(2) 'Consumer' magazines: they cater for all types of leisure interests and include women's, teenage and hobby magazines and comics.

On (1) journalists work closely with experts in the particular field of which they must have/develop some understanding. They write features, report developments, and re-write experts' contributions. Magazine work, however specialized, can be a way into newspaper work – especially for graduates (preferably science or technology) with writing ability.

Consumer magazines employ feature writers, sub-editors and departmental editors more than reporters, but organization varies enormously. Consumer magazines also use freelances more than do newspapers. Editors' work includes originating feature ideas and selecting and briefing outside contributors, both freelance journalists and specialists who are not journalists. This, in contrast to newspaper journalism, is an expanding market.

Freelance Journalism

Freelances are either 'generalists' – feature writers who write on any subject – or specialists. On the whole, only experienced journalists with staff experience, and particularly those with specialist knowledge which is in demand (technology, consumerism, child development, education, for example), succeed.

Specialists – teachers, engineers, lawyers, with writing ability and topical ideas – also do freelance journalism as a sideline, but this is becoming more difficult.

Prospects (all journalism) On newspapers reasonable only for exceptionally determined and talented people, as the market is shrinking; better on trade, technical and consumer magazines. Work on a journal dealing with one particular subject, whether physiotherapy or municipal affairs, is good experience and can be a stepping stone to more general journalism. There is some scope in broadcasting (see p. 534) for experienced reporters. Science and engineering graduates have reasonable scope on the increasing number of publications which deal with various aspects of science and technology (especially information technology/computing) and which try to attract both specialist and lay readers.

Pay: Medium to high (see p. xxiii).

Training

Newspapers

Either:

1. *Direct entry traineeship*: Upper age limit 24. After 6 months' probation, it takes 3 years for entrants with 5 O-levels; 2½ years for entrants with 2 A-levels; 2 years for graduates. Acceptance depends largely on paper's policy and candidate's suitability, rather than on academic qualification. Candidates must apply direct to editors of *provincial* (including suburban) dailies and weeklies. The London-based *nationals* do not normally take trainees. (When applying for traineeship it is advisable to submit samples of work done: an article specially written for the particular paper, which shows the Editor that the applicant has identified the paper's style, is better than work done for school or university paper, though that can be sent too.)

During training trainees attend 28-week block-release courses. Trainees must pass the National Council for the Training of Journalists' proficiency test. Subjects studied: English usage; relevant law; public administration; shorthand (which remains important despite new technologies: reporters may now feed copy directly into a central computer, but they still take notes in the traditional way); interpretive reporting (interviewing, fact-gathering methods, etc.); current affairs; sub-editing skills. (Graduates do not have to study all subjects.)

Papers are supposed to offer trainees a 'schedule of experience', which should cover work in all departments including new technology production methods, but this is by no means always forthcoming. Training tends to be best in newspaper groups which run in-company training schemes jointly with the NCTJ.

Even if training is bad, it is very difficult to 'break indentures' or switch employers; it is therefore advisable to find out as much as possible about the training before accepting a traineeship.

2. *1-year full-time pre-entry courses*: 2 A-levels required.

Over one third of entrants to newspaper journalism now take such courses, at colleges of further education. Courses shorten subsequent apprenticeship by several months. A few candidates are sponsored by newspapers; the majority are accepted after having been interviewed by the NCTJ, to which applications must be made. (Grants are not mandatory (see p. xxv).)

Or:

3. *Post-graduate course* at the Centre for Journalism Studies, Cardiff University and at the City University, London. Graduates from these courses also have to start as trainees, but they take the NCTJ's proficiency test after only 1 year's training.

4. *One 18-month post-graduate course* at the South Glamorgan Institute of Higher Education. Graduates from this course can take the proficiency test after 18 months.

Theoretically it is not possible to get on to a London-based national newspaper without provincial paper traineeship. However every year a few, perhaps 2 or 3 (*not more*) exceptionally gifted graduates manage to go straight from university on to a national newspaper. They tend to be economists or scientists, accepted because of their specialist knowledge. (See also **Late start**.)

Magazines
Two courses at the London College of Printing: entry requirements for both 1 A-level, 4 O-levels including English language or literature (the majority of successful candidates have higher qualifications):
1. *1-year pre-entry course* for periodical (any type) journalism.
2. *2-year BTEC* (see p. xvi) *HND Business Studies* with journalism option.

The London College of Fashion runs a Higher Diploma in Fashion with a journalism option (1-year full-time). Entry usually via the College's own Diplomas in Fashion or in Clothing (see Fashion, p. 197), with A-level English and 4 O-levels, one of which must be a foreign language.

Magazine journalism training is much less tightly structured than newspaper training and entry is still largely with specialist knowledge (especially scientific/technical/computing, but also other expertise, from drama to sport, education to law) and with writing/editing ability. Quite a few arts graduates are editing technical journals. An industry-wide Editorial Training Scheme now operates in a growing number of publishing houses. Jobs which offer the training are worth taking even if less well-paid than jobs without training, especially if the training – as it usually does – covers new technologies and at least *discusses* electronic publishing.

Personal attributes The different jobs demand different talents and temperaments, but all journalists need a feeling for words, the ability to express themselves lucidly and concisely; wide interests; an unbiased approach; a pleasant easy manner so that shy inarticulate people will talk to them easily; a certain presence so that busy, important people do not feel they are wasting their time answering questions; powers of observation; ability to sift the relevant from the irrelevant; ability to absorb atmosphere and to sum up people and situations quickly; an inquiring mind, great curiosity; the ability to become temporarily interested in anything from apple-growing to Zen Buddhism; resourcefulness; resilience; tact; willingness to work very hard; punctuality; a fairly thick skin (interviewees can be rude). *For senior jobs*: organizing ability.

Late start *Newspapers*: Entrants between 24 and 30 do not become trainees but 'follow a programme of training agreed between employers and the NCTJ'. Entrants over 30 do not get trained but are taken on as

specialists, i.e. because of their expertise – not as general reporters/subs.
Magazines: Quite possible for specialists.

Position of women

Newspapers: While the proportion of women trainees has increased considerably over the last few years (43% in 1983), their share of senior jobs has increased very little indeed; yet there is no shortage of applicants (as there is in some other careers where women do badly). Women have no more difficulty than men getting apprenticeships, but there seems to be discrimination at subsequent levels (on newspapers, not magazines). Women also still tend to have 'women's stories' allocated to them. They are not given the varied experience (city page writer; foreign correspondent; assistant to news editor; sub-editor, etc.) which is vital for top jobs. However, this is slowly changing, especially on provincial papers.

Women still have to be considerably better journalists, more determined and more undauntable than their male colleagues, to get beyond middle-level jobs.
Magazines: No problem.

Career-break: Near-insurmountable problems as reporter on *newspapers.* Only well-above-average women who had proved their value to the paper before the break have much hope of returning after several years away. Many women turn to freelancing or edit, on a freelance basis, small organizations' or professional magazines: this is almost a cottage industry and badly paid. Fewer problems for feature writers, sub-editors.

Few problems on *magazines*.

Part-time: Mainly as freelance. A few openings on trade journals, usually a few days a month rather than regular part of day.

Further information

National Council for the Training of Journalists, Carlton House, Hemnall Street, Epping, Essex CM16 4NL (for pre-entry-courses only)
Newspaper Society, Training Department, Whitefriars House, 6 Carmelite Street, London EC4Y 0BL
Periodical Training Trust, Imperial House, 15–19 Kingsway, London WC2BN 6UN

Related careers

Advertising – Information Work – Photography – Public Relations – Television, Film and Radio

Landscape Architecture and Design

Entry qualifications Vary according to training, but for Membership of Landscape Institute: 3 O-levels, 2 A-levels, including a maths or a science and an English subject. The other subjects must include either geography, history or a foreign language. See **Training** for graduate entry.

The work A landscape architect is concerned with the planning and design of the outdoor environment. Working with architects, civil engineers, planners or landscape contractors, she tries to minimize the aesthetic damage done to the scenery by, for example, industrial development or new housing estates. She plans factory sites in country areas and determines how best to blend new motorways into their surroundings so that they are as unobtrusive as possible. She works on land reclamation, tree preservation, and the control of mineral workings. She designs layouts for open spaces, anything from spacious grounds for new hospitals to small private gardens, play- and recreation grounds. She may site and design picnic areas in country parks or lay-bys on motorways.

She is responsible for inviting tenders from contractors, and for supervising the subsequent work, seeing that it is carried out satisfactorily and within a fixed budget. She is also responsible for specifying the right type of plants to achieve the desired appearance at all times of the year: this means balancing the amount of maintenance funds available in a public park, for example, with the amount of maintenance needed by the particular plant. Her knowledge of horticulture must be extensive.

Some landscape architects work in private practice, or for landscape or horticultural contractors, but the majority are employed by ministries, new town corporations and local authorities. In public employment, they are usually responsible to planning officers or architects, with less freedom than in private practice to carry out their own designs.

Prospects Fair. The demand for qualified landscape architects is growing as the need to make the best of our remaining countryside is becoming more widely appreciated. Some opportunities in EEC countries.

Pay: Medium to high (see p. xxiii).

Training *Either*: 4-year full-time course at a school of landscape architecture, attached to a university or polytechnic. *Or*: Architectural or town-planning course (see pp. 50 and 549), followed by a university diploma or certificate course in landscape architecture, either 2 years full-time or longer part-time.

Alternative method of entry:
Training courses in landscape architecture are limited, but it is possible to get into landscape architecture/design by training in a variety of allied disciplines, such as, for example, geography, geology, planning, soil science, plant sciences, rural environment studies, art and design, horticulture, and then learn on-the-job, working in a landscape architect's or developer's office. Initial training should preferably be at degree level, but there is always some limited scope for people with a flair for design and horticulture who are willing to combine some practical work with designing. This overlaps with gardening/garden design. (See Horticulture, p. 24.) Some private courses, which do not lead to membership of the Landscape Institute, are available.

Personal attributes Visual imagination; flair for design; a keen interest in design and in horticulture; a knowledge of how people live in town and countryside; ease of expression, both in drawing and writing; the ability to work well with other people; a good business head (for private practice).

Late start As vacancies on landscape architecture courses are scarce, young applicants are given preference, but see alternative method of training (which, however, is even longer). With experience of related work – e.g. architecture, or business experience plus experience of gardening or horticulture or an interest in the environment, this could be a good second career, on a self-employed basis. (See Working for Oneself, p. 560.)

Position of women Women were among founder members of the Institute. Now about 30% of members and 50% of students are women – considerably more than 10 years ago. There has never been much discrimination in this career.

Career-break: Women who have kept up with developments should have no problems, but few have returned so far.

Part-time: Occasional opportunities in employment; possibility of running small consultative practice – but part-time work likely to be sporadic rather than regular.

Further information

The Secretary, Landscape Institute, 12 Carlton House Terrace, London, SW1Y 5AH

Related careers

Agriculture and Horticulture – Architectural Technician – Architecture – Art and Design – Town and Country Planning

Law

Barrister – barristers' clerk – justices' clerks' assistant – legal executive – solicitor

Barrister

Entry qualifications First- or second-class honours degree (any subject).

The work Barristers plead in courts and give advice on legal matters in Chambers (the term used for barristers' offices). They are consulted by solicitors on behalf of their clients: they do not normally see clients without a solicitor being present. Barristers clarify points of law and use their critical judgement in deciding what legislation and what precedents are relevant in any particular case. Their expertise helps clients, but barristers are first and foremost concerned with points of law, not with helping individuals: their relation with clients is far more formal than that of solicitors.

Barristers normally specialize *either* in *common law*, which includes criminal work (the greatest proportion: it covers any case of law-breaking, however minor the offence), divorce, family, planning and commercial law; *or* in *chancery* work, a much smaller branch which covers conveyancing, trusts, estate duty, taxation, company law.

In *common law* the emphasis is on pleading in court ('advocacy'); in *chancery* on work in Chambers, drafting 'opinions' and advising. *Common law* work appeals, therefore, more to people who enjoy verbal battles and the court's somewhat theatrical atmosphere; *chancery* work appeals to those who enjoy the challenge of intellectual problem-solving.

Common law barristers usually join one of the 6 'circuits' into which England and Wales are divided for legal administration purposes; they may then plead in provincial courts as well as in London.

Prospects Good only for barristers with very good contacts and/or exceptional determination. The Bar is a small (about 4,800 practising members) club-like community. Organization and procedure have not changed for centuries, which causes problems. Barristers still practise their profession only under traditional constraints: they *must* practise from a 'tenancy' in Chambers, the Bar's professional accommodation which, in London, will usually be in one of the 4 Inns of Court (they are rather like non-resident Oxbridge colleges; the bar student must join one of them at the beginning of her training). In recent years the number of barristers has increased enormously, with scarcely any more tenancies being available; yet a newly-qualified barrister has to find Chambers which will offer her a tenancy. This depends entirely on contacts and luck: there is no system of allocating tenancies. From 1984 only a limited number, to be reviewed annually, is admitted to the essential vocational course (950 people in 1984).

Unlike other professionals, a barrister may not go into partnership nor be employed by another barrister: once in practice, a barrister is, financially, on her own. She must wait for briefs by solicitors or be given work by the *barristers' clerk* (see p. 244) who 'distributes' work which comes to the set of Chambers rather than to a particular barrister in the Chambers. Barristers at first often supplement their income by coaching, or other work, unless they have enough money to live on for the first year or so. Many barristers never attempt to practise at the Bar (others try to, but cannot get into Chambers or get work); instead they become legal advisers in industry, or in local or central government. Such work is usually more easily available. It is far less precarious than the Bar, and in industry and commerce can lead to board-level jobs, but the work is not as varied as, nor has it the glamour of, being at the Bar.

The Civil Service offers a variety of jobs: barristers work in ministries as legal advisers; in the Lord Chancellor's office on the administration of the courts; with the Law Commission which keeps English law under constant review; in the Law Officers' Department which advises the government on points of domestic and international law; in the Office of the Parliamentary Counsel on drafting legislation and parliamentary motions – this work involves attending sittings of both Houses; or as Justices' Clerk, advising the lay Justices (JPs) in magistrates' courts. Justices' Clerks have close day-to-day contact with the public.

Barristers, after at least 7 years' practice, are eligible for appointment (by the Lord Chancellor) as Chairmen of Industrial Tribunals. These Tribunals deal with unfair dismissal, redundancy payments and other matters relating to employment generally. Under the Sex Discrimination Act they also now hear complaints from persons who believe they have been discriminated against in terms of equal pay, promotion, acceptance for a particular job and other employment matters. Chairmen are appointed to regional panels and sit on Tribunals within a given area. Appointments can be full-time or part-time (i.e. some lawyers carry on with their practice as well).

In the EEC countries and elsewhere abroad barristers may work as legal advisers. There is no equivalent in the EEC and hence no mutual recognition of legal qualifications.

Pay: Very low to start with. Medium to very high later (see p. xxiii).

Training

The structure has changed. Training now consists of an *Academic Stage* and a *Vocational Stage*.

The *Academic Stage* replaced the traditional Part I Bar Examination. To complete this Stage, students either take a 'Qualifying Law Degree', which is basically one which covers the 6 'core' subjects (see Solicitor, **Training**, p. 249), or they take a degree in another subject followed by the Diploma in Law at the City University or the Polytechnic of Central London which are 1-year full-time courses covering the 6 core subjects. It is necessary to obtain a Certificate of Eligibility from the Council of Legal Education before obtaining a place for the Diploma Course. Holders of the solicitors' CPE (see p. 250) may be exempt, at the Council of Legal Education's discretion, from the Bar's *Academic Stage*.

Law degree courses vary greatly in emphasis on particular aspects of law. All include the 'core subjects', but it is important to relate content to one's interests and plans: for example some courses concentrate more on international and/or EEC law; some on family and welfare law; some on tax and/or company law; some are geared more to private practice, some more to public service. Consult CRAC *Degree Course Guide*, see p. xlix.

The *Vocational Stage* remains the responsibility of the Council of Legal Education. Courses, which last about 1 academic year, are held at the Inns of Court School of Law. All prospective barristers must *take* the Vocational Stage examination. But attendance on the Vocational course is compulsory only for those who intend to practise in Chambers, i.e., not for barristers who intend to become advisers or assistants in industry, local or central government, etc. However, it is advisable to attend a course and become qualified to practise at the Bar (which means plead in the courts). Vocational Stage training includes some specialization in a particular branch of law, for example landlord and tenant, hire purchase and sale of goods, local government and planning, family law. It also includes instruction in pleading in court and drafting. Students may no longer repeat subjects in the Bar examination which they have substantially covered in their degree studies.

After having passed the Bar examination, barristers who want to practise at the Bar must complete a year's 'pupillage' in Chambers; during the last 6 months of that year they may 'accept instructions' from solicitors, which means they may be able to earn a little.

All Bar students must join one of the 4 Inns of Court and 'keep terms' by dining in the Hall of their Inn a certain number of times. The purpose of this is to make contacts with practising barristers and to be initiated into the traditional ways of the Bar.

Scotland: Training and organization differ. English qualifications do not entitle one to practise at Scottish Bar and vice versa.

Personal attributes A confidence-inspiring personality; power of logical reasoning; gift of expression; a quick brain; capacity for very hard work; tremendous self-confidence; some acting ability, or at least a sense of drama and relish for verbal battles in front of critical audiences; physical stamina; a good voice; resilience. *For women*: indifference to seeing male colleagues, even if less able, get on better.

Late start Entrants over 25 may obtain a Certificate of Eligibility to read for the Diploma in Law if they have the required GCE standard or equivalent and have had considerable experience or shown exceptional ability in an academic, professional, business or administrative field. In addition, mature entrants must show that they intend to practise at the Bar of England and Wales or use the qualification in their profession in the United Kingdom. Mature students who are accepted to read for the Diploma in Law must take 8 subjects over 2 years. Permission to prepare for the Diploma Examinations externally by part-time study or correspondence course may be granted.

Position of women Entrenched attitudes and methods of working make this one of the most difficult professions for women to succeed in. Sex discrimination legislation made it – theoretically – impossible for Chambers to admit only a quota of women or none at all (which was the situation till 1976), but discrimination is difficult to prove as there are no established criteria – such as examination results, etc. – according to which pupils are taken on and tenancies granted to applicants. (Women have no problems getting into the Civil Service and industry or commerce.)

Once in Chambers, a *far* greater proportion of women than men concentrate on 'small work' (minor criminal cases) because that is all they can get. 14 out of 512 QCs (Queen's Counsel) are women, and it is from QCs (successful barristers) that the higher judiciary is chosen. There are 3 women High Court Judges among 99 men. The proportion of practising women barristers was about 4% in 1970, and about 11% in 1983.

Only 5% of applications to the Lord Chancellor for appointment to Industrial Tribunals are from women (which is a fraction higher than the proportion of women actually appointed). The Lord Chancellor's office says there has been no noticeable increase in applications from women since the passing of the Sex Discrimination Act (and Tribunals' extended scope).

In the last 10 years 2 Bar Council committees have looked into the position of women barristers; neither has achieved anything much. The existence of discrimination was however admitted. In 1978 the second committee sent a letter to all Heads of Chambers 'reminding them of the need to conform with both the letter and the spirit' of the Sex Discrimination Act.

Women barristers' earnings still lag far behind their male colleagues' (even in the case of women barristers with unbroken full-time careers).

Career-break: There are problems in keeping a tenancy while not working at all. Women barristers have to try and reduce their workload rather than have a complete break of more than a few months, unless they had built up a successful practice before the break, or have a very sympathetic Head of Chambers. (See Civil Service, p. 129, for opportunities for returners; in industry and commerce, arrangements vary.)

Part-time: As practising barrister, under-employment rather than regular part-time which is impossible to arrange; there may be opportunities as legal adviser in industry.

Further information

Council of Legal Education, 4 Gray's Inn Place, London WC1R 5DX
Scotland: Faculty of Advocates, Parliament House. Edinburgh EH1 1RF

Related careers

Accountant – Civil Service – Legal Executive – Solicitor

Barristers' Clerk

Entry qualifications

3 O-levels including an English subject.

The work

This small profession has changed little over the past 100 years or so. Barristers' clerks 'manage' Chambers and the barristers working in them (see Barrister, p. 240). The *senior clerk*'s job is a unique mixture of power-behind-the-throne and humdrum clerking. She negotiates fees and other matters relating to briefs coming to Chambers with solicitors (from whom the briefs come). Clerks play a particularly important role in 'building up' young barristers: some briefs come to Chambers rather than to individual barristers and it is the senior clerk who decides which of the young barristers is to be given the brief.

Senior clerks usually have *junior clerks* who make tea, carry barristers' books and robes to court, type Opinions and Pleadings. There is no career structure and *no hope whatever* of progressing to becoming a barrister, but as senior clerks get a commission on all their Chamber's barristers' earnings they often earn more than some of the barristers for whom they are clerking.

Prospects Keen competition for openings.

Pay: Very poor for junior clerks; high to very high for senior clerks (see p. xxiii).

Training On-the-job, with lectures. Clerks now normally take the Barristers' Clerks Association examination, after 4 years' clerking.

Personal attributes Very great self-confidence and presence; tact; willingness to tackle any kind of menial office job; respect for tradition and the established professional and social pecking order, in which barristers are a long way above clerks; interest in the law.

Late start Upper age for starting is normally 20; people who worked as legal secretaries very occasionally switch to clerking at any age: i.e. barristers are not willing to train late entrants; secretaries would know what clerks' duties are.

Position of women About 12% of clerks are women. *Very* few women are senior clerks. See *Barrister* for male-oriented atmosphere at the Bar.

Career-break: Return to work would be *very* difficult.

Part-time: Limited opportunities, and none for senior clerk. (No logical reason for this.)

Further information Barristers' Clerks Association, 2 Crown Office Row, Temple, London EC4 7AS

Related careers *Civil Service – Legal Executive – Secretarial and Clerical Work*

Justices' Clerks' Assistant

Entry qualifications 3 O-levels; many enter with higher qualifications. 'A good standard' of English (in practice this means O-level English). (Ability to type is an advantage.)

The work Justices' Clerks' Assistants work in Justices' Clerks' offices, attached to magistrates' courts. (Justices' Clerks are either solicitors or barristers.) They are employed by magistrates' courts committees. Assistants first do general office duties. As they progress they prepare warrants, licences for betting offices and public houses, make out orders and notices to people who have been fined, supervise the receipt and payment of maintenance money, deal with the enforcement and receipt of fines and fixed penalties and help with accounting procedures, which may be computerized. Later they may sit in court with the Justices' Clerk or a court clerk to assist with the administration of the court. They have a great deal of contact with the public. Senior assistants may become court clerks and deputize for the Justices' Clerk in the magistrates' court. Court clerks do administrative work but need considerable legal knowledge. Some – *very* few – become articled to Justices' Clerks and qualify as solicitors. They must, of course, have the necessary entry qualifications (see Solicitor, p. 248).

Prospects Fair for first jobs. Promotion may be fairly slow, and also depends on Assistants' willingness to move to another office.

Pay: Medium (see p. xxiii).

Training On-the-job training with some short residential courses. For promotion to court clerk (minimum age 22 and at least 2 years' service): 3-year part-time courses at some polytechnics, plus short residential courses.

Personal attributes Interest in law and court procedures; a conscientious approach to office work; ability to deal discreetly and sympathetically with the public; good figure-work for accounting.

Late start Quite common.

Position of women Approximately 75% are women.

Career-break: Possible

Part-time: Very unlikely at the moment, but no reason why part-time and job-sharing should not be tried.

Further information The Home Office, Room 419, Queen Anne's Gate, London SW1H 1AT

Related Careers *Barristers' Clerk – Legal Executive – Police*

Legal Executive (formerly Managing Clerk)

Entry qualifications 4 academic O-levels. (A-level law shortens the training.)

The work A legal executive works for a solicitor in much the same way as a junior executive works for a managing director: she is responsible for a strictly limited section. The solicitor is in overall control, makes contact with clients and lays down policy. The legal executive often specializes in one particular branch of the law – probate, conveyancing, litigation, company law, etc. She works out the details as they apply in each particular case – looking up references in law books, preparing documents, interviewing witnesses, and conferring with clients on points of detail. In small practices, or when managing a branch office, she may also be involved with the whole spectrum of work.

Although she cannot speak in open court, she appears before Registrars or Masters of the High Court or in the County Court on summonses in the course of proceedings. She may also appear before a Judge in Chambers or before a magistrate.

Prospects Fair. The Law Society grants some exemptions from its exams to Fellows of the Institute of Legal Executives (see Solicitor, p. 248). This is therefore a career for those who are interested in law but unable, or unwilling, to become solicitors.

Pay: Varies – according to type and size of solicitor's practice and seniority (see p. xxiii).

Training On-the-job, together with part-time training at day-release or, more often, evening classes, or by approved correspondence course, for the Institute of Legal Executives' Parts I and II examinations. The syllabus includes general legal subjects and practice and procedure, and allows for specialization in one branch of the law. Training time varies from 2 to 4 years.

Personal attributes Sufficient powers of concentration to detect relevant details in a mass of complex documentation; patience and perseverance; self-confidence and ability to discuss matters with all types of people from criminals to judges.

Late start Over-25s do not need the O-levels; many decide to become legal executives only after having been legal secretaries for many years.

Position of women This used to be an all-male profession; now 60% of members of the ILE are women. However, solicitors tend to be conservative, and women legal executive students have to have more drive than men to get the breadth of experience which is essential for passing exams and getting promotion.

It is possible to prepare for the ILE exams while being employed as clerk or secretary: many women have done this, in the hope of getting a more responsible job once they have passed the exams.

Career-break: Should be no problem for people who keep up with legislative changes.

Part-time: Some opportunities for jobs and also for training.

Further information The Institute of Legal Executives, Kempston Manor, Kempston, Bedford MK42 7AB

Related careers *Barrister – Barristers' Clerk – Company Secretary – Solicitor*

Solicitor

Entry qualifications A degree or high A-level grades, i.e. 2 A-levels (min. B and C) at one sitting or 3 A-levels (min. C at one sitting, B and 2 Cs at two sittings). O-levels to include English.

The work A solicitor is a confidential adviser to whom people turn for legal advice and information in a vast variety of personal and business matters. As everyday life becomes more complex, the solicitor is increasingly asked to help in matters where common sense, wisdom and an objective approach are as important as legal knowledge. Whenever possible a solicitor tries to settle matters out of court. When lawsuits are necessary, she represents her client in the lower and county courts. In the High Court (and at assizes) she briefs counsel (see Barrister, p. 240). But it is always the solicitor, not the barrister who discusses problems with her clients.

Solicitors tend to specialize in, for example, company law; taxation, conveyancing or in what is called 'heavy commercial work'; in EEC or international law; or in family law – divorce, custody of children, etc. In recent years some solicitors have begun to specialize in social welfare law and/or women's rights (sex discrimination legislation has increased scope and demand here), and also in consumer legislation.

There is no need to specialize to the exclusion of all other types of work: very much depends on the type and organization of the partnership a solicitor joins. About 80–90% of solicitors are in private practice. A small proportion work in neighbourhood law centres, usually in poor areas, where they deal largely (but not only) with social welfare and tenancy matters. It is also possible to set up on one's own and wait for clients to come, but this requires capital and contacts.

A solicitor interested in the law, rather than in people *and* the law, may become a legal adviser in the Civil Service (see also Barrister, p. 240; these jobs are open to barristers and solicitors) or in local government, or in commerce and industry, where the work involves vetting contracts and other documents and general advising. There is more security than in private practice, but there may be less variety. More time is spent in discussion with other professional people and less in meeting members of the public, but there are the usual advantages of working in large organizations.

Solicitors can now become judges after many years' experience.

Prospects Fair. It is not always possible to get exactly the kind of work envisaged, where one wants it, but solicitors have so many kinds of work to choose from that they are likely to find something congenial. Lawyers – barristers and solicitors – of at least 7 years' practice are eligible for appointment (by the Lord Chancellor) as Chairmen of Industrial Tribunals. These Tribunals deal with unfair dismissal, redundancy payments and other matters relating to employment generally. Under the Sex Discrimination Act they also hear complaints from women who believe they have been discriminated against in terms of equal pay, promotion, acceptance for a particular job and other employment matters. Chairmen are appointed to regional panels and sit on Tribunals within a given area. Appointments can be full-time or part-time (i.e. some lawyers carry on with their practice as well).

Solicitors may work as legal advisers abroad, but cannot set up in practice.

Pay: High to very high (see p. xxiii).

Training Training now consists of an *Academic Stage* and a *Second (Vocational) Stage*. These are the training methods:

1. Taking an 'approved' (by the Law Society) law degree which means

one that covers the 6 'core' subjects: Constitutional and Administrative Law, Contract, Torts, Criminal Law, Land Law, Trusts. (For differences in course emphasis and content see Barrister, p. 242.) Law graduates then go on to the *Second Stage*. This comprises a 1-year full-time course at a College of Law or Polytechnic, for the Final examination, and 2 years' service under articles. Total training thus takes at least 5 years and 9 months.

2. Graduating in any subject, and then taking a 1-year full-time course at a College of Law or Polytechnic which covers the 6 core subjects and leads to the 'Common Professional Examination' (the title is confusing as, since the solicitors' change of policy on entry requirements, the barristers have abandoned the 'Common' (with the solicitors) examination and have their own 'Diploma in Law' instead). Students then take the Finals course and examination and serve under articles exactly as do law graduates, except that they may serve the 2-year term of articles *before* the Finals course. The total training thus takes at least 6 years and 9 months.

3. For non-graduates over 25 who have a professional qualification or work experience acceptable to the Law Society: taking a 2-year course for the CPE in up to 8 subjects. They then complete the Second Stage like graduates.

4. For school-leavers and non-graduates under 25: taking a 1-year full-time course for the Solicitors' First Examination (SFE) which covers 4 core subjects. They then serve under articles for 5 years, taking remaining core subjects, plus 2 others, by part-time or correspondence course. They then take the 1-year Final course and examination and serve the last 18 months under articles.

5. Fellows of the Institute of Legal Executives (see p. 247) must pass, or obtain exemption from (in up to 3 subjects), the CPE, then *either* attend Finals course and take examination *or* serve 2 years under articles before taking Final examination.

6. Holders of the Justices' Clerks' Assistants' Diploma (see p. 245) must pass or obtain exemption from the CPE, then complete the Second (Vocational) Stage.

Holders of the barristers' Diploma in Law (see p. 242) are admitted to the solicitors' Second Stage, so it is possible to start training for the Bar and then switch to solicitor-training (but there are very few Diploma in Law vacancies).

NOTE: Training under articles varies greatly. In specialized firms clerks do not get the breadth of experience required for choice of work later; and in some firms clerks are used as general assistants rather than trainees (i.e. having work criticized; sitting in on principals' discussions with clients, etc.). It is important to investigate what training is given before accepting articles.

Level of pay bears no relation to the training given: some firms which provide excellent training pay a lot better than others which use articled clerks as general dogsbodies.

Personal attributes Capacity for absorbing facts quickly; logical reasoning; ability to see implications which are not obvious; ability to come to grips with an intricate problem; a good memory for facts and faces; tact; patience; clear and concise expression in writing and in speech; sound judgement of character; an understanding of human behaviour; a personality that inspires confidence.

Late start Entrants over 25 are allowed, at the Law Society's discretion, to take the CPE by part-time or correspondence course; GCE requirements may be relaxed. Articles are difficult to find.

Position of women About 43% of trainees now entering into articles, and 34% of those finally qualifying, are women. A large proportion of women solicitors then go into the Civil Service, industry and commerce, local government, etc. Only 12% of solicitors holding Practice Certificates are women; and most solicitors employed in private practice, and all full partners in practice, *must* hold such Certificates. While the proportion of women qualifying as solicitors has increased about threefold in the last ten years, the proportion holding Practice Certificates has only just doubled.

Women occasionally encounter difficulties getting articles, especially with the type of firm in which they can gain wide experience, so they have to be more determined than men to have equal chances of getting fully qualified. But the situation has improved in the last few years.

There are some firms still, especially those doing important commercial work, which prefer not to have women partners, but other firms welcome women colleagues. It seems that old-fashioned senior partners often *imagine* that clients would object to women solicitors, but in fact clients very rarely do so; once in practice, women solicitors are readily accepted by clients.

About 5% of applications to the Lord Chancellor for appointment to Industrial Tribunals are from women (which is a fraction higher than the proportion of women actually appointed). The Lord Chancellor's office says there has been no noticeable increase in applications from women since the passing of the Sex Discrimination Act.

Career-break: No problem for women who keep up with legislative changes. The Association of Women Solicitors is running occasional *refresher courses*.

Part-time: Reasonable opportunities, mainly in private practice, but not necessarily very regular work/hours (also on Industrial Tribunals).

Further information

The Law Society, Law Society's Hall, 113 Chancery Lane, London WC2A 1PL
Association of Women Solicitors, c/o The Law Society (address above)
Scotland: Law Society of Scotland, Law Society's Hall, 26–27 Drumsheugh Gardens, Edinburgh EH3 7YR (training in Scotland differs from that in England and Wales)

Related careers

Accountant – Barrister – Civil Service – Justices' Clerks' Assistant – Legal Executive – Trading Standards Officer

---

Librarianship and Information Science

Chartered librarian – information scientist

Information technology has had an enormous impact on the work done by librarians and information scientists.

The division between *Chartered Librarian* and *Information Scientist* is now blurred. Job titles often owe more to tradition than to logic. For example, a scientific learned society is likely to employ a 'librarian' who is a scientist and therefore able to cope with specialized inquiries. A multinational corporation's 'information department' is likely to be run by an 'information scientist' or 'information officer' or 'director of information' who might well be a chartered librarian.

Librarians and information scientists serve the same basic purpose: they organize and make available published material (printed or, increasingly, computerized, 'electronically-published' material on video, discs, cassettes, etc.). They also know how to ferret out information which is not readily available. In theory, the information scientist is more likely to be a specialist in the subject her special library/information department deals with and is more concerned with analysing the information; the librarian is more likely to be an organizer and communicator of general published information. In practice, titles are used arbitrarily, and the difference between the two jobs is mainly one of emphasis, working environment and proportion of time spent on different aspects of the work.

Computerized information storage and retrieval systems are becoming more widely used in all types of libraries – including public ones – but especially in information departments. 'Data banks' (electronic versions of reference books, catalogues and other items of information) can now be connected to and 'accessed' by terminals in hundreds of locations. Introducing and making the best use of chip-based information-disseminating inventions is an important aspect of both chartered librarians' and information scientists' work. The term '*informatics*' is beginning to be used for all aspects of electronic information storage, retrieval, dissemination systems, and their implications and their physical development. Informatics specialists are expected to understand the technical side of computer application to information work. At the moment, informatics specialists are still often electronics or computer experts with an interest in library/information work. But this is such a new, unorthodox and rapidly changing job area that librarians/information scientists with an interest in and understanding of electronics could well go into 'informatics'.

Training for the two overlapping careers is often, but not necessarily, identical. It is advisable therefore to look at the careers together and then to consider their different characteristics, and methods of training.

Chartered Librarian

Entry qualifications Degree. See **Training**.

The work About 60% work in public libraries; about 30% in academic/educational establishments (schools, colleges, universities, research organizations, medical schools); the remainder work in industrial and commercial concerns' 'information departments'/'special libraries' (see *Information Scientist* below).

The public library service generally is trying to get rid of its image as a stuffy old-fashioned institution; libraries are extending their 'information point' role and act as advice centres. Librarians have to know what services – social, consumer, commercial, entertainment – are available and how people can use them. So while librarians must of course be interested in books, they must be equally or even more interested in the community's social and economic activities. Organization of individual library services varies in detail.

A *Chief Librarian* is in charge of a central library, branches, and the various activities organized by the service. The chief librarian, with her deputy, is responsible for buying books; how much freedom she has to use the limited cash as she thinks fit, depends on the local authority's library committee, and on the chief librarian's strength of personality.

Each branch is run by a *Branch Librarian* who may or may not be a subject specialist. (In a large library service there are also 'group librarians' in charge of several branches.)

Specialist Librarians advise on the purchase of books within their speciality, and they usually do 'extension work'. The *music specialist* organizes record evenings and perhaps recitals; the *science specialist* organizes 'projects' for children (jointly with the children's librarian) and lectures and exhibitions for the general public and for students; the *literature specialist* organizes poetry readings and may liaise with local dramatic societies. All specialists take part in projects to reach 'new' library users.

The *Cataloguer* does classifying and indexing of new stock and she probably evaluates new computerized systems; there are many, and views on their relative advantages and disadvantages differ. Electronic information storage, classification and retrieval systems, making distant – and often vast and specialized – library services' stocks accessible to local readers, are revolutionizing libraries. Systems are changing fast, and so is the cataloguer's role; it increasingly overlaps with that of the reference librarian.

The *Reference Librarian* deals with inquiries on a vast variety of subjects. Some are straightforward queries, answers to which are available in reference books; others need research. Reference librarians now often try and make their services known to sections of the local community; for example exporting or manufacturing firms have to know about political and economic conditions of countries to which they may want to export, and the reference librarian can provide the necessary information. She may also provide books and information for ethnic minorities. 'Electronic search' equipment is increasing the reference librarian's scope enormously – and also the need for her to understand how developing information technology can be used.

The *Children's Librarian* is responsible for the choice and arrangement of her stock. She organizes a wide range of 'extension activities', such as story afternoons, puppet clubs, scrapbooks for exchange with children's libraries abroad, discussion and review afternoons (when the children review books for their own and younger age groups), and all sorts of activities which help children to appreciate books and library services. She liaises with schools and may help to stock school libraries. She cooperates with teachers on special 'projects', and she teaches children how to use libraries and reference books. Of all specialists, the Children's Librarian has the greatest freedom of action. She does not normally become a branch librarian but concentrates on her speciality either in a branch or, later, in charge of the whole children's library service.

The *Readers' Adviser* (titles vary) helps readers who cannot find their way around or who want to investigate a particular subject. She also acts as a guide to the varied library facilities, and shows readers how to use the catalogue (especially the new computerized ones).

Prospects Limited. Library services are affected by public spending cuts, and new technologies used for cataloguing and such routine work as sending out 'overdue' letters are severely reducing the number of assistants needed.

Training *Either* 3-year (a few 4-year) degree course, *or* 1-year post-graduate course, *or* 2-year post-Dip. HE course lead to membership (after several years' practical library experience) of the Library Association.

Course titles, as well as emphasis on different aspects of librarianship/information science vary enormously; titles do not necessarily show where course emphasis lies. On some 'Librarianship' courses, new information technologies are given as much course-time as on some 'Library and Information Science' courses. Prospective students are advised to study course prospectuses carefully before choosing a particular course. Some courses prefer students to have worked as a trainee or assistant in a library before starting the course.

Personal attributes Wide interests; curiosity; ability to make the first approach to diffident people, and a liking for superficial contact with large numbers of strangers; patience with their tastes and questions; a good memory (a photographic one is a help); a methodical approach; a logical mind; organizing ability. For *children's librarian*, an insight into young minds; the ability and patience to interest the less enthusiastic child. There are many different facets of library work and therefore room for people with only some of these qualities.

Late start No age bar but see **Prospects**.

Position of women Overall a much higher proportion of women, but this is reduced in senior posts.

Career-break: As there are more newly qualified librarians than there are jobs, there may well be difficulties.

Part-time: Few opportunities in public libraries at the moment. Some scope in educational libraries. Some job-sharing schemes are working; more could be started.

Information Scientist

Entry qualifications Nothing rigidly laid down but generally a degree or similar qualification, preferably in a scientific/technological subject. A broad-based degree is usually more useful than a specialized one. See **Training**.

The work As a career in its own right information science is fairly new. As it is no longer possible for the individual scientists, engineers, economists or indeed experts in almost any field to keep track of all the new information relevant to their subject, a growing number of industrial and commercial concerns and research organizations have set up information departments (also called 'special libraries'). An information scientist collects, indexes and classifies material. This involves scanning but not necessarily reading a large number of journals, papers, handouts, etc. Information scientists also abstract information and circulate it to those members of their organization to whom it might be of interest. In fact an information scientist is the link between (a) information that is available somewhere and (b) the person who wants it, or who would find it useful if he knew it existed. The information officer does not necessarily wait to be asked for information; her duties may include keeping specialists up to date with relevant information as it becomes available. She may also have to do research in other libraries and obtain information by telephone or correspondence, or via electronic information points like Ceefax, Prestel, etc.

Information scientists, unlike librarians, are expected to have sufficient specialist knowledge to be able to discuss the subject their organization is dealing with in some depth.

The work increasingly involves dealing with or organizing computerized information storage and retrieval techniques and equipment. Information scientists (and indeed chartered librarians) now often work on the production of public 'on line' data banks (see Computing, p. 131). This involves various aspects of publishing (both electronic and traditional print); database design, and teaching users how to use the new equipment.

Some information scientists (and librarians) are involved in developing the wider use of 'viewdata' systems. With these new computer-based devices, information provided by government, and by commercial and professional organizations, can be 'called up' to appear on television screens or on special visual display units in libraries, offices, etc. Information can be continuously updated by the suppliers – so the information scientists and librarians are re-thinking their traditional cataloguing systems.

Information departments vary in size: some are streamlined, run by highly qualified people; others were started in a haphazard way. Industrial information departments are normally in London and industrial areas; but a number of the government ones, such as the one for the Atomic Energy Authority, are in the country. The work is sometimes very rushed, and information may be urgently required after office hours. Status varies: some information officers are considered as essential to their organization as the experts themselves; others do not rank so high.

Prospects Fair mainly for scientists and engineers, possibly also for economists and other specialists with added information scientist qualifications.

Pay: Medium to high (see p. xxiii).

Training (1) and (2) lead to the widest choice of jobs:

1. Science or engineering degree or BTEC Higher award followed by a 1-year full- or 2-year part-time post-graduate course in information science.

2. Degree in information science (or studies) which combines theory of information dissemination, storage and retrieval techniques;

communication techniques; library organization, etc., with science studies. Any 2 A-levels may be acceptable, but GCEs must usually include a science and a maths subject and a language other than English.
3. Degree in library studies.
4. An economics, business studies, or social science degree followed by a post-graduate course in information science or studies.
5. Assistant in an information department and taking a part-time course in information science.
6. Experience as reference librarian in public library (see above, p. 255).

A reading knowledge of a foreign language is useful, especially one that is not widely studied, such as Chinese and Russian.

Personal attributes Curiosity; an interest in a variety of related topics without the desire to delve too deeply into any one; a methodical approach; a high degree of accuracy; a pigeon-hole mind which retains apparently irrelevant information; staying-power for long, possibly fruitless search; a friendly manner which induces busy experts to answer queries willingly and helpfully; resourcefulness; interest in electronic information systems; capacity to switch instantly from one topic to another; ability to cope with frequent interruptions when doing jobs which require concentration.

Late start Opportunities possibly for science and engineering graduates who can top up their existing qualifications with specialist training.

Position of women As in all new professions where there is no tradition to break down, women have equal opportunities.

Career-break: Should be no problem, if well qualified and up-to-date. Short courses, though not intended as *refresher courses*, can be used as such.

Part-time: Some opportunities for people with specialist qualifications and/or experience. Job-sharing should be possible.

Further information Education Officer, ASLIB, 3 Belgrave Square, London SW1X 8LP
Education Officer, Library Association, 7 Ridgmount Street, London WC1E 7AE
Institute of Information Scientists, Harvest House, 62 London Road, Reading RG7 5AS

Related careers *Archivist – Bookselling – Museum work – Publishing*

Linguist

Bilingual secretary – interpreting – translating – teaching – BBC – Diplomatic Service – industry

There is no such career as 'linguist' as such: a knowledge of languages on its own does not lead anywhere special. Apart from teaching, it is useful only if combined with either technical–scientific and/or almost any other specialist knowledge, or with secretarial skills, or with extremely exceptional talent. In almost any professional area from archaeology to zoology languages can be useful.

Main Possibilities

Entry qualifications

1. *Bilingual secretary*: normally 4 O-levels, including a modern language and an English subject.
2. *Interpreting*: complete command of at least 2 foreign languages.
3. *Translating*: complete command of at least 1 foreign language plus specialist knowledge.
4. *Teaching*: see p. 520.
5. *Information Work*: see Information Scientist, p. 256.
6. *International Accountancy, Banking and Finance*: at least 1 foreign language to degree level.

NOTE: For language degree, O-level Latin is often required.

Bilingual Secretary

The work See Secretarial Work, p. 454.

Interpreting

The work *Conference Interpreters*

At international conferences, interpreters may do *either* 'simultaneous' *or* 'consecutive' interpreting. They must be exceptionally proficient in at least 2 of the UN official languages; an additional knowledge of one or more of the less common languages is a help. Simultaneous interpreters relay the meaning of a speech, often on complicated subjects, almost instantaneously. The technique can be learned, but the talent and temperament are inborn. Consecutive interpreters relay a speech as a whole, or in large chunks, after each speaker. This requires as much skill as simultaneous translating.

A conference interpreter invariably translates *into* her own language; she is expected to have complete command of 3 of the official languages (i.e. those used by the United Nations Agencies), namely English, French, Spanish, Chinese, and Russian. In practice, this usually means that as well as French and German, or French and Spanish, an interpreter has one of the more unusual languages.

Some interpreters are employed by international agencies; others are freelances and are booked for a particular conference. Most of the year is spent travelling to and from New York, Geneva, Paris and London, living in hotels. The life may be luxurious, but it is extremely hectic, with very long irregular hours. Most conference interpreters now are specialists.

Specialist Interpreters

Have some specialist knowledge (such as engineering, information technology, computing, physical science or economics), plus proficiency in a foreign language, and usually do translating as a main job, interpreting as a sideline (see below, Translating on a freelance basis).

General Interpreters

Most of them take tourists around London. They are very few in number. Most of them are accredited guides (i.e. they need a considerable historical knowledge of London or other places) and are on the books of hotels and travel agencies for occasional assignments – it is a pleasant sideline, but not a career in itself.

Some also work for industry, for the courts and for conference organizers.

Prospects Poor, except for the exceptionally gifted, and exceptionally lucky. Most successful interpreters are men, and competition for the very few jobs available is very keen. Far more interpreters than jobs.

Pay: High to very high (see p. xxiii).

Translating

The work Translators must be able to translate idiomatically and to write lucidly and concisely – being bilingual is not sufficient. They translate into their mother-tongue, unless it can be shown that another language has wholly taken the place of this as a language of habitual use.

They need a very good education and specialist knowledge of

preferably a range of related subjects. Most translations have some specialist content – contracts require some legal knowledge; scientific articles some understanding of the subject-matter; specifications (for construction work, of anything from ships to atomic power stations) need some technical knowledge. Translators often have to discuss phrases and technical jargon with engineers, scientists, lawyers, etc., to get the sense absolutely right; translating is therefore often teamwork.

Government departments, and industrial, commercial and research organizations often have translating departments, which employ specialists in particular fields, and sometimes non-specialists, who have, for instance, Chinese or Arabic, as well as 1 or 2 of the more usual languages.

Translating agencies employ specialists, and people who have unusual languages, often on a freelance basis. They like to have on their books a large number of people with widely different specialities and languages, on whom they can call at a moment's notice. There is increasing scope in translating instruction manuals for consumer goods manufacturers.

Much is rushed deadline work, especially for freelances.

Prospects Good only for those with up-to-date specialist technical/scientific knowledge and/or unusual languages.

Pay: Medium to high (see p. xxiii), but varies enormously according to specialist knowledge.

Abroad: Fair opportunities, but depending on other special qualifications.

Teaching

See Teaching, p. 520, for details.

Other Possibilities

BBC

Most of the work in the foreign language section is done by nationals of the various countries; very few linguists are employed and those need thorough political and economic knowledge of the country concerned. Monitors listen to and précis broadcasts in over 30 languages. The work is very intensive and it is shift work. Few openings.

Diplomatic Service

Proficiency even in several foreign languages is no entry qualification on its own (see Civil Service, p. 125).

Industry

Language ability of at least A-level, preferably degree level, together with a knowledge of the social and political institutions of the country concerned, *and* appropriate qualifications in the relevant specialist area, are required for jobs in Britain, and may lead to work abroad.

Personal attributes (for linguists generally)

These vary according to the job, but all linguists must have an agile mind, interest in current affairs, a knowledge of cultural and social structures not only of their own country but of any country in whose language they specialize. They should be willing to take responsibility, for even in comparatively subordinate jobs (such as a secretary's) they may be the only person equipped to judge the correctness of a translation; they need the ability to concentrate for long stretches and to work well with others. Conference interpreters also need a calm temperament, exceptional physical stamina and the ability to snatch a few hours' sleep at any time.

General language training

1. 1- and 2-year full-time diploma courses at further education colleges
Candidates need 1, sometimes 2, A-levels, including 1 in a foreign language, and another language to at least O-level. Course content varies but is likely to include economics; social structure of the countries concerned; commercial practice; overseas marketing; interpreting technique.

2. CNNA or university degree
The content and approach of individual degree courses vary considerably; in some the approach is cultural, the emphasis on literature; others, particularly CNAA degrees, are more practical in content, and prepare students for work in commerce and industry by including more about the economy, the institutions, and the social climate of the country concerned. A number of degrees – university and CNAA – combine a language with a branch of engineering or science, or with such subjects as economics, international relations or law, marketing, computer science or business studies. Most honours courses include a year abroad and last 4 years.

3. Post-graduate courses
These courses are usually at polytechnics. Some are for scientists who need to know a language; others for linguists who want to be interpreters and/or translators.

4. Living and working abroad

This is usually in addition to and not instead of (1) and (2), and an *au pair* job on its own is not enough. It should be supplemented, or followed by, one of the courses for foreigners at various foreign universities. These last from 2 weeks to several terms; there are also some part-time classes, mainly in capital cities.

NOTE: The Institute of Linguists holds examinations in interpreting and translating, but it does not organize (or advise on) training. Examinations are at 5 levels: the Preliminary and Grade I Certificates are intended for those who study at evening classes or by radio or television, for pleasure and perhaps to be able to make themselves understood on holidays abroad. They are not for candidates who want qualifications which might help to get a job.

The Grade II Certificate is roughly equivalent to A-level, but more practical and less academic in content. It is accepted in lieu of A-levels for CNAA and many university degree courses.

The Intermediate Diploma is awarded to students who have practical knowledge of a language and who will probably have had 2 years' post-A-level part-time study, or taken a full-time course, studied abroad, and/or been in a job such as abstracting in a special library.

The Final Diploma is awarded to students who can use the language to 'near native' standard in communication between educated people with considerable knowledge of the political and cultural scene of the country where the language is spoken; and who also have either special knowledge of a particular subject (perhaps trade with the country concerned) or a special ability, such as technical translation, to near-professional standard.

The Final Diploma is recognized as degree level by the Civil Service and similar employers.

The Institute of Linguists does not run courses, but many courses at polytechnics and colleges (and some schools) prepare students for these examinations.

Late start Translating possibly; interpreting unlikely.

Position of women Rather more men than women are professional translators and interpreters, but women who do have the right knowledge and aptitude do well; women tend to be better than men at languages, but they fall down on the necessary specialist knowledge which usually requires long training.

Career-break: Unless very well established, return might be difficult for *interpreters*, as competition very keen. *Translating*: No need to give up all contacts while raising family.

Part-time: Theoretically, there should be a good deal available as translating and interpreting are so often done by freelances. However, more linguists are seeking work than are needed and much of the work has to be done quickly – which means it is not regular part-time work, but a few days' or weeks' rushed full-time work every now and then.

Further information

For courses abroad: individual embassies
Central Bureau for Educational Visits and Exchanges, Seymour Mews House, Seymour Mews, London W1H 9PE
Institute of Linguists, 24a Highbury Grove, London N5 2EA

Related careers

Careers in which a knowledge of languages leads to better jobs:
Accountancy – Civil Service – Engineering – Hotel Work, *p*. 97 *– Information Officer – Scientist – Secretarial Work – Teaching – Travel Agent*

Local Government

Entry qualifications Entry is at all educational levels; increasing proportion of *graduate* entry.

The work Local government officers carry out the policies laid down by the elected local councils and are responsible for administering local services. Services are organized in departments; normally each is run by a person with relevant professional qualifications. (However, there is a tendency for a Chief Executive to be in overall charge of the multi-disciplinary team of heads of departments. She may have any type of professional qualification, but must be a top-flight administrator and coordinator, and must enjoy public functions – she has to attend many.) Departmental staff have relevant professional, administrative, technical or clerical qualifications or skills. Education, libraries, social services, planning, architecture, housing, legal, unicipal engineering, finance, are the main departments. Not all local authorities provide all services.

Local government was reorganized some years ago. Small authorities are now merged into fewer, larger ones. This has meant improved career structures within individual authorities. While in the past it was usually necessary to move to another authority for promotion it is now quite normal to be promoted within an authority, though this may still mean, in the case of large authorities, having to commute, or move, to another part of the authority's area.

Local government in England and Wales is structured in tiers. At the moment there are 6 Metropolitan (large urban conurbations) and 47 Non-Metropolitan County Councils; the second-tier authorities are 36 Metropolitan and 333 Non-Metropolitan District Councils. (London is a special case, with the Greater London Council as the top tier and 32 London Boroughs and the City of London as the second tier.) This structure may soon change.

Top-tier authorities' powers tend to be wider than the second tier's: for example, education and social services and overall planning are top-tier responsibilities. However, in some cases top-tier (County) authorities delegate powers to second-tier authorities. Housing and some planning functions may be shared by top- and second-tier authorities. The division of functions is very complicated indeed, but by and large there is more 'grass roots' involvement with the community at second-tier level; but top-tier authorities may offer better decision-making scope. It is quite common to move from second- to top-tier authority and vice versa in the course of one's career, so there is no need to decide at the outset on preference for either type of authority; but it is important to inquire into a particular job's scope.

Careers fall into 3 main groups: firstly those that can be followed both inside and outside local government, the most important ones being: accountancy, architecture, computers, engineering, horticulture, librarianship, law. Secondly, those that are entirely or largely local government careers, the most important ones being: planning, housing management, environmental health, social work, education (teaching, careers guidance), trading standards (consumer protection). (See individual sections.) Thirdly, there is scope in *general administration*. Administrative officers do committee work, supervise and organize the day-to-day running of departments, introduce and implement modern management techniques. They work closely with their professional colleagues – social workers, architects, housing managers, etc. – and relieve them of administrative duties, at which professional experts are not necessarily any good.

Senior staff attend council and committee meetings and advise on and discuss policy with elected councillors. Although there are many similarities with the Civil Service, local government service gives more opportunity of seeing the effects of one's work. Whether it is social work, building schools, or keeping the files which deal with playgrounds, the work is closely linked with the life of the community.

Facilities for further study are good. Day-release is usually granted for courses leading to qualifications, whether GCE or professional. Officers may be seconded to full-time courses.

There is a tradition of 'upward mobility' in local government; many senior professional posts are today filled by people who qualified entirely by studying part-time by day-release and evening class. However, as more and more school-leavers go on to full-time training, recruitment policy is changing. It is still *possible* to start at 16 with a few O-levels and to study part-time right up to professional qualifications. But this is now *very* rare indeed. Entrants are usually qualified in their chosen profession if it is one of those which can be followed both outside and inside local government. 'Administration' entry is more flexible. See **Training**.

Staff are divided into divisions. However, no two authorities are *exactly* alike in organization.

Training *Individual professions* (e.g. environmental health, planning, etc.): see individual entries.

Administration and clerical work (usual structure)

Clerical Division: Entrants normally have at least 3 or 4 O-levels or BTEC General award (see p. xvi). The higher the entry qualifications, the higher the entry 'grade'. Individual local authorities set different minimum entry requirements. For some jobs specific skills – for example secretarial, or word processing – are required.

All entrants are encouraged to work for further qualifications, and day-release is normally granted. There are opportunities to progress to administrative work.

Administration: Again, local authorities' requirements vary, but normally entry to the Administrative Grade is now with 2 A-levels or with BTEC National or Higher National awards (see p. xvi) or with a degree. Graduate entry is increasing. The qualification for *senior* administration jobs is now the Institute of Chartered Secretaries and Administrators' Diploma (see Chartered Secretary and Administrator, p. 106). Administrative Officers study for this qualification by part-time day- or block-release or correspondence course. In exceptional circumstances they may be sent on 1-year full-time courses. Some enter with the ICSA Diploma.

Many local authorities run graduate trainee schemes.

Once qualified, administrators are frequently sent on post-graduate/post-experience courses in, for example, computer applications, social or financial administration or personnel management.

Graduates with a social administration degree may get promotion more quickly than others; but degree subject is not normally specified for 'graduate entrants' jobs.

Prospects Limited at the moment by public expenditure cuts.

Pay: Medium to very high (see p. xxiii).

Personal attributes Depends on the particular type of work. *For all jobs*: interest in local affairs; *for purely administrative work*: ability to deal with people; capacity for picking out the relevant facts from a mass of detail; organizing ability; ability to work as one of a team. *At senior level*: willingness to carry into effect decisions taken by councillors whether one agrees with them or not.

Late start Career-changers and returners with relevant experience are welcome, in theory, and are also accepted for administration training. However, in practice, young entrants may be given preference – it depends on individual authorities' attitudes.

Position of women Women do well in the various careers (see separate entries) up to middle level, but only very few reach the top (see Town and Country

Planning, Social Work, etc.). The President of the Society of Chief Executives stated publicly as long ago as 1976: 'This [the small proportion of women in top jobs] simply will not do, and we, the Chief Executives, are the only people who can do something about it.' (Out of 487 chief executives then, 2 were women. There was only 1 in 1983.) He advocated a 'deliberate policy of promoting more women to senior posts'. So far no such policy has been implemented, though it has been discussed.

It is probably true that fewer women than men are willing to move from one local authority to another to gain the breadth of experience required for top jobs (but – as they see little hope of getting to the top anyway – they do not have men's incentive to move).

Career-break: It varies from one local authority and one profession to another. No bar on returners, but no encouragement given either.

Part-time: See separate career entries. None in general administration, so far. Some authorities have job-sharing schemes.

Further information

Town Hall or Council office
Local Government Training Board, Arndale House, Arndale Centre, Luton LU1 2TS

Related careers

Civil Service

Management in Industry and Commerce – Management Consultancy

Entry qualifications Nothing specific (see **Work** and **Training**), but a degree or professional qualification is advisable.

The work Any system of operations which provides a product or a service is controlled by managers. A hierarchy of managers is sandwiched between the overall policy-makers at board or equivalent level and the 'doers'. At one end of the scale, managers work closely with the policy-formulators and indeed help formulate policies, at the other end they work closely with the people who carry out the various tasks. Management is a vast and confusing field, with vague terminology. Management is not a career in the usual sense, but an activity, the purpose of which is to make the best use of available resources – human, money, material, equipment – in order to achieve a given objective. Managers, with the help of people working for them, decide how to achieve given objectives, and then get things done: management consists largely of enthusing subordinates into doing things as efficiently as they – the managers – would wish to have done them themselves.

One aspect which applies to all types and levels of management is communication: managers spend between 70% and 90% of their time talking to people, in conference, on the phone, in one-to-one discussion. That applies whether a manager manages a whole or part of a department store; an international sales force; a large export department or a small section of one; an engineering workshop; a manufacturing company, or a shop.

Virtually all managers start as specialists in something. (Anyone who controls the work of other people 'manages'; therefore most people as they rise in the job hierarchy spend more time on managing than they did at first, and less time doing whatever they originally trained for.)

If one's aim is management in business, the careers to choose are 'business functions', such as *accountancy* (p. 1), *production* (Engineering, p. 168); *purchasing and supply* (p. 404); *marketing*

(p. 283); *personnel* (p. 358); *shipbroking and freight forwarding* (p. 473) or one of the so-called 'management services': *operational research* (p. 345); *computing/information technology* (p. 131); *work study* (p. 557). Confusingly, *engineering* (p. 168), though not a business function, can lead to senior management more quickly than any of the business functions. It deserves to be considered as a way into senior management in both industry and commerce much more than it is.

Levels of management: There is no very clear distinction between junior, middle, and senior management; rising from one to another does not necessarily depend on gaining further qualifications (although such qualifications are very useful indeed and often essential, having got them does not automatically lead to the next step on the management ladder).

Most people who choose a management career think of senior, and general, managers – but they are the smallest management section.

Junior managers are the easiest to define. A junior manager is usually responsible for controlling the work of a number of people who are all doing the same work – usually work in which the junior manager is trained (or at least which she is able to do) herself. For example a supervisor fitter is a skilled fitter; a word-processing supervisor is a word processor operator or secretary (see p. 451); a factory production line supervisor has worked on the production line (though possibly as a graduate engineer gaining experience). Junior managers organize the flow of work, and sort out minor problems (often including subordinates' personal ones). In the office of, say, an export department, a junior manager might be responsible for ensuring that documentation relating to goods for one or two countries is dealt with correctly; on the shop-floor she might take responsibility for one or two production lines, which could mean about 100 people. Junior managers are also the link with middle management.

Middle management spans a wide range of jobs and levels of responsibility. The step from junior to middle management is the most crucial on the management ladder: while junior managers are responsible for people all doing the same kind of work, middle managers are responsible for coordinating a number of junior managers who are either all doing slightly different jobs, or for a larger group of people in the same field. This means that a junior manager who wants promotion must usually first broaden her experience and 'move sideways' before moving up. This experience-broadening is part of 'management development' (see Personnel Management, p. 358) and should be built into managers' training, but in very many firms young managers have to plan their own career-paths rather than rely on the personnel manager to do it for them. This is partly what makes 'management' such a difficult career to plan: it is not necessarily qualifications, but varied experience – and luck, drive and initiative – which matter.

The majority of managers remain middle managers always, gradually taking responsibility for a wider range of activities or for bigger departments. For example a sales manager in charge of a regional sales force is a middle manager and remains so even when she becomes responsible for a larger sales force, or a more important – in cash-terms – region. A manager in charge of a mail order firm's dispatch department, responsible for a large sum of money and for the firm's reputation for reliability, is a middle manager, and she might still be a middle manager when she oversees the dispatch *and* the packing departments. However, in another firm she might be a senior manager: it depends on a firm's organization, and their interpretation of what senior management is.

A vital and growing 'senior-middle management' area is 'management of change'. Managers must be aware of the organizational and technical as well as the human aspects of automation. Introduction of new technologies – whether robots in a factory or desk-top computers in an office – is a 'socio-technical' problem. There is as yet no one tried and tested way of tackling this development. While in some companies consultants in 'organizational change' or 'organizational behaviour' (usual backgrounds: academic research plus/or extensive business experience) may be called in to advise; more often managers – departmental, office, production, personnel, it varies enormously – have to cope. Managers may have to deal with employees' fears of new and unknown working practices, with the 'de-skilling' of some jobs and the need for retraining for others, with 'slimming down' the workforce and with the search and training for new job opportunities. 'Planning for change' is evolving into a management specialism or at least a new management task. It involves analysing where, how, when, why and whether new technologies should be introduced and if so, what preparation for a smooth transition from old to new working patterns must be made. No one person is likely to know enough about the various types of machines on the market to choose the equipment most suitable for each particular purpose. 'Planning for change' involves close cooperation with computer and other specialists.

Senior Management: Anyone responsible to the board is definitely a senior manager: all heads of departments – personnel, production, finance, marketing, etc. And coordinators, the general managers, are senior managers. They base important planning and policy decisions on information and advice from specialist senior managers.

Some terms used in management jargon:

Line Management: A line manager is the manager in charge of whatever the organization's principal activity and main purpose is. In a manufacturing industry it is the production manager; in retail it is the store manager; in an air freight charter company it is the person selling aircraft space. (The term 'line' is apparently derived from 'being in the firing line' – the line manager is the one who tends to get shot at when things go wrong.)

General Management: General managers coordinate the work of several specialist departments (or functions), for example personnel, production, accountancy, etc. They are usually a specialist in one of the functions for which they are responsible, which one is immaterial.

Executives and Managers: The distinction is vague. Broadly, managers are responsible for controlling other people's work, which executives are not necessarily: for example, a legal adviser is a senior executive, but not a manager. But middle or senior managers may also be called executives.

Managers and Administrators: Again the distinction is vague. What is called management in industry is often called administration in the public sector. The terms are often interchangeable (in terms of activity), but 'administrators' are more likely to be concerned with the smooth running of a department or organization without making any changes; whereas 'managers' are expected to choose the most efficient (or 'cost-effective') of various alternative routes to achieve an objective. Management implies more decision-making. But as in the whole of the management field, different people mean different things by the same terms.

Prospects Management covers such a vast range of jobs that it is impossible to generalize. However, it can be said that there is a shortage of *good* managers (especially with a technical background), but that on the whole entry is very competitive indeed. Graduate candidates on the whole stand a better chance than others. About one third of vacancies are for 'any discipline' graduates; where the discipline is specified, engineering/technological degrees are most in demand with computing subjects and then business studies next. First jobs are in large firms' *production* (see p. 171); *marketing and sales* (see p. 283); *purchasing and supply* (see p. 404) departments, and in small and medium firms where specialisms are not necessarily so clearly defined. (There are numerically more openings in small and medium-sized firms than in the large, household name 'first choice' companies).

Employers prefer management trainee applicants who have had some work-experience – if not on a sandwich placement, then in holiday or temporary employment. Having worked abroad – in whatever capacity – can also be an advantage. It follows that it may be advisable to take almost any job even if it is not a 'management' one, to gain experience of the work environment.

Pay: Medium to very high (see p. xxiii).

Training This is not neatly structured as it is for the professions. No specific qualifications entitle the holder to any level or type or title in management.

Senior Management
(a) A degree or specialist qualification (see **Work**, above), for example in accountancy (p. 1); engineering (p. 168); law (p. 240).

(b) 4-year sandwich degree in Business Studies. Courses include practical experience in industry or commerce (or public authority) which gives students an insight into the real world of work and enables those who do not enjoy the atmosphere, or find the pace too exacting, to change to some other graduate career. Employers welcome Business Studies graduates because they have had work experience, know what to expect, and have a basic understanding of business.

Sandwich courses come in two versions: 'thick sandwich' students normally spend 2 years at college, then 1 year in paid and supervised work experience, with a final year at college (but some students start with a year's practical work). 'Thick sandwich' students are usually sponsored. They spend their work experience period with their sponsor and normally get a job with their sponsor after graduating. 'Thin sandwich' students usually divide their first 3 years between college and work experience and spend the whole final year at college. They are not sponsored and spend work experience periods in a variety of work environments. They gain a wider range of experience, but do not acquire so much in-depth knowledge of any particular aspect of business. Neither type of sandwich course is 'better' than the other, though people who know exactly what kind of work they want to do eventually may prefer the sponsored 'thick sandwich'. Colleges (usually polytechnics) normally run *either* 'thick' *or* 'thin' sandwich courses – rarely both kinds. There are also some part-time Business Studies degrees, mainly for people in relevant employment, though occasionally people who have had previous relevant experience may be accepted. These courses can then be useful for people who want to return to or switch to a business career while still in other employment. Some 'mixed mode' courses enable students to combine 1 or 2 years' full-time study with 2 or 3 years' part-time study.

Business studies syllabuses vary. All provide a systematic introduction to management and to the various business functions; most courses specialize in a particular branch or management function – for example, marketing or international marketing; industrial relations; export management; manpower planning; finance; organizational behaviour, etc. Some courses are more suitable for people interested in, for example, 'human resources management'; others for those interested in business economics/finance; or in transport management, a growing field. Titles alone do *not* precisely describe a course's emphasis. Students should study the CRAC *Course Guide*, CNAA *Directory of First Degree and Dip. HE Courses*; *Which Degree*, and individual course prospectuses.
Entry requirements: Normally any 2 A-levels and 3 O-levels, including

English and maths. Only a few courses require A-level maths; and a few (those which specialize in international marketing or European business administration) a modern language. Courses accept the BTEC National awards (see BTEC, p. xvi) in lieu of A-levels. Mature candidates may be accepted with experience in lieu of qualifications.

(c) Any degree. About one third of graduate vacancies notified to the graduate careers advisory services are open to graduates from *any* discipline. Vacancies which specify disciplines, most frequently specify a technological subject (including computing), with Business Studies degrees next in order of preference.

(d) *Post-graduate and post-experience training* (includes post-relevant professional qualification and post-BTEC Higher National award – see below). Courses fall into two main groups:
(i) Courses in general management; and (ii) courses leading to specialist qualifications such as personnel management, international marketing, transport, or production, or export management, etc. Both types of courses can be either full-time, or part-time while in relevant employment.

General management courses are more likely to be full-time. The best-known courses are at the graduate business schools in London, Cranfield and Manchester, but there are a great number of others. Courses last 1 or 2 years. Many are suitable also for people who have been working for a few years but have no academic or professional qualifications, and for people who have been out of employment for some time (women who raised families mainly) as well as for mid-career changers.

Courses may lead to higher degrees (Master of Business Administration – MBA, MSc., or M Phil.) in Management Sciences, Administrative Management, Industrial Management, etc. Titles vary and do not necessarily indicate a particular emphasis or content. Prospective students should look at CRAC *Graduate Studies* and carefully study course Prospectuses.

The CNAA Diploma in Management Studies is the largest single management training scheme. Courses are available at many polytechnics and colleges. The 2-stage course structure is very flexible – the DMS can take 9 months' full-time; or 2 or 3 years' day- or block-release or evening study. As the two stages are usually separate units, it is usually possible to switch from one mode of attendance to another; for example, take stage 1 by evening study only, then get sponsored by an employer or TOPS (see p. xlvi) for a full-time stage 2 course. The scheme is intended primarily for people with a few years' middle-management experience. Entry qualifications are *either* HND/C, degree, equivalent professional qualifications; and, often, minimum age 23, *or* minimum age 27 with at least 4 years' relevant experience in lieu of academic qualifications.

All DMS courses update students' knowledge of management techniques and aim to improve their management skills. Most courses also specialize either in a 'management function', for example, personnel; export marketing; production management; or in an 'operational area', for example, recreation/leisure management; transport management; public administration; education administration. Like other vocational training (rather than academic education) courses, DMS course contents are constantly changing to meet employers' and students' requirements.

Recently some Business Studies degrees, post-graduate and post-experience courses have started offering options in 'small business' management, for people who want to work in small firms or who want to set up and run their own small show. (See Working for Oneself, p. 560.)

Below degree-level training

BTEC (see p. xvi), Higher National Diplomas and Certificates. Higher National Diploma courses are usually 2-year full-time or 3-year sandwich. Higher National Certificates are usually taken by day- or block-release while in appropriate employment (see Employers' Training Schemes, below). *Entry qualifications*: 1 A-level and 3 O-levels, or BTEC National Award (see below). Some colleges ask for additional qualifications. All BTEC Courses cover what are called 'central themes': (a) money – basically financial consequences and implications of decisions taken; (b) people – how to get on with and manage them; (c) communication – overlaps with (b) and broadly means making sure everybody in an organization understands what others are doing and why. It involves explaining actions and proposals clearly, in writing and verbally; (d) numeracy and application of new technology to problem solving. This involves learning how to 'quantify' plans, problems and situations, and developing an analytical approach. BTEC's 'central themes' approach should enable students to be flexible and adapt to the different kinds of jobs everyone is likely to be doing throughout their working lives.

On top of the 'central themes', BTEC students specialize in a career group. Each group has 'core modules', plus 'option modules' to suit each student's and (local employment) requirements.

The 3 business-related groups are:

(a) *Business and Finance*: covers non-specialized work in a wide range of commercial, manufacturing, service and financial organizations. Options include personnel; stock control; data processing; transport management; purchasing; insurance; banking; and building societies. This group is also a suitable choice for students who want to go into small or medium-sized organizations, where functions are not as specialized as in large ones; for those who are not sure yet exactly where their interests lie; or for those who want to specialize in financial areas of work.

(b) *Distribution* (wholesale, retail, mail-order); Travel and Tourism (see p. 555); also Hotel and Catering (see p. 91): Most courses are part-time for people in relevant employment. If not locally available, students take the Business and Finance Studies course and add Distribution, etc. options.

(c) *Public Administration*: For students who want to work in local and central government; public utilities (electricity, water authorities, etc.); health service administration; police. (For the vague distinction between Management and Administration, see p. 272 above.)

BTEC Higher National awards may lead to complete, and certainly to partial, exemption from relevant professional bodies' 'intermediate' examinations; for example, BTEC Business and Finance HND leads to the Institute of Bankers' and Chartered Institute of Insurance's final examinations. Increasingly, professional bodies in the commercial field accept, or require, BTEC Higher National awards instead of their own 'Stage 1' or 'intermediate' examinations. The advantage from the students' point of view is that they can postpone narrow specialization till they know more about all the related specializations, and that they can more easily switch specializations in mid-career. (For range of BTEC HND specializations see *Compendium of Advanced Courses in Colleges of Further and Higher Education.*)

Qualifications likely to lead to junior management (at least in the first instance; they can be stepping stones to middle management).

(a) BTEC National Diploma (2 years full-time or 3 years sandwich) or BTEC National Certificate (at least 2 years, possibly 3, by day- or block-release while in relevant employment).

Entry qualifications: Normally 4 O-levels, or BTEC General Award at credit standard. Students cover the BTEC 'central themes' and also study four 'core modules' and two 'option modules' for the National Certificates (see options for the National Diploma). National Diplomas and Certificates lead to partial exemptions from some professional bodies' exams (not from final ones) and are accepted by many professional bodies, and for many degree courses, in lieu of A-levels.

(b) BTEC Certificate in Management Studies (CMS). A 1-year part-time course for managers and potential managers. Minimum age usually 21, but most students are older; candidates normally have at least 5 O-levels or a BTEC National Award, or extensive experience. (Candidates over 25 who have had at least 3 years' supervisory or management experience may be admitted without academic qualifications.) Most courses are 'generalist' – but there are some specialist ones, e.g. National Health Service, Local Government and Recreation Management. The course is intended for people who want to progress up the management ladder and have to acquire specific knowledge as well as general education/training to be able to analyse and understand management processes and practices.

Employers' Training Schemes: Many firms (mainly large ones) and nationalized industries run training schemes. Entry is at various levels either for training, with day-release, for a professional qualification, or, for professionally qualified people – in whatever subject, but specially accountancy or engineering – as 'graduate trainee' or 'management trainee'. Schemes vary enormously in content, quality and usefulness to the trainee. In some firms, trainees learn only how to be of use to that particular organization, in others they get a thorough management training. Detailed research is necessary. Increasingly, large organizations especially take only, or mainly, graduates for training schemes likely to lead to senior or even senior–middle management. Retail chains are the exception – they often groom A-level entrants for top jobs. Entry to good training schemes is *very* competitive.

Personal attributes

Numeracy, business acumen, the ability to get on well with and be respected by people at all levels in the hierarchy; natural authority; willingness to take the blame for subordinates' misdeeds; self-confidence; unflappability in crises; organizing ability. *For senior management*: an analytical brain; ability to see implications and consequences of decisions and actions taken; ability to sift relevant facts from a mass of irrelevant information; enjoyment of power and responsibility; a fairly thick skin to cope with unavoidable clashes of temperament and opinion; resilience, courage, entrepreneurial flair; boundlcss ambition; ability to take snap-decisions without worrying about it afterwards; physical and mental energy.

Late start

See above – post-graduate courses and DMS. A few companies, so far mainly in retail and in catering, are encouraging women of 30-plus to become management trainees. Candidates are expected to have a degree, or professional qualification, or relevant experience which is usually selling or secretarial; but a few companies realize that women who have managed a home, family, voluntary work and/or hobbies of some kind have in fact been 'project managers', i.e. they know how to bring different strands together.

Position of women

Women are faring worse in industrial/commercial management than in the professions. 43% of the total workforce are women, but only 2·3% of the British Institute of Management's members are women. BIM members are middle and senior managers and normally must have degrees or professional qualifications to be eligible for membership. (This figure is a far better indicator of women's share of responsible management positions than census and labour force survey figures which give women's share of management jobs variously as between 5% and 18%. These figures include supervisory and junior management jobs.) The majority of women managers – all levels – are in service industries like retail or catering rather than in wealth-creating manufacturing; and in personnel rather than in 'sharp end' functions like production or financial management. Yet manufacturing industry is desperately short of *good* managers, and for today's 'participative' management style establishing and maintaining good personal relationships with a wide variety of types of people is considered one of the most important management qualities. Women are supposed to be 'good with people', so it is illogical that so few are managers. As industry now realizes that it cannot afford to waste half the nation's management potential simply because it happens to be held by females, several research projects (and many conferences) have been funded in recent years by government and industry to find out (a) why women are making such slow progress in industry (it is not just discrimination; it is clearly more complicated than that), and (b) what can be done to get more women managers. (In 1982, 7072 men and only 1614 women went from university into industry.)

Various research projects have identified (or, perhaps, confirmed?) that there are three basic and interrelated reasons why women do badly in this traditionally male area:

1. *Organizational causes*: Traditional career paths were designed for men, and have not been adapted to take account of women's different requirements and life patterns.
2. *Assumptions* which do not stand up when tested: for example it is still widely believed that women management trainees/graduates leave their first employer sooner than their male colleagues, and before they have 'paid off' the money invested in their training. But this is not so. Statistics show that women leave to have babies after about 7 years; men switch companies after between 5 and 7 years. (The chairman of a big company said recently that he would much rather lose a manager because she was about to have a baby than because he/she was going to work for a competitor.)

Another false assumption: women's alleged worse absentee record. Women employees *as a whole* take more time off, but the lower the level of responsibility, the higher the level of absenteeism; *far* more women have lowly jobs, so far more take time off. At middle and senior management level, women's record equals men's. Other assumptions which research has disproved include: women are more emotional at work; men do not want to work for women. Broadly, research has proved that discrimination founded on false assumption persists, but is *very* slowly diminishing.

3. The third and most intractable reason why women do badly in management lies in *women themselves*: their attitudes, aspirations, qualifications. Women lack confidence and ambition; they need to do more strategic career-planning than men and in fact do less. This ties up closely with (1) above – career structures are planned for men: in most companies young men are *assumed* to want to go up the ladder – their careers are almost automatically 'developed'; they are sent on courses and given broadening experience which fits them for promotion. Women have to *ask* for 'career development', to be sent on courses and given broadening experience (this applies at all levels of management, especially junior management). Women therefore have to be much more highly motivated in order to get as far as men do automatically.

Women find themselves in two kinds of chicken-and-egg situations: (a) if they push themselves forward, they are dubbed aggressive – and that is unacceptable in women managers. If they do not push themselves forward, they are far less likely than men to be given the training/experience essential for promotion. (b) Women have few 'role models'. As so few women are in top jobs, few girls know, or know of, anyone with whom they can identify; whom they can emulate. They feel they will not be promoted anyway; so they do not try. They do not try, so they do not get promoted.

Women are also less likely than men to have the kind of qualifications which help to get on in management: 3% of women but 20% of men university students started technology-based degrees in 1983; yet about two thirds of graduate jobs in industry are for people with such degrees. Proportionately fewer women than men choose business management studies degrees (though *any* A-levels are acceptable). Far fewer girls than boys have the sort of qualifications which enable them to start as technicians on the shop-floor, and get day-release for technical qualifications which can then lead to supervisory work and junior management.

The research projects also found that women's careers 'take off' later than men's. Only when the employer *and the woman herself* seem sure that she will take her career seriously will she be given, or press for, appropriate training. There is evidence, too, that women are less likely to apply for promotion or training than men with equal qualifications and/or experience. Again – lack of self-confidence and of role-models means that women need stronger personalities or more ambition (and push) than their male colleagues to do equally well.

The most important, though not startling, proposal for attracting more women into industry and commerce is that career structures must take account of women's 'broken career-pattern'. No blueprint for action has been produced, but, almost by stealth, forward-looking companies are setting precedents: they are making *ad hoc* arrangements for women managers to return after a few years' break (the statutory maternity provisions have not helped much: most women managers want to take a longer period off work). Arrangements for working part-time, often two or three days a week, or term-time only, rather than short (school-hours) days, are being tried out.

For women with above-average qualifications and self-confidence, prospects are now quite good. Employers like to be *seen* to be complying with equal opportunities legislation and they also realize that women, who still have to prove themselves, tend to work harder and be more committed to succeeding than men of comparable ability. The – regrettably few – women who go into the 'sharp end' business functions such as finance or production do particularly well, probably because only women with above-average self-confidence and ability take up jobs in areas which are still very much male preserves.

At present, women are more likely to do well in large than in small companies. The big companies stress that 'recruitment ratios reflect application ratios'. Not enough women graduates apply for management training.

To help women gain the confidence and the social skills needed to progress, special courses for women have been set up. Most are organized by the Industrial Society and some other, smaller organizations. Course titles vary from *Putting Yourself Across* to *Getting Going* or *Assertiveness Training*. All courses stress the need for women to learn how to assert themselves without being aggressive, and explain the vital difference between being aggressive which is a Bad Thing for women in business and being assertive (broadly, confident and polite yet firm) which is a Good Thing. Courses include role-playing, workshops, seminars. Some general management courses offer special scholarships to women; some large companies sponsor women to attend 6-week or longer courses. (For list of management courses for women write to Equal Opportunities Commission, Overseas House, Quay Street, Manchester M3 3HN.)

Career-break: Schemes for helping women resume their management careers have been discussed for some years now. For example it has been suggested that returners should have an 'industrial tutor' or 'mentor' – someone in the organization (not necessarily a woman) who helps her pick up the threads. Then there are an increasing number of courses specially for returners. They range from 2-day workshops which concentrate largely on confidence-building to 12-week full-time management-technique-updating courses at polytechnics. In addition, some post-graduate or post-experience (including senior secretarial experience) courses give special scholarships to women or make special arrangements to attract more women students. *All* post-graduate and post-experience courses are useful for potential returners and usually accept women who have been away from their jobs for some time: Returners' maturity, life-experience and managing home, family (and specially voluntary work) are recognized as being valuable in management jobs. The Diploma in Management Studies (see **Training**) can be particularly useful for returners – and it can be taken full-time (with TOPS grants) or part-time.

Course organizers report that the numbers of women returner-applicants is disappointing – probably not all potential students know about courses in their area. Some courses set up specially for returners have folded because of lack of applicants. Post-graduate and post-experience courses still have few women applicants. For example in 1983 only 18% of applicants for the London Business School's Master's Programme were women. Still only 5% of the Business Graduates Association members are women – and membership ensures that graduates can keep in touch with developments in business. So while at present a career-break still hinders women's promotion prospects considerably, women do not seem to do as much as they could to ease their return.

Part-time: Few opportunities at present; possibly more in future.

Further information

No one specific information point; see various business functions and Universities' and polytechnics' prospectuses.
CRAC Course Guides: *Which Degree*

Management Consultancy

This is, usually, a 'second career' – see below.

The term 'management consultant' is often used rather loosely for people without specific qualifications who advise on business matters. However, the Institute of Management Consultants says that only professionally qualified people who have had at least 5 years' management experience are able to carry out 'the consultancy function' efficiently. The IMC defines the work as 'identifying and investigating problems concerned with policy, organization procedures and methods; recommending appropriate action and helping to implement recommendations'.

Management consultants are, basically, troubleshooters. They may, for example, be called in by a food manufacturer to investigate the reasons for the company's declining market-share. Before producing a plan of action to improve matters, the management consultants (either one or a team of specialists) thoroughly research the firm's organization, its potential, *and* the competition. They might then suggest the company should widen, or narrow, or change, its product-range; or they might recommend changes in the company's marketing strategy, its management structure, its industrial relations policy, the introduction of new technology – or a combination of any of these and perhaps other strategies. The work requires a thorough understanding of business practice and organization, of economic and technological trends, experience in gathering information and in dealing with people at all levels within an organization.

Management consultants also advise non-profit-making organizations such as charities, local authorities, arts centres: in fact any organization which is either being criticized for lacking in efficiency, or which realizes it could improve its working pattern.

Because the field is so wide, consultants tend to specialize, either in one type of organization – manufacturing (possibly one particular type, say, engineering or high technology or food); hotel/catering; local authorities; or in one 'function' – accountancy; production; or – and this is a recent development – in 'managing change' (see also Management, p. 271), i.e. helping to organize the smooth transition from traditional to new technology-based working patterns.

Consultants are, or work closely with, specialists in various fields – systems analysts, engineers, production managers, etc.

The work requires ability to work as one of a team as well as to take independent decisions which may well be opposed by the people they affect; self-confidence; persuasive powers; ability to express complex matters concisely and simply.

A few management consultancies take on graduates (any discipline) to do 'leg and desk research' (i.e. collect information from people and printed sources), but the normal way in is with a professional qualification *and* management experience.

Position of women There are very few women management consultants – so few women have got the necessary management experience! However, a (relatively) large proportion of women have specialized in 'managing change' in offices, and in advising on the implementation of equal opportunities policies.

Further Information Institute of Management Consultants, 23/4 Cromwell Place, London SW7 2LG

Related careers *Accountancy – Computers – Engineering – Marketing – Operational Research – Personnel – Purchasing and Supply – Shipbroking and Freight Forwarding – Work Study*

Marketing and Selling

Consumer goods and services marketing – industrial marketing – international marketing – selling – export

Entry qualifications Nothing specific; for Institute of Marketing's qualification: 1 A-level, 4 O-levels including English or 3 years' experience at age 21 or BTEC National. Considerable *graduate* entry.

The work Effective marketing is the key to profitability at home and essential for Britain's trading position in the world economy, i.e. for export. Marketing goods and services is as skilled an occupation, and as important, as producing them. But marketing is a vague term, used loosely to cover a range of activities. Different establishments interpret the term differently, and titles vary enormously – brand manager; product manager; development manager; marketing executive; marketing manager; export manufacturing manager, etc. Titles do not necessarily indicate any particular level of responsibility or scope.

The Institute of Marketing defines the purpose of marketing as follows: 'Marketing is the management process responsible for identifying, anticipating and satisfying customer requirements profitably' – at home and, vitally important, abroad.

Marketing people (sometimes called 'marketers') find out what customers want or, more importantly, can be persuaded to want, at what price, and then relate potential demand to the company's ability to produce whatever it is, get it to the 'point of sale', and do all that profitably.

Marketing involves researching the market and analysing research results – which involves devising and organizing surveys and interpreting the results; discussing results with accountants, production, distribution and advertising people. Marketers may suggest the company adapt its existing products to cope with the competition's better products, or with changes in buying habits, or they may think up a totally new product and help to develop and launch it, or they may introduce a better after-sales service.

All these activities have always been carried out in business, but as business has become more complex and professionalized, with decisions being based on researched facts and, above all, figures rather than guesswork and experience, the 'marketing function' has become a 'business profession' and even a degree subject.

Marketing is often split into *consumer goods and services marketing*; *industrial marketing*; and *international marketing* (which could refer to either, and is part of the export business).

In all these activities, marketing involves several types of work: detailed research to establish customers', and potential customers', needs, and potential needs: what type of customers, where, might buy at what price, with how effective an after-sales service, etc. Whether it is yet another washing powder or, in industrial marketing, a new piece of office machinery or computer, a new magazine or a food product, the procedure is basically the same. In *industrial marketing*, an engineering or science background is useful, but people switch from one kind of marketing to another. In *international marketing*, a thorough understanding of other nations' cultural as well as social and economic set-up is vital (and of course speaking the relevant language). Perhaps the most crucial among several other marketing activities is *sales forecasting*. How many cars with what particular features will country X be willing to buy in 2, 5, 10 years' time?

Marketing people must always base their conclusions on researched social and economic trends, which include statistics – though marketing has a glamorous image, the basis of it is the correct interpretation of statistics.

Though the majority of marketing people work in large, often multi-national, companies, increasingly medium and small companies are separating the marketing function from general business management.

Selling is both a career in itself, and an essential part of (and the best way into) marketing. The two are closely linked: *Marketing* finds out what customers want and helps to put the goods/services on the market; *Selling* is concerned with finding and dealing with customers for the product/service.

There are different kinds of selling – and various ways of categorizing sales staff. A useful division is between consumer goods selling, and specialized selling. In consumer goods selling (this totally excludes retail and door-to-door selling), sales representatives, or reps, sell to wholesalers and/or, more usually, to retailers. Selling to retailers involves 'merchandising', which means helping the retailer to maximize sales, by promotion campaigns, suggesting ideas for improving shop display, etc. Reps may also advise retailers on new sales techniques, shop display, etc. There is a hierarchy in consumer goods selling, with the field sales supervisors and area sales managers in charge of reps, and sales managers and directors at head office directing the whole sales operation.

Speciality or technical or industrial selling is usually done by staff with technical background and perhaps production management experience (see p. 171). An engineering background is particularly useful (see Engineering, p. 168). The speciality selling process differs totally from consumer goods selling: purchasing decisions are made not by shop-keepers or store buyers, but technical and financial experts. To effect one sale may take months of negotiations, and extensive after-sales service. Speciality sales staff do not necessarily sell only standard products – whether it is a large piece of machinery or machine tools – they may agree for their company to modify a product or produce a 'one-off' piece of equipment.

A sales rep may form part of a team, or be the only rep in the firm. She may have a 'territory' in this country which may require her to be away from home for several days most weeks, or it may be a territory near home – it depends on the kind of product (how many potential buyers there are within an area). Export sales executives of course travel extensively.

Prospects Depend on economic climate. However, the importance given to marketing in business has grown enormously in recent years. Poor marketing in the past is blamed for poor business performance. This applies particularly to international marketing. As exporting is becoming more and more essential for economic survival, international marketing is becoming a vital function in many more businesses. Marketing people have good prospects of going to the top in general management.

Pay: High to very high (see p. xxiii).

Training There are various ways into marketing – the most usual way to start is as sales rep. Production (see Engineering, p. 171) people often move into marketing (which is usually better paid). Many graduates go straight into marketing as assistants.

While working as trainee or whatever the title, marketing staff can take part-time courses for the Institute of Marketing's Certificate and Diploma examinations.

As *Export Marketing* is a growing specialization, some trainees work for the Institute of Export's examination, by day-release or correspondence study. The syllabus adds export procedure and principles of export management to marketing methods, principles and procedures.

Pre-entry training is either by Business Studies degree with marketing option; or by specialized marketing degree. These degrees either link marketing to a specific area such as chemicals or textiles or engineering; or concentrate on international marketing and export. An engineering or science degree is a good way into speciality selling.

There are also BTEC Higher awards (see p. xvi) with marketing export options, and distribution options.

Personal attributes *Marketing*: A high degree of business acumen and of numeracy; a little gambling instinct; self-confidence; ability to assess the effects of events; ability to stand perhaps unjustified criticism when forecasts turn out wrong, due to unforeseeable causes; social awareness and interest in social and economic trends; ability to communicate easily with colleagues and clients, whatever their temperament and their degree of expertise.

Selling: Numeracy; extrovert personality; ability to establish instant rapport with people; judgement; sensitivity for gauging right approach to customers; indifference to the occasional rebuff; enjoying being alone when travelling; willingness to be away from home a lot.

Late start Not advisable to start from scratch, but people with technological or business qualifications can switch to marketing.

Position of women This is an area in which personality counts more than qualifications. Women have good prospects if they fit the employer's idea of what the 'right type' for any particular job is. In other words, they still have to be better, and more highly motivated, than the men with whom they compete. In export marketing their scope is limited because employers fear that in many countries saleswomen and women negotiators are not acceptable. Graduate women stand much better chances than school-leavers, who tend to be offered secretarial jobs 'with a view to progressing in marketing', and then do *not* progress. Graduate sales reps who are good at their job say they are at an advantage: they tend to be noticed and 'trained up'. So far, however, there are very few women sales directors (except in cosmetics, etc.). Potentially it could be a promising area. Especially in specialized *selling*, more women would be genuinely welcome in many organizations. Companies say that not enough women graduates apply. The proportion of female graduates *accepted* is slightly higher than that of males accepted. Probably women who do apply are more highly motivated. It is too early to say, however, what women's promotion prospects to senior sales management positions are.

Career-break: It is not likely that in this competitive field it will be easy for any but the best and most determined women to return to what is essentially still a young and a men's career. Women with technological or science degrees or experience stand the best chances in industrial marketing.

Part-time: Only in backroom research – very few openings indeed.

Further information Institute of Marketing, Moor Hall, Cookham, Maidenhead, Berks, SL6 9QH
Institute of Export, World Trade Centre, London E1 9AA

Related careers *Advertising – Management in Industry and Commerce – Public Relations – Retail Management*

Medical Laboratory Scientist

In the National Health Service, the title is now Medical Laboratory Scientific Officer, but especially for people in training, the term 'technician' is often used.

Entry qualifications Science A-levels, but see **Training**.

The work Medical laboratory scientists and technicians are concerned with laboratory investigations for diagnosis and treatment of disease, and research into its causes and cure. While training, medical laboratory technicians and scientists work under the overall direction of senior staff who have specialized in the application of their particular discipline to medicine. Work is done in hospitals, universities, blood transfusion centres, public health laboratories, veterinary establishments and pharmaceutical firms. In hospitals, there may be some contact with patients. It varies according to specialization.

Medical laboratory scientists specialize in: clinical chemistry: the analysis of blood and other biological materials; medical microbiology: the isolation and identification of bacteria and viruses from patients with infections, or in water and foodstuffs; haematology and serology: the study of blood; histopathology and cytology: the study of tissues removed during surgical operations and at post-mortem examinations, and in investigations for the early detection of cancer.

Prospects Fair but best for graduates. Scientists can move from one type of laboratory to another; some scope abroad.

Pay: Medium to high (see p. xxiii).

Training Theory and practice differ:

In theory it is possible to start with O-levels in biology or human biology, chemistry, physics and maths and a subject proving an adequate standard of English. Such entrants can take either a 2-year day- or block-release course while in relevant employment, for the BTEC National Certificate in Science. They can then go on to the BTEC Higher National Certificate in Medical Laboratory Sciences after a further 2 years.

Alternatively, students with the above O-levels can take a 2-year full-time BTEC National Diploma in Science and then a 3-year sandwich BTEC Higher National Diploma in Medical Laboratory Sciences, and *then* apply for a job.

Holders of A-levels in *either* chemistry and another science or maths *or* biology and another science or maths provided chemistry has been studied at A-level, can start immediately with the BTEC Higher part-time or full-time course.

In practice it is *highly* unlikely that anyone with fewer than two science A-levels (one of which should be chemistry) and good supporting O-levels will now get a training vacancy which will lead to membership of the IMSL – and such membership is essential for a job as Medical Laboratory Scientific Officer. An increasing proportion of entrants are graduates. For biochemists, degrees are now mandatory. Relevant degree disciplines are chemistry, microbiology, biological sciences, physics, and biochemistry.

There are now also vocational degrees in Medical Laboratory Sciences and in Bio-Medical Sciences, but these limit graduates' job-choice more than do other, less vocationally-orientated, science degrees. Graduate IMLS students normally are eligible for IMLS membership after 1 year's practical experience. Certain IMLS-approved degrees exempt students from further (day-release) study.

Personal attributes An interest in the medical applications of science; scientific aptitude and technical skills; patience; liking for experimental and for routine work.

Late start Possibly for those with up-to-date science and willingness to work for very low pay while on day-release. Better opportunities for career-changers from related fields (nurses, for example).

Position of women The ratio of men to women is approximately 10:7 (among those aged over 24 years, approximately 10:5 and among those aged 16–24 years, approximately 7:5).

Career-break: Opportunities for returners if they have kept up with developments.

Refresher courses: A few 'updating' lectures, but would not help people who are out of touch; some useful evening courses.

Part-time: Few opportunities. No reason why job-sharing (see p. xxiv) should not be tried.

Further information

Institute of Medical Laboratory Sciences, 12 Queen Anne Street, London W1M 0AU
Council for Professions Supplementary to Medicine, 148 Kennington Park Road, London SE11 4BC

Related careers

Medicine – Pharmacy – Radiographer – Science Technician – Scientist – Technician Engineer

---

Medicine

General practice – community medicine – hospital service – research and teaching – industrial medicine

Entry qualifications Precise requirements vary between medical schools but usually 3 A-levels, in chemistry, physics, biology, zoology or maths, lead to exemption from the 'First MB' course (which most medical schools do not run now). But applicants with other good A-levels, even if entirely on the arts side, may be offered a place on condition that they obtain 3 good science A-levels (i.e. they are offered a conditional place 1 or 2 years ahead). 2 O-level sciences and O-level maths are essential for this conditional acceptance.

Doctors can work in a variety of settings:

General Practice (Family Doctor)

The work This absorbs about half of all those who qualify. The vast majority work in contract with the National Health Service. They may also take private patients; but these account for a very small proportion of the general practitioner's work.

A GP spends from 2 to 5 hours holding surgeries on weekdays and visits patients when necessary. She must be available for emergency calls at all times or arrange for someone to stand in for her. The majority of GPs work in some form of partnership, either with a doctor whose surgery is nearby, or with one or several doctors in 'group practice', sharing premises and the services of a secretary-receptionist, and possibly of a nurse and/or health visitor or social worker. Such arrangements solve the problem of isolation which used to affect single-handed young GPs who missed discussion with a colleague.

GPs spend much time discussing patients' personal problems which are often the real cause of symptoms. Perhaps the main difference between general practice and hospital work (working in medical specializations) is that general practitioners 'treat the person, not the illness'. The therapeutic value of 'talking to the doctor' is great; general practitioners must be as much interested in helping people cope with their problems as in medical science.

In many areas there are now part-time hospital appointments for general practitioners. This enables GPs to combine general practice with specializing in one aspect of medicine. These GPs' hospital jobs are *not* 'training posts' (see below, **Training**, post-graduate). Unemployment has risen, but not as sharply as in hospitals.

Prospects Vary from one geographical area to another, but good on the whole. British qualifications are recognized in Eire, most Commonwealth countries and in EEC countries.

Pay: Medium to high, depending on size of practice (see p. xxiii).

Community Medicine (formerly Public Health)

The work Community medicine is primarily concerned with preventive medicine. It deals with health problems as they affect whole communities and particular geographical, occupational and age groups. For example, inhabitants of certain areas may need attention because of air pollution dangers; workers in certain industries may need regular checks because of occupational hazards; schoolchildren, expectant mothers, the old and the handicapped need special provision.

Community physicians' work also includes the overall administration, planning and development of the 3 branches of the health service (environmental health, personal health, community care); the development of comprehensive information; and health education services. Community physicians also act as advisers to local authorities, which retain responsibility for running school, environmental and some personal health services.

Environmental health covers infectious disease control and prevention (regular immunization and special immunization campaigns); food and other hygiene inspection; prevention of insanitary conditions in restaurants, shops, housing (including overcrowding); control of noise nuisance and air pollution. The day-to-day work is carried out by environmental health officers (see p. 192).

Personal health services cover provision of ante-natal, post-natal and child health clinics; midwifery; home nursing, district nursing services (see separate entries); care of handicapped children.

Community care covers provision for the care of the mentally ill and handicapped who live at home or in hostels; support in the home by social workers; day centres for the elderly and handicapped; social clubs; hostel accommodation and organization; cooperation with local voluntary organizations in the mental health field.

Prospects This is an expanding field, but job prospects are affected by public expenditure cuts.

There is some confusion about the similarities and differences between the new community physicians' work – and therefore prospects – and that of the traditional local-authority-employed public health doctors. Amongst the latter were many women who staffed clinics; this provided excellent opportunities for part-time work. But the new community medicine specialists, by definition, are concerned with groups rather than individuals. Clinics are not likely to be staffed by *community* medicine specialists, but by GPs or by specialists in paediatrics, geriatrics, etc. There are opportunities for part-time sessional clinic work, but for that community medicine is not the speciality to choose. Mature entrants (returners) are very welcome.

Pay: High (see p. xxiii).

Hospital Service

The work At the top are consultants who have specialized in a particular field of medicine, such as child health or obstetrics or surgery. There are over 40 specialities. Training under the consultant, and doing most of the day-to-day routine work, are senior registrars, registrars, and house officers. Most of them are studying for various specialist examinations. Students usually decide on a particular specialization during their general medical training, not before. Hospitals attract doctors who like working in teams with other medical staff.

Prospects Vary greatly from one speciality to another. Unemployment amongst doctors has gone up sharply, especially in the London area. In many fields there are far more senior registrars than there are consultant vacancies. Prospects are better in 'shortage' specialities, such as radiology; psychiatry. Consultants may take private patients, but private practice makes up a very small proportion of the work of all but a minority of consultants. During training doctors should be prepared to change their minds about eventual speciality, if it seems advisable.

Pay: Low to very high for a consultant (see p. xxiii).

Research and Teaching

The work Research into new forms of treatments and new drugs and their effects is done in hospitals, research establishments and drug firms. Doctors can, and usually do, combine clinical and scientific work, but there are also research appointments, often including some teaching, for those who are interested in the scientific side of medicine rather than 'patient contact' (see Science, p. 426).

Prospects Fair.

Pay: Medium to high (see p. xxiii).

Industrial Medicine or 'Occupational Health'

The work Industrial medical officers give medical check-ups to employees and work with personnel departments. They also do research into occupational health, studying the effects of diverse environmental conditions on health and efficiency of the staff.

Prospects Fair.

Pay: High (see p. xxiii).

Abroad (all doctors): To work in EEC countries, it is essential to speak the relevant language fluently. The developing countries do not offer as much scope as is generally supposed, but there are some opportunities, mainly in paediatrics, obstetrics, and preventive medicine.

Training (all doctors) This is in 2 parts: pre-registration and post-registration. Doctors must obtain a 'registrable qualification'. There are several, each signified by different initials; all are essentially of equal value.

The basic course takes 5 or 6 years. It usually falls into 2 parts. The first is the *pre-clinical* course, which lasts 2 years and covers anatomy, physiology and biochemistry. The work consists of lectures, laboratory work and a great deal of reading. The *clinical* course lasts 3 or 4 years. Students are attached to a succession of consultants in different specialities (firms). They have contact with patients, take case histories and, under supervision, make diagnoses and give treatments. The clinical course is extremely hard work, with little spare time.

Before students get their registrable qualification they must spend a 'pre-registration year' as full-time resident junior house officer in hospital. (At this stage they start earning.)

Post-registration training is essential, very hard work, and rather haphazard. Everybody has to arrange their own succession of hospital 'training posts', each training post has to be 'accredited' as such by the relevant Royal College (for example a training post in surgery has to be accredited by the Royal College of Surgeons). Post-registration training in a succession of accredited training posts as house officer, registrar, senior registrar takes from 3 to over 10 years (it depends mainly on the specialty chosen). During this period of full-time work, doctors study for specialist examinations.

In 1982, 3-year post-graduate training for principals in *general practice* became compulsory. It consists of 2 years in a choice of specified full-time hospital and community medicine posts, and 1 year as a full-time trainee in general practice (or the equivalent on a part-time basis).

Personal attributes The ability to take responsibility and to make vital decisions after weighing up all the relevant factors; self-confidence; conscientiousness; resourcefulness; the energy and stamina to work hard for long and often irregular periods; great powers of concentration; above-average intelligence; good health.

Especially for general practitioners and the hospital service: patience with people unable to express themselves clearly; sympathy without emotional involvement; understanding of and liking for all types of people and tolerance with human weaknesses.

For research: patience for long-term projects and an inquiring mind.

Late start Individual medical schools vary in their policies on accepting mature candidates, so one has to inquire from several before giving up – if determined to start; it becomes very difficult if over 30. Length of training is not normally reduced even for qualified nurses or people with other related qualifications.

Position of women Proportions of women as practising doctors in some fields (1982):

	Consultants in:	*Registrars* in:
General Surgery	0·9%	5%
Paediatrics	16%	37%
Obstetrics and Gynaecology	11%	26%
Psychiatry (child and adolescent)	38%	54%
Psychiatry (mental handicap)	25%	36%
Geriatrics	9%	15%

General practice (principals): 18%; trainees about 50%.

Present training patterns (see **Training**, post-graduate), established long before there were many women doctors, are more suitable for men than women who wish to combine medicine with child-rearing. Yet 44.8% of entrants to medical school in 1983 were women, and by the late 80s the proportion is expected to be 50%. The male/female proportion of entrants to medical school reflects that of applicants very fairly: there is no discrimination at the entry stage, but indirect discrimination is built into the traditional training and employment pyramid. Some women still complain about discriminatory attitudes in some medical schools and hospitals. It is essential for women to plan their careers carefully (including spacing of their children) and to follow definite aims with determination.

If a profession's structure is unsuitable for half its members, that structure must change. The Medical Women's Federation has fought for years for more part-time post-graduate training posts and some have existed for 10 years. In 1979 the DHSS issued an important Memorandum which stated: 'It is important that optimum use is made of all our doctors and dentists including those only able to work part-time for domestic or other reasons. It will be particularly important to provide posts for women doctors and dentists who wish to complete their training or to work part-time while they raise their families.' The DHSS action was not taken in order to be fair to women, but to reduce the wastage among expensively trained women doctors who give up work/further training in their thirties.

The Memo gave details of arrangements agreed between the DHSS and the profession, which should make it 'neither easier nor harder to obtain a post in a given specialty' for people who can train only part-time.

Implementation of the DHSS proposals – i.e. the setting up of part-time training posts and their 'accreditation' as training posts – still depends on regional health authorities' and the various Royal Colleges' willingness to adapt existing training patterns. Part-time posts are available mainly in shortage subjects (for example, geriatrics, paediatrics, radiology) rather than in prestigious specialties where competition is very keen even for full-time training-post applicants.

The DHSS Medical Manpower Division is monitoring the scheme. If regional health authorities and Royal Colleges do not increase part-time training posts, it will 'reconsider the situation'.

Once qualified, women specialists probably have no more difficulty getting full-time consultants' posts than men (i.e. it depends on their specialty and the part of the country in which they want to work); but there are at present very few part-time top jobs and far more men than women consultants combine part-time hospital posts with private practice. In specialties where full-timers are expected to be on call 24 hours a day (surgery or obstetrics for example), far fewer women than men can compete. Experiments with job-sharing and similar arrangements have shown that such schemes can work well. Most women doctors work full-time. If they choose part-time work in hospitals they should realize that part-time posts are usually 'non-career'.

In *general practice* women can choose whether they want to work part- or full-time. Most practices today very much want a woman partner, and part-time work does not necessarily affect career prospects.

Career-break: Some attempt has been made to adapt career patterns to women's needs. Under the DHSS's Doctors Retainer Scheme, women who, because of domestic commitments, work less than 2 sessions a week, and who intend to return to medical practice when they are more free again, receive an annual retainer of £155 (1984). In return, they undertake to keep up their Registration, to read a professional journal, attend at least 7 'education' sessions a year, and take at least 12 paid service sessions a year.

It is possible (though complicated) to do the *post-registration training* (see above) in part-time training posts, but it is almost impossible to resume training if the break was made *before* completing the pre-registration year as resident junior house officer.

Refresher courses: With the help of the Medical Women's Federation and Postgraduate Dean's committee, *ad hoc* arrangements can often be made.

Part-time: See **Position of women**.

Further information

The British Medical Association, BMA House, Tavistock Square, London WC1
Medical Women's Federation, Tavistock House North, Tavistock Square, London WC1

Related careers

Dentistry – Medical Engineering – Nursing – Occupational Therapy – Ophthalmic Optician – Orthoptics – Osteopathy – Pharmacy – Physiotherapy – Science – Social Work – Veterinary Surgeon

NOTE: Applicants who fail to get a training place should decide whether what attracts them to medicine is dealing with people, or the scientific aspects. Such careers as nursing or physiotherapy do not offer comparable scope. Another science which may lead to medical research may be a more satisfying second choice than one of the auxiliary medical careers.

NOTE ON ALTERNATIVE MEDICINE: In September 1983 a group of NHS doctors formed the British Holistic Medical Association. Holistic medicine aims to treat the patient as a whole, rather than as a series of parts, and concentrates on a preventive and educational approach. The Association hopes to form a bridge between conventional medicine and alternative therapies which have become increasingly popular in recent years. These include osteopathy (see p. 353), chiropractic, naturopathy, herbal medicine and acupuncture. None is as yet recognized by the NHS and many different organizations offer training (standards may vary). Most require A-levels for entry and most have their own systems of registration and codes of practice. There is no central source of information. The following are some useful addresses:

Anglo-European College of Chiropractic, 13–15 Parkwood Road, Boscombe, Bournemouth BH5 2DF

National Institute of Medical Herbalists, 48 Forest Road, Tunbridge Road, Kent TN2 5EY

British College of Naturopathy and Osteopathy, 6 Netherhall Gardens, London NW3 5RR

The Traditional Acupuncture Society, 115 Loxley Road, Stratford-upon-Avon, Warwickshire CV37 7DS

Merchant Navy

Engineer officer – deck (navigating) officer – radio officer – catering officer – assistant purser – children's hostess – nurse – stewardess – ship's doctor

Entry qualifications *Engineer, Deck and Radio Officers*: normally 4 O-levels including maths, English and physical science. *Catering Officer*: BTEC Hotel and Catering Operations (but see **Training**).

The work

Engineer Officers

They are responsible for ships' engines including heating, pumps, etc. They ensure that the ship sails smoothly and efficiently; supervise repairs at sea and overhauls in port. When on watch, the engineer monitors the engines, now usually done with computerized equipment. Modern ships' engine-rooms are clean, airy and contain a mass of electronic equipment. They have nothing in common with old-fashioned boiler rooms.

Engineer Officers are in charge of and responsible for the work of engine-room staff; so managing people is part of the job, as of all ships' officers.

Deck (Navigating) Officers

They navigate the ship. In port they are responsible for efficient loading and unloading, which involves both mathematical and common-sense problem-solving, especially in ships which carry a variety of cargo, simultaneously or in succession. They are responsible for controlling large numbers of seamen; in port they may negotiate with stevedores and others concerned with loading and unloading.

Deck Officer is a step on the ladder to becoming Captain or Master.

Radio Officers

They maintain communications between ships and between ship and shore. Systems vary according to size and age of ship, from morse to satellite-assisted transmitters. They may also operate radar, close-circuit TV and depth-sounding apparatus. In highly automated ships – most of the supertankers and container ships – there may also be an Electronics Officer, who could be either an engineer or a radio officer.

Catering Officer (called Purser or Hotel Manager on cruise liners; sometimes Chief Steward on tankers, etc.)

Responsible for purchase, storage, preparation (supervision) of food, meal service, maintenance of accommodation. On liners, they are also responsible for passengers' banking, information and entertainment services.

Prospects Very poor. Virtually no recruitment at the moment. Conditions at sea have changed dramatically. The bulk of merchant navy tonnage now consists of tankers, supertankers, container ships and other bulk-carriers. Over half of these vessels are less than 5 years old, and living conditions for crews are far better than they used to be (and still are on passenger liners). Everything is being done to minimize boredom and irritation which tends to arise when groups of people live and work together in a close community. Vessels now often have single or double cabin accommodation, TV rooms, spacious lounges. Life at sea in modern ships is a mixture of modern technology and traditional hierarchy. Modern vessels have family accommodation so that officers can bring their wives.

Pay: Medium to occasionally high (see p. xxiii).

Training 1. *Engineering Cadets (trainee officers employed by shipping company)*

(a) With 4 O-levels to include maths, physical science and English: 4-year course for BTEC National Diploma and Higher National Diploma. A few opportunities exist for those with less than the above qualifications to follow a (possibly longer) BTEC National Higher or National Certificate course. All cadets take the Department of Transport Class 4 Certificate examination at the end of the training.

(b) With A-level maths and physics studied, and a pass in one of them: 3½-year sandwich for BTEC Mechanical Engineering (Marine).

(c) With A-level maths and physics: BSc in Marine Engineering.

2. *Navigating Cadets (trainee officers employed by shipping company)*

(a) With 4 O-levels including maths, physics and English: about 3½ years for BTEC Diploma in Nautical Science, leading to D. Tp. Class 3 Certificates or, with lesser qualifications, leading to Class 4 and 5 Certificates.

(b) With A-level (subjects as above): 2½-year 'accelerated cadetship' leading to D. Tp. Class 3 Certificate.

(c) With 2 or 3 A-levels (1 in physics or maths) and 3 O-levels: B.Sc. Nautical Science, 5- to 6-year sandwich course.

3. *Radio Officers (employed normally by radio companies)*
Unlike cadets they must get their qualification, the General Radiocommunications Certificate, *before* going to sea. They need O-levels in maths, physics and English and then take a 2-year basic Certificate or, more usually, 3-year full-time course for the City and Guilds Final Technician's Certificate and the Department of Trade Radar Maintenance Certificate.

4. *Catering Officer*
Boys start as Catering Rating. Women are not accepted at National Sea Training College for catering training; they start higher up the ladder with Hotel and Catering Operations BTEC award (see p. xvi).

Other Opportunities at Sea (very limited):

5. *Assistant Purser*
Must be over 21, have good shorthand/typing, a foreign language, 4 O-levels.

6. *Children's Hostess*
Must be RSCN (Registered Sick Children's Nurse, see p. 328) or teacher.

7. *Nurse*
Must be experienced RGN (see p. 325) and over 26.

8. *Stewardesses on ferries and passenger liners*
Employmennt largely seasonal, experience of domestic work in hotels and a foreign language useful. Not a career with prospects.

9. *Ship's Doctor*
Newly qualified doctors often work as ship's doctors for a few months. So far *very* few women, but on vessels with adequate accommodation theoretically no bar.

Personal attributes

For women: self-sufficiency, as being the only, or one of two or three women among large groups of men, can be lonely; indiffference to standing out in a crowd and therefore being constantly 'on show'; practicality; resourcefulness; ability to supervise and control men at work; gregariousness; willingness to take orders and accept one's place in the hierarchy, coupled with ability to take responsibility and make instant decisions.

Position of women

It is on ships with this type of accommodation that most women officers and cadets sail. There are some female *ratings*, but as most deck and catering ratings are trained initially at the Sea Training College, where girls are not admitted, female ratings can only enter the Merchant Navy by applying for a *job*, not for training. Their hopes of promotion to Petty Officer and beyond are slim. However, girls are being recruited as *Deck Officer Cadets* by a number of companies and a few are being considered as *Engineer Cadets*. There have been women *Radio Officers* for some years. More women would be welcomed as Deck, Engineer and Radio Officers. *Catering Officers* have rather less scope, mainly because the majority of Catering Officers come up through the ranks, after training at the Sea Training College.

In November 1980 the first woman got her Master's Certificate which qualifies her to be Master – Captain – of a foreign-going vessel. There are now about 100 women Deck and Engineer Officers in the British Merchant Navy – more than in any other Western merchant fleet.

Further information

Individual Shipping Companies.

Related careers

Services – Shipbroking

Meteorology

Entry qualifications *Scientific Officers*: A degree in maths, electronics, physics, meteorology, computer science or a BTEC Higher award (see p. xvi) in applied physics or a mathematical subject.

Assistant Scientific Officers: At least 4 O-levels including English language and maths or physics or general science. Many have better qualifications.

The work The Meteorological Office is responsible for weather forecasts for the Forces, Civil Aviation, the Merchant Navy and government departments, public corporations, local authorities, the press, television, radio, industry, as well as the general public. It also does research.

Scientific Officers

Entrants with good honours degrees do research; others become forecasters or support scientists (see Science Technicians, p. 441). Shift work may be necessary.

Assistant Scientific Officers

They do a variety of jobs. At airfields they read meteorological instruments, record the information and then pass it to Air Traffic Control (see p. 111) for transmission to aircraft, and, in international code, by teleprinter for national and international use. They plot weather maps and graphs and answer telephone inquiries as well as pass on warnings of impending bad weather to such bodies as local authorities and others who need such information. They also do statistical and computational work; some are trained as computer programmers. They must be prepared to work anywhere (often in isolated locations) in the United Kingdom, and move when required. They must work unsocial hours if necessary. They may have to do shift work.

Prospects Competition for vacancies is very keen. Once in, there are reasonable prospects for promotion if a higher qualification in a relevant subject is gained. (Day-release may be granted.) There are now also a few opportunities for experienced meteorologists outside the Civil Service, to supply oil rigs with forecasts, for example.

Pay: Medium to high (see p. xxiii).

Training Initial training at residential Meteorological Office College is 4 weeks for Assistant Scientific Officers and up to 5 months for Scientific Officers, followed by on-the-job training.

Personal attributes Self-sufficiency; the ability to work in a team; great interest in science.

Late start There are no age limits, but young entrants are preferred.

Position of women At the moment the ratio of men to women is 11 to 1; among new entrants it varies between 4 to 1 and 7 to 1. Few women at the top.

Career-break: Women are eligible for re-instatement (see Civil Service, p.129), though need for mobility and to work unsocial hours prevents most mothers from returning. Also weather forecasting and reporting procedures are changing all the time and potential returners must have kept in touch through extensive reading and attending lectures.

Part-time: Few opportunities, but job-sharing is under discussion.

Further information The Secretary, Meteorological Office, Met 0 10 Recruitment, London Road, Bracknell, Berkshire, RG12 2SZ

Related careers *Science*

Modelling

Live – photographic – commercials

Entry qualifications No educational requirements. Minimum height requirements usually: for women: live modelling 5 ft 8 ins, photographic modelling 5 ft 6 ins. For men: 5 ft 11 ins.

Live

The work A showroom or house model, is employed on a permanent basis by wholesale, retail or couture houses, or works as a freelance. A show model works freelance during the fashion collections and at other shows during the year.

The designer usually 'builds' his/her originals on models who have to stand for hours while cloth is being draped and pinned. Modelling clothes to customers involves changing outfits at top speed – and yet looking cool and perfectly groomed. Freelances are busy only for a few weeks each in spring and autumn when the trade shows its collections to press and buyers. Then models have to rush from one show to the next.

Photographic

The photographic fashion model may work in cramped studios; in August she may swelter in heavy tweeds; in December she may pose by the sea in a bikini. She dashes from one appointment to another, carrying all accessories she may possibly need – she usually has to provide her own. She has irregular meals. There is the very occasional Mediterranean cruise or flying visit to a foreign city when exotic backgrounds are used for a magazine fashion feature, but these usually come the way of top models only.

She is booked for photographic sessions and is normally freelance. The work may be for fashion articles, mail order catalogues, or advertisements. A versatile model can display anything from tights to toothpaste, diamonds to deodorants. Some, especially the few top international models, work exclusively in fashion.

TV Commercials

In TV commercials and films the work is now nearly always done by actors and actresses (i.e. Equity members, see Acting, p. 11).

Television commercials are made under film studio conditions, and may take anything from half a day to several days to make. Most of the time is spent waiting while shots are 'set up'. The actual 'takes' are done quickly, but each one may be repeated over and over again.

Prospects *Live model*: She may earn less than the photographic model, but her working life is longer – if she keeps her figure.

Photographic model: There are rarely more than a dozen top models at any time, and only the most versatile, who can virtually change their whole appearance and personality to meet changing fashion trends, last more than a few years; photographers then start searching around for new faces. Currently the demand is for schoolgirls, for whom the work is very temporary. Many photographic models started as live models.

Even if successful, a short working life, especially for women. If a model is put under exclusive contract for one product, and appears in advertising campaigns to promote it, she may earn a large salary for a year and become famous; but because her face has become associated with one product, she will not be used for another product for some time afterwards.

Some lucky and intelligent women eventually get jobs as fashion consultants or commentators, in public relations, in retail stores or on magazines; a few remain – or come back later – as 'older' or 'mature' models, for whom there is a small but steady demand. Men usually start modelling a bit later in life than women. They should qualify in some other work first, to which they can return if their 'type' goes out of fashion or they get too old.

Pay: Low to very high (see p. xxiii).

Entry and training There are several methods of entry: (a) by direct approach to wholesalers' showrooms; (b) through a photographer or fashion editor; (c) (most likely) through a good model agency. If they think someone has potential they will arrange test shots, make-up lessons and training in how to wear and show clothes; how to walk; and how to pose for the camera. A few agencies run schools, but it is essential to choose carefully: one sign of a good one is that it rejects applicants who show little chance of succeeding in this highly competitive and over-glamorized field. Good schools turn down well over half the applicants. Applicants should beware of private establishments calling themselves modelling academies. These are more properly called 'grooming' schools, which can help to give a girl confidence. Whatever they claim, no school can teach someone to be a model.

There is one course run by the local education authority. It is held at the London College of Fashion and lasts 1 year full-time. Girls must have 3 O-levels and must be between 5 ft 6 ins and 5 ft 8 ins. Syllabus includes English, German, French, anatomy and hygiene, knowledge of materials, business studies, salesmanship, history of costume, model training, an appreciation of clothing manufacture, millinery and accessories, hairdressing and beauty culture.

A note on male models: men do not need special training – agencies can see from a snapshot whether a man has modelling potential. If he has, the agency will teach him the necessary tricks of the trade. Male models should be about 6 feet tall and have a chest size of 38 inches. They should be older than women when they start. Like women, men need to be versatile and willing to promote all sorts of goods apart from clothes.

Personal attributes Shape and looks currently fashionable; for photographic models, good bone structure and elusive photogenic quality. A strong feeling for clothes and the moods which go with them – the casual air for tweeds and sportswear, the regal air for furs and jewellery; the faculty for lending glamour to even the dullest clothes, in fact, some acting talent; a flair for fashion trends, to be always ahead with the newest hair-dos, make-up, etc.; iron constitution; total reliability; visual imagination; unwavering self-confidence; indifference to being turned down by photographers; adaptability; infinite patience; perseverance; ability to remain calm and keep smiling and to appear interested, however bored or tired.

Late start Not recommended for women – see *Career-break*.

Career-break: There are some jobs for 'mature' models, but fewer even than for young ones.

Part-time: Most work is part-time, except for top photographic models, and permanent showroom models.

Further information No central organization.

Related careers *Acting – Advertising – Fashion – Journalism – Photography*

Motor Mechanic

Entry qualifications Nothing rigid; none required for courses leading to City and Guilds exams (see p. xx) but employers are in buyers' market and prefer people with CSE in maths or a technical subject.

The work Mechanics work *either* in garages to which vehicles are brought for servicing or repair *or* for organizations owning fleets of vehicles. Organization of work varies according to type and size of garage/workshop. For example, in a small roadside garage a mechanic might deal with customers direct and then carry out whatever servicing/repair is required; in a large garage a reception engineer or service manager (who may or may not be a promoted mechanic) would instruct the mechanic what to do. Mechanics occasionally take a mobile repair van to a broken-down vehicle. Work varies from quick and easy repairs to long jobs involving diagnosing faults and doing complex repairs, possibly calling on the help of colleagues with other special skills, for example, auto-electricians.

In workshops where organizations' fleets of vehicles are serviced, mechanics have contact mainly with other mechanics and there tends to be a hierarchy; in repair/service garages there is more contact with the general public and less of a hierarchy.

Workshops and garages are usually noisy and often cold and, naturally, the work involves getting dirty.

Prospects Good for trained mechanics.

Pay: Medium to high (see p. xxiii).

Training Traditional apprenticeships are now rare. Instead, employers offer 1-year, annually renewable, 'traineeships', or simply take on trainees or juniors – titles vary. Most employers grant day- or block-release for study of the City and Guilds certificates for, usually, Light or Heavy Vehicle Mechanics, Vehicle Electricians, Vehicle Bodybuilders, Light Vehicle Repairs, and Motor Cycle Mechanics. If day- or block-release is not granted, mechanics are strongly advised to go to evening classes – theoretical training must complement on-the-job experience as motor vehicle technologies are constantly changing and getting more complex.

City and Guilds Certificates (which can only be taken by people in relevant employment) are in three parts. Normally everybody takes Parts One and Two which leads to recognition as a craftsman/woman. Each Certificate course usually takes 1 year by day- or block-release; at least 2 by evening study only, but individual colleges' arrangements vary. Part Three is taken by people who want to specialize, and covers eight short modules, in, for example, automatic transmission, electrical components, heavy vehicle air brakes, etc. Students make up their own package of modules according to interest and local requirements (and availability at local colleges). The modules can be taken over a period of years – Certificates are issued for each individual module.

Entrants with at least three CSE Grade 3 (in practice colleges usually demand higher qualifications) can also study for BTEC (see p. xvi) awards. The courses are rather more theoretical and, in the motor repair trade, are of no greater value – possibly less valuable than the City and Guilds Certificates. It is likely that overlapping BTEC and City and Guilds courses will eventually merge; the availability of two similar courses is due to historical developments rather than logic or need.

Personal attributes Mechanical aptitude; ability to work as one of a team and also to take responsibility. There is scope for backroom work and for mixing-with-people work; ability to work under pressure. Indifference to getting dirty and cold.

Late start People who have had relevant experience in motor mechanics or similar work may enter directly into the Part Two City and Guilds examination – each case is judged on its merits.

Position of women *Very* few women at the moment – because *very* few apply. Those who do apply are usually highly motivated, and for that reason do not often have difficulties being accepted. (Women who believe they are refused jobs because of their sex should get in touch with the Equal Opportunities Commission, see p. xxxii.)

Career-break: Too early to say what effect it might have.

Part-time: Very rare at present, but it, and job-sharing, should be easy to organize, especially at garages which are open longer than the normal working day.

Further information City and Guilds of London Institute, 76 Portland Place, London W1N 4AA

Museums and Art Galleries

Entry qualifications

For assistants: In theory 4 relevant O-levels plus reading knowledge of at least 1 foreign language; most have far higher qualifications.

For conservation officers and technical assistants: A science degree and/or art-school training (not necessarily at degree level, depending on the work).

For assistant keepers and research assistants: A relevant good honours degree, or diploma in art history usually followed by post-graduate study, plus a reading knowledge of at least 1 foreign language. Specialist knowledge may, in exceptional cases, be acceptable as an alternative qualification.

Degrees in subjects such as English literature, or languages, do not normally lead to museum work. See **Training**.

The work

Professional museum staff are usually called keepers or curators. Duties vary according to type and size of museum or art gallery. Most of the work, except that on the technical side, is concerned either directly or indirectly with helping the public to understand and enjoy the exhibits, and to induce more people to visit the museum. The work is by no means mainly backroom research; it is a combination of research, administration, and public relations. It may not involve direct contact with people, but it is certainly concerned with their interests.

The traditional museum skills were *research*, *classification*, *conservation* and *identification*, now the most important museum skill is *communication*. Museums and art galleries are trying to shed their image of solemn shrines devoted to earnest study of art and history; they are becoming more welcoming places which visitors want to go on visiting and which fit into children's learning-by-discovery process (see Teaching, p. 520). Saturday clubs, junior centres, weekend seminars and various other 'participation' schemes are run for children and adults by museum education officers (titles vary). Many of these are experienced teachers with a flair for showmanship (and for controlling children in a free-and-easy atmosphere). Individual schemes vary greatly and include, for example, studios for art and craft work; making and playing with replicas of old toys; examining scientific instruments; 'acting out' or thinking up stories about paintings on show; joint projects with local history, archaeology, conservation societies, as well as with local radio stations, or local authority planning and architects departments.

In some museums a good deal of time is spent answering the public's questions, both personally and by letter. Objects brought in for identification may range from live insects to old paintings and pieces of pottery dug up in the garden.

Conservation officers work on the restoration, repair, protection and conservation of exhibits. Senior conservation officers are scientists by training, art historians by inclination: their work is a unique combination of scientific work, art appreciation and knowledge of art history. Senior conservation officers may research into new methods of conservation. The practical work is done by conservators, technical assistants, or craftspeople who have had art-school training but not to degree level.

Most large museums are staffed by Civil Servants. In local authorities' small museums, qualifications required vary. Jobs in private art galleries are nearly all at secretarial level. A flair for business and dealing with clients may, occasionally, lead to more responsible work.

Prospects Not good. There is great competition for few vacancies. Promotion to senior posts is slow, and may require moving to another museum.

Pay: Medium (see p. xxiii).

Training A variety of full-time and part-time courses exists in conservation. Specializations range from masonry and antique clocks to archives and monumental stained glass. Entry requirements vary; most courses are heavily over-subscribed (and may change from time to time). The following are the main courses:

After entry into museum work:

(a) On-the-job with tutorials and short courses, for the Museums Association's Diploma. Syllabus covers museum administration, collection, preservation, preparation and storage techniques. Studies are related to the branch of museum work in which the student specializes, such as art, archaeology, ethnography, natural history, etc.

(b) If mainly concerned with conservation and restoration: Part-time day-release for Museums Association's Certificate which is in 2 parts: (i) City and Guilds Science Laboratory Technician's Certificate; (ii) course on museum techniques which is recognized by Museums Association.

(c) Technical assistants doing purely practical work may take the Museums Association's Technical Certificate after 3 years' work.

Before entry into museum work:

(a) Post-graduate (any degree) courses in Museum Studies, which lead to partial exemption from Museums Association's Diploma.

(b) Institute of Archaeology's (London University) degree in Conservation (normally chemistry at A-level required). Syllabus covers applied chemistry, archaeological draughtsmanship, photography, conservation technology, recording systems, care and restoration of pictures.

There is a waiting list for vacancies; applicants frequently go into museum laboratories as juniors and take this course later. It may then be possible to take it in 2 years instead of 3.

Personal attributes Intellectual ability; a love of knowledge for its own sake; organizing ability; visual imagination; a lively curiosity; an understanding of laymen's interests and tastes; communication skills; patience for waiting for the right job and promotion.

Late start No objection in theory; entry requirements to Museums Association's Diploma might even be relaxed, but young entrants likely to be taken in preference for junior jobs.

Position of women The ratio of men to women is about 6 to 4 amongst assistant keepers and keepers, but there are very few women museum directors.

Career-break: No objection in theory but keen competition from young post-graduates might cause problems.

Part-time: No (though there is no reason whatever why this should not be possible).

Further information Museums Association, 34 Bloomsbury Way, London WC1A 2SF
Local museums
UK Institute for Conservation, c/o Conservation Dept., Tate Gallery, Millbank, London SW1P 4RG (send sae with inquiry)

Related careers *Archaeology – Archivist – Art and Industrial Design – Information Officer – Librarian*

Music

Performing – teaching – recording studios – music therapy – administration – musical instrument technology

Entry qualifications

Acceptance at music colleges depends on performance at audition. For most performers, except for singers, intensive musical training must have started by their teens at the latest.

For teaching, see p. 520. For degree courses at least 2 A-levels and 3 O-levels, with, usually, A-level music.

Performing

The work

The provincial, the BBC symphony orchestras, and opera houses normally employ orchestral players on a full-time basis; the London-based national orchestras are made up largely of freelance musicians who are, however, booked regularly and paid a fee for each session. They undertake to do a certain percentage of their work for the orchestra and can then take on other sessions outside. Singers may be salaried members of a chorus or freelance.

Most freelance musicians, however devoted to serious music, are glad to work as 'session players' on TV commercials, film background music and other light music recording sessions, etc. A violinist may play in a concert at the Festival Hall on one evening and the following day in a TV jingle recording session.

A freelance musician has to fit in work as it comes. The work may fluctuate from three daily sessions (3 hours each) over a long period, to no work for many weeks. Long practice at home is always necessary. TV, radio, live concerts or recording sessions are arranged well in advance, and accepting bookings requires careful judgement. Once a date is booked, it is unwise to break it, even if a better engagement is offered.

The musician's work is physically exhausting, and may include travel over long distances, combined with rehearsals and nightly performances, often in cold or overheated halls. An engagement for a season with a ballet or opera company may involve 5 performances a week with as many rehearsals, and practice at home. The atmosphere amongst musicians is usually friendly, although the competition is keen.

Part-time teaching, either privately or in schools, gives many freelance musicians a supplementary income. However, it is often difficult to fit in performing engagements with teaching.

Teaching

As the main job this is quite a different career. Teachers are employed in primary and secondary schools. They teach music either full-time in one school, possibly with a second subject, or part-time in various schools, and/or youth clubs and evening institutes run by the local education authority.

There is scope for imagination and initiative. The music teacher's main job is to promote interest and enthusiasm, as only a few pupils take music examinations. She may start an orchestra, or record evenings; organize record libraries, visits to concerts, etc.

Recording Studios – Sound Engineering

For broadcast sound engineering see Television, Film and Radio (p. 534). Sound engineers (not to be confused with qualified engineers) in recording studios are responsible for the overall recording quality and for interpreting the producer's ideas. They need a grasp of basic physics and electronics in order to understand their equipment, but they do not need great technical knowledge to start with (most enter as tape operators or assistant engineers). Some highly qualified and experienced sound engineers may be called music technologists. They apply advanced science and technology to the creation and reproduction of sound. They work on the design and manufacture of equipment, as well as in recording studios and broadcasting.

Prospects *Orchestral performing*: Not very good at the moment. It is estimated that only about 1 in 10 of music students who finish their full training (itself restricted to the good students) eventually makes a living as a performer. Only one in many hundreds becomes a soloist. Good luck is nearly as important as talent.

Singing: A good deal of evening and weekend work in cities which have choirs.

Pianists: Particularly poor performing prospects because they are restricted to solo-playing or accompanying.

String players: Better numerical opportunities in orchestras.

Pop, folk and jazz: A short career for most performers.

Teaching: Fair. There is a shortage of music teachers in some areas.

Composing: Not a career in the usual sense. Those who have the talent need a full musical training (composing is included in some courses).

Sound engineering: Difficult to enter as record companies in recession.

Really good engineers always in demand and a few become producers. Limited openings as yet for music technologists as still a relatively 'new breed'.

Pay: *For performers*: Depends entirely on ability and luck. *For teachers and recording studios*: Medium (see p. xxiii).

Training

Either 3–6 year full-time graduate course at a college of music; the period of training need not be decided at the outset. Students choose *either* the teaching *or* the performing course after the first year, but it is sometimes possible to switch from one to the other later in the course.

The syllabus normally includes a principal subject and a second study subject. Instrumentalists play two instruments. Singers may either take an instrument as a second study or they may take speech training, or speech and drama. Other subjects included are music appreciation, theory and history of music, aural training, choral and opera study, orchestra practice, and often a language.

Or a BA in Music. Most degree courses are largely academic and theoretical. At some universities music can be taken as a subject in a general arts degree.

To teach music in schools, courses must be followed by 1-year course of professional teacher training (see Teaching, p. 520). At some colleges music can be taken as a main subject in a BEd course. Instrument teachers do not necessarily need professional teacher training.

Sound engineers learn on-the-job and via in-service courses. A few are given day-release for the only part-time course in Sound Studies (at North London Polytechnic). Music technologists need a degree in physics, electronics or a combined music/physics degree.

Personal attributes

For performers: Apart from outstanding talent, the qualities of perseverance, resilience, courage, and indifference to setbacks; the ability to work as one of a team; a pleasant manner; good health; very wide musical interest; good sight-reading speed; willingness to work outside the musical field between engagements. *For teachers*: As for teaching (p. 527), plus creative imagination and initiative.

Music Therapy

This is a small but growing field. Music therapists work with physically or mentally handicapped children and adults. Music can contribute to the development and treatment of handicapped and maladjusted people in various ways – by helping to relax their bodies and minds, as a mental stimulus, and as an emotional outlet. Autistic children, for example, and severely withdrawn adults, who do not respond to any other form of activity and cannot form relationships, often benefit greatly from listening to, and making, music.

There are 1-year full-time post-graduate courses in music therapy. Candidates must have had at least a 3-year full-time musical education or have a music degree. Some work full-time in one hospital, most do 'sessions' in several centres. The work needs maturity and sensitivity.

Music Administration

There is much more to running an orchestra, opera house, festival or regional music or arts centre, than most prospective musicians (and audiences) realize. An Arts Administration course (see Art and Design, p. 69) can be useful, but is not essential. Administrators are employed by orchestras, operas, concert managers, agents and concert halls. Their specific responsibilities and degree of decision-making varies, but they may cover anything from transport to publicity; finance to bookings. They must combine exceptional organizing ability; flair for public relations and programme-building. Though they would not normally be entirely responsible for programme-building, they often have to persuade artistic decision-makers to include the right amount of popular items in programmes to ensure the necessary minimum of 'full houses' during a season. Music administrators need not be music specialists. Previous experience in public relations, journalism, marketing or finance can be just as useful as a music degree.

Musical Instrument Technology

For musical young people who want to learn a craft, there is some limited scope in *musical instrument technology*, which means repairing and making musical instruments. There are 2- and 3-year courses leading to City and Guilds certificates and college certificates and a 4-year BTEC Diploma/Higher Diploma course for 16-year-olds with, normally, 3 GCEs, preferably including maths and any craft subject. Students usually specialize in 1 group of instruments: piano (including tuning); early keyboard instruments; woodwind; strings; fretted instruments (lutes, guitars). All these specializations are craft-workshop-based. Another specialization is electronics (BTEC only), related to the manufacture and repair of musical equipment – it is electronic-lab based and requires ability to cope with physics. This offers probably the best prospects.

There is a steady demand for *piano tuners*. Training is *either* as above in musical instrument technology, *or*, for those with fewer qualifications, there are traineeships with 3-year block-release for City and

Guilds certificate in String and Keyboard Instrument Manufacture (i.e. pianos and harpsichords).

Position of women

About 10% of Musicians Union members are women (and virtually all professional performers are union members); but normally more than half of music students are women. Women orchestral players were barred until very recently from several of the well-known orchestras (with the exception of harpists), and even now the proportion is below 10%. Women musicians have suggested that auditions should be held with performers playing behind a screen so that the sex of the players is not known. However, the suggestion has not been widely taken up, if at all, and women still appear to be discriminated against – though it is probably impossible to prove discrimination.

Career-break: It is unlikely that performers can resume orchestral playing after a long gap unless they kept up with serious daily practice; but there should be no problem returning to teaching.

Part-time: *Performing*: work as freelance is possible in many areas – but work tends to be sporadic rather than regular part-time. *Teaching and music therapy*: part-time should be possible, but not necessarily exactly where one wants it.

Further information

For early training: Local Education Authority music adviser.
For music colleges: Department of Education and Science, Elizabeth House, York Road, London SE1 7PH; *Scotland*: Scottish Education Department, St Andrews House, Edinburgh 1
For music therapy: British Society for Music Therapy, 69 Avondale Avenue, East Barnet, Herts EN4 8NB
For musical instrument technology:
London College of Furniture, 41 Commercial Road, London E1 and other individual college prospectuses

---

Related careers

Dancing – Teaching – Television, Film and Radio

Nursery Nurse/Nursery Officer/ Nanny

Nursery classes and schools – day nurseries – residential nurseries – hospitals – private nanny – children's hostess

Entry qualifications None laid down for National Nursery Examination Board's Certificate, but most colleges demand as least 2 O-levels; most entrants have more; some have A-levels.

The work Nursery nurses look after children under 7. They are primarily concerned with healthy children (they are now often called nursery officers), but in this context 'healthy' may include 'disturbed' and also physically and mentally handicapped.

Nursery nurses' functions cover very much more than physical care and supervision of young children. Young children learn through play and through communicating with other children and with adults; they need adequate stimuli and individual attention to ensure their healthy intellectual, emotional and social development. When nursery nurses read to children, talk to them individually, discuss, say, their painting efforts, and generally help them to enjoy nursery activities they are, in effect, teaching.

Nursery nurses work in various settings:

1. *Nursery classes and schools* (for 3 to 5s) and *infant schools* (5 to 7s), run by local education authorities. Nursery nurses help organize play activities; read to and play with children. Usually 1 nurse is responsible for a small group of children. A qualified *nursery* or *infant teacher* (see p. 521) is normally in charge.

2. *Day nurseries*, run by social services departments for under-5s (mainly 3 to 5s) who are at risk socially, physically or emotionally; and for children where both parents have to go out to work or for other reasons cannot satisfactorily look after them during the day. There are now very few places for children whose parents merely think that nursery is a Good Thing; such children either go to private day nurseries (which also employ nursery nurses) or play groups, which usually cannot afford paid staff.

A large proportion of children in day nurseries are disturbed so work is very demanding. Occasionally staff involve mothers in the nursery's activities – largely to help mothers understand the children's needs and development. Staff may also do unofficial 'casework' (see Social Work, p. 476).

3. *Residential nurseries*, also run by social services departments for under-5s who cannot be looked after at home: they are 'in care' either short-term because of a parent's illness, a new baby, temporary homelessness, etc., or long-term because of family breakdown, mother's death, etc. Whenever possible, healthy young children in long-term care are placed in foster-homes, so that a relatively large proportion of those in residential care are disturbed or physically or mentally handicapped, and they may have behaviour problems: for example be disruptive, bad-tempered, unresponsive.

Usually, each nurse is responsible for her own small group – it may be only 2 or 3 children. Staff try and establish a family atmosphere. (Residential nurseries may be housed in a small family house, on an estate.) Staff do not have to live in, though they usually have to be on duty and sleep in some nights.

4. In *hospital*, nursery nurses help to look after babies in maternity wards, and on children's wards they amuse and feed children. Actual nursing is done by registered nurses (see p. 322).

5. The largest single group – over one third (1983) – work in private families, as '*nanny*'. This is a recent development, due (a) to the cutback in public sector jobs, and (b) to the increasing number of families in which both parents go out to work and need someone to look after their children in their absence. Present-day nanny-ing is very different from the traditional nanny's work who took charge of children whose mothers had no time or inclination to look after their children themselves. Today's nannies share the care of the children with their parents.

A variety of working patterns is emerging: some live-in nannies take charge of a young child or 2 or 3 children all day, and then in-between the end of the school day and a parent's return from work (and perhaps during the school holidays), they may look after several school children whose parents share the nanny's salary. Other nannies work 2 days for one family, 3 days for another if the mothers concerned are themselves part-timers and only need part-week nannies. Work in a family differs from that in institutions in that nannies are on their own: nobody to ask for help in emergencies, and much of the time no other adult to talk to. The work is both more responsible and lonelier. It may also be less hard work. Most nannies do some housework or at least cook for the children while the parents are at work.

6. A *very* small proportion work in hotels and holiday camps as *children's hostesses*.

Prospects *Daily nannies*: Very good. *Public sector* jobs: not very good because of public spending cutbacks. But nursery nurses who take the new post-Certificate courses will have fair promotion prospects and become officers in charge of nurseries of all kinds, at home and abroad.

Experienced nannies can get jobs abroad. They can later often get into public sector work as family-experience proves they can take responsibility.

Pay: Good in private families; not very good in public sector work.

Training

1. The usual methods: minimum age 16. A 2-year course at colleges of further education for the National Nursery Examination Board's Certificate. Students spend three-fifths of their time at college, two-fifths on 'placements' working with children. Most placements are in public sector nurseries, etc., but since 1982, colleges often include days-only placements in private families. The mother – or father if he looks after the children – must have been a teacher, nurse, nursery nurse or social worker for the placement to be acceptable as a 'teaching placement'. Students do not normally have sole charge of children or get experience of 24-hour care and do not get 'the feel' of being a nanny where both parents work.

The NNEB syllabus includes the study of care and of the social, emotional, physical and intellectual development of children from 0 to 7; children's social, emotional and physical needs to ensure normal development; causes of and dealing with physical and mental handicap and disturbed behaviour; importance and significance of play, companionship, communication; promotion and maintenance of health (including nutrition and prevention and control of infection); organizing play activities (which includes things like making toys from egg-boxes, etc.); patterns of family life and social institutions – and changes in both; how the social services work; arts and crafts; some general studies. The syllabus was updated recently and now includes rather more on the changing patterns of family life; on the situation created by both parents going out to work; on the relationship between the nanny in a private family and her employers and it also includes subjects to help students develop their own personality and interests. In fact, despite the unusual (for this type of demanding syllabus) starting age, the NNEB Certificate is being upgraded in professional terms and now caters both for students who just want to look after children and for those who want to make a career in child-care. (Further changes are under consideration.)

In 1983 the first few pilot post-Certificate courses were introduced. Courses are planned to last at least 2 years, on a day- or block-release basis and students can specialize in special groups, such as handicapped or disturbed children, ethnic minorities, or in nursery-management. Tutor-courses are also planned (at the moment, teachers on nursery nursing courses are usually social workers or nursery nurses who have taken Further Education Teacher's courses

(see Teaching, p. 531). (Another way of learning to be a nanny: work as mother's (or parents') help.)
2. 18–24-month courses at the 3 private Association of Nursery Training Colleges. Students must be at least 18; most look after children privately, to make sure they like the work, in-between school and college. Private colleges prepare students for the NNEB examinations and for their own diplomas.
NOTE: The National Association for Maternal and Child Welfare runs courses which, though not recognized as a qualification for public sector work, leads to work as mother's (or parents') help and nanny. Courses last 1 or 2 years and apart from general child-care also include O-level subjects for students who want to improve their general education. Course structure, length and content vary; some courses are integrated into the school curriculum, others are parallel with NNEB courses, at FE Colleges. No entry qualifications are laid down.

Personal attributes A way with young children; patience; imagination; willingness to take responsibility and to work hard at routine chores; ability to work well in a team; interest in mental, social and physical development of children.

Late start It is difficult for mature students to get training places; special courses for mature students were phased out, but a few determined career-changers have got training places and done well.

Position of women About 97% women's occupation; no reason at all why this should remain so – men welcome on courses and in jobs.

Career-break: No problems for people who are able and willing to work long day and residential nursery hours or as daily nannies.

Part-time: Little opportunity at present in social services department nurseries and in infant nursery schools and classes, but growing opportunities as daily nanny – working for women who are themselves working part-time.

Further information National Nursery Examination Board, Argyle House, 29–31 Euston Road, London NW1
National Association for Maternal and Child Welfare (NAMCW), 1 South Audley Street, London W1Y 6JS
Local authority education or social services departments

Related careers *Nursing – Social Work – Teaching*

Nursing

Registered general nurse – registered sick children's nurse – enrolled nurse – registered mental nurse – registered nurse for the mentally handicapped – occupational health nurse – district or home nurse – health visitor – midwife

'Nursing' covers a range of jobs which vary widely in terms of levels of responsibility, professional qualifications required, environment worked in. There is therefore scope for people with widely differing aims, interests, abilities. Some nurses, for example, concentrate entirely on practical bedside nursing; others manage whole hospital groups' nursing services (jobs which equal top executives' in industry in terms of power, pay, and responsibility). Then there is scope for people interested in the impact of new technologies on nursing procedures; for those interested in psychiatry, in the sociological and psychological aspect of patient-care, or in preventive medicine in the community. Nurse-training can also lead to jobs not directly concerned with the care of the sick, both in and outside the hospital (for example specialist publishing; management and administration).

Nursing is *not* a second-choice career for people unable to get into medical schools (or put off medicine by the long training). The two professions are complementary and suit people with very different aims and personalities. A vital difference is that the doctor's contact with the patient is fleeting and episodic, while the nurse must establish and keep up a relationship with the patient (this applies even to nurses who after a few years' ward-nursing opt for other specializations). Nurses are team workers, doctors are not. The nursing scene has changed greatly in recent years. More than any other profession, nursing has been affected by women's wider choice of occupation and it has now to compete for the right applicant with other professions. Today's nurses are professionals who want a caring job, but nevertheless expect better conditions of work than their predecessors did. They now work a 37½ hour week; most live out and those who live in nurses' homes are free to come and go as they wish; instead of autocratic matrons there are approachable – and often quite young – senior nurses. *Very* gradually, pay is creeping up. In some hospitals or wards nurses are called by their first name both by patients and by senior nurses. The doctor–nurse relationship has changed too. The extent of change depends of course on personalities and seniority of nurses and doctors in each case, but there is generally today much more joint decision-making, and more mutual respect for the other's function. Within each of the specialist nursing professions there are opportunities for working in a variety of environments.

The patient–nurse relationship is changing too: nurses – at least in up-to-date hospitals – no longer 'nanny' patients, instead the emphasis is, at least in theory, on 'consultation between equals'.

However, nurses' work is much more difficult to define than other professionals' because there are so many, and some contradictory, facets to it. For example, as the nurse must establish a relationship with her patients, she must be prepared to do basic bedside nursing-chores. Yet the nurse is also a highly-trained professional, who takes vital decisions and uses highly sophisticated equipment.

General, *sick children*'s, *enrolled* and *psychiatric nurses* work mainly in hospitals; *occupational health nurses*, *home* or *district nurses*, *midwives* and *health visitors* work mainly in the community and tend to work more independently, away from the sheltered hospital atmosphere.

Prospective nurses can ask local hospitals to show them round, or even spend a day in the various types of hospital, to see for themselves.

Entry qualifications

On 1 July 1983 the organization of the nursing profession, and nurse titles, changed. Enrolled and registered nurses as well as midwives and health visitors are now organized by one body, the United Kingdom Central Council for Nursing, Midwifery and Health Visiting. The UK Central Council lays down minimum entry requirements and examination standards, but individual English, Welsh, Scottish and Northern Ireland 'National Boards' are free to set their own standards as long as they are not *lower* than those set by the UKCC. National standards may change from time to time as local conditions change; so prospective nurses, midwives and health visitors must check current local requirements.

New Titles

Registered General Nurse/RGN – formerly State Registered Nurse/SRN
Registered Mental Nurse/RMN – same as before
Registered Nurse for the Mentally Handicapped/RNMH – formerly Registered Nurse for the Mentally Subnormal/RNMS
Registered Sick Children's Nurse/RSCN – same as before
Registered Midwife/RM – formerly State Certified Midwife/SCM
Registered Health Visitor/RHV – formerly Health Visitor/HV
Enrolled Nurse (General)/EN(G) – formerly State Enrolled Nurse/SEN or Enrolled Nurse/EN in Scotland and Northern Ireland
Enrolled Nurse (Mental)/EN(M) – formerly State Enrolled Nurse (Mental)/SEN(M)

Enrolled Nurse (Mental Handicap)/EN(MH) – formerly State Enrolled Nurse (Mental Subnormality)/SEN(MS)

There are now two 'levels of training': 'first level' for registered nurses, midwives and health visitors; 'second level' for enrolled nurses.

Entry requirements from January 1986 for first level training (i.e. all registered nurses, midwives, health visitors): 5 O-levels *or* 'the required standard' of pass at the UKCC's new own entry test. It is expected that the 'required standard of pass' will vary according to the type of nurse training applicants want to start. For example, people wanting to do mental handicap nursing will not need to reach the same *academic* standard as do registered general nurses; but the former must have the 'relevant competencies' – i.e. they must have the personal qualities needed for looking after the mentally handicapped (see **The work**, p. 332, below). Individual schools of nursing – quite apart from National Boards – will continue to be free to ask for higher than the minimum standards.

Schools of nursing attached to teaching hospitals have asked for A-levels for some years now, sometimes even for 2 sciences at A-level.

The UK Council does not lay down specific subjects amongst the 5 O-levels, but first level applicants will probably be expected to offer *at least* one science and English (or Welsh as applicable).

Second level training from 1986: In theory, no entry requirements. In practice, it is highly likely that, as now, most schools of nursing will expect at least two good CSEs, possibly including a science.

In practice, entry requirements will continue, as at present, to depend on the supply and demand situation. (City and Guilds Foundation Course in Community Care normally counts as one O-level for both levels of training.)

Until 1986: The minimum entry requirements for *first level training* are 2 O-levels including English or Welsh language or literature and proof of a satisfactory standard in 5 other subjects; or 3 O-levels, one of which must be English or Welsh language or literature. In practice the vast majority of accepted student nurses have had higher entry qualifications for some years now (see above).

Enrolled nurse (*second level training*) until 1986: No specific requirements. In practice, most schools of nursing expect 2 O-levels or exceptional personal qualities.

Also *graduate* entry. See **Training**.

Working in Hospital

Registered General Nurse – RGN (formerly State Registered Nurse – SRN)

Entry qualifications See p. 324.

The work Nurses now apply what is called 'the nursing process': they are trying to get away from the image of nursing as a collection of separate tasks – from giving out bedpans to doing the round with the consultant. Instead, 'patient care' now comprises assessing, discussing, and planning for individual patients' needs – and then putting the plan into operation. Normally, every nurse is, on each duty round, allocated a number of patients to look after. That includes accompanying consultants on their rounds as well as ensuring that the patients are washed, sent for treatment, etc. To carry out the 'nursing process', nurses need extensive knowledge for a variety of highly complex, responsible tasks. These include: administering a vast array of drugs in the right dosages and understanding what side effects to watch out for; using highly sophisticated machines on the wards and in coronary and other intensive care units; keeping records on patients and knowing at all times what changes if any have occurred in their patients' condition; organizing the ward team; discussing patients' conditions with relatives and doctors; helping distressed patients to come to terms with their situation; trying to allay anxious patients' fears. A nurse may have to decide whether a patient's condition warrants sending out an emergency call for the doctor, and she may suggest in discussion with the doctor that the social worker (see p. 476) should come and help sort out a patient's domestic problems. She also helps with the teaching of nurses in training.

Prospects NHS cuts have affected employment opportunities: especially newly-qualified nurses have to search for jobs. However, once in hospital, a nursing qualification can lead to a variety of jobs. At the top of the hierarchy, nurses, jointly with doctors and administrators, are now responsible for running hospital and community health services (see Health Service Administration, p. 214). Staff nurses can choose whether to stay on the wards, or to go into teaching, administration or clinical specialization.

On the wards, in *clinical nursing*, responsibilities are extending as treatments become more sophisticated, requiring nurses to have technical skills and theoretical knowledge of a high professional order.

Clinical nurses can become specialists in theatre work, intensive care units, children's or geriatric nursing, and do research into new techniques and procedures. Specialist nurses may be in charge of numbers of specialist wards or units within a group of hospitals and act as clinical consultants to junior staff and colleagues.

Nurse-teaching is a vitally important nursing specialization suitable for nurses interested in teaching skills and training methods and organization. Nurse-tutors take various courses which academically are at university-lecturer standard and so are at the same level in the hierarchy as Nursing Officers in charge of a group of hospitals.

The third specialization is as *nurse-manager*. She is not as much directly concerned with patient-care as with the smooth and efficient running of a complex organization. The work resembles management in commerce and industry; a large number of people carry out a variety of vital, interrelated activities which have to be coordinated. These 'managers' may have greater job-satisfaction than managers at that level in industry, because the end-product is the well-being of patients. Nurse-managers normally take a succession of management courses, some of them general senior management courses, attended by managers from industry as well; the principles of management are the same, whatever the organization to be managed. Managers work in the hospital and in the community.

Nurses who want to move out of hospital can become *health visitors*, *occupational health nurses*, *district nurses*, *midwives*, or work for general practitioners' group practices. There are also opportunities for nurses with several years' experience, in the Services (see p. 466), in health education – lecturing to schools, various clubs, etc., and doing research in nursing or in medicine; in journalism and in the Civil Service, and in agency nursing.

Pay: Medium (see p. xxiii).

Abroad: RGN qualifications are now accepted in the EEC and most other countries.

Training

The basic training takes just over 3 years at about 225 schools of nursing, which are based on hospitals. The broad curriculum is laid down, and the individual schools' 'training programmes' are approved by the National Boards (see above, p. 323) which are in charge of nurse education and training. Training must now include several weeks each in psychiatric, geriatric, obstetric and community nursing (i.e. nursing outside the hospital). Organization of individual training programmes varies from one hospital to another. Ideally student nurses should be students first and nurses second. While it is generally agreed that nurse training must always be on-the-job, the success, and the method with which schools solve the dilemma of their dual responsibility – to patients and to students – varies greatly.

It is quite illogical that, while prospective degree students carefully consider where to study their subject and finally choose after having studied 'course comparison guides' and university or polytechnic prospectuses, nurses tend to choose where to train rather haphazardly and to go by the advice of someone who trained years ago. Prospective nurses should at least consult the *Directory of Schools of Nursing*, write for a number of prospectuses and visit several schools before making their final choice.

Nursing as a degree subject

It is envisaged that about 5% of nurses in future should be graduates (this proportion has not been reached yet). There are now about 24 courses which lead to a degree either *in* Nursing plus Registration, or to a degree in the social or the natural sciences *as well as* Registration. Nursing as a degree subject is still in the experimental stage and the two ways of graduating are on trial. The main differences between the two types of degrees are (a) the Degree *in* Nursing is shorter – it takes about four years, and (b) all students on the course are going to be nurses. The degree which combines nursing with another subject (a) takes four and a half to six years; (b) it qualifies students in a specific degree subject other than nursing and thus leads to two qualifications; (c) nurses study together with students who are not going to be nurses. (The drop-out rate among nursing degree students is around 14% – the normal degree studies drop-out rate; compared with more than double the drop-out rate from traditional (often haphazardly chosen) nurse training.)

Three part-time (day/block-release) degrees in nursing for qualified RGNs exist; and eight shortened (2-year) courses for graduates with 'relevant' degrees. It is up to individual nursing course directors to decide what is a relevant subject – but it is normally one which includes social or natural sciences.

Graduate nurses are not necessarily promoted more quickly – they start as staff nurses like other RGNs, but their dual qualification widens their opportunities in nursing and outside it. A graduate nurse is eligible for any 'graduate job' where degree subject is not specified (and that covers one third of all graduate jobs in industry and commerce).

Likely changes in training

Training may change in the next few years. Nothing is definite yet, but proposals include lowering of minimum age to 17; *all* entrants, regardless of entry qualifications, to start with common 18-month Certificate course; post-Certificate courses to lead to variety of Registration and post-Registration qualifications and specializations; more degrees in nursing.

Personal attributes Common sense, practical bent; sympathy for the sick and the old without sentimentality; an interest in medicine without morbid curiosity about illness; sensitivity coupled with a certain amount of toughness so as not to get too emotionally involved; organizing ability; patience; a sense of humour to put up with the inevitable occasional short tempers and difficult people; ability to know when to be firm – and how to be firm but not rude; powers of observation; initiative; ability to take responsibility one moment and to do exactly as told the next; good health.

Registered Sick Children's Nurse – RSCN (Paediatric Nursing)

Entry qualifications See p. 323.

The work This is much the same as for RGN plus keeping children amused, and dealing with relatives rather more. Nursing sick children can be both more rewarding and more arduous than nursing adults. Many children stay only for a very short time; others stay for longer because they are very seriously ill and/or suffer from a rare condition which has to be assessed. Increasingly, paediatrics is very much concerned with detection and follow-up of physical and mental handicap. Some paediatric nursing is highly specialized, with nurses having taken post-qualification specialized training.

Modern children's wards are run to resemble home conditions as much as possible. Visiting is now normally allowed at all times; rigid tidiness and regimentation is frowned upon. Mothers or fathers often stay in hospital with their young children and/or help to bath, feed and generally look after their children.

Prospects Fair. Jobs for children's nurses are not as readily available as they used to be. There are a few jobs in hotels, with airlines, as nannies at home and abroad, in boarding schools and as school nurses.

Pay: Medium (see p. xxiii).

Training Separate training for RSCNs has been stopped. There are now 2 ways of training for sick children's nursing: (1) a combined 4-year course for RGN/RSCN; (2) a 13-month post-registration (i.e. post-RGN) training for the Register of Sick Children's Nurses.

Personal attributes The same as for the general nurse; plus extra patience and a way with children. A sick children's nurse must be able to talk to children on their own level. Many of the best children's nurses come from big families. Good powers of observation are essential, as small children cannot explain their ailments.

Enrolled Nurse (General) – EN (G) (formerly State Enrolled Nurse – SEN)

Entry qualifications See p. 323.

The work Enrolled nurses undertake routine nursing duties of a standard no less high than that of their registered colleagues, but different in the range of functions performed and the degree of responsibility.

They do most of the bedside or practical nursing, in fact most of the work generally thought of as the essence of nursing: giving immediate attention to patients' well-being. Their work is complementary to that of the RGN, though it requires less medical knowledge and carries less responsibility.

The work of ENs often overlaps with that of RGNs; especially, but not only, with that of student nurses. Their working hours and conditions are exactly the same as those of RGNs. They share RGNs' social facilities, dining rooms, nurses' homes, etc.

ENs can also specialize in Mental Handicap Nursing and in Mental Illness Nursing (see p. 330). A large proportion work in geriatric wards where, in practice if not in theory, they may be in total charge.

Prospects Fair. There are opportunities for promotion to senior enrolled nurse for those who have been on the Roll for at least 3 years. A senior enrolled nurse's responsibilities are similar to those of the staff nurse. A wide choice of post-enrolment training courses prepares the EN for specialized work, including work in district, psychiatric or geriatric nursing. In fact ENs have scope in the whole field of clinical nursing careers, but not in teaching, administration, and health visiting. *(No opportunities abroad.)*

Pay: Medium (see p. xxiii).

Training ENs train for 2 years *either* in general *or* in one of the two kinds of psychiatric nursing (see below and p. 330). Training is almost entirely practical, on the wards. Pupils watch, are told what to do, and then do it. In the second year there is an 'assessment': senior hospital staff observe and assess the way pupils carry out their duties; the only written test is a simple one taking about 1¼ hours. ENs in training are called 'pupil nurses'. ENs who want to become RGNs must take another 2-years' training.

Nursing Auxiliaries do not take any systematic training or examination. They assist nurses in most hospital wards and clinics. They can work full- or part-time.

Personal attributes Above all a wish to look after other people and to do things for them; a practical nature; the ability to get on well with all kinds of people and to work well as one of a team; good health.

Psychiatric Nurse (see also Enrolled Nurse, p. 329)

There are two separate Registers:
1. Registered Mental Nurse (RMN), which is nursing the mentally ill.
2. Registered Nurse for the Mentally Handicapped (RNMH).

Entry qualifications See p. 323.

1. *Nursing the mentally ill (RMN)*

The work Nursing patients who have suffered a breakdown, but who in the majority of cases will recover. This form of nursing differs very much from general nursing. It differs, too, from most people's picture of it, and from what it was like even a few years ago. In recent years there have been great developments in the treatment of mental illness and in mental hospital atmosphere generally. The number of violent patients has drastically decreased; the proportion of geriatric patients is increasing.

Most psychiatric patients are up and about all day. Many go out to shop, to visit friends, some even to work. Others walk about and busy themselves in the hospital's often extensive recreation rooms, workshops and gardens. Very few wards are locked.

Ninety per cent of patients are 'voluntary' (now called 'informal'). Most patients stay for only a few weeks, though some come back fairly regularly for further treatment. As most mental illness takes the form of an exaggeration of our normal moods of depression, elation, or aggressiveness, patients tend to be much the same as anyone else in behaviour and appearance.

Nurses do little physical nursing, except in geriatric wards and for patients with physical complaints. Psychiatric nursing is often less *physically* exhausting than general nursing, but emotionally it is more demanding.

For many patients an important part of their treatment lies in the contact with a friendly nurse. The inability to 'communicate' with other people is part of most mental illness: nurses help a great deal towards patients' recovery by talking to them and, above all, by listening.

In good psychiatric hospitals the atmosphere is relaxed and informal. Patients and staff live in a friendly so-called 'therapeutic' community with nurses establishing and maintaining personal relationships as an essential part of the treatment. Patients are treated as individuals and are encouraged to share with the staff responsibility for running wards and for the active social life of the hospital. The aim is always to minimize the institutional atmosphere.

At informal meetings with staff the patients are encouraged to discuss and even criticize treatment, to talk about their difficulties and to help each other with their problems. At staff-only meetings, after ward-meetings with the patients, even the most junior nurse has a chance to discuss patients, treatments and new methods with consultants and senior staff.

In many hospitals there are joint wards for male and female patients; male and female nurses cooperate in their care.

Psychiatric nursing can of course sometimes be harrowing. Nurses must always remember that their patients' selfishness or childishness is a symptom of their illness. Teamwork among the staff helps a great deal, and during their training nurses learn to recognize and handle the emotional aspect of their work.

There are an increasing number of day-hospitals for patients well enough to live at home but still in need of contact with nurses, occupational therapy and perhaps psychiatric treatment.

Most hospitals work on shift systems and staff know well in advance when they will be free. Nurses may live out, but as psychiatric hospitals are often in country areas this is not always practicable. Nurses' homes are usually comfortable; each nurse has her own room. There are normally no petty restrictions; nurses are treated as responsible people. Staff come from all over the world, and the staff's social clubs are polyglot. Recreational facilities are usually good; occasionally licensed premises are provided for staff.

Often nurses do not wear uniform, to emphasize the 'normal' atmosphere. The atmosphere in psychiatric hospitals is far more democratic than in general hospitals. The proportion of male nurses is much greater than in general nursing.

Prospects Fair. Psychiatric nurses can also work outside the hospital, in community care, visiting patients who live at home, and at day-hospitals and centres.

Pay: A little higher than RGN (see p. 326).

Training Minimum age for training 18; Scotland 17½.

The course is organized much like the RGN general training (see

p. 326). The syllabus covers: human development and behaviour from infancy to adulthood, deviations from normal behaviour, human biology, psycho-physical disturbances; physical illness and bedside nursing; the principles and practice of psychiatric nursing; psychology and enough elementary psychiatry to understand patients' symptoms and treatments; organization of day-care centres and community care, nursing care of the mentally and physically sick; the art of listening and 'counselling'; nursing care in relation to physical methods of treatment such as drugs, neurosurgery.

One of the degree courses (see above) leads to RMN nursing.

Personal attributes Curiosity about what makes people behave as they do; emotional stability; patience and perseverance; the ability to listen well and to be genuinely concerned without becoming emotionally involved; interest in outside work to keep a sense of proportion; a sense of humour; a gregarious nature; good physical and mental health.

2. *Nursing the mentally handicapped (RNMH)*
Mentally handicapped patients are 'backward' and immature; their mental development has been arrested either before birth or at an early age.

The work Mentally handicapped patients are cared for in special hospitals. Some stay there all their lives, but the tendency today is to provide hostels and day-centres so as to enable as many patients as possible to live outside the 'institutionalizing' hospital atmosphere. This means that patients *in* hospital tend to be the more severely handicapped. It also means that these nurses can work as community nurses in hostels and day-centres for the mentally handicapped, and visit patients in their homes.

Nurses help patients to develop as far as their capacity allows. For example, it is an achievement in some cases to teach a patient to dress and feed himself; others can be taught to do domestic or other simple tasks, go out to work, and live at home.

Most mentally handicapped persons behave like happy children. The majority become devoted to those who look after them and understand their ways. Showing love and affection is a great part of this type of nursing.

The emphasis in mental hospitals is on creating as normal a community as possible, simulating normal everyday life with work, school, holidays, leisure, sports, clubs, etc. Nurses establish relationships with patients and reassure, comfort and support them and help them to become as independent as possible, so that as far as possible patients can eventually leave hospital and live in the community.

Prospects As for RMN.

Pay: A little higher than RGN (see p. 326).

Training Training is organized very much like that for RGN (see p. 326). The syllabus is similar to that for nursing the mentally ill, but with special emphasis on mental handicaps, and on physically handicapped children and adults. The nurse gradually gains experience with patients in different age groups, from babies upwards. She works in the nursery where children learn play-occupations such as painting, doing simple exercises to music, and she works with adults.

It is also possible to take a 13-month post-registration course for the Register of Nursing the Mentally Handicapped. One degree course leads to RNMH (see p. 327).

Personal attributes Affectionate nature; a practical approach; patience; gentleness; interests unconnected with the work; ability to be genuinely concerned without becoming emotionally involved. Those who like looking after small children and animals often enjoy this work.

NOTE: There are also 'Nursing Assistants' in both branches of psychiatric nursing. They help with the practical work of keeping patients occupied and can work full- or part-time. They do not have systematic training.

Bridging the Gap

The time between leaving school and starting training can be spent looking after children or doing the kind of work which brings school-leavers into contact with people. Working as a shop assistant, in a factory or in a café, for example, might be valuable.

There are also pre-nursing courses at some further education colleges, lasting 1 or 2 years. Subjects studied include English and arithmetic, human anatomy, physiology, community care and basic nursing skills. Courses include visits to hospitals, to give some idea of the atmosphere.

Nursing Outside the Hospital

Occupational Health Nurse

Entry qualifications RGN training (see pp. 326) and staff nurse experience.

The work The occupational health nurse works in factories, stores or wherever there is a large number of employees. The work is above all preventive. She advises on diets, keeps an eye on the disabled, discusses worries with those who ask her to, deals with accidents and sudden illness. She gives regular minor treatment, such as injections and dressings, and advises both on health problems generally and on those peculiar to a particular industry, e.g. skin or respiratory diseases caused by certain types of work.

She usually keeps medical records of all employees and assists at the medical examination of prospective employees. She often arranges for such ancillary services as chiropody, eye-testing, physiotherapy. She may discuss safety measures on the shop-floor with management, shop steward and factory inspector (see p. 195).

She works closely with the personnel department. If an employee's work is deteriorating, she helps to find the psychological or physical cause. For those with physical disabilities she helps to find suitable jobs. She discusses work satisfaction problems generally, from canteen facilities to staff holidays, from the rearrangement of desks or workbenches in the toolshop, to the rearrangement of duties in the typing pool and overtime arrangements on the shop floor.

In large concerns there may be a medical department; more often there is one occupational health nurse working for the personnel director or the visiting medical officer.

Unlike other nursing jobs, normal office hours usually apply. OHNs usually belong to firms' social and sports clubs, and generally benefit from any available welfare facilities.

Prospects Occupational health departments are expanding.

Pay: Medium (see p. xxiii).

(ENs can work in Occupational Health as 'first aiders' and take an Occupational Practice Nurse course.)

Training RGN training (p. 326) followed by a 6-month full-time non-resident or longer day-release course leading to the Occupational Health Nursing Certificate. The syllabus includes industrial organization, factory and allied legislation, toxic hazards, psychology and occupational health nursing techniques.

Applicants for this course must have had good experience in out-patient and accident and emergency departments.

Personal attributes As for general nursing, with a special interest in industrial health, safety problems, and human relationships at work. The ability to work independently and to discuss matters easily both with workforce and management is essential.

District or Home Nurse

Entry qualifications RGN training (see p. 326), plus staff nurse experience.

The work The home nurse undertakes skilled nursing duties for patients not ill enough to be in hospital but needing nursing care and/or support and advice. She visits acute and chronically ill patients and elderly people at regular intervals to keep an eye on them. She also helps permanently disabled patients to learn to use new aids, and advises relatives on routine nursing tasks. When necessary she puts people in touch with social workers or gets in touch with them herself.

Home nurses work closely with local general practitioners, who advise on whom to visit and the treatment required, and with hospitals. As there is a tendency for patients to be discharged from hospital as early as possible, home nurses are undertaking more and more technical nursing procedures, such as changing dressings for post-operative patients, taking out stitches, observing and reporting on patients' progress.

District nursing is expanding. An experienced nurse often leads a team which includes enrolled nurses and nursing auxiliaries. To provide a 24-hour service, nurses work shifts: only in rural areas does the district nurse now provide a one-person constant service.

Prospects Fair. Since the reorganization of the Health Service and the bringing closer together of hospital and community nurses (which includes health visitors and midwives), home nurses may, for example, do some out-patient or other clinic sessions in hospital. This means they have both the independence of the home nurse and the companionship and chance to talk shop which hospital work offers. Some district nurses specialize; for example, in work with diabetics; people with psychiatric problems.

Pay: Medium (see p. xxiii).

Training The basic RGN training followed by a 6 -month non-residential course for Certificate in District Nursing. The training includes learning how to adapt hospital nursing techniques to nursing under possibly primitive home conditions; the nursing of illness met infrequently in hospitals; the teaching of home care to patients' relatives; the organization, scope and availability of the social services; counselling.

Enrolled nurses may take a special course and have to satisfy the authorities that they are suitable for the work. Most ENs in home nursing are over 30.

Personal attributes

As for general nursing, plus organizing ability. The home nurse must wish to work independently and to use her experience and ability in the community, rather than in the sheltered atmosphere of the hospital. She should be resourceful, friendly, and a good listener. She needs a wide interest in the community in which she lives and works, and tolerance of other people's way of life. She should know when to be critical and when to accept her patients' own standards of cleanliness, etc., as the best they can achieve.

Late start

Nursing schools and hospitals welcome mature entrants; but over-30s are often advised to take the 2-year EN training.

Position of women

NURSING GENERALLY: About 1 nurse in 10 is male. A disproportionate number of senior jobs are held by men; this is not necessarily due to discrimination: because of demographic changes (more men than women in below 35 age groups, hence fewer spinsters), there are now not enough childless women to fill the top jobs, which are too time- and energy-consuming for most women with children.

However, some women with young children *are* moving up through the nursing hierarchy and into top jobs in a way which was quite unheard of only a few years ago. They either worked right through, taking only their statutory maternity leave, or they took a few years off but kept in touch, or worked part-time for a few years, before going back to full-time work which is still essential in senior nursing jobs.

For a profession which has traditionally relied on single, dedicated women to fill senior jobs, there has been surprisingly little discussion on how to reorganize the job-structure so that women with children can more easily get to the top.

Career-break: Should not present any problem (but see above). *Refresher* training arrangements vary from place to place. If none is available, local Health Authorities could be asked to make arrangements. There are also various post-Registration courses which enable RGNs to take up one of the specialized types of work.

Interrupted training: Students who did not finish their RGN training before the career-break have to ask the appropriate National Board (see above) whether they may resume where they left off, or have to start training again from scratch. The length of the 'gap' largely determines how much training has to be repeated.

Part-time: At the moment there are fair opportunities up to staff nurse. At ward sister level, part-time starts to be difficult. However, as *some* ward sisters successfully run their wards on a part-time basis, it is obviously possible to do so. It is illogical that full use is not made of retired nurses who would gladly return to work part-time. With some prodding from nurses themselves, more senior jobs (both in clinical nursing and in administration) should be available. Also, 'Nurse Banks' now operate successfully in most parts of the country. Nurses who cannot work regularly 'go to the bank'. They notify the days and times they could work, the senior nurse concerned then says whether or not the bank nurse is needed for any of these times. The bank nurse may also be approached if there is a staffing crisis to see if she would be free to help out. There is no contract of employment and the scheme operates rather like a nursing agency. Many nurses with domestic responsibilities prefer this loose arrangement to regular part-time work, but bank nurses cannot normally get further than staff nurse.

Occupational health nursing: Men are beginning to train for this. Older entrants are very welcome; there are good opportunities for RGNs (and in certain circumstances, with extra training, ENs) to train for occupational health nursing. Courses may be available under TOPS (see p. xlvi).

Part-time training: 3-year EN courses widely available, but only one or two RGN and psychiatric courses. Again, as it is *possible* to train nurses part-time, more opportunities *could* be created if there were strong demand.

Health Visitor

Entry qualifications

5 O-levels plus RGN training with midwifery or obstetrics.

The work

Health visitors are professionals in their own right. They organize their own work.

The purpose of health visiting is the prevention and early detection of physical and mental ill health. Health visitors give health care advice, identify the need for and if necessary mobilize other sources of help. The important difference between health visitors on the one hand and nurses and social workers on the other is that the latter meet clients only when something has gone wrong.

The health visitor visits all new-born babies and their families as a matter of routine. She gives practical advice to young mothers at home and in clinics and checks the child's development. She tries to see all under-5s every few months. Usually that is all that is needed. However, her home-visits may act as an 'early warning system', she may notice signs of stress or disorder before these develop into problems.

For example, a young mother who gave up the companionship at work just before the child was born may feel lonely, and guilty for not being a radiant mother; the health visitor helps by discussing her feelings and by suggesting ways of coping with the problem. Other matters which might develop into problems but for the health visitor's early advice are older children's health or behaviour, or marital difficulties.

Health visitors also visit patients recently discharged from hospital; mentally ill or handicapped people who are cared for at home; the elderly; anyone who may be referred to them by social workers, doctors, a neighbour even. They also provide health teaching on a variety of subjects in many settings.

In all cases, health visitors are concerned with the family as a whole, not only the ill or disturbed member of the family. They may be based in doctors' practices, or work from health centres or offices, or from home. They are employed by local Health Authorities (see Health Service Administration, p. 214). They work very much more independently than nurses.

Prospects Fair. Some opportunities to go up the nurse-administration ladder, and in health visitor teaching after one year course.

Pay: Medium (see p. xxiii).

Training For RGNs with midwifery or 3 months' obstetrics experience: 1-year full-time course. Subjects include: social aspects of health and disease; psychology; social studies (with special reference to the family as a social institution); organization of statutory and voluntary services.

Personal attributes Interest and belief in preventive medicine and social advice; understanding and sympathy with social pressures and with people, whatever their temperament, background, life-style, competence; desire and ability to use expertise in the community and to work independently rather than in the sheltered hospital atmosphere; tolerance; patience.

Late start Possible to start the whole training, up to about 30. TOPS awards (see p. xlvi) for post-RGN course. Some GCE requirement relaxations.

Position of women This was a female occupation till recently; now there are some men. It is too early to say whether, as in nursing, a disproportionate number of men will aim at the administrative and teaching posts, and also whether men will be acceptable as advisers to young mothers.

Career-break: No problem.

Part-time: Good opportunities.

Midwife

Entry qualifications 5 O-levels including English language and a science, but see **Training**. Minimum age 20.

The work This differs from nursing in that a midwife's patients are not ill. The whole approach to the work is different. A midwife gives ante- and post-natal advice and instruction and delivers babies. It is her job to take full responsibility for the actual delivery in straightforward cases, and to call the doctor in case of complications. She also looks after the health of the mother and child for the first few weeks after the child's birth.

Most deliveries now take place in hospitals and therefore most midwives now work – or are based – in hospitals, and combine hospital and domiciliary work. They are also responsible for hospitals' 'special care nurseries' and babies' intensive care units where premature and sick babies are looked after. This work involves using highly sophisticated equipment.

Domiciliary midwives deal mainly with ante- and post-natal care. Midwifery often involves dealing with women's post-natal depression. Generally there is now more emphasis on the psychology of child birth in midwifery work than even a few years ago. For example, midwives are very much involved in the hospital-versus-home-confinement debate.

A small number of midwives work in private maternity homes or in private practice, attending the patients of non-NHS doctors.

Prospects Depend on training: fair for midwives who are RGNs. They can also work in EEC and other European countries and in the developing countries and the Commonwealth.

Pay: Medium (see p. xxiii).

Training *Since 1983:*

Two methods (almost all new entrants now choose the RGN training – it leads to a wider choice of opportunities):

1. RGN training (p. 326) followed by 18-month midwifery training.
2. Minimum age: 17. 3-year full-time training for the Registered Midwives Certificate. Pupil midwives do deliveries under supervision in hospital conditions, receive theoretical instruction in midwifery and in the care of the infant, and learn basic nursing techniques. Practical training includes at least 3 months' experience with a district midwife. This is the most crucial training period. Pupil midwives learn how to manage without hospital facilities and how to adapt often unsatisfac-

tory home conditions for a safe delivery. It is, however, extremely difficult to find a training vacancy.

Although training takes longer, much useful experience is gained by taking a midwifery course after nurse training.

Personal attributes Much as for RGN (see p. 328) and for home nurses (p. 336), with of course a special interest in babies. Willingness to work very irregular hours, and the ability to snatch sleep at any time of day, are essential.

Late start Good opportunities, both for qualified nurses and to start from scratch.

Position of women Almost 100% women's profession at the moment, but under the Sex Discrimination Act, arrangements were made for men to be trained. So far only very few have trained.

Career-break: No problem; *refresher courses* are available and obligatory every 5 years.

Part-time: Good opportunities – no part-time training.

Further information (all nursing careers)

United Kingdom Central Council for Nursing, Midwifery and Health Visiting, 23 Portland Place, London W1N 3AF

English National Board, Victory House, 170 Tottenham Court Road, London W1P 0HA

Scottish National Board, 22 Queen Street, Edinburgh EH2 1JX

Welsh National Board, Pearl Assurance House, Greyfriars Road, Cardiff CF1 3AG

The National Board for Northern Ireland, 216 Belmont Road, Belfast BT4 2AT

Related careers *Medicine – Nursery Nurse – Personnel Management – Social Work*

Occupational Therapy

Entry qualifications 1 A-level (in practice usually 2), 5 O-levels, including a science and an English subject. Also *graduate* entry.

The work Occupational therapists treat patients suffering from physical or mental disorders by whatever form of training or activity is likely to contribute to their recovery.

The therapist receives guidance from the patient's doctor on the 'objective' of the treatment, which means the degree of recovery the patient may be expected to achieve. She then plans the treatment to suit the individual patient, taking into account the physical, social, economic, and psychological circumstances.

The main branches of the work, which often overlap, are:

Rehabilitation of Physically Disabled People

For work: this often involves cooperation with physiotherapists. For a man with severe hand injuries, for example, the occupational therapist and the physiotherapist together work out a scheme of gradual retraining for a specific job.

The occupational therapist usually gets in touch with employers to make sure that patients are trained for work which is locally available.

For independence: to lessen the psychological effect of their disability, special gadgets may have to be designed for patients. A partially paralysed woman, for example, may be shown in a specially built hospital 'kitchen' how to cook from a wheelchair, possibly using long-handled saucepans. Men and women learn how to dress by using special gadgets to put on shoes and take clothes off hangers, etc.

(a) *Teaching handicapped children*
The children are taught to feed themselves, to play, and to walk, possibly with special aids.

(b) *Visiting patients at home*
An old lady who recently left a geriatric ward may be visited to see how

she manages her disability, with the special attachments to her chair and cooker.

(c) *Occupying bedridden and long-stay patients in hospital*
Activities range from embroidery done in bed, to woodwork or making Christmas decorations. Some of the work in hospital workshops is done for payment under contract with outside firms.

Rehabilitation in Psychiatric Hospitals, and in the Psychiatric Departments of General Hospitals

Work is done in cooperation with psychiatric staff (see Psychiatric Nursing, p. 330). The occupational therapist works out a 'social programme' for each patient. Severely disturbed patients may have to be coaxed into taking some interest in the world around them and in their own appearance. Some may need encouragement to talk at all, others may be helped by a visit to the hospital's hairdressing salon, or by a walk in the hospital grounds.

The second step may be encouraging the patient to socialize. Group activities are organized by patients with the help of the occupational therapist and range from whist-drives, dances, and play-readings to outings to the seaside.

Art therapy (see also Art and Design, p. 67) may also be done by the occupational therapist, though artists may help with this work.

The next step for the patient coaxed back from apathy is to help her become independent. The occupational therapist may run a special 'flat' in the hospital where patients housekeep and invite staff and other patients to tea. Patients about to leave hospital need help in adjusting to the world outside, and the occupational therapist may take them out shopping, to a Jobcentre or even an employer. She helps to organize work done by patients in hospital garden, kitchen, and workshop. It is also her job to find firms willing to place contracts for work to be done by patients. It is important that patients should work with a purpose, and not just be aimlessly occupied.

The occupational therapist may choose the setting in which she wishes to work. This may be a mental hospital where, in a 'therapeutic community' setting, she takes part in research projects on new methods of treatment; in a general hospital with or without a psychiatric ward. It may be a day-hospital for mental patients; a hospital for spastic children; an orthopaedic hospital; an industrial rehabilitation centre; a child guidance clinic; or a prison. About 20% of occupational therapists now work with local authority social services, visiting people at home and running, or helping at, day-centres.

The occupational therapist is always an important member of the team of professional people helping patients to return to normal health. Her day-to-day work is very responsible since she usually works on her own, even in large hospitals where there are several other occupational therapists.

OT Helpers help in hospitals and in social services departments. They do not get systematic training but are members of the OT team. They can specialize in work with the handicapped, with long-stay patients in hospital and, above all, in work with the elderly who account for an increasingly large proportion of OT patients.

Prospects Fair. Public spending cuts have reduced opportunities, but there are shortages in some areas. Qualifications are recognized in the Commonwealth, most other English-speaking countries, and in the US. There are some opportunities in the EEC for those who speak relevant languages.

Pay: Medium (see p. xxiii).

Training 3–3½ years full-time at an occupational therapy school. About 1 year is spent working in different types of OT settings.

The emphasis in training has shifted from the mainly craft teaching to psychological aspects of the work. The syllabus includes anatomy, physiology, psychology, medicine, surgery (theoretical only), and psychiatry. Under 'occupational techniques' come practical work such as 'self-help' (which is concerned with helping disabled patients back to independence in everyday life), organizing recreational and cultural activities, art and craft work, and the theory and underlying principles of occupational therapy for physical and mental disabilities.

NOTE There is now at the Central London Polytechnic a part-time day- and block-release degree course for *qualified* occupational therapists, physiotherapists and remedial gymnasts in employment. It is useful for people who want to do research and/or explore the possible advantages of joint training for the various 'therapy' professions. It is also likely to be useful for people who want to practise in EEC countries where similar professionals take degree-equivalent qualifications. (OT degree courses are under discussion.)

Personal attributes Organizing ability; the ability to explain things clearly to all types of patient; adaptability and judgement to find the right approach to psychiatric patients; resourcefulness, patience, cheerfulness, good powers of observation; some dexterity; an interest in practical work, and a fairly strong scientific bent.

Late start Some opportunities up to mid-thirties; shortened training occasionally possible for related professionals such as nurses, psychology graduates.

Position of women Traditionally an all-female profession, now about 35 men annually among 800 entrants.

Career-break: No problem. *Refresher courses* available.

Part-time: Good opportunities for basic grade jobs, but virtually none for promotion. No reason why this should be so.

Further information College of Occupational Therapists, 20 Rede Place, London W2 4TU

Related careers *Physiotherapy – Psychiatric Nursing, p. 330*

Operational Research

Entry qualifications Degree in a subject requiring numeracy such as maths, engineering, natural sciences, economics, statistics, computer studies, business studies.

The work Operational researchers apply mathematical and statistical methods to the solving of organizational and management problems. They set up a 'mathematical model' of the system they intend to improve, incorporating such factors as risk and chance in given situations, following different courses of action. They can then predict, and compare, the outcome of alternative decisions. This technique enables management to base its plans and decisions on something more reliable than hunch and experience. Even if there is no one perfect solution in a given situation, operational researchers can forecast in which aspect one course of action will produce different results from another. Operational research is used in any field in which a number of variables have to be taken into account in decision-making – and this covers virtually the whole world of work – industry, government, commerce. (Operational research is a 'management service' (see Management, p. 269).)

For example, in planning a chain of supermarkets, shopping 'peaks and valleys' cause problems: to avoid check-out queues completely on Fridays and Saturdays would mean allocating vast amounts of floor-space and staff to check-out positions, which would be idle most of the week. Operational research workers examine the variables which affect the cost-effectiveness of various levels of expenditure on staff, equipment, floor-space for check-out positions and balance it against what they work out is an acceptable level of queueing (i.e. what length of queue will customers put up with before they go to the competition?).

Other problems in which operational research measures and then balances various factors include levels of stock to be carried in the supermarket; sorting out public transport problems or hospital waiting lists; allocating resources among competing projects in a manufacturing company. Or, if a set of products can be manufactured in a number of factories spread over the country, 'OR' workers determine where how much of each product should be manufactured to minimize production and delivery costs.

The attraction of operational research is that it deals with problems which affect everyone in the community and that it enables operational research workers to work in whatever type of environment appeals to them. Operational research combines working closely with people at all levels and in most areas of organization (invariably a large one), either extracting information or discussing research results, with concentrated desk-work.

Prospects Good. This is an expanding field, but jobs tend to be available mainly in cities.

Pay: High (see p. xxiii).

Training *Either*: (1) degree which includes operational research in, for example, economics, maths, business studies or computer studies; *or*: (2) post-graduate operational research course. Pre-entry training is usually followed by on-the-job training with in-house or outside short courses.

Personal attributes Numeracy, logical and analytical mind; ability to get on well with people at all levels within an organization and to explain complicated matters clearly. There is also room, however, for backroom-research types.

Late start Only for people with suitable degree and industrial experience.

Position of women As in all new career areas, where there is no tradition to break down, women who try to get in do very well, but relatively few women – even of those who have the right first degree – have tried to get into OR, possibly because its mathematical content tends to be over-emphasized, and its 'communication-content' under-emphasized.

A very small proportion of applicants to post-graduate OR courses are women; more would be welcome.

Career-break: Should be no problem for those who keep in touch; updating courses available to all operational research workers can be adapted as *refresher courses*.

Part-time: Not at the moment, but might be possible on a project basis, for experienced people.

Further information Operational Research Society, Neville House, Waterloo Street, Birmingham B2 5TX

Related careers *Actuary – Computers – Engineering – Insurance – Management in Industry – Mathematical Science, p. 437*

Optical Work

Dispensing optician – ophthalmic optician (optometrist)

All opticians must be registered with the General Optical Council. There are two kinds of careers for opticians:

1. *Dispensing optician*, who supplies spectacles, contact lenses and other optical appliances;
2. *Ophthalmic optician*, who also tests eyesight and prescribes whatever spectacles are necessary.

Dispensing Optician

Entry qualifications 5 O-levels including maths or physics, English, plus 1 other science subject.

The work Dispensing opticians do not do any sight-testing or other eye-examination. They interpret the prescription of the ophthalmic surgeon or optician and use complex apparatus to measure for, fit, and supply spectacles, contact lenses, and artificial eyes. All such work requires calculations of distance and angles, etc. Equally important are the selling and 'cosmetic' aspects of the work. Dispensing opticians discuss with patients (a term opticians use in preference to customers) which type of frame is the most flattering in each case.

Most dispensing opticians also deal with other types of optical instruments, supplying apparatus to ophthalmic surgeons, opticians and laboratories, and selling sunglasses, opera glasses, microscopes, etc. to the general public.

Dispensing opticians can also get managerial jobs in 'prescription houses' (firms which make lenses to prescription) and in firms of dispensing opticians which manufacture optical instruments.

Prospects Fair. A dispensing optician usually starts as an assistant but later may manage a shop, or practice, in which ophthalmic opticians or surgeons do the eye-testing.

Dispensing opticians have at least as great a variety of jobs and settings to choose from as ophthalmic opticians. In relation to their educational qualifications and the length of their respective trainings, they do better financially – a dispensing optician manager may in fact earn more than a practising ophthalmic optician.

Pay: In hospital: low to medium; in commercial employment (which includes sight-testing opticians' practices or shops): medium to high (but longer working hours than in hospital). (See p. xxiii.)

Training *Either* (and recommended): a 2-year full-time course at a technical college, plus 1 year's practical experience.
Or: 3 years' work as a trainee with a dispensing optician, plus theoretical instruction, either part-time day-release or, since part-time classes are very few, by correspondence course, with some attendance at a college.

Both methods of training lead to the qualifying examinations for Fellowship of the Association of Dispensing Opticians and membership of the Faculty of Dispensing Opticians.

The syllabus covers optical physics, the anatomy and physiology of the eye, the interpretation of ophthalmic prescriptions, the necessary measurements and adjustments for frames, and the recording of facial measurements. The full-time course includes business practice.

Personal attributes Some manual dexterity; interest in salesmanship and in fashion; ability and enjoyment in dealing with flow of people.

Late start No special problems, but see **Prospects**.

Position of women Steady increase of women entrants over last few years; now women account for just under 50%. Many are in charge of high-street shops staffed by men.

Career-break: No problem: occasional *refresher courses* though not intended primarily for returners.

Part-time: As assistant, yes; not as manager, but there is no reason why job-sharing should not work.

Ophthalmic Optician (Optometrist)

Entry qualifications 2 or more often 3 science A-levels plus O-levels which must include English and physics or physics with chemistry and a biological subject if physics and biology respectively are not offered at A-level. Most degree courses insist on A-level physics.

The work The main duties of an ophthalmic optician are examining eyes; measuring vision defects with the help of optical instruments; and working out lens-prescriptions for short- or far-sightedness and astigmatism. Some opticians now test sight with computerized equipment instead of using the traditional methods.

Ophthalmic opticians do not treat patients with diseased eyes. If they find something is wrong which spectacles cannot cure, they refer the patient to an ophthalmic surgeon. They are concerned with optics, not with medicine; their work is essentially scientific, not medical, but they are taught to treat the human being, not simply a pair of eyes. The work combines dealing with people (without getting to know them) and applied science.

Ophthalmic opticians work either in general practice, doing mainly sight-testing, or in hospital, where they see more intricate eye conditions and assist ophthalmic surgeons with investigations and treatment of eye disease, and with research.

General practice may mean seeing patients in 'rooms' – possibly in the optician's own home; it may mean managing and/or owning an optician's practice and doing all the dispensing work as well; and frequently it means doing the ophthalmic work in a shop managed and/or owned by a firm of ophthalmic or dispensing opticians which owns several practices.

Prospects Very good.

Pay: High (see p. xxiii).

Training 3 years for a BSc degree plus 1 year's clinical experience in paid employment (in Scotland 4-year CNAA degree course).

In 1980 the three former professional bodies, the Worshipful Company of Spectacle Makers, the British Optical Association, and the Scottish Association of Opticians, ceased conducting examinations and founded a new single examining body for ophthalmic optics, The British College of Ophthalmic Opticians (Optometrists). The syllabus includes physical optics, optical instruments, anatomy and physiology, abnormal and pathological conditions of the eye, refraction. After passing the College's Professional Qualifying Examination and completing a pre-registration year, students can apply for registration with the General Optical Council. Registration is obligatory for practitioners.

Personal attributes An interest in physics and maths; patience; manual dexterity; a liking for meeting a flow of new people; a confident manner especially with old people and children; organizing ability.

Late start This is a long training and courses are oversubscribed, therefore only applicants with up-to-date knowledge of science likely to be accepted. But there should be no problem getting jobs.

Position of women (ophthalmic work)

Women have been accepted for a long time and have no problems getting good jobs. The proportion of registered practitioners is still under 22%. But in 1983 116 women and 109 men started ophthalmic optics courses at university. The *proportion* of women students choosing optics is far larger than the proportion of men doing so. Optics is probably the easiest profession to do successfully with largely part-time work. Women ophthalmologists have also found it relatively easy to return to full-time work after a spell of part-time work.

Career-break: If one has kept up with developments, no problem.

Refresher courses: Updating courses available for all ophthalmic opticians.

Part-time: Fair opportunities.

Further information

The Association of Dispensing Opticians, 22 Nottingham Place, London W1M 4AT
The British College of Ophthalmic Opticians (Optometrists), 10 Knaresborough Place, London SW5 0TG
Faculty of Dispensing Opticians, Apothecaries Hall, Blackfriars Lane, London EC4

Related careers

Orthoptics

NOTE (March 1984): Forthcoming legislation may change opticians' employment patterns, but not their training.

Orthoptics

Entry qualifications 5 O-levels and 2 A-levels, including English language, maths and a science subject.

The work Orthoptists work with ophthalmic surgeons. They are responsible for the diagnosis, investigation, treatment and progress-monitoring of patients who have defects of binocular vision, e.g. squint, double vision or related vision conditions. The orthoptist's role is expanding. The importance of early diagnosis and treatment of children is increasingly recognized. Orthoptists therefore work on screening programmes for pre-school age children. Special equipment and special skills enable orthoptists to assess the visual abilities of even very young children – some patients are under a year old. Orthoptists also deal with children who have reading difficulties. They must be able to build up relationships with children of all ages and with their parents.

Other patient-groups include the physically and mentally handicapped; people who have had accidents or strokes; multiple sclerosis sufferers; and the elderly who can be helped to achieve their maximum visual potential. The latter client group is increasing in size as the proportion of elderly people in the population is increasing.

Orthoptists thus deal with a very wide age-range; with a wide range of conditions, and in a range of settings – in hospitals, in paediatrics, school, geriatric and neurological clinics or departments. Patients are referred by neurologists, general physicians, paediatricians, and other specialists.

Equipment used for diagnosis and treatment is highly sophisticated. Its use requires great technical skill. The need for getting clients of all ages to cooperate and do exercises – both in the clinic and at home – requires orthoptists to have great understanding of people of all types, and considerable communication skills.

Prospects Fair – but depend on NHS expenditure levels. There are two types of courses for qualified orthoptists to become Demonstrators and Teachers of Orthoptics. Limited scope for orthoptists in private practice (mainly in London). British qualifications are accepted in most countries; scope for people in the EEC if they speak the relevant language.

Pay: Low to medium (see p. xxiii).

Training

For State Registration which is required in all jobs: 3 years full-time at schools attached to hospitals. Syllabus includes general anatomy and physiology; child development; anatomy and physiology of eye and brain; optics; diseases of the eye and the principles of eye surgery; practice of orthoptics.

Students gradually gain clinical experience working with patients of all ages.

Personal attributes

A scientific bent; powers of observation, deduction and persuasion; understanding of people of all ages and temperaments; ability to work as one of a team, and also independently; communication skills.

Late start

The orthoptists insist on normal GCE qualifications and schools tend to prefer school-leavers; however, determined candidates in their 20s or 30s may be admitted for training especially if they have had experience of dealing with children.

Position of women

This is still a virtually all-female profession, but no reason why it should remain so. (1983: 1 male orthoptist!)

Career-break: Depends on (a) whether orthoptist kept up with developments, and (b) on level of vacancies. Young entrants tend to be given preference.

Refresher courses: Short 'up-dating' courses.

Part-time: Fair opportunities, but no promotion to head of department; no job-sharing schemes so far (see p. xxiv).

Further information

British Orthoptic Society, Tavistock House, North, Tavistock Square, London WC1H 9HX

Related careers

Dispensing Optician – Ophthalmic Optician

Osteopathy

Entry qualifications 2 A-levels, including preferably chemistry and either biology or zoology; and 3 O-levels, English language to be included at either level.

The work An osteopath uses manipulative methods of treatment for the correction of derangements of the bony and muscular structures of the body, and makes a special study of the spine in relation to health and disease. Osteopathy does not include the curing of organic disease but it covers the treatment of some organic functional disorders. The majority of patients need treatment because of stiff joints, slipped discs, etc. Patients are occasionally referred to osteopaths by doctors who recognize the value of osteopathic treatment for certain disorders, but the majority of patients come through personal recommendation.

Osteopaths are not recognized by the National Health Service because they do not have orthodox medical qualifications. The normal procedure is first to obtain experience as an assistant to an osteopath or at a clinic, then to start one's own part-time practice in addition, and perhaps finally to concentrate entirely on one's own practice. However, many GPs now recommend osteopathy treatment to their patients.

Prospects The profession is small, but interest in osteopathy is growing.

Pay: Medium to very high (see p. xxiii).

Training 4-year full-time course at British School of Osteopathy in London. The syllabus includes anatomy, physiology, osteopathic theory, practice and technique, diagnosis, pathology, applied anatomy, applied physiology, preventive medicine, biochemistry, dietetics and bacteriology. Students are then ready to take the qualifying examination, the Diploma of Osteopathy. Subject to character references, this enables them to become members of the General Council and Register of Osteopaths.

Personal attributes Confidence-inspiring manner; skilful, gentle, yet strong hands; physical strength; good health.

Late start Some relaxation of GCE requirements if candidates considered suitable; shortened courses for people with relevant qualifications (e.g. physiology degrees, medicine). Late entrants have no difficulty getting patients once trained. About 15% of students are mature entrants.

Position of women

About 25% of osteopaths are women, and about 35% of osteopathy students. Experienced osteopaths, women and men, say that it is not a job for small and/or delicate women: they would find some of the work physically impossible. But on the whole women osteopaths have no problem getting patients.

Career-break: The vast majority of women osteopaths continue working part-time from home throughout their career. Post-graduate refresher courses available.

Part-time: Very good opportunities.

Further information

British School of Osteopathy, 1–4 Suffolk Street, London SW1Y 4HG
General Council and Register of Osteopaths at the same address

---

Related careers

Medicine – Physiotherapy

Patent Agent (Chartered) and Patent Examiner

Entry qualifications Science or engineering degree; fluency in French and German desirable.

Patent Agent

The work This is a mixture of legal and scientific/technological work. A patent agent advises inventors, and others connected with inventions, on the validity and infringement of patents at home and abroad.

She makes 'searches' for clients to ensure that their inventions really are new, and prepares detailed specifications, descriptions and formulations of claims which 'cover' the invention. She files and negotiates the application for a patent on behalf of her client at the Patent Office. Having assisted in the creation of a patent, she may have dealings with its commercial application. She deals not only with patents for processes and products, but also with 'Registered Designs' and 'Registered Trade Marks'.

The majority of agents specialize in, for example, chemical or mechanical inventions or electronics – a very important area – or in designs and trade marks. Patent agents work in private practice, or for industrial organizations or government departments. It is usual to start as an assistant doing searches in the Patent Office and other libraries.

Patent agents' work has increased in scope and complexity since the coming into force of the European Patent Convention. In addition to preparing and processing patent applications in this country and corresponding with patent agents abroad to obtain similar protection for clients' inventions, patent agents now draft patent applications for submission to the European Patent Office in Munich. Processing of applications may necessitate travel to Munich for hearings with EPO examiners. There are also opportunities to travel to other countries.

Prospects Fair, both in this country and in the EEC.

Pay: Medium to high (see p. xxiii).

Training Students now train for the examinations of both the (British) Chartered Institute of Patent Agents and the European Patent Office.

Candidates who pass either examination may only practise before the relevant patent office, although candidates passing the European examination will receive partial exemption from the British examination. For both examinations candidates train with a patent agent; for the British examination for three years; for the European examination, four years. In each case the syllabus covers European law and practice (and British, where this differs from the European practice); drafting of patents and interpretation and criticism of patent specifications. Some documents in the European examination are in French or German.

Preparation for examinations is by private study. The Chartered Institute arranges lectures and tutorials. Some technical assistants never qualify yet nevertheless do very well, but they cannot become partners in private practice firms.

Personal attributes Curiosity; an analytical mind; a good memory; a scientific bent; the ability to assimilate facts quickly and to reason clearly, both verbally and in writing; liking for concentrated desk work.

Late start There are difficulties getting training vacancies.

Position of women Women make up 4% of Chartered patent agents and 25% of students, so numbers are increasing.

Career-break: Return only possible if legal and technological changes/developments kept up with. (No one seems to have returned yet.)

Part-time: Very limited opportunities in employment, but possible to run small private practice, at least in theory, for experienced patent agents with good contacts.

Further information Chartered Institute of Patent Agents, Staple Inn Buildings, London WC1V 7PZ

Patent Examiner

Entry qualifications First- or second-class honours degree in a scientific, engineering or mathematical subject; plus ability to read French and German is useful.

The work Patent examiners work in the Patent Office in London, and examine applications for patents. They are Civil Servants (see p. 120).

An examiner's work involves detailed examination of the description of an invention; making a search through earlier specifications to ascertain the novelty of the invention; classifying and indexing the features of the invention; writing a report embodying her findings; and, if necessary, interviewing the inventor or his agent to discuss any objections. The work requires an analytical and critical mind. Each examiner works in a specialized field. Training is on the job.

Prospects Limited.

Pay: Medium to high (see p. xxiii).

Personal attributes As for Patent Agent.

Late start Possible for people with relevant (technological) degrees and experience.

Position of women 10% of senior staff; about 50% of entrants are women.

Career-break: Presents problems – few vacancies; need to keep up with developments; competition from new graduates.

Part-time: Not at present.

Further information The Patent Office, 25 Southampton Buildings, London WC2

Related careers *Civil Service – Engineering – Scientist*

Personnel Management

Entry qualifications For Institute of Personnel Management's membership examination: *either* 2 A-levels and 3 O-levels and minimum age 20; *or* 2 years' relevant work experience and minimum age 23. About half of all entrants are *graduates*. See **Training** for alternative method of entry.

The work Personnel officers (titles vary and are not necessarily any indication of scope and level of responsibility) are part of the management-team. Their primary aim is the efficient utilization of human resources. The Institute of Personnel Management says that personnel management is not a job for people who primarily 'want to work with people'. It is not the personnel manager's job to manage people, but 'to provide the specialist knowledge or service that can assist other members of the management-team to make the most effective use of the human resources – people – of the organization'.

Personnel management used to be considered an offshoot of social work; it is certainly that no longer. The average personnel officer spends no more time in one-to-one discussions with individuals who need advice than do solicitors or accountants. 'Personnel' is a 'management function', like buying, marketing and production. Its challenge is to interpret conflicting views and objectives to people at various levels in an organization, some of whom have divergent interests.

Personnel officers are employed not only in industry, but also in hospitals, local and central government: the efficient use of human resources is equally vital to profit-making and to non-profit-making organizations. The range of jobs is very great indeed. In a large organization employing say 70,000 people, at several sites, a personnel director may have a staff of 70, some of whom specialize in one aspect of the work; in a small organization one or two people might do everything.

Main personnel specializations:

Recruitment, training and management-development: the latter means assessing individuals' potential, identifying and planning their career paths accordingly; this may include use of psychological testing and assessment methods. Training is a very important specialization, especially with the introduction of the YTS (see p. xxvii) and changes in work patterns due to new technologies.

Manpower planning: involves close cooperation with all levels of management as well as with recruitment and training colleagues.

Wage and salary administration: covers *job evaluation* (and equal pay administration) and involves detailed study of the tasks that make up individual jobs within the organization, in order to establish salary gradings. 'Wage and salary administration' sounds misleadingly like a desk-bound routine job; but it can be one of the most non-routine and controversial specializations.

Industrial relations, the most challenging of personnel specializations, means above all establishing and maintaining lines of communication between an organization's various interest groups. It involves discussing, with shop stewards and management, 'worker participation' schemes; implication of new legislation (of which there is a constant flow); mergers; implementation of new technologies.

Health and safety, sometimes called *employee services*, covers all welfare aspects. It may now include personal counselling services; responsibility for canteens, etc., as well as sophisticated job satisfaction improvement schemes and cooperation with manpower planning, training and other personnel specialists.

Not all personnel departments necessarily divide personnel functions in the same way; there are many variations on the theme.

Personnel workers who get to the top normally have had experience in several specialist fields, but there are few hard and fast rules. A specialist training officer in a large and/or progressive organization may have greater scope, responsibility and status (and salary) than a personnel director in charge of all specialist functions in another organization. It is impossible to generalize about career-paths, but it is probably best for those aiming at top jobs to get experience in large organizations, where they have the chance of working on a wide range of problems using a variety of personnel techniques.

Prospects Fair for personnel officers with industrial relations experience, willingness to be mobile and IPM qualifications. Many organizations with establishments in different towns expect personnel officers to move around the country. It is quite usual to move from one employer to another, not necessarily remaining in the same type of organization, for example from factory to hospital, store to local government, etc. However, with the introduction of new technologies more personnel people stay *either* in manufacturing *or* in service industries.

Pay: Medium to high (see p. xxiii).

Training A new examination structure has been introduced. It is divided into 3 stages. Stages 1 and 2 students either take a 1-year full-time course (mainly at polytechnics) or they study 3 years part-time, normally while in relevant employment (but see **Position of women**). Stage 3 can only be taken while in relevant employment.

BTEC Higher National award holders (see p. xvi) and graduates qualify for partial or total exemption from Stages 1 and 2 exams; the extent of exemption depends on subjects studied for previous qualification.

It is possible to prepare for IPM exams by correspondence course, preferably, but not necessarily, while in relevant employment.

For people in personnel work who do not have any A-levels there is a Foundation course which leads to student membership of the IPM and later to admittance to Stages 1, 2 and 3 courses. In other words, there is a possibility for people without the normal entry qualifications to catch up and qualify.

Graduates with a social/behavioural science degree or post-graduate qualification may get on well without IPM qualifications. They must acquire the necessary knowledge (legislation, training techniques, industrial relations procedures, etc.). Some employers do not mind whether efficient staff have IPM qualifications or not. However, qualifications *are* required by an increasing proportion of employers. They are particularly valuable for women who want to return to work after the child-rearing gap.

Personal attributes A flair for seeing all sides of a problem and interpreting each side's point of view to the other; a good memory for names and faces; at least an absence of dislike for figure-work, preferably a liking for it; interest in management; lack of prejudice and a fair-minded approach; tact; detachment; an understanding of people of all types, age, race and background, and the ability to gain their confidence and respect; organizing ability.

Late start Some opportunities for mature entrants who have had relevant experience; IPM runs up-dating courses.

Position of women There were proportionately far more women personnel managers in the past, when personnel work was largely concerned with welfare. As emphasis changed from 'dealing with people' to improving the efficient working of an organization, men took over top jobs and it became customary for women only to look after women personnel – i.e. women only remained in top jobs, if at all, in stores and other places where most of the staff were female. No figures are available (job titles give little indication of level of responsibility) but women are now definitely very much in the minority at head of department level, though many do well as training specialists and in small and medium-sized organizations. There are very few women with industrial relations experience, which is essential for most senior jobs in large organizations. Some women have difficulty getting jobs in which to gain such experience, but others are unwilling to move to where such jobs are available – often in the industrial cities. Lack of role models, and the image of industrial relations as 'all confrontation' keeps many young women from choosing this vital specialization. Yet women who have tried have done well in it.

Career-break: Personnel workers are able to return to the work if they have kept up with legislation and other personnel work developments. They can take part-time courses or correspondence courses, mentioned in **Training**, to update their knowledge.

Refresher courses: See **Late start**.

Part-time: Very few opportunities, but recently some determined returners have convinced employers that part-time *works*. Job-sharing (see p. xxiv) should be possible but has apparently not been tried.

Further information Institute of Personnel Management, 35 Camp Road, London SW19 4VW

Related careers *Careers Officer – Factory Inspector – Management in Industry – Retail Management*

Pharmacy

PHARMACIST: retail – hospital – industrial; PHARMACY TECHNICIAN

Pharmacist

Entry qualifications 3 A-levels including chemistry and two chosen from a mathematical subject, physics and a biological science. The subject not offered at A-level should be offered at O-level. In practice, an English O-level is essential.

The work Pharmacists work in 3 distinct fields: *retail*, *hospital*, and *industry*. Students do not need to decide which branch of pharmacy they want to go into until after qualifying.

Retail Pharmacists (usually called 'chemists' – a title pharmacists discourage)

Pharmacists dispense or supervise the dispensing of prescriptions. They act as a link between doctors and their patients, by explaining the effects and the correct use of medicines.

Most medicines are now available ready-made but pharmacists still make up the occasional prescription in the dispensary. They are also responsible for the safe and correct storage of a variety of medicines and some chemical substances. They are legally required to keep records such as the controlled drug registers.

Pharmacists may also deal with the buying and selling of cosmetics, toiletries, etc., and the training of shop staff. In larger pharmacies, and particularly in chains of pharmacies, the pharmacist has the choice of remaining involved with the dispensing and sale of medicines, or of becoming more involved with the commercial side.

But their role is changing. As more and more new drugs come on the market, both doctors and patients are making more use of pharmacists' thorough knowledge of the composition, action and interaction of new drugs. Many doctors ask pharmacists' advice – or at least their views – on the best way to use which new drugs for what particular condition. Pharmacists have more time to keep up with pharmaceutical developments than doctors. Also, patients increasingly ask pharmacists' advice for minor ailments and their opinion on whether they should consult their doctor. Pharmacists are well qualified to know when medical advice must be sought and when a simple remedy (which may be cheaper than one on prescription!) is all that the patient needs.

Because pharmacists are becoming more involved with 'community health care' their professional association is now trying to change the traditional term 'chemist' to 'community pharmacist'.

Prospects Good. Pharmacists are now more often managers of pharmacies or of dispensing departments than owners of their own business. 'High Street' chemists' shops are declining in number.

Abroad: Qualified pharmacists can practise and get jobs fairly easily in some countries of the Commonwealth; mutual recognition of qualifications in EEC countries may soon apply, but jobs are not easy to get.

Pay: Medium to high (see p. xxiii).

Hospital Pharmacists

The work Particularly suitable for those interested in the science of pharmacy. Hospital pharmacists dispense, and supervise the dispensing of, prescriptions for out-patients; they advise patients on the proper use of their medicines; they issue medicines for use within the hospital and they work closely with doctors and nurses to ensure that medicines are used safely, correctly and economically. They advise on doses and side effects of drugs and are often involved in clinical trial work on new drugs. Most medicines used in hospital are ready-made, but some preparations are made up in the pharmacy department. Hospital pharmacists are responsible for supervising the manufacturing process and for checking the quality of manufactured products. They also have a teaching role – they assist with the training of student pharmacists, and student pharmacy technicians; and they lecture to doctors and nurses.

Some hospitals now offer a 24-hour pharmacy service, provided by pharmacists who live in when on duty.

Hospital pharmacists' role is also changing – at least in some hospitals. Pharmacists may accompany consultants on ward rounds and may be consulted on the best drug to use in any particular case. Young doctors often ask pharmacists' advice and pharmacists may be asked to check patients' drug-charts, so there is more patient-contact than in the past.

Prospects Good, with a definite career structure. There is work which involves contact with people, and backroom work. Hospital pharmacists work in a community, with the opportunity of meeting people in similar jobs.

Pay: Medium to high (see p. xxiii).
(*Part-time* work comparatively badly paid.)

Industrial Pharmacists

The work They work in laboratories of pharmaceutical and related firms and on the production and development of new drugs and the improvement and quality control of existing drugs. As in other scientific work (see p. 426), pharmacists work in teams, often together with scientists from other disciplines. Some jobs involve mainly desk-work such as providing information to doctors and the preparation of data on new products for the Licensing Authority. Those with a bent for salesmanship can become representatives, visiting doctors in their surgeries and in hospital, providing information on their companies' products and they may become marketing executives which is an expanding area.

Prospects There is scope for the quiet backroom type content with semi-routine work, for the team-leader with a bent for pursuing new lines of thought and for those who want to go into general management, marketing and, above all, pharmaceutical sales.

Pay: Medium to high (see p. xxiii).

Training 3-year degree course. The syllabus includes: *pharmacognosy* – the study of medicinal plants and animal and mineral sources of drugs; *physiology* – study of the structure and functions of the human body; *pharmacology* – the effect of drugs; *pharmaceutical chemistry; pharmaceutics* – study of the preparation of medicines; general principles in the practice of pharmacy in the 3 branches; ethics and laws governing pharmaceutical practice.

After graduating, students must obtain 1 year's pre-registration experience in pharmacy, which must include at least 6 months in retail or hospital practice before they are eligible to apply for registration as pharmaceutical chemists.

Personal attributes *For all pharmacists*: A strong scientific bent; meticulous accuracy; a strong sense of responsibility; a calm, logical mind; ability to concentrate; organizing ability.
For retail and industrial pharmacists: A flair for business; ability to deal with semi- and untrained staff; a liking for people.
For industrial pharmacists: An inquiring mind; ability to work as one of a team; infinite patience.

Late start No upper age limit for training or jobs, but previous science-based work (perhaps as a technician) desirable.

Position of women This is a very promising career for women; 33% of registered pharmacists are women (compared with 23% in 1969) and in 1983 55% of first year pharmacy students were women. Proportionately more women work in hospitals (where they have equal promotion chances) than in retail and in industry. But that is by choice: they are welcome as retail pharmacy managers (the majority of clients are women) and also in sales and marketing.

Career-break: Should be no problem. *Refresher courses* available (intended mainly for practising pharmacists, but useful for returners). In some cases the Department of Health will even pay costs of refresher course.

Part-time: Fair opportunities in retail and in hospital.

Further information Pharmaceutical Society of Great Britain, 1 Lambeth High Street, London SE1 7JN *or* 36 York Place, Edinburgh EH1 3HU

Related careers *Medicine – Pharmacy Technician – Scientist (Biochemist, p. 433; Chemist, p. 432)*

Pharmacy Technician

Entry qualifications In theory 3 CSE Grade 3 including maths or a science; in practice most colleges and most employers demand higher qualifications – usually now 4 O-levels including at least one science – often chemistry is specified.

The work This varies from one job to another. In retail, technicians help out on the selling side, they also assist the pharmacist with dispensing (but work always under the supervision of qualified pharmacists who must check prescriptions, etc.). In hospitals and industry, technicians have more chance to do responsible and varied work. They assist with experiments, with interviewing patients, and they may liaise with other departments, etc. The role of the technician in the NHS and in industry is changing: as in other science-based jobs (see Science, p. 442) technicians now often do jobs which overlap with graduates, but there will always be a considerable difference between the project-leader type and level of work, and technicians', who implement proven techniques. While using their judgement and expertise, they do not take ultimate responsibility or do original research.

Prospects There is a limited demand for pharmacy technicians.

Pay: Medium (see p. xxiii).

Training This is changing. Technicians now study, by day-release or block-release, for the BTEC National Certificate in Pharmaceutical Sciences. The Certificate is in two stages. Stage I is intended as the final award for retail pharmacists (some of these may not get day-release and must study at evening classes). Technicians in the National Health Service and in industry usually go on to Stage II. Length of the full, two-stage Certificate course depends on entry qualifications (and also on local colleges' course organization). Normally CSE Grade 3 entrants take 3 years; entrants with 4 O-levels including a science complete Stage I and II in 2 years. Stage II need not be taken immediately after Stage I: technicians can 'top up' their Stage I Certificate after a few years' gap.

In some colleges the City and Guilds Technicians' Certificate (2 years' day- or block-release) will still be running for some years. It normally leads to Stage I of the new BTEC Pharmaceutical Sciences Certificate.

The old-established Worshipful Society of Apothecaries' examination, for *retail* pharmacy technicians only, is also still available. Students take the City and Guilds or the BTEC Stage I course and they then complete one year's practical training and pass an oral and practical examination before they are awarded the Apothecaries' Certificate.

Some of the large companies and chains of pharmacies have their own in-house training schemes. These do not *necessarily* count as equivalent of even the BTEC Stage I course and may, therefore, make job-switching, or returning to work after a gap, more difficult. Trainees offered in-house without day- or block-release training should try and get details of in-house training schemes and discuss their value with the local college or hospital pharmacy department.

Personal attributes Meticulous accuracy; a scientific bent but not necessarily great academic ability.

Late start Depends on local supply and demand position. Entrance requirements may be waived; but school-leavers may be given preference.

Position of women The vast majority of technicians are women.

Career-break: Returners' opportunities depend on supply and demand position.

Part-time: Fair opportunities.

Further information

Society of Apothecaries, Blackfriars Lane, London EC4
City and Guilds of London Institute, 76 Portland Place, London W1N 4AA

Related careers

Retail Management – Science Technician

Photography

PHOTOGRAPHER: creative photography (general practitioners, advertising, fashion, photo-journalism and press) – industrial and scientific – medical; PHOTOGRAPHIC TECHNICIAN

Photographer

Entry qualifications

No definite educational requirements for photography as such. For the British Institute of Professional Photography's Vocational Examination: 4 O-levels.
For the Professional Qualifying Examination: 2 A-levels and 5 O-levels, see **Training**.
For medical photography: 4 O-levels.
For press photography: 4 O-levels and 1 A-level.
Most, but not all, London photographers are specialized, but in the provinces one studio often does all types of work.

Creative Photography

General practice

The work

Approximately half of all photographers work in general photographic studios found in most high streets. The bulk of their work consists of portraiture, groups and commercial services. Portrait subjects include, increasingly, pets; some photographers specialize in children.

Photographers prefer their subjects to come to the studio to be photographed, because it is easier to arrange the lighting there. However, there is an increasing demand for portraits in the home, garden or workplace, especially in the case of children's portraits. The 'natural' portrait is much more popular today than the formal one. To produce not just a good likeness, but a characteristic portrait, photographers must have considerable understanding of, and insight into, human nature; they must be able to put sitters at ease so that their expression is natural.

Weddings and other group photographs (e.g. sports and social clubs) form another important part of the work. Wedding photography now offers more scope for 'creative' pictures in a less formal style than it used to. Commercial work is mainly for publicity purposes – for local companies, estate agencies, architects, etc. who do not have enough work to employ a staff photographer.

Prospects Reasonable. One way in for the keen amateur is to help a busy studio with Saturday weddings.

Pay: Medium to high (see p. xxiii).

Advertising

The work Very varied. Although advertising photographers may often be given exact instructions about what to photograph and what effect to aim at, they are also expected to suggest their own ideas for new angles. Many advertisements are records of everyday life – whether it is of a child eating breakfast, or a woman getting out of a car – and involve both work with models and persuading ordinary people to agree to be photographed.

Advertising photographs are taken either by the photographic departments of advertising agencies, by photographic studios (i.e. several photographers working as partners, sharing darkroom and office facilities, or salaried photographers and assistants working for an employer), or by freelance photographers. Most do some catalogue work; some studios specialize in mail-order photography (and may be owned by the mail-order company).

Prospects This is the best paid and hence a very competitive branch; success depends entirely on ability, efficiency and the right personality.

Pay: Medium to very high (see p. xxiii).

Fashion

The work Although advertising includes fashion photography, some photographers specialize in fashion. Most fashion photography is done by specialist studios or freelances who are commissioned by editors, fashion houses, or advertising agencies; they usually work under the direction of a fashion expert.

Prospects This is the most sought after branch and hence *very* difficult to enter.

Pay: High (see p. xxiii).

Photo-journalism (feature photography) and press photography

The work Photo-journalism is, essentially, telling a story in pictures, and therefore a journalistic sense is needed. Feature photographers may work with reporters as a team, or may be freelances, or work for studios. Only a tiny minority are on editorial staffs. It is very varied work, and leads to assignments at any time and in any place – photographing VIPs at home, or life in foreign parts, or schools at work – anything that makes a story. Hours are irregular.

There is more hard, hurried work than glamour in newspaper photography, which consists almost entirely of single news pictures. A press photographer must be versatile in taking all kinds of subjects. On small provincial papers she may have to do the developing. She must know what makes a good news picture; be able to write an accurate caption; work well with a reporter; be very quick and often work under difficult conditions. Hours are irregular.

Prospects Not good. The market for photo-journalism is small and getting smaller. Most work as freelances and may specialize, e.g. in travel. For press photography there are always more candidates than jobs. Some possibilities for photographers in other branches to sell work to newspapers or press agencies.

Pay: Medium to high (see p. xxiii).

Industrial and Scientific

The work This is the most varied branch of photography. Clients include manufacturing companies, research organizations, government departments, higher education establishments, the police and HM Forces. Examples of the work: making photographic progress reports in laboratories; recording the various stages of manufacturing processes; photographing building sites. Industrial photographers also take pictures for house magazines, exhibition stands and instructional purposes. Most of these photographers are salaried employees; some work as freelances or for studios (see General practice).

Prospects Better than in all above branches.

Pay: Medium to high (see p. xxiii).

Medical

The work Most teaching hospitals and medical research institutions employ medical photographers, who make still and cine records of work done in operating theatres and research laboratories, and of particular cases among patients. Photographers must not be squeamish.

As part of a team of hospital workers, medical photographers enjoy the comradeship and friendly atmosphere of hospital life. Of all careers in photography this is the least hectic, least tough, most companionable and worst paid.

Prospects Good. There is some demand for medical photographers.

Pay: Low to medium (see p. xxiii).

Training *All Photography*

Study can be part-time, while working as a junior in a studio, or, increasingly, full-time. The main courses are:

1. With CSE or some O-levels, *either* 2-year full-time or 3-year part-time for City and Guilds in General or Scientific and Technical Photography;
Or full-time courses leading to college diplomas or certificates;
Or DATEC validated courses, 1–3 years (see p. 64).
2. With 4 O-levels (including English language, maths or a science), a full-time 2-year or part-time 3-year course in the photographic department of a technical or art college leading to the Vocational Examination of the British Institute of Professional Photography.
3. With 1 or 2 A-levels, 2-year full-time or 3-year part time course for DATEC Higher award.
4. With 2 A-levels and 5 O-levels (including English language), a full-time 3-year or part-time 4-year course leading to the BIPP Professional Qualifying Examination.
5. With 2 A-levels and 3 O-levels, including chemistry, a degree in Photographic Science and Technology.
6. With 2 A-levels and 3 O-levels, several Photography or Photography, Film & Television or similar degree courses.
Some degrees lead to the PQE of the BIPP. Several Art & Design degrees (see Art & Design, p. 63) have special photography options.
Press Photography
Either: 1-year pre-entry course organized by National Council for Training of Journalists (see Journalism, p. 234);
Or the NCTJ's 3-year traineeship (see Journalism, p. 234).
Medical Photography
With O-levels or preferably A-levels, or after general photography course, entry as trainee in a hospital medical photography department. Then either private study for BIPP Basic and Higher Medical Photography examinations *or* part-time or block release for Modules 1 and 2 of Institute of Medical and Biological Illustration, leading to the Diploma in Medical Illustration.

Photographic Technician

The work The processing and printing of films is an extremely important aspect of photography and one in which backroom types are happiest. Most work nowadays is in colour and is increasingly automated (black-and-white film is still mainly processed on a 'hand' line). The work requires considerable concentration and technical knowledge, especially of the complex chemistry of colour film; without these skills a photographer's assignment worth hundreds or even thousands of pounds could be ruined. Technicians may take turns at all the jobs: processing, transparency-making, enlarging, printing and mounting, or may stick to one or two. Experienced technicians can learn more specialized skills, e.g. retouching, or making duplicate transparencies. Apart from laboratories which service professional photographers, there are 'photofinishing' companies which process film taken by amateurs (e.g. holiday snapshots).

Prospects Good. There is a shortage of good technicians; there is a greater demand for technicians than for photographers. Photofinishing offers most openings to school leavers.

Pay: Medium to high (see p. xxiii).

Training Usually starting as a junior or trainee in a photographic laboratory, and studying by day-release and/or evening classes for City and Guilds or DATEC (see p. 64) examinations. Alternatively, technicians can take one of the full-time courses. There is one DATEC Higher Diploma course in Photographic Technology.

Personal attributes *Needed by all photographers in varying degrees*: Visual imagination; eye for detail and composition; patience; perfect colour vision; artistic sensitivity; creativeness; trust in their own judgement (photographers, unlike other craftsmen and artists, do not usually know whether they have done a good job or not until it is too late); good powers of observation; ability to work quickly, under pressure, surrounded by crowds – in all kinds of unfavourable circumstances; ability to work well with others while keeping to their own individual style; originality; unusual inventiveness (for advertising and fashion photography); business sense (for arranging appointments, sending out bills etc.), as very few can afford secretaries; willingness to 'sell' themselves; a manner which encourages people to cooperate.

Press photography: News sense; ability to remain calm and unmoved, however tragic or unpleasant the circumstances.

Medical photographers: A scientific bent; tactful and reassuring manner; total lack of squeamishness.

Technicians: A scientific bent; manual skill; an eye for detail; patience.

Late start Press photography: upper age 24. A number of photographers have worked in other fields before taking up photography. The main drawback is poor salaries of trainee or assistant photographers.

Position of women There are now a fair number of well-known women photographers, although very few have reached the top in the advertising field. Women still have a little more difficulty than men getting in, especially to press photography.

Career-break: Depends on stage reached before the break and type of work done. Possibly difficult to return to best-paid and most competitive fields, but it should be possible to return to some kind of photography and/or to do some freelance work even while raising a family.

Part-time: Fair opportunities, especially as freelances.

Further information

British Institute of Professional Photography, Amwell End, Ware, Herts SG12 9HN
City and Guilds of London Institute, 76 Portland Place, London W1N 4AA
Institute of Medical and Biological Illustration (IMBI), 27 Craven Street, London WC2

Related careers

Art and Design – Television – Fashion – Journalism

Physiotherapy

Entry qualifications 2 A-levels, 5 O-levels, including an English and 2 science subjects one of which must be physics.

The work A physiotherapist uses exercises and movement, electrotherapy, ultrasound, short-wave diathermy, manipulation and massage to treat the injured, the sick, and the convalescent of all ages for a large variety of conditions.

Chartered physiotherapists normally only treat patients if their doctor suggested physiotherapy should be given. Some doctors give exact directions for treatment. Others state the 'objective' (the therapeutic aim); the physiotherapist decides on the type of the treatment.

Patients too ill to be moved are treated in bed; others, such as post-operative patients, may have to be helped to walk properly again. Post-paralysis cases are taught to make their healthy limbs or muscles do the work, as far as possible, of paralysed ones, and how to use partially paralysed limbs.

The work can be physically strenuous as it involves lifting and supporting patients, but physiotherapists learn to lift heavy weights without strain. In fact 'lifting' is one of the things they teach: patients needing treatment for strained backs are taught to lift correctly.

Some patients do exercises in water and the physiotherapist works with them in heated swimming pools.

Some patients are treated in groups, but most individually. In all cases, the physiotherapist must use her judgement. She must know how far to coax a patient into doing an uncomfortable exercise, and she must adapt treatment to suit each patient. A physiotherapist uses tact and encouragement together with specialist knowledge. She may have to explain to a patient why it is important that exercises are done regularly at home, to persuade children to cooperate; or to allay patients' fear of electrical treatment.

The vast majority work in hospital physiotherapy departments. They work the usual office hours, but may have to do some evening clinics, 'on call' night work and weekend duties.

Some specialize and work in hospitals or clinics for the elderly, in orthopaedic or chest hospitals, or with disabled children only, in homes, hospitals or in schools; or part-time in schools or maternity clinics. Work in the community is of increasing importance.

There is also room for physiotherapists who do not wish to work only with the sick and injured. Some sports clubs employ physiotherapists (often part-time) to keep their members fit, and to treat minor injuries; large industrial and commercial organizations employ a physiotherapist to do largely preventive work: to see that typists' desks are the right height for comfort, health, and therefore efficiency; to show typists how to sit without strain; to teach sales assistants to relax while standing; to teach porters to carry without strain, and so on.

Prospects Good. There is a world shortage of physiotherapists, especially of physiotherapy teachers, but promotion prospects vary.

An experienced physiotherapist can set up in private practice, treating patients either in her own treatment rooms or in patients' homes. But this needs good contacts with local doctors and capital to buy equipment and see her over the first few months. Qualifications are recognized in many countries abroad but EEC countries and the USA require a degree.

Pay: Medium (see p. xxiii).

Training *Either* 3-year full-time course at training schools attached to hospitals and recognized for training by the Chartered Society of Physiotherapy; *or* 3- or 4-year degree course. Degrees were introduced only recently and at present there are only two such courses. It is intended, however, that physiotherapy, like some other professions supplementary to medicine, should become an all-graduate profession. Degree course students normally need two science A-levels or at least one science A-level and a *very* good science O-level. The syllabus of the degree and the non-degree course is much the same. In both cases, for the first few months, training is mainly theoretical; after that it is a combination of theory and practice, with students treating patients under the supervision of trained physiotherapists/teachers. Theoretical training covers physics, physiology, anatomy, movement, manipulation, electrotherapy; conditions for which the therapy is indicated; how to handle patients – both physically and psychologically.

The main difference between the two types of training is that degree students are expected to have a more thorough science background and therefore need to spend less time on absorbing facts. They will have more 'thinking time', and more time to devote to the psychological aspects of their work. They may also study a particular aspect of physiotherapy in greater depth. Above all, as undergraduates they have more opportunity to mix with students from other disciplines. There are several post-registration courses for people who want to specialize in work with specific patient-groups, such as geriatrics, orthopaedic patients, patients with specific disabilities; or in specialisms such as, for example, manipulation.

Personal attributes Enough interest in science and medicine to keep up to date with new developments; a sympathetic yet objective approach to the sick and disabled; ability to work as one of a team and to take responsibility; good health.

Late start Although it is known that mature entrants give longer service and are more highly motivated, schools restrict the number of entrants over 25, and will not normally take anyone over 30. However, GCE entry requirements may be relaxed for late entrants. Courses may be shortened for members of the other remedial professions, graduate nurses and other graduates with relevant degrees, and for PE teachers.

Position of women The vast majority are women, but a disproportionate number of men are heads of physiotherapy schools.

Career-break: Returners are welcome; *refresher* training is usually arranged on an in-service, *ad hoc* basis; promotion tends to be impeded by career-break.

Part-time: Good opportunities in many areas, though usually only at junior level: few departments promote part-timers, but this may change as the generation of unmarried heads of department is beginning to retire and the majority of young physiotherapists are married.

Further information Chartered Society of Physiotherapy, 14 Bedford Row, London WC1R 4ED

Related careers *Science Technician (Hospital) – Occupational Therapy – Remedial Gymnast – Speech Therapist*

Police

Entry qualifications

Minimum age 18½ (cadets from 16); minimum height for women 162 cm (5 ft 4 ins) approximately; for men 172 cm (5 ft 8 ins) approximately. No specific educational requirements; applicants with fewer than 4 O-levels, including English language and maths, take an entrance examination in these subjects. (Entrants without GCEs may have difficulty passing the qualifying examination for promotion to sergeant; see **Prospects**.) Considerable *graduate* entry.

(*For special graduate entry scheme*, see **Training**.)

A few cadet schemes for 16–18-year-olds.

The work

Police work is a unique mixture of important decision-making, independence, teamwork, variety, and routine. The primary purpose of policing is the prevention of crime, not the apprehension and chasing of criminals. Police officers' uniformed, routine presence on the beat, as well as their presence in crowds or wherever trouble is expected, acts as a deterrent to (at least some) potential law-breakers.

Police officers start with 2 years on the beat. In most areas the 'unit beat' system now operates. Like the old village policeman, the unit beat officer tries to be known by and know people on her regular 'patch' and to improve communication between the police and public. This means patrolling on foot or bicycle, not in cars. She has considerable say in arranging her working hours to suit the needs of her area; for example in a quiet suburb she might be around in the early afternoon when mothers fetch children from school and burglars get busy; in a 'rough' area she might be around at pub closing-time.

A typical 'unit' has 2 'resident' police officers; a detective constable and a panda may 'cover' 2 units. All these officers are in touch with each other and the station by personal radio. They can summon instant assistance and ask the station for information or advice.

While patrolling, police officers are on the look-out for missing persons, 'persons behaving in a suspicious manner', stolen and unlocked cars, and generally take note of – and may talk to the station about – anything which seems not quite right. Even when nothing happens, police officers are working.

After about 2 years, police officers may specialize (but it may take longer till a vacancy in the chosen specialization occurs). The main divisions are:

Traffic work, including mobile patrolling; vehicle inspection and giving expert evidence in court; jointly with local authority analysing causes of accidents and of traffic chaos, and working out improvement schemes. This involves research, negotiations, and operating computerized control systems. Work also includes detection of motoring offences.

CID: Occasionally includes working on big newsworthy crimes, but most of it is painstaking attention to detail, collecting and piecing together bits of apparently unimportant evidence. CID officers work closely with the uniformed branch (there is now much more interchange between the two branches than there used to be). The work also includes crime prevention (advising the public on how to make their homes, offices, cars, shops, etc, burglarproof); criminal records, 'scene of crime' and fingerprinting experts (see also Forensic Science, p. 449). CID officers do a lot of interviewing – not only of suspects, but also house-to-house inquiries covering whole areas.

Mounted branch, *dog handling*, *river police* are small specializations which appeal to people who choose the police because of the active, outdoor life; *Community relations* and *juvenile liaison* are specializations for those who choose the police because they want to help solve social problems. In fact most police work involves dealing with and trying to alleviate tensions in society.

From sergeant upwards, policing includes a considerable amount of 'man-management', ensuring as far as possible that every officer's special abilities and interests are made use of. The work also includes more paper-work and requires extensive knowledge of the law. For example when a suspect has been arrested and is brought to the station by the constable, the station sergeant (or possibly an inspector) is responsible for seeing that charges are correctly set out, the prisoner is formally charged and given whatever facilities he is entitled to (contacting his solicitor, for example).

Prospects All promotion is from the ranks. Constables can take the Sergeant's qualifying exam after 2 years (it is a stiff exam, requires hard work, mainly in one's own time) but it normally takes 5 years to make sergeant. The inspector's (equally stiff) exam can be taken after 2 years as sergeant. (However, even after passing exams, promotion is not automatic: vacancies are not always available.) It generally takes 12 years from entry to make inspector. In the Metropolitan force most promotion to sergeant and inspector is by competitive examination. After inspector, promotion is on merit, without further exams.

By no means all constables try to become sergeants; there are a number of jobs for them apart from beat constables; for example becoming 'collator' – collecting and filing information relevant to the area and answering fellow officers' queries about anything from the name of a local vet to numbers of stolen cars (and details of missing persons).

See **Training** for fast promotion for selected *graduates*.

Pay: Medium to high (see p. xxiii).

Training Initial training in the Met. is now 20 weeks; since January 1984 provincial training lasts 14 weeks (plus 1 week induction). Subjects include law; liaison with social services; courts and policing procedures; and crime prevention. Role-playing exercises are carried out to teach, for example, how to deal with traffic accidents, street fights, domestic disputes, hooliganism; how to take statements from shocked suspects. Topics include some sociology, psychology and training in community relations to enable officers to understand the underlying causes of contemporary problems such as racial tension and vandalism, and how to deal with them. Self-defence and physical education play an important part in training.

After the initial course the officer is posted to a station. At first she patrols together with an experienced officer. For the first 2 years she is on probation. Throughout her career she attends specialist (e.g. community relations) and/or promotion courses. Officers who show potential for senior rank may be sent on the residential 'Special Course' at Police College. This lasts 12 months; teaching is at university level. Promotion to at least superintendent eventually is more or less guaranteed. A number are awarded scholarships to university.

Under a special *graduate entry scheme*, selected graduates are accepted, with a near-guarantee of admission to the Special Course after their 2 years on the beat (which is essential grass-roots). They are likely to be inspectors after about 6 years from joining, and promotion prospects after that are very good indeed. In Scotland the accelerated training scheme for graduates is slightly different.

Personal attributes A sense of proportion and outside interests to avoid developing a biased view of humanity; a sincere but not too critical interest in other people's ways of life; understanding of and sympathy with human weakness; ability to combine sympathy with firmness; a sense of humour; an observant eye and a cool head; the ability to make quick decisions, shoulder responsibility and yet accept discipline; the ability to work as one of a team; physical courage; a liking for being out of doors in all weathers; good health (especially good feet); willingness to move for promotion.

Late start Normal upper age 30, but at Chief Constables's discretion whether to accept older candidates.

Position of women

Ratio of female to male police officers is 1 to 10, but about a third of police cadets and recruits are women.

Women have had equal powers and duties for a long time, but until recently they had their own promotion structure, apart from their male colleagues', and they tended to work largely with women and children. Now, they are totally integrated and compete for promotion and specialization on theoretically equal terms with male colleagues. It is too early to say how 'equal' their chances of top jobs now are, but it is quite likely that as a result of integration a smaller proportion of women officers will be promoted to senior jobs. They undoubtedly have to be above average in 'man-management' ability and have much more drive than men, to be put in charge of a busy station – which is usually an important step on the promotion ladder. Women will now not automatically do the social-work part of policing – dealing with women and children in trouble, and liaising with social workers – but many may well go on concentrating on this type of work. It is up to individual senior officers to decide how to make 'the best use of each officer's abilities', and many senior officers still consider women particularly suitable for the social-work aspects of policing.

As individual Forces' policy about promoting women police officers depends ultimately on the Chief Constable's views, women could ask for details about numbers of women and their distribution in the specializations and ranks before applying to any particular Force. There is no need to join one's local Force.

Career-break: Returners are welcome up to about 30; older returners' chances depend on Chief Constables' views (and shortage of young applicants). Chances better for sergeants and inspectors than for constables.

Part-time: No opportunities at the moment. (No reason why experienced officers should not try to change this situation.)

Further information

Local police headquarters

Police Recruiting Department, Home Office, Queen Anne's Gate, London SW1

Scotland: Police Division, Scottish Home and Health Department, St Andrew's House, St James Centre, Edinburgh EH1 3DE

Related careers

Environmental Health Officer – Factory Inspector – Services – Social Work

Politics

Member of Parliament – agent

This is not a career in the usual sense; prospective politicians must first prove their ability in some other area before they stand any chance of attracting votes. Politics is included here simply because so many young people want to know how to get into it.

Entry qualifications Part-time voluntary work in constituency parties or on local councils is the proving ground of loyalty and the essential starting point of any political career.

Member of Parliament

The work There are 650 MPs. The House of Commons sits in the afternoon and evening for an average of 35 to 40 weeks a year. Sessions often last late into the night. An MP spends most of her time listening to and, if she wishes, participating in debate. Mornings are spent in committee (where much of the most important parliamentary work is done), answering constituents' letters, seeing visitors, researching. If at all possible, MPs spend a day a week or frequent weekends in their constituencies, holding 'surgeries', arranging and holding meetings. They must find time to attend social functions, open bazaars, be interviewed by the press, TV, radio, and attend weekend meetings.

Most MPs carry on with some kind of job which can be fitted in with their busy parliamentary schedule; many are journalists, some lawyers, trade union officials, business people. MPs have very little free time indeed. Though vacations are long, they have to attend to constituency matters all the year round.

Prospects Impossible to predict. In marginal constituencies an MP is very insecure; even in a safe seat the unexpected can happen at the next election; MPs may also fail to be re-adopted by their constituencies. Most MPs hope to hold office eventually, but only a small proportion ever do so. It depends partly on their ability and hard work, but also on luck – mainly whether their party is in office, and whether their views on particular issues are acceptable to the party leader.

Pay: Medium (see p. xxiii).

Selection and training

A candidate must normally have been a member of her party for at least 2 years. Many learn the business of politics – debating, dealing with constituents' problems, canvassing, collecting relevant facts, making speeches – by being (unpaid) local councillors. Prospective Labour candidates must be members of a trade union, if eligible.

The methods of selection are, with minor variations, basically the same for the three main parties. In general, candidates must first be approved by the central or regional party organization; only Labour candidates have to be cleared by their local party first. All candidates go through a number of selection interviews where they prove their knowledge of current affairs and their debating and speaking skills.

First-time candidates tend to be given hopeless seats to fight, so that they gain experience and prove that they have the enthusiasm needed to campaign successfully.

Personal attributes

Strong political faith and convictions; self-confidence; resilience; considerable debating skills; great physical stamina; willingness to work unsocial and long hours and to give politics priority over other interests/activities; thick skin to cope with personal attacks.

Late start

Women: although maturity is an asset a woman candidate of 40 who competes for adoption with a man of 30 is probably at a disadvantage. It is very difficult for women to win: if they are very young, adoption committees fear they will have babies (which is more of a temporary hindrance in politics than in other work).
Men: no special problem.

Position of women

Women MPs have numbered between 19 and 30 for many years now. Nothing like as many women as men put themselves forward as candidates, even though women are very active as voluntary party workers. The long hours, the need to be absent from home and the lack of crèche facilities make politics a difficult career for women with children and/or with husbands who are not equally committed to politics or at least to running home and family in their wives' absence. It is probably harder for women to be adopted in the first place: a woman candidate has to be of better calibre than a man to stand equal chance of adoption. There is no indication that women candidates fare worse than men in parliamentary elections (which may of course be due to the fact that women candidates generally *are* of above-average ability). All parties genuinely want more women MPs – as long as they are exceptionally good. Once in Parliament, women are very successful in terms of holding office in relation to their numbers, and they are very active on committees.

Proportions of women in politics have not changed much over the years. There are still only 3% of women MPs; 17% of local councillors are women; 16% of European Parliament Members.

The 300 Group (formed in 1980) is trying hard to persuade more women to enter politics (its name was chosen to indicate that at least 300 MPs ought to be women). The Group is supported by all parties and by prominent women in public and professional life who are not politicians but see advantages to be gained by everyone if more women were in decision-making positions. The Group runs seminars, gives lectures to schools, and individual advice, also by letter, to anyone (also men) who wants to get into politics at any level, in any party.

Constituency Agent

The work Agents are paid or unpaid constituency officials (not all constituencies have paid full-time agents). An agent is responsible for efficient constituency organization, for checking electoral registers, for membership and fund-raising drives, for organizing meetings and MPs' visits and general local party matters. She normally has mainly voluntary helpers.

Selection and training Potential full-time agents must have worked for the party for at least 2 years. Before being eligible for appointment, Labour Party workers take a correspondence course and an examination for the Diploma in Electoral Law and Party Organization. Tory workers have a minimum of 15 months' training working with a qualified agent while taking the examinations for the Associate Membership of the National Society of Conservative and Unionist Agents. Liberal Party training is less formal, but their agents also have to learn relevant law and organization during a residential crash course.

Prospects There are not many posts, but all parties welcome more applicants. Promotion can be either to a key constituency, or to a regional or central office post. Agents' work is grist to the mill for anyone wanting to become an MP eventually, but a certain period of time has to elapse before an agent may stand as candidate in a constituency in which she was an agent.

Pay: Low to medium (see p. xxiii).

Personal attributes Much as for MPs, plus considerable organizing ability, and ability to make volunteers work hard.

Late start No problem.

Position of women In the Liberal Party, about half the agents are women, rather fewer in the Labour and Tory parties, more in the SDP, but this is entirely due to the proportion applying. There is no discrimination in this (usually badly paid or voluntary) work.

Part-time: Possible in theory; in practice part-time agents tend to be volunteers.

Further information

Local or central party organizations.

Related careers

Acting – Barrister – Economics – Journalism – Teaching

NOTE: *On the fringes of politics: Trade union* organizer or researcher. The majority of paid trade union officials are recruited from unpaid union officials; but occasionally sociology, economics and other graduates are taken on as researchers, or possibly as organizers.

Printing

Entry qualifications See **Training**.

The work Printing has been called the 'meeting place of art and science', but above all it is an industry. It uses a variety of technological processes to create a product of visual impact. The product may be books, newspapers, packaging, postage stamps, writing paper, record sleeves or reproductions of old masters: it is always a form of communication. Some printing processes are centuries old, but printing technology has changed enormously in the last few years and continues to change. For example, computer typesetting is now often used for text, and electronic scanners are used in the production of coloured illustrations. In many cases, alternative methods are available, and *production controllers* or *managers* (titles and precise functions vary) have to decide, with the client, on the most advantageous methods in any particular case, weighing up such factors as relative speed, cost, quality.

Apart from working in printing production, technicians and technologists also work in research and development on new machinery, paper, inks.

Prospects Very poor at craft level, better at technician, technologist and management levels.

Pay: High (see p. xxiii).

Training *Craft*: Two systems now exist, one for occupations within the National Graphical Association (NGA), another for those within the Society of Graphical and Allied Trades (SOGAT). Since August 1983 NGA entrants follow a training agreement which replaced the traditional time-serving apprenticeship. This is intended for school leavers, older entrants and existing staff needing re-training – there is no upper age limit. Those under 18 take a 2-year City and Guilds Certificate course (part-time or block-release) and cover 15 modules, to include broad-based skills together with specialization in one of three areas: origination (preparation for print); printing; and finishing. In-company training may last longer, depending on trainee. Some take a printing foundation course first.

SOGAT entrants follow a 4-year apprenticeship. Candidates for both schemes have to go through a selection process and may or may not be sponsored while training.

Technician: Increased technology has meant greater demand for highly skilled workers. Entry qualifications for craft and technician training overlap and promotion from craft to technician level is encouraged. Most common routes are:

1. Traineeship/apprenticeship followed by 1–2-year full-time course for BTEC National Certificate.
2. With 4 O-levels (including maths and English) 3-year (occasionally 2) block-release course for BTEC National Certificate.
3. 1-year foundation course followed by either BTEC National Certificate or Diploma (Diploma usually requires 3–4 O-levels).
4. With A-level mathematics, physics or chemistry *or* BTEC National award, part-time or sandwich study (2–3 years) for BTEC Higher award.
5. With 2 or 3 A-levels including at least one science (preferably chemistry), entrants can take a 4-year BSc in Printing Technology.
6. Art school training (see Art and Design, p. 63), with specialization in Graphic Design or Typography, can also lead to printing jobs.

Personal attributes

Depends on type and level of work, but generally some visual imagination; interest in machinery; practicality; some dexterity; indifference to being the only, or one of a few, women in an all-male setting.

For managerial jobs: organizing ability; ability to work under pressure; being a self-starter.

Late start

Possible in theory at craft level under new NGA training scheme. Should also be possible for design-trained people.

Position of women

This is one of the most traditional industries (especially newspapers). Women make up nearly one third of the workforce, but very few are in skilled occupations. There now are a few women craft and technician apprentices, but women still meet prejudice on the shop-floor and have greater difficulties getting sponsored apprenticeships than men. However, the same proportion of women as men pass the selection tests. The flexibility of the new training scheme, together with changes in the traditional structure of the industry resulting from new technology, should improve women's prospects. At the technology level there is no valid reason whatever why women should not succeed; they have no difficulty getting onto degree or BTEC Higher Diploma courses. Art school trained women are doing quite well in typography and production/design.

Career-break: Return to work is likely to be difficult because of technological changes and shortage of jobs. A few re-training courses exist.

Part-time: Few opportunities in printing: possibly as freelance typographer.

Further information

British Printing Industries Federation, 11 Bedford Row, London WC1R 4DX
Institute of Printing, 8 Lonsdale Gardens, Tunbridge Wells, Kent TN1 1NU

Related careers

Art and Design – Engineering – Publishing – Science

Prison Service

Prison officer – assistant governor

Entry qualifications

Prison officer: minimum age 21. Minimum height 5 ft 6 ins (5 ft 7 ins in Scotland); women normally 5 ft 3 ins.

No specific education requirements. Selection is by short written test and interview.

Assistant governor: minimum age 21.

No specific qualifications laid down, but in practice entry is with a degree or comparable qualification.

The work

This is basically social work, with the emphasis on training, not punishing, prisoners. The important aspect is dealing with people with problems, not just locking and unlocking cells. Staff, who are no longer called 'warders', are expected to take a personal interest in the prisoners, to talk to them as one human being to another and to help their rehabilitation by fostering their self-respect and gaining their cooperation. Prisoners are often in trouble through force of circumstances rather than real criminality, and day-to-day contact with firm but understanding officers is a vital part of their rehabilitation. Although some prisoners are abusive and violent, the majority are not disruptive and just want to finish their sentences as quickly as possible. Overcrowding causes problems and new prisons are being built to help ease the pressure.

There are five different types of establishment: remand centres, mainly for young offenders and persons awaiting trial or sentence; local prisons, to which convicted prisoners are sent initially for assessment; training prisons, open, closed or maximum security, which have facilities for training prisoners in a range of skills; Youth Custody Centres, which are training centres for juveniles between 15 and 21; and detention centres, which provide a tough regime for 14- to 21-year-olds serving shorter sentences than those in Youth Custody Centres. Scottish prisons are organized slightly differently.

Prison work is, of course, often depressing but, like other types of social work, it can be very rewarding and is of real value to the community.

Staff accommodation is normally provided, but increasingly prison staff live out and receive an allowance in lieu of accommodation.

Prison staff can either buy meals in the mess or cook the
inevitably on a shift basis.

Prison Officer

Daily routine varies from prison to prison. Prison officers must be willing to serve in any type of institution, although they have a certain amount of choice. They are concerned with the training, rehabilitation, control and routine supervision of prisoners at work in the kitchen, laundry, workshop, gardens or farm; in their cells; at exercise and during recreation. They escort individual prisoners to and from courts and hospitals and accompany visitors to the visiting room. They work as part of a team, together with medical staff, welfare officers and specialist instructors and teachers. They must see that prisoners who seem to have specific problems discuss these with senior staff. In certain establishments they may take part in 'group counselling' when a group of prisoners and staff discuss personal and general problems. There are opportunities for specialization. Prison officers who can teach a skill or trade (anything from engineering to art and craft) may become *trades officers*. Those interested in nursing and health care can train to become *prison hospital officers*. Others become *dog handlers* or *electronic security experts*.

Assistant Governor

Some are promoted from prison officer but the majority are recruited from outside the Prison Service. Of these two thirds are new graduates. The selection board looks for candidates with a good understanding of social problems and modern methods of dealing with them. A degree in any subject or experience of management in a social setting (for example, personnel work, social studies, institutional management) is an advantage. The precise nature of the work depends on the type of establishment, but it is primarily managerial. The assistant governor is usually in charge of a 'wing' or 'house', and is responsible for managing inmates' general rehabilitation and welfare. She organizes, or helps to organize, work and leisure activities (lectures, concerts, etc.), keeps records of prisoners' progress and problems, and is involved in parole matters.

Prospects Very good. There is a shortage of prison staff at all levels. Over half of prison officers gain some promotion and they can climb up the ladder to assistant governor if they are able to absorb the necessary degree-level academic training. Assistant governors with exceptional ability may be promoted to prison governor. Promotion usually means transfer to another establishment.

Pay: Low to medium; high for governors (see p. xxiii).

weeks in preliminary training at a prison or Youth … working closely with experienced officers, followed by …ng at a Prison Officers' Training School. Academic and …struction is given in subjects appropriate to the work, e.g. …ssification, dealing with people with problems, escort and …uties, supervision of inmates at work and play, security.

…ant governors: Entrants under 24 work for about 1 year as prison …cers. Training during the first 2 years as assistant governor consists … practical experience alternating with theoretical training at Prison Service College. Subjects include psychology, sociology, social casework and group work, management, rehabilitation of prisoners.

Personal attributes Leadership: this is difficult to define, but for example a young person who enjoyed taking an active part in organizing at school or youth club probably has it; a sense of right and wrong, without being censorious; a genuine desire to help people in trouble and the ability to understand and sympathize with people's failings without necessarily condoning them; the ability to find the right approach to all types of people; immense patience with people at their most unbearable; interests entirely outside prison work to help keep a sense of proportion; a friendly, naturally happy disposition.

Late start *Prison officer*: Entry up to 49½ (normally 42 in Scotland). *Assistant governor*: Entry normally up to 35. A *few* people with relevant experience in other spheres are appointed above this age.

Position of women Prison officers normally work with inmates of their own sex; assistant governors may work with both sexes. As there are relatively few women's prisons, women assistant governors are more likely to serve in men's establishments than vice versa. Although far fewer women than men apply for assistant governor posts, a much higher proportion of those who do are accepted.

Career-break: No problem (if there is a local prison).

Part-time: Virtually none.

Further information Home Office, Freepost, London SW1E 5BX

Scotland: Establishment Officer, Scottish Home and Health Department, St Margaret's House, London Road, Edinburgh EH8 7TG

Related careers *Personnel Work – Police – Social Work*

Psychology and Psychotherapy

PSYCHOLOGY: educational – clinical – occupational – social – experimental; PSYCHOTHERAPY: counselling

Psychology

Psychologists are concerned with the systematic study of human behaviour. They must not be confused with psychiatrists, who are medically qualified specialists who give treatment to the mentally sick and disturbed.

Entry qualifications Usually 2 or 3 A-levels, including at least 1 science or maths; maths and a science at O-level if not at A-level (requirements also vary according to whether the course leads to a BSc or BA).

The work There are many specializations. The main job areas are educational, clinical and occupational psychology; among the main research areas are social and experimental psychology. But titles given to research areas vary and overlap. Educational and clinical are the most clearly-defined job areas; occupational psychology is the most diversified; social psychology the least clearly defined, and experimental psychology overlaps most with other specializations.

Educational Psychology

Educational psychologists advise teachers, parents, doctors and social workers on children's and young people's adjustment and learning problems. Assessment involves sessions with the 'problem' child as well as, usually, its parents and teachers, and a thorough study of the subject's background and environment. Various established techniques, such as ability tests and 'personality schedules' are used. Treatment may include individual counselling sessions with child and/or parents and advice to parents and teachers on the 'management' of the problem. Apart from advising when problems have arisen, educational psychologists do preventive work, such as organizing in-service courses for teachers and social workers, talking to groups of parents, to 5th- and 6th-formers, and to youth clubs.

They are employed by local education authorities and work in school/county psychological services and child guidance clinics. They have considerable autonomy right from the start.

Clinical Psychology

Clinical psychologists help handicapped people to come to terms with their problems. Therapeutic work is carried out with children and adults, in individual counselling sessions and in groups; in hospitals; in therapeutic communities (see Psychiatric Nursing, p. 330); at day-centres (see Social Work, p. 476), and in family groups. The wide range of problems treated includes physical and mental handicap; phobias (including children's inability to face school); neurological and obsessional disorders; sexual difficulties; reading and writing difficulties.

Clinical psychologists organize, coordinate and cooperate in vocational guidance for the handicapped, rehabilitation, training and retraining programmes for patients with physical or neurological and mental handicap. They set up systems for job analysis, assess and evaluate the work potential and the progress of patients. The broad types of therapeutic work undertaken are behaviour therapy, psychotherapy and counselling, rehabilitation and training. Most clinical psychologists work in hospitals, some in child guidance clinics. They work in close collaboration with neurologists, psychiatrists and other specialists.

Occupational Psychology

Occupational psychologists study people as workers. They advise on how people can both enjoy and be efficient in their work by giving vocational guidance to both children and adults. They set up selection procedures for employers and develop training schemes; they help in the organizing of work itself by devising new methods of doing jobs, and they advise on the design of tools and machines so that they are easy to use. They also research into and advise on psychological implications of organizational structures and proposed changes, aiming at improving both job satisfaction and productivity (this is now called 'organizational psychology, and overlaps also with social psychology).

Occupational psychologists have developed techniques for collecting information from people about what they like doing and what they are good at, as well as what they find difficult and unpleasant. They match this information against that collected by detailed studies of the actual work involved in the jobs concerned. They are very much involved with 'managing change' of working practices in offices and manufacturing (see Management, p. 271).

Other occupational/social psychology specializations are concerned with retirement: pre-retirement counselling and training and generally looking into problems connected with the growing proportion of retired people in the community; with mid-career changes necessitated by changes in job opportunities; with problems connected with women's changing career-patterns and aspirations.

Social Psychology

This is a wide-ranging and diffuse research specialization. Social psychologists are, broadly, concerned with the behaviour, attitudes and interaction of individuals and groups: what causes whom to behave in what manner; what effect do events, media presentation, individuals and groups' actions have on other individuals and other groups within the community. They investigate, for example, the causes of, and possible cures for, football hooliganism; or the voting behaviour of individuals and groups. They work with occupational sociologists on training methods for both managers and for young people, and on organizational structures. They look into the effect of television on different groups in the community, and they may look into the problems of integration of ethnic minorities into the community, and into the attitudes to, and effect of, class differences among adults and children. Research projects may stem from the psychologist's own idea or they may be commissioned by the police, the Home Office, industrial relations consultants, a football club, a market research organization, etc. Social psychologists use observation, interviews, questionnaires and literature searches to collect information.

Titles now used for what comes under the vague and wide social psychology umbrella include *community psychology* – concerned with such problems as vandalism and squatting, and *child psychology* concerned, for example, with comparing the development of children raised in foster homes with that of children raised in their own families. This might be research done in conjunction with, or for, educational psychologists.

There is no social psychology career structure. Social psychologists' research is usually done in universities, often on short-term contracts.

Experimental Psychology

Research psychologists who specialize in experimental psychology help to solve a wide range of problems that affect people by applying both the accumulated psychological knowledge about people and the special experimental methods that have been developed to study human behaviour. These problems range from designing road signs that can be seen at speed, designing easy-to-use aircraft controls to prevent accidents due to pilot error, finding out how well older people can learn new jobs, developing clothing for special work, to planning houses, offices, and playgrounds for children. In all this work experiments are planned, information is collected and analysed, and conclusions are drawn to enable someone to make decisions that in some way affect people. As well as solving problems experimental psychologists are always trying to extend the scope of psychology by carrying out experiments to find out more about people and how the human brain works. This may include work with animals.

Experimental psychologists usually work in teams with other scientists; mainly in government and university research, often on short-term contracts.

Psychotherapy

Psychotherapy is not a career to go into straight from school or university. Maturity and 'experience of life' are essential even to be accepted for training.

(a) *Adult psychotherapy*: 'Adult psychotherapists' help patients by 'talking through' their psychological or emotional problems. Patients include people who feel they need to gain a better understanding of their own personality, who have suffered bereavement or are depressed for other reasons, and people who are mentally disturbed or ill. There are various 'schools' of psychotherapy: the term is now used to cover different methods of treatment which vary greatly in depth, intensity and basic philosophy.

(b) *Child psychotherapy*: This is a form of treatment for children who suffer from behaviour disturbances which are psychological in origin. Psychotherapists must build up a good relationship with their patients – verbal communication usually has to be supplemented with playing, drawing, painting – and with patients' parents. Most children are seen individually; some are treated in groups.

Child psychotherapists work at child guidance clinics; young people's advice centres, where their patients are adolescents rather than children and the work involves listening and sorting out problems; and with educational psychologists in the National Health Service.

Prospects *Psychology*: There is a small but steady demand (see **Training** for need for post-graduate training for specializations). Psychology degrees can lead to industrial relations and other personnel functions and generally to jobs in industry where 'dealing with people' is important. With post-graduate training it also leads to Social Work (see p. 477).

Psychotherapy: Adult psychotherapy: The demand, especially outside London, is growing, but this is a very small profession and opportunities in the NHS are very limited indeed, so practitioners rely almost entirely on private patients. Good contacts with local GPs are essential.

Child psychotherapy: Overall demand is growing, but although local education authorities and the NHS need more child psychotherapists, expenditure cuts have severely affected job prospects.

Pay: Medium to high (see p. xxiii).

Training

Psychology: 3- (sometimes 4-) year degree course. The composition of the courses varies: some lead to BA, some to BSc. Topics usually covered include: experimental study of such mental processes as thinking, learning and perceiving; animal behaviour; physiology of the nervous system; development of children; social relationships and their effects on personality; mental disorder; applications of psychology to the study of society, industry, and education; techniques of testing and experiment. Students also do a great deal of statistics, laboratory work, and often work with animals.

There is no need to decide what branch of psychology to specialize in till after the course. Post-graduate courses are essential:

Educational and *clinical* psychologists take post-graduate Diploma or Master's degree courses (possibly part-time or 'sandwich') which last 1 to 3 years. Those intending to take a post-graduate qualification in educational psychology must usually have at least 2 years' teaching experience.

Occupational psychologists normally take a 2-year full- or part-time Master's degree or Diploma course.

Experimental psychologists may get 'in-service' training while working for a higher degree by doing research on a special topic.

Psychotherapy: *Adult psychotherapists*: Training varies according to 'school' of psychotherapy – there are several training organizations. All require students to have had previous qualifications and relevant experience, and all psychotherapists must undergo personal analysis (for which they must pay themselves).

The usual qualifications needed for psychotherapy training are:

(a) medical qualification; *or*

(b) psychology degree or a degree containing a substantial psychology component; *or*

(c) social work qualification or (exceptionally) counselling experience and qualification (see below); *or*

(d) teaching qualification and counselling experience.

Child psychotherapists: students must normally have a psychology degree and experience of working with children.

All psychotherapy training starts with a year's probationary work. If accepted for training, students then spend at least 4 years on intensive, time-consuming training. Training is a mixture of theory and practice. During the latter part of the training, students may be allowed to be paid for treating patients. There are a few salaried training posts, especially for child psychotherapists.

Personal attributes A detached interest in individuals' and communities' behaviour rather than personal involvement; an interest in scientific method; the ability to work well on one's own and also to cooperate with people from different backgrounds; patience; numeracy.

Late start Degree course entry requirements may be relaxed for mature students, who are welcome on degree courses, but proof of adequate knowledge of maths at least is essential, and the training is a very long one. Psychotherapy *is* a 'late start' career.

Position of women In psychotherapy women far outnumber men; in other specializations about 45% of professionally qualified psychologists and about 50% of post-graduate students are women. Far more women then men – about twice as many – take psychology degrees, but women then do not necessarily take further training. Women have no more difficulties in getting jobs than men.

Career-break: Depends on competition from newly-qualified people. There are (limited) opportunities to train as counsellor (see below).

Part-time: Some employment opportunities.

Further information The General Secretary, The British Psychological Society, St Andrew's House, 48 Princess Road, Leicester LE1 7DR

Psychotherapy
London Centre for Psychotherapy, 19 Fitzjohns Avenue, London NW3
Tavistock Clinic, Belsize Lane, London NW3
British Association of Psychotherapists, c/o 121 Hendon Lane, London N3 3PR
Association of Child Psychotherapists, Burgh House, New End Square, London NW3

Related careers *Personnel Work – Psychiatric Nursing – Social Work – Sociology – Teaching*

COUNSELLING: This is not usually a career in itself, rather an activity for people with certain skills, qualifications and experience. Counsellors listen to, and help clients cope with, personal problems. It is a form of psychotherapy but counsellors are not as highly qualified, and do not probe as deeply, as fully trained psychotherapists. Counselling is part of social workers', personnel officers', doctors' and teachers' jobs; very few people are employed entirely as counsellors, although some schools and other education establishments employ qualified teachers or social workers who have taken a counselling course; so do some voluntary organizations. The latter usually specialize in a type of 'client group', for example, people become marriage counsellors, student, youth or alcoholics' counsellors. Counselling of this type is usually done by volunteers or as a part-time job for a small fee. There are a few post-graduate counselling courses at universities and polytechnics or run by voluntary organizations, but there are far more qualified counsellors than job vacancies.
Further Information: British Association for Counselling, 37a Sheep Street, Rugby, Warwickshire CV21 3BX

Public Relations

Entry qualifications None are specified, see **Training**.

The work A public relations officer (now often called 'public affairs' officer or executive) acts as a link between client and public; it is her job to present the client's image in more general terms than an advertising campaign. She provides factual stories about the client or his product to newspapers, magazines and television, thus keeping the product or the service in the news and creating a 'favourable climate or image'. She answers journalists' questions about her client's product, views or services, and may take journalists to see a client or his business. She arranges parties, exhibitions and other projects to 'put over' a client, and gives talks to interested groups – schools, women's organizations, etc.

She deals with inquiries (and also complaints) from the public.

Public relations officers work either in a public relations firm (several partners each with their own accounts and a shared office and staff), or in a public relations department of an advertising agency, or in separate press and public relations departments of individual organizations – from stores to public utilities and government departments. This last type of work is increasing. (The title here may be Information Officer.) More and more organizations employ staff to answer questions and generally to see that the public is informed about their functions and activities. Today, local authorities, trade unions, employers' federations, and professional organizations such as the British Medical Association employ public relations or information officers.

Prospects There is no security in P.R. work; far more people want to do this sort of work than there are opportunities.

Pay: Medium to very high (see p. xxiii).

Training School-leavers enter either as secretary in a public relations firm or department or via journalism (see p. 230), or with some specialist knowledge, for instance of engineering (see p. 168) or marketing (see p. 283).

Specific – not obligatory – training for students in relevant employment: part-time (mainly evening) study, for about 2 years, for the CAM (Communications, Advertising and Marketing) Foundation's Certificate. Syllabus covers public relations principles and practice; business organization; organization, technical and policy aspects of the media; communication principles and methods. The Certificate is followed by a further year's part-time study for the CAM Diploma in Public Relations.

Entry requirements for the Certificate course are:

2 A-levels and 3 O-levels; *or* BTEC National award (see p. xvi);

or: 1 year's experience in a public relations office plus 5 O-Levels;

or: 3 years' experience plus employer's recommendation. (In other words, late developers and others who get no school qualifications can eventually catch up.)

The majority of P.R. people have not taken the CAM training. Experience and aptitude are far more important than paper qualifications.

Personal attributes Ability to get on exceptionally well with people of all kinds, whether hard-hitting journalists or timid members of the public; enterprise and initiative; good news sense; sense of salesmanship; a calm temperament; ability to write and speak well and persuasively; imagination; tact; ability to keep polite under provocation and/or pressure.

Late start Only advisable for people with special expertise.

Position of women Women do very well in P.R., some of the top jobs being held by women. This is one career area where starting as a secretary is a useful way in.

Career-break: No problem for women who were firmly established before the break. Many work from home, perhaps having only one client for a year or so then gradually increasing their workload.

Part-time: Some opportunities, especially working from home or for small, non-commercial (i.e. usually voluntary) organizations.

Further information Institute of Public Relations, 1 Great James Street, London WC1N 3DA

CAM Education Foundation, Abford House, 15 Wilton Road, London SW1V 1INJ

Related careers *Advertising – Fashion – Information Officer – Journalism – Marketing – Secretarial Work*

Publishing

Editorial – production – marketing – book packaging

Entry qualifications In practice a degree or comparable qualification and/or specialist knowledge/experience; art school training for some aspects of production. In specialist publishing, such as educational, scientific, or art, editorial assistants normally have a degree in a relevant subject. In general publishing, a graduate's degree subject is normally irrelevant.

The work Book publishing is an industry (one of the smallest in the country), not a profession. It requires business acumen and an interest in marketing (see p. 283) as much as creativity and literary flair. The function of publishing has been described as extending the author's idea into a finished book and getting it into readers' hands – in other words publishing involves the organization of production, marketing and distribution as much as literary effort.

Publishing houses vary greatly in size, from large ones with overseas branches, producing hundreds of titles a year, to those run on a shoestring with a handful of employees and a small yearly output. Some publishers specialize in educational, scientific, art books, paperbacks.

All publishers select and commission manuscripts, design the appearance of the books, have them printed and bound, and promote and sell the finished copies, but the internal organization of houses varies. The process is usually divided into 3 main departments (apart from the usual commercial ones such as accounts). The division of work is more rigid in some houses than others; in small houses everybody may have to do anything that needs doing (a good way of learning).

The 3 main publishing departments or 'functions' are:

Editorial

Main duties are selecting and commissioning manuscripts; getting outside specialist readers' opinions; preparing MSS. for the printer; liaising with authors, possibly suggesting changes; dealing with contracts, copyright, subsidiary rights (these may be separate departments). Editorial departments also deal with new editions of existing books.

An editorial director or chief editor (titles and responsibilities involved vary greatly in different houses) is usually in charge. Individual editors may each be responsible for books on a special subject, or for a range of subjects. The editor may initiate a book on a special subject, select the author and deal with the project right through. The number of books one editor deals with at any particular moment varies according to type of firm and type of book, and so does the amount of contact the editor has with the author.

Editorial assistants or 'copy-editors' deal with 'copy preparation'; checking facts and references, spelling, punctuation, and possibly doing some rewriting, proof-reading and correcting. Again, responsibilities and duties vary greatly.

Production

The production department receives the edited manuscript and decides, in consultation with the editor, on the appearance of the book, on the shape, typeface, paper, illustrations, etc.; and it deals with printers, paper merchants, and binders, etc. Production staff must understand something of costing and marketing and of the various types of illustration and typographies. But above all they must understand the new printing and production technologies which are drastically changing established production methods. Technical and textbook publishers may employ their own illustrators, but most artwork is commissioned from outside studios.

There are training courses in book production and design, and some vocational art courses include book design and production (see Art and Design, p. 58).

Marketing

In some ways the most important publishing activity, marketing or 'promotion' is responsible for planning, researching for, and preparing review lists, sales campaigns, writing 'blurbs', and for the representatives who call on bookshops, schools, libraries, etc. to give information on forthcoming books and to collect orders. In addition, marketing people in many houses now often initiate projects. A topic may be suggested from inside the department or from outside. On the basis of a 'feasibility study' – researching the market, costing, mainly – it is decided whether to go ahead and, jointly with editorial, get the book commissioned, or whether to abandon the idea. This is a good department in which to learn how publishing works.

Book Packaging

A small, but growing development outside traditional publishing is book 'packaging'. Packagers are marketing people. They find an idea which has mass-appeal, commission an author and art work and produce a dummy-copy of the book. They then offer it to publishers, usually in several countries. 'Packages' are usually highly illustrated; a 'bank' of pictures is printed separately and then overprinted with the translated text with the minimum production expense. Promotion, selling and distribution are done by the publishers who buy the 'packaged book'. Packagers' overheads are lower than traditional publishers' and it is therefore easier to start up as a packager than as a publisher. But good contacts, publishing experience and ideas are essential.

Prospects Very limited opportunities, especially in general publishing; more scope in technical, scientific, educational. First editorial job is usually as editorial assistant ('assistant editor' may mean the same thing). It is usually necessary to move to another firm for a better job.

Pay: Low to medium (see p. xxiii).

Training See under **Work**.

A few firms run training schemes. Pre-entry courses exist at a few polytechnics, but they are less useful than a degree.

Personal attributes Creative ability; interest in social as well as literary trends; ability to see books as a marketable commodity; some writing ability; critical judgement; common sense; resilience; good business sense; willingness to take responsibility and make decisions; ability to get on well with a wide variety of types of people.

Late start Difficult because of the competition from young graduates, but possible in technical and educational publishing for people with technical/ scientific background.

Position of women There are far more male than female editorial directors and publishing house board members but women do well in 'senior middle' jobs, especially in marketing, also as children's and educational book editors. Among copy-editors and editorial assistants women greatly outnumber men. Many women go into publishing as secretaries hoping to become editors; some do, although far more remain in junior editorial jobs.

Career-break: It should be possible (and it is advisable) not to give up completely, even temporarily.

Part-time: Experienced proof-readers, copy-editors, editors may be able to do sporadic freelance work.

Further information

Individual publishing houses

Related careers

Art and Design – Bookselling – Information Work – Journalism – Librarian

Purchasing and Supply

Entry qualifications For professional qualification: 2 A-levels, 3 O-levels, including English language and a quantitative subject; or BTEC National award. Also *graduate* entry. No specific qualifications for mature entrants with relevant work experience (see also p. 405), but see **Training**.

The work The purchasing officer is responsible for ensuring regular supplies of materials, tools, components, equipment – anything other departments in her organization may require to function efficiently. This may be raw materials, office equipment, machine components. She searches out most suitable supplies and negotiates terms and delivery dates. She may have to decide, at times, when to agree to pay more than budgeted for in order to get supplies which are in short supply; this would probably be decided jointly with production manager and accountant. She is a vital link between the various departments which need supplies, and the suppliers – her success depends largely on maintaining good relationships with suppliers and on negotiating advantageous terms.

She may travel all over the world – and should be able to speak foreign langauges; she must be aware of technological, social, economic and political developments which might affect price levels and availability of supplies.

Purchasing officers work mainly, but by no means only, in industry, where purchasing is a 'management function'. They can switch from one type of buying to another: commodity knowledge is not vital as specialists give purchasing officers detailed specifications; for example, machine tools or electronic equipment can be bought by a purchasing officer who previously bought raw materials for a food manufacturer. However, many purchasing officers do stay in one type of buying, and a technical background (engineering qualification for example) is useful in many jobs.

Purchasing managers, in charge of departments, are also responsible for holding stocks, stores administration and possibly preservation of stocks (which may involve deciding how far forward supplies can be bought in), weighing up price rises and possible future shortage against possible spoilage and storage costs. They must be conversant with contract and negotiation procedures in this country and abroad.

Purchasing officers in the non-industrial sector are often called supplies officers and are concerned, for example, in the National Health Service, with buying a vast range of equipment from beds to disposable towels for several hospitals within a district or regional health authority. They work closely with medical staff. In education authorities they work closely with heads of schools and education officers.

Prospects Quite good. Medium-sized organizations where buying used not to be a specialist function now often employ purchasing specialists; purchasing is one of the functions which can lead into general management (see p. 269).

Pay: Medium to high (see p. xxiii).

Training The Institute of Purchasing and Supply's Professional Examinations Scheme is in two parts – the Foundation and the Professional stages. Most Foundation stage students qualify via BTEC courses (see p. xvi). Holders of Business Studies degrees and BTEC Higher awards are eligible for exemption from the Foundation examination. The syllabus includes business procedures, buying methods, economics. For the Professional stage examination which is set by the IPS students may specialize in marketing, structure, planning and control of public sector work; commercial procedures and techniques; materials and production planning and control. All take general purchasing subjects.

A 'second-tier' qualification, for school leavers with 4 O-levels and mature entrants with at least 2 years' experience in purchasing and/or stores work, is now available. Study, by day-release, leads to the Certificates of the Association of Supervisors and in Purchasing and Supply. These Certificates qualify holders to enter the IPS Foundation examination training.

Personal attributes Numeracy; organizing ability; practical approach to problem-solving; considerable business acumen and some gambling spirit; ability to establish friendly relationships quickly; judgement to gauge the right approach to individual suppliers; awareness of technological changes and their implications for purchasing.

Late start Good opportunities. Part-time evening and short full-time courses available; people with previous work experience are welcome. The IPS Professional Examination and the Diploma in Management Studies (see p. 274) are available under TOPS (see p. xlvi). Graduates and others with relevant experience are granted substantial exemption from IPS exams, and GCE requirements for those over 26 are waived.

Position of women

At the moment there are very few women indeed, but there is no logical reason for this – women have long been established as buyers for retail stores, which is much the same kind of work. Women who have gone into purchasing are doing well – a number are in engineering purchasing. The main reason why there are so few women in this field is because they don't know about it or imagine they need specialist knowledge.

Career-break: Should not present problems, but keeping in touch with world economic conditions and commercial law is vital. Short Institute courses can be used as *refreshers*.

Part-time: Some opportunities. Scope for job-sharing schemes though none seem to have been started.

Further information

Institute of Purchasing and Supply, Easton House, Easton the Hill, Stamford, Lincs PE9 3N2

Related careers

Commodity Broking – Management in Industry – Quantity Surveyor – Retail Buying – Shipbroking

Radiography

Diagnostic – therapeutic

Entry qualifications 2 A-levels, 2 O-levels. English and maths *or* physics to be included, at either level; *or* BTEC Sciences (see p. 445).

The work Radiography has 2 branches: diagnostic and therapeutic.

Diagnostic Radiographer

She works with medically qualified radiologists and takes X-ray photographs to assist doctors in diagnosing diseases and injuries. Doctors normally give only brief instructions: the radiographer is expected to know exactly how to use the X-ray apparatus, to understand the theory behind X-ray photography, and how best to radiograph the relevant part of the patient's body. She therefore needs a considerable knowledge of anatomy, physiology and physics.

Normally she works in X-ray departments, but occasionally she takes X-rays during an operation, when it is particularly important to take quick, accurate pictures. She also works on the wards using mobile equipment.

The diagnostic radiographer normally sees each patient only once or twice and will meet a large number of people on a rather fleeting basis.

Therapeutic Radiographer

She gives treatment by means of X-ray, radium and other substances under the direction of a medically qualified radiologist. The latest advances of science are used to help cure disease, and the work involves using new and powerful substances and methods.

Treatment is given to seriously ill and worried patients, possibly over a long period of time. The therapeutic radiographer's duties are therefore twofold: firstly the actual treatment, and secondly establishing a friendly relationship with patients to give them confidence. The effect of radiotherapy is permanent: once given, it cannot be undone; the therapeutic radiographer's responsibility is heavy. She needs extensive knowledge of human anatomy and physiology and of radiation physics. Because of constant changes, therapeutic radiographers frequently take short updating courses.

Exposure to X-rays can be dangerous, but X-ray departments are equipped with safeguards which ensure that operators are not harmed in any way. Protective clothing is worn and operators are never within reach of the actual X-ray beams. The controls are operated from outside the treatment rooms so that the radiographer is never exposed to radiation; treatment rooms are lined with material which the X-rays cannot penetrate.

Prospects Good. There is a shortage of radiographers, especially therapy specialists. The majority work in hospital. There are a few posts with specialists in private practice; these may be better paid, but the work is lonelier than in hospital. There are also some openings with mobile X-ray units. For both these jobs previous hospital experience is necessary. Radiographers can earn their living in most countries of the world, provided they speak the appropriate language. The College of Radiographers now also runs courses for qualified radiographers who want to work in such new areas as Medical Ultra-Sound and other forms of 'imaging', which are concerned with diagnostic and treatment methods for various diseases.

Pay: Medium (see p. xxiii).

Training 3 years full-time, at a training school attached to a hospital, for the College of Radiographers' Diploma, which is essential for employment. The first year is common to both types of radiography and includes physics, hospital practice, anatomy and physiology, some supervised practical work. During the second and third years diagnostic radiographers concentrate on radiographic photography; therapeutic radiographers on radiotherapy.

Students can take a further 18 months and acquire a dual qualification, but very few students do so.

Degree courses are in the planning stage.

Personal attributes A strong scientific bent; a steady hand and a sharp observant eye; a genuine liking for people and a desire to help the sick; a confident manner; patience; calmness; firmness and a sense of humour; ability to take responsibility and to work well with others; good health.

Late start Possible for people whose maths and physics are up to date.

Position of women Until recently about 90% of radiographers were women; now there are 25% men. Men have a disproportionate share of top jobs.

Career-break: No problem, but re-training essential – extent depends on length of break (changes in procedures and equipment are drastic and rapid).

Refresher courses: Arranged on *ad hoc* basis, on demand; no organized ones.

Part-time: At the moment opportunities are limited, but there is no reason why work should not be organized on a part-time or job-sharing basis (see p. xxiv).

Further information

College of Radiographers, 14 Upper Wimpole Street, London W1M 8BN

Related careers

Photography – Science Laboratory Technician – Scientist

Recreation Management – also called Leisure and/or Amenity Management

Managers/administrators

Entry qualifications None laid down. In practice, for managers, professional qualification and/or administrative experience; for instructors, PE teaching qualification or expertise in a particular sport plus flair for instructing.

The work This is a fairly new career. It has developed piecemeal as more sports and leisure centres were established. Some local authorities set up multidisciplinary leisure departments to cover indoor and outdoor sports, the arts, community and children's play facilities, as well as municipal entertainments and libraries. Most divide responsibilities between two or more departments; often sports and leisure centres are run as separate entities. Altogether there are now over 500 multi-purpose sports centres. Local government is by far the largest employer of recreation staff; others include the Sports Council, and company sports and social clubs and tourism, catering and leisure companies. The work also covers promoting and organizing drama, music and other entertainments at arts centres, theatres and concert halls.

Managers/Administrators

Job titles vary and can be misleading and do not necessarily indicate levels of responsibility and scope for work. However, a recreation department, or a large sports/leisure centre, usually has a director or manager. Assistant managers are responsible for the operation of particular amenities, e.g. swimming baths and the events organized in the baths, all outdoor sports, or perhaps entertainments in the authority's parks. A large sports centre may have two deputy directors, one in charge of organizing activities and the other in charge of administration and finance. At the next level, assistant managers are responsible for certain areas of the work, such as bookings (a centre may be used by 10,000 people a week), stores (1,000 pieces of equipment may be loaned to users in a week), or supervision of the work of assistants and specialist instructors. Supervisors or recreation assistants look after the day-to-day running of activities, working in shifts to cope with the long hours of opening.

The senior manager, whatever her title, is primarily an administrator. She calls on assistants for specialist advice; for example, before organizing musical events in the parks, she would consult a musician to advise her on choice of programme and performers; before setting up judo classes, she would get judo experts' advice. A senior manager must be able to switch her attention instantly from, say, organization of an Easter parade or a miniature golf course to that of a nature trail; from reorganizing the booking system to hygiene and safety of a paddling pool. She must be a good publicist to attract all sections of the public – as one of the main reasons why local authorities spend money on providing leisure facilities is to attract young people who might otherwise, for lack of something better to do, vandalize property or annoy the neighbourhood in some other way with antisocial behaviour.

As most local authorities now have leisure and recreation departments (titles vary) recreation management, whatever its exact title, is also a local government administrative job (see Local Government, p. 265). At the moment, most people in those departments started as administrators, though it varies. In future, it is likely that, like other local government officers, they will be specialists. Already several officers at or near the top in these departments are people who started by running leisure/sports centres and/or took specialist training (see below).

Prospects This is a growth area. As more people have more leisure – enforced or otherwise – the need for more sports and leisure centres is still generally accepted; despite public expenditure cuts more centres are being set up. Local authorities vary in the priority they give to recreation facilities; some consider them a luxury, others believe they are essential. So jobs are not evenly distributed throughout the country.

Instructors' jobs are usually easier to get than managers'.

Training Training is still haphazard. However, in 1983 the Institute of Leisure and Amenity Management – ILAM – was formed and ILAM's own courses, taken by correspondence or day-/block-release plus short residential courses, are likely to become the normal way into recreation/leisure management.

ILAM training will cover 'the philosophy of leisure and recreation' (broadly – its importance in the community; problems of attracting people; coping with diverse interests and aims of clients, etc.); administration and management; specialisms: environment and amenity;

sports and recreation; entertainment and tourism; arts and culture. It is planned that study for the Associate Membership examination should take 2 years for entrants with 2 A-levels or equivalent (or relevant experience); or 1 year for graduates.

The majority of students are likely to be in relevant employment while studying for the ILAM exam, but people in other kinds of work who want to go into Recreation/Leisure Management may be accepted for training if their present job contains a 'management element'.

Other training courses:
With a degree (any discipline) and, usually, relevant experience: MSc in Recreation Management or similar area of study.
With a degree, or several years' relevant experience: Diploma in Management Studies (see Management, **Training**, p. 274) with recreation management option.
With 2 A-levels: BSc in Physical Education, Sports Science and Recreation Management or BA Combined Studies with recreation option (only a few such courses exist).
With 1 A-level (in practice usually 1 passed and another one at least studied, if not passed): BTEC Higher National Diploma with relevant options (see BTEC p. xvi).
Horticultural, Landscape Architecture and some Agriculture College qualifications also include aspects of recreation management; Arts Administration (see p. 69) can also lead to Recreation Management. As the subject covers such diverse types of jobs, different types of training may be useful and lead to exemption from at least part of the ILAM Associate or Membership examinations.

Instructors: Nothing rigid. Either sports training as above, or proof of proficiency in chosen sports; for example, for swimming instructors lifesaving certificates. (See Sport, p. 493.)

Personal attributes

Management: Good organizing abilities; practicality; ability to make different specialists work as a team; interest in the needs of all sections of the community; confidence in dealing with members of the public (even when they are impatient or boisterous).
Instructors: Teaching ability; enthusiasm; stamina.

Position of women

As there are no traditions, there are no barriers against the promotion of women to be broken down. Many women do well as instructors and as managers.

Career-break: should be possible, but keen competition for jobs and the fact that it is a young person's field may cause problems.

Part-time: As specialist instructor.

Further information

ILAM, Lower Basildon, Reading, Berks RG8 9NE

Related careers

Horticulture – Local Government – Museums and Art Galleries – Public Relations – Sport – Teaching

Religious Ministry
Main religions in Britain

Entry qualifications Normally 3 O-levels and 2 A-levels. Provisions for those who lack these qualifications, especially mature entrants (see **Training**), but must show evidence of ability to undertake academic study.

The work *Ordained ministry*: Many duties are common to all denominations and include: holding services, preaching, conducting marriages and funerals. Less formal but equally important is 'pastoral care', such as visiting the sick, comforting the bereaved and helping individuals with their religious and personal problems. Like family doctors, priests receive many confidences and try to help their parishioners to come to terms with their weaknesses and circumstances. They must also find time for solitary prayer and study. Rabbis in addition play a large social and sometimes political role in their communities.

Traditionally, ministers have been appointed to one congregation. Nowadays many work in team ministries, particularly in inner cities, within which individuals may specialize, e.g. in youth-and-community work. Many serve as hospital chaplains and some are responsible for the administration of schools. Others become chaplains in colleges, the Forces, industry, prisons.

The Roman Catholic and Anglican churches have *religious communities*; in some members are committed to a life of prayer and contemplation, in others they help to run schools, hospitals or residential homes.

Lay ministry: Many churches train and employ lay workers, both stipendiary and non-stipendiary (paid and unpaid). They assist ordained ministers in services and pastoral work and may also be responsible for particular branches of the ministry, such as teaching or counselling.

Prospects Reasonable, but never very well-paid. Some senior posts exist in all churches, both spiritual and administrative.

Training All candidates have to go through a rigorous selection process to assess their 'calling' and suitability. Training is followed by a probationary period and does not lead automatically to ordination.

Church of England (Ordained ministry)

Graduates under 29: with theology degree, 2-year full-time at theological college; with degree in any other subject, 3 years and may include theology degree.
Non-graduates under 25: either 4-year combined degree/training course, or a 2-year part-time training scheme followed by 3 years at theological college (known as the Aston scheme).
Non-graduates 25–30: 3-year full-time, in some cases following Aston scheme.
Graduates and non-graduates over 30: normally 2-year full-time or 3-year part-time course.

Stipendiary lay ministry
As for ordained ministry, except for the Church Army, which runs own 3-year course for trainee officers.

Roman Catholic Church

6-year full-time course of academic study combined with pastoral training. May include theology degree. Course length may be reduced for graduates and mature entrants.

In the Church of England and the Roman Catholic church *religious orders* carry out their own training.

Church of Scotland (Ordained ministry)

Under 23: with Scottish university entrance qualifications *either* 4-year degree course in Divinity plus 2 years further study *or* degree in any subject followed by 3-year course leading to degree or licentiateship in theology.
Aged 23–40: 5-year training incorporating degree or licentiateship depending on academic qualifications.
Aged 40+: 2-year course for graduates, 3-year for non-graduates.

Lay ministry
Aged 18–23: with minimum 3 Ordinary and 2 Higher Grades (SCE), 2-year foundation course plus specialist training.
Over 23: Individual training programme.

Methodist Church

Under 30: with minimum 4 O-levels and Accredited Local Preacher

qualifications, 3-year full-time course. Those with university entrance requirements may take degree.
Aged 30+: 2-year full-time or (if married) 3-year part-time course.

Baptist Union

With 5 O-levels and 2 A-levels: 4-year full-time training course leading to degree or diploma in theology.

Course may be 3 years in some cases.

New pattern of training currently under discussion will combine part-time study with part-time ministerial duties.

United Reformed Church

Graduates under 30: 3-year full-time course.
Graduates over 30: 2-year full-time course.
Non-graduates aged 21–30: with good academic qualifications and 3 years' responsible employment experience, 4-year full-time course which may include degree.
Non-graduates over 30: 3- or 4-year full-time course.
Aged 55+: Shortened training available.

Jewish Faith

Orthodox
Either 3–4-year post-A-level course at Talmudical college, followed by rabbinic training, *or* (more commonly) 3-year degree course at Jews College followed by 3–5 years' rabbinical training. Those not wishing to be rabbis can be ordained as Reverend following degree.
Other training courses: Bachelor of Education in Jewish Studies for intending teachers; Cantorial course for conductors of services.

Progressive (Reform and Liberal)
A degree in any subject followed by 5-year full-time course for rabbinical ordination at Leo Baeck college.

A 2-year full-time teacher training course exists for those wishing to teach at religion school.

Personal attributes Total sense of vocation and conviction that no other kind of work will give personal satisfaction. Desire to share faith with others; good intellect; ability to relate to all members of the church however well or poorly educated. Good health and stamina, mental and physical; open-mindedness and genuine desire to serve others without discrimination; willingness to be continually 'available'; self-discipline and self-sufficiency – although at the centre of the church ministers are always slightly 'set apart'. Emotional stability. Ability to work on own and as part of a team. Administrative skills.

Late start All denominations make provision for mature entrants (see **Training**).

Position of women The status of women varies widely between denominations. The Roman Catholic and orthodox Jewish faiths exclude women from ordination. The Progressive Jews ordained the first woman rabbi in 1976. The Church of England ordains women as deaconesses, but not as priests, but there is a strong pro-ordination movement within the church. The Church of Scotland and the Free Churches have traditionally allowed women to be ordained, although some still feel that they have to be intellectually better qualified than men to receive the same acceptance by the congregations. Many women seek ordination later in life.

Part-time: Some opportunities.

Further information

Church of England: Advisory Council for the Church's Ministry, Church House, Dean's Yard, London SW1P 3NZ
Roman Catholic: The Secretary, The Commission for Priestly Formation, Archbishop's House, Westminster, London SW1P 1QJ
Church of Scotland: Church of Scotland Department of Education, 121 George Street, Edinburgh EH2 4YN
Methodist Church: The Candidates Secretary (Division of Ministries), Room 75, 1 Central Buildings, Westminster, London SW1 9NH
Baptist Union: Department of Ministry, The Baptist Union, 4 Southampton Row, London WC1B 4AB
United Reformed: The General Secretary, The United Reformed Church, 86 Tavistock Place, London WC1H 9RT
Jewish Religion: *Orthodox*: London Board of Jewish Religious Education, Woburn House, Upper Woburn Place, London WC1H 0EP
Progressive: Leo Baeck College, The Manor House, 80 East End Road, London N3 2SY

Related careers *Social work – Teaching*

Remedial Gymnastics and Recreational Therapy

Entry qualifications 5 O-levels plus 1 A-level, preferably including a science subject. Minimum age for training 18.

The work Physiotherapists learn about remedial gymnastics during their training, but remedial gymnasts do not train in physiotherapy.

Remedial gymnastics and recreational therapy involve the treatment of disease and injury using various forms of physical exercise, games and recreational activities. Remedial gymnasts give treatment at any stage in the process of physical rehabilitation. They treat patients either individually or in groups. They work in general and special hospitals, in gymnasia, rehabilitation units, special schools, increasingly in sports and leisure centres, and very occasionally in private practice. They may also work in institutions and clinics for children suffering from cerebral palsy or similar conditions.

Prospects Fair; there is a shortage of remedial gymnasts but jobs are not necessarily available where they are wanted.

Pay: Medium (see p. xxiii).

Training For State Registration, which is essential for most jobs, 3 years, including 2 years full-time at special colleges. The third year is spent in hospitals and is salaried. Syllabus includes anatomy, physiology, physical education, the principles and practice of exercise and recreational therapy, care of the mentally and physically disabled.

Personal attributes Great interest in sport and games; organizing ability; a liking for people of all types and the ability to win their confidence; very good health; a wish to help the sick and injured.

Late start Upper age limit about 35. Physical education teachers and Services physical training instructors take a 24 months' course.

Position of women This used to be an all-male profession; but the ratio now is about 3 women to 1 man.

Career-break: Return easy up to about 35. Some in-service *refresher training*.

Part-time: Some opportunities.

Further information

College of Remedial Gymnastics and Recreational Therapy, Pinderfields General Hospital, Wakefield, Yorkshire WF1 4DG
The Secretary, Society of Remedial Gymnasts, University Hospital of Wales, Health Park, Cardiff CF4 4XW

Related careers

Physiotherapy – Teaching

NOTE (March 1984) Remedial gymnasts are merging with physiotherapists (see p. 374). Last intake of remedial gymnast students 1984 or 1985.

Retail Management

Department stores – chain stores – multiples – supermarkets – franchising – mail order – store management – buying

Entry qualifications Nothing rigid; all educational levels, but considerable and growing *graduate* entry (see **Training**, p. 423).

The work Retailing is one of the largest industries in the country and one of the few career areas where getting on does not necessarily depend on passing examinations.

The industry is constantly adapting to changing life-styles and new technologies. For example, shopping hours are lengthening in many shops because more women go out to work and cannot shop during the traditional working day; computerization and 'rationalization' (less personal service; more part-timers for peak-hour work; fewer leisurely periods for full-timers) has led to a reduced total workforce but, proportionately, more management opportunities.

No industry-wide career-structure exists. Titles, and responsibilities attached to titles, vary from one company to another, and so do recruiting and promotion procedures.

The main types of 'retail outlet': *supermarkets*; *department stores*; *variety chain stores*; '*multiples*' (specialist chains); *co-operatives*; *independents*. The categories are not as clear-cut as they used to be. Supermarkets and multiples may 'diversify', i.e. sell more than one type of merchandise; some department stores give houseroom to specialist shops – for example, photographic equipment; some independents have joined together for bulk-buying purposes; out-of-town *hypermarkets*, like traditional department stores but looking like giant supermarkets, offer 'one-stop shopping' – everything under one roof, but at rock-bottom prices, cash-and-carry only and the emphasis on fast turnover rather than on attracting regular customers as in department stores.

Fairly new and growing is '*franchising*': a group of outlets – mainly food and fashion – is centrally controlled and sells to 'franchisees' the right to use its name and image, and to sell its centrally-bought merchandise. Within certain guidelines, franchisees then run their own shows. *Mail order* is another growth area. It divides into two kinds: the traditional 'catalogue companies' which sell through part-time agents; and the new 'direct-mail', 'direct response' or 'direct marketing' companies. These sell through advertising in the press and/or through small catalogues sent to likely customers. This is a sophisticated, high-risk business, more a marketing operation (see Marketing, p. 283) than traditional retailing. Success depends on selecting a few sure-fire items for sale, the right advertising media and the right people to send catalogues to.

In traditional retailing, buying and selling organization varies from one company to another. For chain stores, multiples and supermarkets buying is usually done centrally: identical merchandise is allocated to stores which are also given display and promotion guidelines. In department store groups and some multiples, buying is also done centrally, but individual outlets still have their own distinctive character and do not necessarily all sell the same merchandise. In a few department stores, individual buyers buy for their own departments which they may also manage.

Most people go into retailing because they want to be buyers. Nearly everybody starts, and most stay, in selling. A few people, mainly specialists, such as *fashion graduates* (see p. 204) and *food technologists* (see p. 447) are recruited as trainee-buyers.

Starting on the shopfloor – the 'sharp end' – is essential to learn about customer-relations and trading principles. There usually is a varying hierarchy from sales assistant, via section, department, specialist (transport, staff, distribution, etc.), deputy to store manager, and after that perhaps area manager. At any time after the first few weeks or months (it varies), individuals may be offered a buying-traineeship. Speed, and likelihood of promotion, varies from company to company, and according to age and ability.

Store managers coordinate the various retailing functions: stock control; security; staff deployment; maximizing profit per square metre of premises; dealing with customers' complaints and queries; liaising with head office, etc. Supermarket and department store work differ greatly; supermarkets are much more hectic places with emphasis on fast-moving goods; managers must make their own, quick decisions whether it is a staff, delivery or customer problem. In department stores, managers have such 'support services' as personnel, distribution, complaints departments on the premises and there is more emphasis on personal service. Hypermarkets and multiples again make different demands. Ideally, prospective retailers should decide which type of atmosphere and work is right for them. In practice, there may not be much job choice, but one can switch from one type of retailing to another: basic retail expertise is a 'transferable skill'.

Staff management may have its own hierarchy, parallel with store management, and it may be a step on the store management ladder (see Personnel Management, p. 358).

Buying is very different from its image of spending other people's money on items one likes. It consists of selecting from suppliers' existing lines and also, jointly with manufacturers, developing new ideas, and adapting existing lines and prototypes bought or seen abroad. Developing 'own brand' lines is expanding. Buyers work closely with marketing and production specialists and with store managers. Buying policies are based on methodical analysis and interpretation of past sales figures, on economic forecasts, on demographic trends (the present ageing population and the reduction in the number of school-age children have important implications for buyers); on life-style changes (the trend for more casual than formal clothing; the fashion to drink out of mugs rather than cups; the increase in foreign travel and resultant interest in foreign food and drinks, etc.). Buying is a commercial activity and requires communication and negotiating expertise and number-crunching, as well as flair for guessing next year's preferences. It involves complex decision-making. For example, a buyer may find a very efficient and inexpensive spindryer with an unsatisfactory after-sales service. She must weigh up whether performance and price advantages out-weigh after-sales service disadvantages – and be able to justify her decision if customers complain.

Commodity knowledge – expertise in one type of merchandise – used to be all-important; then managerial and commercial expertise determined promotion and buyers easily switched from buying one type of merchandise to another. Now, commodity knowledge, at least in 'high-tech' consumer goods, textiles and food, again seems to matter more; but it varies from company to company.

Head office jobs include general management (see Management, p. 269) and store planning: what type of shop/store is likely to be successful where, when and why, in 1995? This is a mixture of crystal-ball gazing, statistics, technological and economic forecasting, psychology and sociology. It is a growth area.

Retailing also offers good opportunities to systems analysts and other computer experts (see Computing, p. 131) as more companies adopt computerized 'point of sale' and stock-control systems and are preparing for 'electronic fund transfer' and computer-based armchair shopping.

Prospects Very competitive entry for management training schemes. Employers tend to recruit more well-qualified (i.e. *at least* 4 O-levels) entrants than they need for even junior management jobs. A-level and graduate entrants have, on the whole, better chances of acceptance for management training than O-level entrants. But, whatever the entry qualifications, once in retailing, personality and suitability for the job count above all.

There is less scope for promotion in independent shops, but the experience might be useful for getting on a company training scheme (see also Working for Oneself, p. 560). Supermarkets now offer widest scope.

Training

There is no one way of training for retail management. Systems vary according to type and policy of company. As stated above, progress does not necessarily depend on passing examinations. Nevertheless, training is essential for going up the management ladder: entrants should try and find jobs with firms which grant day-release for BTEC (see p. xvi) Distribution Certificates or similar awards and/or run systematic in-house training and/or send staff who are potential senior managers on outside courses or at least encourage correspondence courses.

Finding a job with training requires researching the job-market. However, *any* retailing experience can be useful, and if no job with built-in training is available, taking a job and going to evening-classes for BTEC certificates or the DMS (see Management, p. 274) can be a step on the retailing management ladder.

Few companies grant day-release automatically. Even well-known large companies' training schemes vary; this is typical of a good one:

Entrants with few or no qualifications: entry as sales assistant; encouragement, but no compulsion or right to day-release. Subsequent promotion according to suitability and available vacancies. (Entrants have to compete with better-qualified colleagues.)

Entrants with 4 or 5 O-levels including maths and English language: as above, but with greater encouragement to take day-release and systematic 2 or 3 years' in-house training.

Entrants with 2 A-levels for supermarket management; 1 A-level for department store management: 12 to 24 months' management training. Within 6 to 12 months entrants are likely to manage a section – i.e. have got into junior management.

Graduate entrants and people with relevant experience: approximately 18 to 20 months' training for assistant branch or department management or equivalent.

Multiples' traineeships are usually shorter than department and supermarket ones.

There are 'bridges' from one entry-level scheme to another. A 16-year-old entrant without any qualifications but 'potential' (and that includes making immediate superiors *notice* the potential!) may, at 21, have caught up with a graduate-entrant and compete on equal terms for management jobs, and be considered on equal terms for further management courses.

Some companies, especially the large ones, send junior and middle managers on external management courses and/or grant block-release for the new (1983) Certificate in Retail Management. A Diploma in Retail Management and a Retail Business Administration Certificate are being planned.

There is also a BTEC Certificate in Management Studies with a Distribution option. This is a part-time day- or block-release course, but can also be taken by 'distance learning' (see p. xlii), the eighties' version of the correspondence course.

Some companies have elaborate in-house management schemes. Because of those companies' reputation for efficient retailing, such courses can be just as useful on the job-market as Certificates and Diplomas awarded by outside bodies (but thorough research is essential: not all in-house schemes are as useful outside those companies' stores as they may look on paper).

Pre-entry training:
Retailing is best learnt while in a retailing environment, but if there are no suitable vacancies, a second choice for prospective retailers are pre-entry courses:
For entrants with few or no school-leaving qualifications: BTEC General Diploma (Distribution), 1-year, full-time, usually leads to the type of job which 4/5 O-level entrants would apply for, or to BTEC National Diploma.
For entrants with usually 4 O-levels including maths and English language or BTEC General Award: 2-year, full-time course for BTEC National Diploma (Distribution). Diploma holders normally compete with A-level entrants for jobs.
For entrants with at least 1 A-level (and often another studied if not passed) and 3 O-levels; passes to include maths and English language or BTEC National Award: BTEC Higher National Diploma (Distribution) or (Retailing).
For entrants with 2 A-levels and at least 3 O-levels, including English and maths or BTEC National: Business Studies degree with Retailing/ Distribution option.

Candidates over 19 may be admitted to all courses with fewer than the specified qualifications.

Personal attributes Numeracy; an outgoing personality; an interest in both people and things; organizing ability; communication skills; commercial sense. For *store management*: leadership qualities; ability to delegate and take decisions quickly and to keep calm in crises; physical stamina. For *buyers*: interest in social and economic trends; negotiating skills; objectivity to be able to judge the relevance of one's own taste and gauge that of customers.

Late start Good opportunities. Most companies positively welcome people who have had work experience, and will train people of up to about 35 for management.

Position of women Considering that the vast majority of sales assistants, and of customers, are women, surprisingly few women are in senior management. But the situation is improving, more women are moving up the ladder faster. Chain store management, until fairly recently a male preserve, is now open to women. Women do relatively well in multiples. Women buyers are no longer confined to fashion and similar areas. But there are still very few women in supermarket management. The reason given is that managers may have to help humping heavy goods; however, it is unlikely that there is much work which is too hard for any but the most delicate females. Because retailing is such a diffuse industry, women in retail have no forum as have, for example, women in banking or medicine.

Career-break: Most companies encourage returners and provide refresher training.

Part-time: Opportunities at sales assistant level; very few women at management level, but in at least one large group, experiments with part-time senior managers are in progress. With lengthening shopping-hours, several managers share store management anyway, so it is quite possible to arrange part-time management work. Buying, too, could, in theory, be done on a flexible but not necessarily full-time basis. In store-planning and other head office work, enterprising individuals are creating their own part-time and job-sharing opportunities.

Further information The Secretary, National Association of Colleges in Distributive Education and Training, c/o College for the Distributive Trades, 30 Leicester Square, London WC2H 7LE

Related careers *Hotel work – Managers in Industry – Personnel work*

Science

Two career types: **Practising Scientist** and **Science as Background Expertise**

Scientist – science technician – food science and technology – forensic science

Main functions or activities: research and development – analysis and investigation – sales and service – marketing – production – technical writing
Main branches: physics – chemistry – biological sciences – environmental sciences – mathematical sciences – materials sciences

Entry qualifications

Scientists normally need a degree, but the borderline between scientist and senior technician – BTEC Higher award holder (see p. xvi) – is often blurred, many of the latter have degrees.

Precise degree course requirements vary from one course to another. In general:

For *physics, cybernetics and applied sciences* degrees, A-levels must include physics and mathematics.

For some *mathematics* degrees, A-levels must include pure and applied maths.

For *chemistry* degrees, chemistry and physics and/or mathematics A-levels are preferred, but other combinations may be acceptable.

For *biological sciences*, biology, a physical science – preferably chemistry – and mathematics are ideal; other combinations may be acceptable.

For *some* science degrees biology may only be accepted as a third A-level: if only 2 A-levels are offered they must both be in sciences more relevant to the degree subject.

In general – though there are exceptions – polytechnics are more likely than universities to accept applicants with only 2 A-levels.

For *BTEC Higher National Diploma*: 1 relevant A-level passed and another studied at A-level; for *BTEC Higher National Certificate*: either BTEC National award or 2 relevant A-levels passed (but individual subject Certificate courses may vary requirements).

The work

All jobs are based directly or indirectly on scientific or technological developments. More to the point, all jobs are likely to be affected by today's or tomorrow's scientific developments or their exploitation.

'Scientific literacy' – an understanding of what science is about and how it affects virtually every aspect of industrial society – is an advantage in most jobs, and is essential in many, however remote from school-room science.

A science qualification is, of course, often a vocational qualification, but it need not be by any means. The image of the white-coated, lab-based scientist as the only, or even the main kind of, science professional, is quite out of date.

Scientists can choose: they can become 'science practitioners' or 'practical scientists' and use their scientific training and education in all kinds of science jobs. In research, they can push out the frontiers of knowledge even further – in space and astronomical investigations; interaction of energy and matter in lasers; optical fibres; bioengineering, etc. – there is a vast variety of research areas. Then there is work for scientists who want to solve problems thrown up by scientific developments: advances in medical science have led to over-population and food-shortages; excessive use of energy requires alternative sources; chemical industries have led to pollution of the environment. Biotechnologists, chemists and other specialists investigate and try to alleviate undesirable but inevitable side-effects of innovation. And then there is of course the vast, mainly physics-based, information technology industry and its spin-offs, to give just a few examples.

The nature of practising scientists' work ranges from laboratory-centred 'boffin' research to 'people-centred' activities like technical selling (see p. 430) or people-and-technology-centred work in production (see p. 429) or profit-centred work in marketing and other commercial functions. (See below for details of the various 'functions', and of the main science specialisms or 'branches'.)

But scientists can equally choose not to practise as scientists, but to use their understanding of science as a tool with which to do other kinds of jobs – in commerce, industry, the public service – more effectively. People who have scientific curiosity but are not sure whether they want to be scientists, can choose a science qualification confident in the knowledge that their scientific background will be a door-opener into a variety of jobs in many different settings. For example a scientist who goes into stockbroking or merchant banking is better able to assess a new high-technology company's chances of success, or the advantages or disadvantages of a merger between two science-based companies, than someone without a scientific background who has to go by hunch, or someone else's advice. An Administrative Civil Servant is better at advising ministers on, for example, the implications of rapidly changing technology when discussing the future of, say, transport, or the Health Service, or defence expenditure, than someone without a scientific background.

(The Civil Service very much wants to attract more scientists as Administration Trainees (see p. 121) – the potential high-flyers in the Civil Service.) In publishing, to choose a very different example, a scientist will be at an advantage over a non-scientist when judging the implications of electronic publishing – and the speed with which electronics might severely affect traditional 'print' publishing. There are dozens of similar examples.

In industrial and commercial management (p. 269) and in marketing (see p. 283), science graduates are welcome. About a third of all employers' vacancies for graduates are open to graduates from any discipline: the employers buy graduates' 'trained minds' rather than their specific knowledge. Increasingly, when recruiting any-discipline graduates, in practice, employers prefer science or technology to arts graduates. The formers' scientific literacy is useful at a time when science and technology impinge on so many aspects of every organization. Scientists' analytical approach to problem-solving is invariably useful even when the problem is not a scientific one. Scientists with communication skills are above all badly needed to close the communication gap: to explain basic relevant scientific facts, trends and implications to their scientifically-illiterate colleagues (many of them in very high places). Finally, for people who want to set up in business on their own (see Working for Oneself, p. 560), a science background is extremely useful (though it will have to be complemented with business-knowhow).

Practising scientists' work can be divided in two ways: by the types of activities or 'functions' and by the various 'branches' or science-specializations:

Research and Development

Research is the lifeblood of science, enlarging existing knowledge and stimulating the growth of new branches. *Development* translates research findings into new – or improved – products and processes. The two overlap.

The terms 'pure' and 'applied' are often used to describe the type of research undertaken. In this context 'pure' research means increasing knowledge for its own sake and 'applied' research is 'goal-orientated' – directed towards solving technical problems, improving national defence or prestige; or 'wealth creating'. Science research is very expensive to carry out, much of it is sponsored, by industry or government, and is goal-orientated. Some university departments may fund 'pure' research from their resources or through research studentships which lead to higher research degrees (M Phil or PhD).

Most research is teamwork, with several scientists, often from several disciplines, and technicians, working under a team-leader. The work may be divided into projects; several scientists are then responsible for their own project within the overall framework.

Personal attributes Above-average intelligence; willingness to work patiently for long hours (or even months) and persevere with tricky problems; creativity; ability to work in a team and to take decisions and stand up for them if things go wrong; ability to communicate findings effectively; great powers of concentration; stubborn persistence in the face of disappointing research results. Industrial researchers must be willing to change direction – at however interesting a point in their research – in the interests of the company's profitability.

Analysis and Investigation

Routine tests and investigations are carried out in all fields of science. In chemical research, for example, analysis of intermediate compounds enables scientists to keep track of chemical changes that are taking place. In manufacturing industry, the composition of both raw materials and products is monitored by analysing samples in *quality control* laboratories. In the food industry, regular checks are made on biological and chemical purity of foodstuffs. In pharmaceuticals the safety of drugs, beauty preparations and food additives is investigated. Before such products can be marketed, substances are tried out on experimental animals to see whether there are any toxic side-effects. In the agrochemical industry, new fertilizers and pesticides are given field trials; the chemicals are used on experimental plots in various parts of the country – and sometimes overseas – so that scientists can determine how performance is affected by different soils and climates.

Many analytical techniques are automated; most routine testing is carried out by technicians (see p. 441). The professional scientist trains and supervises technicians, and initiates, organizes and oversees projects and researches into new experimental methods.

Personal attributes Interest in applied science; methodical approach; patience; ability to organize other people and their work; ability to communicate effectively with highly specialized colleagues and with trainee technicians; observation to recognize the unexpected.

Production (see also Engineering, pp. 171, 178)

The central activity in industry is organizing production. That involves supervising the people who operate the industrial plant. Production managers (titles vary) are a vital link in the chain of command from chargehand to production director, and between production and other departments. Their main function is to see that production runs smoothly and is as efficient as possible. That means they must keep up with technological developments and arrange for and supervise the installation of new, computerized, equipment as necessary. Hours can be long and irregular, and they may include some shift-work – but this is by no means so in all plants. Production managers usually have a small office, but they spend little time in it. The work involves daily contact with other professionals and managers from other departments as well as with shop stewards, etc.

Production professionals are equally concerned with managing people as with the exploitation of new technologies. The largest opportunities are for chemists. Production managers, or whatever the title of persons in charge, are normally graduates; technicians work under them. Production specialists can switch from one type of plant to another; and they can later go into *marketing* or *general management*.

Personal attributes Willingness to accept responsibility and take decisions; ability to keep calm in a crisis; leadership skills to motivate and organize plant operatives; practicality; ability to get on well with people at all levels in the industrial hierarchy; interest in the commercial application of science.

Technical Sales and Service

Two closely related activities: selling a science-based product and providing a technical back-up service for the customer. The product might be a sophisticated scientific instrument, an industrial chemical, a drug or a pesticide. The customer could be a research scientist, an industrial manager of a tiny or a large concern, a pharmacist or a farmer, i.e. a person with a lot of or no scientific knowledge. The technical saleswoman or 'rep' needs a thorough knowledge of the product, its uses and limitations. The kind of technical service a company provides depends on the nature of its products. A technical service scientist representing a plastics manufacturer deals mainly with customers who mould plastics into containers. She would investigate complaints and answer technical queries (and perhaps suggest new ways of using the material). She acts as a link between the research laboratories and the sales staff.

A representative for a pharmaceutical firm visits doctors and pharmacists and informs them about new drugs. She also provides feedback to her company on doctors' opinions of its products. In agricultural service industries reps may sell fertilizers, pesticides, animal health products to farmers and give advice about how they should be used (see Agriculture, p. 24).

Representatives are usually given a 'territory'; its size depends on what they sell and whether it is a country area or town: some reps may be away from home all week; others come home every night. Many work from home and only go to the office occasionally.

Personal attributes Outgoing personality; liking for meeting a succession of people; a thick skin for the occasional rude customer; sensitivity to gauge the right approach (long-winded, brief, aloof, friendly, etc.); ability to communicate facts effectively to customers who may be much more, and may be much less, knowledgeable than the rep herself; self-sufficiency for possibly long hours of lone travelling.

Technical writing

A technical writer assembles a package of scientific or technical information for a particular readership. The work is often done on a contract basis; specialist firms hire out technical writers to client companies for the duration of a particular writing project. This may concern, for example, a set of handbooks and instruction manuals to accompany a complex piece of electronic equipment which is being marketed by an electronics manufacturer. Two 'packages' may have to be written: one in simple language for operatives or chargehands who have only to know how to operate the equipment; and another package aimed at technical managers who want to know more technical details and may need to be able to repair or adjust the equipment. In the pharmaceutical industry, writers prepare 'case histories' of new drugs (experiments done, etc.) for submission to the Committee on Safety of Medicines.

Technical copywriters (see Advertising, p. 18) may write promotional material for science-based products. This is an expanding field, particularly in electronics, engineering generally and pharmaceuticals.

Personal attributes Wide scientific/technological interests and knowledge; an inquiring mind; ability to search out information and sift the relevant – for the particular purpose – from the irrelevant; ability to explain complex matters lucidly and concisely; a scientific grasshopper mind, to switch from one type of subject to another; liking for desk-work.

The Main Branches of Science

The classification of science into content areas is constantly changing. Most people are familiar with physics, chemistry and biology but as scientific investigation gets more complex, or is applied for different purposes, so different classifications may arise: a 'sub-set' of one of the main disciplines may be identified for more detailed study (e.g. astronomy – the study of extra-terrestrial systems, or virology – the study of viruses). An overlapping area of two main disciplines may emerge as worth studying in its own right (e.g. biophysics, biochemistry) or an interdisciplinary area may be identified, usually problem-orientated (practical rather than academic) and develop its own concepts and methods of study (e.g. cybernetics, environmental sciences, materials science, biotechnology).

Physics

Physics – the study of matter and energy – lies at the heart of science. It is closely related to chemistry; *chemical physics* – the study of materials and molecules – is a subject in its own right. *Biophysics* – the physical properties of living matter – has assumed greater importance as biological knowledge has grown. Many aspects of *engineering* and *materials science* are 'applied' aspects of physics. So the physicist, who always has a sound mathematical background, has a wide choice of occupations and settings in which to work.

Most industrial openings occur in engineering and related industries – especially in electronics, telecommunications and computing; other opportunities exist in chemical and allied industries, oil industry, public utilities (gas, electricity, Post Office). In the Civil Service physicists work on problems ranging from design of naval ships to recycling industrial waste. (See also *Biomedical Engineering*, p. 177.)

The *medical physicist*, one of a team of specialists concerned with the diagnosis and treatment of disease, uses radiotherapy and diagnostic radiology, radioactive isotopes, ultrasonics and many other physical methods to help doctors cure patients. In *occupational hygiene*, physicists help prevent damage to people's health by monitoring potential hazards from radiation, dust and other sources in working environments. (See also Environmental Sciences, especially *geophysics* and *meteorology*.) There are very limited opportunities for physicists (and for mathematicians) to branch out into *astronomy*. Research into such aspects of astronomy as satellite communications systems or the structure of the universe is done at government, university, and some commercial telecommunications (i.e. electronics) research laboratories. In *computer* design and manufacture, physicists play an important part.

Chemistry

Chemistry – the study of the composition of materials, their properties and how they change and react with other materials – occupies a central position in the basic sciences. It forms the basis of, for example, the manufacture of metals, pharmaceuticals, fertilizers, paints, synthetic fabrics, dyestuffs, plastics, paper, cosmetics, herbicides, pesticides and many other products.

It has links with both physics and biology and contributes to 'applied' science areas such as *food science*, *forensic science*, *materials science*, pharmacology and pharmacy. So someone with an interest in chemistry has a wide choice of employment. The big chemical manufacturers, oil, drug and cosmetic companies are the biggest employers of chemists. In the Civil Service, chemists in the Science Group work on road-surface, building materials, nutrition, pollution, and other research; in the general Civil Service they are welcome as Administration Trainees (see Civil Service, p. 121) – using their expertise in an advisory capacity and as background knowledge. A few chemists work on restoration and research in museums (see also *Biotechnology* below).

Biological Sciences

Biology can be subdivided into 4 major disciplines – the study of: plants (*botany*); animals (*zoology*); micro-organisms (*microbiology*); chemistry of living matter (*biochemistry*). However, as the interdependence of plants and animals is increasingly recognized, more emphasis is being placed on biology as an integration of botany and zoology. More specialized biological sciences deal with particular groups of living organisms – viruses (*virology*) and insects (*entomology*) for instance, and with particular biological processes such as the functioning of the body's organs (*physiology*) or the mechanisms of heredity and variation (*genetics*).

Botany and Zoology

Most opportunities occur in the public sector – mainly in the Civil Service Science Group, agricultural and medical research, and in conservation. A small number of biologists work in the Health Service, for water authorities and museums. In industry there are limited opportunities in pharmaceuticals and agrochemicals.

The most marketable aspects of botany and zoology are those related either to medical and pharmaceutical research (such as parasitology and physiology), or to agriculture and horticulture (such as plant pathology and entomology). Opportunities in *marine and freshwater biology* and *general ecology* are very limited.

Biochemistry and Microbiology

Biochemists and microbiologists have much better career prospects than botanists or zoologists; there is a steady demand from industry (mainly food and pharmaceuticals), from medical research, the Health Service, specialist research organizations and, to a lesser extent, agricultural research and the Civil Service Science Group.

A *biochemist* working for a pharmaceutical company might study the action of a new drug on experimental animals or (helped by a microbiologist) investigate biochemical aspects of the production of antibiotics by fermentation. *Hospital biochemists* work alongside medical colleagues and technicians as members of a team; they supervise routine biochemical testing (see Medical Laboratory Scientist, p. 288), do research, and may also teach clinical biochemistry to doctors and nurses.

Microbiologists often specialize in bacteriology and virology and become experts in plant or animal diseases. In the food industry and in environmental health laboratories they check samples for pathogenic microbes and investigate spoilage. In oil companies they explore ways of producing synthetic protein by feeding bacteria with the by-products of petroleum refining.

Biotechnology is not an academic discipline but covers processes which use multi-disciplinary approaches to problem-solving in science-based industries. It is mentioned here because of its impact on industry, as well as its frequent mention in the press, and hence careers-choosers' interest in it.

Biotechnology is, very broadly, the application of biological organisms, systems and processes in manufacturing industry – mainly but not only in the food, fertilizer, animal feedstuffs and pharmaceutical industries. It has also been described as 'factory farming of bugs' or microbes – the smallest living organisms which are then put to industrial uses. 'Genetic engineering' is just one aspect of biotechnology: it is, again very broadly, the manipulation, using scientific techniques, of genes. Biotechnologists work in a vast variety of science-based jobs, for example on the development of synthetic proteins; of new strains of wheat; of hormones and drugs. They also work on pollution control, and on the generation of new sources of energy from such varied natural materials as plant tissue and animal waste products. The usual way into biotechnology is via a science degree – preferably chemistry, biochemistry or microbiology – followed by post-graduate study. Some basic science degrees now offer 2nd- or 3rd-year biotechnology options but these degrees are also likely to have to be followed by post-graduate study. Employment prospects are uncertain: though this is an industrial growth area, it is possible that there will only be jobs for very brilliant scientists at the top of the tree and for lab. technicians (see Science Technician below, p. 441).

Environmental Sciences

The environmental sciences are fashionable. Concern with pollution, dwindling natural resources and threatened plant and animal species has given a fresh impetus to the scientific study of the environment. *Conservation* and *ecology* (the study of how plants and animals interact with their natural surroundings), together with *meteorology*, *oceanography*, *geology* and *geophysics*, are important environmental subjects.

Environmental science is often (and best) a *post*-graduate specialization: scientists take a first degree in a traditional subject and then either graft on an appropriate post-graduate course or get trained by employers in environmental aspects of their subject. *Meteorologists* and *physical oceanographers* usually have degrees in physics or maths; biologists normally specialize in ecology before becoming conservationists. *Geology* graduates are the exception: they can go straight into geological work without further training. *Geophysicists* usually build their specialist knowledge on a foundation of physics, geology or engineering. But there is an increasing number of first degree courses in environmental subjects – either joint honours (such as physics and meteorology) or broad-based integrated courses in environmental sciences.

Geology and Geophysics

Geology is the study of the structure and history of the earth; *geophysics* is concerned with its physical properties and, in particular, with the application of physical techniques to solve geological problems. Geologists locate, and then extract, oil, natural gas, minerals, useful rocks and underground water in the earth's crust. The first stage of exploration often entails making a geological map of a region and then following this up with an aerial survey to provide greater detail of the terrain.

Geophysical techniques are widely used in geological exploration. In *seismic surveying*, for example, shock waves from a small underground explosion set off by geophysicists bounce off the rock layers and are recorded by instruments. By analysing the data with a computer, geophysicists can unravel the underlying geological structure.

Geologists and geophysicists are employed by oil companies, the mining industry, the Institute of Geological Sciences (part of the Natural Environment Research Council – NERC), by specialist contractors and consultants, and the Civil Service Science Group. Geologists also work for civil engineers who construct dams, reservoirs, roads, etc.; for the Nature Conservancy Council; and, a few, for museums.

Field geologists often work in remote parts of the world, under difficult conditions.

Meteorology and Oceanography (see also Meteorology, p. 303)
Meteorology and oceanography – concerned with the atmosphere and the oceans – are closely related. The physics and dynamics of atmospheric and oceanographic processes have much in common; the oceans exert a powerful influence on the weather. At honours degree level, *meteorology* and *physical oceanography* are highly mathematical; numerical methods are widely used in modern weather forecasting.

The Meteorological Office also carries out research into such topics as the physics of cloud formation and energy exchange between atmosphere and oceans. Scientists are usually involved either in *forecasting* or in *research*.

Research in physical oceanography is undertaken at the Institute of Oceanographic Sciences (part of the Natural Environment Research Council – NERC). Topics include studies of waves, tides, currents and general circulation of ocean water. NERC also investigates the ecology of deep-water organisms, the composition of the sea-floor, *marine biology* subjects. Oceanographic work is done partly in the laboratory and partly at sea.

Conservation
Nature conservation used to mean protecting unusual plants and animals and their habitats. Now, many human activities have an environmental impact. Crop protection chemicals, for example, can upset the balance of ecological systems. If herbicides are used to control aquatic weeds, dead plants consume oxygen while decaying. As a result, fish and other organisms may die through lack of oxygen. A pipeline laid across country may disturb plant and animal life around it; an open-cast mine may leave a permanent scar on the countryside. Modern conservationists, recognizing the importance of protecting flora and fauna, are concerned with the wider problems of preserving the countryside as a whole.

The Nature Conservancy Council is responsible for conserving the wildlife and physiographical features of Great Britain. The Council manages over 100 National Nature Reserves and several thousand Sites of Special Scientific Interest, and advises farmers, landowners, local authorities, industrialists and others on conservation matters. Scientists (mainly botanists, zoologists, geologists and geographers) are employed as Assistant Regional Officers. The Nature Reserves are run by Wardens (often non-graduates) who are experienced conservationists. Research is carried out by the Institute of Terrestrial Ecology under the aegis of the Natural Environment Research Council.

Cybernetics

The original definition of cybernetics as 'control and communication in the animal and the machine' now extends to activities as different as landing a man on the moon, and using 'natural enemies' to kill pests. In a cybernetic system – such as a thermostat keeping a room at constant temperature – one thing controls another which reacts on the first to form a feedback loop. Since feedback processes operate in man-made control systems as well as in economics and biological systems, the term cybernetics is interpreted differently by people in different scientific spheres.

Cybernetics courses with a strong technological slant – containing such topics as feedback control theory and computer technology and application – are particularly suitable for a career in computer-based automatic systems (those used in navigation and air traffic control, for instance). Courses with a strong theoretical element – including the mathematical theory of cybernetics, artificial intelligence, biological and human cybernetics, for example – could lead to a career in computer design, systems analysis, operational research or planning.

The cybernetic aspects of industry – such as computer technology and applications – are expanding enormously.

See also Computer Scientist (p. 131).

Mathematical Sciences

Mathematicians – pure and applied – are much in demand. They work in commerce – in finance and in actuarial work (see Actuary, p. 15) for example – in science-based activities and in computers (see p. 131).

In the manufacturing industry and in the Civil Service they may work on translating problems into mathematical terms (making 'models'), working out solutions and then expressing the results in non-mathematical form. Sometimes the mathematical models are so complex that a special technique called *numerical analysis* is used to solve them. Some mathematicians specialize in numerical analysis; others become expert in operational research (see p. 345).

Statisticians – including mathematicians who have specialized in statistics – work in industry, medical, social and agricultural research, and in the Civil Service (Science Group and general). They are concerned with the design of experiments, questionnaires and surveys and with the analysis and interpretation of results. Wherever computers are used – and that, see Computing (p. 131), is in virtually every field of activity – statisticians process and interpret data and help design and improve systems. There is also scope for statisticians in marketing and market research where they design surveys to establish demand for goods and services. The majority of statisticians need a scientific background; some need social science expertise (it is easier to switch with a science background to statistics in social sciences than to switch with a social science background to statistics in science).

Materials Science

Materials Science covers *metallurgy*, *materials science* and specialist subjects such as *paper*, *textile*, *rubber*, *plastics technology*. Materials science is a relatively new subject which includes elements of *metallurgy* but deals also with polymeric materials (plastics and man-made fibres), and other composite materials, together with ceramics, glass and natural fibres.

For metallurgists and materials scientists most opportunities occur in engineering and allied industries, mainly metal manufacturing and electronics. Plastics, textiles, paper and rubber industries have traditionally recruited graduates in physics, chemistry and engineering and specialists in the various specific technologies. But there are now good opportunities for materials scientists to use their interdisciplinary approach in these industries, as well as in the newer ones concerned with composite materials: polymers reinforced with glass or carbon fibre, for example, and others still in the experimental stage. Materials science leads to wider choice of job than paper, rubber, plastics and other technology specialization.

Materials scientists are in short supply.

Prospects generally These vary considerably from one branch to another and they may change from one year to the next. Physicists are in greatest demand (mainly in the expanding electronics industry, see p. 175), but mathematicians, cyberneticians and some applied scientists are also in great demand, followed by chemists, biochemists and microbiologists. Botanists, zoologists and environmental science graduates are least in demand. However, scientists can often switch to another, related field (this may involve a post-graduate course).

The question whether a broad-based or a specialized degree leads to better prospects is impossible to answer in a general way: it depends on an individual's adaptability, motivation, specialization, on changing economic circumstances and on technological developments.

Prospects in the various types of work or *functions* vary mainly according to economic climate. In research and development, cutbacks tend to bite much earlier than in production and analysis and investigation. Technical writing and technical sales are expanding functions. However, scientists only specialize in a subject *after* graduation. (But some degree subjects are more likely to lead to one function, some to another: for example *applied* scientists are much more likely to be in demand in production than, for example, botanists, and a broad-based integrated course is not likely to lead to research.)

Scientists often start in laboratory work (*research and development, analysis, investigation*) and then move into *production*, *technical sales and service*, or *writing*; or they may use their science background in *marketing* (see p. 283); in *information work* (p. 253) or in *patent agency* (p. 355) or *operational research* (p. 345). Physics and mathematics *teachers* are much in demand: prospects for other science teachers are reasonable (in schools: higher education teaching prospects are bleak).

A science degree is not necessarily a vocational qualification, though it is so often believed to be just that. It is a way into all kinds of 'graduate jobs' – in industry, commerce, the Civil Service. Most employers of graduates welcome science graduates and arts graduates alike (except of course for specific professions); many even now prefer graduates with a scientific/technological background, because their special knowledge *might* be useful in management, and in explaining scientific facts and developments to their scientifically illiterate colleagues: and in any case, science graduates' minds are as trained as arts graduates' – and it is very often the 'trained mind' which employers want when they employ graduates.

Career prospects are generally much better for graduates who have at least a reading knowledge of a foreign language (at the moment especially German or Russian). Anyone who wants to work in EEC countries must be fluent in the relevant language and/or have specific experience. Short-term contracts possible in developing countries.

Pay: Medium to high (see p. xxiii).

Training Normally a degree. Science courses consist either of a detailed study of a single subject, with supporting ancillary subjects, or of a study of two distinct disciplines in a joint honours course, or of a cluster of several related disciplines, such as biological sciences. There is a continuing need for specialists, but a 'generalist' scientific education possibly leads to a wider choice of jobs especially for 'non-practising' scientists; its built-in flexibility enables the scientist to change direction if, for example, that should be desirable or necessary after a career-break, or because supply and demand in a specialization have changed.

For *research* a first or upper second honours degree is required. A first degree may have to be followed by a career-orientated postgraduate course. First degree course emphasis varies greatly. Some courses are very much more practical and vocational in approach and construction than others, and prospective students need to do careful research in publications like *Which Degree*, *CRAC Degree Course Guides*, Course Prospectuses.

Most CNAA and some university degrees are 4-year sandwich

courses, with a year spent at work. This may be an advantage to people who want to go into industry: their experience of the work situation during their training reassures employers that the applicant at least knows what a working environment is like.

BTEC Higher awards (see p. xvi) or Dip. HEs normally lead to senior technicians', not to professional scientists' jobs, but the distinction between scientist and technician is often blurred.

BTEC Higher award students can complete their professional training by taking a further 1-year full-time or 2-year part-time (day-release) training for the Graduate Membership of the Royal Institute of Chemistry's examination, which is of graduate standard. There are several equivalent professional Institutes and examinations in other branches of science.

Once in a job, training, or at least learning, continues. This may or may not lead to a further qualification.

Late start Degree course requirements in terms of O-levels and A-levels may be relaxed, but candidates' knowledge of maths and science has to be up-to-date; many late entrants first take evening classes, to freshen up their school sciences, etc. Opportunities limited.

Position of women The number of women scientists remains relatively small; the proportion of women taking science degrees is rising more slowly than the proportion taking science O- and A-levels (and *that* is rising slowly). A far greater proportion of women than of men with 3 science A-levels is trying to get into medicine – one of the most competitive disciplines – than into other science-based degree courses. Industry would welcome more women scientists in research, as well as in technical sales, marketing, production.

In 1983 15% of university students starting physics courses and 28% starting chemistry were women. More women than men – i.e. a much larger *proportion* of women – started botany degrees which carry little weight on the job market. Only 18% of university students (and about 19% of polytechnic students) starting computer science courses were women. When choosing science-based courses women do not plan ahead as realistically as do men. For example 45% of students starting medicine in 1983 were women; yet medicine is, after veterinary science, the most difficult course to get on to: science degree courses are nothing like as oversubscribed.

A few universities and polytechnics now arrange 'conversion' courses, allowing entrants with good science O-levels but without the usually-required A-level, to prepare for science degrees. Some of these courses ceased after 1 year's trial because of insufficient demand – probably not enough women knew about them.

Career-break: Return only possible if one has kept up with developments, and even then some areas, such as research and development, would probably be difficult to get back to. But it is possible to use a science degree to switch to technical writing or information work (see p. 256) or teaching (science teachers are still in demand). A few firms now provide opportunities for women who want to keep in touch, by arranging regular visits to labs, home-based projects or part-time work. But such schemes are still very few. Individuals can *ask* for arrangements to be made! Another way of keeping up with developments is taking a short Open University course (see p. xliv).

Part-time: Not many opportunities at the moment, except in technical writing (and then it is spasmodic rather than part-time) and in physics and mathematics teaching (see p. 520).

Further information

Biochemical Society, 7 Warwick Court, Holborn, London WC1R 5DP
Royal Society of Chemistry, 30 Russell Square, London WC1B 5DT
Institute of Biology, 20 Queensberry Place, London SW7 2DZ
Institute of Mathematics and its Applications, Maitland House, Warrior Square, Southend-on-Sea, Essex SS1 2JY
Institute of Physics, 47 Belgrave Square, London SW1X 8QX
Division of Cybernetics, Brunel University, Kingston Lane, Uxbridge, Middlesex UB8 3PH
Institution of Geologists, Burlington House, Piccadilly, London W1V 9HG
Civil Service Commission, Alencon Link, Basingstoke, Hants RG21 1JB
Nature Conservancy Council, 19–20 Belgrave Square, London SW1X 8PY
Natural Environment Research Council, Polaris House, North Star Avenue, Swindon, Wilts SN2 1EU
BTEC, Central House, Upper Woburn Place, London WC1H 0HH

Science Technician

Entry qualifications

Nothing rigid. They vary according to the job's and to colleges' requirements; from a few CSEs with at least one science to 2 science A-levels or even a degree. (The Civil Service requires 4 O-levels including a science, maths and English language.) For BTEC awards (see p. xvi) the minimum entry qualifications are theoretically 3 CSEs Grade 3 in appropriate subjects. Most colleges, and employers, believe that students need higher qualifications to be able to cope with technician jobs and courses (see **Training** for people with lower qualifications).

The work *Laboratory technician*, *assistant*, *technical assistant*, *research assistant*, *scientific assistant*, *technical officer*, *assistant scientific officer* are all titles used to describe people who perform science-related procedures and techniques under the overall supervision of scientists. As scientific investigations become more complex laboratory technicians become more important and the variety of jobs is growing. They are essential team-members, not unskilled bottle-washers. Their tasks range from mundane routine to work which overlaps very much with that of professional scientists.

They may work in any of the functions and branches described under Science, p. 426.

There are 4 main settings: hospitals, industry, education, Civil Service.

Hospitals

Apart from medical laboratory scientific and assistant scientific officers (see p. 288), there is a variety of *physics*-based technician jobs, some of which involve regular, some occasional and some no patient-contact. The jobs fall into two overlapping groups: *medical physics technician* and *physiological measurement technician*. These technicians' career structure is less clear and their scope more limited than the *biology/chemistry*-based technicians' work (see Medical Laboratory Scientist, p. 288).

Medical physics technicians broadly deal with 'imaging' equipment – X-ray machines; scanners; ultrasound; isotopes and similar matters (including computers), and with medical electronics generally. They may administer tests, i.e. have some patient-contact; or they may be wholly or largely concerned with maintenance, development and design (modification) of equipment – i.e. no or very little patient-contact. The very expensive and advanced imaging equipment is only available in teaching and large district hospitals, hence few medical physics jobs.

Physiological measurement technician is an umbrella term for technicians who administer a variety of diagnostic tests (i.e. it is work with constant patient-contact) such as hearing (audiology); heart function (cardiology); brain activity. In theory, physiological measurement technicians carry out a range of tests and, later, complex investigations. In practice the vast majority of these technicians administer one type of test, say cardiograms (ECGs) or electroencephalograms (EEGs, i.e. brain activity) throughout their working lives. In many hospitals the term 'physiological measurement technician' is in fact unknown. This is often work with job-satisfaction for people who want patient-contact rather than a structured career with prospects. Many audiology, cardiology, etc. technicians are part-timers who do this work as a *late-start* job.

Theory and practice of training differ too. In theory, school leavers with 4 O-levels, including 2 sciences (one must be physics) and English take a BTEC National Certificate in physics or electronics with special options while working as student technicians, and can then go on to take a BTEC Higher National Certificate. In practice at least medical physics technicians now usually need a physics or electronics or similar degree (a third class will do) or at least a BTEC Higher National award, to get a hospital job. In theory there is day-release for a BTEC National Certificate but there are only 8 courses in the whole of the UK for medical physics and physiological measurement technicians.

There is now a state registration scheme as there is for medical laboratory scientific officers, but as employers do not ask for physics-based technicians to be state registered, there is no incentive for individuals to take the necessary exams. However, the fairly new Association of Medical Physics and Physiological Measurement Technicians is hoping physics-based technicians will in due course become as accepted as a profession in its own right as are medical laboratory scientists and technicians now. At present, non-graduates who want hospital technician jobs have more scope in biology/chemistry-based medical laboratory work (see p. 288) than in the fast-changing and developing physics-based area.

Industry

Very varied work most of which falls into two broad categories: *quality control*, and *research and development*.

In *quality control* ('QC'), during the production of chemicals, detergents, plastics, cosmetics and other manufactured goods and in the food processing industry, the technician tests, for example, the purity and/or nutritional value of foodstuffs. In the pharmaceutical industry she helps with tests on drugs and medicines. In electronics, technicians may test computer circuitry or the quality of television and radio components (their work overlaps with that of engineering technicians, see p. 182).

In *research and development* technicians assist scientists with all types of research (see Science, p. 426). They may use new equipment and help modify it and they adapt standard procedures to suit particular experimental work.

Higher Education Establishments

Technicians work in science faculties, in research institutes and medical schools. They prepare work for lectures; and they help with research.

Technicians may prepare specimens for lectures in microbiology, histology, zoology, botany or geology, using for example techniques for culturing bacteria, or prepare thin sections of rocks or fossils for microscopical study, etc. In a chemistry faculty the technician is concerned with the assembly, care and maintenance of apparatus, and the preparation of bench reagents used for demonstration and experiment. She may, in research, use such techniques as flame photometry, spectro-photometry, chromatography, or use radio-isotopes.

Schools, Sixth Form and Tertiary Colleges, Colleges of Further Education

Technicians help teachers and lecturers. This used to be rather a menial job but conditions and prospects have now improved considerably. The work combines science with dealing with children and young people; it covers preparing, setting out and maintaining demonstration materials and apparatus as well as helping students and pupils in the classroom.

In smaller establishments there may only be one technician; in one day the technician could then help in and prepare for classes in physics, chemistry and biology. In large establishments several technicians work under the direction of a chief technician, and there are opportunities for progress, with training, to a more senior post, and to specialize in either biology, chemistry, or physics.

Science Group of the Civil Service

Technicians are called Assistant Scientific Officers. They are part of a team led by a scientist engaged in research in any of the scientific disciplines.

There are over 100 laboratories where scientists carry out fundamental research, investigate new techniques and equipment, ensure that standards of safety are maintained. Technicians provide support to research and project teams. Their work includes making observations of experiments, logging data, summarizing results for interpretation. For example, they may measure jet-pipe temperatures of a helicopter engine; determine the nitrogen content of animal fodder; test for drugs for police investigations; make weather observations at an airport.

Animal technicians work in all the settings, but particularly in pharmaceutical research. In 'animal units' they are concerned with breeding, husbandry, and housing of laboratory animals and with associated research. Animal technicians must be fond of animals and have an aptitude for handling them but they must not be sentimental about their charges: the animals are well looked after, but the reason for their being in the lab is for experiments to be carried out with or on them – so some are inevitably going to die unpleasantly.

Prospects (technicians generally) Good, but they vary according to changing situations, geographic area, area of specialization, level of qualification. Best prospects probably for well-qualified physics-based technicians. They are at present wanted above all throughout the information technology 'hardware' industries as well as elsewhere. For biology/chemistry-based technicians, fair prospects in pharmaceuticals, agricultural chemicals and similar industries and hospital medical research. People with low school-leaving qualifications but interested in the job should try and improve their qualifications if they cannot get student-technician jobs. On the whole there is a growing range of jobs which are loosely called 'science technician'.

Pay: Low to high (see p. xxiii).

Training Usually on-the-job with day- or block-release for BTEC National Certificate (see p. xvi) in the biological sciences, physics or chemistry with specialist options to fit in with their work. Technicians can switch specialization by adding option modules to basic Certificates. There is a great variety of options. Not all specialist subjects are available at all colleges – it depends largely on local job opportunities. Length of training varies mainly according to entry qualifications. With 4 O-levels including a science, maths and an English subject, part-time training normally takes 2 years; with 3 Grade 3 CSEs in relevant subjects it takes 3 years (not all colleges have facilities for lower-entry-level students).

Students with fewer than 3 Grade 3 CSEs can work for a City and Guilds Science Laboratory Assistant (or Technician, the latter is slightly more theoretical in content) Certificate by part-time study while in relevant employment. With experience, they may then be able to go on to BTEC National Certificate training.

Pre-entry training: There are full-time and sandwich BTEC National Diploma courses normally lasting 2 years in all the BTEC Certificate subjects. Entry requirements for these courses are, in most colleges, 4 O-levels, including a relevant science, maths and an English subject. There may be full-time 'catching up' opportunities for students who want to become science technicians but lack appropriate O-levels.

Higher or Senior Technician training
Students with BTEC National Certificates containing sufficient units (see p. xvi) or BTEC National Diplomas can take a BTEC Higher National Certificate (part-time) or BTEC Higher National Diploma (full-time or sandwich). Again, there are a great many specializations.

Direct entry requirements to Higher National Certificates and Diplomas vary according to main subjects. For example, for the Applied Biology Higher National Awards the following requirements now normally apply: 2 A-level science passes one of which must be a biological science *or* maths and a biological science at A-level. Chemistry must at least have been *studied* at A-level. For *Physics* and *Chemistry* Higher National awards: A-level in relevant science (i.e. Physics for Physics award plus 'evidence of substantial study beyond O-level' of two other sciences; maths must of course always be offered at O-level if not included in A-levels). So for direct entry to Higher National awards, 3 sciences must have been studied beyond O-level.

Personal attributes generally Manipulative skill; patience; scrupulous attention to detail; a sense of responsibility; willingness to take orders; ability to work both independently and as one of a team.

Late start Not much scope; school-leavers tend to be given preference. But adults can take full-time BTEC science courses, and see Physiological Measurement Technician, p. 442.

Position of women There are about equal numbers of males and females, but far more men are senior technicians mainly because fewer women have physics at A-levels. As a result more women go into dead-end low-level technician jobs where they do not get – and often do not ask for – day-release for further qualifications. Women with physics O- and A-levels do as well as men.

Career-break: As this is a rapidly changing area, only technicians who systematically keep up with developments can return, but there are up-dating opportunities, partly through the Open University (see p. xliv).

Part-time: Very limited scope – but no reason why work should not be done part-time and by job-sharing.

Further information
Institute of Animal Technicians, 5 South Parade, Oxford OX2 7JL
City and Guilds of London Institute, 76 Portland Place, London W1N 4AA
BTEC, Central House, Upper Woburn Place, London WC1H 0HH

Related careers *Engineering Technician – Medical Laboratory Scientist – Physiotherapy – Optical Work – Orthoptics*

Food Science and Technology

Entry qualifications All educational levels, see **Training**.

The work *Food science* is concerned with the chemical and biological nature of food and its behaviour under natural conditions, during processing and during storage. *Food technology* is the application of relevant sciences, including engineering, to the processing, preservation and development of raw materials and manufactured foods. Food scientists and technologists work in quality control and product development departments (see Science, p. 426) of food companies which make anything from fish fingers to fruit cake or canned soup. They also work for flavour makers, public analysts, or in research centres where experiments with new food products using unorthodox materials (such as seaweed, or plankton) may be carried out. Some work in research and development on 'fast foods' and 'systems catering' (see Catering, p. 91) monitoring the behaviour of foods as new technologies are used. Some work together with *biotechnologists* (see p. 434). Some research jobs are for food *scientists*; production jobs tend to be held by *technologists*; but there is no clear-cut division between the two and both types of specialists are found in most job areas. There are jobs for technicians and for professional scientists and technologists: the division between senior technician and scientist/technologist is often blurred.

Prospects Generally good: the industry is less affected than many by economic slumps. Its diversity provides opportunities to specialize. The broad-based training allows for flexibility. As in other industries, technologists now often move into top general management (see line management, Management in Industry, p. 271).

Pay: Medium (see p. xxiii).

Training *Technician level*: With 3 CSEs Grade 3 *in theory*, but in practice usually 4 O-levels including a science, maths and a subject testing use of English, BTEC award in Food Science/Food Technology with various options. Courses can be part-time day-release (3 years for CSE entrants; 2 for 4 O-level entrants) or full-time (4 O-level entry only), 2 years; or sandwich (4 O-levels only), 3 years.

With 1 science A-level passed and another studied to A-level (more often two passed, in practice) one of which should be chemistry and the other either physics, maths or biology, and 3 O-levels (including chemistry if not at A-level): BTEC Higher award, part-time, full-time or sandwich. BTEC award holders may go on to take Higher awards.

Graduate level: with 2 – or sometimes 3 – science A-levels which must include chemistry (precise requirements vary) degrees in various aspects of food science. Degree titles vary and do not necessarily indicate precise differences in syllabus. The National College of Food Technology (Reading University) awards the only Food Technology degree. Degrees vary in emphasis and content: some are more commercially orientated (combining food science and marketing for example); some are more science-based; others put more emphasis on relevant technologies; yet others on management.

While food science and technology degrees are strictly vocationally orientated, *science* and *engineering* graduates (see p. 426 and p. 181) can also get into the food industries and then take post-graduate qualifications, either by part-time or full-time study. There are post-graduate courses in Food Science; Food Analysis and Composition; Food and Management Science; Food Microbiology; Food Engineering; Biotechnology.

Personal attributes A meticulous approach to technical problems plus an interest in people as consumers and changing tastes and eating habits. For many jobs a real interest in food is desirable, as is the ability to work as part of a team. For *management careers*, ability to organize people and work, to work under pressure and to take decisions.

Late start Some opportunities for those with fairly recent chemistry O-level.

Position of women There is still some bias against women in production jobs where they are in charge of a lot of men, but they have little difficulty in entering other areas.

Career-break: Provided people stay in touch through professional institutes there should be no problem.

Part-time: Very little scope at present.

Further information Institute of Food Science and Technology, 20 Queensberry Place, London SW7 2DR

Forensic Science

Entry qualifications

Scientific Officers: BTEC Higher award (see p. xvi), or degree in a scientific, engineering or mathematical subject.

Assistant Scientific Officers: At least 4 O-levels, including English language *and* a science or maths subject, or BTEC award in Science.

The work

Forensic scientists and their assistants (technicians) are a kind of scientific detective. They apply scientific knowledge to the investigation of crime or suspected crime. They work closely with the police and examine material obtained from the scene of a crime, using the standard experimental techniques to examine and identify traces of soil, paint, glass, etc.; identify drugs; determine the quantity of alcohol in blood samples, etc. They use sophisticated analytical techniques, including chromatography, ultra-violet and infra-red spectrophotometry and neutron activation analysis. They are employed by the Home Office in its central research establishment and in regional laboratories. Most of the openings are for *chemists* and *biologists*, with occasional opportunities for physicists, geologists and others.

Biologists identify body-fluid stains and determine blood groups. They use identify hairs, fibres, seeds and fragments of plant and animal tissues. They use microscopes – including scanning electron microscopes – and increasingly, molecular biology techniques.

Some forensic scientists specialize in working on documents and inks investigating alleged forgeries; others become experts on firearms or explosives. They spend most of their time in the laboratory, but may visit the scene of a crime to collect material, and may appear in court as expert witnesses.

Prospects

Good for promotion from one Civil Service grade to another.

Pay: Medium to high (see p. xxiii).

Training

Normally on-the-job under the supervision of experienced scientists, with day-release for BTEC Higher award.

Personal attributes

As for scientists, plus willingness to be exposed to some sordid aspects of crime and to withstand gruelling cross-examinations in the witness box.

Late start

No upper age limit in theory; in practice competition from young entrants very stiff.

Position of women

Few women at the moment, but only because very few have applied. See Civil Service (p. 129). At present, the top job in forensic science is held by a woman.

Career-break: See Civil Service. Also need to keep up with scientific/legal developments.

Part-time: See Civil Service. In practice none at the moment but no reason why this should remain so. Job-sharing should be possible but has not been tried.

Further information

The Civil Service Commission, Alencon Link, Basingstoke, Hants RG21 1JB

Secretarial and Clerical Work

Secretary – specialist secretary – shorthand- and audio-typist/word processor operator – clerk – supervisor/trainer – customer support representative

Entry qualifications Various educational levels: minimum usually 4 O-levels including English language; but see **Training**.

The work Office work consists largely of handling information – searching for, producing, passing on (verbally or in print) facts and figures, questions and answers, messages and instructions. 'Information Technology' (IT) which broadly describes the equipment and systems used to process, transmit, file or otherwise handle information electronically, is changing the nature of office work. But fear of the unknown has tended to exaggerate IT's effect. The 'paperless office' is not about to take over overnight. The workforce is shrinking – especially at the lower, unskilled end where automation is drastically reducing the scope. But secretaries and people who produce and handle text will still be needed even when managers have their own desk-top computers on which they can call up information and which they can use to communicate with each other, customers, clients, etc. IT also creates some new jobs. The main jobs:

Secretary

Titles have no precise meaning: executive secretary, private secretary, personal assistant are used indiscriminately. Some of the most high-powered secretaries prefer to call themselves merely 'secretary'; some 'personal assistants' just do junior executives' typing and telephoning.

The confusion over titles arose because traditionally there is no promotion ladder and career-structure, and no precise definition of the secretary's work or of the differences between *personal assistant*, *secretary*, *shorthand-* or *audio-typist*, or *word processor operator* and *clerk*. Differences between these jobs are considerable, but in employers' and employees' minds they are blurred, which leads to disappointment and frustration on both sides of the desk. However, with the wider choice of career opportunities for women, fewer able women are now willing to stay in jobs without prospects of advancement. Mainly for that reason, some organizations are now introducing something resembling career-structures (see **Prospects**). For example, the difference between 'personal assistant' and 'secretary' is now often being taken seriously. A secretary follows her boss's instructions; when she fully understands the department's work, she becomes a 'personal assistant' and in that capacity makes her own decisions. For example, as a sales manager's secretary she would, if a sales representative falls ill, ask her boss to whom the sick person's work should be allocated. As personal assistant she would re-allocate the work herself, without asking her boss.

Another development which is changing the secretarial scene is the 'team secretary' (in another office, she might be called an 'administrative assistant'). She 'manages' a group of, say, several junior architects in an architectural partnership, or overseas marketing people in an export department. She organizes her charges' appointments, travel schedules, etc., and keeps track of their various projects and assignments. If the head of the department or partnership wants to know where X is, or how project Y is progressing, the team secretary knows the situation.

Both personal assistant and team secretary are in fact junior/middle management jobs but they are not necessarily recognized as such (see Management, p. 269, and **Position of women**, p. 462).

The traditional secretary usually still works for one person or perhaps two. (This is of course the 'office' secretary, not the administrator in charge of an institution, learned society or similar organization.) It is the secretary's task to husband her boss's time and energy so that he or she can concentrate on whatever the job is at that moment.

The secretary acts as buffer between her boss and callers and phone calls, and takes minor decisions on her/his behalf. She must understand her boss's work well enough to know when to act on her own initiative and when to ask for instructions. This is one of the most challenging secretarial skills. Secretarial duties may involve:

1. Acting as link between individuals and various sections in an organization; this could be departments in a university, company or store, or individuals in a management-team, and may involve writing memos, ringing people up, going to see them.
2. Collecting information from a variety of printed and personal sources – this involves knowing where to go for whatever the information required, perhaps telephoning trade associations or government departments.
3. Preparing agendas for meetings and collecting documents supporting the various items, distributing the papers at the right time to the right people; taking minutes at meetings, editing them and writing them up.
4. Looking through the day's mail and deciding which letters the boss has to deal with personally and which ones she can cope with herself;

summarizing lengthy letters and documents; drafting her own replies to some letters and presenting them to her boss for approval and signature.

5. Making travel arrangements and arranging meetings, at home or abroad, for several busy people: this is a time-consuming task which requires meticulous attention to detail and may involve international trunk calls and lengthy correspondence until finally a time and place suitable to everyone has been agreed upon.

The amount of typing or word-processing a secretary does varies. In a large office she may only deal with her boss's confidential correspondence, other matters being dealt with by a 'junior secretary' or someone from the typing-pool or word-processing unit. She may be in charge of one or several juniors, or cope single-handed.

The extent of automation still varies from one office to another, but it is increasing everywhere. The new technologies mean that secretaries and bosses both have access to numerous types of computerized equipment. As well as enabling bosses to do *their* job more effectively, secretaries will be able to perform many administrative tasks more effectively than hitherto. They will also be able to relieve their bosses of administrative tasks, and possibly take over part of the boss's main task. The availability of data-processing equipment – and opportunities to use it – should, in theory, enable capable secretaries to take part in executives' decision-making tasks, e.g. financial forecasting and analysis and production progress charting; or assessing customer response. The *potential* for merging the two roles – that of the manager/executive and the secretary – now exists. How much, in practice, the secretary will be able to exploit the potential depends on the boss's willingness to let go of responsibilities, the secretary's initiative, and a host of imponderables.

Traditional secretarial tasks which are, increasingly, computerized, include arranging meetings; booking conference rooms; recording and instant dispatch of voice and text messages; maintenance of lists, e.g. personal addresses, business contacts (with background information), internal telephone directories; 'unstructured information', e.g. product descriptions; training records; filing and retrieval; travel arrangements.

Invariably, being a secretary is a self-effacing job. A good secretary rarely gets the kudos she deserves when, thanks to her efficiency, a crisis is avoided, but she is likely to be blamed if things go wrong – say if she forgets to remind her boss of an appointment which she/he too had forgotten and which is written down in the appointments diary.

Specialist Secretary

Though there is no *need* to decide on any specialization before training, there are 3 specializations for which special training is useful but not essential.

1. *Medical Secretary*: She works in hospital, for one or several consultants; in consultants' private consulting rooms; or for general practitioners. She requires knowledge of medical terminology and of health and social services organization. In hospital, secretaries have less contact with patients than in consulting rooms and general practice, but they have more companionship. In GPs' group practices the work involves organizing/administration.

2. *Farm or Agricultural Secretary*: Farm secretaries deal with the paper-work which modern farming entails. They fill in forms, keep accounts, keep and analyse records, and deal with correspondence, often on their own initiative. Only very big farms employ full-timers; most need part-time help. So farm secretaries either work as free-lances, spending a number of days a month on different farms, or they are employed by farm-secretarial agencies and are sent out to different farms. The work is varied, as it involves working on different types of farm; and it requires experience and self-confidence because farmers, unlike other employers, usually know less about the work to be done (accounts, filling in VAT and other forms) than their secretaries. Specialist training is a great advantage.

Both medical and farm secretaries now often use computers; doctors' secretaries to keep patients' records; farm secretaries to record, for example, cows' milk yield in relation to expenditure on various foodstuffs.

3. *Bi- or Multilingual Secretaries*: They translate incoming mail; then may compose their own letters in a foreign language from notes dictated in English, but most outgoing mail is written in English. They sometimes read foreign journals and search for and translate or summarize relevant articles. Occasionally they may act as interpreter. Their scope varies: some secretaries hardly use their languages at all; others are relied upon totally by their mono-lingual bosses. Foreign Office secretaries must be proficient in 1 language but many never use that knowledge even when working in embassies abroad (see Civil Service, p. 125). There are commercial opportunities abroad for truly bi-lingual secretaries with, occasionally, the relevant shorthand. International organizations usually require previous senior secretarial experience. Overall, the greatest demand is for French/English, German/English and French/German/English, mainly in international marketing and in export. There is a small, steady demand for Spanish, for other European languages, and for Russian.

At home, foreign shorthand is rarely required; in order to master it, it is essential to be *absolutely fluent* in the language(s) concerned. For most linguist-secretary jobs a grasp of the relevant country's economic and social set-up is far more important than shorthand and 100% speaking and writing fluency.

Shorthand- and Audio-Typist/Word Processor Operator

Many so-called secretaries are really typists or word processor operators. They work for a number of people, often in a typing-pool or central word processing unit or 'station', and not for individuals as secretaries do. Their job is far more impersonal, concerned with producing texts efficiently and economically rather than dealing with people and all the various jobs the secretaries cope with. It is work for people who like getting on with the job without having to talk much to their bosses; but it can be a step to secretarial work too.

The demand for *shorthand*-writers is still great. There are still many executives who insist on dictating to an individual rather than into a machine.

Copy-typists have virtually disappeared. Offices now either use photocopying or similar machines or word processors.

The term 'word processor' has caught on and is now firmly established. However, most manufacturers would have preferred 'text processors' because the equipment's strength lies in processing texts.

A word processor basically consists of a typewriter-like keyboard connected to a visual display unit (VDU) which looks like a TV screen, and to a 'memory' in which previously 'keyed-in' texts are stored, coded, filed ready for 'retrieval', i.e. for future use either in further printed texts, or for 'call up' on VDU screens. The keyboard is usually connected to equipment which prints the text; it may be connected to other VDUs, either in an office next door, or in one, or several, offices hundreds of miles away. An operator or indeed a manager/executive could be transmitting a message instantly to other VDUs as well as producing the text in printed form.

There is no need to understand how a word processor works any more than there is a need to understand how a television works. It is only necessary to know which key to press to achieve which result. The operator 'keys in' text much as she would type it. The text then appears on the screen.

(Word processors may also be linked to other data-processing equipment, see Computing, p. 131.)

Briefly, the word processor's main advantages over typewriters are these:

1. It enables the operator to correct mistakes easily and quickly.
2. It can produce any number of perfect 'top-copies' instantly.

3. It can automatically file, code, sort and have ready for future use not only whole printed texts but individual paragraphs or sentences or lists of names and/or addresses.
4. It can combine individual sections with new texts and/or with lists of addresses, or with other sections of text stored in the 'memory'.

The preparation of original letters, memos, reports is not any quicker on a word processor than on an electric typewriter operated by a competent typist. Word processors will not totally replace typewriters. They are 'cost effective' and therefore useful when (a) texts have to be amended several times, as happens frequently in offices where reports/memos/letters are drafted by one person and then circulated for approval/amendment by others; (b) where reports are highly complex and, even though composed by one person, are likely to need several drafts before the final version is ready; (c) in offices from which long and complex documents, which vary only *slightly* in content, are sent out in their hundreds. For example solicitors' documents sent to clients often contain several standard paragraphs, as well as original ones; the same applies to estate agents, banks, mail order firms, etc.; (d) in offices where hundreds of standard letters have to be produced, each looking like top copies.

Word processors are used differently in different organizations. There is no agreement yet on which is the best method of using this new technology. In some offices several word processors are combined in one central 'station' or 'unit', all the organization's work being processed there; in other offices each department has its own word processor, and several people use it; in some cases each secretary has her own individual word processor. The tendency now is away from central word processor units and for secretaries to use, or share the use of, a word processor as well as, possibly, a typewriter. Word processor operators, if they are good at the job, tend to get bored and job-hop; so good employers organize the work so that the word processor operating work is shared out between secretaries – i.e. each job has varied content. However, there are also many jobs which involve word processor operating only.

Clerk

This may involve some typing and/or word processing and/or using computers (see Computing, p. 131). Clerks' work varies even more than secretarial work. Some clerks work on their own all day; others are in constant contact with colleagues and/or the public. A clerk in a travel agency may send out brochures to customers or hand them out over the counter; in a mail order firm, however computerized the system, she may check incoming orders to see whether the right postal orders are enclosed; in a hospital or commercial office a junior may do nothing but photocopy. She may work in a post-room, collecting and distributing mail from and to various departments and individuals. In a personnel department, she may work on computerized staff records, entering details about absence, wage increases, etc. In large organizations, whether town hall, store or manufacturing company, there is often a computerized filing system. In a small office a clerk may still do 'old-fashioned' filing, answer the telephone, make the tea and do some typing/word processing. The extent to which clerks' work has been affected by the introduction of computerized equipment varies enormously. At the moment, many offices still rely largely on the old-fashioned methods of entering and updating facts and figures, transmitting messages, collecting and distributing information. But this is changing. For example in insurance offices, when updating clients' policies, clerks first have to look for the file, then re-type part of the policy and file it again. With computerized equipment however, the clerk keys in the reference code, the policy is 'called up' (appears on) the video display unit, the clerk keys in the necessary amendments and, at the press of a few buttons, the policy is amended as required, printed, *and* stored in the equipment's memory – the electronic file. Any telephone inquiry dealt with by clerks, whether from a supplier in a manufacturing industry or an airline customer, is dealt with now by keying in the question and getting the answer instantly on the VDU.

Clerks may also become telephonists or receptionists. The receptionist's job may be rather more complex than it appears – receptionists are expected to have a good knowledge of who does what in the organization so that they can direct callers to the right person or department.

Prospects *'Real' secretaries*: Good for those able to cope with modern office equipment. They can still pick and choose the environment they want to work in, whether the City, a public institution or a professional office – say, accountants' or solicitors'. There are some possibilities in fashion, in public relations, in travel, employment, and estate agents – in areas where specialist training is not expected – for going up the management ladder. *Very* few secretaries in television manage to jump the abyss between secretarial and creative work.

Secretarial work used to be the best way into management generally, but there are much better ways now (see Management, p. 269). The vast majority of secretaries remain secretaries throughout their working lives. Promotion usually still means becoming secretary to someone higher up in the hierarchy – for example, from secretary to sales manager to secretary to finance director to secretary to managing director to secretary to chairman. In this promotion system, expertise gained in one job tends to be fairly useless in the next, therefore the opportunities for independent work, for becoming PA (or *acting* as PA at least) or executive, tend to be less in the new job than they were in the previous one. Many secretaries find that the higher up in the hierarchy their boss, the less the boss is likely to delegate. So secretaries who want a career and not a job need to find out far more details about what an advertised job involves than do people who go into structured careers with accepted work-content, qualifications, promotion prospects, etc.

Secretaries who have word processing experience can become **Supervisors/Coordinators/Trainers**. They are the buffer between the users ('text originators') and the operators; they schedule work as it comes in and they appease users whose text cannot be dealt with instantly. They may also diagnose and possibly deal with minor equipment faults and deal with the equipment suppliers if things go seriously wrong. This job can lead to, or be combined with, 'in-house training' – work which involves training new word processor operators and persuading managers to learn what the equipment can and cannot do; writing manuals; advising office managers by evaluating the many different types of machines when new ones are to be bought. This type of job is still evolving. It always involves contact with a large variety of people, its exact content varies according to size, type and ideas of the employing organization.

Secretaries who want to get out of the office atmosphere and yet use their office technological and work experience can become **Customer Support Representatives** with manufacturers. They demonstrate equipment to prospective clients and later provide a 'handholding' and trouble-shooting service for companies which have bought their equipment. This work, in turn, can lead to Selling and Marketing (see p. 283) for word processing equipment manufacturers. See also Working for Oneself, p. 560.

Bilingual secretaries: They get jobs easily, but not necessarily with much scope for using their language proficiency. Graduates are often overqualified. O-level or A-level language plus knowing how to use a dictionary is often all that is needed, even when the job was advertised as for a linguist. There are more secretaries who want to work *abroad* than there are jobs available. However, good linguists with about 3 years' secretarial experience can get jobs in EEC countries and elsewhere, mainly in British or multinational companies' offices.

Medical secretaries: Secretarial growth area.

Farm secretaries: Good opportunities in most rural areas.

Typists: Word processing equipment is reducing demand drastically, but see **Training.**

Clerks: Poor. Electronic equipment is rapidly reducing demand.

Pay: *Secretaries*: medium to high; *Clerical work*: low to medium; *Word processor operators*: high (see p. xxiii).

Training No set pattern. A secretary should still learn shorthand, at least at 90–100 words per minute (and transcribe it adequately), and audio-type at 50 words per minute. She must be able to spell. She must know how to use, and where to find, sources of reference. She needs a good grasp of who does what in the commercial world, in the community, in government. She must be able to draft and summarize letters, reports, etc. – both verbally and in writing.

Where, and how, she acquires the 'secretarial core skills' is totally immaterial. Certificates and Diplomas awarded by colleges, the Royal Society of Arts, the London Chamber of Commerce and Industry, Pitman's, for example, and specialist ones by the Association of Medical Secretaries, are useful when there are more applicants than vacancies. Qualifications secure a first interview, but they count for far less than impression made at interview.

A 6th-form education, A-levels in such subjects as geography, English, economics, and quickly learning to do shorthand, typing and then word processing, is far more useful than leaving school at 16 and taking a 2-year secretarial course. O-level English language is essential: a degree is rarely an advantage. Even when an employer specifies 'graduate secretary', an intelligent, well-informed 6th-form leaver is usually acceptable. There are so many graduate secretaries simply because arts graduates cannot think of anything else to do – not because many secretarial jobs are so intellectually demanding that only graduates could fill them. Graduate secretaries do not even have significantly greater chances of getting into management than 6th-form leavers.

There is a tremendous variety of secretarial courses, but there is no pecking order, no 'best buy'. Most education and training for secretarial/general office work and word processing is sadly disorganized and out-of-date, with several overlapping qualifications. Certain qualifications, such as the Royal Society of Arts', are well known and carry considerable weight, but individual colleges, teaching methods and equipment vary enormously. At this stage in the 'office revolution', when new office equipment and routines are being widely introduced, a course for a good qualification at a college with antiquated equipment, and teachers who know little of present-day office practice, may be less useful than a course in a college which arranges visits to modern offices, and which has teachers who understand 1980s office technology, even if the college only awards its own diploma.

One cannot even judge the usefulness of secretarial courses by their entry requirements. There are some courses which only accept entrants with at least 2 A-levels (some even insist on a degree) which *may* lead fairly quickly to senior secretarial jobs. But it is quite likely that students who take these courses would have got equally far, equally quickly, if they had merely taken a short sharp typing-only course.

Courses fall into broad categories, each with many variations; and often with various optional subjects:

1. Courses for students with 2 A-levels or with degrees or comparable qualifications, lasting between 3 and 9 months; a 3 months' crash course, learning the core skills, should be sufficient.
2. 6-month to 2-year courses for students with 4 or 5 O-levels. Unless 2-year courses include something like medical, legal, farm or linguist secretarial work, or A-level study, 2 years is unnecessarily long.
3. 1- or 2-year courses for students with 3 to 5 O-levels. They often include O- (or A-) level study. Courses are likely to lead to clerical rather than secretarial jobs in the first instance.
4. Courses for students with 'a good general education' (no specific passes). These are not strictly speaking *secretarial* courses (whatever their title!). They should last 2 years and include general educational subjects if they are eventually to lead to secretarial work.
5. 1-year courses in English, shorthand, typing, office routine, lead to *clerks*' and *typists*' jobs (also applies to commercial courses at school).
6. BTEC courses (see p. xvi), part-time or full-time, 2 or 3 years normally. Broadly, 'General' awards – no specific entry requirements – lead to clerical work; 'National' awards – 4 O-level entry – lead to secretarial work. General awards should include Introduction to Keyboarding and its Application options, and National awards should include Word/Information Processing options.

However, adequate word processing is not available at all colleges. Many lack up-to-date equipment and/or teachers who understand the new technologies. Applicants with good typing skills can still get jobs: they may then be given in-house word processing training. However, as employers are often in a buyers' market now, applicants who are familiar with word processors are at a distinct advantage in the job market. For that reason, private word processing schools have proliferated over the last few years. Their courses vary enormously in quality; some use out-of-date equipment and/or provide insufficient 'hands on' w.p. experience and/or are unnecessarily long. Good courses normally last only about one week full-time (or longer part-time/evenings only) *and they only accept students who can type*. So before signing on for a private school w.p. course, it is essential to make sure that it is a good one. On the whole, courses attached to well-known secretarial agencies are a wise choice. Most of them have been started to ensure the agency has a pool of well qualified people on its books rather than to make a profit; they are run 'at cost' (late 1983: between £50 and £100). Until very recently, it was thought that, as there are about 150 different types of word processors, it would be best to teach the basic concept of word processing rather than to run 'machine-specific' courses. Now agency-attached courses normally teach on the two or three types of machines in widest use. Word processor operators who then get jobs where they have to use a different type of machine, get short 'conversion training' on the job. In any case on-the-job training goes on for some time: it takes quite a few months for a word processor operator to be really proficient at the job.

Specialist Training
Bi- or multilingual secretary: Entry requirements from 'O-level pass' or 'A-level standard' in the relevant language to language degree. Most courses last 2 years. Prospective secretary-linguists who intend to take a language degree should look out for degree courses including 'area studies' – which means the course covers the relevant country's history and social and economic institutions, etc. That type of knowledge is also very important for getting jobs abroad with commercial firms and international agencies.

Medical secretary: With 4 O-levels including English language, 2-year full-time course; with 1 A-level, 1-year full-time course for *Diploma for Medical Secretaries*. With two O-levels one of which must be English language; 1-year full-time course for *Certificate in Medical Reception*. This can be converted into Medical Secretaries' Diploma by taking part-time day-release or evening courses. TOPS courses (see p. xlvi) are also available, and home-study for the two qualifications is possible, if there is no course available locally.

Part-time courses leading to the *Diploma in Practice Administration* (approved by the British Medical Association and the Royal College of General Practitioners) are available for persons holding the Certificate in Medical Reception plus at least 1 year's experience; for those holding the Diploma; and for experienced secretaries who have not taken the Certificate or Diploma examination but have several years' experience of the work and hold a 'Letter of Recognition' (from the Association of Medical Secretaries).
Details from Association of Medical Secretaries, Tavistock House North, Tavistock Square, London WCIH 9LN.

Farm secretary: 2-year course. Farm secretaries' courses at Agricultural Institutes *or* general secretarial course with Farm Accounts.

Personal attributes

Secretaries who hope (probably in vain) to become executives: exceptional organizing ability, self-confidence, determination and ambition, a logical brain, business acumen, willingness to take responsibility *and* willingness to take orders; ability to communicate easily with people at all levels of education and status in the organization; willingness to work long hours.
Personal assistants: the above qualities without the ambition and business acumen; the willingness to take responsibility must be

coupled with the willingness to remain in a supportive role; a sympathetic manner, a desire to be of use to others; ability to ignore getting undeserved blame when things go wrong and not getting well-deserved praise; indifference to seeing less able 'executives' have higher status and pay, and more responsibility.

Typists/word processor operators: wanting to get on with one's work without involvement with people and in the organization's business; accuracy.

Clerks: depends on type of job – some require a liking for quiet backroom work dealing with paperwork; others a liking for dealing with people; most require attention to detail and willingness to do as told.

Late start Secretarial work is easy to start late. While there are *some* employers who will not consider anyone over 35, there is a growing number of employers who *prefer* the over-35s.

3-month to 1-year courses geared to mature students are available under TOPS (see p. xlvi) (including specialist secretary's courses).

Position of women This is still almost 100% women's work, but recently some men have become secretaries. Some word-processing unit supervisors and customer support representatives are male graduates who come into the organization with computing experience or as management trainees.

Career-break: Should be no problem for secretaries with word processor operating experience.

Refresher courses: Available under TOPS (see p. xlvi). Post-experience BTEC (see p. xvi) units on Using Word Processors and Supervising Word Processing are being introduced. These will be useful for people returning after a gap.

Part-time: Good opportunities for word processor operators. Not quite as good for secretaries, who are expected to be available whenever the boss wants them. However, even here part-time work is gradually becoming accepted, but part-timers are never likely to have as wide a choice of jobs as full-timers. The fewer the hours they are willing to work, the more restricted the choice of job.

Part-time can be anything from 6 hours a week, to 4 full days; 2 or 3 full, or 3 or 4 half days are the most usual. A flexible number of hours, to suit both secretary and employers and varying week by week, is sometimes possible. A new variation on the part-time theme is job-sharing; 2 women do one job, either handing over to each other – overlapping perhaps in the middle of the day – or leaving each other detailed notes, anything which minimizes the disadvantage of lack of continuity. There are a few jobs which can be done in term-time only, leaving mothers free during the children's holidays; and occasionally some 1 week (or fortnight) on, 1 week (or fortnight) off jobs.

'*Temping*' is a kind of part-time work. It is particularly suitable for actresses, artists, models, etc., people who have to 'fill in' while waiting for their own kind of work; for mothers who cannot get a term-time-only job, and for secretaries and typists who prefer a frequent change of environment to getting involved with one set of people and one type of work. Temps normally work for agencies who send them to employers on a weekly or daily basis; only those with very good contacts and experience can work as freelances.

Further information

No central organization. Local education authority for lists of local courses (and see Medical Secretaries, p. 461).

Related careers

Chartered Secretary – Computing/Information Technology – Health Service Administration – Linguist – Management – Personnel Work – Public Relations – Working for Oneself

The Services (Women's Only) (WRAC, WRAF, WRNS)

NON-COMMISSIONED RANKS: technical – clerical and communications – catering and stores – medical and dental – miscellaneous trades; COMMISSIONED RANKS: including cadet entrants and permanent and short service commissions – nursing

Women's opportunities are increasing steadily. For example, in the WRNS, women compete successfully with men at the Royal Naval College, Dartmouth. In 1983 one woman became Assistant Naval Liaison Officer responsible for looking after arrangements for British and foreign ships visiting London. Another woman became Commander of an RAF operating station. In the WRAC a woman was in charge of 40 male officers on a technical and command skills course.

Non-Commissioned Ranks

The Services are, to a great extent, self-contained communities, and offer many different jobs. The Woman's Royal Naval Service, the Women's Royal Army Corps, and the Women's Royal Air Force need secretaries, telephonists, drivers, photographers, people to look after welfare, etc.

Apart from jobs which can be done both in the Services and elsewhere, there are the Service careers, concerned with the defence of the country. Women work on radar, aircraft, and radio maintenance, meteorology, gun sites, and communication systems.

Entry qualifications Minimum age for WRNS and WRAF, 17, WRAC, 17½. The Services often rely on aptitude tests and interviews, and do not demand O-levels for all jobs. There are some opportunities to study for O-levels in the Services.

The work and training Junior ranks in the Women's Services lead very much of a community life, both on and off duty. They are rarely alone, they may share bedrooms for 2 to 4 people, but their quarters normally have comfortable sitting-rooms. Discipline and regulations are no longer as rigid as they used to be, and officers, far from being formidable, are usually specially chosen for their pleasant personalities and their ability to get on with and understand other, younger, women. Many officers are themselves in their early 20s. The amount of free time given is generous. Civilian clothes may be worn in off-duty hours, and dances, concerts, films, and games are frequently organized. In all three Services, most women work with men and may share a mess with them. Airwomen and Wrens may live out.

The three Services encourage girls to continue their education. There is no compulsion to do so but promotion normally depends on passing examinations. In the WRAC and the WRAF especially, students may be given time off for study in duty hours.

After an initial period of service at home there is a chance but no guarantee of a foreign posting. Individual preferences are taken into consideration as far as possible.

Recruits sign on for a 'Notice Engagement'. This means that after completing 18 months' service from age 18 or completion of training, whichever is the later, they can at any time give 18 months' notice to end their engagement. Therefore they can, if they wish, serve for a minimum of 3 years. In all Services release can be obtained on marriage or compassionate grounds. In the WRAF it is possible in some areas to sign on for what is known as 'local service', which means living at home, and working at a local Royal Air Force station. Married women often do local service.

Every recruit starts with a few weeks' basic training. This is usually followed by specialist training for the chosen category.

In all three Services recruits are given interviews and tests *before* acceptance: they are 'entered' only if there is a vacancy in the category for which they seem suitable.

The type of work does not necessarily vary greatly between the three Services.

The various careers are called 'employments' in the WRAC and the WRAF, and 'categories' in the WRNS. There are a large number, and to most of the trades and categories there are many branches. Broadly they fall into 5 main groups:

1. Technical, including Transport
2. Clerical and Communications
3. Catering and Stores
4. Medical and Dental
5. Specialists including Provost (military police), Physical Training Instructor, Kennel Maid/Groom, Photographer.

Technical

Acceptance is *either* on the basis of aptitude test; *or* on O-level maths and/or physics, and geography; for WRNS photographers, O-levels maths or CSE Grade 1 Photography is acceptable.

In all Services, servicewomen operate electrical and electronic equipment. They send and receive messages by teleprinter, plot and record positions of ships and aircraft. Women also train as radio and radar mechanics, and in the WRAF as technicians in the various trades, and repair complicated instruments. In the WRNS and the WRAF they work in control-towers of air stations, logging times of incoming and outgoing aircraft and recording aircraft movement. In the WRAC they work on gun positions, spotting and recording shell bursts. Delicate equipment is used to measure the speeds at which shells travel and the work requires great accuracy.

In the WRNS and in the WRAF servicewomen work on the maintenance of aircraft. Other technical trades and categories include tracers, draughtsmen, electricians, aircraft and electronic technicians, instrument mechanics, and weapon analysts.

Specialized training is given after acceptance.

Clerical and Communications

Acceptance depends on an aptitude test.

Recruits are taught office work to suit the demands of their particular Service. Suitable recruits are given further training, and specialize in accounts, shorthand, coding and decoding morse, teleprinting or switchboard operating. Entrants with secretarial training or experience stand a good chance of early promotion in the WRAC and WRAF.

Catering and Stores

Acceptance depends on an aptitude test.

Cooks work in men's, women's and mixed messes. These may range in size from a small officers' mess at an outlying station, to one for hundreds of people.

Duties include meal-planning, ordering, budgeting, some diet-cooking. There is scope both for the untrained keen to learn, and for those with relevant qualifications. Stores work covers food, clothing, furniture and technical items. (See also under Commissioned Ranks, p. 468).

Medical and Dental

See p. 323 for new nursing titles.
Acceptance: *either* on O-levels or A-levels, as required for equivalent jobs in civilian life, *and/or* on suitability tests.

The three Services differ:

(a) QUEEN ALEXANDRA'S ROYAL ARMY NURSING CORPS (QARANC): Trains girls for Registration, Enrolment, dental clerk assistants, dental hygienists, medical clerks and ward stewardesses. It offers 5 training schemes, much the same as those given in civilian hospitals and medical schools.
(i) For girls with minimum 5 O-levels, including English language or history, maths or science, and 1 other subject: 3-year Registered General Nurse. Training is exactly the same as in civilian hospitals (see p. 324) but it takes place in military hospitals at home and/or abroad. Registered General Nurses may be recommended for commissions.
(ii) 2-year Enrolled Nurse (see p. 329) training is the same as in civilian hospitals, but takes place in military hospitals.
(iii) Dental clerk assistant, dental hygienist. Both categories are trained at the Royal Army Dental Training Centre and then work in Army dental departments at home and overseas.
(iv) Medical clerks are trained in clerical duties with particular emphasis on medical terminology. After training they are employed in Army hospitals at home and overseas.
(v) Ward stewardess (hospital housekeeping service).
No GCE requirements for (iii), (iv) and (v), except dental hygienist, who needs 4 O-levels including English language and biology.

(b) QUEEN ALEXANDRA'S ROYAL NAVAL NURSING SERVICE (QARNNS): trains girls for Registration and Enrolment. The WRNS also trains dental hygienists and dental surgery assistants.

(c) PRINCESS MARY'S ROYAL AIR FORCE NURSING SERVICE (PMRAFNS): takes and trains ENs at RAF training hospitals. A qualified RGN may apply for a commission in the PMRAFNS. The WRAF offer training for medical assistant, dispenser, physiotherapist, laboratory technician, hygienist, radiographer, operating theatre technician, dental surgery assistant, and dental hygienist. There are also openings for professionally qualified entrants to most of these trades.

Other Miscellaneous Trades and Categories in the Services

(a) Administration.
(b) Driver: no previous experience necessary.
(c) Bandswoman (WRAC only): acceptance based on audition and having reached grade 6 in main instrument.
(d) Photographer: aptitude rather than previous training required mainly in the WRAF.
(e) PT Instructior: all Services train their own PT Instructors.
(f) Policewoman: no previous experience necessary.

Prospects Promotion prospects to NCO vary according to trade or category, but are generally good for girls able to take responsibility. Servicewomen with good educational qualifications and the right personal attributes are encouraged to apply for commissions and have a good chance of acceptance for officer training (see Commissioned Ranks, below).

Fair chance of being posted abroad.

Pay: Medium (see p. xxiii).

Personal attributes An equable disposition; a gregarious nature; ability to mix and work well with people of all ages and both sexes and to take discipline without resentment; adaptability to new people and places; a spirit of adventure.

Further information See end of section, p. 471.

Commissioned Ranks

The work All officers specialize in a branch of work, such as administration or telecommunications or catering. In most establishments women officers work with their male colleagues as part of a team. They may also be responsible for the discipline and welfare of the servicewomen in their unit, but in any case are expected to take an active interest in the welfare of those (male and female) working under them.

Men and women usually share the officers' mess. Messes are not unlike hotels, with dining-rooms and lounges, and staff to do the chores. Each officer has her own bedroom. Senior officers also have their own sitting-rooms. During working hours officers wear (individually tailored) uniforms; off duty they wear civilian clothes. Outside duty hours they can normally come and go as they like.

Training Three ways:

1. By promotion from the ranks.
2. By direct entry into a Permanent Commission (except for WRNS), for women who intend to spend all their working lives in the Service.
3. By direct entry into a Short Service Commission, which varies from 2 to 8 years. The method of selection is by oral and written tests or exercises, and interview.

Details for the three Services:

WRAC

Entry qualifications

Minimum age 18 years 5 months. Upper age limit varies according to type of commission.
(a) for Permanent Regular Commission – 5 O-levels and 2 A-levels. Passes must include English language, maths and either a science or a foreign language, and not more than one non-academic subject.
(b) for Short Service Commission – 5 O-levels including English language, maths or a science and not more than one non-academic subject.
Graduates are eligible for all types of commissions.

Training

Candidates for all types of commissions complete a 25-week course at the Royal Military Academy, Sandhurst. Instruction is both academic and practical and covers a wide field of general and military subjects. More specialized training may be given after a period of commissioned service.

The following Army Corps offer permanent employment to suitably qualified WRAC officers: Royal Engineers, Royal Signals, Royal Corps of Transport, Royal Army Education Corps, Army Catering Corps, Royal Army Ordnance Corps, and Royal Electrical and Mechanical Engineers.

WRAF

Entry qualifications

Minimum age 18.
(a) Officer entry into Permanent and Short Service (4–6 years) Commissions: a degree, or professional qualification, is required for the engineering, administration (education, catering and physical education specializations), medical and dental branches. Degrees or suitable civilian experience may also confer 'officer entry' status for other branches.
(b) Cadet entry: 5 O-levels, including English language and maths, for aircraft and fighter control, photographic interpretation, supply and administration (secretarial specializations) branches.
(c) Officers commissioned from the ranks normally require entry qualifications as in (a) or (b).

Training

1. Officer entrants are commissioned on entry and receive 4 months' training at the Officer Cadet Training Unit. This is followed by professional training for their branch.
2. Cadet entrants enter as officer cadets and receive 4 months' training at the Department of Initial Officer Training. They are then commissioned and receive professional training for their branch.

WRNS

Entry qualifications

Direct entry into Short Service Commission: Age on entry 20½–26. Degree or comparable qualification in a field relevant to the branch in which the candidate wants to specialize, plus 5 months' service as a rating gaining general service experience.
Cadet entry: Minimum age on entry 18½. 2 A-levels, 5 O-levels, including English language and maths.
Rating entry: Minimum age 20. 5 O-levels including English language and maths, followed by 1 year as rating before selection for officer training.
All officers complete an Officer Training Course at the Royal Naval College, Dartmouth. Further training follows, either on a specialist course or on-the-job at a Naval establishment.

The three Services welcome, and commission, General Registered Nurses. In the Army there are also often vacancies for radiographers and physiotherapists.

Prospects (all Services)

Promotion prospects are good – if only because the marriage rate is high.
In the WRNS promotion is automatic to second officer and thereafter by selection.
In the WRAC promotion for efficient officers is automatic up to and including Captain; above that promotion is by selection after examination.
In the WRAF (as in RAF) promotion up to Flight Lieutenant is by time, thereafter by examination and selection.

Undergraduates are eligible for WRAC or WRAF sponsorship during their studies.

The three nursing services all offer direct promotion from the ranks and Direct Entry Short Service Commissions to General Registered Nurses. In QARANC and QARNNS commissions are also sometimes offered to non-nursing personnel for employment in the administrative, welfare and personnel management field. Opportunities for overseas postings vary between the Services.

Pay: Medium to high (see p. xxiii).

Personal attributes

For all officers: initiative; qualities of leadership; organizing ability and/or special skills; the ability to get on with both men and women at all Service levels; an understanding of the problems of young people; a reasonably gregarious personality; spirit of adventure.

Late start

Varies according to type of work and previous qualifications, but generally upper ages for joining are: WRAC, 33; WRNS, 28; WRAF, 39.

Position of women

The Sex Discrimination Act does not apply to the Services. In the Navy and Army, men's and women's Services are separate entities, with separate promotion structures, so equality of opportunity considerations do not apply. In the RAF there is an integrated career pattern by branch or trade and the principles of the Act are followed where possible.

Career-break: In theory return is possible, but it rarely applies to married women, owing to mobility requirements.

Further information

Ministry of Defence, Lansdowne House, Berkeley Square, London W1X 6AA, or nearest Army Careers Information Office.

For the WRNS and the WRAF the recruiting offices are called Careers Information Offices: Addresses are available at post offices, careers offices and local telephone directories.

Related careers

Nursing – Police

NOTE: The Services is the only section in this book in which careers for men and women are very different (the Sex Discrimination Act does not cover the Forces). The information given here only applies to women's career opportunities. There is no space to cover *both* sexes' opportunities, and information for men is readily available from the Services and from local education authority careers officers.

Shipbroking, Airbroking, Freight Forwarding and Exporting

Entry qualifications All educational levels; in practice at least 4 O-levels. Also *graduate* entry.

Shipbrokers, airbrokers and freight forwarders are concerned with the efficient and economical movement of goods from one part of the world to another. The shipbroker uses only ships, the airbroker only aircraft, the freight forwarder uses any means of transport. The work is a vital part of world trade and at the centre of the country's commercial activities.

Shipbrokers

They match up empty ships with cargoes and negotiate terms on behalf of their clients. This process is known as 'fixing', and is rather like solving a giant jigsaw puzzle. The shipbroker may use a regular cargo run or charter a ship for a single voyage or a series of voyages, or a part of a ship's freight space. She also acts as agent for shipowners when their ships are in port and deals with customs formalities, loading documentation, arrangements for the crew and any problems that may crop up. Shipbrokers also buy and sell ships for their clients.

Shipbrokers often work long and irregular hours, as they have to be in telephone contact with people all over the world during *their* working hours.

The Baltic Exchange in the City of London is the world's only shipping exchange. The 700-odd members comprise shipbrokers, grain traders, and others concerned with shipbroking. They meet 'on the floor of the Exchange' to trade (see also Commodity Markets, p. 499) and exchange mutually useful shipping information.

Airbrokers

They also match cargoes (and people) and carriers from and to all parts of the world. Air-chartering is done mainly by telephone; airbrokers rarely meet each other or see the aircraft they are chartering or the people whose goods or clients they are carrying. They may also buy and sell aircraft and equipment for their 'principals'. Work can be very hectic, as charters may be arranged only a day or so before take-off. However, most of the work is carefully planned ahead. The variety of aircraft for charter is much smaller than the variety of ships; the variety of cargo carried is growing steadily. The bulk of air-chartering is still concerned with two types of cargo: (1) people – aircraft are chartered 'on time charter' to tour operators or, for example, construction firms which transport personnel to and from the Middle East; and (2) perishable foods. Airbroking is still evolving, with airbrokers constantly looking for new business – especially to and from and in the Middle East, Far East and Africa.

Freight Forwarders

They arrange transport of all types of freight to and from anywhere in the world. They search out the most efficient method or combination of methods of transport in each particular case, evaluating respectively the need for speed, security, refrigeration; the fragility of the goods, etc. Goods may be sent by traditional methods such as rail, or something more modern such as container ship or jumbo jet, or by a combination of several modes of transport. The freight forwarder must be well acquainted with the advantages and disadvantages of the various methods of transport (which she is likely to learn by experience and from colleagues rather than from the transporters themselves), and with the intricacies of freight handling and storage and the different techniques and arrangements in the various ports and airports all over the world. She must make it her business to find out routes which, though possibly longer in mileage, may be more efficient because turn-round arrangements in some ports and airports are quicker than in others.

She is also responsible for documentation, such as Bills of Lading, import and export licences, and for specialized packing and warehousing.

Some freight forwarders specialize in certain commodities or geographical areas; others in certain methods of transport and/or types of packing or warehousing.

Prospects Depend largely on world trade conditions: both ship- and airbroking have been affected by the recession. London is one of the world's largest shipping, air chartering and freight forwarding centres and specialized freight forwarding is an expanding industry. There are some opportunities for experienced shipbrokers and for freight forwarders to work *abroad* for a spell.

Pay: Medium to high (see p. xxiii).

Training On-the-job. Experience is the most important part of training. While there are specific institutes – the Institute of Shipbrokers, the Institute of Transport (for airbrokers), the Institute of Freight Forwarding, the Institute of Export – students now normally first take a Business and Technician Education Council (BTEC) award (see p. xvi for various levels of award). This is a more broadly based and a more useful qualification if a broker or freight forwarder has or wants to change to another commercial function later in her career. With a BTEC National award or Higher National award, students can then take the specific Institutes' final examinations. Previous experience in airline operations is a useful qualification for airbroking.

A few big charter firms take graduate and occasionally A-level trainees.

There are also relevant Export Management options in some Business Studies degrees and post-graduate management courses.

Then there is a Foundation Course in Overseas Trade for entrants with at least 4 O-levels including English and preferably maths. The FCOT course covers Part 1 of the syllabuses of the Institute of Export, the Institute of Freight Forwarders, and also of the Society of Shipping Executives.

Although foreign languages are not required for any of the examinations, fluency in at least 1 language is a great advantage.

Personal attributes Interest in commercial geography and world trade; a practical approach; a liking for paperwork, a good telephone manner; *especially for ship- and airbroking*: an entrepreneurial spirit and ability to win people's confidence.

Late start Possible only for people with related industrial or commercial experience (correspondence courses available).

Position of women On the whole firms are reluctant to appoint women to responsible positions because, they say, shipbrokers and freight forwarders deal with countries in which women are not at all equal, and a woman negotiator might therefore lose the firm some business. However, there is no reason why women should not succeed in this field – practicality and getting on with people easily are important ingredients, and women are supposed to be good at both. In airbroking, which is a newer career area where there were no traditions to break down, the few women who have tried have done well.

Career-break: Might not present any problems for experienced shipbrokers/freight forwarders – except that methods of transport change rather rapidly and competition from young people is very keen.

Part-time: Not at the moment – no reason why it should not be possible.

Further information

Institute of Chartered Shipbrokers, 24 St Mary Axe, London EC3A 8DE
Baltic Air Charter Association, The Baltic Exchange, St Mary Axe, London EC3A 8BU
Institute of Freight Forwarders Ltd, Suffield House, 9 Paradise Road, Richmond, Surrey TW9 1SA
Institute of Export, World Trade Centre, London E1 9AA

Related careers

Management in Industry – Purchasing and Supply – Stock Exchange – Travel Agent

Social Work

Casework – groupwork – social services departments – hospitals – child guidance clinics – education welfare – residential social work (including children's homes) – probation work – community work

Entry qualifications Vary according to age and type of course; see **Training**, but about half of entrants are *graduates*.

The work Social workers help individuals and families who have personal, social and environmental problems with which they cannot cope on their own. The precise terms of reference, the most effective way of organizing social work – and what areas of 'helping people' constitute social work – are issues which have been debated for years and will go on being debated and changed.

About ten years ago the former social work specializations, child care, medical and psychiatric social work, work with elderly and handicapped people, were integrated into one social work profession. (In England and Wales probation still keeps its separate entity, but not in Scotland.) Social workers are now 'generically' trained, i.e. trained to work with any type of social work problem and any age range (any 'client group').

The range of work done and settings worked in by individual social workers are therefore much wider than they used to be. Nevertheless, there is still scope for anyone who wants to work mainly with a particular client group – for example, the elderly or children – or who wants to work in a particular setting – in a hospital, residential, or day-centre, or with foster parents and children. Local authorities' social services departments are organized in geographical 'area teams', and it is the *teams* which are generic, i.e. able to cope with any situations. Within area teams workers can often specialize in work with a particular client group. Many voluntary organizations specialize in working with particular client groups and their families.

Social work can be frustrating: often problems arise from causes beyond the clients' or the social workers' control, such as bad housing or unemployment. Social workers are increasingly involved with questioning social policies which are often responsible for clients' situations, and with articulating clients' needs. Whether problems are caused by personal inadequacy, bad luck, ill health, the housing shortage or a combination of circumstances, there are rarely neat solutions. Social workers must accept that scope for improvement is often limited. They help their clients sort out what can and cannot be changed, to accept the latter and concentrate on improving the former.

Most social workers use two main 'social work methods': *casework* and *groupwork*.

Casework

Casework continues to be the main social work method. It involves establishing a relationship of trust and understanding with the client, jointly identifying the client's problem and then 'working through it' to resolve it or to enable the client to live as normally as possible in the circumstances. Social workers always try and work themselves out of a job: however serious a client's problem, the social worker helps her client to remain or become independent and not to rely on the social worker's permanent support.

Clients' problems may be short-term and practical – arranging for a braille course for someone who is going blind; arranging for a child to be taken into care while the mother is seriously ill – or they may be long-term, and possibly requiring daily contact at least over a period, for example supporting a family with many problems; or a disturbed child in foster-care.

In most area teams, 'intake' workers see new clients who may then be allocated to other social workers.

Caseworkers often work with whole families: for example, to help a client understand what led up to a situation (the first step towards resolving it) – whether it is a child's delinquency, despair due to disability, alcoholism, or whatever – the social worker may have to be involved with several members of a family, also with those who are not aware of, or do not want to be involved with, whatever the problem is. This is known as 'family casework'.

Groupwork

Groupwork is a far newer method of social work; it is used much less than casework, but its use has been increasing in the last few years. In groupwork a number of clients share their similar problems, for 'therapeutic' reasons. Some people find it easier to discuss personal problems with fellow-sufferers rather than in a one-to-one situation with the social worker; through talking about their experiences and anxieties under the guidance of the social worker, clients help themselves and each other. Groups may be depressed patients, physically handicapped people, disturbed or retarded youths, etc. Not all groupworkers agree with 'labelling' of clients and some now use groupwork to help clients with various kinds of problems.

Groups can also be practical (and then the work may overlap with community work, see below, p. 481). Young mothers on a new estate may be brought together to avoid their isolation and loneliness developing into serious psychological problems, and/or to encourage them to start a playgroup, etc.

Another form of groupwork takes place in Intermediate Treatment Centres. Children in trouble with the law may be given a community-based alternative to custody, while continuing to live with their families. They attend the IT centre where they are given the opportunity to benefit from new personal relationships, to take part in various activities and to develop new interests.

Social workers work in a variety of settings:

Social Services Departments

Most work in local authorities' social services departments. Their hours are often irregular – clients have to be visited in the evening or at weekends; someone usually has to be on emergency stand-by in case of crises – anything from getting an abandoned baby into a foster home to coping with an evicted family. The social worker plans her own work within the team and has a great deal of scope for decision-making.

Most spend about two-thirds of their time seeing clients; the rest writing up reports, or in discussion with colleagues. This is a very important part, when having to take such vital decisions, for example, as whether to leave a baby with a neglectful mother or whether or not there is a danger of 'non-accidental injury' (baby-battering).

Possible post-training specializations include adoption and fostering; the elderly and/or handicapped; psychiatric patients discharged from hospital but still needing support; working with children whom the Courts have put under Supervision Orders – which means children would be living at home but the social workers would be responsible for them. This may involve occasional, or almost daily, contact.

Hospitals

Most hospitals have a social work department or team of social workers led by a Principal Social Worker. Although hospital social workers are employed by local authority social services departments, they are also members of the hospital team, together with medical colleagues. They assist patients and their families in coping with social and psychological problems which might impede the patient's recovery if left unattended. When working with an orthopaedic surgeon, for example, work may involve organizing help at home for a mother about to be discharged after a hip-replacement; when working with obstetricians, the social worker may help an unmarried mother work out her own and her baby's future – both in practical and psychological terms. Often she may have to help patients and their relatives come to terms with disabling or terminal illness; she may also cope with practical matters such as organizing home helps for new mothers; or meals on wheels for geriatric patients. Hospital social workers liaise with social workers in area teams.

Hospital social work is relatively more of a 9 to 5 job than any other social work, and it does not usually require as much vital on-the-spot decision-making.

Child Guidance Clinics

Much smaller numbers of social workers work in child guidance clinics, where they are part of multi-professional teams with psychiatrists, psychologists and other professionals, helping in the diagnosis and treatment of disturbed children. This may involve intensive long-term casework with both children and their parents.

Education Welfare Officers/ School Social Workers

Another small group are education welfare officers or school social workers, acting as link between school and home. They are alerted by teachers when children first show problems such as truancy or learning difficulties. They visit parents and hope to diagnose and deal with the cause of the problem, or refer children and parents for help to other agencies.

Social Work in Residential Centres

Residential work is really a misnomer: it is the *client* who is residential: by no means all workers in residential establishments have to live in, and to confuse matters even more, 'residential work' may include work in day-centres. Residential homes and day-centres vary in size, purpose, client group. They can be for old people; the physically or mentally handicapped; for various groups of children: nurseries, older children, hostel for adolescents; single mothers; ex-prisoners.

There is a general trend away from residential care to providing more domiciliary services and day-centres.

Residential child care officers are the most clearly defined group of residential workers. They work in community homes (the comprehensive term for children's homes, including former approved schools, reception centres, remand homes, hostels for adolescents), in residential schools and homes for handicapped children. A wide variety of titles are given to similar posts including residential child care officer, residential care officer, residential social worker and houseparent.

The majority of children in residential care are 'deprived'; they tend to react with suspicion and hostility to new faces: social workers must be able to understand the underlying causes of the children's behaviour, to know how to help them. The work varies according to the extent of the children's deprivation and disturbance, and social workers can choose the type of home they want to work in. In a 'family'-type home for six or a dozen children of different ages, several may be quite happy and in care for a short time while their mother is in hospital; in some homes most children suffer from some emotional disturbance, and duties include observing the children's behaviour, their relationships with, and response to, other children and adults.

Residential social workers in children's homes also organize such activities as drama, art and sport. Hours are necessarily long, but regular off-duty times are arranged.

Residential social work (residential care) can mean very different levels and types of work – from housekeeping-plus-sympathy as assistant, to highly skilled diagnostic social work support and rehabilitation. The same qualifications for both residential and fieldworkers (see **Training**) now apply. Residential work also provides excellent pre-training job opportunities.

Probation Work

Probation officers are social workers attached to the Court; their function is, broadly, to help older delinquent children, young people and adults who have been in trouble with the law, to lead more satisfactory lives.

The challenge of probation work is that it involves working towards change: in individuals – helping them towards a life which is both more satisfying for them, and for the community – and in society (experiments with alternatives to prison constitute such change), which may have treated individuals badly. The probation officer has a dual role: she must win and keep her client's confidence and yet must protect society from potentially harmful citizens; she must at times exert authority and yet not lose her client's trust. Probation officers are attached to Courts in England and Wales, but in Scotland local authority social work departments are responsible for work with adult offenders. Work involves:

Social Inquiry Reports: To help the Court decide the best method of dealing with an offender, the probation officer inquires into the offender's background. This may involve having several exhaustive talks with the offender and possibly his/her family, to find out what circumstances led up to the offence and to enable the offender, possibly for the first time ever, to think about the whys and hows of his or her life. On the basis of the probation officer's report, the Court may decide not to send the accused to prison, but to use one of the alternatives to prison:

Probation Orders: Offenders who are put on probation become the probation officer's clients. They report to her at regular intervals and discuss with her any problem – job, housing, relationship with family or boy/girlfriend – anything which has any bearing on the client's way of life. While some clients are only too glad to have someone sympathetic to listen and advise, others are very difficult to make contact with and deal with.

Community Service Orders where offenders are required, under supervision, to do work which is of benefit to the community. Work may consist of helping in homes for the disabled; decorating old people's homes; building adventure playgrounds. Others are *Supervisory Orders* and *Attendance Centres*, where offenders under 21 may be required to attend and be given appropriate occupation or instruction under supervision.

Prison Welfare and After-Care: Probation officers may work in prisons (then they are called prison welfare officers) or in remand centres. They help prisoners keep alive links with their families (they may visit prisoners' families) and help them plan their future.

Voluntary organizations such as the NSPCC Family Service Unit or the Invalid Children's Aid Association and a number of similar organizations also employ trained social workers, and they may offer practical pre-training experience.

Community Work

If casework and groupwork are methods of working with individuals with problems, community work can be said to try to nip problems in the bud. As a 'social work approach' it is still evolving. Different community workers all see their jobs differently; many do not see it as 'social work' at all. Terminology is confused and confusing; terms of reference of, and training for, community work are vague and varied and changing.

Broadly, the community worker tries to improve the quality of life of the community in which she works. She is part information point, part link with the local authority, and other organizations which could be of use to the community, but whose services are not necessarily known to the majority of people. In order to make herself known in the community, the community worker makes it her business to meet as many people as possible. Having discovered what issues people are concerned about – or which may lead to problems – she may bring together people with similar concerns: for example, parents of children with educational problems, and help them form a parent-teacher association. She helps people to help themselves by giving advice and information. She also advises people to know what their rights and options are: she may advise old age pensioners to apply for benefits they are entitled to, or shoppers that they can refer their shoddy shoes to the consumer protection people. She may work closely with immigrant communities and community relations officers. Her terms of reference are vague and wide and call for initiative and insight, tact, and understanding.

Community workers initiate social action and help communities peacefully and lawfully to change the local *status quo*. It is a tricky job at times, as their loyalties may be divided between the community which needs better services or amenities, and their employers, the local authority, which is short of cash.

By no means all local authorities employ community workers; many are employed by voluntary agencies. Community workers may have had social work training or relevant experience. The job requires great judgement, experience and maturity.

Prospects (all social work)

Though there is a shortage of social workers in many areas, level of recruitment depends on level of public expenditure. On the whole, however, the greatest difficulty is getting pre-training practical experience in social services agencies, which is required for admittance to most social work training courses. Most opportunities for such vital experience are in residential social work.

Pay: Medium to high (see p. xxiii).

Training

The pattern of courses allows for different routes to qualification. To qualify as a professional social worker the Certificate of Qualification in Social Work (the CQSW, awarded by the Central Council for Education and Training in Social Work) is required. Several types of courses lead to this qualification. Which type to take depends mainly on candidates' academic qualifications and on the stage in their lives at which they decide on social work.

Courses within each category also vary in emphasis on particular aspects – groupwork, community work, mental health, hospital, probation, residential, etc. Candidates should look at latest course curricula before choosing a course if they are interested in a particular social work setting or approach.

Course types leading to the CQSW
Minimum age 20, although most entrants are older and have had relevant experience (for example, in residential or day-centres as unqualified assistants). Courses leading to the CQSW are available for non-graduates, graduates and undergraduates at polytechnics, universities and other educational institutions. Courses are full-time and half the training is practical work.

Courses for non-graduates normally last 2 years full-time. (In Scotland there is also one course, which lasts 3 years, where students can start at 19 instead of 20.)

Candidates aged 20–24 must normally have at least 5 O-levels including English or Welsh. In England and Wales many colleges normally require A-levels (in Scotland, SCE O grades and 'Highers').

Candidates aged 25 and over do not need formal educational qualifications but must show evidence of ability to study at an advanced level, such as recent part-time or evening studies in an academic subject.

There are also a few 3-year extended courses for people with family commitments which prevent them from taking other courses.

Courses for graduates last either 1 or 2 years. Graduates with 'relevant' degrees, diplomas and certificates can take 1-year CQSW courses. Individual CQSW courses decide which pre-professional awards are 'relevant'; they usually require studies to have covered social administration and practical work in social service agencies. As from September 1985 new previous study requirements for admission to 1-year CQSW courses will apply. Applicants will also need a minimum 1 year's practical experience.

Graduates with 'non-relevant' degrees take *either* 2-year CQSW courses; *or* a course leading to a 'relevant' post-graduate diploma in social administration or social studies followed by a 1-year CQSW course.

Degree courses leading *also* to the CQSW last 4 years.

Preliminary Training: For 16-year-olds with a few or no GCEs: 2-year courses at further education colleges leading to Preliminary Certificate in Social Care (PCSC). Students spend about half the time on general education; most work for O- (possibly A-) levels; and half learning about the social services, about people and how the social services help them. Students spend some time in day and residential settings such as playgroups, day-centres, children's homes and homes for the elderly and handicapped.

The PCSC courses are an *introduction* to, rather than training in, professional social work; they lead to jobs in day and residential settings, but with experience, there is a possibility of becoming professionally qualified by attending a CQSW or Certificate in Social Service (see below) course.

All CQSW, and many CSS courses include some teaching about *work with the deaf and blind*. Some CQSW courses and CSS options emphasize these areas of work. There are also post-qualifying study opportunities for people wishing to specialize in these areas.

Community work: About half the CQSW courses include community work, but there are also specific community work courses which do *not* lead to the CQSW – in other words they qualify students for community work but not for 'orthodox' social work. Most full- and part-time courses are at post-graduate level, but candidates with relevant experience may be accepted. Courses are held at polytechnics and universities. Length: 1 or 2 years.

Certificate in Social Services (CSS): Training leading to CCETSW's Certificate in Social Service is designed to qualify non-social worker staff in the personal social services, including many staff in residential homes and special schools, social work assistants, volunteer and home help organizers and managers, senior staff and instructors in day services. Most students are employees on in-service training. Minimum age 18. If under 21 entrants need 5 O-levels or relevant experience. The courses, which consist of 3 units, last at least 2 years. All CSS students complete a common unit and choose 1 of 4 standard options, relating to either children and adolescents, adults, the elderly, or communities. Within her standard option each student develops her particular interests in, for example, the under-5s or 'handicaps'. She also takes a special option to develop further one specific aspect of the work.

CSS training does *not* normally lead on to professional social work training.

Personal attributes

The desire to help people irrespective of one's own personal likes and dislikes; the ability to communicate with every level of intelligence, cultural or social background or emotional state; perseverance in the face of apparent failure when clients/groups show no sign of improvement or appreciation of efforts made for or on behalf of them; stability; a ready understanding of other people's way of life and point of view; sympathy and tolerance of human failings; the ability to take an interest in other people's problems without becoming emotionally involved; a sense of humour; wide interests unconnected with social work (to keep a sense of proportion); patience and empathy.

Late start Mature entrants are welcome on all types of courses. Over-25s (sometimes over-30s) are accepted on 2-year CQSW courses without the normal GCE qualifications; acceptance depends on course tutors' assessment of candidate's ability to cope with the course.

Courses specially for mature entrants and those with domestic responsibilities:

1. For candidates aged 30-plus: 2-year CQSW courses. Some places are reserved for prospective probation officers. Courses are geared to people with 'experience of life' but not necessarily high educational attainment, though graduates also take these courses.
2. 3-year CQSW courses for people with domestic responsibilities. Students work short days, have school holidays – hence the extra year. Flexible GCE requirements.
3. Extended 2-year course at London University Extra Mural Department for holders of relevant degree or diplomas.

Position of women Women do well up to senior social work level, then proportionately far fewer go up the ladder – while there are more women than men in social work, the proportion of women heads of departments is small.

Career-break: Returners are welcomed. *Refresher* training mainly on in-service basis.

Part-time: Not as many opportunities as one would have thought. Local authorities vary in their attitudes: some go to any lengths to enable women with children to work part-time; others take young full-timers rather than more mature and experienced part-timers. However, as the proportion of single women over 50 is decreasing, social work, like other professions with large proportions of women, may well have to make it easier for married women to return to work on their own (i.e. often part-time) terms.

Further information *CCETSW Information Services*: Derbyshire House, St Chad's Street, London WC1H 8AD; 9 South St David Street, Edinburgh EH2 2BW; 14 Malone Road, Belfast BT9 5BN; West Wing, St David's House, Wood Street, Cardiff CF1 1ES.

Related careers *Careers Officer – Nursery Nurse – Nursing – Personnel Officer – Police – Prison Work – Teaching – Youth-and-Community Work*

Sociology

Entry qualifications 2, or more often 3, A-levels and 3 O-levels; maths or statistics and English language or English at either level.

The work Sociology is often confused with social work, but there is a vast difference between the two. Social workers deal with individuals with problems (see Social Work, p. 476); sociologists try to understand how society functions: they study the conditions under which problems arise and develop, and why they do so. Sociologists research and develop theories and 'concepts', and try and find solutions or at least ameliorations to problems. Social workers need some understanding of sociology; but sociologists do not need the professional social workers' skills of coping with individuals' problems.

Sociology is the study of social relationships, groupings and structures. It is concerned with relationships between individuals and between groups; and with the interaction of individuals' and groups' peculiarities, characteristics and with conditions imposed upon them by custom, social institutions, events, changes in society. Topics studied include, for example, race relations, the relations between unions and management, between the sexes, between parents and children. Sociologists also investigate the organization and function of, and changes in, such institutions as the family, political parties, places of work, village or urban communities.

Sociologists examine how individuals behave in any given group – at home, in the neighbourhood, in the club, in the 'gang'. They examine how individuals in these various groups, and the groups themselves, 'interact', i.e. behave towards each other. For example, the same person is a manager at home, a colleague at work, a customer in a shop, a chairperson at a local amenity group. In each of these roles she meets different people and behaves in a different way. The sociologist studies these 'behaviour patterns'.

Sociologists are also increasingly concerned with the effects of technological developments. Their knowledge of how groups react to given situations; their suggestions on how, for example, to cope with people's natural fear of change, is invaluable when changes of established working patterns have to be implemented. As by no means all concerns which are changing over to new technologies – word processors in offices, robots in manufacturing – foresaw that there would be human (as well as technical) problems, sociologists are often called in to 'rectify mismanagement of change'. Dealing with 'socio-technical' problems resulting from using new technologies has produced a new and important field of work for sociologists.

Sociologists collect information in a variety of ways, mainly by observation and interviewing. Observation may involve participating in the work of an institution or an organization such as a factory or a youth club, or it may mean moving into an urban or rural community and joining in the life of that community. Interviewing can sometimes be combined with observation but is often carried out independently using systematically prepared sets of questions. Apart from this fieldwork, there is the collation, analysis, interpretation and presentation of the information collected. Statistics and computers are used extensively.

Sociology is closely allied to and overlaps with other social sciences such as social psychology (p. 393), economics (p. 163), and social anthropology. In the past anthropologists have concentrated on studying the primitive societies, and sociologists the modern ones, but today the difference between these two disciplines is not as clear-cut.

Prospects There are more sociology graduates than jobs/training for which a sociology degree is useful. A sociology degree is never a vocational qualification, but it can be the basis for further specific training and for certain kinds of jobs with on-the-job training. The best scope used to be in public sector work, mainly social work and planning. Now, more sociologists go into industry, to work in industrial relations or other personnel specializations (see p. 358) and generally on questions related to organizational and technological change. There are some opportunities in market research and marketing, and the police welcome sociologists' understanding of human behaviour.

Pay: Depends on job.

Training Honours degree in sociology or a combination of social sciences. There are also some courses which combine sociology with arts or with modern languages. On some Business Studies degrees sociology is a major option.

The choice of the right course is important, and complicated: the wording used to describe courses varies, and the combination of subjects covered and the emphasis given to the different aspects of sociology cannot necessarily be deduced from the title given to a particular course. It is essential to study up-to-date prospectuses, and to consult the *CRAC Degree Course Guide* before choosing a course. It is not wise to go by the experience of people who read sociology even recently, because of the many changes and innovations in this field.

During their first year, students study the rudiments of the social sciences generally: economics, politics, social institutions, social and/or economic history, psychology, statistics, geography. During the second and third years they concentrate entirely on sociology or choose 2, occasionally 3, subjects from among: sociology, economics, geography, social administration, politics, philosophy, and statistics. There are also a few courses where sociology can be combined with physics and/or maths, engineering, education, management studies, computer studies.

Degree courses are largely theoretical; fieldwork is not normally an integral part of the course. During vacations, or before starting her studies, the student is expected to do some work which brings her into close contact with unfamiliar aspects of life. Such work could be, for example, as a hospital orderly, a factory worker, or a helper in a youth club.

Personal attributes A deep but detached interest in how people live, think and behave; a scientific approach to contemporary social problems rather than emotional involvement; the ability to get on well with all kinds of people at all levels of intelligence, at least sufficiently well to interview them successfully; above-average intellectual ability; an analytical, logical brain; the ability to discuss and write lucidly, and some mathematical ability.

Late start Many mature students study sociology. Maturity helps in work which centres around understanding human behaviour, but as jobs are scarce young graduates tend to be given preference.

Position of women Depends entirely on type of job: on the whole women sociology graduates do not encounter special problems. As the degree is a preparation for a wide variety of jobs, it could be a useful preparation for women who intend to return to work after a break and who are not quite sure what they want to do eventually. More women than men take sociology degrees.

Career-break: Should not cause any problems as long as people keep up with developments. But see **Prospects**.

Part-time: Occasional research assignments.

Further information British Sociological Association, 10 Portugal Street, London WC2A 2HU

Related careers

Economics – Health Visitor – Market Research – Personnel Management – Town and Country Planning – Police – Psychology – Social Work – Work Study

Speech Therapy

Entry qualifications 2 A-levels and 5 O-levels. Subjects should normally include English, a science subject, maths, a foreign language. Some courses specify certain sciences at A-level.

The work A speech therapist assesses and treats defects of voice, speech and language. Children may have an articulation problem or be excessively slow in learning to talk. Stammering can afflict people of all ages. In hospital clinics therapists work with children and adults who may have lost the ability to speak through brain damage (e.g. a stroke) or disease. Patients who have had their larynx or voice box removed have to be taught an alternative method of sound production.

Every patient needs a different approach – in helping each case therapists must apply their knowledge of phonetics, psychology, anatomy and physiology, neurology, acoustics, and their common sense.

Speech therapists work in clinics, special schools or in hospitals. Some patients are treated in groups, most individually. Most speech therapists work on their own, some as members of a team. In rural areas considerable travelling may be necessary.

A speech therapist meets a great many people – teachers, social workers, doctors, psychologists, as well as her patients. The work is very demanding and responsible.

Prospects Good, but jobs are not available everywhere. Some opportunities in Commonwealth and English-speaking developing countries.

Pay: Medium (see p. xxiii).

Training This is now an all-graduate profession.

3- or 4-year degree course syllabus includes: speech pathology and therapeutics; phonetics; linguistics; anatomy and physiology; psychology; neurology. Students are given an insight into related fields, such as physics of sound; paediatrics; the social services; plastic surgery in relation to speech therapy; audiology; diseases of the ear, nose and throat. During practical work in hospital and in school clinics students first observe then assist with treatments.

There is a 2-year Diploma course for graduates in psychology, linguistics or other relevant subjects. Both methods are equal in job-getting terms.

Personal attributes Understanding of people, whatever their age, temperament, background, and mood of the moment; desire to help; ability to detect personal problems which may have a bearing on the cause and treatment of the defect; tact; unlimited patience. Because much of the work is with children, and sometimes with emotionally disturbed ones at that, the knack of gaining children's confidence; a pleasant voice – young patients are apt to imitate; a sensitive ear to detect slight sound differences; a calm manner and stable temperament; good command of concise written English for reports and notes to guide parents. *For senior posts*: organizing ability.

Late start Possible: over-25s may be accepted with lower-than-normal entrance qualifications. Jobs should be no more difficult than for the young entrant.

Position of women This used to be an all-female job: now the ratio is about 25 women to 1 man.

Career-break: No problem. *Refresher courses* available, but essential to keep up with ever-increasing knowledge.

Part-time: Some opportunities, but not for head of department jobs.

Further information College of Speech Therapists, 6 Lechmere Road, London NW2 5BU

Related careers *Acting – Social Work – Teaching (Speech and Drama, p. 527).*

Sport

Professional sport – football – cricket – tennis – golf – horse racing – teaching – administration

Entry qualifications No formal educational qualifications. For degree courses in sport or recreation studies: 2–3 A-levels.

The work Sport can be divided into three main career areas, although many people combine 2 or more:

1. *Players* or *participants* who are paid professionals. This guide is concerned only with those sports in which it is possible to earn a living, although the professional/amateur distinction is frequently blurred or has disappeared altogether.
2. *Teaching* or *coaching* children or adults.
3. *Administration* (which overlaps with Recreation Management, see p. 410).

Professional Players

In most cases those with sufficient talent will have been spotted well before they leave school. People whose job it is to find and nurture talent will have discovered potential players through schools, youth clubs, local and county teams. In general it is too late to start serious training for a sporting career after leaving school (exceptions are horse and motor racing which cannot be started while at school). For most young people sport has to remain a recreation.

Training *Football* (boys only)

Most start as apprentices with football clubs on leaving school. Some will have been signed with clubs as 'associated schoolboys'. During the apprenticeship football training is combined with various duties: helping prepare kit for the team, cleaning boots, doing odd jobs around the ground. Most are encouraged to take day-release classes to further their education. By age 17½ to 18 the club will have decided whether or not to offer a contract: the majority are not good enough and leave the game by their early 20s. Under YTS (see p. xxvii) 600 places for school leavers are being provided by the Footballers' Further Education and Vocational Training Society.

Cricket (boys only)
Most county cricketers are recruited straight from school, having already played trial matches. For a few seasons they play in club and second XI matches. If they are good enough to qualify for the first team they may be offered a contract by the county: they agree to play exclusively for the club in exchange for a salary. Only a handful of players can expect winter employment on overseas tours. The rest have to find other employment in the close season (a few play professional football). Most have stopped playing by age 40, although top players may stay in the game as coaches, umpires or managers.

Tennis (boys and girls)
Promising players follow a national training scheme run by the Lawn Tennis Association. Most will have started playing at age 8 or 9 and are selected first for regional training. The best are then sent for weekend (and some term-time) courses to the LTA's training centre at Bisham Abbey, Bucks. They take part in regular national and international tournaments and receive financial support from several different organizations. They can become full-time players by age 16/17 and it is usually clear by age 20/21 if they are good enough to make it their career. In any one year, only around a dozen men and women make a full-time living and only a handful earn very large sums. A few gain scholarships to the United States at 18/19 years, many become coaches.

Golf
There are two kinds of golfing professional: the tournament player and the club professional (the total membership of the Professional Golfers' Association (PGA) is 2,600, of whom under 200 are tournament players). Some start out as club professionals and hope to turn to tournament playing when their game is good enough and they can apply for a 'player's ticket' (this is done by playing in a special tournament and only about one in five is successful). Only a handful are successful enough to earn large sums through winnings and commercial sponsorship. The club professional works at a club, running the shop, repairing equipment and giving lessons. The job requires a high level of playing ability, thorough knowledge of the game, business flair and organizing ability. Aspiring club pros must find a position as assistant to a full club pro. They then follow a 3–5-year planned programme of work (covering all aspects of the business) together with on- and off-the-job instruction. They must be prepared to work long hours and to receive only a small salary while learning. There is now a post-qualifying correspondence course leading to the PGA Diploma in Golf Management.

Places for aspiring club professionals are available under YTS (see

p. xxvii). Women's golf is a growth area (there are around 65 tournament players) and they have their own association.

Horse Racing

There are two kinds of races – flat and National Hunt (over jumps). Flat jockeys must weigh under 7 stone at age 16. Training is through a national apprenticeship scheme; recruitment is carried out by the British Racing School (formerly the Apprentice Training School). The whole course lasts 10 weeks, after which apprentices are placed with trainers as stable lads (term applies to girls as well as boys). Riding in races takes up a small part of their time – they are mostly concerned with feeding, grooming, exercising and mucking out the horses. A very small number become successful jockeys – the unsuccessful many remain as stable lads. National Hunt jockeys are heavier (about 10 stone) and start racing later, normally after experience in point-to-point races.

There is a clear distinction between amateur and professional jockeys, with many more races for amateurs. Women to date have done better over jumps than they have on the flat but their racing history is comparatively short. They have only been allowed to ride as professionals on the flat since 1975 and over jumps since 1976. The problem is that only likely winners are given rides and until they have had some more successes and proved themselves to be winners, they will not be chosen.

Further information

British Racing School, Snailwell Road, Newmarket, Suffolk
Football Association, 16 Lancaster Gate, London W2 3LW
Lawn Tennis Association, Barons Court, West Kensington, London W14 9EG
Professional Golfer's Association, Apollo House, The Belfry, Sutton Coldfield, West Midlands B76 9PT
Test and County Cricket Board, MCC, Lord's Ground, London NW8 8QN

Teaching and Coaching

Coaches in individual sports work at varying levels, from national teams to youth clubs, from private sports clubs to local authority evening classes. A great many coach part-time or even voluntarily, while following another paid occupation. Full-time paid coaches are nearly all ex-professionals or leading amateurs. Some combine playing with coaching. As well as having great technical expertise they need the ability to be able to get the best from players, to know when to sympathize and when to put on pressure. The relationship between player and coach is crucial to success. All the sports governing bodies run courses for coaches and instructors.

Further information

The Sports Council, 16 Upper Woburn Place, London WC1 0QP

Sports Administration (excluding Recreation Management – see p. 410)

Most sports governing bodies have a very small paid staff. Apart from the usual secretarial and clerical posts, the administration of organizations such as the FA or Lawn Tennis Association is carried out by people with proven expertise. These are either former players or managers, or people with a business or public relations background who can help to bring in sponsorship. There may be occasional openings for people with degrees in sports science or recreation management.

Prospects (sports generally)

A sports person's active career is necessarily short. After this a minority manage to find work in some way connected with their sport (coaching, managing, promoting products), while the majority have to look elsewhere for employment. Therefore it is essential that anyone considering a sporting career should look ahead and reach as high a standard academically as possible while at school or college to enable her to take up another training later. In some cases this means combining a course of further or higher education with part-time playing (e.g. as some cricketers do).

Pay: Top achievers in all sports enjoy a high income, but anyone who becomes a professional footballer or tennis player in the hope of earning a fortune is likely to be disappointed. Most receive a very moderate income, while expenses (equipment, travelling) can be very heavy.

Personal attributes

Total dedication and single-mindedness; strong competitive urge and will to win; high level of physical fitness and mental and physical stamina; ability to respond positively to criticism; resilience and will-power to cope with injuries and setbacks.

Position of women

Sport is different from any other work area. The Sex Discrimination Act does not apply to private clubs which are excluded from the Act altogether and, as most sport is organized by clubs, those who choose to can refuse women as members; also sporting competition may be confined to one sex where the 'average' woman is at a physical disadvantage to the 'average' man (i.e. football, not darts or horse racing). The outstanding girl or woman who is good enough to merit a place in a male team and who may be the best available player can be barred and so is unable to experience the highest level of competition. All too often girls who are good at sport at school are considered rather unfeminine, while boys who are good at it are highly valued. Girls are often automatically assumed to be worse at sport whereas certainly at primary school sex differences are negligible (and it is at this age that serious interest and training in most sports needs to start). Men's events are generally more prestigious, better sponsored and carry higher prize money than women's. Very importantly, the media takes very little notice of women's sporting achievements, whether amateur or professional. However, the situation is improving little by little and no potentially outstanding sportswoman should be put off. In certain sports the gap is narrowing between male and female achievements and each year sees a new 'first' for a woman.

Related careers *Recreation Management – Teaching*

Stage Management

Entry qualifications None specified.

The work The stage manager and her team are responsible to the director, during rehearsals, for the implementation of her/his instructions. This usually includes such things as the recording of actors' moves and other stage directions in the prompt book; collecting props, sound effects, etc. for the director's approval; relaying of the director's requirements to the scenic, costume and lighting departments; ensuring that the actors are in the right place at the right time for rehearsals, costume fittings, etc. During the run of the play the stage manager is in charge of everything on stage and backstage, and is responsible for seeing that each performance keeps to the director's original intention. The stage manager may also conduct understudy rehearsals. She often works all day and is in the theatre until the lights go out. Stage managers are engaged by theatrical managements for one particular production, or for a repertory season, or occasionally on a more permanent basis.

Prospects Fair. There is a shortage of trained and experienced stage managers. Many directors start as stage managers. First jobs are the most difficult to find.

Pay: Low to medium; very occasionally high (see p. xxiii).

Training Full-time stage management courses at drama schools for 1–2 years. Admission to the courses is by interview and only those who are interested in stage management for its own sake or as preparation for work as a producer or director, but not as a stepping-stone to acting, are accepted.

The subjects studied include history of drama and theatrical presentation; literature; the elements of period styles; stage management organization and routine: play study; carpentry; stage lighting; voice; movement; make-up.

Note: Stage management training does *not* lead immediately to work in television and films, but, if supplemented with experience, it may do so. See also Arts Administration course, p. 69.

Personal attributes Organizing ability; natural authority and tact for dealing with temperamental and anxious actors; a practical approach; ability to deal with emergencies from prop-making to mending electrical equipment; calmness during crises; interest in the literary and technical aspects of theatrical production; the ability to speak well – both lucidly and concisely; visual imagination; a genuine desire to do stage management in preference to acting – frustrated actors do not make good, or happy, stage managers.

Late start Should be good opportunities – maturity helps in a job which involves organizing others.

Position of women Proportions of men and women have always been fairly equal; women are welcome in the profession and do well in it.

Career-break: Should be no problem if good experience before the break – and if willing to work all evening *and* often during the day.

Part-time: Sporadic rather than part-time.

Further information Local theatre; drama schools.

Related careers *Acting – Teaching (Speech and Drama, p. 527) – Television, Film and Radio*

Stock Exchange and Commodity Markets

STOCK EXCHANGE: Stock jobbers – stockbrokers – investment analysts – administration staff. COMMODITY MARKETS: Dealers – market clerks – commodity brokers – research staff

Entry qualifications Nothing rigidly laid down: but at least maths and English O-level normally expected (see **Training**). *Graduate* entry usual for *investment analysts* and *research staff*.

The work *The Stock Exchange*

The Stock Exchange is a market at which individuals and institutions with money to invest buy stocks and shares in private companies and Government Securities, and where companies raise money by selling their shares. These 'securities', as they are called, may be in established firms or may be created when a company is formed, or following a merger. There are a few provincial offices; nearly all Stock Exchange people work in London.

The Stock Exchange is less of a 'closed' institution than it used to be. This is partly because of increasing competitiveness with overseas markets and partly because improved information technology has made dealing more international. Data is readily available on computer and the actual completion of paperwork (the 'settlement') is faster and more efficient.

The commodity markets

London is one of the world's main commodity trading centres, both for 'physical' commodities, that is raw materials, as well as 'futures', which concern the promise (or contract) to buy or sell a certain quantity of a commodity at a future date at a price agreed in advance. That means a producer or purchaser of, for example, sugar, who invests a large sum of money in planting or in buying a crop, will minimize losses – and gains – if the price fluctuates because of changes in supply and demand between the times of planting and of harvesting the crop. Speculators neither produce nor use the commodity, but hope to make a profit by buying and selling 'contracts' at what they hope is the right time. 'Soft' commodity markets (sugar, cotton, etc.) are housed at the Corn Exchange (except for grains at the Baltic); five metal markets at the

Metal Exchange. Physical trading is no longer carried out on the floor, but directly between companies; but futures markets are conducted by an 'open outcry' system, in which dealers sit in a ring at the Exchange calling out their bids and offers.

Current moves to change the structure of the market may in time affect the roles of jobbers, brokers etc., but they are presently as follows:

Jobs in the Stock Exchange

1. *Stock jobbers* are wholesalers of shares, specializing in certain sectors of the market. They buy and sell to stockbrokers and other jobbers 'on the floor' of the Exchange, never directly to the public. Some now have police-type radios while 'on the floor' to communicate with their office.
2. *Stockbrokers* are agents who advise their clients on which securities to buy or sell at any given time. They deal with jobbers on behalf of their clients. Most large firms of stockbrokers delegate the actual dealing on the Stock Exchange floor to *authorized clerks* (who are not members of the Stock Exchange). Brokers spend much time talking to clients and studying information provided by the research department's investment analysts. Jobbers and brokers training to become authorized dealers spend some time as juniors, or 'blue buttons'. They sit in the dealing room relaying information and instructions to and from the dealers by phone or two-way radio.
3. *Investment analysts* are mainly employed by broking firms to provide the information on which to base advice to clients. They analyse company accounts and economic reports and confer with senior management of companies in order to assess trends and forecast market movements. Most specialize in one section of the market. (Investment analysts also work for merchant banks.)
4. *Administration staff* process the transactions arranged by the brokers and jobbers. Routine work is done by computer; the rest is highly specialized and involves the preparation of documents and calculating and arranging payment of commission and taxes.

Jobs in the Commodity Markets

1. *Dealers*, or market traders, carry out the actual trading in the dealing ring, as described above.
2. *Market clerks* work for the market organizers themselves and chalk up the trading moves on a large blackboard as dealing is in progress. They usually progress to dealing.
3. *Commodity brokers* advise clients on when to buy and sell which goods at what price (like stockbrokers).

4. *Research staff* (like investment analysts) collect and analyse data with which to brief the brokers. They study information on climatic, political and economic conditions, gluts, shortages, price trends and market movements all over the world.

Prospects These are not the most secure of occupations; success depends on the economic climate and on drive and personality. Openings are not plentiful, but, once in a job, promotion prospects for the right type of person are reasonable, regardless of academic achievement. Clerical staff can become authorized clerks, 'blue buttons', brokers and jobbers. Employees who are considered suitable to become members of the Stock Exchange usually receive assistance towards their membership fee – which is considerable – from their sponsoring firms. Commodity dealers usually progress to posts on the 'physical trading' side of their companies. More movement between the stock market, merchant banks and other financial institutions is likely in the future.

Pay: Medium to high (see p. xxiii). Stockbroking firms generally offer lower salaries than jobbers, but give bonuses, as do commodity brokers.

Training Varies. There are no formal training schemes for the commodity markets – junior staff learn on-the-job. Some stockbroking firms operate training schemes for clerks for the Stock Exchange Certificate. Membership of the Stock Exchange, a precondition of partnership, requires a pass in the Stock Exchange Examination, which can be taken in stages over any length of time, and is studied for by correspondence course, day-release (rarely), or private study.

Graduates entering the Stock Exchange or commodity markets are most likely to go into investment analysis or research departments. Useful degrees are statistics, law, economics, modern languages.

Personal attributes Entrepreneurial and gambling instinct; flair for dealing with figures; extrovert personality; ability to communicate easily on the telephone, personally and in writing; mental agility; quick-wittedness; high powers of concentration; exceptional self-confidence; memory for people and figures.

Late start Only if professionally qualified in a related field, such as economics, accountancy, banking.

Position of women The City may appear very much a male preserve, but many women now work there. Opportunities are increasing for women willing to break down sex barriers. Women members of the Stock Exchange now number over 50. There is a steadily increasing proportion at junior levels and among graduates in research and investment analysis.

Career-break: Would present problems except, possibly, in research.

Part-time: Unlikely.

Further information

Public Relations Department, Stock Exchange, London EC2N 1HP
London Commodity Exchange Co., Cereal House, 58 Mark Lane, London EC3R 7NE

Related careers

Accountancy – Banking – Economics – Insurance

Surveying

Chartered surveyor – surveying technician

Chartered Surveyor

General practice surveying: valuation surveyor – estate agent – auctioneer; quantity surveyor – building surveyor – planning and development surveyor – land agent/agricultural surveyor – land surveyor and hydrographic surveyor – minerals or mining surveyor

Entry qualifications

For membership of the Royal Institution of Chartered Surveyors: 2 A-levels, 3 O-levels; maths and an English subject to be included, at either level. For many degree courses, specific A-levels or A-levels from a group of subjects are required. For example maths, or geography or economic geography or a physical science may be asked for. For polytechnic courses, and for some university courses, relevant BTEC National awards (see Surveying Technician, p. 512) are normally acceptable in lieu of A-levels.

For membership of the Incorporated Society of Valuers and Auctioneers: 5 O-levels, including English language and a maths subject.

The work is not *necessarily* mainly technical: in many surveyors' jobs the commercial element is greater than the technical; but technical expertise is essential background knowledge. The variety of jobs is very great.

The work

Surveying is an umbrella term for jobs which are, in varying degrees and in varying proportion, concerned with, to quote the RICS, 'the measurement, management, development and valuation' of virtually anything: oceans, rivers, harbours, earth's surface, all land, and anything that is in or on land or water, whether natural or man-made. Many surveying jobs are also concerned with protecting or improving the urban and rural environment and the efficient use of resources.

The various surveying branches each involve a different mix of technical, commercial, practical, academic ingredients, and different amounts of time spent on dealing with clients, dealing with other professionals, and on office and outdoor work. Each branch, therefore, suits people with different temperaments, interests, aptitudes. For example, the urban estate agent-surveyor has little in common with the hydrographic surveyor charting oceanic depth, or with the planning surveyor doing research into shopping centres.

The professional surveying specializations are grouped into 'Divisions' by the Royal Institution of Chartered Surveyors: General practice which covers valuation, estate agency, auctioneering and urban estate/housing management; quantity surveying; building surveying; planning and development; land agency and agricultural surveying; land and hydrographic surveying; mineral surveying.

The Incorporated Society of Valuers and Auctioneers' qualification covers much the same ground as the RICS's General Practice Division *except* urban estate/housing management. (See also Housing Management, p. 222.)

The main surveying branches:

General Practice Surveying

Valuation surveyor (also called valuer, or simply surveyor)

She assesses the value of any type of property at any particular time. It may be in connection with rating, insurance, death duty purposes, as well as for general commercial purposes. There are various valuation methods; the most commonly used is the 'comparison' method. This is an intricate mixture of basing judgement on ascertainable facts – value of property in the neighbourhood or other similar property; quality, etc., as well as on 'getting the feel'. When assessing the value of residential property, or a row of shops, for example, factors taken into account include possible future development in the area (motorways, one-way traffic schemes, housing estates, parking restrictions); amenities (open spaces; swimming baths; entertainment facilities generally); proximity to schools, shops, transport; noise; as well as type of neighbourhood and informed guesswork as to whether the area is likely to go down/come up; does it have any feeling of community (which might affect quality of school or be of interest to the elderly, etc.).

Valuers also assess contents of houses. Though they are expected to be able to tell a Rembrandt from an amateur's efforts, valuers do not normally assess the value of works of art but call on experts in that field as necessary. If working for a property developer or local authority they may value land. They may inspect, for example, a plot of land which is up for sale, assess its potential in terms of houses, shops, flats, etc., to be built there, and do a rough 'costing' of whatever type of building is being considered.

Apart from working for estate agents, local authorities, property developers and other commercial concerns, valuation surveyors also set up in private professional practice. Work for property developers requires a certain amount of gambling instinct and very pronounced business acumen; local authority valuers' work is more concerned with valuing according to laid-down criteria.

Estate agent

Valuation surveyors (as described above) may be estate agents, but estate agents are not necessarily valuation surveyors. Within surveying, estate agency is the most commercially and least technically oriented specialization and probably the largest in terms of opportunities. There is at the moment no need for estate agents to have particular qualifications (but this may soon change). However, most firms of estate agents have at least one RICS or ISVA qualified partner. Estate agents negotiate the sale, purchase, leasing of property – not only of houses but also of industrial and commercial premises, agricultural and other land. They arrange and advise on mortgages and on implications of rent acts, and on relevant law generally. They manage property for clients, which involves drawing up leases, collecting rents, responsibility for maintenance, etc.

Estate agents' clients may be property managers of vast commercial empires, or first-time house purchasers who need to be guided through the complexities of making the most expensive purchase of their lives. Estate agents may specialize in one type of property (residential, or commercial or industrial), or they may deal with a mixture of types of properties. 'Negotiators', who deal with clients, often specialize in dealing with one type of client. Women are often expected to specialize in dealing with house purchasers, helping them to sort out priorities: few can afford their dream house, i.e. what they want exactly where they want it. Negotiators help weigh up advantages of, say, sunny garden or 'good neighbourhood'; solidly built but no garage; not-so-solid but near shop/school/transport/parks, etc. But most women now make a point of acquiring the knowledge needed to deal with industrial property: are there goods transport/loading facilities; planning restrictions; is there a supply of skilled labour, etc.

Estate agents advise vendors on the price to ask, so they have to understand something about valuation, even if they are not professionally qualified valuers. The work involves a lot of client-contact, of getting about and getting to know an area and being aware of changes in type of locality and its effect on property values.

Auctioneer

Most estate agents are also auctioneers. (Normally estate agents employ different people as negotiators and as auctioneers, but in small firms everybody might do everything.) Some firms specialize in auctioneering commercial, industrial, residential or agricultural property; others specialize in furniture, machinery, works of art. (The few well-known auction rooms where paintings, etc. are auctioned are staffed by art specialists who have learnt about auctioneering rather than by the estate agent-valuer-auctioneer.) An auctioneer outside London may well auction the contents of a house one day, cattle in the local market-place the next, and a row of shops the day after that. Work varies according to whether done in country town or big city. The actual auctioneering is only part of the work: it also involves assessing value and advising vendors on 'reserve price', and it involves detailed 'lotting up' and cataloguing items to be sold.

While some firms of auctioneers, especially in the country, engage people specially for auctioneering and teach them the necessary skills and techniques, it is advisable to train as valuer (see above) as well.

Quantity Surveyor

Quantity surveyors are also called 'building economists', 'construction cost consultants', 'building accountants'.

The quantity surveyor is an essential member of the design team on building projects of any size. She translates architects' or civil engineers' designs into detailed costs – of labour, materials, overheads; and she breaks down all materials and processes to be used into detailed quantities and timing. She evaluates alternative processes and materials and may suggest alternative design technologies and materials to those suggested on the original design. Her thorough and up-to-date knowledge of new construction technologies and materials enables her to find ways of getting work carried out in the most speedy, economical and efficient way, without impairing the design. Calculations involved may be very complex – for example future maintenance costs have to be considered when evaluating the use of alternative materials and processes. Calculations are usually done with computers.

Quantity surveyors are normally appointed by the designer of the project, i.e. the architect or civil engineer. Because of soaring costs and constantly changing technologies, the quantity surveyor's status in the design team has risen enormously in the last few years. Although the architect/civil engineer still has the last word, the quantity surveyor's suggestions for modifications are taken very seriously indeed. Sometimes a quantity surveyor is appointed the project manager.

The quantity surveyor is responsible for cost control during the whole project. She advises on cost implications of any proposed variations to the design, makes interim valuations of completed work, checks contractors' interim accounts and settles final accounts. She is also involved with financial administration of contracts for mechanical and electrical engineering and similar services for example, and may be responsible for overall project management.

The quantity surveyor's work is a combination of straightforward figure work, complex calculations, and negotiating skills. She must be able to deal with colleagues from other disciplines, contractors, clients. She spends more time at her desk doing calculations or writing reports and at negotiations than on the building site, but the time spent on the various ingredients of the job varies from project to project, and according to the type of employer and method of working.

About 60% of quantity surveyors are in private professional practice; others work for contractors, consultant engineers, in government departments, local authorities, commercial and industrial firms.

Building Surveyor

Building surveyors make structural surveys of and diagnose type of defects of buildings of all types, for prospective purchasers, vendors, owners, building societies. They assess maintenance costs and control maintenance programmes; they prepare plans for conversion and improvements. They draw up plans and specifications, go out to tender, and may supervise contractors' work and check accounts. They advise on building, planning, health and safety regulations, and they may also be involved with restoration or maintenance of ancient monuments and historic buildings. They spend a good deal of time clambering about on buildings to check roofs, lofts, drains, fire escapes and general structural soundness, so their work requires agility.

Some work in private professional practice; the majority are employed by any type of organization which owns, sells, buys, builds, manages property. This includes housing associations, all types of industrial and commercial firms, local authorities and central government. This is the most practical specialization, with the least office work.

Planning and Development Surveyor

The work overlaps with Town and Country Planning (see p. 548).

Planning surveyors are concerned with the efficient allocation of resources in planning and with planning economics and planning law. The work is largely desk research (including statistics) and communicating with other specialists concerned with planning. A planning surveyor, for example, investigates the economics of a proposed shopping area. That would involve collecting facts and figures from various sources, assessing their implications, and writing up the findings. She might have to find a suitable site for an industrial plant which has to be somewhere within a given area, must be near an inland waterway, near transport and must not be within an area of scenic value. That would not necessarily involve travelling, but consulting maps and relevant organizations.

The planning surveyor also advises clients on planning implications or proposals to buy and develop a property. This could involve visiting the site, taking photographs, and then appraising the proposal from a civic design point of view.

Planning and development surveyors work for planning consultants, local and central government, or as specialists in general practice surveying firms.

Land Agent/Agricultural Surveyor

Terms are confusing. Traditionally, land agents were (usually resident) managers of farms or other rural properties. Though some still are employed in that capacity, more often now firms of agricultural surveyors in professional practice act as land agents and manage a number of farms and rural estates on a contract basis. They do much the same work in rural areas as general practice surveyors do in towns. They may do valuation (including livestock and agricultural plant), estate agency, auctioneering, or they may concentrate on farm management (see Agriculture, p. 24). Increasingly they also advise on alternative uses of land, for recreational purposes such as country parks, caravanning and camping sites, country trails, long-distance footpaths, nature reserves. They would then also implement changes.

Agricultural surveyors may also conduct sales and auctions of country properties, contents of country houses, livestock, agricultural machinery, plant, forests and forest products.

Many agricultural surveyors are in private professional practice. According to the size of the practice, other specialist surveyors (valuers, building surveyors) may be employed. Agricultural surveyors sometimes now do farm business management as well, perhaps employing specialists to advise on mechanization, diversification (see alternative land use above) and other ways of improving farm profits. They are also often involved with conservation issues, trying to reconcile landowners' and conservationists' sometimes conflicting interests.

They also work for ADAS (see Agriculture, p. 28), local government, the National Trust and other bodies which own/manage land.

Agricultural surveying is an unusual combination of business, technical, environmental and agricultural work, and one of the few professional jobs which include getting about the countryside.

Land Surveyor and Hydrographic Surveyor

Land surveyors are surveyors in the strict sense of the word. They must not be confused with land agents/agricultural surveyors. They use sophisticated technologies (including aerial photography) to measure and plot the precise shape and position of natural and man-made features on land for the purpose of map-making, including large-scale maps which are used for engineering constructions. (Before motorways can be sited, for example, or bridges built, the minutest physical details of the area have to be plotted and mapped.)

Land surveyors do not draw maps; that is done by cartographers (see p. 89). Land surveyors work in private practice, or for the government (Ordnance Survey, Ministry of Defence mainly), or for consulting engineers and big contractors. Some work for the Directorate of Overseas Surveys which sends (experienced) surveyors to the developing – and other – countries to survey land, some of which has never been surveyed and mapped before. Some go into Archaeological Surveying (see Archaeology, p. 46).

Hydrographic surveyors are the smallest and most scientific branch. They survey oceans, waterways, harbours and ports for purposes of producing nautical charts which show the precise shape, size, location of physical feature of the sea bed, etc. and hazards, currents, tides, sunken wrecks. The information sent by hydrographic survey ships operating in most parts of the world to the Navy's Hydrographic Department is being continuously revised. Collecting and interpreting information is done with highly sophisticated electronic equipment. British Admiralty Charts are used by seafarers all over the world, and by North Sea oil and gas engineers.

Most hydrographic surveyors are also naval officers. This is fairly tough outdoor work, combined with high technology.

Minerals or Mining Surveyor

This is the smallest specialization. Mining surveyors are responsible for mine safety and for mapping mineral deposits, and are involved with the potential use, value, properties, management and exploitation of mineral deposits, which means combining technical, scientific, managerial and commercial aspects. They are also responsible for minimizing environmental damage to the countryside where mineral deposits are mined.

In this country mining surveyors are concerned mainly with coal mining, but overseas minerals surveying covers a variety of other minerals.

Prospects (all chartered surveyors) Vary according to economic conditions, but are reasonable generally; best opportunities are for general practice, quantity, and building surveyors. Some opportunities in EEC countries (for those who speak the relevant language fluently!), especially for quantity surveyors, who are also in demand in Africa and the Middle East.

Pay: Medium to very high (see p. xxiii).

Training For membership of the Royal Institution of Chartered Surveyors (any surveying specialization) about 70% take full-time 3-year (or 4-year sandwich) degrees or diplomas which lead to full or partial exemption from RICS Membership examinations; others study while in appropriate employment, which takes 5 to 6 years of part-time study. Day-release is often granted in public sector employment. In the private sector, students usually have to study in their own time by correspondence course and evening classes. Quantity surveying students may find it much easier than others to be given day-release.

Choosing a course needs careful research. Some courses allow students to choose between several allied specializations during the second year, but for other specializations, such as mineral surveying, the decision has to be made before starting a course. It is essential to study the RICS's up-to-date lists of exempting degrees and diploma courses in each division. Course titles, especially for general practice, vary and are often misleading. For example there are several different titles for courses leading to General Practice Division exemptions; nor are the titles necessarily an indication of course emphasis.

(Though it is usual to work initially in the specialization in which one qualified, it is quite possible to switch specializations later. In practice some specializations (such as, for example, building and quantity surveying) are more easily interchangeable than, for example, general practice and hydrographic.)

Graduates from any discipline may study for the RICS Graduate Entry Scheme examination by part-time study or correspondence course, while in appropriate employment. Study takes about 18 months to 3 years. Though theoretically an arts graduate could qualify in any of the specializations, most opt for the General Practice Division. Science/engineering graduates might opt for Building or Quantity Surveying. Graduates with related degrees, for example in Building or Planning, qualify for partial exemption if they opt for the Building or the Planning and Development Divisions.

General practice surveyors (i.e. valuers, estate agents, auctioneers) can train *either* for the RICS General Practice Division, as above, *or* for membership of the Incorporated Society of Valuers and Auctioneers (see **Entry qualifications**). ISVA training is *either* by 3-year full-time course (courses only at a few colleges and polytechnics); *or* by day-release; *or* (the most common method) by correspondence course, taking 4 to 6 years, while in appropriate employment.

Personal attributes

Practical approach to problem-solving; ability to inspire confidence in clients; ability to take complex decisions on own initiative and work as one of a team as well; for some jobs – ability to handle labour. *For consultancy and estate agency*: business acumen; liking for being out of doors.

Late start Requires very strong motivation. No problem getting training, but first job may be difficult for over-30s. Depends on previous experience.

Position of women There is no logical reason whatever why there should be so ludicrously few women surveyors. Only 2·2% of qualified RICS members are women, and even of its student members only 7% are women. The ISVA has about 4% women members.

The few women in the profession are doing well, although some have changed employers rather often because promotion was blocked for them. A high proportion has gone into general practice and into teaching (and at least one polytechnic has a woman as head of the surveying department).

Only mining and hydrographic surveying should present any problems. Mining surveyors during training must go down the mines and women are not yet allowed to *work* in the mines (which surveying trainees do not actually have to do), and hydrographic surveyors are trained, partly, by the Navy, on naval vessels. These two are, in any case, a tiny minority of surveyors. No other surveying makes demands on physical strength or presents any hazards with which women, however traditional in outlook, cannot cope as well as men. (Building surveyors go up scaffolding, but women have no worse heads for heights than men.)

In fact much surveying work is concerned with improving the environment and generally the quality of life, and much of it involves dealing with people: even the most traditional-minded of women should find something to their liking in surveying. It is lack of knowledge of what surveyors actually do which keeps women from entering this many-sided profession in greater numbers.

Career-break: Should not be difficult in, for example general practice surveying; possibly more difficult in areas where technologies change rapidly, but here keeping up with developments by reading journals and attending meetings should help. No *refresher courses* so far.

Part-time: Not so far, but no reason why established surveyors should not suggest to their employers that part-time – with flexible hours – should work well.

Further information Royal Institution of Chartered Surveyors, 12 Great George Street, Parliament Square, London SW1P 3AD
Incorporated Society of Valuers and Auctioneers, 3 Cadogan Gate, London SW1X 0AS

Related careers *Agriculture and Horticulture – Architecture – Cartography – Engineering – Housing Management – Surveying Technician – Town and Country Planning*

Surveying Technician (includes Managerial Jobs in the Construction Industry) (see Building, p. 79)

Building surveying technician – quantity surveying technician – general practice technician – land surveying technician – mineral surveying technician – hydrographic surveying technician – agricultural surveying technician

Entry qualifications *Either* 4 O-levels including maths, a science and a subject proving competence in the use of English for BTEC National awards (see p. xvi); *or* 1 A-level passed and another one studied for direct entry to BTEC Higher National awards.

The work Most specializations overlap very much with supervisory and management jobs in the building industry (see p. 79). Titles vary: the term 'technician' may not be used, even when the qualification required *is* a technician qualification.

Individual technicians' work varies enormously: some are desk-bound draughtspersons, some are out and about; all now use computerized procedures and equipment. Some have a great deal of client-contact, some have none. Almost invariably they are part of a team.

The majority work under the overall direction of chartered surveyors, architects, civil engineers or planners. Some of their work is indistinguishable from that done by chartered surveyors: until a few years ago, chartered surveyors qualified almost exclusively by on-the-job plus part-time training, and they had only slightly higher entry qualifications (or even lower ones) – 5 O-levels – than technicians have now. While chartered surveyors' training is certainly much more demanding academically than technicians', many tasks are still the same as they always were and do not require the chartered surveyors' in-depth training. Technician-level qualifications are sufficient for the majority of those 'surveyors' who, while wanting responsibility and professional training, do not aspire to initiate and take charge of complex projects.

Surveying technician specializations:

Building Surveying Technician (see Building Surveying, p. 507, and Building Management, p. 80)

Sub-divisions cover construction and assessment of structures; administration of building regulations; preparations of plans; specification for and organization of work to be carried out by contractors; estimates of cost before projects start; dealing with tenders and contracts and checking and passing contractors' accounts; advising lay public on soundness of construction of property they consider buying (while ultimate responsibility for such advice lies with the employing chartered surveyor, the actual surveying on which surveyors' reports to clients are based is often carried out by technicians – the customer is not necessarily aware of this); advice to property owners on maintenance and repair – this may include drawing up schedules for redecoration, advice on eradication of damp, dry rot, etc.

Building surveying technicians work in a great variety of settings – and under a great variety of titles (for example *building manager, building surveyor, building inspector*). They are employed by virtually any type of organization which owns or is responsible for the building and/or maintenance of property, and by firms of consultants. When they work for building contractors, they may also be called *planning* or *contracts manager*, or *contracts surveyor*. Their work may be mainly organizational – ensuring that manpower and equipment are used efficiently; this means planning all the operations which are involved in completing a contract to build whatever it is. For example, if a firm of building contractors is engaged simultaneously on converting several houses into flats and building office blocks, the contracts planner or manager has to estimate for how long how many workers and which equipment will be required on each job and when the various specialists such as heating engineers, plasterers, electricians, should be where.

While in the past only very large contractors had contract planners, now middle-sized firms often engage such staff (under various titles, and not necessarily *only* engaged on this type of planning).

Another job for building surveying technicians is *site manager*. They are responsible for organization of the sequence and smooth working of operations on site.

Technicians who prefer desk-bound work can become draughtspersons and eventually be in charge of a drawing office. But drawing offices now have fewer vacancies as so much work is computerized and completed more quickly. Many work for estate agents, where they meet the general public (see p. 505).

Quantity Surveying Technician (see Quantity Surveyor, p. 506)

They work out the cost of and calculate payment for the various operations carried out by contractors involved in building operations. There are three main sub-divisions (with rather quaint traditional titles).

1. *Taker Off*: She abstracts and measures from architect's, surveyor's or engineer's drawings every item of labour and materials to be used on a project, and lists them in recognized terms. The information is needed to arrive at 'cost plans' and bills of quantity. The job is almost wholly office-based, and usually involves contact with architects, engineers and surveyors as well as cooperation with other technicians.
2. *Worker Up*: She works out volumes, quantities and areas which have been measured by the taker off, and classifies all items in recognized units. Every item of labour and/or material used on a project is then recorded on the bill of quantities. Other information may be 'banked' for future reference, in computers. Workers up are entirely office-based; they may be responsible for a whole project or section of a project.
3. *Post-Contract Surveyor and Site Measurer*: She divides her time between office and site. Work includes measuring for purposes of producing periodic valuations of work done by contractors, and discussions with sub-contractors employed on the site. Post-contract surveyors may be physically measuring work on site one day, attending a site meeting with a number of colleagues from different building-work spheres the same afternoon, and negotiating final payment with a sub-contractor the next day. They normally have been workers up and takers off before becoming post-contract surveyors. Their job overlaps very much with that of chartered quantity surveyors.

General Practice Technician (see General Practice Surveying, p. 504)

This division covers the work done by chartered general practice and planning surveyors. (At chartered level, there is a separate Planning and Development division.)

General practice technicians may specialize in valuation, estate agency, estate management, town and country planning (see p. 548). Openings are the most varied, ranging from suburban estate agency's or international property company's negotiator (see p. 505) to Inland Revenue or insurance company's valuation technician. This specialization offers scope both to those who are mainly interested in meeting members of the public and to those who want to do mainly drawing or other office work and are interested in combining technical and commercial work.

Land Surveying Technician (see Land/ Hydrographic Surveyor, p. 508)

These work with chartered land surveyors. There are opportunities for work with sophisticated instruments such as electronic distance-measuring equipment, for photographing and tracking man-made satellites, or in aerial photography.

This is one of the most adventurous of technician specializations, with work for oil companies and air survey companies at home or abroad, including Third World countries.

Mineral Surveying Technician (see Minerals Surveyor, p. 509)

This is a small division and involves the preparation of accurate plans in connection with safety, operation and development of mines, and geological formations in connection with mineral deposits. Much of the work is underground.

Hydrographic Surveying Technician (see Land/Hydrographic Surveyor, p. 508)

Making and up-dating charts of seas and coastlines, and profiles of sea beds; 'sign posting', on charts, of shipping lanes. This can be arduous outdoor work on surveying ships and requires practical seamanship; only few draughtsmanship, office-based jobs.

Agricultural Surveying Technician (see Land Agent/Agricultural Surveyor, p. 508)

This work overlaps with agriculture (see p. 24) and land agency. Agricultural surveying technicians have only limited scope.

Prospects Surveying technicians generally are in demand but especially in quantity, general practice and building surveying. In these specializations there are often more opportunities for technicians than for chartered surveyors. Experienced technicians have some opportunities in EEC countries if they speak the relevant language fluently.

There is a 'bridging arrangement' which enables qualified technicians to take RICS examinations and become chartered surveyors (but few want to).

Training (all technicians)

Students choose courses according to the type of work they are in or want to do. However, BTEC courses are flexible and, within related areas, it is usually possible to switch from one specialization or division (see Surveying, p. 503) to another; possibly adding course units.

The main surveying divisions are now covered by two 'generic' course categories:

1. Building Studies: This covers *Building Surveying* and *Quantity Surveying*.
2. Land Use: This covers *General Practice Surveying* (incorporating Valuation and Property Management/Estate Agency); *Land Surveying* (incorporating land, sea and air surveying; cartography); *Planning* (incorporating Town and Country and Regional Planning).

Then there are specialized courses:

Mineral Surveying technicians take *Mine and Mining Surveying* courses; *Hydrographic Surveying* technicians train either at the Royal Navy Hydrographic School, Plymouth (residential) or take special options in BTEC *Land Surveying* courses. There are few training vacancies (and jobs) for mining and hydrographic surveying technicians. *Agricultural surveying* technicians take 2-year residential courses at agricultural colleges (see Agriculture, p. 30).

BTEC Courses are normally taken *either* by day- or block-release, and last 2 years for the BTEC National Certificate and a further 2 years for the Higher National Certificate, *or* they are taken by 2-year full-time study for the BTEC National Diploma, followed by a further 2 years' full-time or 3 years' sandwich study for the Higher National Diploma. It is possible to switch from part-time National to full-time/sandwich Higher National and vice versa. (And there are plenty of opportunities, for the less ambitious, with National rather than Higher National awards.) Entrants with 1 relevant A-level and another subject studied at A-level can go straight into the Higher National Diploma course or into the second year of the National Certificate course.

For the majority of jobs, Higher National awards are as marketable as degrees. For some jobs in the building industry they are in fact preferred because of their practical content and approach.

Personal attributes

Some mathematical ability; interest in finding practical solutions to technical problems; liking for outdoor work; ability to work as one of a team and also to take responsibility, coupled with willingness to work for people more highly qualified than oneself; meticulous accuracy; ability to supervise building-site workers.

Pay: Medium to high (see p. xxiii).

Late start There is no reason why people should not start in their twenties or thirties, especially if they have had some related experience on training; for example, a geography degree; work experience in estate agency, on a building site, with computers.

Position of women The proportion of women members of the Society of Surveying Technicians is minute (though there have been draughtswomen for a long time): well below 1%. However, especially in planning, estate agency (general practice) and quantity surveying, opportunities for women are there; but very few women are applying for training or jobs. Only tradition is keeping this area of employment virtually a male preserve.

In some offices women may still be unwelcome, but there are many more where they are welcome. Training courses invariably welcome women students. (However, women may have problems if they want to train for mineral and hydrographic surveying because of the practical work down the mines and on survey ships.) Women do very well in estate agency as negotiators.

Career-break: It is too early to know how returners would fare, but, if they have kept up with developments, there is no reason why experienced technicians should not return to work. It would probably be easier in general practice and quantity surveying than, say, in agricultural surveying.

Part-time: Not at the moment, except, perhaps, in quantity surveying but no reason why experienced technicians should not try and make their own part-time arrangements, especially in estate agency work.

Further information Society of Surveying Technicians, Aldwych House, Aldwych, London WC2B 4EL
BTEC, Central House, Woburn Place, London WC1H 0HH

Related careers *Architectural Technician – Architecture – Building – Chartered Surveyor – Housing Management*

Tax Inspector

Entry qualifications First- or second-class honours or post-graduate degree in any subject or accountancy qualifications. Maximum age 32. (Some opportunities as Tax Officer, see Executive Officer, Civil Service, p. 123).

The work The Inspector of Taxes' main duty is to examine the accounts of business concerns in order to agree the amount of profits for taxation purposes. This brings her into contact with the whole range of Britain's industry and commerce in her own district. There are Inland Revenue Offices in all areas.

She deals with many kinds of people – accountants, lawyers, industrialists, farmers, small shopkeepers – by personal interview as well as by correspondence. She also represents the Crown before an independent tribunal when she and the taxpayer concerned cannot agree on the tax assessment.

Prospects Generally good, but jobs not available everywhere. Promotion prospects good for people willing to move to where there happens to be a vacancy.

Pay: Medium to high (see p. xxiii).

Training During the first 3 years of service inspectors take part-time training and residential courses to a professional standard and have to pass examinations which qualify for promotion.

Personal attributes Common sense; judgement; administrative ability; keen intellect; the ability to sum up people and situations; impartiality; equanimity; enjoyment of responsibility.

Position of women More than twice as many women as men join as tax officers, but the higher up the ladder, the smaller the proportion of women. At the top, women account for just under 11%. Their poor progress may be partly due to the fact that tax inspectors may have to move to get promotion and women are less prepared to be moved to wherever vacancies occur. But see Civil Service, p. 129, **Position of women**.

Part-time: Some opportunities.

Career-break and *Late start*: See Civil Service, p. 128.

Further information

Civil Service Commission, Alencon Link, Basingstoke, Hampshire RG21 1JB

Related careers

Accountancy – Actuary – Banking – Insurance

Teaching

TEACHING IN SCHOOLS: nursery – primary – middle – comprehensive – secondary modern – technical – grammar – 6th-form – special; SPECIAL SUBJECT TEACHERS: speech and drama – art – craft, design and technology – Froebel – Montessori – music; TEACHING IN FURTHER AND HIGHER EDUCATION ESTABLISHMENTS: further education – higher education; NOTES ON THE SCOTTISH SYSTEM

Entry qualifications

Either 2 A-levels and 3 O-levels (or equivalent) for Bachelor of Education degree *or* any degree for Post-Graduate Certificate in Education (PGCE). *All* teaching candidates, whatever their degree, must have O-level English language and maths (arithmetic is not acceptable in lieu of maths). (See Special Subject Teachers below for alternative qualifications.)

The work

Teaching as a career should not be judged by one's own experience of being taught. The atmosphere and the work differ greatly from one school to the other. It depends on current political and individual local education authorities' policies, partly on Heads and teachers' personalities and views on education theories, and partly on type, size and location of the school. (But differences do not depend as much on type of neighbourhood as people outside education often imagine. There *are* inner-city schools where teachers have difficulties keeping order, but there are also inner-city schools which are calm and well-ordered, and country-town schools with discipline problems.)

New techniques for communicating knowledge and enthusiasm give teachers scope for experimenting. Among these are the use of computers in one form or another in almost any subject; new approaches to the teaching of language, mathematics and science (especially to try and get more girls interested in the latter) and the integration of several subjects, possibly involving 'team teaching'.

The emphasis has for some time now been on encouraging children to learn by experience and discovery rather than 'by rote'. Pupils are encouraged to research into anything from natural to ethnic minorities' social history; or indeed into any topic, from consumer protection to the application of robots in industry, which the children themselves may suggest or which arise out of the news. It is for the teacher to 'use' the children's own interests and to encourage their initiative. However, fashions in education change from time to time and at present there is a tendency again towards a rather more structured curriculum than was fashionable a few years ago. The fact that teaching is now a graduate profession is significant, too: teachers are expected to use their professionalism and creativity to guide children effectively through courses which the children will enjoy *and* which impart knowledge. Teachers need a thorough understanding of conflicting educational theories; of the 'learning process'; of children's intellectual, social and emotional development and of outside influences which affect such development. Teachers must have thought deeply about how social and economic facts of present-day life affect children and their future – and this includes the implications of unemployment for young people.

Teaching offers much wider scope than pupils can easily appreciate: the purpose of school is not just to get as many pupils as possible through as many exams as possible and to make them *want* to learn, it is also to prepare them for a changing society made up of many different cultures; to help them use their leisure constructively and to become and to feel useful members of the community.

Teaching is rather harder work than pupils tend to think. Apart from the need to be 'on their toes' every minute they are in the classroom, teachers have to do a great deal of 'homework' marking and preparing lessons and spend many evenings at parent-teacher meetings. Their holidays *are* long but so are their working hours in term-time.

Teaching in Schools

Nursery Schools and Nursery Classes

(For the 2–5s) Classrooms look like a cross between workshop and nursery, with toys, paints and handicraft equipment, plants and often pets easily accessible. Children make things, play by themselves or in small, informal groups. Teachers encourage the timid and less able, calm down the boisterous and aggressive, tell stories, organize games or acting to music and above all, answer unending streams of questions. Normally, one teacher is in charge of her class for the whole of the school day. Nursery assistants (see p. 318) help in nursery schools and classes.

Primary Schools

(For the 5–11s) Infant classes (for the 5–7s) are much like nursery classes; teaching still takes the form largely of play and 'activities'. Formal teaching starts gradually.

Subjects are integrated into 'projects', the emphasis is on keeping alive and stimulating children's natural enthusiasm for learning and for widening their experience: this is considered just as important as teaching facts and figures. A primary school teacher normally teaches the whole range of subjects to her own class but specialists in science, maths, music and drama may act as 'consultants' to colleagues and do some subject teaching.

Neither nursery nor primary school teachers do much marking of exercise books, but they do a good deal of lesson-preparation.

Middle Schools

The majority are for 8–12s or 9–13s; some cover a shorter age-span. As middle schools are fairly new, teachers have scope for working out new approaches to learning and for using experimental methods.

For the first 2 years, children tend to stay with their class teacher, later they have subject teachers; in some schools, subjects are integrated and several subject-specialists work as a team.

Comprehensive Schools (the vast majority)

They provide courses for pupils of 11 (or following middle-schools from 12 to 13) to 18, of all abilities and interests. (In some areas, pupils transfer to 6th-form college at 16.) The organization of individual schools varies enormously. For example, classes may be streamed (by ability) or unstreamed. Pupils may or may not be divided into sets (according to ability) for certain subjects. Some children work for no examination at all; some for Royal Society of Arts examinations in commercial and computing subjects or for City and Guilds exams in vocational subjects; most work for CSE or GCE O-levels and A-levels. A modification of the secondary-education examination system is under discussion. More vocational subjects may be introduced. The range of subjects taught is extremely wide. It may, for example, include photography; use of word processors; engineering subjects; technical drawing; craft, design and technology (see p. 528); as well as A-level courses in computer studies, astronomy, sociology and, of course, orthodox school subjects at all levels. Staff in comprehensive schools represent a wide range of interests and specializations. In many schools challenging experimental work is being done with older children who are not interested in academic subjects but stay on after 16 because they cannot get jobs.

Secondary Modern Schools (very few now)

Secondary modern schools provide a general education to a minimum school-leaving age. Many pupils do not work for examinations; an increasing number do.

Technical Schools (very few indeed)

They provide courses for pupils of 11 to 16 who want to specialize in vocational subjects. The work previously done in these schools is now done in comprehensives.

The vast majority of teachers work in State schools, but there is also scope in the various kinds of independent day and boarding schools (training requirements are essentially the same).

Grammar Schools (very few now)

They provide academic courses for pupils who intend to go on to higher education.

6th-form or Tertiary Colleges

For academic and non-academic pupils working for O-levels and A-levels or vocational qualifications. The atmosphere is more like college than school. They are increasing in number.

Special Schools

Wherever possible, handicapped children go to 'normal' classes now. Special schools and special classes in ordinary schools provide for various categories of severely handicapped children, including physically handicapped, blind, deaf, maladjusted and educationally subnormal children.

Teachers of deaf and of blind children must acquire an additional qualification, either by in-service training or by a 1-year full-time course of special training. (There is also a 4-year BEd in audiology and education of the deaf, as an alternative to teacher training plus the 1-year special training.) Special training for teachers of Children with Special Learning Difficulties within the ordinary school system is not yet compulsory, but it is strongly encouraged. Courses last from 1 term to 1 year. On some BEd courses, students can specialize in teaching handicapped children, but these courses may be discontinued, as all teachers should first teach normal children and then take 'post-experience' courses in 'TCSLD'.

Handicapped children are taught in much smaller classes. Work with them is as much forming relationships and gaining their confidence and support as formal teaching. Training programmes in special schools for mentally handicapped children and in mental handicap hospital 'schools' are designed to help the children develop self-confidence and the capacity to relate to people around them; to help them move, eat, play and walk as best they can in spite of their handicaps. Mentally handicapped children learn slowly, but they can usually acquire simple skills. Painting, movement to music and creative activities generally play a large part in work with these children.

Prospects (all teachers) For the next few years primary school teachers will be more in demand than secondary school teachers generally. But there is a shortage of maths, physics, chemistry (NOT biology), craft design and technology specialists. Religious education teachers are in short supply in some areas, and so are PE teachers. For others – especially arts specialists – prospects are not good at present. However, once trained (entry to post-graduate training places is competitive – see **Training**), promotion prospects are fair. There are some possibilities to change from school to further education teaching, to doing research into teaching methods (including computer-based learning techniques), to industrial training, and to education administration. There is also some scope for teaching and eductaion administration in the developing countries and for exchange with teachers in Europe and the USA.

Training The Department of Education and Science lays down national criteria for selection of prospective teachers and for course content. Unlike other professions such as solicitors, architects or physiotherapists, the teaching profession does not set its own entrance requirements nor award its own qualifications. The structure of teacher training, and the principles on which it is based, have changed recently. Broadly, secondary school teachers are now expected to qualify to teach special subjects to specific age groups. The principle is unlikely to be rigidly adhered to, but prospective teachers should decide where their interests and abilities lie before starting training. One implication of the new DES criteria is that it is no longer advisable for people to choose a degree subject with few job prospects 'because it interests me' in the knowledge that 'I can always teach'. Graduates in, say, archaeology or history of art, subjects which are not generally school subjects, will find it difficult to get on to graduate teacher training courses (see below).

There are now two *main*, separate routes into teaching: one mainly for primary school teachers – the Bachelor of Education; and one mainly for secondary school teachers – the PGCE (Post-Graduate Certificate in Education).

Primary School Teacher Training

About three quarters of primary school teachers take a 4-year honours (or 3-year ordinary) degree course, for the BEd. Most courses are at colleges/institutes of higher education and polytechnics, a few at universities. The training combines classroom work, professional practice (i.e. theory of education, child development, etc.) and subject-study. Primary teachers usually teach the whole range of subjects to their own class, so subject study is broadly-based. But they are now often also trained to take responsibility for one aspect of the curriculum, for example, science or maths or music. They can then act as 'consultant' to their colleagues, and teach the subject themselves throughout the school. Emphasis on subject specialization varies from one training course to another; prospective teachers must carefully 'research the market' before deciding on a particular course. Apart from the most usual subject specialization, there are also opportunities for specializing in such areas as multi-cultural education; remedial work; English as Second Language, etc. Students usually specialize in teaching either the 5–8s or the 7–11s or sometimes 8–13s – middle school pupils; but there is some overlap. Though trained to teach mainly one age-group, teachers do not have to stick rigidly to teaching that age-group throughout their career; about one quarter of intending primary school teachers take the PGCE after having taken a 'relevant' degree. Preference for degree-relevance being a new development, it remains to be seen how strictly it will be enforced. But, for example, music, maths or science graduates will find it much easier to get onto one of the few primary school teaching PGCE courses than English or history graduates.

Secondary School Teacher Training

DES Guidelines in 1983 stated that in future there should be a 'better match between teachers' qualifications and what they teach'. Secondary school teachers are now expected to have taken a degree in the subject they teach. While it is unlikely that teachers will entirely stick to their degree subject, they will in future be more likely to teach *mainly* the subject in which they graduated.

The qualifications for the majority of secondary school and sixth-form (colleges, etc.) teachers is the Post-Graduate Certificate in Education (unlike most other post-graduate courses, the 1-year full-time course qualifies for a mandatory grant). Courses are run at universities, polytechnics and colleges/institutes of higher education and cover the theory and practice of teaching 11–18-year-olds, plus main-subject study. The equivalent of 1 term is spent on classroom practice (compared with about 3 terms on BEd courses). PGCE courses vary in main-subject emphasis. There are also a number of special interest options in, for example, counselling; careers work; work with non-academic sixth-formers, etc. Candidates who intend to teach practical subjects such as home economics, craft design and technology, physical education, business studies, etc. take either a specialist PGCE or a specialist BEd course. Music and drama teachers can take either a BEd with special options or, if suitably qualified, a PGCE (see also pp. 529 and 527).

Prospective maths and physical science teachers with relevant HNDs (see p. xviii) or equivalent qualifications can take a shortened 3-years' honours or 2-year ordinary, BEd course. (Until 1983 maths and science graduates could teach without taking a professional teaching qualification. That is no longer so. Since January 1984 they, like other teachers, must take a professional teaching qualification to gain 'qualified teacher status'.)

Selection for PGCE Teacher Training

This has been tightened up. Teacher training places have been drastically reduced twice in the last ten years. There are no precisely defined selection procedures, but applicants' suitability for teaching is to be more rigorously assessed than it used to be. Wherever possible – and this applies particularly to PGCE primary school teaching candidates – students should have done some work with children to prove their ability to handle classroom work. Youth club work or some other form of showing 'leadership qualities' is valuable. Practising teachers are now likely to be on selection panels, and, as stated above, applicants' degree subject will greatly affect their chances of acceptance on PGCE courses. Competition for acceptance on PGCE courses is very stiff; for BEd courses, not quite so hard.

A year spent abroad and/or having had a job at home working with children or a cross section of adults is looked on favourably by most selectors.

The Diploma of Higher Education

For those who do not wish to commit themselves to teaching at the outset, there are 2-year full-time or 3-year part-time Dip.HE courses, at the end of which students can decide whether to take a further 1- or 2-year course for BEd or, possibly, another degree or professional qualification.

The Dip.HE is available at non-university higher education establishments; requirements are as for a degree (with exceptions for older entrants).

The Dip.HE enables students to postpone final career and subject decisions. A wide variety of courses is offered. In some colleges students specialize in 1 or 2 subjects, but more frequently, they choose a number of 'modules', usually within a main area of study: for example, sciences or humanities. They must complete a set of modules to obtain the Dip.HE; they can usually go on to study for a further year at the same institution, and get a degree. If the first 2 years contained sufficient relevant modules, the students can usually get a BEd (ordinary) in 3 years (honours in 4); but more years are required if the student changes direction during the Dip.HE/BEd course. The same applies to other degree subjects: it depends on the relevance of the modules studied during the first 2 years whether a further 1 or 2 years for a degree will be required.

Before choosing a Dip.HE course, it is essential to research the variety of courses and to study individual course prospectuses carefully.

Personal attributes A liking for and understanding of children; a desire to help them develop and express their personalities; keen interest in the art and techniques of communicating knowledge by stimulating enthusiasm; patience; a friendly manner coupled with the ability to be firm and keep calm under provocation; energy and organizing ability; a good speaking voice; stamina; leadership qualities.

Special Subject Teachers

Teacher of Speech and Drama

The work The functions of the speech and drama teacher are to help children develop their personalities, widen their interests in literature and drama and enable them to use speech more effectively to communicate. She teaches mime and improvisation; movement; verse-speaking; public speaking and simply holding conversations; playwriting; acting and producing plays. Some of the work with school plays has to be done out of school hours. She also deals with pupils' minor defects in speech and improves articulation. (For helping children with defective speech, see Speech Therapist, p. 490.)

Prospects Fair. An increasing number of primary and secondary schools employ these specialists: there are also opportunities in special schools for backward children, as county drama advisers and in youth clubs, amateur dramatic societies, etc.

Pay and *Further Information* as for Teachers generally.

Training *Either* BEd course in conjunction with (but not, as in the past, entirely at) an approved drama school; *or* BEd course at a teacher training institution which specializes in speech and drama (possibly as one of several option modules).

The composition of courses varies slightly, and a second subject (usually music or English literature) is always studied. All courses include every aspect of play production, verse-speaking, movement, phonetics, English poetry and prose, theory of education, and actual teaching practice as for other teachers (see p. 525).

There are also degree courses in drama. Studies can be combined with related subjects. Syllabuses vary from one university to another, but usually include all aspects of play-production and construction, history and literature of the theatre, theories of acting and production, actual acting, and other practical theatre work. The emphasis in these courses is not on producing actors, but on narrowing the gap between the actor's approach and the literary approach to the theatre.

Art Teacher

Prospects Limited opportunities. There are more candidates for jobs than vacancies.

Training Normal training either for BEd at a teacher training institution which specializes in art or 1-year course of teacher training at art training centres for holders of the degree in Art and Design or of some other advanced qualification in art.

Craft, Design and Technology (CDT) Teacher

The work CDT (at non-exam, CSE, O- and A-level) is still evolving. Course content and emphasis vary greatly and so does the title: it is sometimes called 'Design and Technology' – especially at A-level. Career-choosers should not judge CDT by the old-type handicraft or metal-work, etc., which may pass as CDT in their own school. CDT now covers a wide range of activities from handling and working with traditional and new materials, to seeing through a project from the idea, via choosing material and method, planning progress, designing and constructing the product. The product could be as simple as a coathanger, or as complex as a powered wheelchair designed jointly with A-level Engineering Science students.

CDT also covers learning design principles and thus learning how to tell Good Design from Bad Design (in terms of the product's efficiency and its aesthetics), and it gives students a grasp of technology and its applications. CDT is now accepted as an academic subject for entry to most (technical and non-technical) degree courses.

Prospects Good. There is still a shortage of CDT teachers with up-to-date training.

Training *Either* BEd or PGCE (see **Training** above) with CDT option; *or* for people with technical qualifications at BTEC Higher National level or Advanced City and Guilds certificates plus some practical experience, a 2-year BEd course. 3- and 4-year BEd courses specializing in CDT may admit people with these qualifications and experience into the second year.

CDT teachers must either have O-level maths and English language (as do all teachers) or, in the case of mature entrants, they must be able to 'demonstrate competence' in these subjects. (Post-Graduate Certificate in Education (PGCE) candidates must have a relevant degree (Art and Design, Science, Technology) or must prove their CDT suitability in some other way.)

Froebel Teacher

BEd or post-graduate course at Froebel Institute College, Roehampton Institute of Higher Education, London. The Froebel method of teaching does not differ substantially from methods now generally used in infant teaching, which is why there is only one special Froebel course.

Montessori Teacher

Training for the only internationally recognized Montessori Diploma is given by the Maria Montessori Training Organization, 26 Lyndhurst Gardens, Hampstead, London NW3. Grants are not available. The Diploma does not lead to 'qualified teacher status', i.e. only to jobs in private schools and nurseries, not local authority schools and nurseries. It is advisable, therefore, to add a Montessori qualification to a BEd as private school jobs are not available everywhere.

Candidates must be 18 and must have 7 O-levels or 5 O-levels and 1-A level. The Diploma course normally lasts two years, but can be taken in one year by 'very intensive study'.

Music Teacher

See Music, p. 314.

Late start (all teachers)

In the 1970s, mature students were very much encouraged to train for teaching. Since the drastic reduction in teaching jobs, the situation has changed. There is no official upper age limit and entrants in their twenties are still very welcome, but after that, institutions' attitudes vary. Acceptance depends at least partly on applicants' past experience. A 45-year-old scientist or computer specialist who has worked in industry would be accepted on PGCE courses; a woman of 40 who had spent the last 15 years bringing up a family might find it difficult to get a training place. Mature candidates who *are* accepted do not necessarily have to satisfy the normal teacher training entry requirements.

Position of women

In 1981 (latest available figures) 4·3% of women and 9·7% of male teachers had headships. The proportion of women heads is declining. This is only partly due to the fact that more women than men leave the profession and that many women who stay while bringing up a family are too busy to take on the head's extra responsibilities. In the last few years, as more schools became co-educational and small schools and infant and junior amalgamated, more men were appointed to headships than women; and as teachers' pay improved and unemployment rose, fewer men left the profession: so the trend for more top jobs for men continues. Local education authorities (responsible for appointing heads) state categorically that not enough women with the right experience apply for headships. Women who do apply say that they have to have at least as many years (with as much variety) of teaching experience as men to stand equal chance of appointment. Their 'life experience' and experience of bringing up a family (which may have shortened the period spent actually teaching) is, illogically, not taken into consideration. In higher education, the situation is even more unequal. Only 2·5% of professors are women, while they make up about 20% of lecturers and assistant lecturers.

Career-break: Depends on local supply-and-demand and on individuals' subjects. In theory, returners have always been welcome in schools, but new college-leavers are cheaper to employ and may be given preference when jobs are scarce. However, by the time today's students are at the return-to-work stage, the supply-and-demand situation might be more even.

There are 1-year 'retraining' courses for qualified teachers interested in teaching maths, craft design and technology, business studies and the physical sciences. People with relevant qualifications or experience who are not qualified teachers may also be admitted.

There are some, though limited, opportunities to train as a teacher of English as a foreign language (TEFL). 4 weeks' full-time, or longer, evening-only courses for the Royal Society of Arts Diploma lead to fair opportunities at home and abroad.

Refresher courses: Both short full-time and in-service courses are available.

Part-time: Depends on area and subject. Very little scope for primary teachers: fair scope for maths, music, CDT, science specialists. (Only one part-time BEd course.)

Further information

Department of Education and Science, Elizabeth House, York Road, London SE1 7PH
Central Register and Clearing House, 3 Crawford Place, London W1H 2BN
Handbook of Degree and Advanced Courses in Institutes/Colleges of HE; Colleges of Education, Polytechnics and University Departments of Education (in libraries)

Teaching in Further and Higher Education Establishments

Further Education

Further education colleges cater for a very wide range of students: there is a need for almost every kind of specialist. There are opportunities for graduates, especially in maths, science and technology; for members of professional institutions, and for those who have qualifications and experience in anything from catering to business and engineering. Nurses, art college graduates and scientists are also wanted. General or 'liberal' studies are taught to a wide range of students, from apprentices on day-release to A-level and BTEC Higher Award students. General studies teachers are normally graduates.

Further education teachers need not take special teacher training but they can do so (full- or part-time) at Further Education Teacher Training Centres, and are advised to do so.

Higher Education

A good honours degree plus post-graduate research is the usual qualification. Teaching is almost invariably combined with research. Very few openings except in high technology.

Notes on the Scottish System

The system is different in several respects. The main difference in educational requirements and methods of training and qualifications for those straight from school are:

Entry qualifications

(For admission to college of education courses): Either 4 subjects at the Higher grade; or 3 at the Higher grade and 2 at the Ordinary grade. All students must have a pass in arithmetic or maths or statistics.

Candidates educated in England and Wales must have at least 2 subjects at A-level and 4 at O-level. Passes (at either level) must be in approved subjects and must include English language, English literature and maths. (Candidates who do not have a pass in maths must provide evidence of a reasonable standard in arithmetic or maths.)

Training

Only teachers who have registered with the General Teaching Council for Scotland may be appointed to permanent posts in education authority schools. To be eligible for registration, it is necessary to hold a Teaching Qualification awarded by a Scottish college of education or an equivalent qualification approved by the Council (e.g. an English teaching qualification). From September 1984 primary school teachers as well as secondary teachers must take a degree. There are 3 types of Scottish Teaching Qualifications:

(a) Teaching Qualification (primary education). Awarded to those who complete either a degree course followed by a 1-year course of professional teacher training or a 4-year BEd degree course at a Scottish college of education.

(b) Teaching Qualification (secondary education). Awarded to those who hold an honours degree or ordinary degree that includes passes in 2 graduating courses in a subject taught at school, and who have completed a 1-year academic course of training at a college of education, and to persons who have taken a 4-year BEd degree. Teachers of certain subjects, such as homecraft and physical education, normally obtain this qualification after a 3-year course of training at a college of education which specializes in the relevant subjects. In subjects such as art and music the qualification may also be awarded to those who have relevant qualifications of comparable standard, plus a 1-year academic course of professional teacher training.

(c) Teaching Qualification (Further Education). FE teachers do not need a professional teaching qualification, but for permanent jobs they must have the *entry* qualifications required for professional FE teacher training. In practice this normally means they must have technical or commercial qualifications and experience.

Persons who have successfully completed comparable courses in England and Wales may also be admitted to the Register of teachers.

Holders of Teaching Qualification (primary education) may be appointed to posts in secondary schools in England and Wales, but not to do grammar school or grammar stream work.

NOTE: Honours degree courses in Scotland last 4 years, ordinary degree courses 3 years.

Further information

Advisory Service on Entry to Teaching, 5 Royal Terrace, Edinburgh EH7 5AF

Related careers

Careers Officer – Nursery Nurse – Personnel Work – Social Work – Youth-and-Community Work

---

Television, Film and Radio

Broadcast TV – film and video – national and local radio

The work This whole area has undergone big changes in the last few years and more developments are under way. The video boom, breakfast and cable TV, direct broadcast satellites, digital technology, TV/computer link-up, local radio expansion – all these will have an impact on job opportunities. The greatest expansion is likely to be in non-broadcasting TV, i.e. not what is put on our screens by the BBC or ITV, but home video programmes, training films, sales promotions, etc. Anyone considering entering TV or film work in the future should look beyond what is available in the broadcasting companies as there will be more demand for qualified, experienced and highly motivated staff in these other areas.

There are a large number of different jobs but there is very little a school leaver can do right away. Many jobs are done by people with training and/or experience which in itself has nothing to do with TV or radio. For many jobs a degree or specialist qualification/experience is useful. Selection boards may not *demand* degrees, but the sort of lively-minded people broadcasting and film making needs usually have taken a degree. Candidates with a poor degree but with a good record of extra-curricular activities – university journalism, politics, dramatics, etc. – are more likely to be accepted than studious single-minded people. No particular subject is the most useful, except where academic knowledge is required, e.g. in music or science. Many jobs need well-informed all-rounders. Journalistic experience is very useful.

For entry and training (where applicable) see under each type of work.

Broadcast TV

Apart from normal administrative functions found in any large organization (personnel, computing, accounting, etc.) jobs can be divided into two distinct but at times overlapping areas: *production, presentation and design* and *technical and engineering*.

Production Staff

Producers/Directors
Exact functions vary. Producers are usually responsible for initiating, budgeting, casting, and the shape or 'treatment' of programmes. Directors are responsible for interpreting the idea and actually making the programme. These top jobs are very responsible and are done by specialists in particular fields, such as current affairs, drama, science or technology and with long, often technical experience in the medium. Many work on contracts for particular projects.

The BBC runs a highly competitive (total 21 a year) production training scheme for graduates or experienced journalists. Courses last 2 years and trainees specialize in TV (15 posts), radio (3 posts) or external broadcasting (3 posts). TV trainees are appointed as either assistant producers or researchers. In ITV, trainee directors are usually appointed from existing staff with experience in some aspect of programme making.

Production Assistants (BBC)
They provide organizational support to a programme. They may do some research, they sit with the producer in the gallery checking on timing, cue the inserts of film or tape and are normally responsible for continuity. They have considerable contact with people both inside and outside TV. Where there is no *production secretary* in a department they perform any necessary secretarial duties.

Production Assistants (ITV)
Production assistants provide the organizational and secretarial services for the director, coordinating all the arrangements that go into the making of a programme. Many duties similar to those of production assistants in the BBC.

Production Secretaries (BBC and some larger ITV companies)
Entrants who go straight into TV still often start as secretaries. If they are lucky and very good they may become secretary to a producer. They see to it that the right instructions about make-up, costumes, sets, rehearsal times and studio bookings go to the right people. They type (and often re-type) the shooting script. Not all programmes have a secretary (e.g. drama).

Floor Managers (in BBC known as Stage Managers in outside broadcasts)
They may be involved at the planning stage in advising on design, sound and props. During recording they control the studio floor. They are responsible for discipline of the floor and for safety of staff and

artists. Duties include relaying the producer's/director's instructions to actors and presenters using headphones to keep in touch with the gallery. They are responsible for cueing the actors, which can be a complicated task as they are often working on different sets and cannot see each other. The floor manager has to move around the sets while keeping out of camera shot. A diplomatic, pleasant personality is essential. In outside broadcasts they have to liaise with the general public.
Entry: Nearly all from the ranks of *assistant floor managers*.

Assistant Floor Manager (also Stage Manager ITV)
Similar to assistant stage manager in the theatre. Work varies according to size and type of production, but usually includes making sure that all the props are available, taking charge of the prompt book and mark-ups during rehearsals. Assistant floor managers usually start their on-the-job training with the easier talks and discussion programmes before going on to drama series, etc.
Entry: Candidates are expected to have a background in professional theatre stage management.

Floor Assistants
Give calls to artists ensuring they are in the right place at the right time; generally assist floor manager.
Entry: Generally with theatre background (with BBC initially on short-term contract).

Researchers
Research may be anything from looking through newspaper cuttings and finding a suitable person to be interviewed – not by researcher but by interviewer/presenter – on a news programme, to spending several months researching the background for a documentary or drama series. Researchers must be good all-rounders, able to pick out relevant facts from a mass of material. They usually write 'briefs', which may range from a few questions which an interviewer is to ask on a programme, to exhaustive background material for a documentary scriptwriter. Researchers in current affairs must also be able to think up programme ideas, and they work under tremendous pressure. Specialist researchers, for example for scientific or medical programmes, are often freelances.
Entry: Usually graduates and/or ex-journalists, or by promotion from within.

News Staff, Presenters, Interviewers
Newsroom staff compile and write scripts for the presenters; reporters and correspondents 'get the stories' and present some themselves. The

essence of broadcast news is brevity. TV and radio journalists must be instant fact-selectors and decision-makers. They may be sent anywhere at any time. Editors are senior staff responsible for piecing a programme together.

Entry: The BBC runs a regular training scheme (about 2 years' duration) for entrants between 21 and 25 – about 700 applicants for 12 to 16 vacancies. Entrants are almost invariably graduates (any subject) with keen interest in current affairs, but 'general education' plus proven journalistic ability (i.e. good job on a good paper) are also acceptable. ITN recruits about 4 trainee journalists a year for a 2-year training programme in all aspects of television news.

Other routes into presenting are radio interviewing, journalism (reporters on provincial papers are occasionally given a try-out) and, occasionally, acting.

Design Department

Set Designers

They are responsible for designing the sets down to the smallest accessories in accordance with the producer's concept. The producer calls in the designer when the idea is beginning to take shape. Her interpretation of the atmosphere the producer has in mind and her own suggestions are vitally important to the success of the production.

Design Assistants work with the designer on the technical, rather than creative, tasks. They draw ground plans and make working drawings; draw up specifications; make models of sets; and make or search for props.

Graphic Designers and their *Assistants* create credit titles, 'linking material', captions, maps and general illustrations.

Scenic Artists and *Assistants* paint backcloths and decorative features such as curtains, carpets and portraits.

In the BBC *Visual Effects Designers* and *Assistants* devise, make and operate a wide variety of visual effects and 'illusions'. (In ITV these are nearly always handled by relevant departments, e.g. make-up, vision mixing.)

Entry: Whatever the level of entry qualifications, all first appointments are to the post of assistant. Generally speaking, promotion to designer is from design assistant. All design assistants need degree level qualification in relevant art discipline. Additionally, graphic design assistants normally need commercial art experience (e.g. advertising) following a degree or diploma; scenic artists need wide knowledge of painting, history of art and architecture and interior design; visual effects staff need to be able to work in all kinds of materials, make models and have a basic grasp of physics.

Costume Designers (also called Wardrobe)
They are in charge of hiring, designing and adapting up-to-date and period costumes. They are called in on new productions at an early stage to discuss the costumes and to advise on whether to hire, make or adapt, and to arrange for this to be done. Later they liaise with other designers and make-up staff. They need a thorough knowledge of period styles, but further research is often needed to make certain of representing the exact year or season. *Assistants* help designers in all aspects of their work and may stand in for them, e.g. when filming on location.
Entry: With a theatre or textile design degree and considerable experience in theatre or film costumes. All entrants start at assistant level, from which designers are promoted.

Dressmakers make up costumes under the supervision of designers and make alterations to costumes which are hired or from stock.
Entry: With at least City and Guilds (often BTEC Higher National Diploma required) qualification and (for the BBC) a minimum of 2 years' experience with a theatrical costumier. Knowledge of history of costume an advantage.

Dressers work on last minute ironing and maintenance of costumes and help actors to dress for performance.

Make-up Artists/Designers
Television make-up is highly skilled. It requires the ability to understand and defeat the camera's often unkind effects on faces. It also requires a thorough knowledge of period hairstyles. An experienced senior assistant is usually in charge of each dramatic production and makes-up the star actors. Juniors see to the rest of the cast and also look after the simpler make-up required for non-dramatic productions. Tact and diplomacy are essential.
Entry and training: Requirements vary slightly between companies offering training, but main qualifications sought are A-level standard plus beauty therapy/hairdressing/art school training. Minimum age 20½/21. Experience in make-up in amateur theatre very useful. Courses last 2 years. Basic training is followed by carrying out practical duties under supervision, starting with simpler make-up and hairdressing and gradually learning more intricate techniques, such as creating 'scars' or 'wounds'.

Technical and Engineering Work

This is rather a confusing area as the organizational structure and job titles vary between BBC and ITV companies. Broadly speaking there are two sides to the work: *technical operations* and *electronics and communications engineering*.

Technical Operations

These concern the technical interpretation of the director's instructions and producing the required sound and vision effects which are finally seen and heard. Most TV programmes are pre-recorded. When recording a programme as well as during 'live' transmission, previously recorded and/or filmed material may be slotted in. The operational and technical sides of creating programmes and getting them onto TV screens are highly complex and require creativity, technical expertise and an unflappable temperament.

The BBC is the only company with a *comprehensive* training scheme which provides specialization from the beginning. Some ITV companies run training schemes for particular posts, sometimes in conjunction with other companies, while Thames has a technical training scheme for operational work. All trainees cover the same basic course with emphasis on the particular work they are aiming at. The idea is to produce broadly trained, adaptable people.

There are 3 trainee jobs in *Technical Operations* TV specializations:
1. *Camera Assistants* help in setting up and operating electronic cameras and associated equipment in studios and on outside broadcasts. Promotion is to assistant and later cameraman/woman, vision supervisor, vision controller and ultimately possibly to technical manager responsible for lighting.
2. *Sound Assistants* help in setting up and operating sound recording and reproduction equipment; they 'collect sound effects', and may eventually become sound supervisors responsible for control and balance of the various sound sources which are combined for final transmission. They are London-based in the BBC.
3. *Audio Assistants* do similar work to sound assistants but they work in the regional (smaller) centres, and are also involved in the operation of radio sound equipment.

Entry and training: Minimum age 18 (in practice, maximum about 25). O-levels in English language, maths and physics; *or* English language and a BTEC National Certificate in Electrical Engineering, Electronics or Applied Physics. Applicants must also have a keen interest in, and some 'hobby experience' of, hi-fidelity reproduction, tape-recording music, colour photography, or lighting for amateur dramatics. Ability to read a musical score and/or knowledgeable interest in current affairs are also very useful. Acceptance depends very much on interview.

Normally starts with a 3-months course, BBC-run, and continues on the job with further full-time courses for two to three years. Promotion is not *guaranteed* even when the training has been successfully completed but BBC engineering training is highly valued by all sound and vision recording studios outside the BBC.

NOTE: Candidates with qualifications from Art School TV departments or specialist TV schools, or candidates with music technology qualifications (see p. 314), usually have to start as trainee assistants in Technical Operations. However, there are some opportunities in independent (much smaller) companies or as freelances. BBC training is generally considered the best for all vision and/or sound operational jobs.

Thames TV technical training scheme: Normally aged 20–25 with *either* degree/diploma in film, TV or communications engineering plus 'hobby experience' *or* relevant experience in closed circuit TV, recording studios or equipment manufacturers. There are similar arrangements in other ITV companies.

Vision-Mixer

Up to six cameras may be in operation during a production. The producer in the control room decides which camera's picture to send out to the audience, and tells the vision-mixer, who switches to the selected camera as the order is given. This needs concentration and quick reflexes.

Training Mostly on-the-job for existing TV staff.

Engineering

Some TV engineers work in studios, outside broadcasting, coping with emergency repairs and sudden equipment failure, generally acting as technical 'back-up'. Others are responsible for operation and maintenance of equipment used to route, control and distribute signals from various sound and vision programme sources. All this work can be hectic and needs quick decision-making and a cool head. Other departments are concerned with research, development, planning, installation of a variety of complex equipment (see Engineering, p. 168 for engineering functions). In a time of changing technology they must be prepared to update their knowledge and assimilate new ideas quickly.

Technical assistants (or *technicians*) are the professional engineers' support force (see Engineering Technician, p. 182) and may assist in any of the engineering departments.

Entry and training: Minimum age 18 (in practice maximum around 25). For BBC technical assistants training: O-levels in English language, maths and physics and A-level study of physics and maths.

BTEC National Certificate in Electrical Engineering, Electronics or Applied Physics plus O-level English language *may* be acceptable. Acceptance depends very much on interview. Technical assistants must show that they understand the basic principles of electricity and magnetism and have a good grasp of their practical application. 'Hobby experience' as for technical operations trainee assistants.

Training starts with a 3-months, BBC-run course and continues on the job with further courses for about 2½ years. After satisfactorily completing training, technical assistants are eligible for promotion to BBC engineer posts. The majority of BBC and ITV engineers enter as graduates with degrees in Electrical or Electronic Engineering, Applied Physics or other relevant science subjects, or with BTEC Higher awards in Electronics or Telecommunications (or with relevant HND/Cs). For posts in BBC Research and Design (the same as 'Design' in Engineering, p. 169) minimum entry qualification is now a first- or second-class honours degree. There is also scope for engineers with higher degrees.

Filming for TV

Film camera and sound staff are quite distinct from TV camera and sound staff. A considerable amount of television material is shown on film (but not as much as video); whole programmes are filmed, e.g. schools broadcasts, documentaries; and film is used as an important ingredient of all kinds of programmes – light entertainment, current affairs, children's programmes, plays and series. Camera crews travel a lot and at short notice. There are three basic jobs: *editing*, *camera*, *sound* (titles may vary).

Film Editors

Editors work entirely in the cutting-room, 'editing down' material shot in the studio or on location. A great deal of their work is done on their own initiative, as directors do not have time to be with editors all day. The job is highly creative as it is the editor who shapes and fashions the final programme which audiences see. Editing can lead to directing.

Assistant film editors look after the practical side of running the cutting-room. They do the 'joins', log film on its way out of and back into the studio and laboratories. They learn by watching, and often cut sequences under the editor's supervision. Cutting-room work is almost invariably done under great pressure.

Film Camera Crews
Crews usually consist of 2 to 4. The head of the camera crew is in charge of *lighting*. She works in close cooperation with the director; knows the script thoroughly and arranges the all-important lighting and camera angles for each individual shot, so as to achieve the atmosphere the director wants. Lighting cameraman/woman *can* be an important step to directing film.

Assistant camera crews load and change magazines, make sure the right equipment is available at the right time and place and in working order, and they learn how to operate cameras and lighting equipment. Promotion is pretty slow – it takes about 10 years to reach lighting cameraman/woman status.

Film Sound Recordists/Sound Technicians
They are concerned with dubbing, sound-transfer and above all with mixing sound from various sources. This may include location recordings on tape, and sounds produced by effects machines. Achieving the correct balance, controlling the 'input' from various sources, is a highly skilled job requiring great technical skill and musical creativity.

Assistants manipulate microphones and other recording equipment and learn by watching. Far fewer apply for sound than vision jobs so chances of acceptance are better.

Projectionists operate projection equipment and may also work on dubbing.

Entry qualifications and training

Interest and 'hobby experience' are crucial. There are a number of film/TV courses at art schools, either as part of an Art and Design degree course, or 2/3-year DATEC Diploma courses, or at post-graduate level. Course emphasis (and entry requirements) vary enormously: for example on closed circuit educational television films; on feature or instructional films; with technical or creative bias, etc.

Equally useful in later job-opportunity terms, but more difficult to get into (several hundred applicants for every training vacancy) is the BBC film training scheme (1 year approximately; age 18 to 25). No specific GCE requirements, but several O-levels are in practice essential; above all, candidates must show 'evidence of lively interest in film-making techniques' and know enough about cinematography principles to absorb advanced film training; they also need 'special knowledge of some of the following: photography, the cinema, music, magnetic sound recording, sport, news, current affairs'.

ITV companies look for similarly qualified people normally in their 20s. For camera work a diploma from film school or experience of colour filming is an advantage. For sound work A-level standard in maths and/or physics and/or music are preferred, but the most important qualification is a demonstrable flair for sound. Virtually all promotion to camera work, recordist, editor is from inside the broadcasting organization, i.e. via recruitment into Assistant grade. Once established they often go freelance. The greatest hurdle for those who do not start as assistant is getting a union card, without which they cannot get jobs.

Film and Video Industry

Feature film making has for several years been a depressed part of the industry in Britain. Some major recent successes suggest that it might be looking up, while the future demands of cable TV and the home video market should provide greater opportunities than in the recent past. However, entry into cinema film making will remain very highly competitive. The only real job prospects lie with the growing number of often very small production companies which combine TV film making and, very occasionally, cinema, with the whole range of other productions, e.g. training and advertising films. Video recorders, while not offering the same 'creative' scope as film cameras have very wide and growing applications: sales promotions (e.g. for pop records and at 'point of sale' in shops), sales training, recording ballets for a dance company's repertoire, monitoring the performance of racehorses during meetings. Many companies use only freelance staff as and when they need them and many of these specialize, e.g. in making wildlife films. Studio facilities and sophisticated equipment are often hired from 'facility houses' which do not themselves make programmes.

Entry and training: There is no essential difference between filming for TV and making non-broadcast films. Similarly, people employed in video production do much the same work as those in films. There are no regular, on-the-job training schemes outside TV and there are no jobs which can be done straight from school. Entry is normally via one of the following: TV training and experience; an appropriate diploma, degree or postgraduate course at film school or art college (titles and content vary, so it is essential to study prospectuses); an electronic engineering course (all levels) plus in-service training; specialized knowledge leading to making videos on a particular topic; very occasionally, extensive amateur experience. There is more scope for versatility in video than in film making: people can move from one type of work to another more easily. There is always room in the industry for really good technical people.

Radio

Entry routes and jobs differ between BBC national, BBC local and Independent local radio. Once trained it is possible to move from one to the other.

Production

Many *BBC producers* are highly qualified specialists, e.g. in serious music for Radio 3, or education. Others are appointed after experience in other departments (e.g. research), or as studio managers, or a spell as assistant producer (the latter may have been through the production trainee scheme, see p. 535). Their work is similar to, but less complex than that of TV producers. In *local radio stations*, which are run on a shoestring, a *manager* is in charge (titles vary). She will have a *deputy* or *programme organizer* for day to day organization of output.

Stations have between 2 and 10 producers, and about the same number of station assistants (or programme assistants or junior producers).

Broadly, a *producer* is responsible for initiating and developing programme ideas and for involving the local community. She must therefore know people and issues in the locality in which she applies for a job. She may produce anything from local current affairs to request and phone-in programmes (though there may be some specialist producers). She may also interview, and present programmes.

Station assistants research and prepare programmes and also interview (on and off the air); they are also usually responsible for operation of studio and control-room equipment. Some become producers.

No rigid entry qualifications, but all candidates must have a good microphone voice, be well informed on and interested in a wide range of contemporary topics and trends, both national and local, and have sufficient knowledge to handle recording and transmission equipment. Producers and station assistants are usually given a few weeks' basic training.

Vacancies occur very rarely and candidates should have previous broadcasting experience, e.g. in hospital radio.

News Staff, Reporters and Presenters

Entry and training very similar to TV. Openings for reporters also occur for those who have completed a recognized course in radio journalism.

Production Secretaries are usually recruited from within and duties are similar to those in TV (but involve greater responsibility).

Studio Manager

The only training scheme of any size in radio is that for SM. She is responsible for the technical presentation of programmes, and for achieving the artistic effect the producer wants. The job demands sufficient knowledge of radio to operate the equipment, but not necessarily to understand how it works.

To be able to interpret a producer's wishes, an SM must have wide cultural and current affairs interests. She must be good at dealing with other studio staff, with actors, and with people who come to give talks or be interviewed and who may have no previous broadcasting experience.

SMs may eventually become radio producers, or they may go over to television, perhaps as assistant producers/vision mixers or into sound recording.

Technical and Engineering Services

Technical operators (BBC Radio) are trained via the Technical Operations scheme (see p. 539). Apart from operating and later controlling sound equipment, they are concerned with collecting and 'routing' material. Some later switch to TV, although many people who do radio work as a way into TV stay in radio because it is more interesting than they thought. Engineering staff are either recruited with degrees or diplomas in appropriate disciplines or are trained as *radio technicians* via the Technical Operations scheme.

The National Broadcasting School

Since 1981 the National Broadcasting School (independent, but supported by the Independent Broadcasting Authority) has run courses in various aspects of radio broadcasting. Courses for newcomers to radio are mostly modular and last 12–14 weeks. There are foundation courses in:

(a) *Engineering*: entry with O-level English, physics and science to A-level; or BTEC; or City and Guilds Telecommunications or Electronics; or relevant experience.

(b) *Programming*: entry with 3 O-levels, or 1 year's experience in hospital radio or similar, or 3 years' work experience.

(c) *Journalism*: entry with A-levels, a degree or 3 years' work experience.

Minimum age for all courses is 18.

Apart from stated entry requirements the school aims to select only those people it considers suitable for the work. Grants rarely available. Details from: National Broadcasting School, 14 Greek Street, London W1V 5LE.

Prospects (for TV, film and radio) Competition for all jobs is extremely keen and only the best stand a chance. It is impossible to lay down the best route in a particular case as requirements are so varied and complex. A technical training is often the best starting point, but it can take many years to reach a goal. Personality is important (see **Personal attributes**).

Pay: Varies enormously.

Personal attributes Creative imagination; wide interests generally, a special interest in a particular subject; a clear, quick, logical mind; appreciation of what audiences want; a strong constitution; the ability to work as one of a team and to take responsibility; a sociable nature; a fairly thick skin; tact; calmness in crises; speed of action; self-confidence; determination and persistence; desire to communicate ideas; ability to take criticism.

Late start Fair scope for people with relevant experience and qualifications, especially for experienced journalists and engineers.

Position of women On the programme production side women do reasonably well up to about middle-level jobs (nearly a half are women); but it is only fairly recently that women have started being seen on the screen as reporters and interviewers. Companies are now trying to find more women for this work, so suitable ones should have fair chances, i.e. those with enough commitment to be willing to work long and irregular hours and to be fully mobile (especially if they want to report 'hard' news). There are still very few women indeed in policy/decision-making jobs. Opportunities generally for women have increased in the current expansion, so chances have never been better. On the vast technical side there is only a minute proportion of women. This is only because not enough women have taken science or technical subjects at school, or had the relevant 'hobby experience' which is so useful. Any woman who really wants to get into broadcasting should consider getting in via an engineering degree or technician qualification. She would stand out and be noticed and, generally, receive plenty of encouragement. She might later be able to transfer to programme production. TV companies themselves have taken initiatives to encourage more women to apply for technical jobs, e.g. Thames Television, through its Positive Action programme, is providing basic technical background as part of its internal development and training courses.

Career-break: Depends on how well established before, but in some areas return presents problems. Companies are generous over maternity leave but it is essential to get back to work as soon as possible as there is so much competition.

Part-time: Possibly as freelance on contract basis. Job-sharing schemes have been tried out successfully.

Further information

BBC Appointments Officer, Broadcasting House, London W1A 1AA.
Engineering Recruitment Officer, BBC Broadcasting House, London W1A 1AA
Independent Broadcasting Authority, 70 Brompton Road, London SW3 1EY (for list of individual companies)
National Broadcasting School, 14 Greek Street, London W1V 5LE
Mr G. Mansell, Chairman, Joint Advisory Committee of Training of Radio Journalists (JACTRAJ), 46 Southway, London NW11 6SA

Related careers

Acting – Advertising – Art and Design – Journalism – Music – Photography – Stage Management

Town and Country Planning

TOWN PLANNER: Survey, analysis and research – physical planning; PLANNING TECHNICIAN

Entry qualifications For admission to studentship of the Royal Town Planning Institute: 2 A-levels and 3 O-levels including English language (or use of English), maths, and history or geography or a foreign language.

Town Planners

The work Planners aim to reconcile the community's desire for a high standard of environment for work, home and leisure with the conflicting demands for land from industry, traffic, etc. They are concerned, in broad terms, with civic design, urban renewal, land-use and transportation systems. The majority work in local authorities, some in the Civil Service and some in private consultancy firms. In recent years planning emphasis has changed. Planners have learnt from past experiments; for example instead of large-scale slum-clearance schemes which dispersed long-established communities, planners now recommend rehabilitation of existing houses, to keep 'urban villages' intact; or help re-vitalization of inner-city areas: as factories and inhabitants move out, small workshops are being created out of derelict warehouses and factories to attract light industry and create local jobs. Altogether, the social and economic consequences of planning are researched and considered much more thoroughly now than they were only a few years ago.

The planning process may be broadly broken down into two separate but interrelated functions:

Survey, Analysis, and Research

Involves devising and conducting surveys of the structure, functioning, wishes and needs of communities and assessing problems and aims of urban and regional development. This is social research (see Sociology, p. 486). Physical planners' final plans are based on the outcome of these findings.

Physical Planning

Drawing up development plans and implementing them. When, for example, a twilight area is redeveloped, planners draw up plans for new road networks, for shopping precincts, leisure and recreation facilities, the number and types of schools likely to be needed, etc.

Each county (see Local Government, p. 265) is covered by a *Structure Plan* which outlines planning policy for that area in relation to neighbouring counties' Structure Plans. This is 'regional planning'. A county council planner might collate and analyse information in order to predict, for example, likely levels of need for transport, leisure facilities, schools, if plan 'A', proposing plans for increased industrial development, is implemented.

Structure Plans are mainly written policy statements. District planning authorities draw up *Local Plans*. These fit into a Structure Plan, and go into much more detail. They consist largely of maps and drawn plans. A Local Plan would show, for example, streets which are designated conservation areas; or a plan for small workshops and a shopping precinct. Local planners are also concerned with development control – dealing with planning applications from the public. Very broadly, there is more scope for improving the environment at Structure Plan level planning; but more contact with the general public and such immediate environmental matters as closing roads and re-routing traffic, rehabilitating old houses rather than pulling them down, at Local Plan level.

Prospects They depend on public authority spending levels, i.e. not good at present. There are occasional openings for experienced planners in developing countries, mainly on a short-contract basis.

Pay: High (see p. xxiii).

Training 1. 4-year full-time or 5-year sandwich degree leading to exemption from the Royal Town Planning Institute's Final examination.

2. Graduates (any subject) can take a 2-year full-time or 3-year part-time course leading to exemption from the Royal Town Planning Institute's Final examination.

3. Practical training as trainee in a planning office, with day- or block-release and evening study for the RTPI examinations. Takes at least 6 years, usually more.

4. Practical training as in (3) to First Professional examination, followed by 2-year full-time or 3-year part-time course. Length of training 5–6 years.

5. Full-time training to First Professional RTPI examination followed by traineeship and part-time day-release. Length of training 5–6 years.

Methods (3)–(5) are not recommended: drop-out and failure rates are high, and trainee vacancies are very difficult to get.

After 2 years' practical planning experience, candidates who have passed or been exempt from the RTPI's Final examination qualify for election to Membership as Chartered Town Planners.

Sociologists, geographers, economists, architects, and other specialists concerned with the various aspects of planning also work in planning departments, particularly in counties and big cities. For work concerned with overall strategic planning problems and policy, i.e. for senior posts, however, a planning qualification is essential.

See also Architecture **Training** (p. 50).

Personal attributes A keen interest in other people's priorities and way of life; powers of observation; creative imagination; patience for painstaking research; the ability to work as one of a team as well as to take responsibility; interest in social, economic and environmental developments.

Late start Graduates with relevant degrees (geography, social science, engineering) could start post-graduate training. There is no specific upper age limit, see **Prospects**. An RPTI 'distance learning package' will be available from 1985 for people who want to switch to planning from related careers (architects, geographers, engineers, etc.) in mid-career. It should also be useful for people returning after a *career-break*.

Position of women 10·5% of qualified members but 20% of student members of the RTPI are women. Women do well up to middle-level jobs; *very* few (2 in 1983) are Chief Officers in local government planning departments.

Career-break: Planning priorities and legislation change constantly, so planners must keep up with developments. There are 'mid-career' updating courses and seminars for all planners, which could be useful as *refresher courses*. Returners can also take additional courses, for example in traffic engineering/planning at the returning stage. But see **Prospects**.

Part-time: Experienced planners occasionally do freelance work. Some local authorities have job-sharing schemes.

Further information The Royal Town Planning Institute, 26 Portland Place, London W1N 4BE

Planning Technicians

They are the support staff, assisting with the drawing up of plans; with conducting surveys and with interpreting results. They use computers for the various activities and may be in charge of a department's computer system.

Entry qualifications In practice usually 4 O-levels including maths and a subject involving written English; (in theory 3 CSE Grade 3 are required but employers expect higher qualifications normally).

Prospects Not good at the moment as much technician work is done by graduates who cannot get higher level jobs.

Training On the job with day-release for the BTEC National Certificate (see p. xvi) in Planning, Surveying and Cartography which takes 2 years (with 4 O-levels, 3 with lower entry qualifications), with a further 2 years for the BTEC Higher National award. There is no bridge to full professional planning qualification.

Further information Society of Planning Technicians, 26 Portland Place, London WIN 4BE

Related careers *Architectural Technician – Architecture – Auctioneer – Cartography – Economics – Engineering – Housing Management – Landscape Architecture – Local Government – Surveying*

Trading Standards Officer

Entry qualifications 2 A-levels, 3 O-levels, including English, a maths and a science subject. *Graduate* entry: about 44%.

The work Trading standards officers are employed by local authorities to ensure a fair system of trading between consumers and traders, and between traders themselves. They are responsible for the enforcement of consumer protection legislation, such as the Trade Descriptions Act, consumer credit, and food and drugs legislation. Complaints and investigations may concern, for example: a holiday brochure which misled travellers into expecting a luxury hotel on the beach when in fact they bought a holiday in a guest-house in a back-street; a 'showerproof' coat which does not withstand the briefest of showers; a 'pre-shrunk' shirt which is two sizes smaller after the first wash. Officers ascertain facts, which involves getting expert opinion and/or having articles examined in a testing laboratory, and get matters put right. If necessary, they take offenders to court. They may also investigate complaints from the public about unscrupulous/phoney companies offering products like double glazing, central heating, etc.

They also check the accuracy of weighing and measuring equipment – from the nip used to sell whisky in a pub to the weigh-bridge which weighs lorry-loads in the docks (the Trading Standards Administration developed out of the Weights and Measures Department). They use elaborate electrical equipment to check quantities in, for example, prepacked goods; they use straightforward methods to check that, for example, petrol pumps dispense correct amounts.

Britain's entry into the EEC has greatly affected and expanded the trading standards officer's work, as British quantity and quality control methods have had to be brought into line with Continental practice.

Officers divide their time between dealing with traders and with individuals who have complaints and/or queries; inspection; report writing. The higher up the hierarchy, the greater the management content of the job, the smaller the checking of equipment and quantities element. TSOs meet a great variety of people and have much scope for decision-making.

Prospects This is an expanding area but opportunities depend on local authority spending priorities. It may be necessary to move to get a job and even more often to obtain promotion.

Pay: Medium (see p. xxiii).

Training

3 years on-the-job, with block-release, for the Diploma in Trading Standards. The syllabus covers relevant legislation; structure of trade; trading standards inspection techniques and administration; sampling techniques; quantity and quality control administration.

Late start

People with business or other experience of dealing with people or with the law (police officers, for example) should have reasonable chances. In theory, this is a good 'second career'; in practice young entrants may be given preference when there are more applicants than vacancies.

Position of women

It used to be an all-male preserve, and even now only about 10% are women. This is rather illogical as so much of the work is concerned with women shoppers' complaints. It is a hangover from the days when the trading standards officer's predecessors, the weights and measures inspectors, had to do some (though never very much) heavy physical work – for example, weighing sacks of coal. The Trading Standards Administration genuinely wants more women to take up this work; the few qualified women in this career have done very well.

Career-break: Too early to say whether return to work will be easy; there should be no difficulty in theory if those in temporary retirement keep up with legislation and other developments.

Part-time: Not at the moment – not enough people have asked for it.

Further information

Institute of Trading Standards Administration, Estate House, 319D London Road, Hadleigh, Benfleet, Essex SS7 2BN

Related careers

Environmental Health Officer – Factory Inspector – Home Economics

Travel Agent/Tour Operator

Clerical work – Counter work – Planning

Entry qualifications None for work in a travel agency. 4 O-levels including English for the Institute of Travel and Tourism's examination. To get a good job: a 'tourist country' language; good geography; numeracy.

The work There are 2 types of travel company: travel agents who are the retailers, and tour operators who put together and organize package tours. Travel agents sell tour operators' holidays, as well as tickets for rail, air and coach travel.

Travel Agency: the work can be divided into clerical and counter. *Tour Operators* concentrate on planning – with such sub-divisions as British and foreign, summer and winter; business and holiday; party and individual marketing.

Clerical Work

Keeping elaborate filing systems with cross-references; every member of staff must be able to find quickly details about block and individual bookings.

Each booking involves filling in forms, sending them out, filing, and checking. There may be several letters full of intricate detail. Itineraries and currency-conversion have to be worked out; timetables checked. Minor clerical errors can have disastrous consequences when concerned with clients' holidays. Increasingly, clerks use computerized equipment. See Clerical Work (p. 456).

Counter Work

This is just selling. Clients (never called customers) may know what they want and simply buy a ticket for a train journey, or book a world tour, or want some travel literature. But most have no idea of what they want. Their leisure-time tastes must be summed up, and 'channelled' into what the counter-clerk thinks is the holiday they will most enjoy in a price range they can afford.

The counter-clerk usually has not been to the places she suggests – but she should know, from travel literature or from colleagues, as much about them as posible. She must take trouble with each client;

her responsibility is far greater than that of most other sales assistants. Most people 'buy' only one holiday a year, and if this one is not a success, they will go to another agency next year.

Planning

This is done by directors and 'travel technicians' (i.e. experienced clerks). 'Planning trips' last from 2 to 8 weeks twice a year and are exhausting. 2 or 3 resorts and perhaps 12 hotels may be investigated in a day. Local transport, garage facilities, food, amusements, beaches will be checked and local tourist officials consulted. Planning of the tour later involves checking timetables and maps, costing, and conferring with transport and accommodation services suppliers.

Staff work long hours and most Saturday mornings.

Prospects Ample scope for clerical and counter work; slim chance of promotion to manager of section or agency. There is a high proportion of junior to senior staff, and competition for senior posts is very keen indeed. Opening one's own travel agency needs a great deal of experience and capital.

Pay: Low to medium (see p. xxiii).

Training It is important to check that courses are recognized by ABTA (Association of British Travel Agents) and the Institute of Travel and Tourism.

With O-levels: *either* on-the-job with correspondence course or part-time day-release and/or evening classes leading to COTAC (Certificate of Travel Agency Competence); *or*: 2-year full-time course for BTEC National award with travel/tourism option modules (see BTEC, p. xvi), followed by Higher National award.

The syllabus includes: geography; law; a European language; travel agency operation; 'tourist value'; transportation and administration systems; tourist regions; economics; major festivals and special events; travel.

With A-levels: full-time course, either BTEC, HND or degree. Some Business Studies and some Catering (see p. 105) degrees include tourism or similar options, and there are some post-graduate courses; some also accept BTEC Higher National award holders. At graduate and post-graduate level tourism and catering training and work overlap.

Personal attributes Aptitude for figure work; good judgement of people; a friendly manner; accuracy; organizing ability; common sense; a good memory.

Late start Training posts are very poorly paid and as there are always more applicants than vacancies, not much chance – except for clerical or counter work (*without* day-release).

Position of women There are few women travel agency managers. In large tour operating companies, women are beginning to do well, though they have to have more paper qualifications (and languages) than the men with whom they compete.

Career-break: Opportunities for returners depend on contacts, on having kept up with changes in the industry, and on economic conditions.

Part-time: Normally only seasonal.

Further information ABTA National Training Board, Barratt House, 7 Chertsey Road, Woking, Surrey GU21 5AB
Institute of Travel and Tourism, 53–54 Newman Street, London W1P 4JJ

Related careers *Catering (Hotel Work) – Civil Aviation (Cabin Crew and Ground Staff) – Linguist – Secretarial Work*

NOTE: *Couriers* are normally employed for the season, though some may do secretarial work and/or planning off-season. This is not a career as such but rather a pleasant change for competent secretaries /linguists or simply good organizers. Occasional courses arranged by the International Association of Tour Managers, 397 Walworth Road, London SE17 2AW.

Work Study and Organization and Method

Entry qualifications 4 O-levels, including English and maths, if under 21; an employer's reference if between 21 and 25 and not holding the minimum O-level requirements; if over 25 and without the necessary O-levels, the ability to satisfy a college that she can benefit from the course.

The work Work study is part of management services, which means techniques designed to help management make the best use of all available resources.

Work study officers are concerned with analysing and improving working methods. Originally *work study* referred to work in production, *organization and method* to office work; but the aims and principles are basically the same, and the two types of specialists now form one profession which is very much involved with the implications of the change from traditional office and shop-floor work to the use of word processors and computerized equipment in manufacturing.

The work has two main aspects:

1. *Method study*, which is the analysis of how operations – whether workshop or office – are carried out with the aim of devising improvements (both in terms of productivity and work satisfaction).
2. *Work measurement*, which means using specific techniques to measure the amount of human effort that is contained in any particular job and in the operations contained in a particular job, whether it is work on an assembly line, as supermarket shelf-filler, as shop assistant, as hospital sister or as civil servant. Work measurement plays an important part in settling equal pay matters, where 'work of equal value' has to be defined, and in regrading jobs when new technologies change traditional working patterns. Officers may also be involved in planning re-training courses.

The success of the work always depends on gaining and keeping people's confidence – employees may have to be reassured that no changes detrimental to them will be introduced; employees may resent being 'measured'; managers may have to be convinced that work which *looks* easy is in fact highly complex.

Work study combines dealing with people and technical, analytical work in an unusual way.

Prospects Good for people who have had any kind of industrial or commercial 'work situation experience'. This is, say the Institute, very much a 'second career'. (See **Late start** below.)

Pay: Medium to high (see p. xxiii).

Training The Institute Certificates and Diplomas are taken mainly by part-time evening or correspondence study (sometimes day-release) over a period of about 3 years. The normal way to learn is as assistant to a work study officer, preferably with some past experience of work (in any capacity) – even if only a few months.

Personal attributes Numeracy; common sense; ability to gain and keep people's confidence and to establish good relationships with people at all educational levels, and of all temperaments; methodical approach; reasonably analytical brain; imagination; average intelligence; ability to organize people as well as their work.

Late start Very good opportunities: as mentioned above, this is very much a 'secondary career'; so anyone with any kind of work experience, whether clerical, in retail, catering in hospital or whatever, stands a good chance. There are a number of 3- to 6-month courses under the TOPS scheme which are sadly under-used by women (see p. xlvi).

Position of women The Institute's membership of 17,000 includes 950 women, the majority of whom work in hospitals, local and central government and similar areas concerned mainly with office work; some work in textiles and electronics manufacturing, where there are many women workers. But women with some kind of past working experience, no matter where, who are willing to do a spell in shop-floor production as assistant work study officer, should have no problem eventually getting good jobs (they may have difficulty getting the *first* job). As the work depends so much on common sense, organizing ability and establishing good relations with people, this is an area in which women who have tried have done well; the trouble is that so very few women know about the job.

Career-break: In theory there should be no problems, but too few have tried to be definite about this.

Part-time: Not much scope, but there are occasionally special projects where shift-work has to be studied, and several work study officers may share the working day – this may involve 'unsocial hours'.

Further information

Institute of Management Services, 1 Cecil Court, London Road, Enfield, Middlesex EN2 6DD

Related careers

Careers Officer – Engineering – Factory Inspector – Management

Working for Oneself: Mini-Entrepreneurship

This is not a career in the accepted sense. It is included in this Guide because creating one's own work is an 'alternative career' in today's – and tomorrow's – work pattern. As jobs are no longer available for all, more and more people are finding their own means of earning a living (and not in the 'black economy') – they become *mini-entrepreneurs*.

Entry qualifications See **Personal attributes**

The work The variety of self-generated work is unlimited. It can be broadly divided into three overlapping types of activity: *Providing a service*; *Selling*; *Making*. Most enterprises combine two activities, one of which is the crucial one.

Providing a Service

This requires least capital, involves least risk, covers a vast range, e.g. babysitting, window – or office – cleaning, running a bicycle delivery service – activities based on using one's time, basic skills and possibly basic equipment; *or* repairing videos or motor-bikes, cooking directors' lunches in offices, running a word-processing or computer-programming service – i.e. using specific skills plus equipment and, possibly, premises – kitchen, garden-shed, living-room.

Selling

This may overlap with *Providing a service* or with *Making*, or depend on 'buying-in' goods to sell (or collecting them from friends, etc.). It includes, for example, making sandwiches at home and delivering them to regular customers, running a second-hand clothes or clutter stall, selling 'bought-in' groceries from a mobile shop (probably a battered old van). This kind of selling could be a run-up to opening a shop, restaurant, mail-order business. Selling involves more initial organization and business know-how, capital and risk than *Providing a service*.

Making

This usually overlaps with *Selling* and covers anything from making children's clothes to assembling car roof-racks to manufacturing high tech. components for the computer industry; i.e. it ranges from using talent plus basic skills to using sophisticated skills acquired by apprenticeship to degree course, plus equipment. It requires some capital and probably premises. But if the idea is viable (see below) and the skills are there, finance is available (see below).

The law Far fewer formalities have to be complied with than would-be entrepreneurs tend to fear. Mini-entrepreneurship is fashionable and a Good Thing in bureaucracy's eyes. The spirit rather than the letter of bye-laws has to be observed. It is not permissible to run a saw-mill in one's garden because the noise would annoy the neighbours. It is unlikely that the Environmental Health Officer (from the Town Hall) would forbid sandwiches for sale being prepared in one's kitchen as long as that is clean. Local authorities must be consulted about planning and other regulations, but permission to go ahead is rarely 'unreasonably withheld' in the present climate of encouragement for so-called 'start-ups' – small businesses. Even the Inspector of Taxes and the Department of Health and Social Security, which have to be told, advise and inform rather than hinder. (Many people, for example, fear they will have to cope with VAT if they want to set up in business. In fact few people will reach the annual turnover limit necessary for registration in the first year or two.

Business format Again far fewer formalities in the initial stages than generally believed. The basic formats are (a) *Sole trader*: The Income Tax and DHSS merely have to be informed that the business exists; (b) *Partnership*: If two or more set up a business jointly, a solicitor draws up a straightforward agreement. Both sole traders and partnerships are liable for all the debts they incur should the business fail; (c) *Limited Company*: Requires slightly more formalities, but once set up persons involved are only liable for the money they put into the business should things go wrong; (d) *Cooperatives*: various types; need solicitors' or special agencies' advice (see **Further information**).

Prospects Successful entrepreneurship requires several indispensable ingredients: (a) *A marketable idea*: No idea is good in a vacuum. It must fill a gap in a given market. A bike repair service in a seaside suburb mainly inhabited by retired people would fail; one on a new housing estate some miles from shops and offices etc. stands a good chance (as long as there is no efficient competition); a mobile grocery-van on that housing estate where few shops have yet been opened sounds a good idea; a mobile grocery-van near a large shopping centre does not; a small-van removal service might flourish in bedsitter-land; it would not in a large-one-family-houses suburb. Researching the market is probably the most essential part of preparing to go it alone; (b) *Motivation and commitment*: Mini-entrepreneurs have to be willing to work harder, and more irregular hours, than employees (see **Personal attributes**); (c) *Resources*: If the idea fills a gap in the market and the commitment is there, advice and financial assistance and help with finding premises (if kitchen/garden-shed/living-room are insufficient/unsuitable) are available. Because the powers-that-be agree that in business small is beautiful (at least to start with) and that only an increase in self-generated jobs can reduce unemployment, a plethora of agencies to help 'start-ups' have sprung up over the last few years. The main ones:

Small Firms Service run by the Department of Industry; it is a nationwide information and advice network. Its main task is helping small businesses to become more efficient and grow, but it also gladly advises people who would like to set up their own show but have no idea how to. No question is too trivial or basic. What is VAT? Can I convert the front room into a shop? (The answer is probably 'No', but alternatives may be suggested.) Can I repair bikes in the garage? (Probably 'Yes, if you don't use noisy machinery and have a stream of customers calling'.) Do I need a licence – and if so from whom – to run a TV repair service/riding school/sandwich bar/market stall? (It depends on circumstances and local bye-laws which vary greatly.) The SFS answers some questions by phone but prefers face-to-face interviews because there are usually supplementary questions. The first interview is free, for subsequent 'counselling sessions' a small fee is charged. The SFS provides free and detailed literature on request. A similar, not quite so elaborate, service for people intending to set up in business in rural areas is provided by COSIRA (Council for Small Industries in Rural Areas) and for setting up a pottery, weaving or similar crafts business the Crafts Council will advise (but not in detail).

Then there are an ever-increasing number of *Enterprise Agencies*. They are run and funded mainly by local industry, usually with local authority involvement. Precise titles vary; an organization called *Business in the Community* has an up-to-date list of all such agencies. Enterprise Agencies provide factual information on tax, level of demand, marketing, law, etc. They tend to probe in depth, 'whether the chemistry is right'; does the prospective entrepreneur *really* have the personal qualities (see below) which are essential for success; and are the personal circumstances right? For example, someone without financial commitments/family responsibilities might be encouraged to go ahead with a risky project; someone with a family to keep and/or the slightest symptom of an anxious nature might be persuaded to try something more down-to-earth.

Local enterprise agencies want to encourage small businesses from enlightened self-interest (helping the local economy to flourish) rather than pure altruism. They often help with finding premises – small workshops in converted warehouses for example – and some can help with cash. Above all, they will help with preparing the vital 'business plan' which would-be entrepreneurs must present to the bank – usually the most likely source of finance. The business plan has to show that the prospective business person has worked out the project in detail. That involves defining setting-up as well as the first year's running costs; making a marketing-plan; proving that the customers are there; costing the work and pricing the product or service taking into consideration transport, materials, time, lighting and heating, etc. and allowing for imponderables such as equipment breakdown, illness, theft.

Personal attributes

Imagination; unquenchable resilience; tenacity; decisiveness; organizing ability; being a bit bossy; exceptional stamina; business acumen; enjoying risk-taking – being a bit of a gambler; ability to put up with temporary hardship; resourcefulness; self-confidence bordering on conceit; true enjoyment of hard work; ability to get on well with other people however unreasonable their requests/criticisms/impatience; ability to work under pressure. (Extent of these qualities depends on extent of venturesomeness of enterprise contemplated.)

Training

For most businesses mini-entrepreneurs need special skills. Welders, hairdressers, typographers, software engineers, electricians, electronics engineers (technicians or graduates) – or whatever, are all assumed to have got the skill they intend to 'sell', i.e. which they want to use as the basis for their business. (If necessary, see under individual career headings how to acquire such skills.) But to survive in the tough business world basic business know-how is essential, too.

The meaning of such terms as cash-flow, balance sheets, mark-up and, say, the difference between marketing and market research must be absolutely clear. Some courses are run by local education authorities, mostly at evening classes. They may not be specifically for prospective entrepreneurs: some are in basic book-keeping; basic computer application, etc. A few are day-time courses organized under the '21 hours rule'. That means unemployed people can draw benefit while attending college for a maximum of 21 hours a week.

The majority of courses for prospective entrepreneurs are run under the auspices of the Manpower Services Commission. The main types of courses:

1. *Skills into Business*: Mainly intended for skilled craftspersons and technicians who either were made redundant or did not get a job after finishing training. Courses consist of 9 days' theory at a Further Education College, followed by a month or so of updating/reinforcing the particular skill or trade at either an FE College or a Skill Centre. Built into *Skills into Business* are several counselling and follow-up sessions. People who benefited from the 1983 pilot courses include a welder who was helped to set up a wrought-iron-gates workshop; a hairdresser who set up a mobile hairdressing service in a rural area; an electronics technician who set up a TV/video repair service. Courses likely to be available all over the country in 1985.

2. *Project Full-Employ*: Intended for people with few or no qualifications aged between 16 and 25. Courses combine basic business training with training in a particular skill – from bicycle repairs to signwriting; carpentry to sound and vision recording (the latter for people with at least relevant hobby experience). Courses last about 20 weeks, full-time; trainees qualify for a training allowance. In 1984/5 it is hoped that there will be about a dozen courses around the country.

3. *Self-Employment Courses*: These are short, possibly only 2 days', courses at Further Education Colleges (but sponsored by the Manpower Services Commission) for people whose business idea has passed muster with the SFS or a local enterprise agency but who need an introduction to basic business skills such as how to keep records of outgoings and income. Suitable for people who intend to run their own one-man/woman businesses, either school/college leavers or people who want/have to change from employment to self-employment. Courses were piloted in 1983, likely to be available widely from 1984.

4. *Small Business Courses*: They last from 6 to 10 weeks, starting with college-based grounding in elements of business strategy, followed by a project period when students do their own market research and generally test their business idea. Courses are intended for people who may *start* on their own but intend to employ a few others. Most courses cater for any kind of business idea, but some are specially geared to catering or construction businesses. Trainees receive a weekly allowance. Courses are run for the Manpower Services Commission by universities, polytechnics, colleges, regional management centres and private consultants.

5. *The New Enterprise Programme* is rather more high-powered. Courses, at Business Schools attached to universities, last about 16 weeks and are intended for people with ideas for firms that will expand into sizeable concerns. Computer scientists with software publishing plans; engineers with well-worked-out plans for manufacturing metal

parts on a sub-contracting basis for existing engineering concerns; people with franchising ideas and retail experience (see Retail, p. 420) might, for example, qualify for acceptance – which is very competitive.

To qualify for admittance to the last two courses applicants must be at least 19, have been out of full-time education for two years; be either unemployed or give up their present job (exceptions are made for disabled people); and either have or have the promise of sufficient funds to set up the proposed business (i.e. they must have gone through the SFS or enterprise agency counselling stage and/or persuaded the bank or another financial institution to put up the necessary cash). Trainees qualify for a grant under TOPS (see p. xlvi).

Other courses may be available locally: for example the London Enterprise Agency (LENTA) runs 1-day sessions for anyone starting up or thinking about starting up their own business, as well as 'Linked Weekend Courses' – a programme of 4 weekends, 2 of which are residential. While local education authority and MSC courses are normally free, LENTA 1-day sessions cost £15; the Linked Weekend Courses between £150 and £350 (it depends whether persons qualify for subsidies – most do).

Other local enterprise agencies run similar courses – especially the 1- or 2-day ones. There are also correspondence or 'distance learning' courses but prospective students are strongly advised to check with the SFS or enterprise agency before signing up with any particular distance learning/correspondence college.

Late start

This 'alternative' career is the only one in this Guide where age is a positive advantage. Anyone who has had experience of the world of work scores over school and college leavers when it comes to applying to banks etc. for funds or to other agencies for premises or other help. Career-changers and returners are welcome on courses (only *Full-Employ* has a 25 years-of-age cut-off limit). One scheme, in practice, is in fact much more likely to accept second-career/career-change applicants: namely the *Enterprise Allowance Scheme*. In theory open to anyone over 18 (but numbers are severely restricted), about 85% of applicants are over 25. Under the scheme, people receive a weekly allowance of £40 for the first year to supplement receipts from their business. (Applicants must have available £1000 of their own or the promise of a bank or similar loan for that amount.)

Position of women

Disappointingly few women have so far attended the MSC courses and consulted the advisory services. Just under 10% of those attending LENTA's 1-day sessions in 1983, and about 8% of people helped under the Enterprise Allowance Scheme were women.

A large proportion of home-based catering services and employment, word-processing and similar agencies are believed to be run by women from home. Self-employment could be the answer for many women who feel thwarted in the business world and would like to use their managerial/pulling-various-strands-together talents and experience.

Career-break: Presents problems.

Part-time: No way.

Further information

Small Firms Service, Freefone 2444 in England; 846 in Scotland; 1208 in Wales
COSIRA, 141 Castle Street, Salisbury, Wiltshire
Crafts Council, 8 Waterloo Place, London SW1 4AU
Business in the Community (for Directory of local enterprise agencies), 227A City Road, London EC1
Project Full-Employ, 31 Clerkenwell Close, London EC1 0AT
Cooperatives: Cooperative Development Agency, Broadmead House, 21 Panton Street, London SW1Y 4DR
Courses: local further education college; Jobcentre for local MSC courses

Youth-and-Community Work

Entry qualifications Depend on age and experience. See **Training**.

The work Job definition is again confusing. The youth service comes under the local education authority, not the social services department. Youth workers, youth-and-community workers and community centre wardens or community workers can all be different jobs, or one person may combine the activities. See also Community Work, p. 481.

The *youth worker* is the most clearly defined job, and the oldest established. She initiates a wide variety of activities, usually for the 14–20-year-olds. All interests, from dancing to classical music, sailing to dressmaking, drama to sport, have to be catered for. The youth worker's most difficult tasks are to find the right balance of activities; to let members do as much organizing and planning for themselves as possible; never to let the club resemble an evening institute, and yet to bear in mind that the youth service is 'educational' in the widest sense. She must take an interest in all club members, especially in those who have personal problems. She may occasionally do a little unofficial social casework.

Her duties also include management of premises; recruitment and selection of voluntary helpers; dealing with administration; keeping in touch with social workers; attending committees; trying new methods of attracting 'unclubbables', which may mean going into discos and cafés to meet young people who do not come to youth clubs.

Increasingly, youth workers are '*youth-and-community workers*' and try and involve all ages. Youth clubs are attached to or part of a community centre where citizens of all ages meet for recreation, education or entertainment. Activities may include morning mother-and-toddler clubs; pre-school playgroups; adventure playgrounds; painting or pottery classes for adults; reading classes for illiterates; English for immigrants; discussion groups. This type of work overlaps with community work (see Social Work, p. 481), but it is usually rather more administrative and traditional in aims. The main difference between the work of the new-style community worker and the youth-and-community worker is that the former spends as much time as possible in the community; the traditional 'community centre warden' type of youth-and-community worker is busy in the centre.

Pay: Low to medium (see p. xxiii).

Prospects Depend on current public expenditure levels. Though this is an expanding work area, there are at present more qualified applicants than vacancies, but the situation might well change.

Training This is flexible and ensures that suitable people, whatever their age and educational qualifications, have a chance of qualifying. Though applicants for courses are normally expected to have 5 O-levels plus experience of voluntary or paid (for example, playleader) work with young people and/or other community work, applicants whose practical work experience has shown that they are suitable for the work, may be accepted with lower educational qualifications. Minimum entry age varies from one course to another and again depends on individuals' experience and maturity.

Types of courses

1. 2-year full-time course leading to qualified youth-and-community worker status; minimum age usually 23; occasionally younger.
2. 1-year full-time course leading to qualified youth-and-community worker status for graduates only (any discipline); practical relevant work or voluntary experience essential.
3. Some CQSW (see Social Work, **Training**, p. 482) include youth-and-community work as an option and lead to social worker *and* youth-and-community worker status. Course content and emphasis vary: courses may include more community relations *or* more youth-and-community work. The amount of time devoted to the option also varies, and some CQSW courses which have a youth-and-community work option do in fact rarely lead to good youth-and-community work jobs because students had too little relevant practical experience during the course.
4. A few BEd courses (see Teaching, p. 524) include youth-and-community work options. Again, course content and emphasis should be carefully examined: a BEd course may include youth-and-community work only as a subsidiary subject with little time devoted to it, and in that case BEd graduates wanting to go into youth-and-community work have difficulty in competing with more thoroughly trained graduates from the specific 2-year youth-and-community work courses.

In Scotland, youth-and-community work training takes 3 years, full-time, and entrants must have 2 SCE Highers. People with practical experience who are over 23 may be exempt from the first year of the course. There is also a 1-year course for graduates, teachers and social workers.

Personal attributes An outgoing personality; ability to communicate easily with people who may need 'drawing out'; patience; imagination to put oneself into the shoes of people who feel alienated from society; wide interests in current social and economic trends and problems; organizing ability; feeling at ease with people of all ages; creativity to think up activities (see also Social Work, **Personal attributes**, p. 484).

Late start Mature candidates are welcome on courses. This can be a suitable 'second career' for people changing direction in their 20s or 30s, if they have relevant work or voluntary work experience.

Position of women There are far more men than women in both youth and youth-and-community work. This is not due to discrimination but in the past very few women tried to get into this field. The proportion of women on courses is however rising, and there is no reason whatever why women should not do well in this kind of work.

Career-break: Should not present any problems. Experience of having brought up children – especially teenagers – should be a help. But so far few women have returned after a break.

Part-time: Ample opportunity in youth work; not so much for community relations-type of work at present. No reason why job-sharing should not be tried.

Further information

National Youth Bureau, 17–23 Albion Street, Leicester LE1 6GD
Central Council for Education and Training in Social Work, see Social Work
Council for Education and Training in Youth and Community, Wellington House, Wellington Street, Leicester LE1 6HL

Related careers *Recreation Management – Social Work – Sport – Teaching*

Index

This book uses only the feminine pronoun though the information, unless otherwise stated, applies to both sexes.

MORE ABOUT PENGUINS, PELICANS AND PUFFINS

For further information about books available from Penguins please write to Dept EP, Penguin Books Ltd, Harmondsworth, Middlesex UB7 0DA.

In the U.S.A.: For a complete list of books available from Penguins in the United States write to Dept DG, Penguin Books, 299 Murray Hill Parkway, East Rutherford, New Jersey 07073.

In Canada: For a complete list of books available from Penguins in Canada write to Penguin Books Canada Ltd, 2801 John Street, Markham, Ontario L3R 1B4.

In Australia: For a complete list of books available from Penguins in Australia write to the Marketing Department, Penguin Books Australia Ltd, P.O. Box 257, Ringwood, Victoria 3134.

In New Zealand: For a complete list of books available from Penguins in New Zealand write to the Marketing Department, Penguin Books (N.Z.) Ltd, P.O. Box 4019, Auckland 10.

In India: For a complete list of books available from Penguins in India write to Penguin Overseas Ltd, 706 Eros Apartments, 56 Nehru Place, New Delhi 110019.

Diets and Exercise in Penguins

VOGUE BOOK OF DIETS AND EXERCISE

Barbara Tims

Here is a PRACTICAL guide to achieving and maintaining the right shape and correct weight

*Proportion-control and calorie-control diets to keep within daily limits
*Special food-control diets for limited periods
*Special-object diets designed for extra energy, treatment of cellulite etc.
*A range of exercises designed to appeal to all tastes and athletic abilities – including water shape-ups and Tai Chi
*Fabulous illustrations

JANE FONDA'S WORKOUT BOOK

Pioneered by Jane Fonda in California, this is her extraordinarily successful programme of exercises and advice on diet for today's fitness seeker – *the* book that will help you help yourself to better looks, superb fitness and a more fulfilling lifestyle. Her programme is specially designed to
*Burn calories
*Improve the shape of the body
*Strengthen the heart and lungs and build up muscle stamina and flexibility

'You couldn't do better than follow Jane Fonda's example' – *Woman's Journal*

'Energy and enthusiasm . . . and the intimacy of one woman talking to another' – *Time Out*

ROSES FOR ENGLISH GARDENS

Gertrude Jekyll and Edward Mawley

Gertrude Jekyll brings her garden sense to the best-loved flower of all. In collaboration with Edward Mawley, a practical rose gardener, she shows the nearly limitless possibilities for planting between walls, on pergolas, along wood posts, on verandas, and on trees, never instructing so much as inspiring. To instil practical principles of successful gardening and the experience of her gardening eye to the enthusiastic gardener is her aim.

Edward Mawley provides details for plantings, pruning and propagating different varieties of roses along with defence against disease and ways to exhibit roses for shows.

THE ALLOTMENT GARDENER'S HANDBOOK

Alan Titchmarsh

The creation of a well cultivated and high yielding allotment of fruit and vegetables unsurpassed for quality and flavour is within the grasp of all. Beginning with information on how to acquire an allotment, Alan Titchmarsh describes the use of tools, soil types, and the great variety of growing systems, weed control and fertilisers.

The whole range of everyday fruit and vegetables is covered as well as unusual varieties such as asparagus, kohlrabi and salsify, together with herbs and flowers. Each entry has a summary with a star rating for the amount of effort each crop requires. Advice is given on how to tackle pests, diseases and disorders – and a chart for easy identification of symptoms and the appropriate remedy. Finally there is a useful miscellany of facts and figures, including a sowing and harvesting chart.

Know Your Rights: The Questions and the Answers

WOMEN'S RIGHTS IN THE WORKPLACE

Tess Gill and Larry Whitty

Women and training * Working part-time * Maternity rights * Women and new technology * Paid work at home * Women and employment law * Creches and child-care at work

Whether you're employed in an office, a factory or a school, *Women's Rights in the Workplace* is designed to arm you with the information – and the expertise and confidence – to get a better deal at work. Containing full, up-to-date information on women's jobs, pay and conditions, it is the essential handbook for all working women.

YOUR SOCIAL SECURITY

Fran Bennett

School-leavers and social security * Benefit and one-parent families * Retirement pensions * Family income supplement

In practical question and answer format, here at last is a handbook to guide you through the maze of social security benefit regulations. Whether you are out of work, a single parent, retired, disabled or simply grossly underpaid, this book will give you the essential information to help you claim your rights from the State.

Other volumes in this new Penguin series *Know Your Rights: The Questions and the Answers* cover marital rights and the rights of ethnic minorities.